james halliday

australia & new zealand

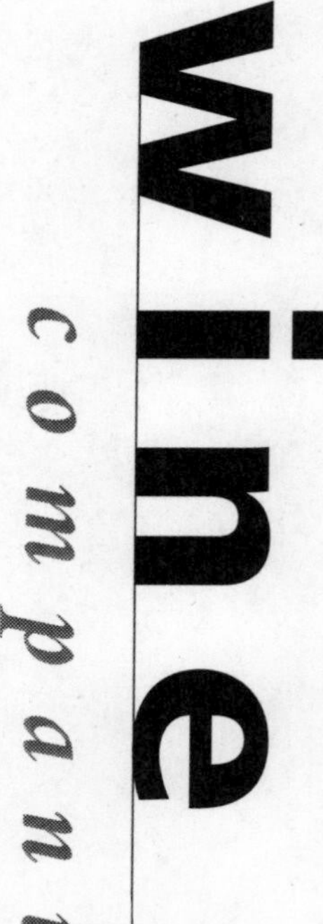

wine companion

1999 EDITION

james halliday

australia & new zealand

wine
companion

1999 EDITION

HarperCollinsPublishers

HarperCollins*Publishers*

First published as *Australia and New Zealand Wine Companion* in Australia in 1997
This edition published in 1998
by HarperCollins*Publishers* Pty Limited
ACN 009 913 517
A member of HarperCollins*Publishers* (Australia) Pty Limited Group
http://www.harpercollins.com.au

HarperCollins*Publishers*
25 Ryde Road, Pymble, Sydney, NSW 2073, Australia
31 View Road, Glenfield, Auckland 10, New Zealand
77–85 Fulham Palace Road, London W6 8JB, United Kingdom
Hazelton Lanes, 55 Avenue Road, Suite 2900, Toronto, Ontario M5R 3L2
and 1995 Markham Road, Scarborough, Ontario M1B 5M8, Canada
10 East 53rd Street, New York NY 10032, USA

National Library Cataloguing-in-Publication data:

Halliday, James, 1938–.
Australia and New Zealand Wine Companion.

1999 ed.
ISBN 0 7322 5852 9.

1. Wine and wine making – Australia. 2. Wine and wine making – New Zealand. 3. Wineries – Australia – Directories. 4. Wineries – New Zealand – Directories. I. Title.

641.220993

Cover inset photograph by Kevin Judd

Set in Bembo 8/10
Printed in Australia by Griffin Press Pty Ltd, Adelaide on 80 gsm Econoprint

5 4 3 2 1 98 99 00

contents

how to use this book

The *Wine Companion* is arranged with wineries in alphabetical order, and the entries should be self-explanatory, but here I will briefly take you through the information for each entry.

winery entries

leeuwin estate ★★★★★
Stevens Road, Margaret River, WA 6285 **region** Margaret River
phone (08) 9430 4099 **fax** (08) 9430 5687 **open** 7 days 10.30–4.30
winemaker Bob Cartwright **production** 40 000 **est.** 1974
product range ($15–67.45 CD) Art Series Chardonnay, Riesling, Sauvignon Blanc, Pinot Noir, Cabernet Sauvignon; Prelude Classic Dry White, Chardonnay, Pinot Noir, Cabernet Sauvignon are lower-priced alternatives, with a non-vintage Prelude blended white the cheapest wine on the list.
summary Leeuwin Estate's Chardonnay is, in my opinion, Australia's finest example based on the wines of the last 15 years. The Cabernet Sauvignon, too, is an excellent wine with great style and character. Almost inevitably, the other wines in the portfolio are not in the same Olympian class, although the Prelude Chardonnay and Sauvignon Blanc are impressive at their lower price level.

winery name Leeuwin Estate

Although it might seem that stating the winery name is straightforward, this is not necessarily so. To avoid confusion, wherever possible I use the name that appears most prominently on the wine label and do not refer to any associated trading name.

ratings ★★★★★

The winery star system may be interpreted as follows:

★★★★★ Outstanding winery regularly producing exemplary wines.
★★★★☆ Extremely good; virtually on a par with a five-star winery.
★★★★ Consistently produces high-quality wines.
★★★☆ A solid, reliable producer of good wine.
★★★ Typically good, but may have a few lesser wines.
★★☆ Adequate.
★★ Hard to recommend.

If the ratings seem generous, so be it. The fact is that Australia is blessed with a marvellous climate for growing grapes, a high degree of technological skill, and a remarkable degree of enthusiasm and dedication on the part of its winemakers. Across the price spectrum, Australian wines stand tall in the markets of the world. I see no reason, therefore, to shrink from recognising excellence. NR = not rated, either because the winery is new or because I have not tasted enough of its wines.

address Stevens Road, Margaret River, WA 6285
phone (08) 9430 4099 **fax** (08) 9430 5687

The details are usually those of the winery and cellar door but in a few instances may simply be of the winery; this occurs when the wine is made at another winery under contract and is sold only through retail.

region Margaret River

The mapping of Australia into Zones and Regions with legally defined boundaries is now well underway. This edition sees radical changes (and additions) to the regional names and boundaries. Wherever possible the official 'Geographic Indication' name has been adopted, and where the registration process is incomplete, I have used the most likely name. Occasionally you will see 'Warehouse' as the region. This means the wine is made from purchased grapes in someone else's winery. In other words, it does not have a vineyard or winery home in the ordinary way.

cellar door sales hours **open** 7 days 10.30–4.30

Although a winery might be listed as not open or only open on weekends, some may in fact be prepared to open by appointment. Many will, some won't; a telephone call will establish whether it is possible or not. Also, virtually every winery that is shown as being open only for weekends is in fact open for public holidays as well. Once again, a telephone call will confirm this.

winemaker Bob Cartwright

In the large companies the winemaker is simply the head of a team; there may be many executive winemakers actually responsible for specific wines.

production 40 000

This figure given (representing the number of cases produced each year) is merely an indication of the size of the operation. Some wineries (principally but not exclusively the large companies) regard this information as confidential; in that event, NFP (not for publication) will appear. NA = information was not available.

year of establishment **est.** 1974

A more or less self-explanatory item, but keep in mind that some makers consider the year in which they purchased the land to be the year of establishment, others the year in which they first planted grapes, others the year they first made wine, others the year they first offered wine for sale, and so on. There may also be minor complications where there has been a change of ownership or a break in production.

price range and product range ($15–67.45 CD) Art Series Chardonnay, Riesling, Sauvignon Blanc, Pinot Noir, Cabernet Sauvignon; Prelude Classic Dry White, Chardonnay, Pinot Noir, Cabernet Sauvignon are lower-priced alternatives, with a non-vintage Prelude blended white the cheapest wine on the list.

The **price range** given covers the least expensive through to the most expensive wines usually made by the winery in question (where the information was available). Hence there may be a significant spread. That spread, however, may not fully cover fluctuations that occur in retail pricing, particularly with the larger companies. Erratic and often savage discounting remains a feature of the wine industry, and prices must therefore be seen as approximate.

The Australian winery prices are for purchase in Australia, in Australian dollars; those for New Zealand are for purchase in New Zealand, in New Zealand dollars.

I have indicated whether the price is cellar door (CD), mailing list (ML) or retail (R). By and large, the choice has been determined by which of the three methods of sale is most important to the winery. The price of Australian and New Zealand wines in other countries is affected by a number of factors, including excise and customs duty, distribution mark-up and currency fluctuations. Contact the winery for details.

product range Particularly with the larger companies, it is not possible to give a complete list of the wines. The saving grace is that these days most of the wines are simply identified on their label by their varietal composition.

summary Leeuwin Estate's Chardonnay is, in my opinion, Australia's finest example based on the wines of the last 15 years. The Cabernet Sauvignon, too, is an excellent wine with great style and character. Almost inevitably, the other wines in the portfolio are not in the same Olympian class, although the Prelude Chardonnay and Sauvignon Blanc are impressive at their lower price level.

My summary of the winery. Little needs to be said, except that I have tried to vary the subjects I discuss in this part of the winery entry.

The vine leaf symbol indicates wineries that are new entries in this year's listing.

wine entries and tasting notes

Leeuwin Estate Art Series Chardonnay

The core of the Art Series Chardonnay is Block 20 (one of five blocks on the estate) with yields never exceeding 2.5 tonnes to the acre, and frequently less than 2 tonnes. Barrel fermentation in the finest French oak, and prolonged bottle maturation do the rest.

1995 Light to medium yellow-green; an exceptionally intense, complex yet fine bouquet with perfectly married nutty barrel-ferment characters running through sweet melon and citrus fruit is followed by an intense, yet elegant palate with melon, cashew, chestnut, citrus and oak spice flavours. Long and penetrating, with excellent acidity, the wine has an indefinite future, however seductive it is now. **rating:** 97

best drinking 1999 – 2010 **best vintages** '80, '81, '82, '83, '85, '87, '89, '90, '92, '94, '95 **drink with** Richer veal, chicken dishes • $67.45

wine name Leeuwin Estate Art Series Chardonnay

In most instances, the wine's name will be prefaced by the name of the winery.

ratings

Two ratings are given for each wine; the ratings apply to the vintage reviewed, and may vary from one year to the next.

Points scale	Glass symbol	
98–100	–	Perfection which exists only as an idea.
94–97	5 glasses	As close to perfection as the real world will allow.
90–93	4½ glasses	Excellent wine full of character; of gold medal standard.
85–89	4 glasses	Very good wine; clear varietal definition/style; silver verging on gold medal standard.
80–84	3½ glasses	Good fault-free, flavoursome; high bronze to silver medal standard.

You will see that nearly all of the wines reviewed in this book rate 84 points (3½ glasses) or better. This is not wanton generosity on my part. It simply reflects the fact that the 1000 or so wines selected for specific review are the tip of more than 5000 tasting notes accumulated over the past year. In other words, the wines described are among Australia's top 20 per cent. NR = not rated.

background The core of the Art Series Chardonnay is Block 20 (one of five blocks on the estate) with yields never exceeding 2.5 tonnes to the acre, and frequently less than 2 tonnes. Barrel fermentation in the finest French oak, and prolonged bottle maturation do the rest.

Like the summary information given in the winery entries, I have tried to vary the approach of my discussions.

tasting note 🍷🍷🍷🍷🍷 **1995** Light to medium yellow-green; an exceptionally intense, complex yet fine bouquet with perfectly married nutty barrel-ferment characters running through sweet melon and citrus fruit is followed by an intense, yet elegant palate with melon, cashew, chestnut, citrus and oak spice flavours. Long and penetrating, with excellent acidity, the wine has an indefinite future, however seductive it is now. **rating:** 97

The tasting note opens with the vintage of the wine tasted. With the exception of a very occasional classic wine, this tasting note will have been made within the 12 months prior to publication. Even that is a long time, and during the life of this book the wine will almost certainly change. More than this, remember that tasting is a highly subjective and imperfect art. NV = non-vintage.

best drinking 1999 – 2010

I will usually give a range of years or a more specific comment (such as 'quick-developing style'), but whatever my best drinking recommendation, always consider it with extreme caution and as an approximate guide at best. When to drink a given wine is an intensely personal decision, which only you can make.

best vintages '80, '81, '82, '83, '85, '87, '89, '90, '92, '94, '95

Self-explanatory information, but a note of caution: wines do change in bottle, and it may be that were I to taste all of the best vintages listed, I would demote some and elevate some not mentioned.

drink with Richer veal, chicken dishes

Again, merely a suggestion – a subliminal guide to the style of wine.

price • $67.45

This is a recommended retail price only. NA = information not available.

australian wineries and wines

wine regions of australia

key to regions

1 Lower Hunter Valley
2 Upper Hunter Valley
3 Hastings River
4 Mudgee
5 Orange
6 Cowra
7 Murray Darling and Swan Hill
8 Riverina
9 Pericoota
10 Hilltops
11 Canberra District
12 Tumbarumba
13 Shoalhaven
14 Far South West Victoria
15 Grampians
16 Pyrenees
17 Ballarat
18 Bendigo
19 Goulburn Valley
20 Central Victorian High Country
21 Glenrowan
22 Rutherglen
23 King Valley
24 Ovens Valley
25 Gippsland
26 Mornington Peninsula
27 Yarra Valley
28 Geelong
29 Sunbury
30 Macedon
31 Northern Tasmania
32 Southern Tasmania
33 Mount Gambier
34 Robe
35 Coonawarra
36 Koppamurra
37 Mount Benson
38 Padthaway
39 Langhorne Creek
40 McLaren Vale
41 Adelaide Hills
42 Eden Valley
43 Adelaide Plains
44 Barossa Valley
45 Riverland
46 Clare Valley
47 Port Lincoln
48 Great Southern
49 Pemberton
50 Blackwood Valley
51 Margaret River
52 Geographe
53 South-west Coast
54 Perth Hills
55 Swan District
56 Burnett Valley
57 Granite Belt

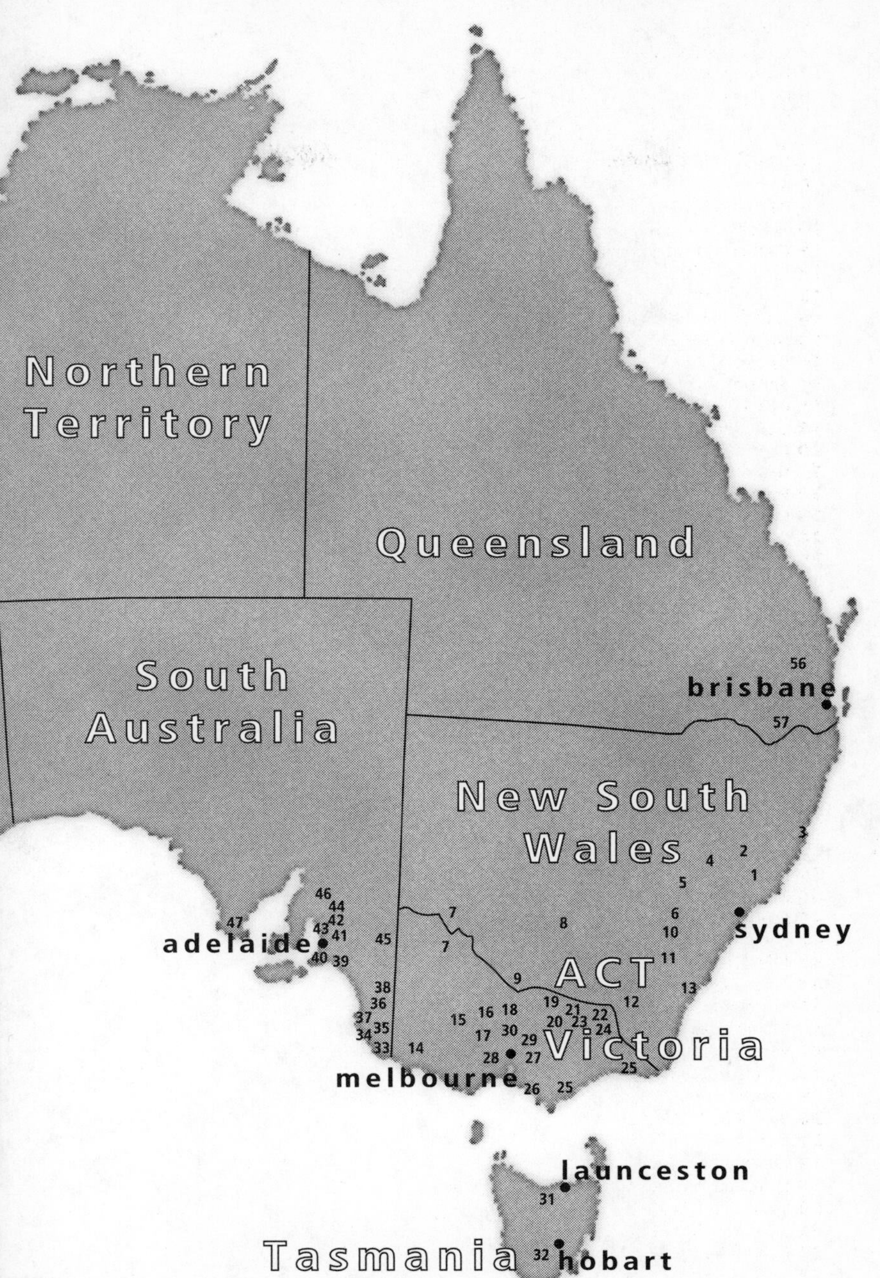
Northern Territory
Queensland
South Australia
New South Wales
ACT
Victoria
Tasmania
brisbane
sydney
adelaide
melbourne
launceston
hobart
1
2
3
4
5
6
7
7
8
9
10
11
12
13
14
15
16
17
18
19
20
21
22
23
24
25
25
26
27
28
29
30
31
32
33
34
35
36
37
38
39
40
41
42
43
44
45
46
47
56
57

abbey vale ★★★★

Wildwood Road, Yallingup, WA 6282 **region** Margaret River
phone (08) 9755 2121 **fax** (08) 9755 2286 **open** 7 days 10–5
winemaker Dorham Mann **production** 8000 **est.** 1986
product range ($14–28 CD) Festival White, Semillon, Dry Verdelho, Sauvignon Blanc, Sunburst Verdelho, Chardonnay, Merlot Shiraz, Cabernet Merlot, Cabernet Sauvignon, Reserve Cabernet Sauvignon; Moonshine Ale brewed on the premises.
summary Abbey Vale has gone from strength to strength in recent years, vinifying an ever-increasing proportion of the production from its large 30-hectare vineyard, and winning a significant number of show awards.

ada river ★★★

Main Road, Neerim South, Vic 3831 **region** Gippsland
phone (03) 5628 1221 **fax** (03) 5623 6723 **open** 10–6 weekends and public holidays
winemaker Peter Kelliher, Chris Kelliher **production** 700 **est.** 1983
product range ($12–17 CD) From Gippsland-grown grapes Chardonnay and Cabernet Sauvignon; from Yarra Valley grapes Traminer, Chardonnay and Pinot Noir; and Pinot Noir drawn from both regions.
summary The Kelliher family first planted vines on their dairy farm at Neerim South in 1983, extending the original Millstream Vineyard in 1989, and increasing plantings yet further by establishing the nearby Manilla Vineyard in 1994. The family also has the Goondalahg Vineyard at Steels Creek in the Yarra Valley under long-term lease, thus providing two distinct wine ranges. Wine production began in 1991, the first wines going on sale in 1995.

affleck NR

RMB 244 Millynn Road off Gundaroo Road, Bungendore, NSW 2621 **region** Canberra District
phone (02) 6236 9276 **open** Weekends and public holidays by appointment
winemaker Ian Hendry **production** 130 **est.** 1976
product range Chardonnay, Pinot Noir, Dry White (Semillon), Sweet White, Cabernet Shiraz, Muscat, Ruby Port.
summary The cellar-door and mail order price list says that the wines are 'grown, produced and bottled on the estate by Ian and Susie Hendry with much dedicated help from family and friends'. The 2.5-hectare vineyard, situated on the shale of the Lake George escarpment, is very much a weekend and holiday occupation for the Hendrys, who lead busy weekday professional lives.

aldinga bay vineyards NR

Main South Road, Aldinga, SA 5173 **region** McLaren Vale
phone (08) 8556 3179 **open** 7 days 10–5
winemaker Nick Girolamo **production** 6000 **est.** 1979
product range ($6.50–14.80 CD) Chardonnay, Sauvignon Blanc, Riesling, Cabernet Sauvignon, Shiraz.
summary The former Donolga Winery has had a name and image change since Nick Girolamo, the son of founders Don and Olga Girolamo, returned from Roseworthy College with a degree in Oenology. Nick Girolamo has taken over both the winemaking and marketing; prices remain modest, though not as low as they once were, reflecting an increase in the quality and an upgrade in packaging.

alkoomi ★★★★★

Wingeballup Road, Frankland, WA 6396 **region** Great Southern
phone (08) 9855 2229 **fax** (08) 9855 2284 **open** 7 days 10.30–5
winemaker Michael Staniford, Merv Lange **production** 40 000 **est.** 1971
product range ($13–50 R) Classic White, Riesling, Chardonnay, Sauvignon Blanc, Late Harvest Riesling, Classic Red, Malbec, Shiraz, Cabernet Sauvignon, Sparkling Alkoomi, Tawny Port.

summary For those who see the wineries of Western Australia as suffering from the tyranny of distance, this most remote of all wineries shows there is no tyranny after all. It is a story of unqualified success due to sheer hard work, and no doubt to Merv and Judy Lange's aversion to borrowing a single dollar from the bank. The substantial production is entirely drawn from the ever-expanding estate vineyards, which by 1998 amounted to 45.5 hectares. Wine quality across the range is impeccable, always with precisely defined varietal character.

Alkoomi Riesling

As with all of the Alkoomi wines, produced from estate-grown fruit. Yet another example of the symbiotic relationship between Mount Barker and Riesling, for it is usually an excellent wine.

🍷🍷🍷🍷 **1997** Light green-yellow; the aromas are clean, light and crisp, in the herbal/lemon spectrum, and none of the passionfruit which is present in many of the region's Rieslings in recent years. The palate is tight and toasty; not a lot of flesh there now, but bred to stay. **rating:** 85

➯ **best drinking** 2000 – 2007 **best vintages** '94, '95, '96 **drink with** Salad • $16

Alkoomi Sauvignon Blanc

Alkoomi has 2.5 hectares of sauvignon blanc, and was one of the first vineyards in the region to experiment with the variety. Some of the early vintages lacked varietal character, but every year since 1995 have displayed great depth of flavour and strong varietal character.

🍷🍷🍷🍷½ **1997** Light yellow-green; a strikingly intense and vibrant bouquet with masses of passionfruit and gooseberry aromas is followed by a surprisingly, but refreshingly, delicate palate, crisp and tingling with good acidity and mouthfeel. **rating:** 92

➯ **best drinking** 1998 – 1999 **best vintages** '95, '96, '97 **drink with** Ginger prawns • $18

Alkoomi Chardonnay

Produced from 5 hectares of estate plantings, and barrel-fermented and matured in a mixture of oak, predominantly French Nevers and Vosges from Seguin Moreau.

🍷🍷🍷🍷½ **1997** Medium yellow-green; a fragrant bouquet with fine melon, citrus and sweet apple fruit aromas is followed by a deliciously fruit-driven palate ranging through melon, apple and cinnamon (the latter from oak); harmonious finish. **rating:** 93

➯ **best drinking** 1998 – 2002 **best vintages** '85, '88, '90, '92, '94, '97 **drink with** Stir-fried chicken with cashew nuts • $23

Alkoomi Blackbutt

A new super-premium release from Alkoomi, first made in 1994 from a blend of Cabernet Sauvignon, Malbec and Merlot, with the first blend made after the components had already been in barrel for 20 months, thereafter being transferred to 100% new French oak for a further eight months before bottling. Only very small quantities are made.

ΥΥΥΥΥ **1994** Still holding red-purple; it has supple yet rich and sweet blackberry, chocolate, cedar and vanilla aromas on the bouquet, leading on to a palate with quite superb fruit, which swallows up the oak and finishes with lingering tannins. **rating:** 94

➯ **best drinking** 1999 – 2005 **best vintages** '94 **drink with** Rare beef • $50

all saints ★★★★☆

All Saints Road, Wahgunyah, Vic 3687 **region** Rutherglen
phone (02) 6033 1922 **fax** (02) 6033 3515 **open** 7 days 9–5
winemaker Terry Barnett **production** 30 000 **est.** 1864
product range ($8.70–45 CD) Chardonnay, Marsanne, Orange Muscat (a winery specialty), Shiraz, Cabernet Sauvignon, Late Harvest Semillon, Late Picked Muscadelle. The real focus is on Classic Release Muscat and Tokay and on Show Reserve Muscat and Tokay.
summary Brown Brothers have spent both time and considerable money on restoring All Saints since acquiring it in 1991. The winery rating principally reflects the Show Reserve fortified wines, but the table wines are more than adequate. An excellent winery restaurant makes this a compulsory and most enjoyable stop for any visitor to the northeast.

All Saints Shiraz

A typically concentrated Rutherglen Shiraz in terms of fruit, but not so typical in terms of the addition of a considerable degree of new American oak. The marriage works well.

ΥΥΥΥ **1996** Strong, deep red-purple; the bouquet is rich and full, with plum and cherry fruit smothered in smooth vanillin American oak. A chewy, rich, dense mouthfilling, indeed mouthstopping, wine which needs years to settle down, but could well prove to be something special in ten years time. **rating:** 86

➯ **best drinking** 2005 – 2010 **best vintages** '92, '96 **drink with** Venison • $16

All Saints Classic Release Tokay

An exceptionally good wine at the price, with an average blend age of eight years. The varietal definition is excellent, the blend a delightful amalgam of old and young material.

ΥΥΥΥΥ **NV** Light golden-brown; rich and sweet malt and tea-leaf aromas with barely perceptible fortifying spirit. The palate is of medium to full weight, with malty/toffee/caramel/tea-leaf flavours, finishing with well-balanced acidity. **rating:** 94

➯ **best drinking** 1997 – 2007 **best vintages** NA **drink with** Try it as an aperitif • $19.50

All Saints Show Reserve Tokay

While some of the best stocks of All Saints were sold to other purchasers before Brown Brothers completed the acquisition of the entire property, certain of the very best material remained. This has in turn formed the base of this show blend, which has an average age of 20 years, and which has already accumulated a large number of trophies and gold medals.

ΥΥΥΥΥ **NV** Deep golden-brown; wonderfully concentrated and rich caramel, toffee and molasses aromas lead on to a sensuously luscious and complex toffee, tea-leaf and butterscotch-flavoured palate. **rating:** 96

➯ **best drinking** 1997 – 2007 **best vintages** NA **drink with** A meal in itself • $55

All Saints Classic Release Muscat

The blend has an average age of ten years, and, even if not showing the same outstanding varietal character as its sister wine, the Liqueur Tokay, is an impressive wine, attesting to the depth of the fortified stocks still held at All Saints. Won two trophies at the 1998 Sydney International Wine Competition, including the Millers Trophy for runner-up to Best Wine of Show. With a price of $19.50 retail, it was placed in the top ten Best Value Wines.

🍷🍷🍷🍷🍷 **NV** Medium tawny with just a hint of brown on the rim; soft, raisiny varietal muscat with fractionally earthy spirit. The palate is quite luscious, with good raisined fruit, starting sweet and finishing with cleansing acidity. **rating:** 90

➩ **best drinking** 1997 – 2007 **best vintages** NA **drink with** Coffee and chocolates • $19.50

allandale ★★★★

Lovedale Road, Pokolbin via Maitland, NSW 2321 **region** Lower Hunter Valley
phone (02) 4990 4526 **fax** (02) 4990 1714 **open** Mon-Sat 9–5, Sun 10–5
winemaker Bill Sneddon, Peter Orr **production** 15 000 **est.** 1978
product range ($14–22 R) Hilltops Riesling, Late Picked Hilltops Riesling, Hilltops Semillon, Semillon, Sauvignon Blanc, Chardonnay, Chardonnay Semillon, Lombardo (Pinot Noir Shiraz blend), Matthew Shiraz, Mudgee Cabernet Sauvignon, William Méthode Champenoise.
summary Unostentatious, medium-sized winery which has been under the control of winemaker Bill Sneddon for well over a decade. Has developed something of a reputation as a Chardonnay specialist, but does offer a broad range of wines of good quality, with an increasing number of wines produced from grapes grown in the Hilltops region.

Allandale Semillon

Utilises 2 hectares of estate plantings, part of which are used for Semillon Sauvignon Blanc and Chardonnay Semillon blends. The best component is released as a straight varietal, made in the classic style without oak influence. An interesting comment on the back label of the '97 says, 'The vintage conditions were both difficult and challenging. Past history has show the wetter years often produce the best Semillons.' A true statement, and certainly true in this instance.

🍷🍷🍷🍷🍷 **1997** Medium yellow-green; a penetrating and full bouquet with lemony/herbaceous varietal character is supported by an attractive minerally undertone. The palate has excellent flavour and length, lively and fresh with lemony characters. Good length and balance. **rating:** 90

➩ **best drinking** 2002 – 2007 **best vintages** '86, '91, '94, '96, '97 **drink with** Summer salads • $15

Allandale Hunter River Chardonnay

Draws upon 3 hectares of estate plantings. At its best, the wine shows excellent use of a mix of French and American oak. The wine is given extended lees contact and taken through partial malolactic fermentation.

🍷🍷🍷🍷 **1997** Quite brilliant yellow-green; the sophisticated and clever use of spicy oak does not hide the peach and melon fruit on an attractively complex bouquet. The palate, likewise, shows lots of oak input, with more of that sweet, almost fleshy fruit; does cloy ever so fractionally on the finish. **rating:** 85

➩ **best drinking** 1998 – 2000 **best vintages** '91, '94, '96 **drink with** Smoked salmon • $17.50

allanmere 

Allandale Road, Allandale via Pokolbin, NSW 2321 **region** Lower Hunter Valley
phone (02) 4930 7387 **fax** (02) 4930 7900 **open** 7 days 9.30–5
winemaker Greg Silkman **production** 7000 **est.** 1984
product range ($15–20 CD) Gold Label Chardonnay, Semillon, Trinity White (Chardonnay, Semillon, Sauvignon Blanc), Cabernet Sauvignon, Trinity Red (Cabernet blend), Cabernet Shiraz. Durham Chardonnay is top-of-the-range Chardonnay.
summary For the time being at least, Newton Potter continues to own Allanmere. While it has a relatively low profile in conventional retail markets, cellar-door sales are flourishing in response to the ever-increasing tourist traffic in the Hunter Valley. No recent tastings.

allinda NR

119 Lorimers Lane, Dixons Creek, Vic 3775 **region** Yarra Valley
phone (03) 5965 2450 **fax** (03) 5965 2467 **open** Weekends and public holidays 10–6
winemaker Al Fencaros **production** 2000 **est.** 1991
product range ($14–22.50 CD) Riesling, Sauvignon Blanc, Chardonnay, Late Harvest Riesling, Cabernets.
summary Winemaker Al Fencaros is a graduate of Bachelor of Wine Science from Charles Sturt University, and was formerly employed by De Bortoli in the Yarra Valley. All of the Allinda wines are produced on site; all except the Shiraz (from Heathcote) are estate-grown from a little over 3 hectares of vineyards.

amberley estate ★★★★

Thornton Road, Yallingup, WA 6282 **region** Margaret River
phone (08) 9755 2288 **fax** (08) 9755 2171 **open** 7 days 10–4.30
winemaker Eddie Price, Greg Tilbrook **production** 35 000 **est.** 1986
product range ($12.50–31 CD) Semillon Sauvignon Blanc, Classic Margaret River Semillon Chardonnay, Semillon, Chardonnay, Chenin Blanc, Nouveau, Cabernet Merlot, Shiraz.
summary Based its initial growth on the basis of its ultra-commercial, fairly sweet Chenin Blanc which continues to provide the volume for the brand, selling out well prior to the following release. However, the quality of all of the other wines has risen markedly over recent years as the 31 hectares of estate plantings have become fully mature.

Amberley Estate Semillon Sauvignon Blanc

A blend of 80% Semillon and 20% Sauvignon Blanc; a portion of the Semillon component is fermented in American oak hogsheads, and left in oak for a further two months. The remaining Semillon and the Sauvignon Blanc is fermented in stainless steel. Has produced an outstanding wine in both 1995 and 1996. The '97 was selected in the Top 100 Sydney International Wine Competition 1998.

1997 Medium to full yellow-green; the bouquet is complex, powerful, fruit-driven with strong tropical fruit. The palate has excellent structure and length, with touches of herb, lemon and mineral, the oak contributing more to the texture than to the flavour. **rating:** 90

best drinking 1998 – 1999 **best vintages** '95, '96, '97 **drink with** Richer Asian seafood dishes • $16

Amberley Estate Shiraz

Strongly flavoured and positively styled wine, first made in 1994, and has since established itself as one of Amberley's showcase wines.

ŸŸŸŸ **1996** Strong purple-red; there is youthful, ripe black cherry fruit and some American oak on the bouquet. A wine which exhibits rather more power than finesse or even varietal character on the palate, but does have all of the building blocks there to flower as it matures in bottle. Lots of tannins and extract, and the components are well balanced. **rating:** 86

⇨ **best drinking** 2001 – 2006 **best vintages** '94, '95, '96 **drink with** Moroccan lamb • $31

anderson NR

Lot 12 Chiltern Road, Rutherglen, Vic 3685 **region** Rutherglen
phone (02) 6032 8111 **open** 7 days 10–5
winemaker Howard Anderson **production** 1200 **est.** 1993
product range ($11–25 CD) Semillon, Chenin Blanc, Doux Blanc, Chardonnay, Soft Cabernet, Shiraz, Cabernet Merlot, Cabernet Sauvignon, Late Harvest Tokay, Sparkling, Fortifieds.
summary With a winemaking career spanning 30 years, including a stint at Seppelt Great Western, Howard Anderson and family have started their own winery, ultimately intending to specialise in sparkling wine made entirely on site.

andrew garrett ★★★★

Kangarilla Road, McLaren Vale, SA 5171 **region** McLaren Vale
phone (08) 8323 8853 **fax** (08) 8323 8550 **open** 7 days 10–5
winemaker Phillip Reschke **production** 127 700 **est.** 1983
product range ($10–16 R) Semillon, Sauvignon Blanc, Chardonnay, Cabernet Merlot, Bold Shiraz, Vintage Pinot Chardonnay.
summary Effectively another brand in the Mildara Blass wine group, with many of the wines now not having a sole McLaren Vale source, but instead drawn from regions across south-eastern Australia. Over the past few years, winemaker Phillip Reschke has produced some excellent wines which provide great value for money, particularly for the smooth, peachy Chardonnay.

Andrew Garrett Chardonnay

A blend of 55% Padthaway, 30% McLaren Vale and 15% Cowra fruit barrel-fermented in a mix of American and French oak hogsheads. Over the past few vintages has been particularly good, a testimonial to the winemaking skills of Phillip Reschke.

ŸŸŸY **1996** Medium to full yellow-green; the effective use of oak together with ripe fig and melon fruit produces a full and complex bouquet. The palate, too, is honest and full-flavoured, the oak judiciously handled. Probably best earlier in its life. **rating:** 84

⇨ **best drinking** 1998 – 1999 **best vintages** '95, '96 **drink with** Loin of pork • $12

Andrew Garrett Bold Shiraz

I'm not too sure about the brand name for this wine, as it recalls a Kaiser Stuhl Bold Red which failed dismally 20 years ago. This is in fact a far better wine than either the name or the price would suggest, and what is more has been given Rolls Royce oak treatment in new French and American oak barrels for 12 months.

ŸŸŸŸ **1996** Strong red-purple; masses of dark cherry fruit with some more briary undertones, and subtle oak on the bouquet. The palate shows rather more vanillin American oak than does the bouquet, but works well, for there is plenty of rich, sweet fruit to justify that oak. **rating:** 87

⇨ **best drinking** 1988 – 2003 **best vintages** NA **drink with** Barbecued red meat • $12

andrew harris vineyards ★★★★☆

Sydney Road, Mudgee, NSW 2850 **region** Mudgee
phone (02) 6373 1215 **fax** (02) 6373 1296 **open** Not
winemaker Simon Gilbert (Contract) **production** 5000 **est.** 1991
product range ($15–40 R) Premium Chardonnay, Shiraz, Premium Cabernet Sauvignon; at the top come Reserve Chardonnay, Reserve Shiraz and Reserve Cabernet Sauvignon; super premium is Shiraz Cabernet Sauvignon The Vision.
summary Andrew and Debbie Harris have lost no time since purchasing a 300-hectare sheep station southeast of Mudgee in 1991. The first 6 hectares of vineyard were planted in that year, and have since been expanded to 90 hectares. A substantial portion of the production is sold to others, but right from the first vintage limited quantities of high-quality wines have been made under the Andrew Harris label (by Simon Gilbert as contract winemaker) which have deservedly enjoyed considerable show success. Releases in transition; no new tastings.

angove's ★★★☆

Bookmark Avenue, Renmark, SA 5341 **region** Riverland
phone (08) 8595 1311 **fax** (08) 8595 1583 **open** Mon–Fri 9–5
winemaker Garry Wall **production** 1 million **est.** 1886
product range ($3.15–45 CD) Classic Reserve Riesling, Colombard, Sauvignon Blanc, Chardonnay, Shiraz, Mondiale Shiraz Cabernet, Cabernet Sauvignon; Mondiale (White), Mondiale Shiraz Cabernet; Sarnia Farm Chardonnay, Cabernet Sauvignon; Floreate; Cheaper Butterfly Ridge varietals and Misty Vineyards generics; also specialist Brandy producer; Fortifieds.
summary Exemplifies the economies of scale achievable in the Australian Riverland without compromising potential quality. Very good technology provides wines which are never poor and which can sometimes exceed their theoretical station in life. The white varietals are best. Angove's expansion into Padthaway has resulted in estate-grown premium wines at the top of the range.

Angove's Sarnia Farm Cabernet Sauvignon

A new venture for Angove's which has hitherto produced almost all of its wines from its Nanya Vineyard in the Riverland, making occasional Limited Release/Winemaker Selection with grapes purchased from various premium areas. 1993 was the inaugural vintage. As with the Chardonnay, gained the name 'Sarnia Farm' with the second release, and which really impresses with its most recent release. It may well be that a maturing vineyard and/or better viticulture is playing a role.

🍷🍷🍷🍷 **1996** Medium to full red-purple; an attractive bouquet with sweet cassis and cedar aromas is followed by a palate which, while only of medium weight, is quite luscious, with sweet cassis/berry fruit supported by sweet oak. Soft tannin finish. **rating:** 87

⇨ **best drinking** 1999 – 2004 **best vintages** '93, '96 **drink with** Beef Provençale • $13.15

---

antcliff's chase NR

RMB 4510, Caveat via Seymour, Vic 3660 **region** Central Victorian High Country
phone (03) 5790 4333 **fax** (03) 5790 4333 **open** Weekends 10–5
winemaker Chris Bennett, Ian Leamon **production** 800 **est.** 1982
product range ($14–30 CD) Riesling, Chardonnay, Pinot Noir, Cabernet Franc.

summary A small family enterprise which commenced planting the vineyards at an elevation of 600 metres in the Strathbogie Ranges in 1982, but which has only recently commenced wine production from the 4-hectare vineyard. As the scarecrow label indicates, birds are a major problem for remote vineyards such as this.

apsley gorge vineyard ★★★★☆

Rosedale Road, Bicheno, Tas 7215 **region** Southern Tasmania
phone (03) 6375 1221 **fax** (03) 6375 1589 **open** By appointment
winemaker Andrew Hood (Contract) **production** 1000 **est.** 1988
product range ($20 ML) Chardonnay, Pinot Noir.
summary While nominally situated at Bicheno on the East Coast, Apsley Gorge is in fact some distance inland, taking its name from a mountain pass. Clearly, it shares with the other East Coast wineries the capacity to produce Chardonnay and Pinot Noir of excellent quality, with skilled winemaking by Andrew Hood doing the rest.

Apsley Gorge Chardonnay

Contract-made by Andrew Hood in tiny quantities since 1994. It is a wine that has grown in stature year by year, with the '96 and '97 vintages both absolutely excellent, and at the top of the Tasmanian quality tree. Interestingly, the only Chardonnay made by Andrew Hood which normally undergoes malolactic fermentation, this being the express wish of Apsley Gorge owners Brian Frankland and Greg Walch. The '97 won a gold medal at the 1998 Tasmanian Wines Show.

🍷🍷🍷🍷🍷 **1997** Light to medium yellow-green; complex grapefruit and other citrus aromas with sophisticated, albeit subtle, oak on the bouquet is followed by a palate with real style. Here melon and grapefruit flavours are balanced by appropriate acidity and just a twist of oak. **rating:** 93

⇨ **best drinking** 1998 – 2002 **best vintages** '96, '97 **drink with** Sugar-cured tuna • $20

aquila estate ★★★

85 Carabooda Road, Carabooda, WA 6033 **region** Swan District
phone (08) 9407 5100 **fax** (08) 9407 5070 **open** Not
winemaker Elaine Washer **production** 10 000 **est.** 1993
product range ($13.95–17.95 R) Semillon, Sauvignon Blanc, Chardonnay, Reflections (white blend), Cabernet Sauvignon, Flame (red blend).
summary Aquila Estate appeared out of nowhere, as it were. It is situated on the Washer family's 15-hectare avocado plantation at Carabooda, north of Perth, which has 4 hectares of estate vines coming into production. Most of the grapes will, however, come from the Margaret River and Boyup Brook regions under long-term contracts. Winemaker and chief executive Elaine Washer is a 25-year-old science graduate with an honours degree in Genetic Engineering. Her brother Stewart is a specialist in DNA research.

arlewood estate NR

Harmans Road South, Willyabrup, WA 6284 **region** Margaret River
phone (08) 9755 6267 **fax** (08) 9755 6267 **open** Fri–Mon 11–4, 7 days during school holidays
winemaker Jurg Muggli (Contract) **production** 2000 **est.** 1988
product range ($13–19 CD) Semillon, Sauvignon Blanc Semillon, Margaret River Classic, Liaison (sweet), Cabernet Sauvignon, Port.

summary Liz and John Wojturski have established their 2.5-hectare vineyard between Ashbrook and Vasse Felix, with contract winemaking. Production has now reached its projected maximum of around 2000 cases.

Arlewood Estate Cabernet Sauvignon

The only red wine from Arlewood Estate but on the evidence of the 1996, an extremely creditable one.

🍷🍷🍷🍷 **1996** Medium to full red-purple; a rich and concentrated bouquet with cassis, berry and spice aromas with well-balanced oak. The palate ranges through flavours of spice, leaf, mint and cassis, finishing with quite firm but not overly aggressive tannins. **rating:** 86

⇨ **best drinking** 2001 – 2006 **best vintages** NA **drink with** Braised beef with olives • $19

arrowfield ★★★

Denman Road, Jerry's Plains, NSW 2330 **region** Upper Hunter Valley
phone (02) 6576 4041 **fax** (02) 6576 4144 **open** 7 days 10–5
winemaker Don Buchanan **production** 100 000 **est.** 1968
product range ($13–21 R) Top-of-the-range Show Reserve Chardonnay, Semillon, Shiraz, Cabernet Sauvignon; Cowra Chardonnay, Merlot, Late Harvest Gewurztraminer; Arrowfield varietals Chardonnay, Semillon Chardonnay, Sauvignon Blanc, Traminer Riesling, Late Harvest Riesling, Shiraz, Cabernet Merlot; Sparkling and Fortifieds; also Simon Whitlam range of Semillon, Semillon Chardonnay, Shiraz, Cabernet Sauvignon.
summary After largely dropping the Arrowfield name in favour of Mountarrow and a plethora of other brands, this Japanese-owned company has come full circle, once again marketing the wines solely under the Arrowfield label. Its principal grape sources are Cowra and the Upper Hunter, but it does venture further afield from time to time.

Arrowfield Shiraz

Arrowfield releases both a Show Reserve Shiraz and a lower-priced varietal Shiraz. Four tastings of each on separate occasions, some in shows and competitions, throughout 1997 left the varietal Shiraz (admittedly from 1995, as opposed to the '94 of the Reserve) a long way in front. The varietal is a quite delicious wine, although one would be hard-pressed to guess that it came – as it apparently does – from the Hunter Valley. The '95 has won a trophy and several gold medals.

🍷🍷🍷🍷🍷 **1995** Medium to full red-purple; a complex, rich and concentrated bouquet with strong black cherry fruit and full-blooded vanillin oak. There is lots of dark berry, dark chocolate and vanilla oak on the palate, which is textured and layered with pronounced yet soft tannins. **rating:** 93

⇨ **best drinking** 1998 – 2003 **best vintages** NA **drink with** Marinated beef • $21

arthurs creek estate ★★★★★

Strathewen Road, Arthurs Creek, Vic 3099 **region** Yarra Valley
phone (03) 9827 6629 **fax** (03) 9824 0252 **open** Not
winemaker Mitchelton (Contract), Gary Baldwin (Consultant) **production** 1500 **est.** 1976
product range ($23.65–25.35 R) Chardonnay, Cabernet Sauvignon.

summary A latter-day folly of leading Melbourne QC, S E K Hulme, who planted 1.5 hectares each of semillon, chardonnay, and cabernet sauvignon at Arthurs Creek in the mid-1970s, and commenced to have wine made by various people, for 15 years before deciding to sell any of it. A ruthless weeding-out process followed, with only the best of the older vintages offered. The Cabernets from the 1990s are absolutely outstanding, deeply fruited and marvellously structured.

Arthurs Creek Cabernet Sauvignon

Since 1992 the winemaking has been carried out by Mitchelton; at the 1994 Victorian Wine Show the '92 Cabernet Sauvignon won the top gold medal in Class 22 (1992 and older Cabernets), the 1992 won a silver medal in Class 18, while the 1994 Cabernet Sauvignon was awarded the trophy for Best Cabernet Sauvignon of Show. One is never quite sure which vintage of Arthurs Creek will be on sale at any one time, but as at early 1998 the '93 and '94 were available, the '95 coming up.

🍷🍷🍷🍷🍷 **1993** Strong, deep and bright red-purple; the bouquet is powerful and dense, with a mix of blackberry, olive, forest and earth aromas; very powerful and concentrated blackberry, chocolate and earth fruit flavours on the palate finish with strong but fine tannins. **rating:** 93

🍷🍷🍷🍷🍷 **1994** Medium red-purple; smooth, blackberry fruit with slightly foresty/briary characters on the bouquet leads into a powerful, concentrated, almost tangy palate with blackberry, briar and mint flavours, and those hallmark tannins on the finish. **rating:** 91

🍷🍷🍷🍷🍷 **1995** Medium to full red-purple; a clean but dense bouquet with blackberry, cassis, chocolate and ripe mint fruit is followed by a wine with wonderful mouthfeel and richness, and sweet, fine tannins running throughout. **rating:** 92

⇨ **best drinking** 2000 – 2010 **best vintages** '82, '87, '89, '91, '92, '93, '94, '95 **drink with** Lamb fillets • $25.35

ashbrook estate ★★★★★

Harmans Road South, Willyabrup, WA 6284 **region** Margaret River
phone (08) 9755 6262 **fax** (08) 9755 6290 **open** 7 days 11–5
winemaker Tony Devitt, Brian Devitt **production** 8000 **est.** 1975
product range ($14–23 CD) Gold Label Riesling, Black Label Riesling, Semillon, Sauvignon Blanc, Chardonnay, Verdelho, Cabernet Sauvignon.

summary A fastidious maker of consistently outstanding estate-grown table wines but which shuns publicity and the wine show system alike, and is less well known than it deserves to be, selling much of its wine through the cellar door and by an understandably very loyal mailing list clientele. All of the white wines are of the highest quality, year in, year out.

Ashbrook Estate Semillon

All of the Ashbrook Estate wines are estate-grown, the Semillon from 2.6 hectares of vines. Fermented in stainless steel, and not given any time in oak, the wine shows the herbaceous style of Margaret River Semillon to best advantage.

🍷🍷🍷🍷🍷 **1997** Light to medium yellow-green; there is excellent varietal fruit on the bouquet, showing perfect balance and ripeness, faintly herbaceous (in the best sense) yet not green. The palate, too, shows a range of flavours from sweet, almost tropical, through to more herbaceous notes. As ever, a very distinguished wine. **rating:** 92

⇨ **best drinking** 1998 – 2003 **best vintages** '87, '92, '93, '94, '95, '97 **drink with** Blanquette of veal • $14

asher NR

360 Goldsworthy Road, Lovely Banks, Geelong, Vic 3231 **region** Geelong
phone (03) 5276 1365 **open** Sat, public holidays 10–5, Sun 12–5
winemaker Brian Moten **production** Minuscule **est.** 1975
product range ($10 CD) Sauvignon Blanc, Cabernet Sauvignon, Malbec.
summary A tiny, semi-home-winemaking operation situated at the picturesquely named Lovely Banks on the outskirts of Geelong.

ashton hills ★★★★☆

Tregarthen Road, Ashton, SA 5137 **region** Adelaide Hills
phone (08) 8390 1243 **fax** (08) 8390 1243 **open** Weekends 11–5.30
winemaker Stephen George **production** 1500 **est.** 1982
product range ($16–25 R) Chardonnay, Riesling, Salmon Brut, Pinot Noir, Obliqua (Cabernet Merlot).
summary Stephen George wears three winemaker hats: one for Ashton Hills, drawing upon a 3.5-hectare estate vineyard high in the Adelaide Hills; one for Galah Wines and one for Wendouree. It would be hard to imagine three wineries producing more diverse styles, with the elegance and finesse of Ashton Hills at one end of the spectrum, the awesome power of Wendouree at the other. The Riesling has moved into the highest echelon.

Ashton Hills Riesling

A wine of unusually consistent style, and which invariably ages slowly. The natural acidity is high, and the fruit always tight and often inexpressive when the wine is young, slowly opening up as it evolves in bottle. These elegant wines are ideal to complement food.

🍷🍷🍷🍷🍷 **1997** Light green-yellow; the bouquet is fragrant, with intense passionfruit and lime aromas, the palate crisp, clean and firm, with lime and mineral flavours. Great acidity and a long finish. Will develop superbly. **rating:** 94

➪ **best drinking** 2000 – 2010 **best vintages** '89, '90, '91, '93, '94, '96, '97 **drink with** Fresh asparagus • $16

Ashton Hills Chardonnay

Like all the Ashton Hills wines, relatively slow-developing, progressively building complexity as it ages.

🍷🍷🍷🍷 **1995** Glowing yellow-green; now has very complex and toasty bottle-developed aroma; the palate shows similar complex, bottle-developed characters with fig and melon fruit under more toasty/buttery characters. **rating:** 87

➪ **best drinking** 1998 – 2002 **best vintages** '95 **drink with** Roast veal • $22

---

ashwood grove NR

Wood Wood, Swan Hill, Vic 3585 **region** Murray Darling and Swan Hill
phone (03) 5030 5291 **fax** (03) 5030 5605 **open** By appointment
winemaker Andrew Peace **production** NA **est.** 1995
product range ($10–12 R) Murphy's Block Classic Dry White and Classic Dry Red; Lady Hamilton Chardonnay, Grenache, Shiraz.

summary The Peace family has been a major Swan Hill grape grower since 1980, and moved into winemaking with the opening of a $3 million winery in 1997. The modestly priced wines are aimed at supermarket-type outlets in Australia and, in particular, at the export market.

ashworths hill NR

Ashworths Road, Lancefield, Vic 3435 **region** Macedon
phone (03) 5429 1689 **fax** (03) 5429 1689 **open** 7 days 10–6
winemaker Anne Manning **production** 100 **est.** 1982
product range ($12–20 CD) Macedon Ranges Cabernet Sauvignon is the flagship; Victorian Riesling and Chardonnay also available.
summary Peg and Ken Reaburn offer light refreshments throughout the day, the property offering scenic views of the Macedon Ranges.

augustine ★★★☆

George Campbell Drive, Mudgee, NSW 2850 **region** Mudgee
phone (02) 6372 3880 **fax** (02) 6372 2977 **open** 7 days 10–4
winemaker Rothbury Estate **production** 5000 **est.** 1918
product range ($10–14 R) Mudgee Semillon, Verdelho, Chardonnay, Shiraz, Cabernet Sauvignon; Settler's Creek Semillon and Chardonnay.
summary The historic Augustine Vineyard, established by the Roth family but purchased by Dr Thomas Fiaschi in 1917, passed into the control of Rothbury Estate in 1993. Wines are available cellar door under the Augustine label, but otherwise only appear as The Rothbury Estate Mudgee range.

Augustine Cabernet Sauvignon

Richly flavoured, juicy in typical Mudgee style and, of course, technically well made.
▼▼▼▽ **1995** Medium red-purple; a soft, gently plummy bouquet with some spice and earth notes. There is lots of sweet, juicy plummy fruit on the palate, rounded off with soft tannins. Nice mouthfeel. **rating:** 84

➾ **best drinking** 1998 – 2003 **best vintages** NA **drink with** Steak and kidney pie • NA

auldstone 

Booths Road, Taminick via Glenrowan, Vic 3675 **region** Glenrowan
phone (03) 5766 2237 **open** Thur-Sun 9–5
winemaker Michael Reid **production** 4000 **est.** 1987
product range ($10–21 CD) Riesling, Traminer Riesling, Chardonnay, Late Picked Riesling, Shiraz, Cabernet, Herceynia Tawny Port, Boweya Muscat, Sparkling Shiraz.
summary Michael and Nancy Reid have restored a century-old stone winery and have replanted the largely abandoned vineyard around it. Gourmet lunches are available on weekends.

Auldstone Cabernet Sauvignon

Made in similar rich, dense and concentrated style to that of the Shiraz. Widely separated tastings in different circumstances come up with some similar taste descriptors for both wines, notably dried prune. Drawn from the heart of 6.5 hectares of estate plantings.

🍷🍷🍷🍷 **1996** Deep red; solid chocolatey, briary and dried prune aromas with varietal earthy overtones on the bouquet; a rich, full dark prune, berry and chocolatey-flavoured palate follows, with a slightly tough finish. **rating:** 84

➾ **best drinking** 2001 – 2006 **best vintages** NA **drink with** Beef in red wine sauce • $14

austin's barrabool NR

50 Lemins Road, Waurn Ponds, Vic 3221 **region** Geelong
phone (03) 5241 8114 **fax** (03) 5241 8122 **open** By appointment
winemaker John Ellis (Contract), Pamela Austin **production** 1350 **est.** 1982
product range ($15–25 CD) Riesling, Chardonnay, Cabernet Sauvignon.
summary A tiny winery, selling part of the production from its 10-hectare vineyard, and having a portion contract-made by John Ellis. Over the years, Riesling has been one of the best wines, the Chardonnay also good.

Austin's Barrabool Riesling

A wine which distinguished itself (on my score sheet, at least) at the 1998 Winewise Small Makers Competition.

🍷🍷🍷🍷 **1997** Medium yellow-green; the bouquet is light but crisp, with fine lime and toast aromas, the palate with interesting lime/lemon tingle flavours; good weight, length and balance. **rating:** 87

➾ **best drinking** 1998 – 2003 **best vintages** NA **drink with** Marinated scallops • $15

avalon vineyard ★★☆

RMB 9556 Whitfield Road, Wangaratta, Vic 3678 **region** King Valley
phone (03) 5729 3629 **fax** (03) 5729 3635 **open** 7 days 10–5
winemaker Doug Groom **production** 800 **est.** 1981
product range ($11–18 CD) Chardonnay, Semillon, Sauvignon Blanc, Cabernet Sauvignon, Pinot Noir, Pinot Noir Méthode Champenoise.
summary Avalon Vineyard is situated in the King Valley, 4 kilometres north of Whitfield. Much of the production from the 10-hectare vineyard is sold to other makers, with limited quantities made by Doug Groom, a graduate of Roseworthy, and one of the owners of the property.

avalon wines NR

1605 Bailey Road, Glen Forrest, WA 6071 **region** Perth Hills
phone (08) 9298 8049 **open** By appointment
winemaker Lyndon Crockett **production** 100 **est.** 1986
product range ($10–14 CD) Chardonnay, Semillon, Cabernet Sauvignon.
summary One of the newer wineries in the Perth Hills, drawing upon three-quarters of a hectare each of chardonnay, semillon and cabernet sauvignon.

baileys of glenrowan ★★★★★

Cnr Taminick Gap Road and Upper Taminick Road, Glenrowan, Vic 3675 **region** Glenrowan
phone (03) 5766 2392 **fax** (03) 5766 2596 **open** Mon-Fri 9–5, weekends 10–5
winemaker Allan Hart **production** 30 000 **est.** 1870

product range ($15–50 CD) Classic Chardonnay, Riesling, Touriga, Shiraz, 1920's Block Shiraz are the principal wines; Warby Range, Founders and Winemaker's Selection Tokay and Muscat; Phantom's Lake Chardonnay and Shiraz were introduced in 1997 in fancy bottles.

summary Now part of the sprawling Mildara Blass empire, inherited via the Rothbury takeover. Has made some excellent Shiraz in recent years, but its greatest strength lies in its fortified wines. It is for these wines that the winery rating is given.

Baileys 1920's Block Shiraz

Baileys was founded in 1870 by Varley Bailey, and in 1920 – to celebrate the 50th anniversary – a special block of shiraz was planted. It is from these vines that the wine is made, first produced in 1991 and immediately proclaiming its class. Only 900 cases of the wine are produced each year.

🍷🍷🍷🍷 **1996** Medium purple-red; a clean and fresh bouquet with black cherry, earth, spice and liquorice aromas is followed by a fresh, firm palate; cherry, spice and liquorice are all there, with crisp acid to close. Very much in the style of this block, unusual in the context of northeast Victoria. **rating:** 87

➩ **best drinking** 2002 – 2016 **best vintages** '91, '92, '93, '96 **drink with** Rare rump steak, venison • $22

Baileys Founder Liqueur Tokay

The midpoint of the Tokays produced by Baileys, coming between Warby Range at the bottom end and Winemaker's Selection at the top end. In the totally distinctive, rich and sweet Baileys' style, with more accent on complexity and less on primary fruit than that of Morris; one of the great classics.

🍷🍷🍷🍷 **NV** Medium golden brown; full, complex sweeter style of Tokay with clean spirit. The palate is rich, full and textured with flavours of butterscotch and sweet biscuit, and a chewy texture, but finishing long and clean. **rating:** 89

➩ **best drinking** 1998 – 1999 **best vintages** NA **drink with** Winter aperitif; summer after dinner • $18

Baileys Winemaker's Selection Old Liqueur Tokay

Made in very limited quantities, and these days released on strict allocation as the popularity of these very old wines has deservedly grown. Made from muscadelle (as are all northeastern Victorian Tokays) and is preferred by many winemakers to Muscat because of its greater elegance.

🍷🍷🍷🍷🍷 **NV** Deep brown; the bouquet shows obvious barrel-aged rancio characters, very complex but still retaining good varietal character. The wine has outstanding structure in the mouth, with complexity apparent immediately the wine is tasted. The flavours run in the cold tea/butterscotch/brandysnap spectrum, finishing with cleansing acidity. **rating:** 94

➩ **best drinking** 1998 – 1999 **best vintages** NA **drink with** After coffee; alternative to Cognac • $50

Baileys Founder Liqueur Muscat

Made from Brown Frontignac, otherwise known as Brown Muscat, and the best known of the fortified wines of northeastern Victoria. As one would expect, in the rich Baileys mould. One of four Muscats produced, starting at the bottom with Warby Range, then Founder Liqueur, then Gold Label and ultimately Winemaker's Selection.

ŸŸŸŸ **NV** Medium red-brown; an arresting bouquet with hints of spice to the sweet, ripe, complex fruit. The same unusual spicy/cinnamon aspects are apparent on the rich and complex palate. **rating:** 88

➯ **best drinking** 1998 – 1999 **best vintages** NA **drink with** After coffee; alternative to Cognac • $18

bald mountain ★★★☆

Hickling Lane, Wallangarra, Qld 4383 **region** Granite Belt
phone (07) 4684 3186 **fax** (07) 4684 3433 **open** 7 days 10–5
winemaker Simon Gilbert (Contract) **production** 5000 **est.** 1985
product range ($11–19 CD) Classic Queenslander (in fact 100% Sauvignon Blanc), Chardonnay, Late Harvest Sauvignon Blanc, Shiraz, Shiraz Cabernet.
summary Denis Parsons is a self-taught but exceptionally competent vigneron who has turned Bald Mountain into the viticultural showpiece of the Granite Belt. In various regional and national shows since 1988, Bald Mountain has won almost 70 show awards, placing it at the forefront of the Granite Belt wineries. The two Sauvignon Blanc-based wines, Classic Queenslander and the occasional non-vintage Late Harvest Sauvignon Blanc, are interesting alternatives to the mainstream wines. Future production will also see grapes coming from new vineyards near Tenterfield just across the border in New South Wales.

Bald Mountain Chardonnay

Produced from 1.5 hectares of immaculately maintained estate plantings. The wine has a very particular and distinctive bouquet which is strongly reminiscent of many Hunter Valley Chardonnays, notably when fermented with a particular type of yeast. It is interesting to see the character also appear in the Granite Belt. As at 1998, four vintages of Chardonnay ('93 to '96 inclusive) were available as part of the Vintage Series Pack then on issue. Of the Chardonnays, the '95 is the best, a fact attested to by its solid show record. However, there is a strong family style which runs through all of the Chardonnays, all of which have had significant show success.
ŸŸŸŸ **1995** Medium yellow-green; a rich, full toasty/buttery bouquet is followed by an equivalently rich buttery/toasty/peachy palate, which has good length and acidity. **rating:** 85

➯ **best drinking** 1998 – 1999 **best vintages** '92, '93, '95 **drink with** Seafood pasta • $11.50

Bald Mountain Shiraz

Two vintages of Shiraz ('93 and '94) were available in 1998, both very attractive wines showing fully ripened fruit.
ŸŸŸŸ **1993** Medium red-purple; sweet chocolate and berry aromas of medium to full intensity are supported by subtle oak on both bouquet and palate. Still quite youthful, well balanced and again with just a trace of lift. **rating:** 85
ŸŸŸŸ **1994** Medium red-purple; sweet, ripe chocolate, cherry and vanilla aromas are followed by a lively chocolate and berry-flavoured palate. A degree of volatile lift is more help than hindrance. **rating:** 86

➯ **best drinking** 1998 – 2003 **best vintages** NA **drink with** Beef in red wine • NA

Bald Mountain Shiraz Cabernet

An estate-grown wine which achieved considerable show success. The two components are picked at the same time and fermented together. The '94, which won a gold medal at the Royal Brisbane Wine Show (in open classes, not Queensland classes), and silvers at Adelaide and Perth (together with a swag of bronze medals) has achieved a higher level of success than any other Queensland-grown red wine in national wine shows. However, there will be no further release until the 1999 vintage, as the cabernet vines had to be replanted after 1994 due to leaf roll virus.

🍷🍷🍷🍷 **1994** Light to medium red-purple; a quite fragrant bouquet with a mix of minty and sweeter berry aromas is followed by a palate with greater weight and richness than the bouquet suggests, fleshed out by a hint of sweet vanilla oak and rounded, fluffy tannins. **rating:** 87

⇨ **best drinking** 1998 – 2002 **best vintages** '94 **drink with** Lamb kebabs • $16.30

baldivis estate ★★☆

Lot 165 River Road, Baldivis, WA 6171 **region** South West Coast
phone (08) 9525 2066 **fax** (08) 9525 2411 **open** Mon–Fri 10–4, weekends, holidays 11–5
winemaker Jane Gilham **production** 6000 **est.** 1982
product range ($9.95–28.95 CD) Wooded and Unwooded Chardonnay, Classic White, Late Picked Semillon, Blue Rock Pinot Noir Cabernet, Cabernet Merlot, Cabernet Sauvignon Reserve.
summary Part of a very large mixed horticultural enterprise on the Tuart Sands of the coastal plain. There is ample viticultural and winemaking expertise; although the wines are pleasant, soft and light-bodied, they tend to lack concentration.

balgownie estate ★★★★

Hermitage Road, Maiden Gully, Vic 3551 **region** Bendigo
phone (03) 5449 6222 **fax** (03) 5449 6506 **open** Mon–Sat 9–5
winemaker Lindsay Ross **production** 17 000 **est.** 1969
product range ($22 R) Estate-produced Shiraz and Cabernet Sauvignon; Premier Cuvée (second, non-estate label), Chardonnay and Cabernet Shiraz.
summary After 20 or so years in Mildara ownership, has finally emerged in its own right, producing consistently strong, characterful Shiraz and Cabernet Sauvignon, with a string of good vintages in the mid-1990s.

Balgownie Estate Shiraz

Produced from fully-mature estate vineyards established in the early 1970s, and with a proud history dating back to that time. After an uncertain period in the second half of the 1980s and early '90s, has returned to form in no uncertain fashion.

🍷🍷🍷🍷🍷 **1996** Medium to full red-purple; powerful and earthy dark chocolate and blackberry fruit aromas introduce a rich and substantial palate. The flavours run through dark chocolate, raspberry and blackberry with soft, chewy tannins and subtle oak on the finish. **rating:** 90

⇨ **best drinking** 2001 – 2008 **best vintages** '91, '93, '96 **drink with** Beef in red wine • $22

Balgownie Estate Cabernet Sauvignon

The best known of the Balgownie wines in the height of its glory days of the mid-1970s, partly because there were so few small-winemaker Cabernet Sauvignons around at the time. After a period in the wilderness, has bounced back to top form.

🍷🍷🍷🍷 **1995** Dense red-purple; the bouquet, like the colour, is dense, with dark chocolate, earth and berry fruit. A somewhat rustic wine on the palate, once again powerful and dense, with earthy/chocolatey flavours. Masses of character and tannins. **rating:** 86

⇨ **best drinking** 2000 – 2008 **best vintages** '75, '76, '80, '94 **drink with** Beef casserole • $22

ballandean estate ★★★

Sundown Road, Ballandean, Qld 4382 **region** Granite Belt
phone (07) 4684 1226 **fax** (07) 4684 1288 **open** 7 days 9–5 pm
winemaker Mark Ravenscroft **production** 9000 **est.** 1970
product range ($7–25 CD) Riesling, Semillon, Sauvignon Blanc, Sylvaner Late Harvest, Dolce Rosso (Cabernet Late Harvest), Granite Range Shiraz, Print Label Shiraz Cabernet Merlot Malbec, Port.
summary The senior winery of the Granite Belt, and by far the largest. The white wines are of diverse but interesting styles, the red wines smooth and usually well made. The estate specialty Sylvaner Late Harvest is a particularly interesting wine of good flavour.

balnarring 

62 Bittern-Dromana Road, Balnarring, Vic 3926 **region** Mornington Peninsula
phone (03) 5983 5258 **open** 7 days 10–4
winemaker Bruce Paul, Stan Paul **production** 1200 **est.** 1982
product range ($11–15 ML) Chardonnay, Riesling, Gewurztraminer, Pinot Noir, Merlot, Cabernet Merlot.
summary Over the years, the wines of Balnarring have been made at various wineries under contract, but have shown a consistent vineyard style, with the red wines in particular possessing exceptional colour and depth of flavour. Winemaking is now carried out by owners Bruce and Stan Paul.

balnaves of coonawarra 

Main Road, Coonawarra, SA 5263 **region** Coonawarra
phone (08) 8737 2946 **fax** (08) 8737 2945 **open** Mon-Fri 9–5, weekends 10–5
winemaker Peter Bissell **production** 8000 **est.** 1975
product range ($17–28 R) Chardonnay, Sparkling Cabernet, The Blend (Merlot Cabernet Franc), Shiraz, Cabernet Sauvignon.
summary Former Hungerford Hill vineyard manager and now viticultural consultant-cum-grape grower Doug Balnaves established his vineyard in 1975, but did not launch into winemaking until 1990, with colleague Ralph Fowler as contract-maker in the early years. A striking new 300-tonne winery was built and was in operation for the 1996 vintage, with former Wynns Coonawarra Estate assistant winemaker Peter Bissell in charge. The expected leap in quality has indeed materialised with the 1996 and subsequent vintages.

Balnaves Chardonnay

Produced from a careful selection from part of the estate vineyards. The clarified juice is barrel-fermented in new Seguin Moreau French oak hogsheads followed by lees stirring for two months, followed by a further two months oak maturation before relatively early bottling.

🍷🍷🍷🍷 **1997** Light to medium yellow-green; fragrant melon, citrus and fig fruit is supported by subtle, gently spicy oak on the bouquet. A well-balanced and structured wine on the palate with melon, citrus and cashew flavours; subtle oak. Tighter than the '96, but still a fraction soft. **rating:** 87

➾ **best drinking** 1998 – 1999 **best vintages** '92, '93, '94 **drink with** Robe crayfish • $17

Balnaves Shiraz

Only produced when seasonal conditions permit; not made, for example, in either 1994 or 1995. Selected from estate-grown grapes from the highest and stoniest part of the Balnaves shiraz plantings. The fermentation is commenced in vinimatic (rotating fermenter) and completed in new and second-use American oak barrels.

🍷🍷🍷🍷🍸 **1996** Medium to full red-purple; a most attractive bouquet, with rich, dark plum, chocolate and other sweet fruit aromas; an almost sumptuous wine on the palate, with rich, dark plum fruit flavours cradled in vanillin oak. **rating:** 92

⇨ **best drinking** 2000 – 2007 **best vintages** '93, '96 **drink with** Cotechino sausages • $18

Balnaves Cabernet Sauvignon

Drawn from a little over 16 hectares of estate plantings, the majority of the grapes are sold to other leading Coonawarra winemakers. As with the Cabernet Merlot, vintages since 1991 have been on the light side, and one also has to wonder whether there is an element of over-cropping. The '96 won the trophy for Best Varietal Cabernet in Show at the 1998 Royal Sydney Wine Show.

🍷🍷🍷🍷🍸 **1996** Medium to full red-purple; the best of the Cabernet family wines produced at Balnaves in 1996, with sweet cassis berry fruit and subtle oak. There is plenty of concentration to the cassis/red berry fruit on the palate, supported by fine, lingering tannins and the same subtly sweet oak as the bouquet. **rating:** 92

⇨ **best drinking** 2001 – 2005 **best vintages** '90, '91, '95, '96 **drink with** Veal chops • $21

bannockburn vineyards ★★★★★

Midland Highway, Bannockburn, Vic 3331 **region** Geelong
phone (03) 5281 1363 **fax** (03) 5281 1349 **open** Not
winemaker Gary Farr **production** 7000 **est.** 1974
product range ($20–100 R) Riesling, Sauvignon Blanc, Chardonnay, Pinot Noir, Saignee (Rosé), Shiraz, Cabernet Merlot, Cabernet Sauvignon.
summary With the qualified exception of the Cabernet Merlot, which can be a little leafy and gamey, produces outstanding wines across the range, all with individuality, style, great complexity and depth of flavour. The low-yielding estate vineyards play their role, but so does the French-influenced winemaking of Gary Farr. A shadow has fallen across the estate in the wake of the death of founder Stuart Hooper in 1997, with the future direction not certain, compounded by the loss (due to hail) of the 1998 crop.

Bannockburn Chardonnay

As with all the Bannockburn wines, 100% estate-grown from plantings made in 1974, 1981 and 1987 which are typically low-yielding and produce fully ripe grapes with very concentrated flavour. Made with what I describe as traditional French techniques, with roughly settled juice, barrel-fermented, natural yeast and natural malolactic fermentation, resulting in wines of great complexity.

🍷🍷🍷🍷 **1995** Medium to full yellow-green; the bouquet is typical, with lots of barrel-ferment, malolactic-ferment and oak inputs on top of richly concentrated fruit on both bouquet and palate. There is an ever so slightly burnt twist to the finish which probably comes from the oak, but does not enhance the wine. **rating:** 88

⇨ **best drinking** 1998 – 2003 **best vintages** '88, '90, '91, '92, '94 **drink with** Rich white meat dishes • $39

Bannockburn Pinot Noir

Widely acknowledged as one of Australia's best Pinot Noirs, made in a very distinctive style with strong French influences from low-yielding vineyards at Geelong, near Melbourne. Winemaker Gary Farr begins making the Pinot Noir in the vineyard, but does not finish his work until the wine is bottled. Even then, a certain degree of patience is required to allow the wine to show its best. There will be no '98 Bannockburn Pinot Noir in the wake of the hail devastation at the start of the season.

🍷🍷🍷🍷 **1995** Medium red; an undeniably complex bouquet with a mix of briary/leafy/forest aromas attesting to the high percentage of whole bunches (and hence stalks) in the fermenter. The palate continues the wholly idiosyncratic style of Bannockburn with a potent mix of briary/foresty/gamey characters over the underlying plum and cherry fruit. **rating:** 88

➾ **best drinking** 1998 – 2002 **best vintages** '84, '86, '88, '89, '90, '91, '92, '94 **drink with** Rare roast squab • $39

Bannockburn Shiraz

Gary Farr has made wine in France every year since 1983. While based at Domaine Dujac in Burgundy, he has closely watched the methods of Rhône winemakers, including Alain Graillot of Crozes Hermitage (who himself worked at Dujac), and this wine is strongly, and very deliberately, Rhône-influenced in style.

🍷🍷🍷🍷🍷 **1995** Medium red-purple; a vibrant and lively bouquet with complex cherry-accented fruit and obvious carbonic maceration spice influences. There is more of the same on the palate, with complex cherry and spice flavours, bright acidity and subtle oak. **rating:** 94

➾ **best drinking** 1998 – 2005 **best vintages** '88, '91, '92, '94, '95 **drink with** Rich game, strong cheese • $29

barak estate NR

Barak Road, Moorooduc, Vic 3933 **region** Mornington Peninsula
phone (03) 5978 8439 **fax** (03) 5978 8439 **open** Weekends and public holidays 12–5
winemaker James Williamson **production** 450 **est.** 1996
product range ($15–17 CD) Chardonnay, Shiraz, Cabernet Shiraz.

summary When James Williamson decided to plant vines on his 4-hectare Moorooduc property and establish a micro-winery, he already knew it was far cheaper to buy wine by the bottle than to make it. Undeterred, he ventured into grape growing and winemaking, picking the first grapes in 1993, and opening Barak Estate in 1996. Old telegraph poles, railway sleepers, old palings and timber shingles have all been used in the construction of the picturesque winery, although it is fair to say the 'sold out' sign goes up for many of the wines as the year goes by.

barambah ridge NR

79 Goschnicks Road, Redgate via Murgon, Qld 4605 **region** Other Wineries of Qld
phone (07) 4168 4766 **fax** (07) 4168 4770 **open** 7 days 10–5
winemaker Bruce Humphery-Smith **production** 10 000 **est.** 1997
product range ($10.50–16.50 CD) Semillon, Ridge Semillon, Ridge White, Chardonnay, French Oaked Chardonnay, Ridge Red, Reserve Shiraz, Cabernet Sauvignon.

summary Barambah Ridge is owned by South Burnett Wines, an unlisted public company, and is a major new entrant on the Queensland wine scene. A winery has been constructed for the 1998 vintage, with an anticipated crush of 150 tonnes. The 1997 wines were made by the omnipresent Bruce Humphery-Smith, winning an array of medals at the annual Sheraton/Courier-Mail Brisbane Queensland Wine Awards, including the trophy and gold medal for Best White Wine (with the 1997 unwooded Chardonnay).

barossa ridge wine estate NR

Light Pass Road, Tanunda, SA 5352 **region** Barossa Valley
phone (08) 8563 2811 **fax** (08) 8563 2811 **open** By appointment
winemaker Marco Litterini **production** 500 **est.** 1987
product range ($17 CD) Valley of Vines Merlot Cabernet Franc Cabernet Sauvignon Petit Verdot, Trinity Ridge Merlot, Mardia's Vineyard Cabernet Franc.
summary A grape grower turned winemaker, with a small list of interesting red varietals, including the Valley of Vines blend of Merlot, Cabernet Franc, Cabernet Sauvignon and Petit Verdot, the only such wine produced in the Barossa Valley.

barossa settlers

Trial Hill Road, Lyndoch, SA 5351 **region** Barossa Valley
phone (08) 8524 4017 **fax** (08) 8524 4519 **open** Mon–Sat 10–4, Sun 11–4
winemaker Howard Haese **production** 700 **est.** 1983
product range ($10–27 CD) Gully Winds Riesling, Semillon, Woolshed Flat Chardonnay, Megan's White (Semillon Chardonnay), Festive Champagne, Millstowe Royale (Sparkling Red), Late Harvest Riesling, Old Home Block (Light Red), Hoffnungsthal Settlement Shiraz, Rostock Red (Shiraz), Cabernet Sauvignon, Port, Sherry.
summary A superbly located cellar door is the only outlet (other than mail order) for the wines from this excellent vineyard owned by the Haese family. Production has slowed in recent years, with the grapes from the 31-hectare vineyard being sold to others, picking up pace again in 1997.

Barossa Settlers Gully Winds Riesling

Made from the best block of riesling on the substantial vineyard.
YYYY **1997** Light yellow-green; the bouquet is of medium intensity with lime and some toast aromas lurking in the background. The palate is well balanced with sweet lime flavours, even a faint touch of peach; long, rich finish. **rating:** 85

best drinking 1999 – 2004 **best vintages** NA **drink with** Sweetbreads • $13.50

barossa valley estate

Heaslip Road, Angle Vale, SA 5117 **region** Adelaide Plains
phone (08) 8284 7000 **fax** (08) 8284 7219 **open** Mon–Fri 9–5
winemaker Fiona Donald **production** 60 000 **est.** 1984
product range ($16–36 R) Classic Dry White, Gewurztraminer, Semillon Chardonnay, Late Picked Frontinan, Alicante Bouchet, Classic Dry Red; Moculta Semillon Sauvignon Blanc, Chardonnay, Shiraz, Cabernet Sauvignon Merlot; Ebenezer Chardonnay, Shiraz, Cabernet Sauvignon Malbec Merlot Cabernet Franc; E & E Black Pepper Shiraz, Sparkling Shiraz.
summary The brand of Valley Growers' Co-operative, is one of the last and largest co-operative-owned wineries in Australia. Across the board, the wines are full-flavoured and honest. E & E Black Pepper Shiraz is an up-market label with a strong reputation and following, the Ebenezer range likewise.

barratt ★★★★★

PO Box 204, Summertown, SA 5141 **region** Adelaide Hills
phone (08) 8390 1788 **fax** (08) 8390 1788 **open** Not
winemaker Jeffrey Grosset (Contract) **production** 350 **est.** 1993
product range ($23–29 ML) Chardonnay, Pinot Noir.
summary Lindsay and Carolyn Barratt purchased the Uley Vineyard, situated at the northern end of the Piccadilly Valley at a height of 500 metres, from the late Ian Wilson in August 1990. Part of the production from the 5.2-hectare vineyard is sold to other makers, with a small proportion being contract-made by Jeffrey Grosset. Both wines are complex and of high quality.

Barratt Chardonnay

Made from hand-harvested grapes selected from particular blocks within the Uley Vineyard, and matured in a mix of new and one-year-old French oak barriques for approximately ten months. Forty per cent of the wine undergoes malolactic fermentation.

🍷🍷🍷🍷🍷 (4½) **1996** Medium to full yellow-green; a very complex, rich, tangy and layered bouquet, quite Burgundian in style, leads into a mouthfilling and rich wine on the palate with very good mid to back palate grapefruit and melon flavours, assisted by subtle oak. **rating:** 92

➾ **best drinking** 1998 – 2003 **best vintages** NA **drink with** Trout mousse • $23

Barratt Piccadilly Valley Pinot Noir

Fermented in tiny, open half-tonne fermenters with footstamping and plunging of whole bunches, and matured in a mix of new and one-year-old French oak barriques for 11 months prior to bottling. The wine is neither fined nor filtered; the 1995 won a gold medal at the 1996 Adelaide Hills Wine Show, topping its class. The '96 topped the Pinot Noir Class at the 1998 Winewise Small Makers Show.

🍷🍷🍷🍷🍷 **1996** Medium red-purple; voluminous, rich and sweet spice and plum fruit on the bouquet is followed by a wonderful palate with dancing spicy/silky cherry and plum fruit. A class act from start to finish. **rating:** 94

➾ **best drinking** 1998 – 2002 **best vintages** NA **drink with** Jugged hare • $29

barretts wines NR

Portland-Nelson Highway, Portland, Vic 3305 **region** Far South West Victoria
phone (03) 5526 5251 **open** 7 days 11–5
winemaker Rod Barrett **production** 1000 **est.** 1983
product range ($10–15 CD) Riesling, Traminer, Noble Riesling, Pinot Noir, Cabernet Sauvignon, Port.
summary The second (and newer) winery in the Portland region. The initial releases were made at Best's, but since 1992 all wines have been made on the property by Rod Barrett.

barrington estate ★★★☆

Barrington Estate, Yarraman Road, Wybong, NSW 2333 **region** Upper Hunter Valley
phone (02) 6547 8118 **fax** (02) 6547 8039 **open** By appointment
winemaker Simon Gilbert (Contract) **production** 20 000 **est.** 1967
product range ($22.50 R) Yarraman Road is the top label with Black Clay Chardonnay and Sandy Slopes Cabernet Shiraz; Barrington Estate is cheaper label.

summary Yarraman Road/Barrington Estate is the reincarnation of Penfolds Wybong Estate, into which Penfolds poured millions of dollars between 1960 and 1978, when it sold the winery and surrounding vineyards to Rosemount Estate. Rosemount removed most of the unproductive vineyards, and used the winery for red wine production until 1992, then converting it to pure storage area. In 1994 Gary and Karen Blom purchased the property from Rosemount after they returned from the United States where Australian-born entrepreneur Gary Blom had a highly successful career; their main investment is the IMAX Theatre in Darling Harbour, but they intend to spend $3–4 million in redeveloping Yarraman Road.

barwang vineyard ★★★★

(vineyard only) postal c/o McWilliam's, Marrowbone Road, Pokolbin, NSW 2321 **region** Hilltops
phone (02) 6963 0001 **fax** (02) 6963 0002 **open** Not
winemaker Jim Brayne **production** NA **est.** 1975
product range ($14.95 R) Chardonnay, Shiraz, Cabernet Sauvignon.
summary Peter Robertson pioneered viticulture in the Young region when he planted his first vines in 1975 as part of a diversification programme for his 400-hectare grazing property. When McWilliam's acquired Barwang in 1989, the vineyard amounted to 13 hectares; today the plantings exceed 100 hectares. Wine quality has been exemplary from the word go, always elegant, restrained and deliberately understated, repaying extended cellaring.

Barwang Chardonnay

From the Barwang Vineyard in the Hilltops region, near Young, New South Wales, purchased from Peter Robertson some years ago, and now significantly expanded. Made in a restrained style, with subtle oak and which evolves steadily but slowly given time in bottle.

🍷🍷🍷🍷 **1997** Medium yellow-green; the bouquet is clean, with gentle fig, peach and cashew aromas, but is not intense. The palate has some elegance, with mineral, cashew and melon flavours, but is very restrained and light. Time in bottle may be its own reward. **rating:** 84

➾ **best drinking** 1999 – 2003 **best vintages** '94 **drink with** Calamari • $14.95

Barwang Shiraz

Overall, the Shiraz has been the best performer in a classy stable. Each vintage has been extremely good, with very clear varietal character, the only problem being a slight hardness in the mouth in the lesser years.

🍷🍷🍷🍷 **1996** Medium red-purple; intense cherry, spice and earth varietal aromas with typically restrained oak follow-through on the palate, with liquorice, cherry and earth flavours and fine-grained tannins to close. **rating:** 85

➾ **best drinking** 2000 – 2005 **best vintages** '90, '91, '92, '93, '94 **drink with** Kraft Australian parmesan • $14.95

Barwang Cabernet Sauvignon

The continental climate of the Barwang Vineyard, marked by cold nights and warm summer days, but with the growing season finishing much later than it does in either the Hunter Valley or Mudgee, produces red wines of considerable flavour, power and extract, exemplified by this wine.

🍷🍷🍷🍷🍷 **1996** Medium red-purple; the bouquet is full and sweet, with complex red berry, vanilla and chocolate aromas, the palate even better, with rich, sweet cassis, berry and chocolate flavours; excellent tannins and structure. **rating:** 90

➯ **best drinking** 2001 – 2006 **best vintages** '89, '91, '92, '93, '96 **drink with** Beef Wellington • $14.95

basedow ★★★☆

161–165 Murray Street, Tanunda, SA 5352 **region** Barossa Valley
phone (08) 8563 3666 **fax** (08) 8563 3597 **open** Mon-Fri 9–5, weekends 11–5
winemaker Craig Stansborough **production** 65 000 **est.** 1896
product range ($11–60 CD) Eden Valley Riesling, Barossa Valley Semillon (White Burgundy), Sauvignon Blanc Semillon, Barossa Chardonnay, Late Harvest, Oscar's Heritage, Grenache, Barossa Shiraz, Mistella, Old Tawny Port; Museum Release Watervale Riesling, Barossa Carbernet Sauvignon.
summary An old and proud label, particularly well known for its oak-matured Semillon (called White Burgundy on the Australian market), which underwent a number of changes of ownership during the 1990s. Overall, a reliable producer of solidly flavoured wines.

basket range wines NR

c/o PO Basket Range, SA 5138 **region** Adelaide Hills
phone (08) 9390 1515 **open** Not
winemaker Phillip Broderick **production** 500 **est.** 1980
product range ($18 ML) A single Bordeaux-blend of Cabernet Sauvignon, Cabernet Franc, Merlot, Malbec drawn from 3 hectares of estate plantings.
summary A tiny operation known to very few, run by civil and Aboriginal rights lawyer Phillip Broderick, a most engaging man with a disarmingly laid-back manner.

bass phillip ★★★★★

Tosch's Road, Leongatha South, Vic 3953 **region** Gippsland
phone (03) 5664 3341 **fax** (03) 5664 3209 **open** 7 days 11–6 summer and autumn
winemaker Phillip Jones **production** 700 **est.** 1979
product range ($24–90 ML) Tiny quantities of Pinot Noir in three categories: standard, Premium and an occasional barrel of Reserve. A hatful of Chardonnay also made; plus Pinot Rosé and Gamay.
summary Phillip Jones has retired from the Melbourne rat-race to hand-craft tiny quantities of superlative Pinot Noir which, at its best, has no equal in Australia. Painstaking site selection, ultra-close vine spacing and the very, very cool climate of South Gippsland are the keys to the magic of Bass Phillip and its eerily Burgundian Pinots. The quality (and longevity) of the '96 wines will only add to the reputation of the brand.

Bass Phillip Pinot Noir

A wine which shows the limitation of any star or symbol rating system because, on the one hand, there is an undoubted quality differential between the standard, Reserve and Premium wines, yet on the other hand, one could not possibly rate this wine at less than the top rating.

Indeed, because it is the most direct and least oak-influenced of the three wines, it is often more pleasurable to drink in its youth.

🍷🍷🍷🍷🍷 **1996** Medium purple-red; the bouquet is redolent of sweet plummy fruit with the forest floor lying underneath. The palate shows a similar mix of ripe plummy fruit together with more earthy/foresty characters, and fully sufficient tannins for ageing. **rating:** 90

➾ **best drinking** 2000 – 2005 **best vintages** '84, '85, '89, '91, '92, '93, '94, '95, '96 **drink with** Slow-cooked Tasmanian salmon • $38

Bass Phillip Premium Pinot Noir

Produced from the oldest vines which are ultra-close planted. The wine receives substantially more new oak than does the standard release.

🍷🍷🍷🍷🍷 **1996** Dark red-purple; an intense, concentrated and ripe dark plum, forest and spice bouquet is followed by an extremely complex, textured and structured wine on the palate with more dark plum, forest and spice flavours. Still tight and closed, and needs a long time (by the standards of Pinot Noir) to evolve. **rating:** 92

➾ **best drinking** 2001 – 2006 **best vintages** '84, '85, '89, '91, '92, '93, '94, '95, '96 **drink with** Venison • $65

Bass Phillip Reserve Pinot Noir

An ultra-scarce single barrel (250 bottles) selection of the best wine in the cellar, and forming part of the wine which would otherwise go into the Premium label. Only released in the best years and, like Romanee Conti, sold on allocation in single and double bottle quantities. It is the reason why many people – myself included – are inclined to say that Bass Phillip makes the best Pinot Noir in Australia.

🍷🍷🍷🍷🍷 **1996** Dark red-purple; an exceptionally powerful, deep yet tightly folded bouquet, with dark plum and spice leads into a power-laden, potent dark plum, forest and briar-flavoured palate. Borders on the unappealing now, so unready is it, but time will create its own magic. **rating:** 94

➾ **best drinking** 2003 – 2010 **best vintages** '89, '91, '94, '95, '96 **drink with** Saddle of hare • $90

beckett's flat NR

Beckett Road, Metricup, WA 6280 **region** Margaret River
phone (08) 9755 7402 **fax** (08) 9755 7402 **open** 7 days 10–6
winemaker B Abbott **production** 1200 **est.** 1992
product range ($13–18 CD) Sauvignon Blanc Semillon, Cabernet Shiraz Merlot, Cabernet Sauvignon.
summary Bill and Noni Ilic opened Beckett's Flat in September 1997. Situated just off the Bussell Highway, at Metricup, midway between Busselton and the Margaret River, it draws upon 8 hectares of estate vineyards, first planted in 1992. Accommodation is available.

belbourie ★★☆

Branxton Road, Rothbury, NSW 2330 **region** Lower Hunter Valley
phone (02) 4938 1556 **open** Weekends, holidays 10-sunset
winemaker Bob Davies **production** 2000 **est.** 1963

product range ($15–16 CD) Barramundi Chardonnay, Belah Semillon Chardonnay, Hermitage.
summary A winery with a rich, and at times highly controversial, history of wine and winemaking, but these days tending more to the conventional. It has always sought to encourage cellar-door and mailing list sales, focusing on monthly wine and food events, and has a loyal clientele.

bellingham vineyards ★★★

Pipers Brook, Tas 7254 **region** Northern Tasmania
phone (03) 6382 7149 **open** By appointment
winemaker Greg O'Keefe (Contract) **production** 700 **est.** 1984
product range ($5.50–8 ML) Riesling, Chardonnay, Pinot Noir, Cabernet Sauvignon.
summary Dallas Targett sells most of the grapes from his 13-hectare vineyard to Greg O'Keefe; a small part has been made for the Bellingham label.

Bellingham Riesling

Until mid-1997 Bellingham had small stocks of the '90, '94 and '96 vintages of Riesling for sale at cellar door. A five-star review for the 1990 in *Winestate* magazine led to the immediate demise of the 1990, but micro stocks of the '94 and slightly better quantities of the '96 were still available in early 1998. The latter vintage received a well-deserved silver medal at the 1998 Tasmanian Wines Show.

🍷🍷🍷🍷 **1996** Medium to full yellow-green; the bouquet is clean and smooth, and moderately intense, the palate following the same track with predominantly lime and toast flavours, and just a hint of Tasmanian mineral underneath. **rating:** 87

⇨ **best drinking** 1998 – 2003 **best vintages** '90, '91, '96 **drink with** Spring rolls • $8

belubula valley vineyards NR

Golden Gully, Mandurama, NSW 2798 **region** Orange
phone (02) 6367 5236 **fax** (02) 9362 4726 **open** Not
winemaker David Somervaille **production** 1000 **est.** 1986
product range Cabernet Sauvignon.
summary Belubula Valley is a foundation member of the Central Highlands Grapegrowers Association, centred on Orange; the vineyard is located on the Belubula River, near Carcoar, and the small amounts of wine made to date have not yet been commercially released. David Somervaille, incidentally, was Chairman of partners of the national law firm Blake Dawson Waldron.

beresford wines ★★★

49 Fraser Avenue, Happy Valley, SA 5159 **region** McLaren Vale
phone (08) 8322 3611 **fax** (08) 8322 3610 **open** Mon–Fri 9–5, weekends 11–5
winemaker Robert Dundon **production** 145 000 **est.** 1985
product range ($8–18 CD) First the Saints range of St Estelle Semillon Chardonnay, St Yvette Chardonnay and St Helene Cabernet Shiraz; then Highwood Sauvignon Blanc, Chardonnay and Shiraz; then Katherine Hills Semillon Sauvignon Blanc, Cabernet Merlot; and lastly the Beresford range of Semillon Sauvignon Blanc, McLaren Padthaway Chardonnay, McLaren Cabernet Merlot.

summary The Beresford brand sits at the top of a range of labels primarily and successfully aimed at the export market. The accent is on price, and the wines do not aspire to great complexity. Quality, however, seems to have improved in the latter part of the 1990s.

berri estates ★★

Sturt Highway, Glossop, SA 5344 **region** Riverland
phone (08) 8582 0300 **fax** (08) 8583 2224 **open** Mon-Sat 9–5
winemaker Paul Kasselbaum **production** NFP **est.** 1916
product range Light Fruity Lexia, Fruity Gordo Moselle, Chablis, Claret, Rosé, White Lambrusco, all in cask form.
summary Strictly a producer of cask and bulk wine with no pretensions to grandeur, and with a substantial part of the production exported in bulk. Part of the BRL Hardy Group.

best's wines ★★★★☆

1 kilometre off Western Highway, Great Western, Vic 3377 **region** Grampians
phone (03) 5356 2250 **fax** (03) 5356 2430 **open** Mon-Fri 9–5, Sat 9–4, Sun and holidays 12–4
winemaker Viv Thomson **production** 25 000 **est.** 1866
product range ($7–38 R) Chardonnay, Riesling, Chenin Blanc, Ondenc, Golden Chasselas, Pinot Noir, Dolcetto, Pinot Meunier, Bin O Shiraz, Thomson Family Shiraz, Cabernet Sauvignon, together with a large range of fortified wines sourced from St Andrews at Lake Boga. Some of these wines are available only at cellar door.
summary An historic winery, owning some priceless vineyards planted as long ago as 1867 (other plantings are, of course, much more recent) which has consistently produced elegant, supple wines which deserve far greater recognition than they in fact receive. The Shiraz is a classic; the Thomson Family Shiraz magnificent.

Best's Bin O Shiraz

One of the more understated classic wines, produced entirely from estate-grown grapes, made with a minimum of artifice and with high-quality fruit, rather than oak, doing the work.

🍷🍷🍷🍷 **1995** Medium to full red; there are fragrant red cherry, berry and cedar aromas on the moderately intense bouquet, followed logically by sweet red cherry fruit and silky tannins on the palate. Subtle oak treatment throughout. **rating:** 87

➭ **best drinking** 2000 – 2007 **best vintages** '62, '70, '77, '78, '85, '88, '90, '91, '92, '94 **drink with** Roast veal, mature cheddar • $27

Best's Thomson Family Shiraz

A magnificent wine first released in late 1994 to commemorate the Centenary of Best's Great Western Vineyards. What might have been a one-off event is now an annual one (vintage permitting) under the Thomson Family label. The '95 is a superb successor to the Centenary vintage, made entirely from vines planted adjacent to the winery in 1867 by Henry Best, and matured in small French oak.

🍷🍷🍷🍷🍷 **1995** Dense red-purple; the bouquet exudes gloriously dense chocolate and black cherry fruit, supported by excellent oak. The exotically concentrated and dense palate has outstanding texture and structure; ripe black cherry and chocolate flavours, subtle but sweet oak and fine tannins complete a great wine. **rating:** 95

➭ **best drinking** 2000 – 2015 **best vintages** NA **drink with** Stir-fried beef • $35

Best's Cabernet Sauvignon

Has been overshadowed by the Shiraz but is a more than useful wine, produced entirely from estate-grown grapes. The '96 is an extraordinary wine with 14.5 degrees alcohol, and 15% Merlot included.

🍷🍷🍷🍷 **1996** Medium red-purple; the bouquet is potent and clean, with cassis and hints of cedar; the palate is powerful, and extremely ripe, with blackberry tinged with cedar and olive. Those olive characters no doubt come from the Merlot. **rating:** 86

⇨ **best drinking** 2001 – 2006 **best vintages** '88, '91, '92, '93, '96 **drink with** Sirloin of beef • $26

bethany wines ★★★★

Bethany Road, Bethany via Tanunda, SA 5352 **region** Barossa Valley
phone (08) 8563 2086 **fax** (08) 8563 0046 **open** Mon-Sat 10–5, Sun 1–5
winemaker Geoff Schrapel, Robert Schrapel **production** 20 000 **est.** 1977
product range ($10–50 CD) Riesling (Reserve Dry, Special Select Late Harvest), Chardonnay, Wood Aged Semillon, Steinbruch, Cabernet Merlot, Shiraz, Family Reserve Shiraz, Grenache Pressings, Old Quarry Barossa Tawny Port, Old Quarry Barossa Fronti (White Port).
summary The Schrapel family has been growing grapes in the Barossa Valley for over 140 years, but the winery has only been in operation since 1977. Nestling high on a hillside in the site of an old quarry, it is run by Geoff and Rob Schrapel, who produce a range of consistently well-made and attractively packaged wines.

Bethany Shiraz

Estate-grown, hand-pruned and hand-picked, and matured for two years in American oak. Since 1988 the wine has had conspicuous show success, winning important trophies with both the '88 and '92 vintages. Seldom less than excellent, the '96 living up to its reputation.

🍷🍷🍷🍷🍷 **1996** Medium red-purple; a rich and complex bouquet with sweet plummy fruit, hints of game and deftly judged oak. The palate is archetypal Barossa, with sweet plum and mint fruit, soft tannins and a comfortable cocoon of oak. **rating:** 90

⇨ **best drinking** 2001 – 2006 **best vintages** '88, '90, '91, '92, '94, '96 **drink with** Mild curry • $19.80

bianchet ★★★

Lot 3 Victoria Road, Lilydale, Vic 3140 **region** Yarra Valley
phone (03) 9739 1779 **fax** (03) 9739 1277 **open** Weekends 10–6
winemaker Tony Inglese **production** 2000 **est.** 1976
product range ($8–17 CD) Traminer, Semillon, Chardonnay, Verduzzo, Pinot Noir, Shiraz, Cabernet Sauvignon, Merlot.
summary Produces very full-flavoured wines sold with considerable bottle age. The style is somewhat rustic, but wine such as that made from the rare Italian grape verduzzo makes the cellar door well worth a visit.

bimbadgen estate NR

Lot 21 McDonalds Road, Pokolbin, NSW 2321 **region** Lower Hunter Valley
phone (02) 4998 7585 **fax** (02) 4998 7732 **open** Weekends, holidays 10–5
winemaker Kees Van De Scheur, Thomas Jung **production** 50 000 **est.** 1968

product range ($10–25 R) Semillon, Chardonnay, Shiraz, Cabernet Shiraz; Grand Ridge Estate is the second label.

summary Established as McPherson Wines, then successively Tamalee, then Sobels, then Parker Wines and now Bimbadgen, this substantial winery has had what might politely be termed a turbulent history. It has the great advantage of having 45 hectares of estate plantings, mostly with now relatively old vines.

Bimbadgen Estate Shiraz

As with the Chardonnay, three vintages were available in 1998 from cellar door.

🍷🍷🍷🍷 **1996** Medium to full red-purple; the bouquet is ripe, with some of the hay/straw aromas encountered in old-time Hunter Shiraz, together with some gamey/boot polish varietal aromas. The palate is powerful, with more of those gamey/liquorice/boot polish characters together with some chocolate and earth flavours. Striking Shiraz. **rating:** 86

➾ **best drinking** 2000 – 2008 **best vintages** NA **drink with** Stewed oxtail • $15

bindi wine growers ★★★★☆

145 Melton Road, Gisborne, Vic 3437 **region** Macedon
phone (03) 5428 2564 **fax** (03) 5428 2564 **open** Not
winemaker Michael Dhillon, Stuart Anderson **production** 800 **est.** 1988
product range ($27.75 ML) Chardonnay, Pinot Noir.
summary A new arrival in the Macedon region, owned and run by the Dhillon family. Specialises in highly rated and stylish Pinot Noir, with help from veteran Stuart Anderson.

Bindi Chardonnay

Bindi produces complex rich and notably long-lived Chardonnay. A four-vintage mini vertical tasting in January 1998 produced top points for the still-youthful, complex and powerful '91 vintage (92 points), followed by the citrussy '94, with an exceptionally long, fine palate (87 points), then a curiously garlicky '95, which I did not like at all (73 points), and the very different '96, most deeply coloured of all of the wines, and showing what appears to be some botrytis influence.

🍷🍷🍷🍷 **1996** Full, developed yellow-green; a voluminous bouquet with peach, apricot, butter and butterscotch aromas is followed by a fleshy, fruity wine, quite reminiscent of some New Zealand Chardonnays, and again pointing the finger of suspicion at some botrytis influence. **rating:** 84

➾ **best drinking** 1998 – 2002 **best vintages** '91, '94, '96 **drink with** Corn-fed chicken • $27.75

Bindi Pinot Noir

A wine which has acquired a cult status not far removed from that of Giaconda. Except in vintages such as '95 (high yielding across most southern Victorian regions, and generally resulting in lighter Pinot Noir) the wine is notable for its strength and – by the standards of Pinot – longevity. The '94 vintage, reviewed in the 1998 edition of *Companion*, has developed superbly over the past two years, with powerful foresty/plummy/earthy flavours to the fore (92 points), while the '93 vintage is another long-lived, powerful wine.

🍷🍷🍷🍷 **1996** Dense red-purple; a rich, deep, solid briar and plum bouquet is followed by a formidably strong palate, with dense plummy fruit. Early in its life, seems to dip slightly and shorten on the finish, but may well change shape if the '94 is any guide. **rating:** 88

➾ **best drinking** 2000 – 2005 **best vintages** '93, '94, '96 **drink with** Squab • $27.75

birdwood estate ★★★☆

Mannum Road, Birdwood, SA 5234 **region** Adelaide Hills
phone (08) 8263 0986 **fax** (08) 8263 0986 **open** Not
winemaker Oli Cucchiarelli **production** 800 **est.** 1990
product range ($11–20 ML) Chardonnay, Riesling, Merlot, Cabernet Sauvignon.
summary Birdwood Estate draws upon 5 hectares of estate vineyards progressively established since 1990. The quality of the Chardonnay is very good indeed.

birnam wood wines NR

Turanville Road, Scone, NSW 2337 **region** Upper Hunter Valley
phone (02) 6545 3286 **fax** (02) 6545 3431 **open** 7 days 10–4
winemaker Simon Gilbert (Contract) **production** 4000 **est.** 1994
product range ($14.95–18.95 CD) Semillon, Semillon Sauvignon Blanc, Chardonnay, Premium Reserve Chardonnay.
summary Former Sydney car dealer Mike Eagan and wife Min moved to Scone to establish a horse stud; the vineyard came later (in 1994) but is now a major part of the business, with over 30 hectares of vines. Most of the grapes are sold; part only is vinified for Birnam Wood.

black george NR

Black Georges Road, Manjimup, WA 6258 **region** Pemberton
phone (08) 9772 3569 **fax** (08) 9772 3102 **open** 7 days 10.30–4.45
winemaker Shelley Wilson **production** 4000 **est.** 1991
product range ($16.50–23 CD) Unwooded Chardonnay, The Captains Release Chardonnay, Late Picked Verdelho, Classic White, Pinot Noir, Cabernet Franc Merlot.
summary A relatively recent arrival on the scene, with particular aspirations to make high-quality Pinot Noir. As with so much of the Pemberton region, it remains to be seen whether the combination of soil and climate will permit this.

blackjack vineyards ★★★

Cnr Blackjack Road and Calder Highway, Harcourt, Vic 3453 **region** Bendigo
phone (03) 5474 2355 **fax** (03) 5474 2355 **open** Weekends and public holidays 11–5
winemaker Ian McKenzie, Ken Pollock **production** 2000 **est.** 1987
product range ($20–25 CD) Shiraz, Cabernet Merlot.
summary Established by the McKenzie and Pollock families on the site of an old apple and pear orchard in the Harcourt Valley. Best known for some very good Shirazes. Ian McKenzie, incidentally, is not to be confused with Ian McKenzie of Seppelt Great Western.

BlackJack Shiraz

Produced from the hillside vineyards of BlackJack, and aged in American and French oak barriques for 18 months prior to bottling. The name 'BlackJack' derives from an American sailor who jumped ship during the gold-rush days of the 1850s and 1860s, and who earned for himself this nickname.

🍷🍷🍷🍷 **1996** Medium red-purple; a strong bouquet, with more weight and dark cherry/berry fruit than the '95. The palate confirms the return to form, with cherry, mint, plum and earth flavours all intermingling. Subtle oak. **rating:** 85

➪ **best drinking** 2000 – 2006 **best vintages** '93, '96 **drink with** Barbecued T-bone • $20

blackwood crest wines ★★☆

RMB 404A Boyup Brook, WA 6244 **region** Other Wineries of WA
phone (08) 9767 3029 **fax** (08) 9762 3029 **open** 7 days 10–6
winemaker Max Fairbrass **production** 1000 **est.** 1976
product range ($10–14 CD) Riesling, Classic White, Sweet White, Shiraz, Cabernet Sauvignon.
summary A remote and small winery which has produced one or two striking red wines full of flavour and character; worth watching.

blanche barkly wines NR

Rheola Road, Kingower, Vic 3517 **region** Bendigo
phone (03) 5443 3664 **open** Weekends, public holidays 10–5
winemaker David Reimers **production** NFP **est.** 1972
product range ($10–16.50 CD) Shiraz, Cabernet Sauvignon.
summary Sporadic but small production and variable quality seem to be the order of the day; the potential has always been there. No recent tastings.

blaxlands wines NR

Broke Road, Pokolbin, NSW 2320 **region** Lower Hunter Valley
phone (02) 4998 7550 **fax** (02) 4998 7802 **open** 7 days 10.30–4.30
winemaker Trevor Drayton (Contract) **production** 400 **est.** 1976
product range ($17–18 CD) Chardonnay, Chardonnay Semillon, Shiraz.
summary Chris Barnes is an industry veteran who has run Blaxlands Restaurant and Wine Centre in Pokolbin for almost 20 years. He is also the owner of 1 hectare each of chardonnay and semillon, the wines from which are included in the comprehensive range of Hunter Valley wines available from the Wine Centre (and the restaurant).

bleasdale vineyards ★★★☆

Wellington Road, Langhorne Creek, SA 5255 **region** Langhorne Creek
phone (08) 8537 3001 **fax** (08) 8537 3224 **open** Mon–Sat 9–5, Sun 11–5
winemaker Michael Potts **production** 60 000 **est.** 1850
product range ($7–27 R) Late Picked Riesling, Chardonnay, Sandhill Verdelho, Malbec, Mulberry Tree Cabernet Sauvignon, Bremerview Shiraz, Frank Potts Cabernet Malbec Merlot, Sparkling, Fortified.
summary One of the most historic wineries in Australia drawing upon vineyards that are flooded every winter by diversion of the Bremer River, which provides moisture throughout the dry, cool, growing season. The wines offer excellent value for money, all showing that particular softness which is the hallmark of the Langhorne Creek region.

blewitt springs winery 

Fraser Avenue, Happy Valley, SA 5159 **region** McLaren Vale
phone (08) 8322 3611 **fax** (08) 8322 3610 **open** Not
winemaker Brett Howard **production** 4000 **est.** 1987
product range ($10.60–13.70 R) Riesling, Chardonnay, Semillon, Shiraz, Cabernet Sauvignon.
summary When it first arrived on the scene, attracted much attention and praise for its voluptuous Chardonnays, crammed full of peachy, buttery fruit and vanillin American oak. Oak also plays a major role in the Semillon and the red wines; a lighter touch might please some critics.

bloodwood estate ★★★★

4 Griffin Road, Orange, NSW 2800 **region** Orange
phone (02) 6362 5631 **fax** (02) 6361 1173 **open** By appointment
winemaker Stephen Doyle, Jon Reynolds **production** 3000 **est.** 1983
product range ($10–25 ML) Riesling, Rosé of Malbec, Chardonnay, Ice Riesling, Cabernet, Chirac (Pinot Chardonnay).
summary Rhonda and Stephen Doyle are two of the pioneers of the burgeoning Orange district. The wines are sold mainly through cellar door and an energetically and informatively-run mailing list; the principal retail outlet is Ian Cook's Fiveways Cellar, Paddington, Sydney. Bloodwood has done best with elegant but intense Chardonnay and the intermittent releases of super-late harvest Ice Riesling.

Bloodwood Estate Chardonnay

Made by Jon Reynolds at Reynolds Yarraman, and has consistently shown that it needs time in bottle to evolve. A delicate style, usually light-bodied but texturally complex, with malolactic cashew notes.

🍷🍷🍷🍷 **1996** Medium to full yellow-green; a complex bouquet with cashew nut, melon and ripe fig fruit together with hints of oak spice. The palate is full, with spicy/bacony oak more evident than on the bouquet, perhaps a fraction intrusive given the fruit weight, but the wine certainly has character, and should develop well. **rating:** 87

➡ **best drinking** 1999 – 2004 **best vintages** NA **drink with** White-fleshed fish • $16

Bloodwood Estate Ice Riesling (375 ml)

So far as I am aware, the last grapes to be harvested in Australia in the years in which the wine is made. 1994 was the previous vintage, with the grapes harvested in July, those for the '97 vintage were picked on June 20. The quality of the wine justifies the patience and faith of the Doyles.

🍷🍷🍷🍷🍷 **1997** Glowing yellow-green; the bouquet shows an exotic mix of tropical peach, apricot and lime fruit; the palate is quite excellent, with intense tropical fruit salad flavours balanced by acidity. **rating:** 90

➡ **best drinking** 1998 – 2002 **best vintages** NA **drink with** Any fruit-based dessert • $25

Bloodwood Estate Cabernet

A wine which attests to the ability of the Orange region to produce late-ripening red wine styles as handsomely as it does Chardonnay.

🍷🍷🍷🍷 **1995** Medium to full red-purple; the bouquet is clean, of medium intensity and fruit-driven with a mix of cassis, olive and herb aromas. The elegant palate shows the cool climate with cassis, mint and olive flavours supported by fine tannins. **rating:** 86

➡ **best drinking** 2000 – 2005 **best vintages** NA **drink with** Rib of veal • $18

blue pyrenees estate ★★★

Vinoca Road, Avoca, Vic 3467 **region** Pyrenees
phone (03) 5465 3202 **fax** (03) 5465 3529 **open** Mon-Fri 10–4.30, weekends and public holidays 10–5
winemaker Vincent Gere **production** 108 000 **est.** 1963

product range ($9.95–29.95 R) Brut, Midnight Cuvee, Chardonnay, Estate Red; Fiddlers Creek Chardonnay, Sauvignon Blanc, Semillon, Pinot Noir, Cabernet Shiraz, Brut. Leydens Vale has recently been introduced as a mid-priced range between the Estate wines and Fiddlers Creek.
summary Notwithstanding its distinguished French ownership, the perseverance of winemaker Vincent Gere, a very well-equipped winery, and lavish marketing expenditure, the former Chateau Remy has struggled. The 1996 renaming of the winery as Blue Pyrenees is a sign of that struggle, and also of a progressive shift in production towards still table wine, a sensible move.

Blue Pyrenees Estate Red

A blend of estate-grown Shiraz, Cabernet Sauvignon and Merlot, packaged in the very distinctive Blue Pyrenees label.

🍷🍷🍷🍷 **1995** Medium red-purple; the bouquet is clean, of medium intensity, with aromas of earth and mint supported by subtle oak. The palate is unexpectedly complex and rich, with ripe, lush damson plum and cherry fruit with hints of spice. Finishes with nice tannins; continues the renaissance begun with the '94. **rating:** 84

⇨ **best drinking** 1999 – 2005 **best vintages** '86, '89, '91, '94 **drink with** Beef Bordelaise • $28

---

boneo plains NR

RMB 1400 Browns Road, South Rosebud, Vic 3939 **region** Mornington Peninsula
phone (03) 5988 6208 **fax** (03) 5988 6208 **open** By appointment
winemaker R D Tallarida **production** 2500 **est.** 1988
product range ($10–18 CD) Chardonnay, Cabernet Sauvignon; Roch Unwooded Chardonnay, Roch Rosé.
summary A 9-hectare vineyard and winery established by the Tallarida family, well known as manufacturers and suppliers of winemaking equipment to the industry. The Chardonnay is the best of the wines so far released.

bonneyview NR

Sturt Highway, Barmera, SA 5345 **region** Riverland
phone (08) 8588 2279 **open** 7 days 9–5.30
winemaker Robert Minns **production** 5000 **est.** 1975
product range ($6–25 CD) Riesling, Chardonnay, Frontignan Blanc, Shiraz Petit Verdot, Cabernet Petit Verdot, Cabernet Blend, Fortifieds.
summary The smallest Riverland winery selling exclusively cellar door, with an ex-Kent cricketer and Oxford University graduate as its owner/winemaker. The Shiraz Petit Verdot (unique to Bonneyview) and Cabernet Petit Verdot add a particular dimension of interest to the wine portfolio.

booth's taminick cellars NR

Taminick via Glenrowan, Vic 3675 **region** Glenrowan
phone (03) 5766 2282 **fax** (03) 5766 2151 **open** Mon-Sat 9–5, Sun 10–5
winemaker Cliff Booth, Peter Booth **production** 4000 **est.** 1904
product range ($6.50–12 CD) Trebbiano, Chardonnay, Late Harvest Trebbiano, Shiraz, Cabernet Merlot, Cabernet Sauvignon, Ports, Muscat.
summary Ultra-conservative producer of massively flavoured and concentrated red wines, usually with more than a few rough edges which time may or may not smooth over.

boroka vineyard ★★

Pomonal Road, Halls Gap, Vic 3381 **region** Grampians
phone (03) 5356 4252 **open** Mon-Sat 9–5, Sun, public holidays 10–5
winemaker Bernard Breen **production** 1500 **est.** 1974
product range ($7.50–12 CD) Chablis and Riesling blends, Dry Rosé, Shiraz, Cabernet Sauvignon, Reserve Port.
summary Out of the mainstream in terms of both wine quality and location, but does offer light lunches or picnic takeaways, and the views are spectacular.

boston bay wines ★★★☆

Lincoln Highway, Port Lincoln, SA 5606 **region** Other Wineries of SA
phone (08) 8684 3600 **fax** (08) 8684 3600 **open** Weekends, school/public holidays 11.30–4.30
winemaker David O'Leary (Contract) **production** 2600 **est.** 1984
product range ($10–17 CD) Riesling, Spätlese Riesling, Chardonnay, Cabernet Sauvignon, Merlot, Baudin's Blend (Magnum), Mistelle.
summary Boston Bay Wines is a strongly tourist-oriented operation which has extended the viticultural map in South Australia. It is situated at the same latitude as Adelaide, overlooking the Spencer Gulf at the southern tip of the Eyre Peninsula. Say proprietors Graham and Mary Ford, 'It is the only vineyard in the world to offer frequent sightings of whales at play in the waters at its foot'.

Boston Bay Cabernet Sauvignon

The 1 hectare of cabernet sauvignon is now 12 years old, and in years such as '91, '93 and '95 produced a wine of distinctive style and quality, although in cooler vintages herbaceous characters tend to take over.

🍷🍷🍷🍷 **1995** Medium red-purple; the bouquet is moderately sweet, with a nice range of cedar, cigar, briar and chocolate aromas, and the palate is – if anything – even more attractive than the bouquet, with cedar, cassis and a touch of bitter chocolate. Good tannin structure. **rating:** 85

⇨ **best drinking** 1998 – 2002 **best vintages** '91, '93, '95 **drink with** Rack of lamb • $14

botobolar ★★★☆

Botobolar Lane, Mudgee, NSW 2850 **region** Mudgee
phone (02) 6373 3840 **fax** (02) 6373 3789 **open** Mon-Sat 10–5, Sun 10–3
winemaker Kevin Karstrom **production** 6500 **est.** 1971
product range ($8–14 CD) Chardonnay, Marsanne, Shiraz, Cabernet Sauvignon; St Gilbert Dry Red and White; Preservative Free White and Red.
summary One of the first organic vineyards in Australia with present owner Kevin Karstrom continuing the practices established by founder Gil Wahlquist. Preservative Free Dry White and Dry Red extend the organic practice of the vineyard to the winery. Shiraz is consistently the best wine to appear under the Botobolar label.

Botobolar Shiraz

The Botobolar vineyard has been granted Certified Organic status by the National Association of Sustainable Agriculture, attesting to the founder Gil Wahlquist's commitment to organic practices, and to the equally strong commitment by his successor Kevin Karstrom. This wine is made from vines planted in 1971, with typically low yield. The waxed top to the bottle is a nice touch, but the wine is of such quality that it in fact needs no marketing gimmickry.

🍷🍷🍷🍷 **1994** Medium to full red, still with a touch of purple; the bouquet is spotlessly clean with a mix of dark chocolate and plum fruit, and only the barest hint of oak. A powerful, fruit-driven wine on the palate with dark berry fruit flavours and soft lingering tannins. Truly delicious. **rating:** 89

➾ **best drinking** 1998 – 2005 **best vintages** NA **drink with** Rich beef stew • $12

Botobolar Cabernet Sauvignon

Like the Botobolar Shiraz, produced from organically grown grapes on the estate vineyard. It is very evident that Kevin Karstrom is a highly accomplished self-taught winemaker.

🍷🍷🍷🍷 **1994** Medium to full red-purple; the bouquet is ripe and full, with the fruit aromas running through plum, dark chocolate, earth and a touch of mint. The palate is full and round, with softly chewy dark chocolate/dark berry fruit, soft tannins and subtle oak. **rating:** 84

➾ **best drinking** 1998 – 2004 **best vintages** NA **drink with** Moroccan lamb • NA

bowen estate ★★★★

Riddoch Highway, Coonawarra, SA 5263 **region** Coonawarra
phone (08) 8737 2229 **fax** (08) 8737 2173 **open** 7 days 10–5
winemaker Doug Bowen **production** 11 000 **est.** 1972
product range ($20–23 CD) Chardonnay, Shiraz, Cabernet Sauvignon Merlot Cabernet Franc, Cabernet Sauvignon, Sanderson Sparkling.

summary One of the best-known names among the smaller Coonawarra wineries with a great track record of red winemaking; Chardonnay and Sanderson Sparkling have joined the band, and the Riesling ended with the '93 vintage. Full-bodied reds at the top end of the ripeness spectrum are the winery trademarks, with a chewy richness uncommon in Coonawarra.

Bowen Estate Shiraz

A wine which has given tremendous pleasure over the years, always crammed full of personality and flavour. Doug Bowen certainly prefers to allow the grapes to ripen fully, sometimes to frightening levels. The ripe style does not always turn me on, but the '94 and '95 did so in spades.

🍷🍷🍷🍷 **1996** Medium red-purple; a clean but surprisingly light bouquet with earthy berry varietal character, and a palate which runs through cherry, briary, leaf and mint flavours, but which utterly belies its 14 degrees alcohol and, for that matter, the reputation of the vintage. **rating:** 84

➾ **best drinking** 2000 – 2004 **best vintages** '86, '90, '91, '92, '94, '95 **drink with** Kangaroo fillet • $21.50

Bowen Estate Cabernet Sauvignon Merlot Cabernet Franc

A relatively new direction for Bowen Estate, and intriguingly made (at least on the evidence of the '95) in a very different style from the normal Bowen Estate reds, earlier picked and with less opulently ripe flavour.

🍷🍷🍷🍷 **1995** Medium red, with just a touch of purple; the berry and earth fruit aromas have an attractive, faintly spicy edge; the palate proclaims its Bordeaux-blend base, with lively flavours and good length to a pleasantly herbaceous finish. **rating:** 87

➾ **best drinking** 1998 – 2003 **best vintages** '95 **drink with** Lasagne • $21.50

boynton's of bright ★★★☆

Ovens Valley Highway, Bright, Vic 3747 **region** Ovens Valley
phone (03) 5756 2356 **fax** (03) 5756 2610 **open** 7 days 10–5
winemaker Kel Boynton **production** 15 000 **est.** 1987
product range ($10–16 CD) Riesling, Semillon, Sauvignon Blanc, Chardonnay, Unoaked Chardonnay, Noble Riesling, Noble Chardonnay, Pinot Noir, Shiraz, Merlot, Cabernet Sauvignon, Port, Vintage Brut.
summary The original 12.5-hectare vineyard expanded almost 16 hectares by 1996 plantings of pinot gris, durif and sauvignon blanc, is situated in the Ovens Valley north of the township of Bright, under the lee of Mount Buffalo. In the early years a substantial part of the crop was sold, but virtually all is now vinified at the winery. Overall, the red wines have always outshone the whites, initially with very strong American oak input, but in more recent years with better fruit/oak balance.

brahams creek NR

Woods Point Road, East Warburton, Vic 3799 **region** Yarra Valley
phone (03) 9560 0016 **fax** (03) 9560 0016 **open** Weekends and public holidays 10–5
winemaker Geoffrey Richardson **production** 1000 **est.** 1985
product range ($12.50 CD) Chardonnay, Sauvignon Blanc, Pinot Noir, Cabernet Sauvignon, Merlot.
summary Owner Geoffrey Richardson did not start marketing his wines until 1994 and a string of older vintage wines are available for sale at cellar door.

brand's laira 

Main Road, Coonawarra, SA 5263 **region** Coonawarra
phone (08) 8736 3260 **fax** (08) 8736 3208 **open** Mon-Fri 9–4.30, weekends 10–4
winemaker Jim Brand, Bruce Gregory **production** NFP **est.** 1965
product range ($14–20 R) Riesling, Chardonnay, Cabernet Merlot, Shiraz, Cabernet Sauvignon.
summary Part of a very substantial investment in Coonawarra by McWilliam's, which first acquired a 50% interest from the founding Brand family, then moved to 100%, and followed this with the purchase of 100 hectares of additional vineyard land. Significantly increased production of the smooth wines for which Brand's is known will follow through to the end of the decade.

Brand's Laira Chardonnay

A relatively recent arrival on the scene for Brand's, the style of which has improved greatly since McWilliam's became involved. These wines tend to develop very well.

🍷🍷🍷🍷 **1996** Light to medium yellow-green; attractive melon, peach and fig varietal fruit is supported by quality oak on the bouquet. Similarly, lively peachy melon fruit, with a slippery feel, is complexed by touches of nutmeg and clove (from oak) on the palate. Nice wine. **rating:** 88

➾ **best drinking** 1998 – 1999 **best vintages** '90, '92, '95, '96 **drink with** Pasta with salmon • $16.95

brangayne of orange ★★★★☆

49 Pinnacle Road, Orange, NSW 2880 **region** Orange
phone (02) 6365 3229 **fax** (02) 6365 3170 **open** By appointment
winemaker Simon Gilbert (Contract) **production** 2700 **est.** 1994
product range ($14–20 ML) Sauvignon Blanc, Premium Chardonnay, Reserve Chardonnay, Shiraz, Merlot, Cabernet Sauvignon.
summary Orchardists Don and Pamela Hoskins decided to diversify into grape growing in 1994, and have progressively established 25 hectares of high-quality vineyards. With viticultural consultancy advice from Dr Richard Smart, and skilled contract-winemaking by Simon Gilbert, Brangayne has made an extraordinarily auspicious debut, emphatically underlining the potential of the Orange region.

Brangayne of Orange Premium Chardonnay

A silver medal winner in Class 3 at the 1997 Liquorland National Wine Show, and well-deserving of that award. Skilful winemaking, subtle use of oak and excellent cool-climate fruit are the ingredients.

🍷🍷🍷🍷 **1997** Medium yellow-green; the bouquet is spotlessly clean, of light to medium intensity, with melon and citrus fruit; almost imperceptible oak. The palate is similarly lively, fresh and clean, with attractive melon and citrus flavours, and a clean finish. **rating:** 87

➯ **best drinking** 1998 – 2001 **best vintages** '97 **drink with** Calamari • $14.15

Brangayne of Orange Reserve Chardonnay

The best chardonnay, picked riper (13.5 degrees versus 13 degrees than the Premium Chardonnay) is barrel-fermented in a mix of Allier and Vosges French oak barriques, before spending five months on lees. Sophisticated winemaking with excellent base material has produced a spectacular first-up wine.

🍷🍷🍷🍷½ **1997** Medium yellow-green; a sophisticated bouquet, subtle yet complex, with melon and cashew aromas is followed by an even better palate. Cashew, fig and melon fruit is supported by quite beautiful oak handling; while by no means a heavyweight, has great development potential. **rating:** 92

➯ **best drinking** 1998 – 2004 **best vintages** '97 **drink with** Flathead fillets • $16.65

Brangayne of Orange Shiraz

An impressive debut from 2.3 hectares of estate plantings. Meticulous attention to viticulture has resulted in perfect ripening of the fruit. Made in tiny quantities, and only briefly available at cellar door, but with increased quantities in the future.

🍷🍷🍷🍷 **1996** Bright red-purple; rich, ripe cherry fruit and vanilla oak on the bouquet are followed by more perfectly ripened cherry/berry fruit flavours on an exceptionally attractive palate for a first-crop wine. **rating:** 88

➯ **best drinking** 1998 – 2003 **best vintages** NA **drink with** Lamb fillets • $20

bream creek vineyard ★★★

Marion Bay Road, Bream Creek, Tas 7175 **region** Southern Tasmania
phone (03) 6231 4646 **fax** (03) 6231 4646 **open** By appointment
winemaker Steve Lubiana (Contract) **production** 2000 **est.** 1975
product range ($14–16 ML) Riesling, Chardonnay, Pinot Noir, Cabernet Pinot, Cabernet Sauvignon.

summary Until 1990 the Bream Creek fruit was sold to Moorilla Estate, but since that time has been independently owned and managed under the control of Fred Peacock, legendary for the care he bestows on the vines under his direction. The site has proved very difficult, but trellis improvements and additional plantings should see a significant increase in production as the years go by.

bremerton wines ★★★★

Strathalbyn Road, Langhorne Creek, SA 5255 **region** Langhorne Creek
phone (08) 8537 3093 **fax** (08) 8537 3109 **open** 7 days 10–5
winemaker Craig Willson, Rebecca Willson **production** 7500 **est.** 1988
product range ($11–28 CD) Sauvignon Blanc Semillon, Botrytised Chenin Blanc, Verdelho, Young Vine Shiraz, Old Adam Shiraz, Bremerton Blend (red), Cabernet Sauvignon.
summary The Willsons have been grape growers in the Langhorne Creek region for some considerable time, with 20.7 hectares of cabernet sauvignon, 15.4 of shiraz, 1.2 of merlot, and around half a hectare each of semillon, sauvignon blanc and petit verdot. They both sell grapes (the major part of the production) and also purchase grapes or wines for the Bremerton Lodge label, which is made under contract – and very competently.

Bremerton Cabernet Sauvignon

Draws upon a little over 20 hectares of estate plantings. Matured in a mix of new and two-year-old French oak barriques.

🍷🍷🍷🍷🍸 **1996** Medium to full red-purple; solid, sweet blackberry and plum fruit aromas lead into an equally solid and sweet plum, blackberry and blackcurrant-flavoured palate, aided by soft, sweet oak. **rating:** 90

➾ **best drinking** 1999 – 2004 **best vintages** '91, '96 **drink with** Steak and kidney pie • NA

briagolong estate ★★☆

Valencia-Briagolong Road, Briagolong, Vic 3860 **region** Gippsland
phone (03) 5147 2322 **fax** (03) 5147 2400 **open** Not
winemaker Gordon McIntosh **production** 400 **est.** 1979
product range ($25 ML) Chardonnay, Pinot Noir.
summary This is very much a weekend hobby for medical practitioner Gordon McIntosh, who nonetheless tries hard to invest his wines with Burgundian complexity, with mixed success. Dr McIntosh must have established an all-time record with the 15.4% alcohol in the '92 Pinot Noir.

brian barry wines ★★★☆

Farrell Flat Road, Clare, SA 5343 **region** Clare Valley
phone (08) 8338 3822 **fax** (08) 8338 3811 **open** Not
winemaker Brian Barry **production** NFP **est.** 1977
product range ($10–25 R) Jud's Hill Handpicked Riesling, Chardonnay, Handpicked Merlot, Handpicked Cabernet Sauvignon; Gleeson's Ridge Shiraz Merlot and Semillon Chardonnay.
summary Brian Barry is an industry veteran with a wealth of winemaking and show-judging experience. His is nonetheless in reality a vineyard-only operation, with a substantial part of the output sold as grapes to other wineries, and the wines made under contract at various wineries, albeit under Brian Barry's supervision. As one would expect, the quality is reliably good.

Brian Barry Jud's Hill Handpicked Merlot

'Hand Picked', so the label proclaims, and a new release for the Jud's Hill label. An interesting wine, with true Merlot varietal character – or as true as one can find it in Australia.

🍷🍷🍷🍷 **1994** Medium red-purple; a quite fragrant and fine bouquet with distinct and correct varietal character showing a mix of leaf and spicy medicinal aromas. An elegant and complex wine on the palate with nuances of leaf, spice and bitter chocolate; soft tannins. **rating:** 85

⇨ **best drinking** 1999 – 2004 **best vintages** NA **drink with** Veal steak • $25

briar ridge ★★★☆

Mount View Road, Mount View, NSW 2325 **region** Lower Hunter Valley
phone (02) 4990 3670 **fax** (02) 4990 7802 **open** Mon-Fri 9–5, weekends 9.30–4.30
winemaker Karl Stockhausen, Neil McGuigan **production** 15 000 **est.** 1972
product range ($17–25 CD) Early Harvest Semillon, Hand Picked Chardonnay, Chairman's Chardonnay, Stockhausen Semillon, Botrytis Semillon, Stockhausen Hermitage, Old Vines Shiraz, Cabernet Sauvignon.

summary Semillon and Hermitage, each in various guises, have been the most consistent performers, underlying the suitability of these varieties to the Hunter Valley. The Semillon, in particular, invariably shows intense fruit, and cellars well. In late 1994, Neil McGuigan created a minor sensation in the industry by leaving the large, public-listed McGuigan Brothers to join the far smaller Briar Ridge.

Briar Ridge Early Harvest Semillon

Judging by the alcohol disclosed on the label, the title 'Early Harvest' Semillon might have been better phrased 'Traditional Harvest'. A little over 11 degrees, it is in fact a full degree above the average alcohol of the great Lindemans' Semillons of the 1950s and 1960s. Semillon reaches flavour ripeness at far lower sugar levels in the Hunter Valley than in any other part of Australia, and is also extremely susceptible to the impact of vintage rain (a common occurrence) so is almost invariably picked 'early'.

🍷🍷🍷½ **1997** Medium to full yellow-green; a clean bouquet, of medium to full intensity with pleasant lemony fruit leads into a generously flavoured, honey and lemon-accented palate. In many ways belies the early harvest tag; not only does it taste ripe, but it has 11 degrees alcohol, which is reasonably high for Semillon from the Hunter. **rating:** 84

⇨ **best drinking** 1998 – 2003 **best vintages** NA **drink with** Crab or shellfish • $17

Briar Ridge Stockhausen Semillon

The prestige Semillon from Briar Ridge, drawn from vineyards at Pokolbin and at Mountview.

🍷🍷🍷🍷 **1997** Medium yellow-green; the bouquet is of medium to full intensity, quite tight and classic, with some minerally characters. The palate, too, is rather tighter, with lively lemony flavours and good length, finishing with crisp acidity. **rating:** 89

⇨ **best drinking** 1999 – 2005 **best vintages** NA **drink with** Flathead fillets • $21

Briar Ridge Chairman's Chardonnay

The flagship Chardonnay from Briar Ridge, barrel-fermented and matured in new French oak for nine months. In some vintages the oak has been somewhat heavy-handed, but not 1997 – a particularly good achievement given the difficult vintage conditions.

🍷🍷🍷🍷 **1997** Medium to full yellow-green; a complex bouquet with pronounced nutty/buttery oak. A powerful wine on the palate with strong oak inputs, but sufficient fruit there to justify that oak; good structure and acidity. **rating:** 88

➾ **best drinking** 1998 – 1999 **best vintages** NA **drink with** Kassler • $21

Briar Ridge Hand Picked Chardonnay

The label proudly proclaims that the grapes were hand-picked, which I suppose is a sign of the times, although still remaining standard practice with the majority of Australia's smaller wineries. A competently made wine in which the barrel-ferment oak influence has been kept under better control than the more expensive Chairman's Selection Chardonnay, which is a touch oaky for my taste.

🍷🍷🍷🍷 **1997** Medium to full yellow-green; a rich, buttery bouquet with some peachy notes and well-handled oak introduces a well-balanced palate with peachy fruit supported by a touch of charry oak, and well-balanced acidity lifting the finish. **rating:** 86

➾ **best drinking** 1998 – 1999 **best vintages** '87, '89, '91, '92, '97 **drink with** Sautéed veal • $17

Briar Ridge Stockhausen Hermitage

Named in honour of veteran winemaker Karl Stockhausen, who spent decades with Lindemans in the Hunter Valley, commencing his winemaking career there in 1960. Now a consultant to Briar Ridge, and brings his vast experience into play.

🍷🍷🍷🍷🍷 **1996** Medium red-purple; an ultra-typical young, earthy Hunter Shiraz bouquet with hints of boot polish and subtle oak is followed by a palate on which red cherry and raspberry fruit comes to the fore. Attractively soft and fine tannins round off a very good young wine. **rating:** 90

➾ **best drinking** 2000 – 2006 **best vintages** '86, '87, '89, '91, '93, '94, '96 **drink with** Braised lamb shanks • $21

bridgewater mill ★★★★

Mount Barker Road, Bridgewater, SA 5155 **region** Adelaide Hills
phone (08) 8339 3422 **fax** (08) 8339 5253 **open** Mon-Fri 9.30–5, weekends 10–5
winemaker Brian Croser **production** 20 000 **est.** 1986
product range ($15–33 R) Sauvignon Blanc, Chardonnay, Millstone Shiraz, Cabernet Malbec.
summary The second label of Petaluma, which consistently provides wines most makers would love to have as their top label. The fruit sources are diverse, with the majority of the sauvignon blanc and chardonnay coming from Petaluma-owned or managed vineyards, while the Shiraz is made from purchased grapes. Curiously infrequent tastings; none recent.

brindabella hills ★★★★

Woodgrove Close, via Hall, ACT 2618 **region** Canberra District
phone (02) 6230 2583 **fax** (02) 6230 2023 **open** Weekends, public holidays 10–5
winemaker Dr Roger Harris **production** 2000 **est.** 1989
product range ($15–18 CD) Riesling, Sauvignon Blanc Semillon, Chardonnay, Vintage Reserve Chardonnay, Shiraz, Cabernet.
summary Distinguished research scientist Dr Roger Harris presides over Brindabella Hills, which increasingly relies on estate-produced grapes, with small plantings of cabernet sauvignon, cabernet franc, merlot, shiraz, chardonnay, sauvignon blanc, semillon and riesling. Wine quality has been consistently impressive.

Brindabella Hills Sauvignon Blanc Semillon

One hundred per cent estate-grown, with the components picked over a range of degrees of ripeness, cold fermented to dryness and early bottled.

🍷🍷🍷🍷 **1997** Light green-yellow; the bouquet has a range of aromas running from herbal through to lime and lemon blossom; medium intensity. The well-flavoured palate shows a similar mix of herbal and riper flavours, no doubt reflecting the varietal mix. **rating:** 85

➾ **best drinking** 1998 – 1999 **best vintages** NA **drink with** Gravlax • $16.50

Brindabella Hills Vintage Reserve Chardonnay

In both 1996 and 1997 the most distinguished of the Brindabella Hills range. The '96 was placed first in the 1998 Winewise Small Makers Competition, and the '97 is of similar class and style.

🍷🍷🍷🍷🍷 **1997** Medium to full yellow-green; a complex bouquet with strong, toasty/charry/cinnamon barrel-ferment oak characters; the palate, likewise, shows substantial high toast barrel-ferment oak input, but does have elegant melon and peach fruit to justify this oak usage, and has a long finish. **rating:** 90

➾ **best drinking** 1998 – 2001 **best vintages** '96, '97 **drink with** Chinese prawns • $18

Brindabella Hills Cabernet

The wine is produced from a blend of Cabernet Sauvignon, Cabernet Franc and Merlot, fermented and hand-plunged in open fermenters, basket pressed, and matured in French and American barriques for two years. The upcoming '96 promises to be even better than the '95.

🍷🍷🍷🍷 **1995** Medium to full red-purple; the bouquet is clean, with sweet, dark berry fruit aromas of medium intensity, supported by sweet oak. The well-modulated palate shows cassis and leaf fruit, with touches of cedary/foresty characters; overall leaves a quite dry impression. **rating:** 86

➾ **best drinking** 1999 – 2003 **best vintages** '90, '91, '93, '95, '96 **drink with** Roast lamb • $18

britannia creek wines NR

75 Britannia Creek Road, Wesburn, Vic 3799 **region** Yarra Valley
phone (03) 5780 1426 **fax** (03) 5780 1426 **open** Weekends 10–6
winemaker Charlie Brydon **production** 1200 **est.** 1982
product range ($12–18 CD) Sauvignon Blanc, Semillon, Cabernets.
summary The wines (from Britannia Creek Wines) are made under the Britannia Falls label from 4 hectares of estate-grown grapes. A range of vintages (stretching back to 1990) were available from cellar door in 1998, with some interesting, full-flavoured Semillon.

broke estate ★★★☆

Wollombi Road, Broke, NSW 2330 **region** Lower Hunter Valley
phone (02) 6579 1065 **fax** (02) 6579 1065 **open** By appointment
winemaker Simon Gilbert (Contract) **production** 5000 **est.** 1989
product range ($14–45 ML) Limited Edition Chardonnay, Sauvignon Blanc, First Edition Cabernets, Limited Edition Cabernets.
summary With a high-profile consultant viticulturist (Dr Richard Smart) achieving some spectacular early results, Broke Estate has seldom been far from the headlines. Contrary to what one might expect, the opulent red wines (rather than the whites) have been the most successful.

broken bago vineyards NR

Nilligans Road, off Bago Road, Wauchope, NSW 2446 **region** Hastings River
phone (02) 6585 7099 **fax** (02) 6585 7099 **open** 7 days 11–5
winemaker Cassegrain (Contract) **production** NA **est.** 1985
product range ($14.50 CD) Chardonnay, Chambourcin.
summary Jim and Kay Mobs commenced planting the Broken Bago Vineyards in 1985 with 1 hectare of chardonnay, and have now increased the total plantings to 12 hectares. The wine is contract-made by Cassegrain, and wine sales commenced in 1996.

brokenwood ★★★★★

McDonalds Road, Pokolbin, NSW 2321 **region** Lower Hunter Valley
phone (02) 4998 7559 **fax** (02) 4998 7893 **open** 7 days 10–5
winemaker Iain Riggs, Dan Dineen **production** 70 000 **est.** 1970
product range ($15–50 R) Semillon, Cricket Pitch Sauvignon Blanc Semillon, Cricket Pitch Unwooded Chardonnay, Graveyard Chardonnay, Cricket Pitch Red, Cricket Pitch Cabernet Merlot, Shiraz, Pinot Noir, Cabernet Sauvignon, Graveyard Shiraz.
summary Deservedly fashionable winery producing consistently excellent wines. Cricket Pitch Sauvignon Blanc Semillon has an especially strong following, as has Cabernet Sauvignon; the Graveyard Shiraz is one of the best Hunter reds available today, the unwooded Semillon a modern classic. In 1997 acquired a controlling interest in Seville Estate (Yarra Valley) and has also been involved in the establishment of substantial vineyards in Cowra.

Brokenwood Semillon

A wine much appreciated by the Sydney market, which ensures that each release sells out long before the next becomes available. It is made in traditional style: in other words, without the use of oak, and unforced by techniques such as skin contact. Most is drunk young as a crisp, quasi-Chablis style, but as tastings show, can develop into a Hunter classic. (Specially made Reserve releases are in the maturation pipeline.)

🍷🍷🍷🍷🍷 **1997** Medium yellow-green; spotlessly clean and smooth, and a great rendition of the variety on the bouquet. The palate is perfectly balanced, with fine, delicate lemony/grassy fruit, with enough character to make it thoroughly enjoyable now, but with the capacity to age and develop beautifully. **rating:** 94

⇨ **best drinking** 1998 – 2007 **best vintages** '85, '86, '89, '92, '94, '95, '96, '97 **drink with** Balmain bugs • $16.50

Brokenwood Shiraz

A blend of McLaren Vale and Hunter Shiraz which demonstrates that cross-regional blending is not the exclusive preserve of the big companies. Nonetheless, it was Roger Warren, master winemaker at Hardys during the 1950s and '60s who first realised the synergies to be obtained from blending Hunter and McLaren Vale Shiraz, and he would no doubt be pleased to see the continuation of the tradition. The wine is matured in a mix of new and one-year-old American oak barriques for 16 months.

🍷🍷🍷🍷🍷 **1996** Strong red-purple; a powerful bouquet with concentrated black cherry, blackberry and chocolate-accented fruit supported by surprisingly subtle American oak. The palate, too, is driven by its excellent fruit flavours, with red and blackberry chocolate-tinged flavours rounded off with attractive oak, appropriate tannins and firm acidity. Should age beautifully. **rating:** 92

⇨ **best drinking** 2000 – 2006 **best vintages** '91, '94, '95, '96 **drink with** Barbecued leg of lamb • $20

Brokenwood Cricket Pitch Red

First made in 1987, taking its name from the fact that the vineyard immediately adjacent to the Brokenwood winery was once the site of a cricket field. The wine in fact has had no greater connection than the name with that vineyard, as it has been sourced from grapes grown in various parts of Australia, typically McLaren Vale, Mount Barker, Cowra, Coonawarra and the Hunter Valley. To add spice to the mix, it is a blend of 48% Merlot, 45% Cabernet Sauvignon and 7% Shiraz. It stands apart from most Brokenwood reds as a smooth early-drinking style.

🍷🍷🍷🍷 **1996** Medium red-purple; the clean and smooth bouquet shows ripe sweet fruit of medium intensity with well-balanced and integrated oak. The palate is clean and well balanced, with lively red berry and mint fruit, subtle oak and fine tannins. **rating:** 87

➯ **best drinking** 1998 – 2003 **best vintages** NA **drink with** Pork spare ribs • $18.50

brook eden vineyard NR

Adams Road, Lebrina, Tas 7254 **region** Northern Tasmania
phone (03) 6395 6244 **open** 7 days 10–5
winemaker Jan Bezemer **production** 800 **est.** 1988
product range ($15–18 CD) Chardonnay, Pinot Noir.
summary Jan and Sheila Bezemer own a 60-hectare Angus beef property which they purchased in 1987, but have diversified with the establishment of 2.5 hectares of vines. Jan Bezemer makes the wine at Delamere, the first vintage being 1993. The vineyard site is beautiful, with viticultural advice from the noted Fred Peacock.

brookland valley ★★★★

Caves Road, Willyabrup, WA 6284 **region** Margaret River
phone (08) 9755 6250 **fax** (08) 9755 6214 **open** Tues-Sun 11–4.30
winemaker Paul Lapsley **production** 8000 **est.** 1984
product range ($18–27 R) Sauvignon Blanc, Chardonnay, Merlot, Cabernet Merlot.
summary Brookland Valley has an idyllic setting, with its much enlarged Flutes Cafe one of the best winery restaurants in the Margaret River region. In 1997 BRL Hardy acquired a 50% interest in the venture, and has taken responsibility for viticulture and winemaking. The move towards richer and more complex red wines evident before the takeover will no doubt continue in its wake.

Brookland Valley Sauvignon Blanc

A wine which has consistently impressed, gaining in power and concentration as the vines have matured. The wine is produced from 2 hectares of estate plantings, and is at the richer end of the Margaret River spectrum – an area noted for producing Sauvignon Blanc with excellent varietal character. Winner of a gold medal at the 1994 Perth Sheraton Wine Awards, while the '95 was one of the stars at the 1996 Sydney International Wine Competition.

🍷🍷🍷🍷🍸 **1997** Light to medium yellow-green; the bouquet is fragrant, with a mix of gooseberry and tropical varietal fruit, the generously flavoured palate with attractively sweet gooseberry, passionfruit and tropical fruit flavours. **rating:** 91

➯ **best drinking** 1998 – 1999 **best vintages** '92, '93, '94, '95, '97 **drink with** Calamari • $21

Brookland Valley Merlot

A wine which does nothing to answer the eternal question asked in Australia: what should Merlot taste like? For all that, a new direction for Brookland Valley, and a variety which does appear suited to the Margaret River region.

🍷🍷🍷🍷 **1995** Medium to full red-purple; abundant sweet vanilla oak submerges the fruit on the bouquet, with some minty notes lurking underneath. A substantial wine on the palate with sweet, minty fruit and lots and lots of oak. I'm not sure this is what the variety is all about, but the wine certainly has flavour. **rating:** 84

➩ **best drinking** 1999 – 2004 **best vintages** NA **drink with** Barbecued beef • $26.95

Brookland Valley Cabernet Merlot

Since the arrival of BRL Hardy on the scene, the already good quality of the Brookland Valley wines has improved. So, in some instances, has the style changed for the better, particularly with the Cabernet Merlot, which is now produced in a much sweeter, softer and fruitier style than hitherto.

🍷🍷🍷🍷 **1995** Medium to full red-purple; there are abundant sweet, smooth dark berry/blackcurrant fruit aromas on the bouquet, with just a touch of oak. The palate is rich, ripe and smooth, with luscious oak a little more evident than on the bouquet, but by no means overplayed. **rating:** 89

➩ **best drinking** 2000 – 2007 **best vintages** '90, '91, '92, '93, '95 **drink with** Char-grilled steak • $27.90

brookside vineyard NR

5 Loaring Road, Bickley Valley, WA 6076 **region** Perth Hills
phone (08) 9291 8705 **fax** (08) 9291 5316 **open** By appointment
winemaker Jane Brook Estate (Contract) **production** NA **est.** 1984
product range ($16 CD) Chardonnay, Cabernet Sauvignon, Sparkling.
summary Brookside is one of the many doll's house-scale vineyard operations which dot the Perth Hills. It has a quarter of a hectare each of chardonnay and cabernet sauvignon, basically selling the wine through a mailing list. It does, however, offer bed and breakfast accommodation at the house with its attractive views of the Bickley Valley.

brown brothers ★★★★☆

Snow Road, Milawa, Vic 3678 **region** King Valley
phone (03) 5720 5500 **fax** (03) 5720 5511 **open** 7 days 9–5
winemaker John Brown, Terry Barnett, Rob Scapin **production** 300 000 **est.** 1885
product range ($9–38 R) A kaleidoscopic array of varietal wines, with a cross-hatch of appellations, the broadest being Victorian (e.g. Victorian Shiraz), more specific being King Valley (e.g. NV Brut and Pinot Chardonnay) and Milawa (e.g. Noble Riesling), then the Limited Release, Family Selection (e.g. Very Old Tokay and King Valley Chardonnay) and the Family Reserve ranges.
summary Brown Brothers draws upon a considerable number of vineyards spread throughout a range of site climates, ranging from very warm to very cool, with the climate varying according to altitude. It is also known for the diversity of varieties with which it works, and the wines always represent excellent value for money. Deservedly one of the most successful family wineries in Australia.

Brown Brothers Family Reserve Chardonnay

The Family Reserve range sits at the top of the Brown Brothers tree, the white wines held back for at least three years bottle age, the Cabernet-based reds for eight years. The Chardonnay is a vineyard selection from the King Valley, barrel-fermented in a mix of new and used French oak barriques, with 70% being matured in oak for eight months prior to bottling.

🍷🍷🍷🍷🍸 **1994** Full yellow, still with a touch of green; a full, complex, pungent bottle-developed bouquet with strong buttery/toasty aromas. The palate, which has reached the peak of its development, has masses of peachy/buttery fruit and attractive toasty oak characters in support. It won three trophies in wine shows in 1997. **rating:** 90

➪ **best drinking** 1998 – 1999 **best vintages** NA **drink with** Veal terrine • $28.85

Brown Brothers King Valley Pinot Chardonnay

A Pinot Noir dominant (typically around 70%) blend with Chardonnay and Pinot Meunier comprising the balance, produced entirely from grapes grown at Brown Brothers Whitlands Vineyard high in the King Valley. Complexity is gained by an extraordinarily broad harvest span extending from early February to late April. The wine undergoes malolactic fermentation before being blended and tiraged, and spends three years on yeast lees prior to disgorgement. Invariably a distinguished wine. The yet to be released 1995 won the Thorp Trophy for Best Sparkling White Wine at the 1998 Royal Sydney Wine Show.

🍷🍷🍷🍷🍸 **1993** Medium yellow-green with excellent fine mousse. The bouquet is complex, with bready aromas of medium to full intensity. The wine has interesting flavour and structure, at once full yet delicate, with biscuity Pinot Noir and Pinot Meunier flavours, finishing with a very dry but classic finish. **rating:** 90

➪ **best drinking** 1998 – 1999 **best vintages** '90, '91, '92, '93, '95 **drink with** Shellfish • $35.35

Brown Brothers Noble Riesling (375 ml)

Traces its origins back to 1934, when the first incidence of botrytis in the riesling at Milawa was noticed by John Brown senior. The wine was made but incorporated into a fortified wine, for there was no market for the style at the time. The first commercial vintage, albeit on a tiny scale, was 1962, the first significant commercial vintage in 1970. But it can legitimately claim to be the first Australian botrytised Riesling commercially released, and the wine has gone from strength to strength, particularly with the 1990's era decision to bottle and release the wine as a fresher, younger style. Recent vintages have been consistent gold medal, and not infrequently trophy, winning wines.

🍷🍷🍷🍷🍷 **1994** Glowing yellow-green; there are intense botrytis-driven fruit aromas of apricot, lime and peach, with apricot and lime predominating on the intense palate. The wine has excellent balance with a long finish aided by ideal acidity. **rating:** 94

➪ **best drinking** 1998 – 2002 **best vintages** '92, '94, '96 **drink with** Sticky date pudding • $18.10

Brown Brothers Classic Release Cabernet Sauvignon

The Classic Release Cabernets are first marketed when five years old. Typically sourced from the best growers in the upper reaches of the King Valley, sometimes with a dash of Shiraz added to the blend. A wide spread of picking dates (from March until May) adds complexity, and the wine is partially barrel-fermented, and then matured for 18 months in a mix of French and American oak, some new, some old.

🍷🍷🍷🍷 **1992** Medium to full red-purple; a fragrant bouquet with a mix of sweet fruit, more leafy notes, and cedar and vanillin oak, which is well integrated. A generously flavoured wine on the palate with sweet fruit, pleasant vanilla oak and soft tannins. **rating:** 89

best drinking 1998 – 2002 **best vintages** NA **drink with** Grilled veal chops • $34.75

Brown Brothers Family Selection Very Old Tokay

While Brown Brothers has always had its own fortified wine programme, and while it is anxious to keep the All Saints programme separate, the quality and complexity of the Brown Brothers releases seems to have increased since the All Saints acquisition. In any event, a lovely wine. The material used to make the wine averages ten years of age, with the oldest components between 20 and 25 years, the youngest between three and four years.

🍷🍷🍷🍷🍷 **NV** Medium to full tawny-red; very complex tea-leaf/plum pudding/malty aromas. High-quality Tokay varietal character on the palate, which is lively and intense, with strong tea-leaf/malt/butterscotch flavours, and good balance. **rating:** 94

best drinking 1997 – 1998 **best vintages** NA **drink with** After coffee • $29.80

browns of padthaway ★★☆

Keith Road, Padthaway, SA 5271 **region** Padthaway
phone (08) 8765 6063 **fax** (08) 8765 6083 **open** At Padthaway Estate
winemaker Contract **production** 30 000 **est.** 1970
product range ($10–20 R) Classic Diamond, Riesling, Sauvignon Blanc, Non Wooded Chardonnay, Verdelho, T-Trellis Shiraz, Redwood Cabernet Malbec, Myra Family Reserve Cabernet Sauvignon, Sparkling Shiraz.
summary The Brown family has for many years been the largest independent grape grower in Padthaway, a district in which most of the vineyards were established and owned by Wynns, Seppelts, Lindemans and Hardys, respectively. A rapidly expanding range of wines is now appearing under the Browns of Padthaway label, the majority being pleasant but very light in body and flavour.

bullers beverford 

Murray Valley Highway, Beverford, Vic 3590 **region** Murray Darling and Swan Hill
phone (03) 5037 6305 **fax** (03) 5037 6803 **open** Mon–Sat 9–5
winemaker Richard Buller (Jnr) **production** 50 000 **est.** 1952
product range ($9.50–14.50 CD) Victoria Chenin Blanc Colombard and Shiraz Grenache Malbec; The Magee Semillon Chardonnay and Cabernet Sauvignon Shiraz; White Label range of Semillon Chenin Blanc, Spätlese Lexia, Rosé, Shiraz, Cabernet Sauvignon; Victoria range of fortifieds including Port, Tokay and Muscat.
summary Traditional wines which in the final analysis reflect both their Riverland origin and a fairly low-key approach to style in the winery. It is, however, one of the few remaining sources of reasonable quality bulk fortified wine available to the public, provided in 22-litre Valorex barrels at $6.50 per litre. Some recent red wines have impressed.

bullers calliope 

Three Chain Road, Rutherglen, Vic 3685 **region** Rutherglen
phone (02) 6032 9660 **fax** (02) 6032 8005 **open** Mon–Sat 9–5, Sun 10–5
winemaker Andrew Buller **production** 5000 **est.** 1921

product range ($16–55 CD) Limited Release Shiraz, Mondeuse Shiraz, Grenache Cinsaut; Premium Black Label range and Museum Release range of old and rare material; Rare Liqueur and Liquid Gold Muscat and Tokay.

summary The winery rating is very much influenced by the recent superb releases of Museum fortified wines. Limited releases of Calliope Shiraz and Shiraz Mondeuse can also be exceptionally good.

Bullers Limited Release Shiraz Mondeuse

Mondeuse was imported into Australia, and specifically to northeast Victoria, around the turn of the century by Francois De Castella, apparently because of its ability to retain acid in warm climates. Brown Brothers released the first Shiraz Mondeuse blend in the early 1960s (perhaps even earlier still) and Bullers have grown the variety for many decades. This is a wholly remarkable wine, a Vintage Port without the spirit, the '96 containing an awesome 15.9% alcohol.

🍷🍷🍷🍷🍷 **1996** Dense red-purple; a dense, ripe and rich bouquet with an impenetrable mix of chocolate and berry fruit. The palate is no less rich, rather like chewing a dark chocolate bar spiced with plums; soft but persistent tannins are an essential part of the wholly imposing architecture. **rating:** 90

➾ **best drinking** 2001 – 2011 **best vintages** NA **drink with** Beef stew • $18

Bullers Liquid Gold Tokay (375 ml)

Repackaged into the slender, clear glass 'olive oil' type of 375 ml bottle much favoured these days, but done extremely well with an attractive label and capsule design. Externalities to one side, a beautiful expression of young Rutherglen Tokay, the sort of wine one should drink, rather than sip – especially on a cold winter's night.

🍷🍷🍷🍷🍷 **NV** Glowing golden brown; totally delicious, sweet tea-leaf and caramel varietal aromas leap from the glass, with the flavour precisely tracking the bouquet. Clean spirit, sweet but not the least bit cloying. **rating:** 91

➾ **best drinking** 1998 – 1999 **best vintages** NA **drink with** Cake and coffee • $18

Bullers Calliope Rare Liqueur Tokay (375 ml)

Both the Rare Liqueur Muscat and Tokay are of extreme quality and of great age, with the older material in the blend dating back to the 1940s, and picked from Bullers' 1920 Rutherglen dryland vineyard. The base wine is over 20 years old, and only 150 dozen 375 ml bottles are released each year to protect the integrity of the base material. Like the Liquid Gold Tokay, very smartly packaged in a 375 ml bottle.

🍷🍷🍷🍷🍷 **NV** Deep golden brown; a classic mix of sweet tea-leaf and crème brûlée aromas is followed by an outstanding palate showing the complexity which only age (and first class base material) can bring; some nutty characters join the tea-leaf and crème brûlée of the bouquet. **rating:** 95

➾ **best drinking** 1998 – 2008 **best vintages** NA **drink with** Strictly unnecessary, a meal in itself • $55

Bullers Liquid Gold Muscat (375 ml)

The sister wine to the Tokay, again featuring relatively fresh material, and again in the style one can drink in generous quantities. Shares the same attractive packaging.

🍷🍷🍷🍷🍷 **NV** Orange-brown; classic raisiny/grapey aromas lead into a young Muscat at its very best, with intense raisiny fruit, just a hint of nuttiness, and finishing with clean spirit. **rating:** 90

➪ **best drinking** 1998 – 1999 **best vintages** NA **drink with** Walnuts and almonds • $18

Bullers Calliope Rare Liqueur Muscat (375 ml)

Emerged from the shadows in spectacular fashion at the 1994 Sydney International Wine Competition, where it won the trophy for Best Wine of Show. A magnificent wine of great age and complexity. Originally released as Very Old Rutherglen Muscat, but now under the Rare Liqueur label, and in the new package.

🍷🍷🍷🍷🍷 **NV** Deep brown with a touch of olive on the rim; full and deep, almost into chocolate, with intense raisined fruit; richly textured, with great structure to the raisined/plum pudding fruit flavours, and obvious rancio age. **rating:** 94

➪ **best drinking** 1998 – 2008 **best vintages** NA **drink with** Strictly unnecessary, a meal in itself • $55

bungawarra NR

Bents Road, Ballandean, Qld 4382 **region** Granite Belt
phone (07) 4684 1128 **open** 7 days 10.30–4.30
winemaker Bruce Humphery-Smith, Jeff Harden **production** 1300 **est.** 1975
product range ($10–16 CD) Traminer, Block Six Chardonnay, Foundation Chardonnay, Festival Red, Paragon (Shiraz Cabernet Malbec), Liqueur Muscat.
summary Now owned by Jeff Harden. It draws upon 5 hectares of mature vineyards which over the years have shown themselves capable of producing red wines of considerable character.

burge family winemakers ★★★☆

Barossa Way, Lyndoch, SA 5351 **region** Barossa Valley
phone (08) 8524 4644 **fax** (08) 8524 4444 **open** 7 days 10–5
winemaker Rick Burge **production** 3500 **est.** 1928
product range ($12–40 CD) Olive Hill Riesling, Olive Hill Semillon, Chardonnay, Muscat Blanc Late Harvest, Clochmerle (Grenache), Old Vines Grenache Shiraz, Draycott Shiraz, Dracott Reserve Shiraz, Draycott Cabernet Merlot; Draycott Sparkling Red, Fortifieds.
summary Rick Burge came back to the family winery after a number of years successfully running St Leonards; there was much work to be done, but he has achieved much, using the base of very good fortified wines and markedly improving table wine quality, with Draycott Shiraz (both standard and Reserve) leading the way.

Burge Family Draycott Shiraz

Produced from the estate-owned Draycott Vineyard (hence the name) which is hand-pruned and yields 2–3 tonnes per acre, depending on the vintage. A classic Barossa Shiraz in traditional style.

🍷🍷🍷🍷 **1996** Medium to full red-purple; a solid bouquet with a mix of dark berry, chocolate, mint and earth aromas supported by subtle oak. Black cherry, mint and chocolate flavours run through a nicely balanced palate with good fruit composition. **rating:** 85

➪ **best drinking** 2000 – 2006 **best vintages** '84, '88, '91, '94, '95 **drink with** Wild duck, or failing that, domestic duck • $16.80

Burge Family Draycott Reserve Shiraz

A similar fruit base to the standard Draycott Shiraz, but given Rolls Royce treatment in new oak. The '96 was runner-up in the Shiraz Class at the 1998 Winewise Small Makers Competition, and perhaps a tad unlucky not to win its class.

1996 Dense full red-purple; the bouquet is dark and concentrated, with brooding black fruits and masses of vanilla oak. The palate abounds with rich, black cherry fruit, spice and lashings of charry American oak bound around it. **rating:** 90

⇨ **best drinking** 2002 – 2010 **best vintages** NA **drink with** Char-grilled rump • $38

burnbrae NR

Hill End Road, Erudgere via Mudgee, NSW 2850 **region** Mudgee
phone (02) 6373 3504 **fax** (02) 6373 3601 **open** Wed-Mon 9–5
winemaker Alan Cox **production** 1100 **est.** 1976
product range ($10–18 CD) Sauvignon Blanc, Chardonnay, Primavera Classic White, Primavera Rosé, Pinot Noir, Shiraz Cabernet Sauvignon Malbec, Vintage Granforte (Fortified Shiraz), Liqueur Muscat.
summary The founding Mace family sold Burnbrae in 1996. No recent tastings.

burramurra NR

Barwood Park, Nagambie, Vic 3608 **region** Goulburn Valley
phone (03) 5794 2181 **fax** (03) 5794 2755 **open** Not
winemaker Mitchelton (Contract) **production** 800 **est.** 1988
product range ($18 R) Cabernet Merlot.
summary Burramurra is the relatively low-profile vineyard operation of the Deputy Premier of Victoria, the Honourable Pat McNamara. Most of the grapes are sold to Mitchelton; a small amount is contract-made for the Burramurra label.

Burramurra Cabernet Merlot

A blend of 80% Cabernet Sauvignon and 20% Merlot grown on the vineyard owned by Victorian Deputy Premier Pat McNamara, and spends 18 months in French and American oak. The striking label depicts Australia's first banknote, which shows the Goulburn Weir adjacent to the Burramurra property.

1994 Medium red-purple; the bouquet is of light to medium intensity, with earthy overtones together with subtle, cedary oak. The palate is clean, relatively light, with reserved briary/leafy flavours. **rating:** 84

⇨ **best drinking** 1998 – 1999 **best vintages** NA **drink with** Yearling beef • $18

calais estates 

Palmers Lane, Pokolbin, NSW 2321 **region** Lower Hunter Valley
phone (02) 4998 7654 **fax** (02) 4998 7813 **open** Mon-Fri 9–5, weekends 10–5
winemaker Adrian Sheridan **production** 11 000 **est.** 1987
product range ($12–30 CD) Chenin Blanc, Semillon, Chardonnay, Reserve Chardonnay, Late Harvest Riesling, Sauterne, Shiraz Pinot, Shiraz, Reserve Shiraz, Cabernet Sauvignon.
summary The '97 white wines entered at the 1997 Hunter Valley Wine Show showed raw oak and other problems, but the '96 Shiraz (gold medal and top in its class) is excellent, with rich blackberry/plum pudding fruit and sweet vanilla oak.

cambewarra estate ★★★

520 Illaroo Road, Cambewarra NSW 2540 **region** Shoalhaven
phone (02) 4446 0170 **fax** (02) 4446 0170 **open** Weekends and holidays Wed-Sun 10–5
winemaker Tamburlaine (Contract) **production** 1500 **est.** 1991
product range ($12–29 CD) Light Chambourcin, Chardonnay (wooded and unwooded), Verdelho, Petit Rouge, Chambourcin, Cabernet Sauvignon, Vintage Port.
summary Geoffrey and Louise Cole founded Cambewarra Estate near the Shoalhaven River on the central southern coast of New South Wales, with contract winemaking competently carried out (a considerable distance away) at Tamburlaine Winery in the Hunter Valley. It had its moment of glory at the 1998 Royal Sydney Wine Show, topping two of the Small Producer classes, although it has had consistent success in other shows over the past few years.

Cambewarra Estate Chambourcin

Chambourcin is a French-bred hybrid which is highly resistant to mildew and rot, and particularly suited to warmer, wetter growing regions. Cassegrain on the north coast of New South Wales has the largest plantings, but they are scattered through various parts of the State. At Cambewarra, as elsewhere, it produces a strongly coloured wine which is typically best consumed when young. Cambewarra makes two versions: one a lighter style, without oak, the other a fuller, oak-matured wine.
🍷🍷🍷🍷 **1997** Vivid purple, almost unreal, though understandable in the context of the variety; a clean and potent bouquet stuffed with juicy blackberry and chocolate fruit aromas. The same flavours repeat on an extraordinary palate; whether this is almost beyond wine and into a caricature is a legitimate question, but it is an extraordinary achievement. Came top in its class at the '97 Rutherglen Wine Show. **rating:** 86

➾ **best drinking** 1998 – 1999 **best vintages** '94, '97 **drink with** Italian cuisine • $15

Cambewarra Estate Cabernet Sauvignon

Half a hectare of estate plantings produced the first vintage in 1996. The wine is matured in French oak, and shows excellent varietal character. The '96 won a gold medal at the 1997 Cowra Wine Show, then going on to win the trophy for Best Table Wine in the Small Producers classes at the 1998 Royal Sydney Wine Show, an exceptional achievement for Cambewarra Estate and the Shoalhaven region.
🍷🍷🍷🍷½ **1996** Medium red-purple; a rich and full bouquet with potent cassis fruit and charry oak is followed by a palate packed with juicy berry fruit. A brawling youth at the moment, but the potential is undeniable. **rating:** 90

➾ **best drinking** 2000 – 2004 **best vintages** '96 **drink with** Illabo lamb • $29

campbells ★★★★

Murray Valley Highway, Rutherglen, Vic 3685 **region** Rutherglen
phone (02) 6032 9458 **fax** (02) 6032 9870 **open** Mon-Sat 9–5, Sun 10–5
winemaker Colin Campbell **production** 35 000 **est.** 1870
product range ($10.95–80 R) Semillon, Riesling, Pedro Ximenez, Bobbie Burns Chardonnay, Silverburn Dry White and Red, Bobbie Burns Shiraz, The Barkly Durif, Malbec, Cabernets, Liquid Gold Tokay, Isabella Tokay, Rutherglen Muscat, Merchant Prince Muscat.
summary A wide range of table and fortified wines of ascending quality and price, which are always honest; as so often happens in this part of the world, the fortified wines are the best, with the extremely elegant Isabella Tokay and Merchant Prince Muscat at the top of the tree. For all that, the table wines are impressive in a full-bodied style; the winery rating is something

of a compromise between that for the fortified wines and for the table wines. A feature of the cellar door is an extensive range of back vintage releases of small parcels of wine not available through any other outlet.

Campbells Isabella Tokay

One of a pair of super-premium fortified wines produced by Campbells, the other being Campbells Merchant Prince Muscat. The Campbells wine is, and always has been, lighter and fresher than that of the other major producers, with more emphasis thrown on the underlying varietal fruit of the wines. It is a question of style rather than quality; these deluxe wines deserve their price.

🍷🍷🍷🍷🍸 **NV** Light tawny-gold; fragrant grapey, sweet tea-leaf aromas with clean spirit; the palate is luscious with sweet juicy berry and tea-leaf flavours, finishing with good acidity and a very clean aftertaste. **rating:** 93

➯ **best drinking** 1998 – 1999 **best vintages** NA **drink with** As fine an aperitif as it is a digestif • NA

Campbells Merchant Prince Muscat

A superbly balanced and constructed Muscat in a distinctly lighter mould than Baileys, Chambers or Morris, the big names of the district. For all that, it has an average age of 25 years, with the oldest component dating back over 60 years. One of those rare Muscats which actually invites a second glass.

🍷🍷🍷🍷🍷 **NV** Light to medium brown; intense but fragrant spice and raisin aromas with clean spirit. The palate is remarkably fresh and light given the age of the wine, with raisin, spice, malt and toffee flavours all intermingling, followed by cleansing acidity. **rating:** 94

➯ **best drinking** 1998 – 1999 **best vintages** NA **drink with** Coffee, high-quality biscuits • $80

canobolas-smith ★★★★

Boree Lane, Off Cargo Road, Lidster via Orange, NSW 2800 **region** Orange
phone (02) 6365 6113 **fax** (02) 6365 6113 **open** Weekends, public holidays 11–5
winemaker Murray Smith **production** 2000 **est.** 1986
product range ($10–20 CD) Chardonnay, Highland Chardonnay, Highland Red, Cabernets, Alchemy (Cabernet blend).
summary after a tentative start with early experimental vintages, Canobolas-Smith has established itself as one of the leading Orange district wineries with its distinctive blue wrap-around labels. Much of the wine is sold from the cellar door, which is well worth a visit.

Canobolas-Smith Chardonnay

Produced from 2.2 hectares of estate plantings at an elevation of 820 metres on Mount Canobolas. The vines are not irrigated, and are grown on red volcanic soils. Each vintage has shown distinct improvement, the '95 and '96 being the best yet.

🍷🍷🍷🍷 **1996** Medium to full yellow-green; the bouquet shows strong barrel ferment inputs, nutty and rich; the palate retains some elegance, notwithstanding the quite assertive barrel-ferment oak characters. There are white peach flavours and the wine has moderate length. **rating:** 86

➯ **best drinking** 1998 – 1999 **best vintages** '94, '95, '96 **drink with** Pasta • $18

cape bouvard NR

Mount John Road, Mandurah, WA 6210 **region** South West Coast
phone (08) 9739 1360 **fax** (08) 9739 1360 **open** 7 days 10–5
winemaker Gary Grierson **production** 2000 **est.** 1990
product range ($15–20 CD) Chardonnay, Shiraz, Cabernet Sauvignon, Sparkling, Port.
summary Doggerel poet-cum-winemaker Gary Grierson draws upon 1 hectare of estate plantings, but also purchases grapes from other growers for the new Cape Bouvard label. The few wines tasted have been light but inoffensive.

cape clairault ★★★★

Henry Road, Willyabrup, WA 6280 **region** Margaret River
phone (08) 9755 6225 **fax** (08) 9755 6229 **open** 7 days 10–5
winemaker Ian Lewis, Peter Stark **production** 8000 **est.** 1976
product range ($13–22 CD) Under the Cape Clairault label Sauvignon Blanc, Unwooded Chardonnay, Semillon Sauvignon Blanc, Riesling, Claireau (sweet white), Clairault (Cabernet blend); under the second Cape label, Cape White, Cape Rose, Cape Late Harvest and Cape Red.
summary Ian and Ani Lewis have been joined by two of their sons and, in consequence, have not only decided not to sell the business, but to double its size, with winery capacity being almost doubled from 85 tonnes to 150 tonnes. Notwithstanding increasing production, demand for the wines is so great that Cape Clairault has withdrawn from export to concentrate on the local market. A vineyard specialty is guinea fowl, not to be eaten (I think), but to control grasshopper plagues.

Cape Clairault Sauvignon Blanc

Cape Clairault has a little over 3 hectares of sauvignon blanc, which in turn accounts for almost one-third of its total plantings. It is, of course, a variety which does very well in the Margaret River region, and provides Cape Clairault with its flagship wine. Over the years some excellent Sauvignon Blancs have been produced under the Clairault label.

🍷🍷🍷🍷🍷 **1997** Light to medium yellow-green; has slightly more bite in a mineral/herbal spectrum than the Semillon Sauvignon Blanc, but in similar style. The palate is firmly but not aggressively structured, with herb and gooseberry flavours on a long finish with very good mouthfeel. **rating:** 91

➾ **best drinking** 1998 – 1999 **best vintages** '93, '95, '97 **drink with** Shellfish • $15.75

Cape Clairault Semillon Sauvignon Blanc

A blend of 70% Semillon and 30% Sauvignon Blanc. Ten per cent of the wine was matured in new French oak, which adds to the texture rather than altering the flavour.

🍷🍷🍷🍷🍷 **1997** Light to medium yellow-green; a most attractive bouquet, with pleasantly sweet fruit ranging through lemon and gooseberry. The palate provides more of the same, with gooseberry and passionfruit characters giving most appealing flavour; good length. **rating:** 90

➾ **best drinking** 1998 – 2000 **best vintages** '88, '91, '92, '93, '95, '97 **drink with** Seafood salad • $15

The Clairault

A variable blend of Cabernet Sauvignon, Cabernet Franc and Merlot, which differs greatly according to the vintage. The philosophy is simply to come up with the best wine from the available components. In 1995 the wine was 90% Cabernet Sauvignon and 10% Cabernet Franc.

🍷🍷🍷🍷 1995 Medium red-purple; a complex and concentrated bouquet, with earthy berry fruit and touches of sweet oak. The quite powerful palate is basically in a briary/earthy mode, although there are some mint and red berry fruit flavours present. Just a fraction abrasive in its presentation. **rating:** 85

➾ **best drinking** 2000 – 2005 **best vintages** '82, '85, '86, '90, '91, '95 **drink with** Margaret River Chevre • $28

cape estate NR

Harvey Road, Denbarker, WA 6280 **region** Margaret River
phone (08) 9857 6046 **fax** (08) 9954 1732 **open** By appointment
winemaker Gavin Berry (Contract) **production** 200 **est.** 1980
product range ($10–15 CD) Sauvignon Blanc, Chardonnay, Cabernet Sauvignon.
summary Cape Estate is owned by Perth architect Peter May and wife Carol. It is in fact the new name for the Shemarin Vineyard established by Rob Bowen in 1980. Since 1994 all the wines have been made at Plantagenet.

cape jaffa wines NR

Limestone Coast Road, Cape Jaffa, SA 5276 **region** Mount Benson and Robe
phone (08) 8768 5053 **fax** (08) 8768 5040 **open** 7 days 10–5
winemaker Derek Hooper **production** 5000 **est.** 1993
product range ($16–18 CD) Unwooded Chardonnay (McLaren Vale), Semillon Sauvignon Blanc, Barrel Fermented Chardonnay (Mount Benson and Padthaway), Merlot (McLaren Vale), Shiraz (McLaren Vale) Cabernet Sauvignon (Mount Benson).
summary Cape Jaffa is the first of the Mount Benson wineries to come into production, albeit with most of the initial releases coming from other regions. Ultimately all of the wines will come from the substantial estate plantings of 20 hectares which include the four major Bordeaux red varieties, shiraz, chardonnay, sauvignon blanc and semillon. It is a joint venture between the Hooper and Fowler families, and the winery (built of local paddock rock) has been designed to allow eventual expansion to 1000 tonnes, or 70 000 cases.

cape mentelle ★★★★★

Off Wallcliffe Road, Margaret River, WA 6285 **region** Margaret River
phone (08) 9757 3266 **fax** (08) 9757 3233 **open** 7 days 10–4.30
winemaker John Durham **production** 50 000 **est.** 1970
product range ($20–44 R) Chardonnay, Semillon Sauvignon Blanc, Cabernet Sauvignon, Cabernet Merlot, Shiraz, Zinfandel, Trinders Cabernet Merlot.
summary Notwithstanding majority ownership by Veuve Clicquot, David Hohnen remains very much in command of one of Australia's foremost medium-sized wineries. Exceptional marketing skills and wine of the highest quality, with the back-up of New Zealand's Cloudy Bay, are a potent combination. The Chardonnay and Semillon Sauvignon Blanc are among Australia's best, the potent Shiraz usually superb, and the berry/spicy Zinfandel makes one wonder why this grape is not as widespread in Australia as it is in California.

Cape Mentelle Semillon Sauvignon Blanc

A wine that has been part of the Cape Mentelle portfolio since 1985, but which in the early years was not particularly exciting. To what extent the Cloudy Bay skills rubbed off is a moot point, but the fact is that in more recent times this has been another faultless wine combining finesse with power.

TTTTT **1997** Medium yellow-green; a complex yet fruit-driven bouquet, with a mix of rich, ripe gooseberry and more lemony fruit supported by subliminal oak. There is masses of flavour on the palate, essentially sweet passionfruit and gooseberry, followed by a pleasantly dry finish which prevents the wine going over the top. **rating:** 94

⇨ **best drinking** 1998 – 2001 **best vintages** '85, '88, '91, '93, '95, '96, '97 **drink with** Fish, Asian cuisine • $20.75

Cape Mentelle Chardonnay

First made in 1988, and immediately established itself as another classic. The 1990 vintage was selected for British Airways First Class; each succeeding year has reached new heights. These are wines of exceptional complexity, Chardonnays made by a red winemaker (but in the best possible way). The 1993 won the George Mackey Award for best wine exported from Australia in 1994; subsequent vintages have all been in the same class.

TTTTY **1996** Medium yellow-green; a rich, full and complex bouquet with ripe, strongly figgy, fruit leads into an even more complex palate in which a range of tangy citrus and melon flavours, at once distinctively Margaret River yet vaguely Burgundian, come into play. **rating:** 92

⇨ **best drinking** 1998 – 2003 **best vintages** '90, '91, '92, '93, '94, '95, '96 **drink with** Tasmanian salmon • $29.80

Cape Mentelle Shiraz

Made its debut in 1981, and over the intervening years has produced some spectacular wines which – to my palate at least – have not infrequently outclassed the Cabernet Sauvignon. The wines typically show wonderful spice, game and liquorice characters reminiscent of the Rhône Valley. Since 1986 a small percentage of Grenache has been included in some years.

TTTTY **1996** Dense red-purple; a marvellously complex bouquet with an array of rich, dark plum and berry fruit with game and boot-polish undertones, quintessentially varietal. The palate, too, is multiflavoured and multilayered with plum, liquorice and berry fruit, supported by lingering tannins. **rating:** 93

⇨ **best drinking** 2000 – 2010 **best vintages** '86, '88, '90, '91, '93, '94, '96 **drink with** Stir-fried Asian beef • $24

Cape Mentelle Zinfandel

Also made its first appearance in 1981, a direct reflection of David Hohnen's early winemaking experiences in California. Despite its exceptional quality, remains the only Zinfandel worth mentioning in Australia; it is most surprising that it has not encouraged others to try.

TTTT **1996** Medium to full red-purple; an intense, riotously ripe, bouquet with dark glossy cherry fruit and spicy highlights. The palate has lots of extract and concentration, ranging through briary, berry, prune, plum and cherry; a slightly hot finish prevents absolute top points. **rating:** 86

⇨ **best drinking** 1998 – 2003 **best vintages** '86, '87, '91, '92, '93, '94, '95 **drink with** Rare char-grilled rump steak • $24

Cape Mentelle Cabernet Sauvignon

The wine which started the Cape Mentelle juggernaut, with the '82 and '83 vintages winning the Jimmy Watson Trophy in successive years. Both style and quality wandered somewhat in the second half of the 1980s, but has steadied (and improved greatly) in the 1990s as David Hohnen has come to terms with the now fully mature vineyard (and it with him).

🍷🍷🍷🍷🍷 **1994** Medium to full red-purple; the bouquet is clean, of medium intensity with perfectly blended blackberry/cassis fruit and cedary oak. The palate provides more of the same, with a harmonious blend of cassis, blackberry and cedar, finishing with soft, lingering tannins. **rating:** 91

⇒ **best drinking** 1999 – 2009 **best vintages** '76, '78, '82, '83, '86, '90, '91, '93, '94 **drink with** Loin of lamb • $43.20

capel vale ★★★★

Lot 5 Stirling Estate, Mallokup Road, Capel, WA 6271 **region** Geographe
phone (08) 9727 1986 **fax** (08) 9791 2452 **open** 7 days 10–4
winemaker Rob Bowen, Krister Jonsson **production** 100 000 **est.** 1979
product range ($11.50–48 R) CV Chenin, Classic White, Unwooded Chardonnay, Sauvignon Blanc Chardonnay, Classic Red, Pinot Noir, Shiraz, Cabernets Merlot; Capel Vale Riesling, Verdelho, Sauvignon Blanc Semillon, Chardonnay, Merlot, Shiraz, Cabernet Sauvignon; 'Reserve Connoisseur' range of Whispering Hill Riesling, Seven Day Road Sauvignon Blanc, Frederick Chardonnay, Kinaird Shiraz and Howecroft Cabernet Sauvignon Merlot; Tawny Port.
summary Capel Vale continues to expand its viticultural empire, its contract-grape sources and its marketing, the last through the recent introduction of a series of vineyard or similarly named super-premium wines. Against the run of play, as it were, the most successful of these super-premiums are the red wines, for I have long admired the elegance and finesse of the Capel Vale whites. The strong marketing focus the company has always had is driven by its indefatigable owner, Dr Peter Pratten.

Capel Vale Whispering Hill Riesling

First produced under the top Reserve label in 1996, and drawn from Capel Vale's Whispering Hill Vineyard at Mount Barker. A particularly powerful wine was made in 1997, picked at 13.5° baumé.

🍷🍷🍷🍷 **1997** Light to medium yellow-green; a quite fragrant bouquet with lime, passionfruit and an extra touch of lift deriving from a touch of botrytis influence. The palate is intense, with lime and passionfruit flavours, and again just an echo of that botrytis on the finish. It is difficult to know whether this adds to or detracts from the wine. **rating:** 86

⇒ **best drinking** 1998 – 2002 **best vintages** NA **drink with** Thai cuisine • $25

Capel Vale CV Unwooded Chardonnay

Drawn from the same spread of vineyard sources utilised by Capel Vale in making its conventional (i.e. wooded) Chardonnays, and neatly puts an argument that regional blending adds to complexity. Certainly one of the better unwooded Chardonnays on the market.

🍷🍷🍷🍷 **1997** Light green-yellow; the bouquet is fragrant, with a mix of passionfruit, melon and white peach. The palate is slightly more herbaceous than the bouquet, but melon and passionfruit flavours do reappear, and while light and crisp, it has pleasant mouthfeel and a harmonious finish. **rating:** 88

⇒ **best drinking** 1998 – 2001 **best vintages** NA **drink with** Terrine of salmon • $14.50

Capel Vale Kinnaird Shiraz

Another prestige wine for Capel Vale from its Whispering Hill Vineyard, grown on granitic soils. The wine spends 18 months in oak; 30% is new French, the balance being two-year-old

French and American oak barriques. The wine was not filtered, but, in a world-first, was fined using (I kid you not) free-range eggwhites. It is presented in the biggest, heaviest bottle imaginable, like a giant tenpin bowling ball. Free-range eggs and bowling balls to one side, this is a terrific wine.

🍷🍷🍷🍷🍷 **1996** Medium to full red, with just a touch of purple. The intense bouquet is clean, with fully ripe sweet cherry fruit and subtle oak swelling into an opulent palate with waves of black cherry fruit and sophisticated spicy oak. **rating:** 94

➾ **best drinking** 2000 – 2010 **best vintages** NA **drink with** Game pie • $48

Capel Vale Howecroft Cabernet Sauvignon Merlot

A blend of 80% Cabernet Sauvignon from the Margaret River and 15% Merlot and 5% Cabernet Franc from Capel. The components were separately fermented, and matured in new French oak for 12 months prior to blending. The wine selected for the Howecroft reserve bottling then spent a further year in barrel before being bottled. Like the Kinnaird Shiraz, presented in a dreadnought-class bottle.

🍷🍷🍷🍷🍷 **1995** Medium to full red-purple; the bouquet is full and complex, with ripe blackberry and chocolate fruit supported by subtle oak. The palate is elegant, yet powerful, with restrained cassis and chocolate fruit flavours, followed by lingering tannins. **rating:** 91

➾ **best drinking** 2000 – 2010 **best vintages** NA **drink with** Rare eye fillet • $48

capercaillie ★★★

Londons Road, Lovedale, NSW 2325 **region** Lower Hunter Valley
phone (02) 4990 2904 **fax** (02) 4991 1886 **open** Mon-Sat 9–5, Sun 10–5
winemaker Alasdair Sutherland **production** 6000 **est.** 1995
product range ($17–25 CD) Semillon, Unoaked Chardonnay, Chardonnay, Dessert Style Gewurztraminer, Hunter Hastings Chambourcin, Orange Merlot, Coonawarra Orange Cabernet Sauvignon Merlot Cabernet Franc.
summary The former Dawson Estate, now run by Hunter Valley veteran Alasdair Sutherland (no relation to Neil Sutherland of Sutherland Estate). The Capercaillie wines, and the Chardonnays in particular, are always extremely full-flavoured and generous.

Capercaillie Hunter Valley Chardonnay

The benchmark for Capercaillie, produced predominantly from 4.5 hectares of chardonnay which is now over 20 years old. Opulent oak handling is part of the style that will appeal more to some than others.

🍷🍷🍷🍷 **1997** Medium to full yellow-green; very strong spicy/clove/nutmeg American oak is the first impression on a strikingly rich bouquet. The palate, too, is driven by sophisticated and largely successful use of American oak, although it does catch up a little on the finish, where coffee/toffee flavours overtake the vanilla and peach of the mid-palate. **rating:** 85

➾ **best drinking** 1998 – 1999 **best vintages** NA **drink with** Spiced chicken • $19

capogreco estate NR

Riverside Avenue, Mildura, Vic 3500 **region** Murray Darling and Swan Hill
phone (03) 5023 3060 **open** Mon-Sat 10–6
winemaker Bruno Capogreco **production** NFP **est.** 1976
product range ($8–12 CD) Riesling, Moselle, Shiraz-Mataro, Cabernet Sauvignon, Claret, Rosé, Fortifieds.

summary Italian-owned and run, the wines are a blend of Italian and Australian Riverland influences; the herb-infused Rosso Dolce is a particularly good example of its kind.

caraboода estate NR

297 Carabooda Road, Carabooda, WA 6033 **region** Swan District
phone (08) 9407 5283 **open** 7 days 10–6
winemaker Terry Ord **production** 500 **est.** 1989
product range ($12.50–16 CD) Sauvignon Blanc, Shiraz, Cabernet Sauvignon.
summary 1989 is the year of establishment given by Terry Ord, but it might as well have been 1979 (when he made his first wine) or 1981 (when he and wife Simonne planted their first vines). But it has been a slowly, slowly exercise, with production from the 3 hectares of estate plantings now supplemented by purchased grapes, the first public release not being made until mid-1994.

carbunup estate ★★★

Bussel Highway, Carbunup, WA 6280 **region** Margaret River
phone (08) 9755 1111 **open** 7 days 10–5
winemaker Robert Credaro **production** NFP **est.** 1988
product range ($12–16 CD) Under the premium Vasse River Wines label: Chardonnay, Semillon, Sauvignon Blanc; under Carbunup Estate label: Verdelho, Shiraz.
summary A relative newcomer, selling part of the grapes produced from the 18 hectares of vineyards, but keeping part for release under the Carbunup Estate and Vasse River labels – strikingly different in design, and giving no clue that they emanate from the same winery. It has had immediate success with its white wines, and in particular its Chardonnay and Semillon.

carosa NR

310 Houston Street, Mount Helena, WA 6082 **region** Perth Hills
phone (08) 9572 1603 **fax** (08) 9572 1604 **open** Weekends, holidays 11–5 or by appointment
winemaker James Elson **production** 500 **est.** 1984
product range ($12–21 CD) Chardonnay, Classic Dry White, Pinot Noir, Cabernet Merlot, Janne Louise Méthode Champenoise, Old Tawny Port, White Port.
summary Very limited production and small-scale winemaking result in wines which can only be described as rustic, but which sell readily enough into the local market. Barrel samples tasted early in the piece were not in proper condition for judging, while bird damage has restricted yields from the Carosa vineyards. However, winemaker (and consultant) Jim Elson has extensive eastern Australian winemaking experience (with Seppelt) so should succeed. No recent tastings.

casella ★★★

Farm 1471 Wakley Road, Yenda, NSW 2681 **region** Riverina
phone (02) 6968 1346 **fax** (02) 6968 1196 **open** Not
winemaker Alan Kennett **production** 700 000 **est.** 1969
product range ($7.95–14.95 R) Under the newly adopted Carramer Estate label Semillon Sauvignon Blanc, Chardonnay, Botrytis Semillon, Shiraz, Shiraz Cabernet, Cabernet Sauvignon.
summary Casella is typical of the new wave sweeping through the Riverina. It draws upon 216 hectares of estate vineyards, selling much of its wine in bulk or as cleanskin bottled wine to

other producers, but also marketing a range of varietals under the Carramar Estate label. Predictably, the Botrytis Semillon is the outstanding release.

Casella Carramar Estate Botrytis Semillon

Fully botrytised semillon was picked at 23° baumé and cold fermented at 12 degrees in stainless steel. A powerful testament to the quality of Botrytis Semillon from the Riverina.

🍷🍷🍷🍷 **1996** Medium to full yellow; rich mandarin, cumquat and apricot aromas precede a wine with complex honeycomb and cumquat flavour, well balanced by firm but not aggressive acidity. If there is any oak in the wine, it is not easy to see it, and it is none the worse for that. **rating:** 85

➾ **best drinking** 1998 – 2000 **best vintages** NA **drink with** Stuffed baked apple • $14.95

cassegrain ★★★☆

Hastings River Winery, Fernbank Creek Road, Port Macquarie, NSW 2444 **region** Hastings River

phone (02) 6583 7777 **fax** (02) 6584 0354 **open** 7 days 9–5

winemaker John Cassegrain, Glenn Goodall **production** 55 000 **est.** 1980

product range ($9.25–27.95 R) Traminer Riesling, Sauvignon Blanc, Semillon, Verdelho, White Pinot, Chardonnay, Rose, Shiraz, Pinot Noir, Cabernet Merlot, Reserve Merlot, Chambourcin, Reserve Chambourcin; Fromenteau Chardonnay; Five Mile Hollow Red and White; Sparkling, Fortified and Dessert Wine.

summary A very substantial operation based in the Hastings Valley on the north coast of New South Wales. In earlier years, it drew fruit from many parts of Australia, but is now entirely supplied by the 162 hectares of estate plantings which offer 14 varieties, including the rare chambourcin, a French-bred cross.

Cassegrain Hastings River Semillon

Produced solely from grapes grown in various vineyards in the Hastings River region, and cold-fermented in traditional large oak vats. Given one month's lees contact and then racked and bottled mid-year. Traditional Semillon making.

🍷🍷🍷🍷 **1997** Medium to full yellow-green; an interesting mix of toast and herb aromas, almost going into tobacco. There is a similar range of honey and herb flavours on the palate, with well-balanced acidity. **rating:** 87

➾ **best drinking** 1998 – 2002 **best vintages** NA **drink with** Oysters • $14.95

Cassegrain Hastings River Chardonnay

The junior of the two Hastings Valley Chardonnays (Fromenteau Vineyard is the top-end release made in tiny quantities) but provides further evidence that chardonnay is well suited to the warm, humid conditions of the Hastings Valley.

🍷🍷🍷 **1997** Medium to full yellow-green; a rich, ripe bouquet with honey, peach and butter flows into a soft fig and peach-flavoured palate which is not, however, particularly focused. **rating:** 82

➾ **best drinking** 1998 – 1999 **best vintages** '96 **drink with** Pasta • $15.95

Cassegrain Reserve Chardonnay

Top-of-the-range Chardonnay from the Hastings River vineyards, given full-blown winemaking treatment, including the relatively lavish use of new oak.

ŸŸŸŸ **1997** Medium to full yellow-green; the bouquet is driven by strong, spicy/toasty barrel-ferment oak characters, with some more creamy fig and peach fruit. There is more of the same on the palate, with abundant spicy nutmeg oak blending with creamy/figgy/honeyed fruit. If you like oak, you will love the wine. **rating:** 86

➪ **best drinking** 1998 – 1999 **best vintages** NA **drink with** Stir-fried prawns with cashew nuts • $27.95

castle rock estate ★★★★

Porongurup Road, Porongurup, WA 6324 **region** Great Southern
phone (08) 9853 1035 **fax** (08) 9853 1010 **open** Mon-Fri 10–4, weekends and public holidays 10–5
winemaker Michael Staniford **production** 4500 **est.** 1983
product range ($13.50–18 CD) Riesling, Late Harvest Riesling, Estate White, Chardonnay, Pinot Noir, Cabernet Sauvignon, Muscat Liqueur.
summary An exceptionally beautifully sited vineyard and cellar-door sales area with sweeping vistas from the Porongurups, operated by the Diletti family. The standard of viticulture is very high, and the site itself ideally situated (quite apart from its beauty). The Rieslings have always been elegant, and handsomely repaid time in bottle. In the most recent vintages the other wines of Castle Rock have improved considerably, with far greater weight and flavour than hitherto.

Castle Rock Riesling

Consistently the best of the Castle Rock Estate wines, and ages wonderfully well. It is easy to overlook the wine in its youth, when it is typically very toasty, very crisp and on the lean side, but flowers with age. The lesson has been learnt again and again, with four- and five-year vertical tastings producing the same result: the wines age superbly, gaining progressively higher points the older they are. In a mini-vertical tasting in January 1998 the point scores for the older vintages went as follows: '96 – 98 points; '94 – 90 points; '93 – 92 points.

ŸŸŸŸ **1997** Light straw-green; the bouquet is, as always, light, faintly spicy and with faint wafts of passionfruit. The palate is very well balanced with lime, spice and mineral flavours, and a spotlessly clean, low phenolic finish. Fresh acid guarantees its longevity. **rating:** 88

➪ **best drinking** 2002 – 2007 **best vintages** '86, '89, '90, '91, '93, '94, '96, '97 **drink with** Seafood salad • $14

Castle Rock Chardonnay

Undoubtedly a slow-developing style, and, like the Riesling, often deceptively light in its youth. Vintage variation, too, plays a role, and some of the wines have lacked concentration. However, both the '94 and '97 are fine wines, the '97 due for release at the end of 1998.

ŸŸŸŸ **1997** Medium yellow-green; showed particularly attractive melon and cashew fruit on both bouquet and palate shortly after bottling, and will undoubtedly go forward from here. The palate is elegant and fine, with citrus and cashew flavours; the wine has what can only be described as a 'dancing delicacy'. **rating:** 87

➪ **best drinking** 1999 – 2004 **best vintages** NA **drink with** Marron or lobster • $18

Castle Rock Pinot Noir

The wine is fermented in open tanks and matured for 12 months in French oak. There is no doubt that Pinot Noir in the Great Southern region is vintage-dependent. Castle Rock regards the '96 as the best Pinot Noir it has made, and it is not hard to see why. Yet, on the other hand, none at all was made in 1997.

🍷🍷🍷🍷 **1996** Medium red, with just a touch of purple; the bouquet is fragrant, with a mix of cherry and plum fruit set against more foresty/earthy characters. There is a similar mix on the palate, with plum, briar and forest flavours and above-average weight and length. A major and pleasant surprise. **rating:** 85

➾ **best drinking** 1998 – 1999 **best vintages** NA **drink with** Smoked quail • $18

cathcart ridge estate ★★

Moyston Road, Cathcart via Ararat, Vic 3377 **region** Grampians
phone (03) 5352 1997 **fax** (03) 5352 1558 **open** 7 days 10–5
winemaker David Farnhill **production** 2000 **est.** 1977
product range ($8–25 CD) Grampians Riesling, Sauvignon Blanc, Chardonnay, Pinot Noir, Rhymney Reef Shiraz, Cabernet Merlot, Merlot, Cabernet Sauvignon; second label is Mount Ararat Estate, with Dry White, Late Picked White, Colombard, Dry Red (Grenache) and Shiraz.
summary Now owned and operated by the Farnhill family; it remains to be seen whether the high reputation that Cathcart Ridge enjoyed in the early 1980s can be restored, although tastings to date have not impressed.

catherine vale vineyard ★★★☆

Milbrodale Road, Bulga, NSW 2330 **region** Lower Hunter Valley
phone (02) 6579 1334 **fax** (02) 6579 1334 **open** 7 days 10–5
winemaker John Hordern (Contract) **production** 520 **est.** 1994
product range ($12.80–14.50 CD) Semillon, Chardonnay.
summary Former schoolteachers Bill and Wendy Lawson have established Catherine Vale as a not-so-idle retirement venture. Both were involved in school athletics and sports programmes, handy training for do-it-yourself viticulturists. Most of the grapes from the 3.5-hectare vineyard are sold to contract winemaker John Hordern; a small proportion is vinified for the Catherine Vale label.

chain of ponds ★★★★☆

Adelaide Road, Gumeracha, SA 5233 **region** Adelaide Hills
phone (08) 8389 1415 **fax** (08) 8389 1877 **open** 7 days 10.30–4.30
winemaker Caj Amadio (Contract) **production** 6000 **est.** 1993
product range ($12–29 CD) Riesling, Semillon, Sauvignon Blanc Semillon, Chardonnay, Novello Rosso, Pinot Noir, Florance Cabernet Merlot, Amadeus Cabernet Sauvignon.
summary Caj and Genny Amadio are the largest growers in the Adelaide Hills, with 100 hectares of vineyards established on a Scott Henry trellis producing 1000 tonnes of grapes a year, almost all sold to Penfolds, but with a small amount made into wine for sale under the Chain of Ponds label. The first vintage was 1993, and the wines first offered for sale in 1995. The full-flavoured white wines have enjoyed consistent show success.

Chain of Ponds Sauvignon Blanc Semillon

First produced in 1997, and met with immediate success, winning a gold medal at the 1997 Adelaide Hills Wine Show.

🍷🍷🍷🍷🍷 **1997** Bright yellow-green; the aromatic sauvignon blanc component is obvious on the bouquet, but on the palate the two varieties mesh neatly together, producing a most attractive wine with excellent flavour and balance. **rating:** 90

➾ **best drinking** 1998 – 2002 **best vintages** NA **drink with** Crab mornay • $19

Chain Of Ponds Chardonnay

Has the winemaker's fingerprints all over it, with the full gamut of winemaking techniques being used. Barrel ferment, lees contact and malolactic fermentation are all evident, but there is the fruit intensity there to support these inputs. The '94 received the trophy for Best Wine of Show at the 1996 Adelaide Hills Wine Show; the '95 and '96 are good, but not in same outstanding category.

🍷🍷🍷🍷 **1996** Light to medium yellow-green; an interesting bouquet, with bready/mealy notes, not particularly rich. The palate, again, is in a finer style, quite long, with secondary bready and minerally characters. **rating:** 84

➾ **best drinking** 1998 – 2001 **best vintages** '94 **drink with** Veal saltimbocca • $25

chalk hill NR

Brewery Hill Road, McLaren Vale, SA 5171 **region** McLaren Vale
phone (08) 8323 8815 **open** 7 days 1–5
winemaker Nancy Benko (Contract) **production** NFP **est.** 1973
product range ($5.90–13 CD) Riesling, Rosé, Shiraz, Cabernet Sauvignon, Port.
summary Established by former research scientist Nancy Benko, but purchased by prominent McLaren Vale grape growers John and Di Harvey in 1996, who have replanted the vineyard and will in due course release a new range of wines, presumably under the Chalk Hill label.

chambers rosewood ★★★★☆

Barkley Street, Rutherglen, Vic 3685 **region** Rutherglen
phone (02) 6032 8641 **fax** (02) 6032 8101 **open** Mon-Sat 9–5, Sun 10–5
winemaker Bill Chambers **production** 10 000 **est.** 1858
product range ($15–75 CD) A range of modestly priced and modestly made table wines, but the real forte of the winery is its Tokay and Muscat, also old Amontillado Sherries and Ports.
summary Bill Chambers is one of the great characters of the industry, but is not given to correspondence or to filling out forms. It remains a matter of record, however, that Bill Chambers makes some of the very greatest, albeit nearly unprocurable, Special Old Liqueur Muscat and Special Old Liqueur Tokay to be found in the northeast of Victoria. No recent tastings; Bill Chambers doesn't believe in wasting wine on wine scribes.

chapel hill ★★★★

Chapel Hill Road, McLaren Vale, SA 5171 **region** McLaren Vale
phone (08) 8323 8429 **fax** (08) 8323 9245 **open** Mon-Fri 9–5, weekends 11–5
winemaker Pam Dunsford (Consultant), Angela Meaney **production** 45 000 **est.** 1979
product range ($11.50–32 CD) Eden Valley Riesling, Unwooded Chardonnay, Reserve Chardonnay, Verdelho, McLaren Vale Shiraz, The Vicar (Cabernet Shiraz), Reserve Cabernet Shiraz, McLaren Vale/Coonawarra Cabernet Sauvignon, Tawny Port.
summary A winery which, in the 1990s, leapt from obscurity to national prominence after a change of ownership, a very large capital injection, and the installation of Pam Dunsford as

consultant winemaker. In the early phases of the growth the wines were superb, but continued growth seems to have taken some of the edge off. It is a reasonable expectation that once growth has slowed, quality will return to the very highest level.

charles cimicky ★★★☆

Gomersal Road, Lyndoch, SA 5351 **region** Barossa Valley
phone (08) 8524 4025 **fax** (08) 8524 4772 **open** 7 days 10.30–4.30
winemaker Charles Cimicky **production** 10 000 **est.** 1972
product range ($15–25 CD) Sauvignon Blanc, Chardonnay, Cabernet Franc, Classic Merlot, Cabernet Sauvignon, Signature Shiraz, Old Fireside Tawny Port.
summary These wines are of very good quality, thanks to the lavish (but sophisticated) use of new French oak in tandem with high-quality grapes. The intense, long-flavoured Sauvignon Blanc has been a particularly consistent performer, as has the rich, voluptuous American-oaked Signature Shiraz.

charles melton ★★★★★

Krondorf Road, Tanunda, SA 5352 **region** Barossa Valley
phone (08) 8563 3606 **fax** (08) 8563 3422 **open** 7 days 11–5
winemaker Charlie Melton, Joanne Aherne **production** 7500 **est.** 1984
product range ($10–28 R) Rosé of Virginia, Grenache, Shiraz, Nine Popes (Shiraz Grenache Mourvedre), Cabernet Sauvignon, Sparkling Red.
summary Charlie Melton, one of the Barossa Valley's great characters, with wife Virginia by his side, makes some of the most eagerly sought à la mode wines in Australia. Inevitably, the Melton empire grew in response to the insatiable demand, with a doubling of estate vineyards to 13 hectares, and the erection of a new barrel store in 1996. The expanded volume has had no adverse effect on the wonderfully rich, sweet and well-made wines.

Charles Melton Rosé Of Virginia

One of the most interesting Rosés currently made in Australia, produced from grenache, and presumably a partial by-product of Nine Popes juice run-off. It has much more fruit flavour than a standard Rosé, at least being more a cross between a standard Rosé and a Beaujolais style. Tremendous summer drinking.

🍷🍷🍷🍷🍸 **1997** Bright crimson fuschia; spotlessly clean cherry-accented bouquet leads into a palate with abundant cherry fruit flavours; very good length and balance, and more weight than the Turkey Flat Rosé of the same vintage. **rating:** 90

➯ **best drinking** 1998 – 1999 **best vintages** NA **drink with** Light Mediterranean dishes • $13.90

Charles Melton Shiraz

Produced from small patches of old low-yielding shiraz scattered across the Barossa Valley, but also showing the sophisticated use of American oak to produce a very modern style.

🍷🍷🍷🍷🍸 **1996** Medium to full red-purple; scented, sweetly ripe, juicy cherry fruit aromas are followed by a ripe but lively palate with black cherry, blackberry and mint fruit; soft tannins and subtle oak. **rating:** 90

➯ **best drinking** 1999 – 2009 **best vintages** '95, '96 **drink with** Spiced lamb • $29.80

Charles Melton Nine Popes

A label which is Australia's answer to California's Bonny Doon, where Randall Grahm is the genius pulling the strings. Charlie Melton is no slouch either, as this blend of low-yielding, dry-grown Shiraz, Grenache and Mourvedre handsomely shows. Melton realised the supreme quality of these vines well before most others, and the market has now caught up with his vision.

🍷🍷🍷🍷🍷 **1996** Medium to full red-purple; a dense and complex bouquet with a mix of chocolate, berry, mint and vanilla oak. There are similarly rich, mouthfilling chocolate, blackberry and mint flavours, with good tannin balance and well-judged oak. **rating:** 94

⇨ **best drinking** 1998 – 2003 **best vintages** '90, '91, '92, '93, '94, '95, '96 **drink with** Full-blooded Italian cuisine • $29.80

Charles Melton Cabernet Sauvignon

Charles Melton is best known for his Shiraz and Rhône-style reds, but also makes an exceptionally good Cabernet Sauvignon, which he skilfully moulds into the winery style one expects of the label without compromising varietal character.

🍷🍷🍷🍷🍷 **1996** Medium to full red-purple; a powerful, ripe dark chocolate, cigar box and cedar bouquet is followed by an exceptionally attractive, ripe textured palate reflecting all of the flavours promised by the bouquet, finishing with good tannins and equally good oak. **rating:** 92

⇨ **best drinking** 1999 – 2010 **best vintages** NA **drink with** Braised ox cheek with demi glaze • $30

charles sturt university winery ★★★★☆

Boorooma Street, North Wagga Wagga, NSW 2650 **region** Other Wineries of NSW

phone (02) 6933 2435 **fax** (02) 6933 2107 **open** 7 days 10–4

winemaker Kirsten Munro, James Kelly **production** 16 000 **est.** 1977

product range ($10–20 R) The precise composition varies from one release to the next, but is divided into two sections: the top-of-the-range Limited Release Series (e.g. Cabernet Sauvignon Shiraz, Cowra Chardonnay, Méthode Champenoise, Cabernet Sauvignon, Botrytis Semillon, Liqueur Port and Liqueur Muscat) and a basic range of lower-priced varietals including Chardonnay, Traminer Riesling, Sauvignon Blanc Semillon and Cabernet Sauvignon Shiraz.

summary Between 1990 and 1996 winemaking at Charles Sturt University was carried out under the direction of Rodney Hooper, who managed to resolve the dual roles of producing commercial wines and teaching students with consummate skill. A far harder task than might appear at face value, and a challenge which the new team of Kirsten Munro and James Kelly has handled with aplomb.

Charles Sturt Limited Release Cowra Chardonnay

Charles Sturt University has only limited vineyards of its own, the primary function of which is for teaching and experimental purposes. It purchases fruit from various parts of Australia, often on an irregular basis, so that the Chardonnays come and go – frustratingly at times. It would be nice to think that this wine becomes a regular part of the roster. The multi gold medal winning '94 vintage was one of the best Chardonnays ever to come from Cowra, and the '96 is not far behind.

🍷🍷🍷🍷🍷 **1996** Medium yellow-green; spicy oak is quite evident on the bouquet, though reasonably well integrated. There is excellent melon fruit in abundance on the palate, with the oak in harmonious support. Exceptional flavour and style for a wine in its price category. **rating:** 90

⇨ **best drinking** 1998 – 1999 **best vintages** '93, '94, '96 **drink with** Prawns, creamy pasta • $16

Charles Sturt University Cabernet Shiraz Merlot
A blend of Cabernet Sauvignon and Merlot grown on Charles Sturt University's own vineyards at Wagga Wagga and Shiraz from Heathcote in Victoria. The wine is matured for 12 months in a mix of American and French oak and represents extraordinarily good value for money.
🍷🍷🍷🍷🍷 **1996** Strong red-purple; a very rich, ripe and full bouquet with abundant dark berry fruit leads on to a rich and concentrated palate with dark cherry and berry fruit flavours with balanced tannins on the finish. **rating:** 90

⇨ **best drinking** 2001 – 2006 **best vintages** NA **drink with** Rare beef • $14

charley brothers ★★★

The Ruins Way, Inneslake, Port Macquarie, NSW 2444 **region** Hastings River
phone (02) 6581 1332 **fax** (02) 6581 0391 **open** Mon-Fri 1–5, weekends 10–5
winemaker John Cassegrain **production** 1600 **est.** 1988
product range ($8.50–12 CD) Semillon, Chardonnay, Semillon Chardonnay, Summer White, Dry Red, Shiraz Cabernet.
summary The property upon which the Charley Brothers vineyards are established has been in the family's ownership since the turn of the century, but in fact had been planted to vines by a Major Innes in the 1840s. After carrying on logging and fruit growing at various times, the Charley family planted vines in 1988 with the encouragement of John Cassegrain, who acts as contract-winemaker. A little over 10.5 hectares of vines have been established.

charlotte plains NR

The Grange, RMB 3180, Dooleys Road, Maryborough, Vic 3465 **region** Bendigo
phone (03) 5361 3137 **open** By appointment
winemaker Roland Kaval **production** 80 **est.** 1990
product range ($16 ML) Shiraz.
summary Charlotte Plains is a classic example of miniaturism. Production comes from a close-planted vineyard which is only one-third of a hectare, a quarter being shiraz, the remainder sauvignon blanc. The minuscule production is sold solely through the mailing list and by phone, but the '96 Shiraz (the second vintage from Charlotte Plains) was awarded four stars in *Winestate* magazine in mid-1997, and judged as the Equal Best Shiraz for Central Victoria.

chateau doré NR

Mandurang Road, via Bendigo, Vic 3551 **region** Bendigo
phone (03) 5439 5278 **open** Tues-Sun 10–6
winemaker Ivan Gross **production** 1000 **est.** 1860
product range ($9–14 CD) Riesling, Shiraz, Cabernet Sauvignon, Tawny Port.
summary Has been in the ownership of the Gross family since 1860 with the winery buildings dating back respectively to 1860 and 1893. All wine is sold through cellar door.

chateau dorrien NR

Cnr Seppeltsfield Road and Barossa Valley Way, Dorrien, SA 5352 **region** Barossa Valley
phone (08) 8562 2850 **fax** (08) 8562 1416 **open** 7 days 10–5
winemaker Fernando Martin **production** 2000 **est.** 1983

product range ($9–18 CD) Riesling, Semillon Chardonnay, Traminer, Frontignac Traminer, Frontignac Spaetlese, Late Harvest Frontignac, Semillon Chardonnay Sparkling Brut, Prima Vera (light red), Limited Release Grenache, Shiraz, Cabernet Sauvignon, Tawny Port.
summary Unashamedly and successfully directed at the tourist trade.

chateau francois ★★★

Broke Road, Pokolbin, NSW 2321 **region** Lower Hunter Valley
phone (02) 4998 7548 **fax** (02) 4998 7805 **open** Weekends 9–5 or by appointment
winemaker Don Francois **production** 700 **est.** 1969
product range ($11 ML) Pokolbin Mallee Semillon, Chardonnay, Shiraz Pinot Noir.
summary The retirement hobby of former NSW Director of Fisheries, Don Francois. Soft-flavoured and structured wines which frequently show regional characters, but which are modestly priced and are all sold through the cellar door and mailing list to a loyal following. The tasting room is available for private dinners for 12 to 16 people. Don Francois has sailed through a quadruple-bypass followed by a mild stroke with his sense of humour intact, if not enhanced. His most recent newsletter says (inter alia) '... my brush with destiny has changed my grizzly personality and I am now sweetness and light ... Can you believe? Well, almost!' He even promises comfortable tasting facilities.

chateau hornsby NR

Petrick Road, Alice Springs, NT 0870 **region** Alice Springs
phone (08) 8955 5133 **fax** (08) 8955 5133 **open** 7 days 11–4
winemaker Gordon Cook **production** 1000 **est.** 1976
product range ($12–17 CD) Riesling, Semillon, Chardonnay, Shiraz, Cabernet Sauvignon.
summary Draws in part upon 3 hectares of estate plantings, and in part from grapes and wines purchased from other regions. Very much a tourist-oriented operation, with numerous allied entertainments on offer.

chateau leamon ★★★

5528 Calder Highway, Bendigo, Vic 3550 **region** Bendigo
phone (03) 5447 7995 **fax** (03) 5447 0855 **open** Wed-Mon 10–5
winemaker Ian Leamon **production** 1500 **est.** 1973
product range ($13–20 CD) Rhine Riesling, Semillon Sauvignon Blanc, Pinot Noir, Shiraz, Cabernets Merlot.
summary After a period of uncertainty, Chateau Leamon is returning to some of its former glory. Ian Leamon is using both locally grown grapes, but also looking to the Strathbogie Ranges for grapes for other wines, including Pinot Noir.

Chateau Leamon Shiraz

Produced from 30-year-old vines grown on the Big Hill Vineyard.
🍷🍷🍷🍷 **1996** Medium red, with just a touch of purple; while only light to medium intensity, the bouquet is quite fragrant, with an appealing mix of leaf, cedar, mint and spice. The palate is similarly multiflavoured with spice (sweet, rather than peppery) to the fore; by no means a heavyweight, but flavoursome. **rating:** 86

➾ **best drinking** 1998 – 1999 **best vintages** NA **drink with** Deep-fried quail • $18

chateau pato ★★★★

Thompson's Road, Pokolbin, NSW 2321 **region** Lower Hunter Valley
phone (02) 4998 7634 **open** By appointment
winemaker Nicholas Paterson **production** 300 **est.** 1978
product range ($14–18 CD) Gewurztraminer, Shiraz.
summary Nicholas and Roger Paterson have taken over responsibility for this tiny winery following the death of their father David Paterson during the 1993 vintage. It is a much-loved, if tiny, Hunter landmark, with vintages back to 1993 available at the microscopic cellar door. On all the evidence, David Paterson's inheritance is being handsomely guarded.

chateau tahbilk ★★★★

Goulburn Valley Highway, Tabilk, Vic 3607 **region** Goulburn Valley
phone (03) 5794 2555 **fax** (03) 5794 2360 **open** Mon-Sat 9–5, Sun 11–5
winemaker Alister Purbrick **production** 90 000 **est.** 1860
product range ($9.95–95 R) Riesling, Chardonnay, Marsanne, Shiraz, Cabernet Sauvignon; 1860 Vines Shiraz is rare flagship, with a Reserve Red released from each vintage.
summary A winery steeped in tradition (with high National Trust classification) which should be visited at least once by every wine-conscious Australian, and which makes wines – particularly red wines – utterly in keeping with that tradition. The essence of that heritage comes in the form of the tiny quantities of Shiraz made entirely from vines planted in 1860.

Chateau Tahbilk Chardonnay

Chateau Tahbilk has quite extensive plantings of chardonnay, both making wine under its own label and selling grapes (and bulk wine) to others. Obviously, Alister Purbrick selects the best material for Chateau Tahbilk's own use, and over the years has produced one or two quite lovely wines, one winning a major trophy at the Sydney Wine Show some years ago. Subtle use of French and American oak is a feature of the style.

🍷🍷🍷🍷 **1996** Medium to full yellow-green; a big fruit-driven wine with ripe buttery/peachy fruit together with a few spicy oak notes on the bouquet. There is lots of mid to back palate flavour, again with pleasantly subtle oak, and finishes with good acidity. **rating:** 85

➾ **best drinking** 1998 – 1999 **best vintages** '91, '96 **drink with** Rotisserie chicken • $16.95

---

chatsfield ★★★★

O'Neil Road, Mount Barker, WA 6324 **region** Great Southern
phone (08) 9851 1704 **fax** (08) 9851 1704 **open** Wed-Sun, public holidays 10–5
winemaker Gavin Berry (Contract) **production** 10 000 **est.** 1976
product range ($14–17 CD) Mount Barker Riesling, Gewurztraminer, Chardonnay, Cabernet Franc, Shiraz.
summary Irish-born medical practitioner Ken Lynch can be very proud of his achievements at Chatsfield, as can the various contract-winemakers who have taken the high-quality estate-grown material and made such impressive wines, notably the Riesling, vibrant Cabernet Franc (as an unwooded nouveau style) and spicy liquorice Shiraz.

Chatsfield Chardonnay

By no means a flashy wine, made in a reserved style, and unequivocally showing its cool-climate background, often seeming more like a cross between Sauvignon Blanc and Chardonnay than anything else. Will mature well with age.

🍷🍷🍷🍷 **1997** Medium yellow-green; gentle fig and cashew fruit is neatly picked up by an attractive hint of spicy oak on a bouquet of light to medium intensity. The palate is well made and balanced, picking up on the finish with a tweak of crisp acidity and spicy oak; not a blockbuster but will develop. **rating:** 85

➾ **best drinking** 1998 – 2002 **best vintages** '87, '89, '90, '93, '97 **drink with** Smoked salmon • $17

Chatsfield Cabernet Franc

The wine is challenging, because it is fermented in tank and taken straight to bottle, without any wood maturation at any stage.

🍷🍷🍷🍷 **1997** Light to medium red-purple; a clean and fragrant bouquet, with lively raspberry and almost citrussy aromas. The palate shows very attractive varietal character through to the mid-palate, but does have a slight leafy bitterness on the finish, perhaps the penalty of taking the wine direct from stainless steel to bottle, but this is the well established style of the wine. **rating:** 86

➾ **best drinking** 1998 – 1999 **best vintages** NA **drink with** Breast of duck • $15

---

chestnut grove ★★★☆

Chestnut Grove Road, Manjimup, WA 6258 **region** Pemberton
phone (08) 9771 4255 **fax** (08) 9772 4255 **open** By appointment
winemaker Alkoomi (Contract) **production** 4000 **est.** 1988
product range ($16.30–21.25 CD) Chardonnay, Unwooded Chardonnay, Verdelho, Pinot Noir, Cabernet Merlot.
summary A joint venture between the Lange family of Alkoomi and Vic Kordic and his family, through to grandson Darren Cook. Initial vintages were slightly weak and dilute, but increasing vine age (and one suspects better viticulture) has resulted in a significant lift in wine quality, particularly with the Cabernet Merlot.

Chestnut Grove Verdelho

Produced from 3 hectares of estate plantings established in 1988. Successive releases have shown increasing flavour and complexity, but right from the word go, clear varietal character has been evident.

🍷🍷🍷🍷 **1997** Light to medium yellow-green; the bouquet is fragrant, with tropical fruit salad aromas providing plenty of character. The palate follows on in fine fashion, with passionfruit and tropical fruit salad flavours, yet finishes pleasantly dry. Excellent example of varietal Verdelho. **rating:** 84

➾ **best drinking** 1998 – 1999 **best vintages** '97 **drink with** Asian seafood • $16.30

---

chittering estate NR

Chittering Valley Road, Lower Chittering, WA 6084 **region** Other Wineries of WA
phone (08) 9273 6255 **fax** (08) 9273 6101 **open** Weekends and public holidays 11–4.30 (Apr–Dec)
winemaker Francois Jacquard **production** 12 000 **est.** 1982
product range ($14.90–21 R) Chardonnay, Hill Top Reserve Chardonnay, Semillon Sauvignon Blanc, Pinot Noir, Cabernet Merlot, Hill Top Reserve Cabernet Sauvignon.
summary Chittering Estate was sold in late 1997, and no information has been forthcoming about its new owner's intentions.

ciavarella NR

Evans Lane, Oxley, Vic 3678 **region** King Valley
phone (03) 5727 3384 **fax** (03) 5727 3384 **open** Mon–Sat 9–6, Sun 10–6
winemaker Cyril Ciavarella **production** 1200 **est.** 1978
product range ($10–14 CD) Chenin Blanc, Late Harvest Chenin Blanc, Chardonnay, Vendemmia (light red), Dolcino (medium-bodied red), Shiraz, Cabernet Sauvignon, Tawny Port.
summary The Ciavarellas have been grape growers in the King Valley for almost 20 years, selling their grapes to wineries such as Brown Brothers. Changes in the grape marketplace led to Ciavarella deciding to make limited quantities of wines, which were first offered for sale from the cellar door in early 1994.

clarendon hills winery ★★★★☆

Brookmans Road, Blewitt Springs, SA 5171 **region** McLaren Vale
phone (08) 8364 1484 **fax** (08) 8364 1484 **open** By appointment
winemaker Roman Bratasiuk **production** 10 000 **est.** 1989
product range ($60–175 R) Chardonnay (Kangarilla Vineyard and Norton Summit Vineyard), Pinot Noir, Merlot, Old Vines Grenache (Blewitt Springs Vineyard and Clarendon Vineyard), Astralis (Shiraz – and the flagship wine).
summary Clarendon Hills produces some of the most startlingly concentrated, rich and full-bodied red wines to be found in Australia, rivalled in this respect only by Wendouree. Roman Bratasiuk is a larger-than-life figure who makes larger-than-life wines. Technocrats may quibble about this or that aspect, but influential judges such as Robert Parker have neither reservations nor problems with the immense, brooding red wines which Bratasiuk regularly produces from small patches of old, low-yielding vines which he ferrets out.

Clarendon Hills Shiraz

Often the best of the current releases of Clarendon Hills, for while it is immensely concentrated and powerful, it is possible both to see the superb varietal fruit which has gone to make the wine, and impossible not to consider drinking it.

🍷🍷🍷🍷 **1996** Medium to full red-purple; the bouquet is solid and dense, with potent briary/chocolatey fruit and oak in restraint. The palate opens with ripe briary berry fruit, and closes with formidable, indeed ferocious, tannins. Like big Italian reds, calls out for rich red meat dishes. **rating:** 86

➯ **best drinking** 2002 – 2010 **best vintages** '90, '91, '92, '93, '96 **drink with** Venison, game • $80

Clarendon Hills Merlot

Roman Bratasiuk achieves things with Merlot that no one else can imitate. Whether this is a good thing or not is an interesting question.

🍷🍷🍷🍷 **1996** Medium to full red-purple; a tremendously powerful, concentrated and dense bouquet with a mix of earthy, briary and spicy notes foreshadows an ultra-powerful palate which takes no prisoners. There is so much structure there, it is hard to see the flesh or really understand where the wine will head over the next ten years. **rating:** 86

➯ **best drinking** 2002 – 2008 **best vintages** '90, '91, '96 **drink with** Char-grilled rare rump • $90

Clarendon Hills Old Vines Grenache

Grenache can all too easily make flabby, cloying sickly sweet red wine, which in many ways is the correlative of unwooded Chardonnay, and is no more attractive, but I remain to be convinced that it is necessary to invest Grenache with as much tannin and structure as one finds in this wine, old vines notwithstanding. Nonetheless, compelling and interesting.

🍷🍷🍷🍷 **1996** Medium to full red-purple; the bouquet shows good varietal character with sweet, ripe powerful fruit, and just a hint of volatility. The palate starts with powerful, concentrated juicy berry fruit, then runs into mouth-ripping tannins. **rating:** 85

➾ **best drinking** 2000 – 2007 **best vintages** NA **drink with** Dinosaur rump • $60

cleveland ★★★☆

Shannons Road, Lancefield, Vic 3435 **region** Macedon
phone (03) 5429 1449 **fax** (03) 5429 2017 **open** 7 days 9–6
winemaker Keith Brien **production** 4000 **est.** 1985
product range ($11–25 CD) Estate Chardonnay, Pinot Noir, Minus Five (Cabernets Merlot), Cabernet Sauvignon, Macedon Brut; Brien Family Selection Muscat Gordo Blanco, Chardonnay Gordo, Shiraz Cabernet.
summary The Cleveland homestead was built in 1889 in the style of a Gothic Revival manor house, but had been abandoned for 40 years when purchased by the Briens in 1983. It has since been painstakingly restored, and 3.5 hectares of surrounding vineyard established. Cleveland has done best with Pinot Noir and Chardonnay, but the occasional Cabernet Sauvignon attests to an unusually favourable vineyard site in a very cool region.

cliff house 

RSD 457, Kayena, Tas 7270 **region** Northern Tasmania
phone (03) 6394 7454 **fax** (03) 6394 7419 **open** By appointment
winemaker Heemskerk (Contract) **production** 2500 **est.** 1983
product range ($15 R) Riesling, Chardonnay, Pinot Noir, Cabernet Sauvignon.
summary Geoff and Cheryl Hewitt established 4 hectares of vineyard in the Tamar Valley area in 1983. After a slightly slow start, the Cliff House wines have really came into their own since 1994.

clonakilla 

Crisps Lane, Off Gundaroo Road, Murrumbateman, NSW 2582 **region** Canberra District
phone (02) 6227 5877 **fax** (02) 6251 1938 **open** 7 days 11–5
winemaker Dr John Kirk, Tim Kirk **production** 1200 **est.** 1971
product range ($14–22 CD) Riesling, Chardonnay, Semillon Sauvignon Blanc, Muscat, Shiraz, Shiraz Viognier, Cabernet.
summary Distinguished scientist Dr John Kirk (among other things, the author of some interesting papers on the measurement of vineyard climate) presides over this tiny winery. Shiraz is the shining star of Clonakilla, leaving the other wines – adequate though they are – in its wake.

Clonakilla Riesling

Made in a consistent style throughout the 1990s, always showing considerable flavour, and quite often exhibiting a not unpleasant character which I can only describe as slightly cosmetic.

🍷🍷🍷🍷 **1997** Bright, light to medium yellow-green; there is quite intense lime/mineral fruit on the bouquet, which is rich but not heavy. The palate is more elegant and restrained than the bouquet suggests, but has excellent balance and flavour, with lime and mineral notes on the moderately long finish. Good Riesling; the best yet from Clonakilla. **rating:** 87

➯ **best drinking** 1999 – 2003 **best vintages** '91, '93, '94, '95, '97 **drink with** Spiced Asian dishes • $14

Clonakilla Shiraz

Now firmly established as Clonakilla's best wine, and indeed one of the best wines to come out of the Canberra District each year. Since 1994 the wine has been a blend of Shiraz, Pinot Noir and Viognier, with the Shiraz component typically accounting for between 80% and 85% of the blend. Interestingly, too, the grapes are not crushed, but are placed as whole bunches in open fermenters, foot-trodden, and the fermentation is completed in new and used French oak barriques.

🍷🍷🍷🍷🍷 **1997** Dark, dense red-purple; an extremely complex bouquet with spice, liquorice and distinct gamey overtones. An enormously powerful and complex wine on the palate, but tasted as a blended barrel sample, and before pre-bottling fining. The rating is approximate only; Tim Kirk thinks the wine may be one of the best yet. **rating:** 90

➯ **best drinking** 1993 – 2000 **best vintages** '90, '92, '93, '94, '95, '97 **drink with** Jugged hare • $18

clos clare NR

Government Road, Watervale, SA 5452 **region** Clare Valley
phone (08) 8843 0161 **fax** (08) 8843 0161 **open** Weekends and public holidays 10–5
winemaker Various contract **production** 400 **est.** 1993
product range ($12.50–16 CD) Riesling, Shiraz.
summary Clos Clare is based on a small, unirrigated section of the original Florita Vineyard once owned by Leo Buring and which produces Riesling of extraordinary concentration and power.

clover hill ★★★★☆

Clover Hill Road, Lebrina, Tas 7254 **region** Northern Tasmania
phone (03) 6395 6114 **fax** (03) 6395 6257 **open** 7 days 10–5
winemaker Shane Clohesy, Dominique Portet, Chris Markell **production** 4000 **est.** 1986
product range ($28 R) Clover Hill (Sparkling).
summary Clover Hill was established by Taltarni in 1986 with the sole purpose of making a premium sparkling wine. Its 20 hectares of vineyards, comprising 12 hectares of chardonnay, 6.5 of pinot noir and 1.5 of pinot meunier, are still coming into bearing, and production is steadily increasing. Wine quality is excellent, combining finesse with power and length.

Clover Hill

A Chardonnay-predominant style given not less than 24 months on yeast lees, and invariably clean, fresh and finishing with pronounced acidity – a testament to the very cool climate in which the grapes are grown.

🍷🍷🍷🍷 **1995** Medium yellow-green, with good mousse; the bouquet is firm, but complex with mineral, citrus, toast and bready/biscuit aromas all present. The palate opens with lemon, citrus and mineral flavours before finishing with bracing acidity. Will undoubtedly benefit from a year or two on cork. **rating:** 86

➯ **best drinking** 1999 – 2002 **best vintages** '90, '91, '92, '95 **drink with** Caviar, shellfish • $28

clyde park NR

Midland Highway, Bannockburn, Vic 3331 **region** Geelong
phone (03) 5281 7274 **fax** (03) 5281 7274 **open** Not
winemaker Scott Ireland **production** 500 **est.** 1980
product range ($25 R) Chardonnay, Pinot Noir, Cabernet Sauvignon.
summary Sold by founder Gary Farr to leading Melbourne hotelier and restaurateur Donlevy Fitzpatrick in late 1994, but as at early 1998 once again on the market. In the meantime, the product range has been increased somewhat.

cobanov NR

Stock Road, Herne Hill, WA 6056 **region** Swan District
phone (08) 9296 4210 **open** Wed-Sun 9–5.30
winemaker Steve Cobanov **production** 10 000 **est.** 1960
product range ($6–10 CD) Chenin Blanc, Chardonnay, Sauvignon Blanc, Verdelho, Shiraz, Grenache, Cabernet Sauvignon.
summary A substantial family-owned operation producing a mix of bulk and bottled wine from 21 hectares of estate grapes. Part of the annual production is sold as grapes to other producers, including Houghton; part is sold in bulk; part sold in 2-litre flagons, and the remainder in modestly priced bottles.

cobaw ridge ★★★☆

Perc Boyer's Lane, East Pastoria via Kyneton, Vic 3444 **region** Macedon
phone (03) 5423 5227 **fax** (03) 5423 5227 **open** Weekends 10–5, or by appointment
winemaker Alan Cooper **production** 800 **est.** 1985
product range ($18–25 CD) Chardonnay, Shiraz, Shiraz Reserve, Cabernet Sauvignon.
summary Nelly and Alan Cooper have established Cobaw Ridge's 4-hectare vineyard at an altitude of 610 metres in the hills above Kyneton complete with self-constructed pole-framed mudbrick house and winery. Wine quality has been variable, but overall Alan Cooper has done extremely well.

Cobaw Ridge Chardonnay

Produced from 2 hectares of estate plantings, and, like all the Cobaw Ridge wines, made and bottled on the estate.

🍷🍷🍷🍷 **1996** Medium to full yellow-green; there is rich, sweet peachy fruit on a bouquet with plenty of character, character which builds on the complex, ripe palate with hints of caramel and butterscotch on top of the peachy fruit. A mouthful. **rating:** 84

➾ **best drinking** 1998 – 2001 **best vintages** NA **drink with** Honey chicken • $25

cobbitty wines NR

Cobbitty Road, Cobbitty, NSW 2570 **region** Other Wineries of NSW
phone (02) 4651 2281 **fax** (02) 4651 2671 **open** Mon-Sat 10–5, Sun 12–6
winemaker Giovanni Cogno **production** 5000 **est.** 1964
product range ($5–14 CD) A full range of generic table, fortified and sparkling wines under the Cobbitty Wines label; also cocktail wines.
summary Draws upon 10 hectares of estate plantings of muscat, barbera, grenache and trebbiano, relying very much on local and ethnic custom.

cockfighter's ghost vineyard ★★★

Lot 251 Milbrodale Road, Broke, NSW 2330 **region** Lower Hunter Valley
phone (02) 9667 1622 **fax** (02) 9667 1442 **open** Not
winemaker Various contract **production** 8000 **est.** 1994
product range ($16–22 ML) Semillon, Unwooded Chardonnay, Chardonnay, Pinot Noir, Shiraz.
summary Like Poole's Rock Vineyard, owned by eminent Sydney merchant banker David Clarke, but run and marketed as a separate venture, with lower wine prices.

cofield ★★★☆

Distillery Road, Wahgunyah, Vic 3687 **region** Rutherglen
phone (02) 6033 3798 **fax** (02) 6033 3798 **open** Mon-Sat 9–5, Sun 10–5
winemaker Max Cofield, Damien Cofield **production** 5000 **est.** 1990
product range ($12–22 CD) Riesling, Chenin Blanc, Semillon Chardonnay, Chardonnay, Late Harvest Tokay, Soft Red, Shiraz, Merlot, Cabernet Sauvignon, Cabernet Merlot, Sparkling, Fortified.
summary District veteran Max Cofield, together with wife Karen and sons Damien, Ben and Andrew, is developing a strong cellar-door sales base by staging in-winery functions with guest chefs, and also providing a large barbecue and picnic area. The quality of the red wines, in particular, is good, and improving all the time.

Cofield Shiraz

Stands out as the best of the '96 red wine releases from Cofield, and a good wine by any standards. Estate-grown, with the vineyard utilising the Scott Henry trellis system which simultaneously increases yield and ripeness.

🍷🍷🍷🍷 **1996** Medium to full red-purple; the bouquet is solid and full with dark berry fruit complexed by hints of liquorice and leather. The palate is in full-on Rutherglen style, but not extractive or excessively tannic; rich and powerful dark chocolate, blackberry and liquorice fruit flavours are there in abundance. **rating:** 86

➾ **best drinking** 2000 – 2006 **best vintages** NA **drink with** Marinated beef • $14

coldstream hills NR

31 Maddens Lane, Coldstream, Vic 3770 **region** Yarra Valley
phone (03) 5964 9410 **fax** (03) 5964 9389 **open** 7 days 10–5
winemaker James Halliday, Philip Dowell **production** 50 000 **est.** 1985
product range ($22–36 CD) Semillon Sauvignon Blanc, Sauvignon Blanc, Chardonnay, Reserve Chardonnay, Pinot Noir, Reserve Pinot Noir, Merlot, Reserve Merlot, Briarston (Cabernet Merlot), Reserve Cabernet Sauvignon.
summary Founded by the author, who continues in charge of winemaking, but acquired by Southcorp in mid-1996. Expansion plans already then underway have been accelerated, with well in excess of 100 hectares of owned or managed estate vineyards as the base. Chardonnay and Pinot Noir continue to be the principal focus, with varietal Merlot coming on-stream from the 1997 vintage.

Coldstream Hills Sauvignon Blanc

1997 was the first varietal Sauvignon Blanc produced by Coldstream Hills. In prior years the Sauvignon Blanc was blended with a greater volume of Semillon to produce a wine labelled Fumé Blanc. Twenty-five per cent of the wine was barrel-fermented in new French oak, the remainder fermented in stainless steel, both at low temperatures. The barrel-fermented portion was removed from oak immediately after the end of fermentation, and the components thereafter blended and bottled. It is a fruit-driven style, with the low crops and warm growing conditions of the 1997 vintage manifest in the wine, which has above-average length and concentration.

1997 Bright green-yellow; the bouquet is concentrated and intense, neither tropical nor herbal, but in the mid-ripeness spectrum of gooseberry and even a hint of blackcurrant. The palate is relatively powerful and rich, with gooseberry fruit flavours particularly evident on the mid to back palate. Firm acidity, but overall not an aggressive style of Sauvignon Blanc. **rating:** NR

➾ **best drinking** 1998 – 2002 **best vintages** '97 **drink with** Salad • $22

Coldstream Hills Chardonnay

Made from Yarra Valley grapes, part estate-grown and part purchased from other Yarra Valley growers. Largely barrel-fermented in a mix of new and used French oak under strictly controlled temperatures. Prolonged lees contact but no malolactic fermentation.

1997 Light to medium yellow-green; the bouquet is already showing some weight, with tangy citrus and melon fruit together with a whiff of barrel ferment and cashew nuances from the malolactic-fermented component. The palate is quite powerful, with nectarine and melon fruit, subtle French oak and again that extra dimension of texture from the concentrated fruit and the malolactic input. **rating:** NR

➾ **best drinking** 1999 – 2004 **best vintages** '86, '88, '91, '92, '93, '94, '96, '97 **drink with** Oven-roasted Blue Eye cod • $24

Coldstream Hills Reserve Chardonnay

Made primarily from estate-grown grapes which are 100% barrel-fermented in a mix of new (over 50%) and used French oak barriques, principally Vosges but with Troncais and Allier also used. Six months lees contact; 20% malolactic fermentation.

1996 Light to medium yellow-green; smooth melon and fig is interwoven through faintly spicy French oak on the bouquet, with just a hint of cashew from the small percentage taken through malolactic fermentation. While tight and restrained, the palate has more weight and freshness than the '95, and should develop extremely well over the next five-plus years. Gold medal at the 1997 International Wine Challenge, London. **rating:** NR

➾ **best drinking** 1999 – 2006 **best vintages** '88, '91, '92, '93, '94, '96 **drink with** Veal, chicken • $36

Coldstream Hills Pinot Noir

Part estate-grown and part sourced from other Yarra Valley growers, with a range of site climates. It is made using the full gamut of Burgundian techniques, including substantial use of whole bunches, foot-stamped and macerated. The primary fermentation is completed in a mix of new and used Troncais (French) oak.

1997 Medium red-purple; there is a classic mix of plum, cherry and forest aromas on the bouquet, supported by the typical subtle, faintly spicy oak. The palate is complex and mouthfilling, with sweet plum and cherry fruit on the mid-palate then a long, silky finish, with touches of spice woven throughout. **rating:** NR

➾ **best drinking** 1998 – 2003 **best vintages** '87, '88, '91, '92, '94, '96, '97 **drink with** Seared or slow-cooked salmon, Asian cuisine • $26

Coldstream Hills Reserve Pinot Noir

Produced entirely from estate-grown grapes, in turn coming mainly from the Amphitheatre Block established in 1985. The same making techniques are used with the Reserve wine as with the standard, the difference being fruit selection and a much higher percentage of new Dargaud & Jaegle Troncais oak barriques.

1996 Strong red-purple; the bouquet already shows considerable complexity, with plum, spice and forest aromas of medium to full intensity. A wine of above-average concentration, with plum, spice and foresty/briary flavours supported by toasty French (Troncais) oak. Considerably richer than the '95, harking back to the '94. Gold medal 1997 International Wine Challenge, London. **rating:** NR

⇨ **best drinking** 1999 – 2007 **best vintages** '87, '88, '91, '92, '94, '96 **drink with** Quail, Asian cuisine • $36

Coldstream Hills Briarston

A blend of 80% Cabernet Sauvignon, 6% Cabernet Franc and 14% Merlot. As with the other wines, part estate-grown, part purchased from other Yarra Valley growers. It is matured in a mix of new and used French oak (predominantly Nevers and Allier, with lesser amounts of Troncais) for 18 to 20 months before bottling.

1996 Medium red-purple; the bouquet shows a mix of redcurrant, cassis, olive and cedary French oak. The palate is typically soft, with a mix of sweet berry and more minty/olive-like flavours. Fine, subtle tannins ripple through the gentle but long finish. **rating:** NR

⇨ **best drinking** 1998 – 2005 **best vintages** '88, '90, '91, '92, '93, '97 **drink with** Lamb with redcurrant sauce • $24

Coldstream Hills Reserve Cabernet Sauvignon

First introduced in 1992, and in fact will only be made in those years in which the quality of the Cabernet Sauvignon is outstanding. Entirely estate-produced from a single-vineyard block, the wine is matured in a high percentage of new Allier and Nevers oak barriques for 20 months. None made in 1996.

1995 Medium red-purple; perfectly ripened varietal cabernet is supported by subtle and well-integrated cedary French oak on the bouquet. The wine is of medium to full intensity with cassis/blackberry fruit, subtle, cedary oak and lingering soft tannins. The excellent balance and easy feel of the wine in the mouth should not deceive, it will in fact be long-lived. **rating:** NR

⇨ **best drinking** 1999 – 2008 **best vintages** '92, '93, '94, '97 **drink with** Rump steak • $33

---

constable & hershon NR

1 Gillards Road, Pokolbin, NSW 2320 **region** Lower Hunter Valley
phone (02) 4998 7887 **fax** (02) 4998 7887 **open** 7 days 10–5
winemaker Neil McGuigan (Contract) **production** 2500 **est.** 1981
product range ($15.50–19.95 CD) Chardonnay, Unwooded Chardonnay, Pinot Noir, Cabernet Merlot, Reserve Cabernet Merlot.

summary Features four spectacular formal gardens, the Rose, Knot and Herb, Secret and Sculpture; a free garden tour is conducted every Monday to Friday at 10.30 am lasting 30 minutes. The 7-hectare vineyard is itself spectacularly situated under the backdrop of the Brokenback Range. Typically offers a range of back vintages spanning five years ex-cellar door or by mailing list.

constables ★★★

Graphite Road, West Manjimup, WA 6258 **region** Pemberton
phone (08) 9772 1375 **open** 7 days 9–5
winemaker Houghton (Contract) **production** NFP **est.** 1988
product range ($10–15 CD) Riesling, Sauvignon Blanc, Chardonnay, Cabernet Sauvignon.
summary Father John and son Michael, together with other members of the Constable family, have established an 11-hectare vineyard at Manjimup. Most of the grapes are sold to Houghton under a long-term contract, and limited quantities are made for the Constable label by Houghton under contract.

cooinda vale NR

Bartonvale Road, Campania, Tas 7026 **region** Southern Tasmania
phone (03) 6260 4227 **open** By appointment
winemaker Andrew Hood (Contract) **production** 300 **est.** 1985
product range ($15–16 R) Riesling, Pinot Noir.
summary The tiny production means that the wines are not widely known, even in Southern Tasmania, and quality has been somewhat variable.

coolangatta estate ★★★☆

1335 Bolong Road, Shoalhaven Heads, NSW 2535 **region** Shoalhaven
phone (02) 4448 7131 **fax** (02) 4448 7997 **open** 7 days 10–4
winemaker Tyrrell's (Contract) **production** 2500 **est.** 1988
product range ($13–17 CD) Sauvignon Blanc, Semillon Sauvignon Blanc, Unwooded Chardonnay, Alexander Berry Chardonnay, Verdelho, Chambourcin, Cabernet Shiraz, Merlot, Cabernet Sauvignon, Vintage Port.
summary Coolangatta Estate is part of a 150-hectare resort with accommodation, restaurants, golf course, etc, with some of the oldest buildings convict-built in 1822. It might be thought that the wines are tailored purely for the tourist market, but in fact the standard of viticulture is exceptionally high (immaculate Scott Henry trellising) and the winemaking is wholly professional (contract by Tyrrell's). The 1991 Chardonnay, incidentally, won a gold medal in the Chardonnay Museum Class at the 1997 Liquorland National Wine Show, an outstanding achievement.

Coolangatta Estate Eileen Chambourcin

Produced from estate-grown grapes. Chambourcin is particularly well suited to the relatively wet and humid conditions of the New South Wales coast, as it is a hybrid with strong disease resistance, and the ability to retain excellent colour.

🍷🍷🍷🍷 **1997** Medium red-purple; rich, dark blackberry fruit aromas have a whisker of what may be charry vanilla oak in the background. On the palate rich, sweet, juicy blackberry fruit on the mid-palate is followed by slightly fierce acid on the finish, suggesting the wine may not have undergone malolactic fermentation. Always best when young and fresh. **rating:** 84

➯ **best drinking** 1998 – 1999 **best vintages** NA **drink with** Pizza • $14

Coolangatta Estate Cabernet Shiraz

A surprise performer (on my score sheet at least) at the 1998 Winewise Small Makers Competition.

🍷🍷🍷🍷 **1996** Medium to full red-purple; the bouquet is quite fragrant with seductive oak, so much so it is difficult to tell whether the spicy characters come from the fruit or the oak.

The palate shows the similarly clever use of sweet spicy oak together with sweet red berry fruit and soft tannins. Good mouthfeel and length. **rating:** 89

➾ **best drinking** 1998 – 2003 **best vintages** NA **drink with** Beef stroganoff • $16

coombend estate ★★★★

Coombend via Swansea, Tas 7190 **region** Southern Tasmania
phone (03) 6257 8256 **fax** (03) 6257 8484 **open** 7 days 9–6
winemaker Andrew Hood (Contract) **production** 400 **est.** 1985
product range ($22–28 ML) Riesling, Sauvignon Blanc, Cabernet Sauvignon.
summary John Fenn Smith has established 1.75 hectares of cabernet sauvignon (together with a little cabernet franc) on his 2600-hectare sheep station, choosing that part of his property which is immediately adjacent to Freycinet. This slightly quixotic choice of variety has been justified by the success of the wine in limited show entries.

coorinja ★★☆

Toodyay Road, Toodyay, WA 6566 **region** Swan District
phone (08) 9626 2280 **open** Mon-Sat 8–5
winemaker Michael Wood **production** 3200 **est.** 1870
product range ($8–10.50 CD) Dry White, Claret, Hermitage, Burgundy, Fortifieds; the latter account for 50% of Coorinja's production.
summary An evocative and historic winery nestling in a small gully which seems to be in a time-warp, begging to be used as a set for a film. A recent revamp of the packaging accompanied a more than respectable Hermitage, with lots of dark chocolate and sweet berry flavour, finishing with soft tannins.

cope-williams ★★★☆

Glenfern Road, Romsey, Vic 3434 **region** Macedon
phone (03) 5429 5428 **fax** (03) 5429 5655 **open** 7 days 11–5
winemaker Michael Cope-Williams **production** 7000 **est.** 1977
product range ($14–25 R) Chardonnay, Cabernet Merlot; d'Vine is second label, Riesling, Chardonnay and Cabernet Sauvignon; winery speciality sparkling wine Macedon R.O.M.S.E.Y.
summary One of the high country Macedon pioneers, specialising in sparkling wines which are full-flavoured, but also producing excellent Chardonnay and Pinot Noir table wines in the warmer vintages. A traditional 'English Green'-type cricket ground is available for hire and booked out most days of the week from spring through till autumn.

Cope-Williams Macedon Ranges Brut

Made entirely from Macedon Ranges grapes, but not estate-grown as is the case with R.O.M.S.E.Y. Brut. A blend of Chardonnay and Pinot Noir which spends two years on yeast lees.

🍷🍷🍷🍷 **NV** Light straw-yellow; a complex and stylish bouquet with a mix of bready/toasty characters deriving from the time on lees, allied with a hint of mandarin. The wine has excellent mouthfeel and balance, with clean citrus/sweet apple fruit flavours and a long finish. **rating:** 88

➾ **best drinking** 1997 – 1998 **best vintages** NA **drink with** Hors d'oeuvres • NA

Cope-Williams R.O.M.S.E.Y. Brut

Made from estate-grown Chardonnay and Pinot Noir, and now fully made at the property. The high altitude, very cool vineyard site produces exceptional quality base wine, and this has been reflected in the illustrious show record of the Cope-Williams sparkling wines over the past few years – a record undimmed by the limited number of entries available to it because of restricted production.

🍷🍷🍷🍷 **NV** Bright full yellow with particularly good mousse; complex bready/yeasty autolysis over fresh citrussy fruit; the palate is complex with a nice blend of crisp fruit and yeast autolysis. The finish is long and the dosage low. **rating:** 89

➾ **best drinking** 1998 – 1999 **best vintages** NA **drink with** Oysters • $23

coriole ★★★★☆

Chaffeys Road, McLaren Vale, SA 5171 **region** McLaren Vale
phone (08) 8323 8305 **fax** (08) 8323 9136 **open** Mon-Fri 10–5, weekends 11–5
winemaker Stephen Hall **production** 25 000 **est.** 1967

product range ($13–40 R) Lalla Rookh Semillon, Semillon Sauvignon Blanc, Chenin Blanc, Semillon, Chardonnay, Sangiovese, Shiraz, Redstone (Shiraz Cabernet Grenache), Diva (Sangiovese blend), Sangiovese, Cabernet Sauvignon; Mary Kathleen (Cabernet blend), Lloyd Reserve Shiraz, Lalla Rookh Grenache Shiraz.

summary Justifiably best known for its Shiraz, which, both in the rare Reserve, and also like standard form, is extremely impressive. It has spread its wings in recent years, being one of the first wineries to catch onto the Italian fashion with its Sangiovese, but its white varietal wines lose nothing by comparison.

Coriole Lalla Rookh Semillon

A very interesting wine which over the past few years has shown strong passionfruit/gooseberry aromas when young, presumably due at least in part to the use of aromatic yeast during fermentation, but is possibly also partly vineyard character. Whatever the answer, it produces wines that are striking and attractive in their youth. The wine is partially fermented in French oak, and spends three months on yeast lees. A change of name in 1997 saw the addition of 'Lalla Rookh' to the name, but the wine remains unchanged.

🍷🍷🍷🍷 **1997** Light green-yellow; the bouquet is quite fragrant and lemony, almost with a touch of Sauvignon Blanc character, and a hint of subtle oak. The palate again shows the clever use of a touch of spicy oak to support the lemony fruit; good flavour and balance. **rating:** 86

➾ **best drinking** 1998 – 2000 **best vintages** '93, '94 '95, '97 **drink with** Salad, seafood • $18

Coriole Shiraz

Produced from estate plantings on red loam over ironstone and limestone subsoils. While the vines are new in comparison to those used to make Lloyd Reserve, they are in fact old by any normal standards, dating back to the late 1960s. This has always been a distinguished wine.

🍷🍷🍷🍷🍷(half) **1996** Strong red-purple; the bouquet is rich and full, with dark plum and cherry fruit supported by subtle oak. The equally rich multiflavoured palate has dark cherry, plum and some minty flavours, finishing with positive tannins. **rating:** 90

➾ **best drinking** 2000 – 2010 **best vintages** '90, '91, '96 **drink with** Steak and kidney pie • $20

Coriole Lloyd Reserve Shiraz

One of McLaren Vale's most distinguished Shiraz wines, with a track record going back to the establishment of Coriole in 1967, based upon 1.3 hectares of vines then 60 years old. Those vines provided the core of fruit over the intervening decades until additional plantings came first into bearing and then into maturity, allowing the introduction of a Reserve Shiraz from 1989 using only those original plantings. The vines typically produce 4 to 4.5 tonnes of grapes, enough to make about 250 cases per year.

1995 Dark red-purple; the bouquet is powerful and concentrated, with dark berry/foresty fruits and subtle oak; the palate shows the same dark cherry and regional bitter chocolate flavours, with quite pronounced tannins and high total extract. Bred to stay. **rating:** 93

➯ **best drinking** 2005 – 2015 **best vintages** '70, '74, '84, '88, '89, '90, '91, '92, '94, '95 **drink with** Ragout of lamb • $40

Coriole Lalla Rookh Grenache Shiraz

In my halcyon days as a university student at St Paul's College, Sydney, the Lalla Rookh was the local (and frequently visited) pub. Only now do I learn the name has an incredibly complicated history, going back to a mythical Indian princess, a steeplechaser ridden by Adam Lindsay Gordon, a sailing ship, the name of one of the Lloyd family vineyards, and a hybrid flower. Behind all this is a blend of 88% Grenache and 12% Shiraz matured for 12 months in a mix of one and two-year-old French oak barrels.

1996 Medium to full red-purple; a richly luscious bouquet with blackberry, plum, spice and vanilla aromas is followed by a concentrated and powerful palate with the same flavours together with a dusting of dark chocolate. There are sufficient tannins for the wine to age well. **rating:** 87

➯ **best drinking** 1999 – 2003 **best vintages** NA **drink with** Rich casserole • $18

Coriole Sangiovese

Together with Montrose, Coriole has been one of the pioneers in the growing and making of Sangiovese in Australia, with no small input from winemaker Peter Hall. 1996 in fact marks the tenth vintage from Coriole. The wine is open-fermented and spends 12 months in old French and American oak barrels. I have not always been persuaded by earlier vintages, but perhaps it was in part due to my reluctance to accept certain aspects of the Sangiovese varietal character as manifested in Australia. Certainly the wine has a fine reputation, and the '96 vintage is good.

1996 Strong, bright red-purple; the bouquet is quite intense, with earthy/black forest varietal fruit, followed by unexpectedly sweet, minty fruit on the early and mid-palate, then showing pronounced tannins on the finish. **rating:** 85

➯ **best drinking** 1999 – 2004 **best vintages** NA **drink with** Osso buco • $15

Coriole Mary Kathleen Cabernet Blend

Second in the Coriole hierarchy after the scarce Lloyd Shiraz, but still very much a super-premium wine. Typically made from roughly equal quantities of Merlot and Cabernet Sauvignon, with a dash of Cabernet Franc (in 1995 45% Merlot, 41% Cabernet Sauvignon and 14% Cabernet Franc) it is a distinguished wine, utterly different from the others in the Coriole stable.

1995 Medium red-purple; a smooth but powerful bouquet with classic dusty cabernet fruit is somewhat unexpectedly followed by a remarkably sweet and luscious palate with masses of dark chocolate and blackberry fruit surrounded by soft, lingering tannins. **rating:** 92

➯ **best drinking** 2000 – 2010 **best vintages** '90, '91, '92, '94, '95 **drink with** Mature cheddar • $26

cosham NR

101 Union Road, Carmel via Kalamunda, WA 6076 **region** Perth Hills
phone (08) 9293 5424 **fax** (08) 9293 5062 **open** Not
winemaker Lyndon Crocker **production** 100 **est.** 1989
product range ($12 ML) Chardonnay, Pinot Noir, Merlot Cabernet.
summary The newest of the Perth Hills ventures, with a microscopic amount of wine available. Both the Chardonnay and Pinot Noir spend two years in French oak barriques before bottling – a long time by any standards.

cowra estate ★★★

Boorowa Road, Cowra, NSW 2794 **region** Cowra
phone (02) 6342 1136 **fax** (02) 6342 4286 **open** 7 days 9–6
winemaker Simon Gilbert (Contract) **production** 30 000 **est.** 1973
product range ($12–15 CD) Chardonnay, Unwooded Chardonnay, Cool Classic Chardonnay, Cool Classic Brut de Brut, Directors Reserve Merlot, Cabernet Rosé, Cabernet Shiraz, Cabernets. The Classic Bat series of Chardonnay, Pinot Noir and Cabernet Merlot is now at the head of the range.
summary Cowra Estate was purchased from the family of founder Tony Gray by South African-born food and beverage entrepreneur John Geber in 1995. A vigorous promotional campaign has gained a higher domestic profile for the once export-oriented brand. John Geber is very actively involved in the promotional effort, and rightly proud of the excellent value for money which the wines represent.

Cowra Estate Classic Bat Cabernet Merlot

The obvious question is 'why Classic Bat' (and a label depicting Victor Trumper). The answer, says John Geber, is because Trumper's unique cricketing style also personifies the very best of Cowra Estate wines: consistency, character and quality. Hmmm. Actually, this is a very decent wine at the price.

🍷🍷🍷🍷 **1996** Medium red-purple; the bouquet is clean, with pleasant chocolate, red berry and earth aromas of medium intensity. The palate is direct, but with plenty of attractive red berry, chocolate and mint-flavoured fruit; subtle oak. **rating:** 85

⇨ **best drinking** 1998 – 2002 **best vintages** NA **drink with** Pizza • $13.90

Cowra Estate Cabernets

As the name suggests, a Bordeaux-blend, which offers a pretty good value at the price. Winner of the Riedel Crystal Trophy for Best Lighter Bodied Dry Red Table Wine of Show at the 1998 Sydney International Wine Competition, receiving strong support from the overseas judges.

🍷🍷🍷🍷 **1996** Medium red-purple; the bouquet is of light to medium intensity, with minty/earthy fruit supported by a touch of vanilla oak. A fairly light but clean palate, with pleasant minty berry fruit, just a touch of oak and soft tannins. **rating:** 84

⇨ **best drinking** 1998 – 1999 **best vintages** NA **drink with** Lasagne • $12

crabtree of watervale ★★★

North Terrace, Watervale SA 5452 **region** Clare Valley
phone (08) 8843 0069 **fax** (08) 8843 0144 **open** 7 days 11–5
winemaker Robert Crabtree **production** 4500 **est.** 1979

product range ($12–16 CD) Riesling, Late Harvest Riesling, Semillon, Watervale Dry Red, Grenache, Shiraz Cabernet, Cabernet Sauvignon, Muscat.
summary The gently eccentric Robert Crabtree has sold his winery to an Adelaide-based syndicate of wine lovers; how many changes are in store I do not know.

craig avon vineyard ★★★☆

Craig Avon Lane, Merricks North, Vic 3926 **region** Mornington Peninsula
phone (03) 5989 7465 **open** Weekends and public holidays 12–5
winemaker Ken Lang **production** 1000 **est.** 1986
product range ($24–32 CD) Chardonnay, Pinot Noir, Cabernet, Cabernet Merlot.
summary All of the wines are sold cellar door and by mailing list. The wines are competently made, clean and with pleasant fruit flavour.

craigie knowe ★★★

Glen Gala Road, Cranbrook, Tas 7190 **region** Southern Tasmania
phone (03) 6223 5620 **fax** (03) 6223 5009 **open** Weekends or by appointment
winemaker Dr John Austwick **production** 500 **est.** 1979
product range ($16–22 ML) Cabernet Sauvignon, Pinot Noir.
summary John Austwick makes a small quantity of full-flavoured, robust Cabernet Sauvignon in a tiny winery as a weekend relief from a busy metropolitan dental practice.

craiglee ★★★★★

Sunbury Road, Sunbury, Vic 3429 **region** Sunbury
phone (03) 9744 4489 **fax** (03) 9744 4489 **open** Sun, public holidays 10–5, or by appointment
winemaker Patrick Carmody **production** 2000 **est.** 1976
product range ($17–23 CD) Chardonnay, Pinot Noir, Shiraz, Cabernet Sauvignon.
summary An historic winery with a proud nineteenth-century record which recommenced winemaking in 1976 after a prolonged hiatus. Produces one of the finest cool-climate Shirazes in Australia, redolent of cherry, liquorice and spice in the better (i.e. warmer) vintages, lighter-bodied in the cooler ones. Maturing vines and improved viticulture has made the wines more consistent (and even better) over the past ten years or so.

Craiglee Chardonnay

Has stood in the shadow of the Craiglee Shiraz, but a vertical tasting late in 1997 with vintages back to 1982 showed it to be a very fine wine in its own right, and with true cellaring potential. Since 1991 the move to barrel fermentation in French oak and the exclusion of malolactic fermentation has both tightened the style, and increased its longevity.

🍷🍷🍷🍷🍷 **1996** Light to medium yellow-green; the bouquet is fresh and delicate, with citrus, melon and peach fruit; integrated and balanced French oak. The palate is smooth, with most attractive butterscotch nuances to the nectarine and melon fruit; impeccable acid balance on a long finish. **rating:** 95

➪ **best drinking** 1999 – 2006 **best vintages** '87, '90, '92, '96 **drink with** Pan-fried veal • NA

Craiglee Shiraz

Produced from 4 hectares of estate plantings, almost invariably producing wines of the highest imaginable quality, with wonderful cherry, pepper and spice aromas and flavours. The wines are fruit, rather than oak-driven; they are immaculately structured, having the fruit weight and vinous sweetness to balance the peppery/spicy tang.

🍷🍷🍷🍷🍷 **1996** Bright red-purple; the bouquet is fresh and lively with the hallmark black cherry and spice fruit aromas, the palate likewise lively and fresh, with spicy flavours and soft tannins. Matured in 40% new French oak. **rating:** 90

➭ **best drinking** 2001 – 2010 **best vintages** '84, '86, '88, '91, '92, '93, '94, '96 **drink with** Italian cuisine • $23

craigmoor ★★★

Craigmoor Road, Mudgee, NSW 2850 **region** Mudgee
phone (02) 6372 2208 **fax** (02) 6372 4464 **open** Mon-Fri 9–4, weekends 10–4
winemaker Robert Paul **production** NFP **est.** 1858
product range ($12.95–13.95 R) Semillon, Chardonnay, Shiraz, Cabernet Sauvignon.
summary One of the oldest wineries in Australia to remain in continuous production, now subsumed into the Orlando/Wyndham group, with an inevitable loss of identity and individuality of wine style, although the technical quality of the wines cannot be faulted.

craigow NR

Richmond Road, Cambridge, Tas 7170 **region** Southern Tasmania
phone (03) 6248 5379 **fax** (03) 6248 5482 **open** Not
winemaker Andrew Hood (Contract) **production** 200 **est.** 1989
product range ($15–19 ML) Pinot Noir.
summary Craigow has substantial vineyards, with 5 hectares of pinot noir and another 5 hectares divided between riesling, chardonnay and gewurztraminer. However, almost all of the grapes are sold, and only a little Pinot Noir is made each year.

crane winery NR

Haydens Road, Kingaroy, Qld 4610 **region** Other Wineries of Qld
phone (07) 4162 7647 **fax** (07) 4162 7647 **open** 9–4 Fri-Tues or by appointment
winemaker John Crane **production** 3500 **est.** 1996
product range ($10–16 ML) Marsanne Verdelho Semillon, Chardonnay, Hillside White and Red, Cabernet Franc, Shiraz Cabernet Sauvignon, Sparkling Burgundy, Vintage Liqueur Shiraz, Liqueur Muscat.
summary Established by John and Sue Crane, Crane Winery is one of several in the burgeoning Kingaroy (or South Burnett) region in Queensland, drawing upon 3 hectares of estate plantings, but also purchasing grapes from other growers in the region. Interestingly, Sue Crane's great-grandfather established a vineyard planted to shiraz 100 years ago (in 1898) and which remained in production until 1970.

craneford NR

Main Street, Springton, SA 5235 **region** Eden Valley
phone (08) 8568 2220 **fax** (08) 8568 2538 **open** Wed-Mon 11–5
winemaker Contract **production** 2400 **est.** 1978

product range ($11–15 CD) Riesling, Chardonnay, Shiraz, Cabernet Sauvignon.
summary A recent change of ownership may herald a revival in the fortunes of Craneford which had suffered from a range of winemaking problems over the past five years or so.

cranswick estate ★★★

Walla Avenue, Griffith, NSW 2680 **region** Riverina
phone (02) 6962 4133 **fax** (02) 6962 2888 **open** Mon-Fri 10–4.30, Sat 10–4
winemaker Ian Hongell **production** 600 000 **est.** 1976
product range ($10–22 R) There are three ranges in two price sectors; at the top come the Premium and Regional Selection ranges (with Autumn Gold Botrytis Semillon off to one side and higher priced again) comprising Barrel Fermented Semillon, Young Vine Chardonnay, Conlon Block Marsanne, McLaren Vale Sauvignon Blanc, Gnarled Vine Barossa Grenache and NV Sparkling Shiraz; then there is the volume-selling Vignette Range of Fruition (White Frontignac), Unoaked Chardonnay, Semillon Sauvignon Blanc, Semillon Cabernet Merlot, Shiraz.
summary Taking full advantage of the buoyant share market and the continuing export success of Australian wines, Cranswick Estate made a highly successful entry to the lists of the Australian Associated Stock Exchanges in 1997. The substantial capital raised will see the further expansion of an already thriving business, firmly aimed at the export market.

Cranswick Estate Autumn Gold Botrytis Semillon (375 ml)

One hundred per cent Botrytis Semillon sourced from a single grower (Pat Zirilli) in Griffith, and given 12 months maturation in oak. Prior vintages have been prolific show medal winners; the '95 has won gold medals at minor shows (Rutherglen and Griffith).

🍷🍷🍷🍷 **1995** Glowing yellow-green; a complex array of cumquat, mandarin and honey fruit aromas come through solid oak on the bouquet, and even more evident oak on the palate. Plenty of total flavour, and finishes with good acid. **rating:** 84

➾ **best drinking** 1998 – 1999 **best vintages** '94, '95 **drink with** Peach tart • $22

crawford river wines ★★★★★

Hotspur Upper Road, Condah, Vic 3303 **region** Far South West Victoria
phone (03) 5578 2267 **fax** (03) 5578 2240 **open** 7 days 10–4
winemaker John Thomson **production** 3000 **est.** 1975
product range ($12–24 R) Riesling, Semillon Sauvignon Blanc, Chardonnay, Classic Dry White, Cabernet Merlot, Cabernet Sauvignon.
summary Exemplary wines right across the range are made by full-time grazier, part-time winemaker John Thomson who clearly has the winemaker's equivalent of the gardener's green thumb. The Riesling is consistently outstanding, the Cabernet-based wines excellent in warmer vintages.

Crawford River Riesling

A wine of consistently good quality over the years, tight and reserved, and fully reflecting the very cool climate in which it is grown. It is 100% estate-grown (as are all of the Crawford River wines).

🍷🍷🍷🍷🍷 **1997** Light to medium yellow-green; the bouquet shows extraordinarily intense passionfruit aromas; you can almost visualise the passionfruit pips in the juice. Similar flavours come through on the striking palate, which is, however, elegant, and with considerable structure. **rating:** 92

➾ **best drinking** 1998 – 2005 **best vintages** '86, '88, '89, '91, '94, '96, '97 **drink with** Antipasto • $19

Crawford River Semillon Sauvignon Blanc

Yet another testament to the winemaking skills, and in particular the white winemaking skills, of John Thomson. It is hard to imagine a more perfect evocation of a blend such as this, with the two varieties seamlessly merging with each other, and reflecting the cool climate.

🍷🍷🍷🍷🍷 **1997** Light green-yellow; a highly aromatic bouquet, crisp and clean, with a mix of herb and gooseberry aromas is followed by an ultra-crisp, tangy and lively palate in brilliant summer seafood style. **rating:** 92

➾ **best drinking** 1998 – 1999 **best vintages** NA **drink with** Crab or shellfish • $17

Crawford River Cabernet Sauvignon

Grown at the extreme edge for Cabernet Sauvignon, and always presents a rather austere, minerally, European cast, but in most years redeems itself with the length of its finish, and the way the flavour builds-up with the second glass.

🍷🍷🍷🍷 **1994** Medium red-purple; the bouquet ranges through leafy/cedar/earthy/briary notes, but then sweetens up with some more chocolatey characters. The palate is extremely long, with considerable briary/earthy grip. It has a character peculiar to the 1994 vintage running across Coonawarra/Padthaway and into southern Victoria, a certain austerity yet strength. **rating:** 85

➾ **best drinking** 2000 – 2006 **best vintages** '86, '88, '90, '91, '93 **drink with** Roast veal • $20

cruickshank callatoota estate ★★☆

Wybong Road, Wybong, NSW 2333 **region** Upper Hunter Valley
phone (02) 6547 8149 **fax** (02) 6547 8144 **open** 7 days 9–5
winemaker Andrew Cruickshank, Hartley Smithers **production** 7000 **est.** 1973
product range ($10–16 CD) Cabernet Rosé, Cabernet Sauvignon, Two Cabernets, Pressings.
summary Owned by Sydney management consultant John Cruickshank and family. Wine quality has definitely improved in the 1990s, although the wines still show strong regional, rather earthy, characters, the label itself likewise doggedly remaining old-fashioned.

cullen ★★★★★

Caves Road, Cowaramup, WA 6284 **region** Margaret River
phone (08) 9755 5277 **fax** (08) 9755 5550 **open** 7 days 10–4
winemaker Vanya Cullen **production** 12 500 **est.** 1971
product range ($15–48 CD) Flagship wines: Chardonnay, Sauvignon Blanc, Reserve Cabernet Merlot; premium wines: Classic Dry White, Blanc de Noir, Velvet Red, Late Harvest Cabernet Sauvignon.
summary One of the pioneers of Margaret River which has always produced long-lived wines of highly individual style from the substantial and mature estate vineyards. Winemaking is now in the hands of Vanya Cullen, daughter of the founders; she is possessed of an extraordinarily good palate. The Cabernet Merlot goes from strength to strength; indeed, I would rate it Australia's best.

Cullen Chardonnay

An exceptionally complex wine which has really hit the heights since 1993; both that vintage and 1994 stand high among the more powerful, structured Chardonnays made in Australia. One hundred per cent barrel fermentation, 100% malolactic fermentation and prolonged lees contact all make their mark.

🍷🍷🍷🍷🍷 **1996** As befits this winery and its winemaker, Vanya Cullen, a wine of great character and presence. Full-on barrel fermentation and maturation characters are woven through rich fig and peach fruit, balanced by reasonably firm acidity on the finish. The best yet from Cullen. **rating:** 95

➯ **best drinking** 1998 – 2003 **best vintages** '93, '94, '96 **drink with** Sweetbreads • $34

Cullen Cabernet Merlot

An estate-grown wine of the highest quality which since 1990 has been arguably the best Margaret River Cabernet Merlot blend. Up to 1995 both a varietal and a Reserve version were made, but as from that vintage the decision was taken to only release one wine. Consistently outstanding.

🍷🍷🍷🍷🍷 **1995** Reserve. Full red-purple; proclaims its class from the first second, with dark berry, dark chocolate and cedar oak skilfully interwoven; the palate is as concentrated as the bouquet promises with ripe, luscious fruit in a dark berry spectrum, perfectly balanced and integrated oak, and equally perfectly judged and controlled tannins. Retasted November 1997 (and subsequently); a once in a decade wine. **rating:** 97

➯ **best drinking** 2000 – 2015 **best vintages** '77, '84, '86, '90, '91, '92, '93, '95 **drink with** Lamb, strong cheddar • $48

currency creek wines ★★★

Winery Road, Currency Creek, SA 5214 **region** Other Wineries of SA
phone (08) 8555 4069 **fax** (08) 8555 4100 **open** 7 days 10–5
winemaker Phillip Tonkin **production** 8000 **est.** 1969
product range ($5–21.25 CD) Dry White, Semillon, Sauvignon Blanc, Chardonnay, Princess Alexandrina Noble Riesling, Gamay, Pinot Noir, Harmony (Shiraz Merlot), Ostrich Hill Shiraz, Cabernet Sauvignon, Sparkling, Fortifieds.
summary Constant name changes (Santa Rosa, Tonkins have also been tried) did not help the quest for identity or recognition in the marketplace, but the winery has nonetheless produced some outstanding wood-matured whites and pleasant, soft reds selling at attractive prices.

curtis NR

Foggo Road, McLaren Vale, SA 5171 **region** McLaren Vale
phone (08) 8323 8389 **open** Weekends 11–4.30
winemaker P Curtis **production** 1500 **est.** 1988
product range ($4–5.50 CD) Riesling, Moselle, Claret, Shiraz Grenache, Ruby Port, Tawny Port.
summary A small and relatively new producer in McLaren Vale, whose wines I have not tasted.

d'arenberg ★★★★☆

Osborn Road, McLaren Vale, SA 5171 **region** McLaren Vale
phone (08) 8323 8206 **fax** (08) 8323 8423 **open** 7 days 10–5
winemaker Chester Osborn, Philip Dean **production** 120 000 **est.** 1912

product range ($10–45 R) Dry Dam Riesling, Dry Land Sauvignon Blanc, Olive Grove Chardonnay, Other Side Chardonnay, Noble Riesling, Peppermint Paddock Chambourcin, Twenty Eight Road Mourvedre, d'Arry's Original Shiraz Grenache, The Custodian Grenache, Dead Arm Shiraz, Old Vine Shiraz, Red Ochre, Ironstone Pressings, High Trellis Cabernet Sauvignon, The Coppermine Road Cabernet Sauvignon; Fortified.

summary d'Arenberg has adopted a much higher profile in the second half of the 1990s with a cascade of volubly worded labels and the opening of a spectacularly situated and high-quality restaurant, d'Arry's Verandah. Happily, wine quality has more than kept pace with the label uplifts.

d'Arenberg The Olive Grove Chardonnay

The name is conjured not from a specific grove of olive trees, but rather the olive trees that abound throughout McLaren Vale particularly along old creek beds and watercourses. Very much a Chardonnay made by a red winemaker, rich and opulent, but which has had considerable success in wine competitions, notably overseas. The '96 vintage won a gold medal at the Chardonnay du Monde competition in Burgundy in 1997.

🍷🍷🍷🍷 **1996** Medium to full yellow-green; a big, rich wine with lots of barrel-ferment characters and abundant ripe, peach and melon fruit on the bouquet. Less fat on the mid-palate than expected, and does have some minerally grip to the finish, helping the overall balance of the wine. **rating:** 85

➪ **best drinking** 1998 – 1999 **best vintages** NA **drink with** Gnocchi • $35

d'Arenberg Dead Arm Shiraz

Part of a veritable cascade of new labels which tumbled out from d'Arenberg in the mid-1990s, and a decidedly strange name for the super-premium flagship of the winery. The name comes from a fungal disease (phomopsis viticola) which attacks vines in many parts of the world, and which can cause one half (or one side) of the vine to die, leaving the other side unaffected (at least for the time being). The older the vines, the more likely the incidence of attack. So much for the name, the wine itself can be absolutely outstanding, bringing together concentrated fruit with 12–18 months maturation in new American oak barriques.

🍷🍷🍷🍷½ **1996** Dense red-purple; the bouquet is spotlessly clean, with concentrated dark cherry and dark chocolate fruit, together with plenty of new oak. A rich and concentrated wine on the palate with more of that dark chocolate fruit, finishing with powerful but ripe tannins. **rating:** 93

➪ **best drinking** 2001 – 2011 **best vintages** '94, '95, '96 **drink with** Marinated beef • $45

d'Arenberg The Footbolt Old Vine Shiraz

Produced from vines dating back as far as 1890 but harvested over a long period to achieve differing flavour and sugar levels to add complexity. Made traditionally in open fermenters, basket-pressed, and aged in a mix of French and American barriques and hogsheads for one year, all of which have been previously used, and which are not intended to impart excessive oak flavour. The adddition of the word 'Footbolt' on the front label has given rise to a world record back label, best read with a microscope and a spellcheck, the latter to tell you that the 'absinent' Joe Osborn was really abstinent.

🍷🍷🍷🍷 **1996** Medium to full red-purple; a clean bouquet, with a mix of berry, earth and liquorice fruit together with just a touch of chocolate and subtle oak is followed logically by the palate, with sweet fruit and oak, earth and liquorice flavours, finishing with moderate tannins. **rating:** 88

➪ **best drinking** 2001 – 2006 **best vintages** '82, '88, '90, '91, '94, '95, '96 **drink with** Smoked lamb with redcurrant sauce • $17

d'Arenberg Ironstone Pressings

An intermittent release from d'Arenberg over the years, but likely to become a permanent part of the scene in the future, being made in both 1994 and 1995. Typically a blend of 85% Grenache and 15% Shiraz, it is not – as the name might suggest – made up of the pressings component of the various Grenache and Shiraz blends and wines made by d'Arenberg. In other words, it contains the usual mix of free-run and pressings material; to the extent it has extra weight, it comes from the late harvesting, with the ripest components nearing 16° baumé – terrorising stuff for the uninitiated.

1996 Medium red-purple; clean, chocolatey/minty/earthy/red cherry aromas with a nice touch of oak on the bouquet. The palate is rich, full and dense, with dusty tannins running throughout, before drying off slightly on the finish. **rating:** 85

best drinking 2001 – 2006 **best vintages** '91, '94, '95 **drink with** Leave it in the cellar • $30

d'Arenberg d'Arry's Original Shiraz Grenache

A classic wine style with an illustrious show record and, as the classic wine entry indicates, dating back to 1961. Made from roughly equal proportions of low-yielding, old vine Shiraz and Grenache, held in a mix of large and small oak (principally old) for ten months prior to bottling. Quite deliberately made in a slightly old-fashioned style, fruit, rather than oak, driven, but none the worse for that.

1995 Strong purple-red; a rich and complex array of aromas ranging through liquorice, chocolate, game and mint lead into a wonderfully accessible and textured palate with sweet berryish fruit, hints of liquorice and game, finishing with soft tannins. The initial confection trap characters have disappeared. **rating:** 93

best drinking 1999 – 2009 **best vintages** '63, '76, '86, '87, '88, '91, '95 **drink with** Jugged hare • $17

d'Arenberg The Custodian Grenache

As with all of the d'Arenberg wines, if you get to read the back label, these background notes will be as superfluous as they are brief. Suffice it to say that grenache has always been a major part of the d'Arenberg red wine production, and the best parcels of old vine grenache are used to produce the wine. It is kept in tank and in large wood for part of the time, before spending six months in new and old American oak barriques, thus putting the major emphasis on the luscious fruit – which is as it should be.

1996 Medium red-purple; a fragrant, juicy style, clean, with a hint of mint and minimal oak on the bouquet; the palate is very strongly juicy and jammy, typical of one of the faces of grenache, but slightly unformed and, early in its life, seems to have been rushed into bottle. **rating:** 82

best drinking 1999 – 2006 **best vintages** '91, '92, '94, '95 **drink with** Ragout of venison • $20

d'Arenberg The Coppermine Road Cabernet Sauvignon

The name comes from a road adjoining the vineyard (which in fact has four different names along parts of its not very great length, which is somehow apppropriate). It spends 18 months in new and used French and American oak barriques.

1996 Medium to full red-purple; a potent bouquet with masses of cassis, blackberry and blackcurrant fruit; clean subtle oak. The palate is rather raw and astringent shortly after bottling, with fairly tough tannins, certainly needs considerable time in bottle; the points may prove to be a harsh assessment. **rating:** 84

best drinking 2004 – 2010 **best vintages** NA **drink with** Leave it in the cellar • $45

d'entrecasteaux NR

Boorara Road, Northcliffe, WA 6262 **region** Pemberton
phone (08) 9776 7232 **open** By appointment
winemaker Alkoomi (Contract) **production** 600 **est.** 1988
product range Chardonnay, Sauvignon Blanc, Pinot Noir, Cabernet Sauvignon.
summary Not to be confused with the now moribund Tasmanian winery of the same name, but likewise taking its name from the French explorer Admiral Bruni D'Entrecasteaux who visited both Tasmania and the southwest coast of Western Australia. Four hectares of estate vineyards, planted on rich Karri loam, produce grapes for the wines which are contract-made at Alkoomi.

dal zotto wines NR

Edi Road, Cheshunt, Vic 3678 **region** King Valley
phone (03) 5729 8321 **fax** (03) 5729 8490 **open** By appointment
winemaker Otto Dal Zotto **production** 900 **est.** 1994
product range ($13.50–14.50 CD) Chardonnay, Merlot, Shiraz, Cabernet Merlot, Cabernet Sauvignon.
summary Dal Zotto Wines remains primarily a contract grape grower, with almost 15 hectares of vineyards (predominantly chardonnay and cabernet sauvignon) but does make a small amount of wine for local sale (and by mail order).

dalfarras

PO Box 123, Nagambie, Vic 3608 **region** Goulburn Valley
phone (03) 5794 2637 **fax** (03) 5794 2360 **open** Not
winemaker Alister Purbrick **production** 17 500 **est.** 1991
product range ($14.95–19.95 R) Riesling, Unwooded Chardonnay, Barrel Fermented Chardonnay, Sauvignon Blanc, Marsanne, Shiraz, Cabernet Sauvignon.
summary The personal project of Alister Purbrick and artist-wife Rosa (née) Dalfarra, whose paintings adorn the labels of the wines. Alister, of course, is best known as winemaker at Chateau Tahbilk, the family winery and home, but this range of wines is intended to (in Alister's words) 'allow me to expand my winemaking horizons and mould wines in styles different to Chateau Tahbilk'.

Dalfarras Sauvignon Blanc

Not all of the Dalfarras wines seem as different in style from those of Chateau Tahbilk as one might expect, but this wine does fit that description, being thoroughly modern rather than thoroughly traditional. A blend of Goulburn Valley and McLaren Vale material, reflecting the partnership between Alister Purbrick and Geoff Merrill. The '96 was the top gold medal winner in the Sauvignon Blanc Class at the 1997 Sydney Wine Show.

1997 Light green-yellow; a light, fresh and clean bouquet with gently herbaceous varietal fruit, and a quite flavoursome palate, with a mix of gooseberry, passionfruit and more herbal flavours. A solid follow-up to the '96. **rating:** 85

best drinking 1998 – 1999 **best vintages** '96 **drink with** Smoked eel • $14.95

Dalfarras Shiraz

While some of the Dalfarras wines do not seem particularly different in style from those of Chateau Tahbilk, this wine certainly does. Matured in new French and American oak barrels for 18 months, and made entirely from Goulburn Valley grapes, it is a rich, sweet and supple style.

🍷🍷🍷🍷 **1995** Medium to full red; the bouquet is not particularly rich or robust, but does have attractive liquorice, game and earth varietal aromas with well-balanced oak. The palate is particularly harmonious and smooth, with berry and liquorice fruit flavours, and seems to have swallowed up the oak in which it was matured. Finishes with soft tannins. **rating:** 85

⇨ **best drinking** 1999 – 2005 **best vintages** NA **drink with** Steak and kidney pie • $16.95

dalrymple ★★★★

Heemskerk/Lebrina Road, Pipers Brook, Tas 7250 **region** Northern Tasmania
phone (03) 6331 3179 **fax** (03) 6331 3179 **open** Sat-Sun 10–5
winemaker Various contract **production** 1280 **est.** 1987
product range ($16 ML) Chardonnay, Sauvignon Blanc, Pinot Noir.
summary A partnership between Jill Mitchell and her sister and brother-in-law, Anne and Bertel Sundstrup, inspired by father Bill Mitchell's establishment of the Tamarway Vineyard in the late 1960s. In 1991 Tamarway reverted to the Sundstrup and Mitchell families, and it too, will be producing wine in the future, probably under its own label but sold ex the Dalrymple cellar door. Its Sauvignon Blanc is consistently Tasmania's best.

dalwhinnie ★★★★★

Taltarni Road, Moonambel, Vic 3478 **region** Pyrenees
phone (03) 5467 2388 **fax** (03) 5467 2237 **open** 7 days 10–5
winemaker David Jones, Rick Kinzbrunner (Contract) **production** 4500 **est.** 1976
product range ($24–35 CD) Chardonnay, Pinot Noir; Moonambel Shiraz, Cabernet.
summary David and Jenny Jones have now acquired full ownership of Dalwhinnie from Ewan Jones, and have three children of their own to ensure the future succession. In the meantime, Dalwhinnie goes from strength to strength, making outstanding wines right across the board. The wines all show tremendous depth of fruit flavour, reflecting the relatively low-yielding but very well-maintained vineyards. It is hard to say whether the Chardonnay or the Shiraz is the most distinguished, the Pinot Noir (made with assistance from Rick Kinzbrunner) a startling arrival from out of nowhere.

Dalwhinnie Chardonnay

Produced from a little under 4 hectares of low-yielding, unirrigated estate-grown vines, with an ancestry going back to the clone introduced in the nineteenth century and discovered at Mudgee in the late 1960s. Barrel fermentation adds to the richness to produce an invariably extremely complex wine.

🍷🍷🍷🍷🍷 **1996** Medium to full yellow-green; a quite complex yet nicely restrained bouquet with melon and grapefruit aromas supported by subtle oak; a long, intense and well-structured palate with melon and grapefruit flavours, finishing with good acidity. Has come together exceptionally well. **rating:** 90

⇨ **best drinking** 1998 – 2002 **best vintages** '87, '88, '90, '92, '93, '94, '96 **drink with** Turkey • $25

Dalwhinnie Pinot Noir

Produced from 2.4 hectares of estate plantings, and a wine which I tasted without any foreknowledge. It came as a total surprise, and it was only when I subsequently read that it was made by Rick Kinzbrunner (of Giaconda) that the pieces fell into place.

🍷🍷🍷🍷🍷 **1996** Medium red; the bouquet is fragrant and extremely stylish, with sappy pinot and obvious whole-bunch fermentation influences. The palate has excellent varietal character, with sappy, cherry fruit and the barest whiff of mint. A tour de force of winemaking given the origin of the grapes. **rating:** 90

⇒ **best drinking** 1998 – 2001 **best vintages** NA **drink with** Game • $30

Dalwhinnie Moonambel Shiraz

An exceptionally concentrated and powerful wine, fully reflecting the low yields and the influence of the quartz, clay and gravel soils. These are not wines for the faint-hearted, positively demanding long cellaring, but having the balance to repay patience.

🍷🍷🍷🍷 **1996** Medium red-purple; the bouquet is clean, with cherry/berry fruit of medium to full intensity, although not especially complex. On the palate powerful cherry, berry and mint fruit flavours are followed by tannins which build on the mid to back palate. Subtle oak throughout. **rating:** 86

⇒ **best drinking** 2002 – 2006 **best vintages** '86, '88, '90, '91, '92, '94, '95 **drink with** Potent cheeses, strong red meats • $35

---

dalyup river estate NR

Murrays Road, Esperance, WA 6450 **region** Other Wineries of WA
phone (08) 9076 5027 **fax** (08) 9076 5027 **open** Weekends 10–4
winemaker Gavin Berry (Plantagenet) **production** 500 **est.** 1987
product range ($10–12 CD) Dry Riesling, Medium Sweet Riesling, Fumé Blanc, Shiraz, Port.
summary Arguably the most remote winery in Australia other than Chateau Hornsby in Alice Springs. The quantities are as small as the cellar-door prices are modest; this apart, the light but fragrant wines show the cool climate of this ocean-side vineyard.

dargo valley winery NR

Lower Dargo Road, Dargo, Vic 3682 **region** Gippsland
phone (03) 5140 1228 **fax** (03) 5140 1212 **open** Mon-Thur 12–8, weekends, holidays 10–8 (closed Fridays)
winemaker Hermann Bila **production** 250 **est.** 1985
product range ($12–14 CD) Traminer, Rhine Riesling, Sauvignon Blanc, Chardonnay, Pinot Noir, Cabernet Sauvignon, Port.
summary Situated in mountain country north of Maffra and looking towards the Bogong National Park. Hermann Bila comes from a family of European winemakers; there is also an on-site restaurant, and Devonshire teas and ploughman's lunches are provided – very useful given the remote locality. The white wines tend to be rustic, the sappy/earthy/cherry Pinot Noir the pick of the red wines.

darling estate ★★★

Whitfield Road, Cheshunt, Vic 3678 **region** King Valley
phone (03) 5729 8396 **fax** (03) 5729 8396 **open** By appointment
winemaker Guy Darling, Rick Kinzbrunner (Consultant) **production** 400 **est.** 1990

product range ($9–16 ML) Koombahla Riesling, Chenin Blanc, Nambucca Chenin Blanc, Koombahla Chardonnay, Pinot Noir, Koombahla Pinot Noir, Nambucca Gamay Koombahla Shiraz, Koombahla Cabernets, Koombahla Cabernet Sauvignon.

summary Guy Darling was one of the pioneers of the King Valley when he planted his first vines in 1970. For many years the entire production was purchased by Brown Brothers, providing their well-known Koombahla Estate label. Much of the production from the 21 hectares is still sold to Brown Brothers (and others) but since 1991 Guy Darling has had a fully functional winery established on the vineyard, making a small portion of the production into wine – which was, in fact, his original motivation for planting the first vines. All the wines on sale have considerable bottle age.

darling park ★★★★

Red Hill Road, Red Hill, Vic 3937 **region** Mornington Peninsula

phone (03) 5989 2324 **fax** (03) 5989 2254 **open** 7 days Jan, Feb-Dec weekends & holidays 11–5

winemaker Kevin McCarthy (Contract) **production** 1000 **est.** 1986

product range ($13.50–15.50 CD) Chardonnay, Pinot Noir, Rosé Clair (a blend of Cabernet, Merlot and Pinot Gris), Cabernet Merlot.

summary John and Delys Sargeant have now opened their cellar door-cum-restaurant at Darling Park, which is open every day through January of each year. The labels are the most gloriously baroque of any to be found in Australia, and would give the American Bureau of Alcohol, Tobacco and Firearms (which governs such matters in the United States) total cardiac arrest.

Darling Park Pinot Noir

Absolutely extraordinary labelling to one side, this is a most attractive Pinot Noir which shows the '97 Mornington Peninsula vintage to good effect.

🍷🍷🍷🍷 **1997** Medium red-purple; a quite complex, fragrant bouquet with plum, black cherry and touches of spice, with a similar display of plum and spice flavours on the youthful, moderately weighted palate. **rating:** 86

➪ **best drinking** 1998 – 2001 **best vintages** NA **drink with** Smoked quail • NA

darlington estate ★★★☆

Lot 39 Nelson Road, Darlington, WA 6070 **region** Perth Hills

phone (08) 9299 6268 **fax** (08) 9299 7107 **open** Thurs-Sun and holidays 12–5

winemaker Caspar van der Meer **production** 2000 **est.** 1983

product range ($12–24 CD) Chardonnay, Semillon Sauvignon Blanc, Shiraz, Cabernet Sauvignon, Ruby Port; also cheaper Symphony (Chenin Blanc), Sonata (Sauvignon Blanc), Vin Primeur and Minuet (Rosé).

summary By far the largest producer in the Perth Hills region, and the best. Winemaking responsibilities have now passed to Caspar van der Meer, Balt's son, who graduated from Roseworthy in 1995 and, after a vintage at Chateau de Landiras in Bordeaux, joined the family business in 1996, returning to Languedoc in 1997 to make a large quantity of wine for the American market. Further improvements in wine quality seem highly probable.

david traeger ★★★

139 High Street, Nagambie, Vic 3608 **region** Goulburn Valley

phone (03) 5794 2514 **fax** (03) 5794 1776 **open** 7 days 10–5

winemaker David Traeger **production** 7000 **est.** 1986

product range ($9–19 R) Verdelho, Shiraz, Cabernet, Reserve Cabernet (premium aged release); Helvetia (available from cellar door only) Riesling, Late Harvest Riesling, Cabernet Dolce.
summary David Traeger learned much during his years as assistant winemaker at Mitchelton, and knows central Victoria well. The red wines are solidly crafted, the Verdelho interesting but more variable in quality.

de bortoli ★★★★

De Bortoli Road, Bilbul, NSW 2680 **region** Riverina
phone (02) 6964 9444 **fax** (02) 6964 9400 **open** Mon-Sat 9–5.30, Sun 9–4
winemaker Darren De Bortoli **production** 3 million **est.** 1928
product range ($3.50–35 CD) Noble One Botrytis Semillon is the flagship wine; Premium varietals under Deen De Bortoli label, and a low-priced range of varietal and generic wines under the Sacred Hill label. Substantial exports in bulk.
summary Famous among the cognoscenti for its superb Botrytis Semillon, which in fact accounts for only a minute part of its total production, this winery turns around low-priced varietal and generic wines which neither aspire to nor achieve any particular distinction. Financial and marketing acumen has made De Bortoli one of the fastest-growing large wineries in Australia in the 1990s.

de bortoli (victoria) ★★★★★

Pinnacle Lane, Dixons Creek, Vic 3775 **region** Yarra Valley
phone (03) 5965 2271 **fax** (03) 5965 2442 **open** 7 days 10–5
winemaker Stephen Webber, David Slingsby-Smith, David Bicknell **production** 100 000 **est.** 1987
product range ($12–55 R) At the top comes the premium Melba (Cabernet blend), followed by Yarra Valley Semillon, Chardonnay, Pinot Noir, Shiraz, Cabernet Sauvignon, Cabernet Merlot; then comes the intermediate Gulf Station range of Riesling, Chardonnay and Cabernet Sauvignon; the Windy Peak range of Riesling, Chardonnay, Pinot Noir, Cabernets, Prestige Cuvée; Montage White and Red.
summary The quality arm of the bustling De Bortoli group, run by Leanne De Bortoli and husband Stephen Webber, ex-Lindeman winemaker. Both the top label (De Bortoli), the second (Gulf Station) and the third label (Windy Peak) offer wines of consistently good quality and excellent value – the complex Chardonnay of outstanding quality. The omission of the (utterly justified) top rating for the winery in the previous edition of this book was entirely inadvertent.

De Bortoli Windy Peak Riesling

Made primarily from riesling grown in the Strathbogie Ranges and the Yarra Valley, often with a small percentage of Yarra Valley Gewurztraminer included. First made in 1989, the wine has garnered a constant stream of gold medals in national wine shows from that time, with the '97 no exception.

🍷🍷🍷🍷🍷 **1997** Light to medium yellow-green; a highly aromatic bouquet with lime tropical aromas. The palate is beautifully modulated and fine, with lime and passionfruit followed by a crisp, dry finish. Outstanding winemaking. **rating:** 90

➾ **best drinking** 1998 – 2003 **best vintages** '90, '92, '94, '95, '96, '97 **drink with** Fresh asparagus • $12

De Bortoli Gulf Station Chardonnay

Achieved immediate fame for De Bortoli when it swept all before it at the 1996 Adelaide Wine Show. This new range, named after the historic Gulf Station on the outskirts of Yarra Glen, shows the winemaking skills of Stephen Webber to full advantage. It also shows just what can be achieved with American oak, a technique previously employed to full advantage by Yarra Ridge. The '96 vintage followed in the path of the '95, winning a gold medal at the 1997 Sydney Wine Show, the '97 repeating the success in 1998.

🍷🍷🍷🍷🍸 **1997** Light to medium yellow-green; the bouquet is smooth, with well-balanced and integrated oak, ranging from earthy mineral characters through to melon and cashew. A stylish palate with attractive melon fruit has a touch of almost biscuity oak. **rating:** 90

➪ **best drinking** 1998 – 2001 **best vintages** '95, '96, '97 **drink with** Yabbies • $17

De Bortoli Windy Peak Chardonnay

Sourced from vineyards in Victoria, but always containing a significant proportion of southern Victorian material, including the Yarra Valley. Over the years has consistently out-performed far more expensive wines in wine shows, and has always represented exceptionally good value for money. Some barrel ferment and lees contact, together with the very clever use of American oak, are all contributors. Smart new packaging introduced for the 1997 vintage does the wine justice, making it appear far above its class.

🍷🍷🍷🍷 **1997** Medium yellow-green; sophisticated, spicy oak handling is the first impression on a complex bouquet, with citrus-tinged fruit coming along thereafter. The palate is certainly driven by oak, but skilfully so, with a texture, feel and flavour way above its price. **rating:** 88

➪ **best drinking** 1998 – 2000 **best vintages** '90, '92, '93, '94, '97 **drink with** Sashimi • $12

De Bortoli Yarra Valley Chardonnay

Made from both estate-grown grapes and grapes purchased from other Yarra Valley vineyards. Usually in a full-bodied style, albeit with restrained oak from partial barrel fermentation. Richly repays cellaring.

🍷🍷🍷🍷🍸 **1997** Medium yellow-green; an extremely stylish yet typical young Yarra bouquet with fine melon, citrus and cashew fruit. The palate is very tight, intense and complex, with tangy citrus/melon fruit, good acid and subtle oak. A brilliant outcome for what was a better red than white vintage. **rating:** 93

➪ **best drinking** 1998 – 2002 **best vintages** '90, '92, '93, '94, '96, '97 **drink with** Yabbies • $22

De Bortoli Windy Peak Pinot Noir

Arguably, the best-value Pinot Noir produced in Australia today. Said to be produced from Victorian-grown grapes, but usually contains a high proportion of Yarra Valley material, sometimes exclusively so.

🍷🍷🍷🍷 **1997** Light to medium red-purple; the bouquet is quite brisk, with earthy/sappy overtones to the cherry and plum fruit. The palate is almost classically austere, with stemmy/foresty notes surrounding plum and mint fruit flavours. **rating:** 86

➪ **best drinking** 1998 – 1999 **best vintages** NA **drink with** Chinese dry-fried shredded beef • $13

De Bortoli Yarra Valley Pinot Noir

In the manner of Socrates dissatisfied, Stephen Webber has until recently pronounced himself unhappy with the De Bortoli Pinot Noirs. However, the '95 won the prestigious Wine Press Club trophy for Best Mature Pinot Noir at the National Wine Show, and both the '96 and '97 wines are better than the '95. Partial cold maceration prior to fermentation, and partial barrel fermentation in 100% French oak are key techniques which have led to the improvement in style.

➪ **best drinking** 1997 – 1999 **best vintages** NA **drink with** Duck casserole • $28

De Bortoli Melba

Made in such tiny quantities as to be barely commercial, but is sold through cellar door in restricted quantities. A super-deluxe selection of the best, sometimes with only one barrel, and named in honour of Dame Nellie Melba. Typically a blend of Cabernet Sauvignon, Shiraz, Cabernet Franc and Merlot.

YYYYY **1994** Medium to full red-purple; the bouquet is very smooth and stylish, with ripe, dark berry fruit aromas together with gently cedary oak. A powerful wine in the mouth, with dark berry fruits, hints of leaf and mint, persistent tannins and quite firm acidity. **rating:** 92

➪ **best drinking** 2000 – 2008 **best vintages** '93 **drink with** Yarra Valley venison • $55

De Bortoli Yarra Valley Cabernet Sauvignon

Like the Shiraz, made from both estate-grown and purchased grapes. A 100% Cabernet Sauvignon (a Cabernet Merlot is also marketed) made using what might be described as traditional French techniques, and matured in a mix of new and used French barriques for 18 months before bottling. Can be outstanding; the 1995 vintage has won five trophies and six gold medals in various Victorian wine shows.

YYYYY **1995** Medium to full red-purple; there is an attractive spicy/nutmeg/earthy edge to sweet dark berry fruit on the bouquet. Neither the bouquet nor the palate show any green herbaceous characters whatsoever, but the cool-grown origins come through in the blackcurrant and mint-flavoured palate. Supported by well-handed oak throughout. **rating:** 91

➪ **best drinking** 2000 – 2009 **best vintages** '88, '90, '91, '92, '94, '95 **drink with** Beef casserole • $28

---

deakin estate ★★★

Kulkyne Way, via Red Cliffs, Vic 3496 **region** Murray Darling and Swan Hill
phone (03) 5029 1666 **fax** (03) 5024 3316 **open** Not
winemaker Mark Zeppel **production** 200 000 **est.** 1980
product range ($9.99–12.50 R) Colombard, Sauvignon Blanc, Sauvignon Blanc, Chardonnay, Alfred Chardonnay, Shiraz, Cabernet Sauvignon, Brut.
summary Effectively replaces the Sunnycliff label in the Yunghanns-owned Katnook Estate, Riddoch and (now) Deakin Estate triumvirate, which constitutes the Wingarra Wine Group. Sunnycliff is still used for export purposes, but does not appear on the domestic market any more. Deakin Estate draws on 346 hectares of its own vineyards, making it largely self-sufficient, producing competitively priced wines of consistent quality.

Deakin Estate Shiraz

Producing an early-bottled red wine from the Riverland and investing it with both flavour and structure is no easy task. In 1997 Deakin Estate succeeded admirably, particularly given the modest price of the wine.

ΥΥΥΥ **1997** Medium to full red-purple; surprisingly concentrated and ripe earthy berry fruit aromas blossom in the glass. The palate, too, shows lots of black cherry, blackberry and raspberry fruit and avoids those hard tanky flavours of many early-bottled reds. **rating:** 84

⇨ **best drinking** 1998 – 1999 **best vintages** NA **drink with** Meat pie • $9.90

delacolline estate ★★★

Whillas Road, Port Lincoln, SA 5606 **region** Other Wineries of SA
phone (08) 8682 5277 **fax** (08) 8682 4455 **open** Weekends 9–5
winemaker Andrew Mitchell (Contract) **production** 650 **est.** 1984
product range ($10–15 R) Riesling, Fumé Blanc, Cabernet Sauvignon.
summary Joins Boston Bay as the second Port Lincoln producer; the white wines are made under contract in the Clare Valley. The 3-hectare vineyard, run under the direction of Tony Bassett, reflects the cool maritime influence, with ocean currents which sweep up from the Antarctic.

delamere ★★★

Bridport Road, Pipers Brook, Tas 7254 **region** Northern Tasmania
phone (03) 6382 7190 **fax** (03) 6382 7250 **open** 7 days 10–5
winemaker Richard Richardson **production** 1500 **est.** 1983
product range ($12–24 CD) Chardonnay, White Pinot Noir, Pinot Noir (Standard, Dry Red and Reserve), Sparkling.
summary Richie Richardson produces elegant, rather light-bodied wines which have a strong following. The Chardonnay has been most successful, with a textured, complex, malolactic-influenced wine with great, creamy feel in the mouth. The Pinots typically show pleasant varietal fruit, but seem to suffer from handling problems with oak and a touch of oxidation.

delatite ★★★★

Stoneys Road, Mansfield, Vic 3722 **region** Central Victorian High Country
phone (03) 5775 2922 **fax** (03) 5775 2911 **open** 7 days 10–5
winemaker Rosalind Ritchie **production** 12 000 **est.** 1982
product range ($17–27.50 CD) Unoaked Chardonnay, Chardonnay, Sauvignon Blanc, Riesling, Late Picked Riesling, Dead Man's Hill Gewürztraminer, Delmelza Pinot Chardonnay, Pinot Noir, Shiraz, Merlot, Malbec, Dungeon Gully, Devil's River (Cabernet Sauvignon Malbec Shiraz), Fortifieds.
summary With its sweeping views across to the snow-clad alps, this is uncompromising cool-climate viticulture, and the wines naturally reflect the climate. Light but intense Riesling and spicy Traminer flower with a year or two in bottle, and in the warmer vintages the red wines achieve flavour and mouthfeel, albeit with a distinctive and all-pervasive mintiness.

Delatite Riesling

Delatite has been a leader in the move to the correct labelling of Rhine Riesling as 'Riesling' but has also swept all before it in recent years. The '92 won a gold medal at the National Wine Show in 1993, while the '93 was named as Wine of the Year in the 1994–95 edition of the *Good Wine Guide*, by Huon Hooke and Mark Shield.

ΥΥΥΥ **1997** Light to medium yellow-green; an intensely floral and striking bouquet with spice and Germanic lime pastille aromas is followed by an equally lively, intense and pungent wine on the palate, with pronounced acidity and an almost peppery prickle on the finish. **rating:** 87

⇨ **best drinking** 1998 – 2003 **best vintages** '82, '86, '87, '93, '97 **drink with** Grilled fish • $17

Delatite Dead Man's Hill Gewürztraminer

A wine that has attracted much favourable comment over the years, particularly from United Kingdom writers. It is exceptionally delicate, with very low phenolic levels, and at times seems to me to be just that little bit too delicate. On the other hand, the style is infinitely better than the heavy, oily versions of Traminer.

🍷🍷🍷🍷 **1997** Light to medium yellow-green; a typically fine and delicate bouquet which, however, has very precise varietal definition, showing spice, rose petal and lime aromas. The palate delivers more of the same on a long, lingering finish punctuated by lime, spice and rose petal flavours. The acid is undeniably brisk but I like it. **rating:** 88

⇨ **best drinking** 1998 – 1999 **best vintages** '82, '86, '87, '93, '94, '97 **drink with** Delicate Chinese dishes • $19

Delatite Malbec

A most interesting varietal from Delatite, a long way removed from the powerful, dense wines of the Clare Valley, but still showing exemplary varietal character, a character which can only be described as jammy, yet not pejoratively so.

🍷🍷🍷🍷 **1996** Light to medium red, with just a touch of purple; a clean and clear bouquet with sweet, juicy/jammy berry fruit is tracked precisely by the palate, again showing jammy berry varietal character. Fine tannins and subtle oak do not get in the way. **rating:** 86

⇨ **best drinking** 1999 – 2003 **best vintages** NA **drink with** Devilled kidneys • $25

demondrille vineyards NR

RMB 97 Prunevale Road, Kingsvale, NSW 2587 **region** Hilltops
phone (02) 6384 4272 **fax** (02) 6384 4292 **open** Fri-Mon 10–5 or by appointment
winemaker Pamela Gillespie, Rodney Hooper (Contract), Gerry Sissingh (Consultant)
production NA **est.** 1979
product range ($15–20 CD) The Dove (Sauvignon Blanc Semillon), Purgatory (Pinot Noir), The Raven (Shiraz) and Black Rose (Cabernet Sauvignon Merlot Franc), together with lesser quantities of cellar-door only wines (from the 'Tin Shed' range).
summary Pamela Gillespie and Robert Provan purchased the former Hercynia Vineyard and winery in 1995. Pam Gillespie has an Associate Diploma in Winemaking and Marketing from Adelaide University – Roseworthy, and has been in the hospitality industry since 1989. Her partner had a remarkable career, and is partway through a Bachelor of Science degree at Sydney University (as a mature-age student) majoring in agriculture. Most of the wines from Demondrille are made at Charles Sturt University, with smaller quantities made on-site with assistance from Gerry Sissingh. Purgatory, though far from a great wine, is not so bad as to deserve its (bizarre) name. Specially created food platters featuring local produce are available at the winery each weekend.

Demondrille The Raven Shiraz

Comprehensively the best of the Demondrille range, and an extremely good wine, made under the direction of Rodney Hooper before he moved on from Charles Sturt University.

1996 Medium red-purple; attractive blackberry and dark chocolate fruit aromas are supported by subtle oak on the bouquet; the palate shows abundant and attractive sweet blackberry, plum and chocolate fruit, again supported by well-balanced oak and tannins. Delicious wine. **rating:** 89

➾ **best drinking** 1999 – 2006 **best vintages** NA **drink with** Rare fillet of beef • $20

dennis ★★★

Kangarilla Road, McLaren Vale, SA 5171 **region** McLaren Vale
phone (08) 8323 8665 **fax** (08) 8323 9121 **open** Mon-Fri 10–5, weekends, holidays 11–5
winemaker Peter Dennis **production** 10 000 **est.** 1970
product range ($13–30 CD) Sauvignon Blanc, Chardonnay, Shiraz, Cabernet Sauvignon, Merlot Cabernet, Mead, Egerton Vintage Port, Old Tawny Port.
summary A low-profile winery which has, from time to time, made some excellent wines, most notably typically full-blown, buttery/peachy Chardonnay.

derwent estate ★★★

329 Lyell Highway, Granton, Tas 7070 **region** Southern Tasmania
phone (03) 6248 5073 **fax** (03) 6248 5073 **open** Not
winemaker Stefano Lubiana (Contract) **production** 300 **est.** 1993
product range ($17.50 ML) Riesling, Pinot Noir.
summary The Hanigan family has established Derwent Estate as part of a diversification programme for their 400-hectare mixed farming property. Five hectares of vineyard have been progressively planted since 1993, initially to riesling, with the first Pinot Noir due from the 1998 vintage.

Derwent Estate Riesling

Produced entirely from 1.5 hectares of estate plantings; typically picked at the end of the first week of May with yields of around 8 tonnes per hectare. Cold fermented to dryness and early bottled.

1997 The bouquet is clean, with a mix of herb, mineral and lime aromas; the palate is well balanced, with lime/lemon fruit of medium intensity, and a fractionally hard finish. **rating:** 84

➾ **best drinking** 1998 – 2001 **best vintages** NA **drink with** Avocado salad • $17.50

devil's lair

Rocky Road, Forest Grove via Margaret River, WA 6286 **region** Margaret River
phone (08) 9757 7573 **fax** (08) 9757 7533 **open** By appointment
winemaker Janice McDonald **production** 20 000 **est.** 1985
product range ($19–30 R) Chardonnay, Pinot Noir, Cabernet Merlot; Fifth Leg Dry White and Dry Red.
summary Having rapidly carved out a high reputation for itself through a combination of clever packaging and marketing allied with impressive wine quality, Devil's Lair was acquired by Southcorp (Penfolds, etc) wine group in December 1996, and production is projected to increase to 70 000 cases after the turn of the century. Readers should be aware that from mid-1997 I have assumed Group Winemaking responsibility (inter alia) for Devil's Lair, although Janice McDonald remains firmly in command of winemaking.

Devil's Lair Fifth Leg Dry White

It is difficult to know whether the cleverness of the label and the marketing exceeds the quality of the wine, or vice versa. Both are excellent, the wine is a blend of 60% Chardonnay, 20% Semillon and 20% Sauvignon Blanc while the label features the 'fifth leg' from the Aboriginal drawing on the main label, and comes replete with the Devil's Lair Email address imprinted on the cork. Understandably, became the darling of the smart café set in 1996.

🍷🍷🍷🍷 **1997** Light green-yellow; a clean bouquet of medium intensity with smooth, gently ripe fruit salad aromas, the Chardonnay influence rounding off the other components. On the palate, too, the Chardonnay influence is to the fore with rounded melon fruit balanced by hints of citrus and lemon. **rating:** 87

⇨ **best drinking** 1998 – 1999 **best vintages** '96, '97 **drink with** Brasserie food • $19

Devil's Lair Fifth Leg Dry Red

A variable blend, with Merlot predominant, followed by Cabernet Sauvignon and some Cabernet Franc. Matured in predominantly used French oak for 15 months. One hundred per cent Margaret River origin.

🍷🍷🍷🍷 **1996** Medium to full red-purple; the bouquet is clean, of medium intensity, with a mix of berry, earth, leaf and mint; subtle oak. The palate has more weight and fruit richness than the bouquet suggests, clean, with fresh red and blackcurrant fruit, finishing with well-balanced tannins. **rating:** 85

⇨ **best drinking** 1999 – 2004 **best vintages** NA **drink with** Yearling beef • $19

diamond valley vineyards ★★★★☆

2130 Kinglake Road, St Andrews, Vic 3761 **region** Yarra Valley
phone (03) 9710 1484 **fax** (03) 9710 1369 **open** Not
winemaker David Lance, James Lance **production** 6000 **est.** 1976
product range ($15–39.50 R) Estate Riesling, Chardonnay, Pinot Noir, Cabernet Sauvignon, Sparkling Diamond; Blue Label Semillon Sauvignon Blanc, Chardonnay, Pinot Noir, Cabernet Merlot.
summary One of the Yarra Valley's finest producers of Pinot Noir, and an early pacesetter for the variety, making wines of tremendous style and crystal-clear varietal character. They are not Cabernet Sauvignon look-alikes, but true Pinot Noir, fragrant and intense. Much of the wine is sold through an informative and well-presented mailing list.

Diamond Valley Blue Label Pinot Noir

The Diamond Valley Blue Label denotes wines made from grapes grown by others in the Yarra Valley, and is roughly half the price of the Estate version. It tends to be lighter in body and less complex than the Estate, but still shows David Lance's sure touch with the variety.

🍷🍷🍷🍷 **1996** Light to medium red-purple; in typical Diamond Valley-style, shows ripe, slightly jammy fruit on the bouquet, with abundant, sweet cherry/plum varietal flavour on the palate. The slight touch of jamminess is not the least bit offensive, simply providing the wine with a distinctive character. The oak influence is subtle. **rating:** 88

⇨ **best drinking** 1998 – 2001 **best vintages** '91, '92, '94, '96 **drink with** Seared salmon • $19.75

Diamond Valley Estate Pinot Noir

Deserves its recognition as one of the greatest of the Yarra Valley Pinot Noirs, invariably generously flavoured, and invariably showing strong varietal character, often in a ripe mould. A prolific trophy winner over the years, and never misses the mark. The secret lies in large part in the estate vineyard, with meticulous viticulture and low yields.

🍷🍷🍷🍷🍷 **1996** Medium red-purple; the tangy, sappy plum and strawberry aromas are of varietal Pinot Noir at its best, supported by just a hint of oak. The intense and complex dark plum fruit of the palate has a high-class underlay of spice and forest; long, harmonious and rich. **rating:** 94

➾ **best drinking** 1998 – 2001 **best vintages** '86, '90, '91, '92, '93, '94, '96 **drink with** Wild duck • $39.50

Diamond Valley Estate Cabernet Sauvignon

In 1995 Diamond Valley took a one-off decision to separately bottle each of the components of the wine which normally goes to make a Bordeaux-blend: namely Cabernet Sauvignon, Cabernet Franc, Malbec and Merlot. It is an interesting exercise for the wine student, or anyone wishing to see what lies behind a blend of this kind. You can even have a dinner party and make a DIY blend as you go along. It just so happens that the Cabernet Sauvignon is by far the best of the four components.

🍷🍷🍷🍷 **1995** Medium to full red-purple; the bouquet is the richest of the four wines, with dark berry fruit touched by chocolate. The palate likewise having another dimension of power with blackberry, cherry and cedar nuances; good tannins, structure and length. **rating:** 89

➾ **best drinking** 2000 – 2007 **best vintages** NA **drink with** Marinated beef • $23.85

---

diggers rest NR

205 Old Vineyard Road, Sunbury, Vic 3429 **region** Sunbury
phone (03) 9740 1660 **fax** 03 9740 1660 **open** By appointment
winemaker Peter Dredge **production** 400 **est.** 1987
product range ($15–20 CD) Chardonnay, Pinot Noir, Shiraz, Cabernet Sauvignon.
summary The Diggers Rest Vineyard was planted in 1987 on the site of the original Schroesberg Vineyard in Sunbury – hence the name of the road. Over 7 hectares of vineyards have now been established, and Diggers Rest is the closest cellar door to Melbourne on the Calder Highway.

domaine chandon ★★★★★

Maroondah Highway, Coldstream, Vic 3770 **region** Yarra Valley
phone (03) 9739 1110 **fax** (03) 9739 1095 **open** 7 days 10.30–4.30
winemaker Dr Tony Jordan, Wayne Donaldson **production** 90 000 **est.** 1986
product range ($12.50–52 CD) Sparkling (Méthode Champenoise) specialist with five sparkling wines: Brut, Blanc de Blancs, Blanc de Noirs, Rosé, Yarra Valley Cuvée Riche; Green Point is export label, also used for still Pinot Noir (with a Reserve version now joining ranks) and Chardonnay; Colonnades is third label for table wines.
summary Wholly owned by Moet et Chandon, and the most important wine facility in the Yarra Valley, superbly located with luxurious tasting facilities (a small tasting charge is levied). The wines are exemplary, thought by many to be the best produced by Moet et Chandon in any of its overseas subsidiary operations, a complex blend of French and Australian style.

Domaine Chandon Green Point Chardonnay

The Green Point varietal table wines have slowly but steadily assumed greater significance in the Domaine Chandon winemaking portfolio. The Chardonnay and Pinot Noir are both sourced from the Yarra Valley, and predominantly (if not exclusively) from estate vineyards surrounding the winery. Right from the outset, the style has been generous and full-flavoured.

🍷🍷🍷🍷 **1996** Medium yellow-green; a full bouquet with sweet buttery/peachy fruit and pronounced French oak. A wine with lots of flavour and presence, with a textured palate attesting to the use of malolactic fermentation and high-quality French oak/barrel-fermentation characters also contributing. **rating:** 88

➾ **best drinking** 1998 – 2002 **best vintages** '92, '93, '96 **drink with** Veal in white sauce • $20

Domaine Chandon Blanc De Blancs

Made entirely from Chardonnay sourced from all over Australia, with a significant contribution from Coonawarra and the Yarra Valley. Usually released between four and five years after vintage, and invariably shows just why French Champagne makers regard Chardonnay as particularly long-lived. The '93 is the best yet under this label.

🍷🍷🍷🍷🍷 **1993** Bright yellow-green; the spotlessly clean bouquet has wonderfully attractive creamy/toasty autolysis characters yet retains tightness, with hints of citrus. The palate is delicate yet flavoursome, with a fine, gently creamy texture and flavours of citrus and ripe pear. **rating:** 95

➾ **best drinking** 1998 – 2002 **best vintages** '90, '92, '93 **drink with** Aperitif, shellfish • $26

Domaine Chandon Blanc De Noirs

The converse of the Blanc de Blancs, made entirely from Pinot Noir; like the Blanc de Blancs, held on lees for over three years before disgorgement. Sourced from numerous southern Australian vineyards, notably the Yarra Valley and Tasmania.

🍷🍷🍷🍷🍷 **1992** Pale straw; the bouquet is still extraordinarily discreet, tight and full, with scents of spice, earth and forest berries. A structured wine in the mouth, with a grain to its texture, showing bread, biscuit and mineral flavours, finishing with brisk acidity. **rating:** 93

➾ **best drinking** 1998 – 2001 **best vintages** '90, '92 **drink with** Hors d'oeuvres • $26

Domaine Chandon Brut

Typically a blend of 48% Chardonnay, 50% Pinot Noir and 2% Pinot Meunier, sourced from the cooler parts of Australia including Victoria, Coonawarra, Tasmania and the Great Southern Region. Up to 50 individual components are used in the blend to produce a wine of exceptional style and complexity. Dosage 6.5 grams per litre. The introduction of a greater component of wine taken through malolactic fermentation has added both creaminess and a certain delicacy to the palate; despite the unfashionable vintage, the '95 is assuredly going to prove the best yet from Domaine Chandon.

🍷🍷🍷🍷🍷 **1995** Distinct straw tinges, typical of Domaine Chandon Brut at the point of its first disgorgement. The bouquet is crisp, clean and youthful, with attractive mineral and apple aromas. The palate is citrus-tinged, with touches of cinnamon spice, and has an almost fairy-like delicacy. Great finish; one of the best young Bruts to so far come from Domaine Chandon. **rating:** 94

➾ **best drinking** 1998 – 2002 **best vintages** '88, '90, '91, '92, '93, '94, '95 **drink with** Ideal aperitif • $26

Domaine Chandon Late Disgorged Brut

A relatively new direction for Domaine Chandon, but then not so surprising given the length of time such wines have to be left on yeast lees. The '92 spent five and a half years on yeast lees before disgorgement and release early in 1998.

🍷🍷🍷🍷🍷 **1992** Bright, pale straw-yellow; the bouquet is spotless, with wonderfully fresh yet exceptionally complex aromas of bread and brioche; powerful yet not heavy. The palate is no less complex, with outstanding balance and composition, ranging through ripe pear, citrus together with hints of spice and cake. The acidity and dosage are perfect. **rating:** 95

➪ **best drinking** 1998 – 2000 **best vintages** '95 **drink with** Caviar, of course • NA

Domaine Chandon Green Point Pinot Noir

Unlike the Domaine Chandon sparkling wines, sourced entirely from the Yarra Valley and principally from the estate vineyards surrounding the winery. Generously flavoured, but perhaps still finding its way in terms of style.

🍷🍷🍷🍷 **1996** Strong red-purple; the medium intensity bouquet is clean, with solid strawberry and plum fruit augmented by high-quality oak. The palate is complex, but relatively advanced, sappy and long, with a hint of tobacco leaf. Just seems to lack the piercing fruit of the best of the '96 Yarra Valley Pinots. **rating:** 84

➪ **best drinking** 1998 – 2002 **best vintages** '96, '97 **drink with** Smoked quail • $20

donnelly river wines ★★★

Lot 159 Vasse Highway, Pemberton, WA 6260 **region** Pemberton
phone (08) 9776 2052 **fax** (08) 9776 2053 **open** 7 days 9.30–4.30
winemaker Blair Mieklejohn, Kim Oldfield **production** 4000 **est.** 1986
product range ($15–22 CD) Chardonnay, Mist (white blend), Sauvignon Blanc, Pinot Noir, Cabernet Sauvignon, Port.
summary Donnelly River Wines draws upon 6 hectares of estate vineyards, planted in 1986 and which produced the first wines in 1990. It has performed consistently well with its Chardonnay.

donovan 

Main Street, Great Western, Vic 3377 **region** Grampians
phone (03) 5356 2288 **open** Mon-Sat 10–5.30, Sun 12–5
winemaker Chris Peters **production** 2000 **est.** 1977
product range ($12–17.50 CD) Riesling, Chardonnay, Shiraz, Cabernet Sauvignon, Chardonnay Brut.
summary Donovan quietly makes some attractively fragrant Riesling and concentrated, powerful Shiraz, most of which is sold cellar door and by mail order with considerable bottle age.

doonkuna estate 

Barton Highway, Murrumbateman, NSW 2582 **region** Canberra District
phone (02) 6227 5811 **fax** (02) 6227 5085 **open** Sun-Fri 12–4
winemaker Malcolm Burdett, Gary Baldwin (Consultant) **production** 2000 **est.** 1973
product range ($10–20 CD) Rhine Riesling, Sauvignon Blanc, Semillon Sauvignon Blanc, Chardonnay, Pinot Noir, Shiraz, Cabernet Merlot.

summary With judicious help from consultants, Lady Janette Murray will continue the work of the late Sir Brian Murray in making some of the best white wines in the Canberra district, and red wines which have improved significantly in recent vintages.

Doonkuna Estate Chardonnay

The best of the two white Doonkuna wines, and usually the best Chardonnay made in the Canberra district, though sometimes shaded by Lark Hill. Invariably well made, with skilled use of barrel fermentation. Bounced back to top form in 1995.

🍷🍷🍷🍸 **1996** Medium yellow-green; a subtle, attractively understated bouquet with tangy barrel-ferment characters is followed by a fuller palate with soft, ripe fig, melon and cashew flavours. Minimal oak; a slightly spongy finish. **rating:** 84

➾ **best drinking** 1998 – 2001 **best vintages** '88, '90, '91, '92, '95 **drink with** Snowy Mountains trout • $16

Doonkuna Estate Cabernet Merlot

The red wines of Doonkuna, and in particular the Cabernet Sauvignon, are generously flavoured wines which have improved markedly over recent vintages. The inclusion of 40% Merlot has seen a label change since 1996.

🍷🍷🍷🍸 **1996** Medium red-purple; a quite fragrant bouquet with berry and mint aromas and some characters associated with dense vineyard canopy. The palate is fresh, with sweet berry and mint fruit supported by quite sweet oak; soft tannins. **rating:** 83

➾ **best drinking** 2000 – 2004 **best vintages** '90, '91, '92, '96 **drink with** Strongly flavoured cheese • $20

dorrien estate NR

Cnr Barossa Valley Way/Siegersdorf Road, Tanunda, SA 5352 **region** Barossa Valley
phone (08) 8561 2200 **fax** (08) 8561 2299 **open** Not
winemaker David Thompson (Chief), Reid Bosward, Wayne Dutschke, John Schwartzkopff
production 750 000 **est.** 1982
product range ($9.95–24.95 CD) Produces a substantial number of wines under proprietary labels for the Cellarmaster group; notable are Storton Hill Riesling, Di Fabio Shiraz and Mums Block Shiraz.
summary Dorrien Estate is the physical base of the vast Cellarmaster network which, wearing its retailer's hat, is the largest direct-sale outlet in Australia. It buys substantial quantities of wine from other makers either in bulk, or as cleanskin, i.e. unlabelled bottles, or with recognisable but subtly different labels of the producers concerned. It is also making increasing quantities of wine on its own account at Dorrien Estate. Mildara Blass acquired the Cellarmaster Group in 1997, and how the winemaking activities of Dorrien Estate will be conducted in the future remains to be seen.

Storton Hill Riesling

Produced from dry-grown grapes from Merv Storton's vineyard in the Eden Valley. Between 1995 and 1997 this wine won a gold and four silver medals at Australian wine shows.

🍷🍷🍷🍷 **1994** Medium to full yellow-green; the bouquet shows developed, toasty honeyed characters in that cross-over phase where one can be unsure whether the wine is Semillon or Riesling; the palate is rich and full, again with toasty honeyed characters predominant and just a hint of lime juice on the finish. Delicious flavour. **rating:** 86

➾ **best drinking** 1998 – 1999 **best vintages** NA **drink with** Grilled pork • $14.95

Di Fabio Shiraz

This wine was made from vines over 50 years of age grown at the Blewitt Springs vineyard and is the first release under the Di Fabio Estate label. Produced from hand-pruned and hand-picked bush vines, the wine spends 18 months in new American oak and was a gold medal winner at the Cowra Wine Show.

🍷🍷🍷🍷 **1995** Dense red-purple; the bouquet is voluminous and rich, literally crawling with American oak. The palate, too, is front-end-loaded with American oak, but there is wonderfully rich fruit encased within that oak. This style has particular appeal for some palates. **rating:** 85

➯ **best drinking** 1999 – 2005 **best vintages** NA **drink with** Beef casserole • NA

Rorhlach Reserve Merlot

The Rorhlach family have been growing grapes in the Barossa Valley for 50 years, although doubtless Merlot has been a relatively recent arrival on the scene. The wine is matured in a mix of American and French oak for 18 months; the '96 won a gold medal at Brisbane in 1997.

🍷🍷🍷🍷 **1996** Medium red; sweet juicy berry aromas intermingle with quite pronounced oak on the clean bouquet. The oak contribution is again quite prominent on the sweet, ripe redcurrant fruit of the palate. Attractive wine, but not particularly varietal. **rating:** 84

➯ **best drinking** 1999 – 2004 **best vintages** NA **drink with** Braised duck • $15.95

Black Wattle Cabernet Sauvignon

This is the first wine to be produced from Cellarmaster's substantial vineyard at Mount Benson, a new region within the Limestone Coast Zone of South Australia. Cellarmaster has much hope for the vineyard, and has spared no expense in the striking, avant-garde packaging.

🍷🍷🍷🍷 **1995** Medium to full red-purple; the bouquet is potent and lively, with a mix of spicy, leafy, briary and cedary aromas. The palate flavours, which are also spicy and leafy, are the indications of a cool vintage in a cool region resulting in grapes which did not fully physiologically ripen. Nonetheless, very interesting. **rating:** 83

➯ **best drinking** 1999 – 2003 **best vintages** NA **drink with** Mature cheddar • $24.95

dowie doole ★★★☆

182 Main Road, McLaren Vale, SA 5171 **region** McLaren Vale
phone (08) 8323 8100 **fax** (08) 8323 0100 **open** Not
winemaker Brian Light (Contract) **production** 2500 **est.** 1996
product range ($18 R) Chenin Blanc, Semillon Sauvignon Blanc, Chardonnay.
summary The imaginatively packaged and interestingly named Dowie Doole is a joint venture between two McLaren Vale grape growers: architect Drew Dowie and one-time international banker Norm Doole. Between them they have over 40 hectares of vineyards, and only a small proportion of their grapes are used to produce the Dowie Doole wines.

drayton's ★★★☆

Oakey Creek Road, Cessnock, NSW 2321 **region** Lower Hunter Valley
phone (02) 4998 7513 **fax** (02) 4998 7743 **open** 7 days 9–5
winemaker Trevor Drayton **production** 100 000 **est.** 1853
product range ($7.50–30 R) Semillon, White Burgundy, Riesling, Chardonnay Semillon, Verdelho, Sauternes, Bin 5555 Hermitage, Pinot Noir, Cabernet Merlot, Cabernet Sauvignon; Oakey Creek Semillon Chardonnay, Semillon Sauvignon Blanc, Traminer Riesling, Hermitage, Shiraz Cabernet. William Shiraz and Joseph Shiraz are top-end releases.

summary A family-owned and run stalwart of the Valley, producing honest, full-flavoured wines which sometimes excel themselves, and are invariably modestly priced. The size of the production will come as a surprise to many, but it is a clear indication of the good standing of the brand.

driftwood estate ★★★★

Lot 13 Caves Road, Yallingup, WA 6282 **region** Margaret River
phone (08) 9755 6323 **fax** (08) 9755 6343 **open** 7 days 11–4.30
winemaker Maria Melsom, Steve Pester **production** 11 000 **est.** 1989
product range ($14–21.50 CD) Classic White, Semillon, Sauvignon Blanc Semillon, Chardonnay, Cane Cut Semillon, Shiraz, Cabernet Sauvignon, Sparkling, Tawny Port.
summary Driftwood Estate is yet another remarkable new entrant on to the vibrant Margaret River scene. Quite apart from offering a brasserie restaurant capable of seating 200 people (open 7 days for lunch and dinner) and a mock Greek open-air theatre, its wines feature striking and stylish packaging (even if strongly reminiscent of that of Devil's Lair) and opulently flavoured wines. The winery architecture is, it must be said, opulent but not stylish.

Driftwood Estate Semillon

Produced from 2.9 hectares of estate plantings, and shows the richness and concentration one expects from Margaret River white wines. The grapes are typically picked at exceptionally high baumé levels for semillon, ranging between 13 degrees and almost 14 degrees.

🍷🍷🍷🍸 **1997** Medium yellow-green; a very rich and complex bouquet with strong tropical overtones to the herb fruit, and an echo of what may be a touch of barrel ferment. The palate is equally complex, with many characteristics of very ripe sauvignon blanc, but does not convincingly carry its 13.7 degrees alcohol. **rating:** 84

➾ **best drinking** 1998 – 2001 **best vintages** NA **drink with** Baked ham • $15.40

Driftwood Estate Chardonnay

Produced from 3.2 hectares of estate plantings; right from the outset, has been made in what might be termed a 'Battleship Galactica' style, even by the at-times exceedingly opulent and concentrated standards of the Margaret River.

🍷🍷🍷🍷 **1997** Medium to full yellow-green; fruit and oak vie for supremacy on both bouquet and palate, with high-quality toasty/nutmeg oak to the fore on the bouquet. A massive, mouth-coating wine on the palate with peachy/buttery fruit and masses of barrel-ferment oak character. **rating:** 86

➾ **best drinking** 1998 – 2000 **best vintages** '94, '95, '97 **drink with** Turkey, veal • $17.10

Driftwood Estate Cane Cut Semillon

The only such wine made in the Margaret River region; the severing of canes on the vine, allowing the fruit to raisin – thereby increasing both sugar and acid levels – is not uncommon in the Barossa and Clare Valleys, and is used in regions where botrytis does not occur. A most successful innovation for the Margaret River.

🍷🍷🍷🍸 **1997** Glowing yellow; the bouquet has rich honey and toffee aromas, with more style and intensity than expected. The palate is similarly rich, with peach and honey flavours balanced by crisp acidity on the finish. **rating:** 84

➾ **best drinking** 1998 – 1999 **best vintages** NA **drink with** Baked apple • $16.10

dromana estate 

Cnr Harrison's Road and Bittern-Dromana Road, Dromana, Vic 3936 **region** Mornington Peninsula

phone (03) 5987 3800 **fax** (03) 5981 0714 **open** 7 days 11–4

winemaker Garry Crittenden **production** 12 000 **est.** 1982

product range ($14–45 CD) Dromana Estate Sauvignon Blanc, Chardonnay, Reserve Chardonnay, Pinot Noir, Reserve Pinot Noir, Shiraz, Reserve Merlot, Cabernet Merlot; Second label Schinus, Riesling, Chenin Blanc, Sauvignon Blanc, Chardonnay, Longest Lunch Brut, Rosé, Pinot Noir; and a newly packaged range of Italian generics Barbera, Dolcetto, Sangiovese, Granaccia, Riserva, Nebbiolo and Rosato under the Garry Crittenden i label.

summary Since it was first established, Dromana Estate has never been far from the headlines. The energetic marketing genius of Garry Crittenden has driven it hither and thither, launching a brief but very successful foray into the United Kingdom market, but since concentrating much of its efforts on a no less successful restaurant and cellar door, with a kaleidoscopic array of wines, first under the Dromana Estate label, then under the Schinus label and in late 1995, a strikingly revamped range of Italian-accented wines.

Dromana Estate Chardonnay

Estate-grown from immaculately tended vineyards, barrel-fermented and given eight months in barriques on its lees. If malolactic fermentation has been used, it is not obvious.

▼▼▼▼ **1997** Medium to full yellow-green; a clean, penetrating citrus blossom and mineral bouquet is followed by a lively, fresh citrussy/tangy palate with neatly balanced acidity. The oak is there, but very much in the background. **rating:** 86

➪ **best drinking** 1998 – 2002 **best vintages** '91, '92, '97 **drink with** Crab • $25

Dromana Estate Reserve Chardonnay

This wine has everything the smartest wine drinker could ever wish for: brilliant and innovative packaging, and the full kit and caboodle of winemaking (or rather, non-winemaking) tricks. Whole-bunch pressed straight to barrel, no yeasts were added, the wine fermenting naturally, and then spending 12 months on lees. It is not filtered, and winemaker Garry Crittenden says it may be slightly cloudy when poured but 'this is a positive attribute'. Why that should be so escapes me, but this is a high-quality wine nonetheless.

▼▼▼▼▽ **1996** Medium to full yellow-green; the bouquet is complex and solid with citrus and nectarine fruit surrounded by hints of charry oak. It is a remarkably smooth wine in both flavour and texture, the fruit and oak harmoniously balanced; good acidity and length. **rating:** 91

➪ **best drinking** 1998 – 2000 **best vintages** '91, '94, '96 **drink with** Kassler • $38

Dromana Estate Pinot Noir

Like the Chardonnay, estate-grown. Also like the Chardonnay, showing to the full the impact of a magnificent vintage in the region.

▼▼▼▼ **1997** Medium red-purple; sweet, full plummy varietal fruit with hints of spice flood the bouquet; the palate is no less attractive, with delicious plum, cherry and spice fruit flavours showing exemplary varietal character. **rating:** 89

➪ **best drinking** 1998 – 2000 **best vintages** '97 **drink with** Grilled quail • $28

Garry Crittenden i Riserva

The top end of the Italian varietal range created by Garry Crittenden; a blend of Nebbiolo and Barbera, principally sourced from the King Valley in Victoria, and which works extremely well.

🍷🍷🍷🍷 **1996** Medium red; attractive cedary/earthy aromas introduce a wine which is in authentic Italian-style, firm and quite tannic on the palate, and formidable to taste without food. The flavours are in the cedary/briary/earthy spectrum, finishing with firm but not abrasive tannins. **rating:** 85

⇨ **best drinking** 2000 – 2004 **best vintages** NA **drink with** Osso buco • $18

Garry Crittenden i Barbera

To my palate, one of the better of the five Italian-style releases under the striking 'i' label. It is made from barbera grown by Arnie Pizzini in the King Valley.

🍷🍷🍷½ **1996** Medium red-purple; the bouquet is strongly varietal, with those typically earthy/minerally notes giving a slightly hard edge. The palate has both extract and concentration, with earthy, brooding dark fruit flavours. A well-made wine with excellent varietal character. **rating:** 84

⇨ **best drinking** 1998 – 2002 **best vintages** NA **drink with** Osso buco • $17

dulcinea ★★★★

Jubilee Road, Sulky, Ballarat, Vic 3352 **region** Ballarat
phone (03) 5334 6440 **fax** (03) 5334 6828 **open** 7 days 9–5
winemaker Rod Stott **production** 800 **est.** 1983
product range ($15–18 CD) Chardonnay, Sauvignon Blanc, Pinot Noir, Shiraz, Cabernet Sauvignon.
summary Rod Stott is a part-time but passionate grape grower and winemaker who chose the name Dulcinea from 'The Man of La Mancha' where only a fool fights windmills. With winemaking help from various sources, he has produced a series of very interesting and often complex wines, the current releases being exceptionally impressive.

Dulcinea Chardonnay

Very competent and tightly controlled winemaking has produced a finely crafted wine. The wine spends six months in French oak. The '96 is a stylish, elegant wine which won a gold medal at the 1997 Ballarat Wine Show.

🍷🍷🍷🍷 **1996** Medium to full yellow-green; the bouquet is relatively light, but has an appealing mix of cashew, melon and dried fig aromas woven through subtle oak. The elegant palate is very tangy and citrussy, with a long, cleansing finish. Tends to challenge rather than soothe. **rating:** 88

⇨ **best drinking** 1998 – 2001 **best vintages** '96 **drink with** Chinese cashew prawns • $18

Dulcinea Pinot Noir

A great achievement, and in many ways a landmark wine for Ballarat Pinot Noir.

🍷🍷🍷🍷 **1997** Bright red-purple; the bouquet is solid, with excellent dark plum and mint fruit, the palate likewise exhibiting considerable power and depth to the dark, plummy fruit. Notwithstanding all that power, not the least bit extractive or heavy, and has the essential softness of good Pinot Noir. **rating:** 87

⇨ **best drinking** 1998 – 2002 **best vintages** '96 **drink with** Roast duck • $18

Dulcinea Shiraz

Produced not from Ballarat-grown grapes, but from Bendigo.

🍷🍷🍷🍷 **1996** Medium red-purple; a very smooth and clean bouquet with black cherry and subtle cedary oak introduces an attractive, mid-weight wine with more cherry and mint flavours. Dips fractionally on the back palate, perhaps. **rating:** 84

➪ **best drinking** 1999 – 2005 **best vintages** NA **drink with** Daube of beef • $16

duncan estate ★★★

Spring Gully Road, Clare, SA 5453 **region** Clare Valley
phone (08) 8843 4335 **fax** (08) 8843 4335 **open** 7 days 10–4
winemaker John Duncan **production** 2500 **est.** 1968
product range ($11–15 CD) Riesling, Chardonnay, Semillon Sauvignon Blanc, Spätlese, Shiraz, Cabernet Merlot Shiraz.
summary The Duncan family has been growing grapes in the Clare Valley since 1968, and first produced wines from its 7.4 hectares of vineyards in 1984. Over the years some attractive wines have been produced, with the Cabernet Merlot and Shiraz usually good.

dyson wines NR

Sherriff Road, Maslin Beach, SA 5170 **region** McLaren Vale
phone (08) 8386 1092 **fax** (08) 8327 0066 **open** 7 days 10–5
winemaker Allan Dyson **production** 2000 **est.** 1984
product range ($10–15 CD) Chardonnay, Sauvignon Blanc Semillon, Pinot Cabernet, Cabernet Sauvignon, White Port.
summary Owned by district veteran Allan Dyson. Typically for the district, Sauvignon Blanc has been one of the more consistent performers in the Maslin Beach portfolio, showing good varietal character and depth of flavour. No recent tastings.

eastbrook estate NR

Lot 3 Vasse Highway, Eastbrook, WA 6260 **region** Pemberton
phone (08) 9776 1251 **fax** (08) 9776 1251 **open** Fri-Sun, public holidays 11–4
winemaker Kim Skipworth **production** 2000 **est.** 1990
product range ($10–17 CD) Chardonnay, Pinot Noir, Cabernet Sauvignon, Port.
summary Established on part of the same former grazing property which also accommodates Salitage, Phoenicia, and Dr Bill Pannell's vineyard. A jarrah pole, limestone and cedar weatherboard winery and restaurant have been built on the site by former Perth real estate agent Kim Skipworth, who is also a shareholder in one of the major Margaret River cheese factories. The wines come from 7 hectares of estate plantings of pinot noir, chardonnay, sauvignon blanc and shiraz.

eastern peake NR

Clunes Road, Coghills Creek, Vic 3364 **region** Ballarat
phone (03) 5343 4245 **fax** (03) 5343 4365 **open** Weekends 10–5
winemaker Norman Latta **production** 1000 **est.** 1983
product range ($14–20 CD) Unwooded Chardonnay, Persuasion (Pinot Rosé), Pinot Noir.
summary Norm Latta and Di Pym commenced the establishment of Eastern Peake, situated 25 kilometres northeast of Ballarat on a high plateau overlooking the Creswick Valley almost 15 years ago. In the early years the grapes were sold to Trevor Mast of Mount Chalambar and

Mount Langi Ghiran, but the 4.5 hectares of vines are now dedicated to the production of Eastern Peake wines. The Pinot Noir is on the wirey/minerally/stemmy side; earlier bottling might preserve more of the sweet fruit.

elan vineyard NR

17 Turners Road, Bittern, Vic 3918 **region** Mornington Peninsula
phone (03) 5983 1858 **fax** (03) 5983 2321 **open** First weekend of month, public holidays 11–5 or by appointment
winemaker Selma Lowther **production** 500 **est.** 1980
product range ($13–18 CD) Riesling, Chardonnay, Shiraz, G'may, Cabernet Merlot.
summary Selma Lowther, fresh from Charles Sturt University (as a mature-age student) made an impressive debut with her spicy, fresh, crisp 1990 Chardonnay. Most of the grapes from the 2.9 hectares of estate vineyards are sold; production remains minuscule.

elderton ★★★☆

3 Tanunda Road, Nuriootpa, SA 5355 **region** Barossa Valley
phone (08) 8562 1058 **fax** (08) 8562 2844 **open** Mon-Fri 8.30–5, weekends, holidays 11–4
winemaker James Irvine **production** 32 000 **est.** 1984
product range ($13–45 R) Riesling, Golden Riesling, Semillon, Chardonnay, Sparkling, Old Hayshed Red, Shiraz, Command Shiraz, Cabernet Shiraz Merlot, Cabernet Sauvignon, Merlot; the Elderton Domain range is in fact the second label.
summary The wines are based around some old, high-quality Barossa floor estate vineyards, and all are driven to a lesser or greater degree by lashings of American oak; the Command Shiraz is at the baroque end of the spectrum, and has to be given considerable respect within the parameters of its style.

Elderton Cabernet Shiraz Merlot

Gold medal winner at the 1997 Royal Adelaide Wine Show.
🍷🍷🍷🍷🍷 **1995** Medium red-purple; somewhat unusually for Elderton, fruit, rather than oak-driven, with classic red and blackcurrant fruit supported by gentle cedary oak on both bouquet and the long palate. **rating:** 91

➪ **best drinking** 2000 – 2005 **best vintages** NA **drink with** Venison • NA

eldredge ★★★☆

Spring Gully Road, Clare, SA 5453 **region** Clare Valley
phone (08) 8842 3086 **fax** (08) 8842 3086 **open** 7 days 11–5
winemaker Leigh Eldredge, Tim Adams (Contract) **production** 4000 **est.** 1993
product range ($12–16 CD) Watervale Riesling, Semillon Sauvignon Blanc, Late Harvest Riesling, New Age Grenache, Blue Chip Shiraz, Cabernet Sauvignon, Port.
summary Leigh and Karen Eldredge have established their winery and cellar-door sales area in the Sevenhill Ranges, at an altitude of 500 metres, above the town of Watervale. Contract-winemaking by Tim Adams has ensured a solid start to the business. The popular Leigh Eldredge collected the trophy for Best Cabernet Sauvignon at the 1997 Royal Adelaide Wine Show.

Eldredge Cabernet Sauvignon

The '95 was a trophy and gold medal winner at the 1997 Royal Adelaide Wine Show.

YYYYY **1995** Strong red-purple; there is a mix of leaf, earth and blackberry aromas on the bouquet. The palate has excellent length and grip, again showing pristine varietal character as the main driving force; the oak is subtle throughout. **rating:** 94

⇨ **best drinking** 2000 – 2008 **best vintages** NA **drink with** Barbecued lamb • $14

eldridge estate NR

Red Hill Road, Red Hill, Vic 3937 **region** Mornington Peninsula
phone (03) 5989 2644 **fax** (03) 5989 2644 **open** Weekends, holidays and all January 10–5
winemaker David Lloyd **production** 1000 **est.** 1985
product range ($15–26 CD) Semillon Sauvignon, Chardonnay, Pinot Noir, Cabernet Merlot.
summary The Eldridge Estate vineyard, with seven varieties included in its 3.5 hectares, was purchased by Wendy and David Lloyd in 1995. Major retrellising work has been undertaken, changing to Scott-Henry, and all of the wines will now be estate-grown and made.

elgee park NR

Wallaces Road, Merricks North, Vic 3926 **region** Mornington Peninsula
phone (03) 5989 7338 **fax** (03) 5989 7553 **open** One day a year – Sunday of Queen's Birthday weekend
winemaker Tod Dexter (Contract) **production** 1500 **est.** 1972
product range ($12–25 R) Chardonnay, Pinot Noir, Cabernet, Cuvée Brut.
summary The pioneer of the Mornington Peninsula in its twentieth-century rebirth, owned by Baillieu Myer and family. The wines are now made at Stonier's, Elgee Park's own winery having been closed, and the overall level of activity decreased. No recent tastings (or sightings).

eling forest winery NR

Hume Highway, Sutton Forest, NSW 2577 **region** Other Wineries of NSW
phone (02) 4878 9499 **fax** (02) 4878 9499 **open** 7 days 10–5
winemaker Leslie Fritz **production** 2000 **est.** 1987
product range ($13.50–20 CD) Eling Forest Riesling, Chardonnay Blend, Catherine Hill, Botrytis Riesling, Furmint, Peach Brandy, Peach Ambrosia, Cherry Ambrosia.
summary Eling Forest's founder Leslie Fritz celebrated his 80th birthday not long after he planted the first vines at his Sutton Forest vineyard in 1987. The vineyards have now been expanded to over 3 hectares, including plantings of the Hungarian white grape varieties harslevelu and furmint, the latter providing the only varietal wine of its kind made in Australia.

elmslie 

Upper McEwans Road, Legana, Tas 7277 **region** Northern Tasmania
phone (03) 6330 1225 **fax** (03) 6330 2161 **open** By appointment
winemaker Ralph Power **production** 600 **est.** 1972
product range ($18 ML) Pinot Noir, Cabernet Sauvignon.

summary A small, specialist red winemaker, from time to time blending Pinot Noir with Cabernet. The fruit from the now fully mature vineyard (half a hectare of pinot noir and 1.5 hectares of cabernet sauvignon) has depth and character, but operational constraints mean that the style of the wine is often somewhat rustic.

elsewhere vineyard ★★★★☆

40 Dillons Hill Road, Glaziers Bay, Tas 7109 **region** Southern Tasmania
phone (03) 6295 1509 **fax** (03) 6295 1509 **open** Not
winemaker Andrew Hood (Contract), Steve Lubiana (Contract) **production** 3000 **est.** 1984
product range ($18–25 ML) Riesling, Chardonnay, Pinot Noir, Méthode Champenoise.
summary Eric and Jette Phillips' evocatively named Elsewhere Vineyard jostles for space with a commercial flower farm also run by the Phillips. It is a mark of the success of the wines that in 1993 some of the long-established flower areas made way for additional chardonnay and riesling, although it is Elsewhere's Pinot Noirs that are so stunning. Steve Lubiana has now added to the reputation by producing the trophy-winning Méthode Champenoise (1995 vintage) at the 1998 Tasmanian Wines Show.

Elsewhere Vineyard Méthode Champenoise

Winner of the trophy for Best Sparkling Wine at the 1998 Tasmanian Wines Show.
🍷🍷🍷🍷 **1995** Medium straw-yellow; a complex bouquet with strong, biscuity notes from the Pinot Noir, together with hints of strawberry. A generously flavoured wine on the palate, with that extra degree of weight which presumably comes from a substantial Pinot Noir component, but with the softness on the finish which so distinguishes the sparkling wines made by Steve Lubiana. **rating:** 89

➪ **best drinking** 1998 – 1999 **best vintages** NA **drink with** Tasmanian salmon • $25

eltham vineyards ★★★

225 Shaws Road, Arthurs Creek, Vic 3099 **region** Yarra Valley
phone (03) 9439 4688 **fax** (03) 9439 5121 **open** By appointment
winemaker George Apted, John Graves **production** 850 **est.** 1990
product range ($14.95–18.95 ML) Chardonnay, Pinot Noir, Cabernet Sauvignon.
summary Drawing upon vineyards at Arthurs Creek and Eltham, John Graves (brother of David Graves of the illustrious Californian Pinot producer Saintsbury) produces tiny quantities of quite stylish Chardonnay and Pinot Noir, the former showing nice barrel-ferment characters.

emerald estate NR

Main North Road, Stanley Flat, SA 5453 **region** Clare Valley
phone (08) 8842 3296 **fax** (08) 8842 2220 **open** 7 days 10–5
winemaker Tim Adams (Consultant), Frank Sheppard **production** 3500 **est.** 1990
product range ($9–12 CD) Rhine Riesling, Unwooded Chardonnay, Shiraz, Cabernet Sauvignon.
summary Don and Gwen Carroll purchased a 33-hectare property at Stanley Flat in 1990. A small existing vineyard was pulled out, and since 1990 20 hectares of vines have been established. Most of the production is sold to leading wineries in the region, a portion being retained for the Emerald Estate wine range.

eppalock ridge NR

633 North Redesdale Road, Redesdale, Vic 3444 **region** Bendigo
phone (03) 5425 3135 **fax** (03) 5425 3135 **open** 7 days 10–6 by appointment
winemaker Rod Hourigan **production** 1000 **est.** 1979
product range ($22.50 CD) Shiraz.
summary A low-key operation now focusing solely on estate-grown Shiraz.

ermes estate NR

2 Godings Road, Moorooduc, Vic 3933 **region** Mornington Peninsula
phone (03) 5978 8376 **open** Weekends and public holidays 11–5
winemaker Ermes Zucchet **production** 500 **est.** 1989
product range ($10–15 CD) Riesling Malvasia, Chardonnay Pinot Grigio, Cabernet Merlot.
summary Ermes and Denise Zucchet commenced planting of the 2-hectare estate in 1989 with chardonnay, riesling, cabernet sauvignon and merlot, adding pinot gris in 1991. In 1994 an existing piggery on the property was converted to a winery and cellar-door area (in the Zucchets' words, the pigs having been evicted) and the modestly priced wines are on sale during the weekends. No recent tastings.

eurunderee flats winery NR

Henry Lawson Drive, Mudgee, NSW 2850 **region** Mudgee
phone (02) 6373 3954 **fax** (02) 6373 3750 **open** Sun-Fri 10–4, Sat 9–5
winemaker Peter Knights **production** 2000 **est.** 1985
product range ($9–15 CD) Riesling Gordo, Sauvignon Blanc, Chardonnay, Shiraz, Merlin Rouge, Liqueur Muscat, Tawny Port.
summary Formerly Knights Vines, now called Eurunderee Flats, although under the same ownership. A small producer making whites of variable quality, and rather better dry red table wines.

evans family ★★★★☆

Palmers Lane, Pokolbin, NSW 2321 **region** Lower Hunter Valley
phone (02) 4998 7333 **fax** (02) 4998 7798 **open** By appointment
winemaker Contract **production** 3000 **est.** 1979
product range ($16–22.50 ML) Pinchem Chardonnay, Howards Chardonnay, Statue Vineyard Sparkling Pinot, Chapel Gamay, Hillside Pinot Noir.
summary In the wake of the acquisition of Rothbury by Mildara Blass, Len Evans' wine interests now focus on Evans Family (estate-grown and produced from vineyards around the family home) and on the Evans Wine Company (a quite different, part-maker, part-negociant business). Len Evans continues to persist with the notion that the Hunter Valley can produce Gamay and Pinot Noir of quality, and irritatingly occasionally produces evidence to suggest he may be half right. There is, of course, no such reservation with the Chardonnay.

Evans Family Chapel Gamay

Len Evans planted gamay in the vineyards surrounding his marvellous house in the Hunter in a gesture of defiance. The vines invariably bear a huge crop but in vintages such as '91 and '96 can produce remarkably attractive wine from this rarely seen variety.

🍷🍷🍷🍷 **1996** Medium to full red-purple; there is quite surprising richness and character to the bouquet with a touch of liquorice and that earthy softness unique to the Hunter. On the palate there is abundant spicy/plummy fruit with echoes of liquorice; a really attractive wine. **rating:** 84

➾ **best drinking** 1998 – 1999 **best vintages** '91, '96 **drink with** Smoked pork hock • $16

evans & tate ★★★★☆

Metricup Road, Willyabrup, WA 6280 **region** Margaret River
phone (08) 9296 4666 **fax** (08) 9296 1148 **open** 7 days 10.30–4.30
winemaker Brian Fletcher, Fi Purnell **production** 100 000 **est.** 1970
product range ($14–35 R) There are two basic echelons: an expanding range of commercial wines including the newly released Tate White (an extraordinary blend of Chardonnay and Grenache) and Tate Red; Western Australia Classic Sauvignon Blanc, Two Vineyards Chardonnay, Gnangara Shiraz Cabernet and Barrique 61 Cabernet Merlot. The top echelon is based on the Margaret River vineyards which produce Chardonnay, Semillon, Sauvignon Blanc, Shiraz, Merlot and Cabernet Sauvignon.
summary Single-handedly changed perceptions of the Swan Valley red wines in the '70s before opening its highly successful Margaret River operation which goes from strength to strength. The most recent expansion has been the establishment of a large vineyard in the new Jindong subregion of the Margaret River, precipitating a flood of other arrivals in that area. The continuing rapid growth of the business has taken edge off the wines which, while immaculately crafted and ever-reliable, lack the concentration and complexity of the very best wines of the region.

Evans & Tate Margaret River Semillon

Has its own light but intensely flavoured style, away from the Margaret River mainstream. Has had conspicuous show success over the years.

🍷🍷🍷🍷 **1997** Medium to full yellow-green; the bouquet is powerful with herbaceous semillon neatly woven through with a hint of spicy oak. The palate delivers more of the same with quite potent semillon fruit and distinct seasoning of spicy/charry oak adding flavour for early drinking. **rating:** 87

➾ **best drinking** 1998 – 2003 **best vintages** '91, '92, '93, '94, '95 **drink with** Marron, yabbies • $19

Evans & Tate Margaret River Chardonnay

Made using the full panoply of winemaking techniques, many borrowed from Burgundy. Part whole-bunch pressed, and part crushed, fermentation is initiated in stainless steel and then transferred to new French oak barriques for the remainder of fermentation. Twenty per cent of the wine is taken through malolactic fermentation, and the wine matured in a temperature-controlled cool room, with prolonged lees contact and stirring. Notwithstanding all of these techniques, typically a more elegant and restrained style than one usually encounters in Margaret River.

🍷🍷🍷🍷 **1996** Light to medium yellow-green; the bouquet is smooth and stylish, with a seamless marriage of melon/citrus fruit and oak. The palate is lively and fresh, with tight citrussy – almost minerally – fruit, less luscious than many of its peers, but more elegant. **rating:** 89

➾ **best drinking** 1999 – 2004 **best vintages** '95, '96 **drink with** Marron or lobster • $35

Evans & Tate Margaret River Shiraz

A 100% estate-grown wine from the Redbrook Vineyard (using the Hermitage name until 1992, but of course made from shiraz). The Margaret River region has not done a great deal with Shiraz overall, preferring to concentrate on other varieties, but this wine shows the potential that the region has for this variety. Matured in a French oak for a quite miraculous two years, given that the wine was bottled and packaged by January 1998.

🍷🍷🍷🍷🍷 **1996** Strong, deep red-purple; the bouquet is rich, ripe and dense with black cherry fruit and a touch of sweet oak. The palate is intense, with black cherry, chocolate and hints of sweet, cedary oak. Well-balanced tannins. **rating:** 90

➾ **best drinking** 2002 – 2006 **best vintages** '86, '88, '90, '91, '92, '93, '95, '96 **drink with** Strong red meat dishes • $25

Evans & Tate Margaret River Merlot

Evans & Tate were one of the first producers in Australia to market a varietal Merlot. The grapes are grown at Evans & Tate's Redbrook Vineyard from now fully mature vines. Partial (10%) barrel fermentation and maturation in a mix of one and two-year-old French oak barriques for 18 months produces an elegant wine.

🍷🍷🍷🍷🍷 **1996** Dense red-purple; very ripe and rich fruit floods the bouquet with chocolate, mint and berry aromas. The palate, too, is sweet, mouthfilling and ripe, with small black fruit flavours, and a smooth, sweet middle palate. **rating:** 91

➾ **best drinking** 2001 – 2006 **best vintages** '95, '96 **drink with** Osso buco • $30

Evans & Tate Margaret River Cabernet Sauvignon

Sometimes produced from 100% Cabernet Sauvignon, but in some vintages with a little Merlot blended in, produced from Evans & Tate's Redbrook Vineyard in the Margaret River. Whether coincidence or not, the arrival of Brian Fletcher lifted this wine into another class and dimension. The wine is matured in French oak barriques for 22 months.

🍷🍷🍷🍷 **1996** Dense red-purple; the bouquet is powerful, with strong, ripe cassis and mint fruit. The fruit-driven palate has abundant red berry, mint and blackberry fruit, with slightly savoury, green undertones. Subtle oak. **rating:** 89

➾ **best drinking** 2002 – 2007 **best vintages** '86, '88, '90, '91, '92, '95 **drink with** Braised ox cheek in red wine sauce • $30

---

excelsior peak NR

22 Wrights Road, Drummoyne, NSW 2047 (postal address) **region** Tumbarumba
phone (02) 9719 1916 **fax** (02) 9719 2752 **open** Not
winemaker Charles Sturt University (Contract) **production** 1150 **est.** 1980
product range ($18–22 ML) Chardonnay, Pinot Noir, Méthode Champenoise.
summary Excelsior Peak proprietor Juliet Cullen established the first vineyard in Tumbarumba in 1980. That vineyard was thereafter sold to Southcorp, and Juliet Cullen subsequently established another vineyard, now releasing wines under the Excelsior Peak label. Plantings total 9 hectares, with 6.5 hectares in production.

eyton-on-yarra ★★★☆

Cnr Maroondah Highway and Hill Road, Coldstream, Vic 3370 **region** Yarra Valley
phone (03) 5962 2119 **fax** (03) 5962 5319 **open** 7 days 10–5
winemaker Matthew Aldridge **production** 10 000 **est.** 1991
product range ($15–35 R) There are now three labels in the range: at the top NDC Reserve Merlot and Shiraz, a tribute to the late Newell Cowan, who effectively founded

Eyton-on-Yarra; the main varietal range under the Eyton label; and the second label range of Dalry Road, the name of the second vineyard owned by Eyton.

summary Now owned and run by the Cowan family, with the energetic and innovative Deidre Cowan overseeing an excellent and capacious restaurant, a sound shell for concerts of every shape and hue, and – of course, the winemaking side of a substantial business.

Eyton-on-Yarra Dalry Road Unwooded Chardonnay

This is the second label of Eyton-on-Yarra, but still drawn from the very substantial vineyard resources available to Eyton. A small percentage is barrel-fermented; a classy wine which shows the winemaking skills of Matt Aldridge to good advantage.

🍷🍷🍷🍷 **1997** Light to medium yellow-green; subtle melon and fig fruit aromas, with barely perceptible oak, lead into a fine, elegant understated yet classic Yarra-style Chardonnay, with citrus and melon fruit, finishing with good acidity. **rating:** 86

➾ **best drinking** 1998 – 2003 **best vintages** NA **drink with** Snapper • $15

Eyton-on-Yarra NDC Reserve Shiraz

The NDC Reserve range (currently Merlot and Shiraz) was created in memory of Eyton's founder, Newell Cowan. The wines are considered to be premium selections, and spend 18 months in oak.

🍷🍷🍷🍷 **1995** Medium red-purple; vanillin American oak is dominant on both bouquet and palate, although there is quite a deal of sweet fruit underneath that oak. An interesting wine, seemingly closer in style to traditional South Australian Shiraz than one normally encounters in the Yarra Valley. Flavoursome, if atypical. **rating:** 83

➾ **best drinking** 1999 – 2004 **best vintages** NA **drink with** Braised beef • $35

fairfield vineyard NR

Murray Valley Highway, Browns Plains via Rutherglen, Vic 3685 **region** Rutherglen
phone (02) 6032 9381 **open** Mon-Sat 10–5, some Sun 12–5
winemaker Andrew Sutherland-Smith **production** 4200 **est.** 1959
product range ($8.50–15 CD) White Hermitage, Riesling, Moselle, Rosé, Light Red, Shiraz, Durif, Cabernet Sauvignon, Fortified.

summary Specialist in red and fortified wines made with nineteenth-century wine equipment housed in the grounds of the historic Fairfield Mansion built by G F Morris. A tourist must. Offers a wide range of back vintages.

faisan estate NR

Amaroo Road, Borenore, NSW 2800 **region** Orange
phone (02) 6365 2380 **open** Not
winemaker Col Walker **production** 500 **est.** 1992
product range ($10–13 ML) Chardonnay, Canobolas Classic White, Britton's Block Cabernet Sauvignon, Old Block Cabernet Sauvignon.

summary Faisan Estate, within sight of Mount Canobolas, and 20 kilometres west of the city of Orange, has been established by Trish and Col Walker. They now have almost 7 hectares of vineyards coming into bearing, and have purchased grapes from other growers in the region in the interim.

farrell's limestone creek

Mount View Road, Mount View, NSW 2325 **region** Lower Hunter Valley
phone (02) 4991 2808 **fax** (02) 4991 3414 **open** Weekends, public holidays 10–5
winemaker McWilliam's (Contract), Neil McGuigan (Consultant) **production** 1000 **est.** 1982
product range ($11–18 CD) Semillon, Chardonnay, Late Harvest Verdelho, Shiraz, Cabernet Sauvignon.
summary The Farrell family purchased 50 acres on Mount View in 1980, and gradually established 18 acres of vineyards planted to semillon, verdelho, chardonnay, shiraz, cabernet sauvignon and merlot. Most of the grapes are sold to McWilliam's, which contract-makes a small amount for cellar-door sales. The quality of the wines is as good as one would expect, with vintages going back to 1989 available in early 1998.

felsberg winery

NR

Townsends Road, Glen Aplin, Qld 4381 **region** Granite Belt
phone (07) 4683 4332 **fax** (07) 4683 4377 **open** 7 days 9–5
winemaker Otto Haag **production** 1500 **est.** 1983
product range ($10–15 CD) Rhine Riesling, Traminer, Sylvaner, Chardonnay, Traminer Rosé, Merlot, Shiraz, Cabernet Sauvignon, Mead.
summary After a prolonged gestation, opened for business in 1991. The wines are made by former brewer Otto Haag. Occasional tastings over the years have not impressed.

ferguson falls estate

NR

Pile Road, Dardanup, WA 6236 **region** Geographe
phone (08) 9728 1083 **fax** (08) 9728 1083 **open** By appointment
winemaker James Pennington (Contract) **production** 350 **est.** 1983
product range ($16 CD) Chardonnay, Cabernet Sauvignon.
summary Peter Giumelli and his family are dairy farmers in the lush Ferguson Valley, located 180 kilometres south of Perth. In 1983 they planted 3 hectares of cabernet sauvignon, chardonnay and merlot, making their first wines for commercial release from the 1995 and 1996 vintages. Both vines confirm the suitability of the region for the production of premium wine.

fergusson

★★★★

Wills Road, Yarra Glen, Vic 3775 **region** Yarra Valley
phone (03) 5965 2237 **fax** (03) 5965 2405 **open** 7 days 11–5
winemaker Christopher Keyes, Peter Fergusson **production** 10 000 **est.** 1968
product range ($14.50–28.50 CD) There are two basic ranges: the lower-priced Tartan Range sourced from grapes grown outside the Yarra Valley, with Sauvignon Blanc, Chardonnay, Semillon Sauvignon Blanc, Shiraz, Sparkling; and three wines in the Estate Range, Victoria Chardonnay, Jeremy Shiraz and Benjamin Cabernet Sauvignon.
summary Best known as a favoured tourist destination, particularly for tourist coaches, and offering hearty fare in comfortable surroundings accompanied by wines of non-Yarra Valley origin. For this reason the limited quantities of its estate wines are often ignored, but should not be.

Fergusson Victoria Chardonnay

Confusingly, Victoria Chardonnay does not indicate an appellation – in other words, that the wine comes from various regions within Victoria – but is named after the Fergussons' daughter, and is made from estate-grown grapes.

🍷🍷🍷🍷 **1997** Medium to full yellow-green; the bouquet is quite developed, with rich, honeyed, toasty overtones to buttery/peachy fruit. The palate is round and ripe, with plenty of mouthfeel, showing the rich buttery/peachy and slightly charry oak characters promised by the bouquet. **rating:** 85

⇨ **best drinking** 1998 – 1999 **best vintages** '90, '92, '93, '94, '97 **drink with** Seafood salad • $28.50

fermoy estate NR

Metricup Road, Willyabrup, WA 6280 **region** Margaret River
phone (08) 9755 6285 **fax** (08) 9755 6251 **open** 7 days 11–4.30
winemaker Michael Kelly **production** 15 000 **est.** 1985
product range ($10.50–26 CD) Sauvignon Blanc, Semillon, Chenin Blanc, Chardonnay, Reserve Chardonnay, Cabernet Sauvignon, Reserve Cabernet.
summary Consistently produces wines with a particular character and style, with the focus away from primary fruit and into secondary flavours, with strong structure; the Americans would call them 'food styles'. Quite deliberately out of the mainstream.

Fermoy Estate Reserve Chardonnay

The Fermoy Estate Reserve range is made in very limited quantities, the Chardonnay around 200 cases. One hundred per cent barrel-fermented in Vosges and Allier oak, with a small percentage of new barrels, and taken through malolactic fermentation. Made in a distinctly European-style.

🍷🍷🍷🍸 **1996** Medium yellow-green; a restrained yet solid bouquet; moderately intense, but not fruity, leads on to a structured wine with pronounced secondary creamy/nutty flavours. There is a slightly bitter grip to the finish, and at no time is the wine lush in its impact. **rating:** 84

⇨ **best drinking** 1999 – 2003 **best vintages** NA **drink with** Veal scaloppine • $26

fern hill estate ★★☆

Ingoldby Road, McLaren Flat, SA 5171 **region** McLaren Vale
phone (08) 8383 0167 **fax** (08) 8383 0107 **open** Mon-Fri 10–5, weekends 10–5
winemaker Grant Burge (Contract) **production** 5000 **est.** 1975
product range ($14.95–17.95 CD) Semillon, Chardonnay, Shiraz, Cabernet Sauvignon.
summary One suspects there have been significant changes since Wayne Thomas sold Fern Hill to the Hill International Group, not all for the better.

fishburn & o'keefe ★★★☆

16 Pioneer Avenue, New Norfolk, Tas 7140 **region** Southern Tasmania
phone (03) 6286 1238 **fax** (03) 6261 4029 **open** 7 days at Meadowbank Vineyard
winemaker Greg O'Keefe **production** 3000 **est.** 1991
product range ($15–25 CD) Riesling, Chardonnay, Pinot Noir, Cabernet Sauvignon, Trout Brut, Sparkling Burgundy.
summary Wine consultant and contract-winemaker Greg O'Keefe, one time winemaker at Normans, has joined forces with Hutchins schoolteacher Mike Fishburn to produce wines

made from grapes purchased from various growers across Tasmania, but with an estate vineyard in the course of establishment. Greg O'Keefe also has an active consultancy and contract-winemaking business in his own right. Has also managed to produce a hard to find Sparkling Shiraz from grapes grown in the Tamar Valley.

Fishburn & O'Keefe Riesling

Greg O'Keefe draws upon vineyards from both north and south Tasmania for his wines, relying entirely upon contract-grown fruit.

🍷🍷🍷🍸 **1997** Medium yellow-green; the bouquet is quite voluminous and floral, with spice and apple aromas. There are similar floral/spicy flavours on the forepalate, together with lime, but the finish, though not sweet, does seem to cloy a fraction, perhaps needing a touch more acid. **rating:** 83

➾ **best drinking** 1998 – 2002 **best vintages** NA **drink with** Tasmanian lobster • $15

Fishburn & O'Keefe Pinot Noir

A solidly structured wine drawn from vineyards in both the north and south of the State.

🍷🍷🍷🍷 **1997** Medium to full red-purple; the bouquet is solid, with deep, plummy fruit, with more of the same on the very substantial palate. Excellent fruit flavour and concentration, but not especially complex; hopefully this will build with time in bottle. **rating:** 85

➾ **best drinking** 1998 – 2002 **best vintages** '94, '97 **drink with** Tasmanian venison • $20

five oaks vineyard NR

Aitken Road, Seville, Vic 3139 **region** Yarra Valley
phone (03) 5964 3704 **fax** (03) 5964 3064 **open** Weekends and public holidays 10–5
winemaker Wally Zuk, Michael Zitzlaff (Consultant) **production** 2000 **est.** 1997
product range ($18–20 CD) Riesling, Merlot, Cabernet Sauvignon.
summary Wally and Judy Zuk purchased the Five Oaks Vineyard in Aitken Road, Seville from Oakridge Estate, which has moved to its new premises on the other side of the Yarra Valley. Wally Zuk, with a background in physics, has completed his wine science degree at Charles Sturt University, spending part of his time working in Sydney and Canberra as a physicist and part as winemaker (with help from Michael Zitzlaff of Oakridge) at Five Oaks.

fox creek wines ★★★★☆

Malpas Road, Willunga, SA 5172 **region** McLaren Vale
phone (08) 8556 2403 **fax** (08) 8556 2104 **open** 7 days 11–5
winemaker Njal (Sparky) Marquis, Sarah Marquis **production** 11 000 **est.** 1995
product range ($14–35 CD) Sauvignon Blanc, Verdelho, Unwooded Chardonnay, Chardonnay, Botrytis Chenin Blanc, Vixen Sparkling Burgundy, Reserve Shiraz, JSM Shiraz Cabernets, Reserve Cabernet Sauvignon.
summary Fox Creek has made a major impact since coming on-stream late in 1995. It is the venture of a group of distinguished Adelaide doctors (three of them professors) with particular input from the Watts family, which established the vineyard back in 1985 (selling the grapes) and whose daughter Sarah is now married to winemaker Sparky Marquis. The Reserve red wines, and especially the Reserve Shiraz, are outstanding and have enjoyed considerable show success.

Fox Creek Reserve Shiraz

Estate-grown; a gold medal winner at the 1997 Liquorland National Wine Show.

🍷🍷🍷🍷🍷 **1996** Strong red-purple; there is masses of powerful, earthy shiraz on the bouquet and a mix of mint, black cherry and earthy varietal fruit on the palate, supported by strong tannins. The oak influence is subtle. **rating:** 90

➾ **best drinking** 2002 – 2010 **best vintages** NA **drink with** Grilled beef • $30

Fox Creek JSM Shiraz Cabernets

JSM are the initials of James Stanley Malpas (born 1873) and are cut into the stone lintel above the present-day tasting room, but which was his house after he had graduated from Roseworthy Agricultural College. The wine is a blend of Shiraz, Cabernet Sauvignon and Cabernet Franc, 70% of which is matured for 12 months in second-use American oak and 30% for 12 months in second-use French oak.

🍷🍷🍷🍷 **1996** Medium to full red-purple; the intense bouquet is fruit-driven with strong earthy berry and chocolate aromas, the palate similarly rich and sweet with a mix of cassis, chocolate, berry and earth flavours. Subtle oak throughout. **rating:** 89

➾ **best drinking** 2001 – 2006 **best vintages** NA **drink with** Rib of beef • $18

Fox Creek Reserve Cabernet Sauvignon

An imperious wine, which spent an awesome 52 days on its skins during the fermentation and post-fermentation maceration period, followed by maturation in new French oak for 12 months. The '96 was a gold medal winner at the 1997 Adelaide Wine Show.

🍷🍷🍷🍷🍷 **1996** Dense red-purple; the bouquet is concentrated and rich, with cassis, berry and chocolate fruit and soft oak. The palate is similarly rich and concentrated, with powerful cassis fruit, some almost chewy chocolate flavours, and strongly structured tannins on a lingering finish. **rating:** 91

➾ **best drinking** 2005 – 2015 **best vintages** NA **drink with** Game pie • $30

frankland estate ★★★★

Frankland Road, Frankland, WA 6396 **region** Great Southern
phone (08) 9855 1555 **fax** (08) 9855 1583 **open** By appointment
winemaker Barrie Smith, Judi Cullam **production** 10 000 **est.** 1988

product range ($18–29.50 R) Riesling, Sauvignon Blanc, Isolation Ridge (Shiraz), Olmo's Reward (Bordeaux-blend of Cabernet Franc, Merlot, Malbec, Cabernet Sauvignon, with Petit Verdot in future vintages), Cabernet.

summary A rapidly growing Frankland River operation, situated on a large sheep property owned by Barrie Smith and Judi Cullam. The 14-hectare vineyard has been established progressively since 1988, and a winery built on the site for the 1993 vintage. The Riesling, Isolation Ridge and Olmo's Reward are consistently good.

fraser vineyard ★★★

Lot 5 Wilderness Road, Rothbury, NSW 2321 **region** Lower Hunter Valley
phone (02) 4930 7594 **fax** (02) 4933 1100 **open** 7 days 10–5
winemaker Peter Fraser **production** 1500 **est.** 1987

product range ($12–15 CD) Chardonnay, Semillon Sauvignon Blanc, Chenin Blanc, Shiraz Malbec.

summary A small, 100% estate operation which offers accommodation at the Claremont Country House recently built on the property, and accommodating groups of up to ten people. Has from time to time made some wonderfully generous and fleshy white wines.

freycinet ★★★★★

Tasman Highway via Bicheno, Tas 7215 **region** Southern Tasmania
phone (03) 6257 8384 **fax** (03) 6257 8454 **open** Mon-Fri 9–5, weekends 10–4
winemaker Claudio Radenti **production** 5000 **est.** 1980
product range ($14–28 CD) Riesling Muller Thurgau, Chardonnay, Pinot Noir, Cabernet Sauvignon, Cabernet Franc.
summary The 4-hectare Freycinet vineyards are beautifully situated on the sloping hillsides of a small valley. The soils are podsol and decaying granite with a friable clay subsoil, and the combination of aspect, slope, soil and heat summation produce red grapes of unusual depth of colour and ripe flavours. One of Australia's foremost producers of Pinot Noir, with a wholly enviable track record of consistency – rare with such a temperamental variety.

Freycinet Chardonnay

Freycinet has produced a remarkable string of vintages between 1993 and 1996 inclusive, with wines of exemplary quality and a richness of texture not often encountered in Tasmania. The wines reinforce the message of the Freycinet Pinot Noir: that the amphitheatre/bowl in which the vineyard is situated provides a unique site climate, and with it, an extra dimension of weight and flavour. The 1996 won the trophy for Best Wooded Chardonnay at the 1998 Tasmanian Wines Show.

🍷🍷🍷🍷🍷 **1996** Medium yellow-green; the bouquet is clean and smooth, with elegant white peach fruit, the palate likewise perfectly balanced, with harmonious fruit and gently nutty oak. Manages to combine complexity with elegance. **rating:** 94

➭ **best drinking** 1998 – 2002 **best vintages** '93, '94, '95, '96 **drink with** Abalone • $24

Freycinet Pinot Noir

The remarkable site climate of the Freycinet Vineyard is primarily responsible for the outstanding quality of the Pinot Noir, although the experience and skills of Geoff Bull, daughter Lindy Bull and Claudio Radenti ensure that the potential quality is maximised. Interestingly, the only red fermenter the winery possesses is a rotary fermenter, which in turn helps in the extraction of both colour and flavour. The '96 continues the trophy-winning streak of Freycinet, winning trophies for Best Pinot Noir and Best Wine of Show at the 1998 Tasmanian Wines Show.

🍷🍷🍷🍷🍷 **1996** Medium red-purple; an exceptionally fragrant and complex bouquet with a range of cherry, plum, leaf, mint and earth, all cascading through on to a rich, fleshy palate, with superb texture and structure running through the very finish. **rating:** 94

➭ **best drinking** 1998 – 2002 **best vintages** '91, '92, '94, '95, '96 **drink with** Duck, hare, venison • $26

fyffe field NR

Murray Valley Highway, Yarrawonga, Vic 3730 **region** Goulburn Valley
phone (03) 5748 4282 **fax** (03) 5748 4284 **open** 7 days 10–5
winemaker David Traeger (Contract) **production** 1000 **est.** 1993

product range ($7–15 CD) Traminer, Riesling, Diamond White, Chardonnay, Brut, Big Rivers Rosé, 2nd Vintage Shiraz, Cabernet (from Langhorne Creek), Shiraz, Tokay, Tawny Port, Tokay and 'Tawny Snort' (a fearsome blend of Tawny Port, Reserve Port and Muscat).
summary Fyffe Field has been established by Graeme and Liz Diamond near the Murray River between Cobram and Yarrawonga in a mudbrick and leadlight tasting room opposite an historic homestead. A highlight is the ornamental pig collection on display.

galafrey ★★★☆

145 Lower Sterling Terrace, Albany, WA 6330 **region** Great Southern
phone (08) 9841 6533 **fax** (08) 9851 2324 **open** Mon-Sat 10–5
winemaker Ian Tyrer **production** 4000 **est.** 1977
product range ($10–27 CD) Riesling, Chardonnay, Müller Thurgau, Pinot Noir, Shiraz, Cabernet Sauvignon.
summary Relocated to a new purpose-built but utilitarian winery after previously inhabiting the exotic surrounds of the old Albany wool store, Galafrey makes wines with plenty of character, drawing grapes in the main from 12 hectares of estate plantings at Mount Barker. The wines always have character and flavour, but are not necessarily technically precise. No recent tastings.

galah wine ★★★☆

Tregarthen Road, Ashton, SA 5137 **region** Adelaide Hills
phone (08) 8390 1243 **fax** (08) 8390 1243 **open** Available at Ashton Hills
winemaker Stephen George **production** 750 **est.** 1986
product range ($6.50–35 ML) Barossa Valley Riesling, Barossa Valley Fume Blanc, Marlborough Chardonnay, McLaren Vale Shiraz, SE Aust Shiraz Cabernet, Barossa Valley Grenache, Clare Valley Cabernet Malbec, Clare Valley Shiraz, Sparkling Shiraz, Galah Brut, Vintage Port.
summary Over the years, Stephen George has built up a network of contacts across South Australia from which he gains some very high-quality small parcels of grapes or wine for the Galah label. These are all sold direct at extremely low prices for the quality.

Galah Wine Sparkling Shiraz

The base for this wine, Clare Valley Shiraz, spent five years in old oak before being tiraged (refermented) and ultimately being liqueured with Shiraz Vintage Port from 1976 and 1981. Not surprisingly, an extremely complex and stylish wine.

YYYY **1992** Medium red; the bouquet has gently sweet, faintly earthy fruit with hints of vanilla, possibly coming from the old oak, possibly just from the age of the base wine. The palate is complex, with earthy Shiraz of medium weight and not too sweet; the wine picks up pace on a long finish. **rating:** 88

⇨ **best drinking** 1998 – 2005 **best vintages** NA **drink with** Cold smoked meats • $35

Galah Clare Valley Shiraz

Although the label makes no mention of it, Stephen George is consultant winemaker at Wendouree in the Adelaide Hills, and it is well known that he has first option on any small parcels not required by Wendouree for its own label. All the hallmarks of having come from that marvellous source.

🍷🍷🍷🍷 **1995** Medium purple-red; a firm, clean bouquet with dark cherry and faintly earthy varietal fruit; subtle oak. The palate is powerful but contained, with strong tannin structure around black cherry and plum fruit. **rating:** 88

➭ **best drinking** 2000 – 2010 **best vintages** '88, '89, '90, '91, '92, '95 **drink with** Venison, kangaroo • $15

Galah Wine Clare Valley Cabernet Malbec

Although, as ever, the precise source of the wine is not stated, it is highly probable it is declassified Wendouree. What does not come up to the mark for Wendouree is better than most mortals would hope for.

🍷🍷🍷🍷🍷 **1994** Medium to full red-purple; the bouquet is wonderfully rich and full, with sweet dark chocolate, dark plum and blackberry fruit, the palate rather more austere, with the Cabernet component dominant, and finishing with persistent, lingering tannins. **rating:** 90

➭ **best drinking** 2004 – 2010 **best vintages** NA **drink with** Braised ox cheek • $15

garbin estate NR

209 Toodyay Road, Middle Swan, WA 6056 **region** Swan District
phone (08) 9274 1747 **fax** (08) 9274 1747 **open** Mon-Sat 10–5.30, Sun 12–5.30
winemaker Peter Garbin **production** 1000 **est.** 1956
product range ($12–15 CD) Chenin Blanc, Chardonnay, Shiraz, Cabernet Merlot, Dessert Wine, Ruby Port.
summary Peter Garbin, winemaker by weekend and design draftsman by week, decided in 1990 that he would significantly upgrade the bulk fortified winemaking business commenced by his father in 1956. The vineyards have been replanted, the winery re-equipped, and the first of the new generation wines produced in 1994.

garden gully vineyards 

Garden Gully, Great Western, Vic 3377 **region** Grampians
phone (03) 5356 2400 **fax** (03) 5356 2400 **open** Mon-Fri 10.30–5.30, weekends 10–5.30
winemaker Brian Fletcher, Warren Randall **production** 2000 **est.** 1987
product range ($12.50–25 CD) Riesling, Shiraz, Sparkling Burgundy, Sparkling Chardonnay, Sparkling Pinot Noir.
summary Given the skills and local knowledge of the syndicate which owns Garden Gully, it is not surprising that the wines are typically good: an attractive stone cellar-door sales area is an additional reason to stop and pay a visit. Shiraz produced from the 100-year-old vines adjoining the cellar door is especially good. Not all the wines are from Grampians grapes; most, indeed, come from South Australia.

Garden Gully Sparkling Burgundy

The label is not specific about the fruit sources for this wine, which still clings to the soon-to-be-outlawed Sparkling Burgundy name. Notwithstanding its relatively short time on lees, a good example of the style.

🍷🍷🍷🍷 **1996** Dark purple-red; a youthful, potent bouquet with rich dark fruit aromas, and a fresh, well-balanced palate of medium weight exhibiting an array of plum, berry and spice flavours. Should develop well with extended cork age. **rating:** 85

➭ **best drinking** 2002 – 2008 **best vintages** NA **drink with** Borsch • $24.80

Garden Gully Shiraz

Produced from the old, dry-grown vineyards surrounding the attractive cellar door. Unquestionably the best of the Garden Gully range, year in, year out.

🍷🍷🍷🍷🍷 **1995** Medium red-purple; the bouquet has a marvellous array of dark chocolate, black cherry and spice fruit, the palate displaying the same flavours with that typical restrained power and super-fine tannin structure of Great Western. **rating:** 91

⇨ **best drinking** 2000 – 2015 **best vintages** '91, '93, '95 **drink with** Barbecued lamb • $17.50

---

geebin wines NR

Channel Highway, Birchs Bay, Tas 7162 **region** Southern Tasmania
phone (03) 6267 4750 **fax** (03) 6267 4601 **open** Not
winemaker Andrew Hood (Contract) **production** 80 **est.** 1983
product range ($10–11 CD) Riesling, Cabernet Sauvignon.
summary Although production is minuscule, quality has been consistently high. The Riesling is well made, but the interesting wine from this far southern vineyard is Cabernet Sauvignon: clearly, the vineyard enjoys favourable ripening conditions.

gehrig estate 

Cnr Murray Valley Highway and Howlong Road, Barnawartha, Vic 3688 **region** Rutherglen
phone (02) 6026 7296 **fax** (02) 6026 7424 **open** Mon-Sat 9–5, Sun 10–5
winemaker Brian Gehrig **production** 5000 **est.** 1858
product range ($8.50–25 CD) Chenin Blanc, Riesling, Chardonnay, Autumn Riesling, Late Harvest, Pinot Noir, Shiraz, Cabernet Sauvignon, Fortifieds.
summary An historic winery (and adjacent house) are superb legacies of the nineteenth century. Progressive modernisation of the winemaking facilities and operations has seen the quality of the white wines improve significantly, while the red wines now receive a percentage of new oak. Another recent innovation has been the introduction of the Gourmet Courtyard serving lunch on weekends, public holidays and Victorian school holidays.

gembrook hill ★★★★

Launching Place Road, Gembrook, Vic 3783 **region** Yarra Valley
phone (03) 9818 5633 **fax** (03) 9818 5633 **open** By appointment
winemaker Dr Ian Marks, David Lance **production** 950 **est.** 1983
product range ($18–22 R) Sauvignon Blanc, Chardonnay, Pinot Noir.
summary The 6-hectare Gembrook Hill Vineyard is situated on rich, red volcanic soils 2 kilometres north of Gembrook in the coolest part of the Yarra Valley. The vines are not irrigated, with consequent natural vigour control. The Sauvignon Blanc is invariably good, sometimes outstanding.

Gembrook Hill Sauvignon Blanc

The wine for which Gembrook Hill first came into prominence, and suited (in terms of wine style) both to the site and climate. It has proved to be a very difficult variety to grow, or at least to crop well, with a tiny production from the 2 hectares of vines. Devotees of the style are pleased that Dr Ian Marks has persevered.

🍷🍷🍷🍷 **1997** Light yellow-green; the bouquet is light and clean. A mix of gooseberry and herbal aromas, palate similarly crisp and clean, with tangy lemony/herb and pear flavours. **rating:** 84

➯ **best drinking** 1998 – 1999 **best vintages** '90, '92, '93, '94, '95 **drink with** Lobster bisque • $22

geoff merrill ★★★★

291 Pimpala Road, Woodcroft, SA 5162 **region** McLaren Vale
phone (08) 8381 6877 **fax** (08) 8322 2244 **open** Mon–Fri 10–5, Sun 12–5
winemaker Geoff Merrill **production** 50 000 **est.** 1980
product range ($14–40 R) There is now an altered product range under the Geoff Merrill label: the Reserve range of Chardonnay, Shiraz and Cabernet Sauvignon; then the Premium wines (although not labelled as such, simply by the variety) of Semillon, Sauvignon Blanc, Chardonnay, Bush Vine Grenache, Shiraz and Cabernet Merlot.
summary The premium brand of the three wines made by Merrill (Mount Hurtle and Cockatoo Ridge being the other two); always given bottle age, the wines reflect the desire of this otherwise exuberant winemaker for elegance and subtlety. In 1998 the product range was rearranged into two tiers: premium (in fact simply varietal) and reserve, the latter being the older (and best) wines.

Geoff Merrill Premium McLaren Vale Semillon

As the label attests, drawn entirely from McLaren Vale vineyards, and to this extent different from many of the Geoff Merrill wines which have a multi-regional source. Stainless steel fermented and early bottled in the traditional Semillon style, and all the better for that.
🍷🍷🍷🍷 **1997** Light to medium yellow-green; the bouquet shows good varietal character with lemon and herb aromas of medium intensity. A well-structured, unforced wine on the palate, with more than sufficient fruit weight to carry its development for many years, while offering enough for immediate consumption. **rating:** 84

➯ **best drinking** 1998 – 2003 **best vintages** NA **drink with** King George whiting • $14

Geoff Merrill Premium Sauvignon Blanc

A new label in the Geoff Merrill range. This particular wine is a blend of 89% McLaren Vale and 11% Padthaway material which (appropriately) has not been given any oak maturation.
🍷🍷🍷🍷 **1997** Light yellow-green; the bouquet is crisp, clean and firm with herbaceous fruit aromas. The palate has good weight and structure, with length and grip to the finish, although the varietal character is in the subdued minerally/herbal spectrum. **rating:** 88

➯ **best drinking** 1998 – 1999 **best vintages** NA **drink with** Seafood • $14

Geoff Merrill Premium Shiraz

A blend of 75% McLaren Vale and 25% Goulburn Valley (doubtless ex-Chateau Tahbilk) grapes which were, in typical Merrill fashion, cold-fermented and then matured in a mix of new and used American oak for 24 months. Very much in the idiomatic style of the maker.
🍷🍷🍷🍷 **1994** Medium red-purple; quite fragrant (as the cold fermentation would suggest), clean and fresh; a marked lemon and vanilla oak influence is also immediately apparent. A well-made, elegant wine on the palate, with fresh berry fruit and nicely balanced oak. **rating:** 87

➯ **best drinking** 1998 – 2003 **best vintages** NA **drink with** Ragout of veal • $17.50

Geoff Merrill Reserve Shiraz

Drawn from old, dry-grown McLaren Vale Shiraz, and first made in 1994. Something of a departure in style for Geoff Merrill, with far greater fruit weight and ripeness than most of the Geoff Merrill reds.

🍷🍷🍷🍷🍷 **1994** Medium to full red-purple; the bouquet is redolent of ripe, dark cherry and liquorice-accented fruit of medium to full intensity. The palate delivers all of the promise of the bouquet with abundant dark cherry and plum fruit supported by soft tannins. Well-handled oak; good structure and weight, and – notwithstanding all this flavour – keeps the core of elegance of the Merrill style. **rating:** 90

⇨ **best drinking** 2000 – 2010 **best vintages** NA **drink with** Kangaroo fillet • $40

Geoff Merrill Reserve Cabernet Sauvignon

Effectively takes over from the wine previously simply labelled Cabernet Sauvignon, sharing with it the multi-regional source and the occasional dash of Cabernet Franc or Merlot. Those sources span Coonawarra, McLaren Vale and the Goulburn Valley.

🍷🍷🍷🍷 **1994** Medium red-purple; a most attractive bouquet with characters and aromas reminiscent of Bordeaux, with a mix of earthy herbaceous characters at one extreme, and cedar and vanilla at the other. The palate has good weight, flavour and structure, with cedar, cassis and olive flavours, finishing with fine tannins. **rating:** 88

⇨ **best drinking** 1999 – 2004 **best vintages** NA **drink with** Rack of lamb • $27

---

geoff weaver ★★★★★

2 Gilpin Lane, Mitcham, SA 5062 **region** Adelaide Hills
phone (08) 8272 2105 **fax** (08) 8271 0177 **open** Not
winemaker Geoff Weaver **production** 5000 **est.** 1982
product range ($14–27 ML) Stafford Ridge Riesling, Chardonnay, Sauvignon Blanc, Cabernet Merlot.

summary This is now the full-time business of former Hardy Group chief winemaker Geoff Weaver. He draws upon a little under 10 hectares of vineyard established between 1982 and 1988; for the time being, at least, the physical winemaking is carried out by Geoff Weaver at Petaluma. He produces an invariably immaculate Sauvignon Blanc, and one of the longest-lived Chardonnays to be found in Australia, with intense grapefruit and melon flavour. The beauty of the labels ranks supreme with that of Pipers Brook.

Geoff Weaver Stafford Ridge Riesling

Produced from 1 hectare of riesling planted in 1982 at an altitude of 540 metres. The wines are unequivocally long-lived.

🍷🍷🍷🍷 **1997** Light yellow-green; the aromas are classic varietal, led by lime with some mineral undertones, tight and intense. The palate has delicate lime and passionfruit flavours running through to a relatively firm, youthful finish. At the very dawn of its life. **rating:** 89

⇨ **best drinking** 2000 – 2007 **best vintages** '90, '93, '94, '96 **drink with** Fresh asparagus • $14

Geoff Weaver Stafford Ridge Sauvignon Blanc

Produced from 1.8 hectares of close-planted but very low-yielding sauvignon blanc planted in 1987. Right from the outset, the quality of this wine has been exceptional, with a purity and intensity of flavour equalled by few other Australian Sauvignon Blancs. It is not wooded, nor does it need to be.

🍷🍷🍷🍷🍷 **1997** Light to medium green-yellow; a fragrant mix of gooseberry and passionfruit aromas of absolute purity lead on to a delicate, yet intense, palate. The wine is beautifully balanced, with crisp acidity; not at all flamboyant, and the sort of wine which can easily be overlooked in the show ring. **rating:** 93

➯ **best drinking** 1998 – 1999 **best vintages** '92, '93, '94, '96, '97 **drink with** Mussels • $18.14

Geoff Weaver Stafford Ridge Chardonnay

The 3.5 hectares of chardonnay at Stafford Ridge are now over 15 years old, producing grapes with great intensity of flavour, but with a particular grapefruit citrus character which has been present since the very first vintage. The wine matures slowly and gracefully, and is always released with several years bottle age.

🍷🍷🍷🍷🍷 **1995** As always, an extremely powerful, intense, cool-climate style that is slow-developing. A complex array of grapefruit, apple and melon fruit aromas introduces a full-bodied palate, with some bottle-developed complexity starting to show, but sustained by fresh acidity. **rating:** 94

➯ **best drinking** 1999 – 2003 **best vintages** '95 **drink with** Sweetbreads • $27

giaconda ★★★★★

McClay Road, Beechworth, Vic 3747 **region** Ovens Valley
phone (03) 5727 0246 **fax** (03) 5727 0246 **open** By appointment
winemaker Rick Kinzbrunner **production** 900 **est.** 1985
product range ($29–39 ML) Chardonnay, Pinot Noir, Cabernet Sauvignon.
summary Wines which have a super-cult status and which, given the tiny production, are extremely difficult to find, sold chiefly through restaurants and mail order. All have a cosmopolitan edge befitting Rick Kinzbrunner's international winemaking experience. The Chardonnay and Pinot Noir are made in contrasting styles: the Chardonnay tight and reserved, the Pinot Noir usually opulent and ripe.

Giaconda Chardonnay

Four hundred and fifty cases of handcrafted wines are produced from a little under 1 hectare of estate vineyard every year. The style of the wine is entirely different from mainstream Australian Chardonnay, relying far more on texture and structure, and far less on primary fruit. An exceptionally distinguished and consistent wine which is the very deliberate product of Rick Kinzbrunner's winemaking philosophy. Made using wild yeasts, and bottled unfiltered.

🍷🍷🍷🍷🍷 **1996** Medium to full yellow-green; a very complex bouquet with an array of toasty nutty bacony aromas to accompany the melon fruit is followed by a no less powerful and complex palate. Very Burgundian in feel and texture, it is already weighty by the normally reserved standards of Giaconda. **rating:** 93

➯ **best drinking** 2000 – 2006 **best vintages** '86, '88, '90, '92, '93, '94, '95, '96 **drink with** Slow-roasted Tasmanian salmon • $39

Giaconda Pinot Noir

As fastidiously produced and as full of character as the Chardonnay. It comes from a little over half a hectare of estate plantings, and is made in tiny quantities. The style has been quite different from the Pinot Noirs of southern Victoria, being much fuller and more robust, with the obvious potential to age well. In recent vintages, the style and flavour has veered more towards Burgundy, and become better and better.

🍷🍷🍷🍷🍷 **1996** Light red, giving no hint of the outstanding character and flavour of the wine. The bouquet is striking, with fragrant sappy, spicy aromas; the palate is extraordinarily long, with silky slippery sappy foresty flavours rippling on and on. Superb with tea-smoked duck, each mouthful better than the previous one. **rating:** 95

⇨ **best drinking** 1999 – 2003 **best vintages** '85, '86, '88, '90, '91, '92, '95, '96 **drink with** Tea-smoked duck • $35

gilbert ★★★★

RMB 438 Albany Highway, Kendenup via Mt Barker, WA 6323 **region** Great Southern
phone (08) 9851 4028 **fax** (08) 9851 4021 **open** Wed-Mon 10–5
winemaker Plantagenet (Contract) **production** 1600 **est.** 1980
product range ($14–18 CD) Riesling, Alira (medium sweet), Chardonnay, Shiraz.
summary A part-time occupation for sheep and beef farmers Jim and Beverly Gilbert, but a very successful one. The now mature vineyard, coupled with contract-winemaking at Plantagenet, has produced small quantities of high-quality Riesling and Chardonnay; the tiny production sells out quickly each year.

gilgai winery NR

Tingha Road, Gilgai, NSW 2360 **region** Other Wineries of NSW
phone (02) 6723 1204 **open** 7 days 10–6
winemaker Keith Whish **production** 400 **est.** 1968
product range Semillon, Shiraz Cabernet, Chandelier (Fortified White), Port.
summary Inverell medical practitioner Dr Keith Whish has been quietly producing wines from his 6-hectare vineyard for almost 30 years. All of the production is sold through cellar door.

glen erin grange NR

Woodend Road, Lancefield, Vic 3435 **region** Macedon
phone (03) 5429 1041 **fax** (03) 5429 2053 **open** Weekends, public holidays 10–6
winemaker Brian Scales **production** 2000 **est.** 1993
product range ($14–26 CD) Gewurztraminer, Chardonnay, Pinot Noir, Mystic Park Macedon Sparkling, Cabernet Merlot.
summary Brian Scales acquired the former Lancefield Winery and has renamed it Glen Erin Grange. The accompanying restaurant is open on Friday and Saturday evenings à la carte and for Saturday and Sunday lunch.

glenara wines ★★★☆

126 Range Road North, Upper Hermitage, SA 5131 **region** Adelaide Hills
phone (08) 8380 5056 **fax** (08) 8380 5056 **open** Sun-Fri 11–5
winemaker Trevor Jones **production** 6000 **est.** 1971
product range ($15–22 CD) Riesling, Chardonnay, Sauvignon Blanc Semillon, Unwooded Chardonnay, Pinot Noir, Shiraz, Cabernet Rosé, Cabernet Merlot, Cabernet Sauvignon, Sparkling, Old Tawny Port.
summary Glenara has been owned by the Verrall family since 1924; the first vines were planted in 1971, the first wine made in 1975, and the winery built in 1988. Has proceeded to produce many good wines, particularly the full-flavoured Rieslings, but also with creditable full-bodied reds.

Glenara Adelaide Hills Riesling

A range of vintages is available at cellar door, showing significant variation in style and quality from one year to the next. The '96 won the only gold medal in the Riesling Class at the 1997 Adelaide Hills Wine Show.

🍷🍷🍷🍷 **1997** Light yellow-green; a light, crisp and minerally bouquet which is very youthful and unevolved leads into a powerful palate with firm lime, lemon and mineral flavours and a slightly chalky finish. Will undoubtedly develop. **rating:** 84

➪ **best drinking** 2000 – 2005 **best vintages** '90, '92, '96 **drink with** Braised pork neck • $15

Glenara Sauvignon Blanc Semillon

A new edition to the Glenara range, showing the Adelaide Hills to full advantage.

🍷🍷🍷🍷 **1997** Light to medium yellow-green; there is a mix of gooseberry, herbal and passionfruit aromas on the medium-intensity bouquet; the extremely harmonious palate showcases all the flavours promised by the bouquet, with a long, pleasing finish. The sort of wine which invites the second glass. **rating:** 89

➪ **best drinking** 1998 – 1999 **best vintages** NA **drink with** Asparagus and prosciutto • $16

Glenara Pinot Noir Bottle Fermented

One unusual feature of this wine is that it is produced from organically grown grapes, albeit made using conventional techniques. Less unusual is its base of 100% Pinot Noir.

🍷🍷🍷🍷 **1995** Salmon pink; a powerful, if fractionally coarse, bouquet, but a much better, well-structured and balanced palate with strong varietal strawberry/spice flavours, good acidity and length. **rating:** 86

➪ **best drinking** 1998 – 1999 **best vintages** NA **drink with** Light Asian dishes • $19

Glenara Limited Release Pinot Noir

Situated in the warmer, western side of the Adelaide Hills as Glenara is, it is not the least bit surprising that its Pinot Noir is very full-bodied. The '96 was good enough to win a silver medal at the 1997 Adelaide Hills Wine Show.

🍷🍷🍷🍷 **1996** Excellent, strong red-purple; the bouquet is solid, with powerful ripe fruit, but tending to dry red in style. Substantial oak input comes through on the palate, but there is solid fruit there to sustain that oak. Will be greatly enjoyed by those who like fuller-bodied Pinots. **rating:** 84

➪ **best drinking** 1998 – 2002 **best vintages** NA **drink with** Strong red meat dishes • $22

glenayr ★★★☆

Back Tea Tree Road, Richmond, Tas 7025 **region** Southern Tasmania
phone (03) 6260 2388 **fax** (03) 6244 7234 **open** By appointment
winemaker Chris Harrington (at Stoney Vineyard) **production** 300 **est.** 1975
product range ($18–20 CD) Riesling, Chardonnay, Pinot Noir, Cabernet Shiraz Merlot.
summary The principal occupation of Chris Harrington is as viticultural manager of the substantial Tolpuddle Vineyard, the grapes of which are sold to Domaine Chandon. Tiny quantities of wine are made from an adjacent 1-hectare vineyard for mailing list sales under the GlenAyr label; chardonnay and pinot noir grapes are also purchased from Tolpuddle Vineyards.

glenfinlass NR

Elysian Farm, Parkes Road, Wellington, NSW 2820 **region** Other Wineries of NSW
phone (02) 6845 2011 **fax** (02) 6845 3329 **open** Sat 9–5 or by appointment
winemaker Brian G Holmes **production** 500 **est.** 1971
product range ($10–15 CD) Sauvignon Blanc, Shiraz, Hill Vineyard Shiraz Cabernet, Cabernet Sauvignon.
summary The weekend and holiday hobby of Wellington solicitor Brian Holmes, who has wisely decided to leave it at that. I have not tasted the wines for many years, but the last wines I did taste were competently made.

glenguin NR

River Oaks Vineyard, Lot 8 Milbrodale Road, Broke, NSW 2330 **region** Lower Hunter Valley
phone (02) 6579 1009 **fax** (02) 6579 1009 **open** At Boutique Wine Centre, Broke Road, Pokolbin
winemaker Robin Tedder (Contract) **production** 7000 **est.** 1993
product range ($16–18.50 R) Semillon, Unwooded Chardonnay, Barrel Fermented Chardonnay.
summary Glenguin's vineyard has been established along the banks of the Wollombi Brook by Robin, Rita and Andrew Tedder, Robin and Andrew being the grandsons of Air Chief Marshal Tedder, who was made Baron of Glenguin by King George VI in recognition of his wartime deeds. Glenguin was in fact a Scottish distillery which continues to produce a single malt, but there is no other connection between the two Glenguins.

gloucester ridge vineyard ★★★

Burma Road, Pemberton, WA 6260 **region** Pemberton
phone (08) 9776 1035 **fax** (08) 9776 1390 **open** 7 days 10–5, later on Saturdays
winemaker John Wade **production** 5000 **est.** 1985
product range ($14–22.50 CD) Pemberton White, Late Harvest Riesling, Sauvignon Blanc, Aurora, Chardonnay, Pemberton Red, Pinot Noir, Cabernets.
summary Gloucester Ridge is the only vineyard located within the Pemberton town boundary, within easy walking distance. It is owned and operated by Don and Sue Hancock; quality has varied, but as the Sauvignon Blanc shows, can be good.

gnadenfrei estate NR

Seppeltsfield Road, Marananga via Tanunda, SA 5353 **region** Barossa Valley
phone (08) 8562 2522 **fax** (08) 8562 3470 **open** Tues-Sun 10–5.30
winemaker Malcolm Seppelt **production** 8000 **est.** 1979
product range ($8–20 CD) Riesling, Semillon, Traminer Riesling, White Frontignan, Shiraz Grenache, Tawny Port, Brut.
summary A strictly cellar-door operation, which relies on a variety of sources for its wines, but has a core of 2 hectares of estate shiraz and 1 hectare of grenache. A restaurant is open for morning teas, lunches and afternoon teas.

golden grape estate NR

Oakey Creek Road, Pokolbin, NSW 2321 **region** Lower Hunter Valley
phone (02) 4998 7588 **fax** (02) 4998 7730 **open** 7 days 10–5

winemaker Neil McGuigan (Consultant) **production** NFP **est.** 1985
product range ($15–21 CD) Premier Semillon, Gewurztraminer, Sauvignon Blanc, Semillon Verdelho, Happy Valley Chardonnay, Five Star (light fruity), Frizzante Rosé, Mount Leonard (Cabernet Sauvignon), Domaine Springton (Shiraz), Classic Red, Fortifieds.
summary German-owned and unashamedly directed at the tourist, with a restaurant, barbecue and picnic areas, wine museum and separate tasting room for bus tours. The substantial range of wines are of diverse origins and style. Most of the wines entered at the 1996 Hunter Valley Wine Show failed to trouble the scorers, but were well-enough made, and had flavour.

golders vineyard NR

Bridport Road, Pipers Brook, Tas 7254 **region** Northern Tasmania
phone (03) 6395 4142 **fax** (03) 6382 7250 **open** By appointment
winemaker Richard Crabtree **production** 200 **est.** 1991
product range ($18–20 CD) Pinot Noir.
summary A Pinot Noir specialist with 1.5 hectares planted, and worth watching in the future. The wine is available for sale at the Delamere cellar door.

Golders Pinot Noir

Winemaking runs in the family, it seems, for Richard Crabtree is Robert Crabtree's (of Watervale in the Clare Valley) brother. His 1995 Pinot Noir, sourced from Craig Hogarth's small vineyard at Pipers Brook, is his first wine, and a creditable effort, followed up by an even better '96.

🍷🍷🍷🍷 **1996** Medium to full red-purple; the bouquet is clean, with smooth plummy fruit with clear varietal character and good intensity. The palate, too, has abundant plummy fruit, and is well balanced and structured. **rating:** 88

➯ **best drinking** 1998 – 2001 **best vintages** '95, '96 **drink with** Quail • $18

goona warra vineyard ★★★☆

Sunbury Road, Sunbury, Vic 3429 **region** Sunbury
phone (03) 9740 7766 **fax** (03) 9744 7648 **open** 7 days 10–5
winemaker John Barnier **production** 2500 **est.** 1863
product range ($15–22 R) Semillon, Chardonnay, Black Cygnet Chardonnay, Pinot Noir, Cabernet Franc, Black Cygnet Cabernets, Black Widow Brut, Tawny Port.
summary An historic stone winery, established under this name by a nineteenth-century Victorian premier. Excellent tasting facilities; an outstanding venue for weddings and receptions; Sunday lunch also served. Situated 30 minutes drive from Melbourne (10 minutes north of Tullamarine airport).

goundrey ★★★★

Muir Highway, Mount Barker, WA 6324 **region** Great Southern
phone (08) 9851 1777 **fax** (08) 9851 1997 **open** Mon-Sat 10–4.30, Sun 11–4.30
winemaker Keith Brown **production** 187 000 **est.** 1978
product range ($16–26 R) Chenin Blanc, Classic White, Unwooded Chardonnay, Cabernet Merlot, Cabernet Sauvignon; Reserve range of Riesling, Sauvignon Blanc, Chardonnay, Pinot Noir, Shiraz, Cabernet Sauvignon; second label Fox River Classic White, Chardonnay, Classic Red.

summary Under the ownership of Perth businessman Jack Bendat, not to mention the injection of many millions of dollars into vineyard and winery expansion, Goundrey grows apace. There seems to be a widening gap between the quality of the Reserve wines (usually, but not invariably, outstanding) and the varietal range (workmanlike). This may be no bad thing from a commercial viewpoint, particularly if the differential is reflected in the price, but does make an overall rating difficult.

Goundrey Reserve Pinot Noir

There is no doubt that Pinot Noir in the Mount Barker region is an on-again, off-again affair, at least in terms of varietal character. Plantagenet succeeded in 1994, but not in 1996, in which year it was Goundrey's turn to do so.

YYYY **1996** Medium purple-red; a fragrant spicy/stalky bouquet shows good varietal character, as does the palate with its interesting spicy/foresty flavours. There is clear-cut varietal character evident all the way through the wine. **rating:** 85

➾ **best drinking** 1998 – 2000 **best vintages** '96 **drink with** Spiced quail • $24

Goundrey Reserve Cabernet Sauvignon

Over the past 20 years, the wine which has performed most consistently has been Goundrey Cabernet Sauvignon. Generous, rich and long-lived, it typifies the region. The '96 was a gold medal and trophy winner at the 1997 Liquorland National Wine Show, and is an excellent wine.

YYYYY **1995** Medium red-purple; the lush bouquet is flooded with ripe blackberry fruit and high-quality oak; the palate is similarly full of perfectly ripened cassis cabernet fruit, with exemplary structure and equally good oak in support. A great wine, but the '96 may prove to be every bit as good. **rating:** 95

➾ **best drinking** 2000 – 2010 **best vintages** '81, '85, '87, '90, '92, '95, '96 **drink with** Fillet steak • $25

gralyn cellars ★★★☆

Caves Road, Willyabrup, WA 6280 **region** Margaret River
phone (08) 9755 6245 **fax** (08) 9755 6245 **open** 7 days 10.30–4.30
winemaker Graham Hutton, Merilyn Hutton **production** 1700 **est.** 1975
product range ($16–36 CD) Riesling, Classic Dry White, Late Harvest Riesling, Shiraz, Michael Hutton Shiraz, Late Harvest Cabernet, Cabernet Nouveau, Cabernet Shiraz, Cabernet Sauvignon, and an extensive range of fortifieds including White Port and Tawny Port.
summary The move from primarily fortified wine to table wine production continues, and does so with considerable success. The red wines are made in a distinctively different style from most of those from the Margaret River region, with a softness and sweetness (in part from American oak) which is reminiscent of some of the better-made wines from the eastern States.

Gralyn Michael Hutton Shiraz

Made by and named after son Michael Hutton, produced from 20-year-old shiraz vines, and matured in a mix of new French and American oak. The 1994 vintage won a silver medal at the Perth Show in open competition against wines from all over Australia; the '95 did even better, winning silver at both the Perth Show and – even more significantly – the Sheraton Wine Awards. The '96 repeated almost exactly the performance of the '95.

🍷🍷🍷🍷 **1996** Medium to full red-purple; a rich, full and ripe bouquet with complex black cherry/gamey varietal fruit leads into a very good palate, with liquorice, boot polish and game varietal flavours supported by well-handled vanillin oak. The best yet under this label. **rating:** 86

⇨ **best drinking** 2000 – 2005 **best vintages** '94, '95, '96 **drink with** Strong red meat dishes • $36

grant burge ★★★★

Jacobs Creek, Tanunda, SA 5352 **region** Barossa Valley
phone (08) 8563 3700 **fax** (08) 8563 2807 **open** 7 days 10–5
winemaker Grant Burge **production** 80 000 **est.** 1988
product range ($12–70 R) Has recently moved to a series of vineyard-designated varietal wines including Thorn Vineyard Riesling, Virtuoso Sauvignon Blanc Semillon, Kraft Vineyard Sauvignon Blanc, Zerk Vineyard Semillon, Barossa Ranges Chardonnay, Lily Farm Frontignac, Filsell Shiraz, Hillcott Merlot, and Cameron Vale Cabernet Sauvignon. Top-of-the-range red are Meshach Shiraz, The Holy Trinity (Grenache Shiraz Mourvedre) and Shadrach Cabernet Sauvignon; Oakland is cheaper second label.
summary As one might expect, this very experienced industry veteran makes consistently good, full-flavoured and smooth wines chosen from the pick of the crop of his extensive vineyard holdings, which total an impressive 200 hectares; the immaculately restored/rebuilt stone cellar-door sales buildings are another attraction. The provocatively named The Holy Trinity (a Grenache Shiraz Mourvedre blend) joins Shadrach and Meshach at the top of the range.

Grant Burge Barossa Ranges Chardonnay

First released under this label in 1993, and made an immediate impact, winning a cascade of gold medals and a number of major trophies. Attractive fruit and sophisticated oak handling were the key, and although subsequent vintages have not scaled the same heights, the wine is seldom less than good.

🍷🍷🍷🍷 **1996** Medium to full yellow-green; a quite complex bouquet with softly spicy/charry oak and sweet fruit. The palate has pleasant soft peach and nectarine fruit in abundance, with appropriate oak in support. **rating:** 85

⇨ **best drinking** 1998 – 1999 **best vintages** '93, '94, '96 **drink with** Char-grilled octopus • $19.80

Grant Burge Meshach Shiraz

First made in 1988, and the signature wine of the Grant Burge range. Named in honour of Meshach William Burge, Grant Burge's great-grandfather. It is produced from 65-year-old vines grown on the Filsell Vineyard, which also gives its name to the gold and trophy-winning varietal wine which sits alongside Cameron Vale. The '95 was a trophy and gold medal winner at the 1997 Royal Adelaide Wine Show.

🍷🍷🍷🍷 **1994** Medium red-purple; as ever, vanillin oak is the dominant force in the bouquet, but there is sweet, medium weight fruit present. The palate is likewise saturated with oak, but once again has attractive chocolate and berry fruit lurking underneath. Very well made if you like this much oak; the upcoming release of the '95 is excellent, with much more fruit (or less oak). **rating:** 85

⇨ **best drinking** 1999 – 2005 **best vintages** '88, '90, '91, '92, '95 **drink with** Braised beef • $70

Grant Burge The Holy Trinity

A new super-premium wine from Grant Burge, presented in a custom-made bottle with the Grant Burge seal embossed in the glass. Wine and the church have had a long history together, which is just as well given the name of this wine, and its launch date on 7 June 1998, which was Holy Trinity Sunday. The Trinity in the wine is Grenache, Shiraz and Mourvedre.

🍷🍷🍷🍷 **1995** Light to medium red-purple; the bouquet is clean, smooth, with gently sweet berry aromas of light to medium intensity. An attractive, fruit-driven wine, silky smooth and sweet and not too jammy; the texture is very much akin to that of a Southern Rhône Valley red. **rating:** 89

⇨ **best drinking** 1999 – 2003 **best vintages** NA **drink with** Jugged hare • NA

green valley vineyard NR

Sebbes Road, Forest Grove via Margaret River, WA 6286 **region** Margaret River
phone (08) 9384 3131 **open** Sat, public holidays 10–6, Sun 10–4
winemaker Clive Otto **production** 3000 **est.** 1980
product range ($12.50–25 CD) Chardonnay, Riesling, Müller Thurgau, Dolce (Chenin Blanc), Cabernet Sauvignon.
summary Owners Ed and Eleanore Green commenced the development of Green Valley Vineyard in 1980. It is still a part-time operation, with the wines made by contract, but production has grown steadily from the 7.7 hectares of vines, and the Cabernet Sauvignon has been a consistent medal winner.

greenock creek cellars NR

Radford Road, Seppeltsfield, SA 5360 **region** Barossa Valley
phone (08) 8562 8103 **fax** (08) 8562 8259 **open** Wed-Mon 11–5
winemaker Michael Waugh **production** 1500 **est.** 1978
product range ($13–16.50 CD) Chardonnay, Shiraz, Cabernet Sauvignon.
summary Michael and Annabelle Waugh are disciples of Rocky O'Callaghan of Rockford Wines, and have deliberately accumulated a series of old dryland, low-yielding Barossa vineyards, aiming to produce wines of unusual depth of flavour and character. They have handsomely succeeded in this aim. They also offer superior accommodation in the ancient but beautifully restored two-bedroom cottage 'Miriam's'; Michael Waugh is a highly skilled stonemason.

grevillea estate NR

Buckajo Road, Bega, NSW 2550 **region** Other Wineries of NSW
phone (02) 6492 3006 **fax** (02) 6492 3006 **open** 7 days 9–5
winemaker Nicola Collins **production** 3000 **est.** 1980
product range ($10–15 CD) Rhine Riesling, Sauvignon Blanc, Chardonnay, Gewurztraminer, Merlot, Family Reserve Cabernet Sauvignon.
summary A tourist-oriented winery which successfully sells all of its surprisingly large production through cellar door and to local restaurants.

grosset ★★★★★

King Street, Auburn, SA 5451 **region** Clare Valley
phone (08) 8849 2175 **fax** (08) 8849 2292 **open** Wed-Sun 10–5 from 1st week of September
winemaker Jeffrey Grosset **production** 7500 **est.** 1981

product range ($13–32 R) Watervale Riesling, Polish Hill Riesling, Semillon Sauvignon Blanc, Piccadilly Chardonnay, Gaia (a Cabernet blend), Noble Riesling, Reserve Pinot Noir.

summary Jeffrey Grosset served part of his apprenticeship at the vast Lindeman Karadoc winery, moving from the largest to one of the smallest when he established Grosset Wines in its old stone winery. He now crafts the wines with the utmost care from grapes grown to the most exacting standards; all need a certain amount of time in bottle to achieve their ultimate potential, not the least the Rieslings and Gaia, among Australia's best examples of their kind.

Grosset Polish Hill Riesling

A finer, crisper and more elegant wine than the Watervale, with more lime and citrus fruit, albeit less generous. Since 1985 the Molloy Vineyard has been the major source, but as from 1994 estate plantings also contribute. Like the Watervale, made with neutral yeasts and without the use of enzymes. Always brilliant.

🍷🍷🍷🍷🍷 **1997** Light to medium yellow-green; a very fragrant bouquet with a distinct minerally edge to the herb and spice fruit. The palate is intense but fine, with tremendous grip and length to the finish; tighter and less evolved than the Watervale, but will literally flower with time in bottle. **rating:** 96

➾ **best drinking** 2002 – 2010 **best vintages** '82, '86, '87, '90, '93, '94, '96, '97 **drink with** Grilled South Australian whiting • $18.95

Grosset Watervale Riesling

Made from hand-picked grapes grown on a single vineyard established on red clay over limestone at an altitude of 450 metres. It is a richer, fuller style than the Polish Hill River wine, and tends to be slightly earlier maturing. All of the recent vintages have been made bone-dry, with deliberately neutral yeast influence.

🍷🍷🍷🍷🍷 **1997** Light to medium yellow-green; vibrant lime, spice and herb aromas on the bouquet announce a wine with an almost fleshy feel in the mouth, with glorious mid to back palate weight; typically elegant, yet very long. **rating:** 96

➾ **best drinking** 2000 – 2007 **best vintages** '81, '86, '90, '93, '94, '95, '96, '97 **drink with** Thai soup • $14.95

Grosset Semillon Sauvignon Blanc

Other than the Tim Knappstein Fumé Blanc, which incorporates Lenswood fruit from the Adelaide Hills, this is by far the best example of its kind from the Clare Valley. Immaculate winemaking produces a very fine, elegant, crisp seafood style. Composed of Semillon from the Clare Valley and Sauvignon Blanc from the Adelaide Hills. Typically only 750 cases made.

🍷🍷🍷🍷🍷 **1997** Light to medium green-yellow; a perfectly weighted bouquet with gently sweet gooseberry fruit together with some passionfruit nuances is followed by a perfectly balanced wine running through sweet, honeyed Semillon and gooseberry-accented Sauvignon Blanc flavours. **rating:** 94

➾ **best drinking** 1998 – 2004 **best vintages** '93, '94, '95, '96, '97 **drink with** Shellfish • $20.95

Grosset Piccadilly Chardonnay

Since 1994 Jeffrey Grosset has sourced his Chardonnay from Piccadilly in the Adelaide Hills, and labelling it as such. In a far finer style than the preceding Clare Valley wines, and – one would imagine – a longer future. Forty per cent of the wine is taken through malolactic fermentation.

🍷🍷🍷🍷 **1996** Medium yellow-green; a mix of melon and ripe pear fruit is supported by perfectly balanced and integrated French oak. The same harmony and integration continues through on the palate, with its array of nectarine, pear and melon fruit flavours, and gently spicy oak. **rating:** 93

⇨ **best drinking** 1998 – 2003 **best vintages** '96 **drink with** Gravlax • $26

Grosset Reserve Pinot Noir

A single vineyard wine, produced from grapes grown in the Piccadilly Valley of the Adelaide Hills region. Only 150 cases were made, and another powerful testament to the winemaking skills of Jeffrey Grosset.

🍷🍷🍷🍷🍷 **1996** Full red-purple; a very intense and powerful bouquet showing whole-bunch carbonic maceration characters in the background leads into a multiflavoured palate with a mix of forest floor, tomato vine and black cherry fruit characters, not dissimilar to the great Burgundies of the Domaine de la Romanee Conti. **rating:** 94

⇨ **best drinking** 1997 – 2001 **best vintages** NA **drink with** Wild duck • NA

Grosset Gaia

A blend of 85% Cabernet Sauvignon, 10% Cabernet Franc and 5% Merlot, typically made in amounts of less than 1000 cases. Shot to stardom with the initial vintage of 1990, and has not faltered since.

🍷🍷🍷🍷🍷 **1995** Medium purple-red; the bouquet is as spotless and immaculate as ever, with wonderful blackberry/cassis fruit; the same sweet cassis/blackberry fruit is the dominant feature of a supple palate, with perfect oak handling and integration, finishing with fine, lingering tannins. **rating:** 95

⇨ **best drinking** 2000 – 2010 **best vintages** '90, '91, '92, '94, '95 **drink with** Game pie • $31.95

grove hill NR

120 Old Norton Summit Road, Norton Summit, SA 5136 **region** Adelaide Hills
phone (08) 8390 1437 **fax** (08) 8390 1437 **open** Sunday 11–5
winemaker Roman Bratasiuk (Contract) **production** 500 **est.** 1978
product range ($18–25 ML) Riesling, Chardonnay, Marguerite Pinot Chardonnay.
summary Grove Hill is situated on the site of a heritage property established in 1846 with the original homestead and outbuildings and held by the same family since that time. The wines from the 3 hectares of vineyards are made in the full-frontal (and unpredictable) style one expects from Roman Bratasiuk.

habitat NR

Old Canobolas Road, Nashdale, NSW 2800 **region** Orange
phone (02) 6365 3294 **fax** (02) 6362 3257 **open** At Ibis Wines
winemaker Phil Stevenson (Contract) **production** 120 **est.** 1989
product range Pinot Noir.
summary The Habitat vineyard is situated on the northern slope of Mount Canobolas on deep-red basalt soil at an altitude of 1100 metres, making it one of the highest – if not the highest – vineyards in Australia. In prior vintages the grapes were sold to Charles Sturt University to make sparkling (and table) wines.

haig NR

Square Mile Road, Mount Gambier, SA 5290 **region** Mount Gambier
phone (08) 8725 5414 **fax** (08) 8725 0252 **open** 7 days 11–5
winemaker Katnook (Contract) **production** 500 **est.** 1982
product range Chardonnay, Late Harvest Chardonnay, Pinot Noir, Shiraz Pinot, Fortifieds.
summary The 4 hectares of estate vineyards are planted on the rich volcanic soils near the slopes of the famous Blue Lake of Mount Gambier. I have neither seen nor tasted the wines.

hainault ★★☆

255 Walnut Road, Bickley, WA 6076 **region** Perth Hills
phone (08) 9293 8339 **fax** (08) 9293 8339 **open** Weekends
winemaker Celine Rousseau **production** 2300 **est.** 1980
product range The Terroir Range of Mount Barker Chardonnay, Bickley Vale Semillon, Pemberton Pinot Noir; also lesser-priced BV range of Unwooded Chardonnay, Sauvignon Blanc, Cabernets.
summary Perth public affairs consultant Bill Mackey and wife Vicki purchased Hainault from founder Peter Fimmel in late 1995 and have since increased plantings to almost 7 hectares, also installing Celine Rousseau, a highly credentialled French-born and trained oenologist, as winemaker. The increased production is now being actively marketed in Perth, in conjunction with Deep Dene Estate, part-owned by the Mackeys.

halcyon daze ★★★

Lot 15 Uplands Road, Lilydale, Vic 3140 **region** Yarra Valley
phone (03) 9726 7111 **fax** (03) 9726 7111 **open** By appointment
winemaker Richard Rackley **production** 250 **est.** 1982
product range ($14–30 ML) Riesling, Chardonnay, Pinot Noir, Cabernets; also Sparkling.
summary One of the lower-profile wineries with a small, estate-grown production which in fact sells the major part of its output of grapes from its 6.5 hectares of vines to others. Immaculate viticulture ensures that the grapes have a strong market.

hamelin bay ★★★★

Five Ashes Vineyard, RMB 116 McDonald Road, Karridale, WA 6288 **region** Margaret River
phone (08) 9758 6779 **fax** (08) 9758 6779 **open** By appointment
winemaker Eddie Price, Greg Tilbrook (Contract) **production** 5000 **est.** 1992
product range ($15.40–20.50 CD) Sauvignon Blanc, Semillon Sauvignon Blanc, Chardonnay, Merlot, Shiraz, Cabernet Sauvignon.
summary The 25-hectare Hamelin Bay vineyard, established by the Drake-Brockman family, has enjoyed outstanding success with its first wine releases from the 1996 and 1997 vintages. For the time being its wines are contract-made, but a winery with cellar-door sales facility is due to be opened in the year 2000.

Hamelin Bay Sauvignon Blanc

First made in 1996, but not made in 1997 (the Sauvignon Blanc was blended with Semillon in that year). Estate-grown and stainless steel fermented.

🍷🍷🍷🍷 **1996** Medium yellow-green; a quite powerful and intense bouquet with a mix of herb and grass aromas is followed by a palate with plenty of depth, the flavours running from asparagus through to gooseberry, finishing with firm authority. **rating:** 85

➯ **best drinking** 1998 – 1999 **best vintages** NA **drink with** Char-grilled octopus • $18

Hamelin Bay Semillon Sauvignon Blanc

A blend of 50% Semillon and 50% Sauvignon Blanc, with 5% barrel-fermented in American oak, the remainder in stainless steel. 1997 was the first vintage, winning a gold, two silver and two bronze medals in wine shows in 1997.

🍷🍷🍷🍷½ **1997** Medium yellow-green; a fragrant bouquet with Sauvignon Blanc the dominant partner, and providing sweet gooseberry fruit over a more grassy undertone. The palate has good balance and fruit ripeness, with Sauvignon Blanc again driving the wine. **rating:** 90

➯ **best drinking** 1998 – 1999 **best vintages** NA **drink with** Tempura • $18.10

Hamelin Bay Chardonnay

Between 25% and 50% of the wine is barrel-fermented in French oak, the remainder in stainless steel, lees contact and partial malolactic fermentation then follow. A light-bodied but well-constructed style.

🍷🍷🍷½ **1997** Medium yellow-green; a fragrant bouquet with delicate white peach and nectarine fruit together with subtle oak is replicated on the palate. Light-bodied, but the flavours and mouthfeel are pleasant. **rating:** 84

➯ **best drinking** 1998 – 1999 **best vintages** NA **drink with** Lemon chicken • $20.50

hanging rock winery ★★★☆

The Jim Jim, Jim Road, Newham, Vic 3442 **region** Macedon
phone (03) 5427 0542 **fax** (03) 5427 0310 **open** 7 days 10–5
winemaker John Ellis **production** 20 000 **est.** 1982

product range ($10–44 CD) Macedon Cuvée V, Colemans Gully Riesling, The Jim Jim Sauvignon Blanc,Victoria Semillon Sauvignon Blanc, Victoria Chardonnay, Reserve Swan Hill Chardonnay, Late Harvest Riesling, Late Harvest Gewurztraminer, Central Highlands Pinot Noir, Victoria Cabernet Merlot, Gralaine Merlot, Victoria Shiraz, Picnic Red and White.

summary The Macedon area has proved very marginal in spots, and the Hanging Rock vineyards, with their lovely vista towards the Rock, are no exception. John Ellis has thus elected to source additional grapes from various parts of Victoria, to produce an interesting and diverse style of wines. The low-priced Picnic White and Picnic Red, with the striking label, have been particularly successful.

Hanging Rock Victoria Semillon Sauvignon Blanc

A blend of Semillon grown in Geelong and the estate Jim Jim vineyard together with Sauvignon Blanc from the Strathbogie Ranges. Cool fermented and early bottled, it is by a considerable distance the best of the Victoria range released in 1998.

🍷🍷🍷🍷 **1997** Light straw-yellow; an absolutely correct and crisp tangy/minerally bouquet is followed by a crisp, clean, gently tangy palate with considerable length. A restrained but stylish wine which shows its cool-grown origins to best advantage. **rating:** 87

➯ **best drinking** 1998 – 1999 **best vintages** NA **drink with** Shellfish • $15

Hanging Rock Picnic White

The distinctive gingham check label of the Hanging Rock Picnic White and Red is an exceptional piece of label design. From time to time, the wine can be equally striking, as this Colombard/Chardonnay blend was in 1997.

1997 Light green-yellow; a lively, lifted bouquet with passionfruit aromatics is followed by an equally lively palate, with more of those passionfruit accents, and a nicely balanced flick of residual sugar. Smart winemaking. **rating:** 84

➯ **best drinking** 1998 – 1999 **best vintages** NA **drink with** Café food • $9

hankin estate NR

Johnsons Lane, Northwood via Seymour, Vic 3660 **region** Goulburn Valley
phone (03) 5792 2396 **fax** (03) 9353 2927 **open** Weekends 10–5
winemaker Dr Max Hankin **production** 1500 **est.** 1975
product range ($7–22 CD) Semillon, Sauvignon Blanc, Premium Dry White, Rosé, Shiraz, Shiraz Cabernet Malbec, Cabernet Sauvignon.
summary Hankin Wines is a strictly weekend and holiday operation for Dr Max Hankin. Intermittent tastings over the years have revealed full-bodied if somewhat rustic reds typical of the central Goulburn Valley.

hanns creek estate NR

Kentucky Road, Merricks North, Vic 3926 **region** Mornington Peninsula
phone (03) 5989 7266 **fax** (03) 5989 7500 **open** 7 days 11–5
winemaker Tony Aubrey-Slocock **production** 1500 **est.** 1987
product range ($18–25 CD) Chardonnay, Rosé, Pinot Noir, Cabernet Shiraz, Cabernet Sauvignon.
summary Denise and Tony Aubrey-Slocock have established a 3-hectare vineyard on the slopes of Merricks North. After an uncertain start, with contract-winemaking moving around, Kevin McCarthy took control, and wine-style steadied.

hanson ★★★

340 Old Healesville Road, Yarra Glen, Vic 3775 **region** Yarra Valley
phone (03) 9439 7425 **fax** (03) 9435 9183 **open** Not
winemaker Dr Ian Hanson **production** 600 **est.** 1983
product range ($19–22 ML) Pinot Noir, Cabernets, Cabernet Franc, Cabernet Sauvignon.
summary Dental surgeon Ian Hanson planted his first vines in the late 1960s close to the junction of the Yarra and Plenty Rivers; in 1983 those plantings were extended (with 3000 vines), and in 1988 the Tarrahill property at Yarra Glen was established with ten further acres. The wines all now bear the Hanson label.

happs 

Commonage Road, Dunsborough, WA 6281 **region** Margaret River
phone (08) 9755 3300 **fax** (08) 9755 3846 **open** 7 days 10–5
winemaker Erl Happ, Frank Kittler **production** 12 000 **est.** 1978
product range ($13–27 CD) Dry table wines are Classic (Semillon Chardonnay), Marrime (Semillon Chenin Blanc), Chardonnay, Margaret River Red, Shiraz, Merlot and Cabernet Merlot; sweet table wines are Fuschia, Topaz and Late Picked Verdelho; fortifieds are Fortis

(Vintage Port), 10 Year Fortis (Tawny), Garnet (from Muscat à Petit Grains), Pale Gold (White Port) and Old Bronze (Muscat). In 1994 a Preservative Free Red was also made.
summary Former schoolteacher turned potter and winemaker Erl Happ is an iconoclast and compulsive experimenter. Many of the styles he makes are very unconventional, the future likely to be even more so: the Karridale vineyard planted in 1994 has no less than 22 different varieties established. Merlot has been a winery specialty for a decade.

harcourt valley vineyards NR

Calder Highway, Harcourt, Vic 3453 **region** Bendigo
phone (03) 5474 2223 **fax** (03) 5474 2293 **open** 7 days 10–6
winemaker John Livingstone **production** 2000 **est.** 1976
product range ($12.50–25 CD) Chardonnay, Riesling, Barbara's Shiraz, Cabernet Sauvignon.
summary Traditional producer of rich, full-bodied red wines typical of the district, but sporadic (and largely outdated) tastings since ownership changed preclude evaluation. No recent tastings; however 1996 Barbara's Shiraz has won two gold and two silver medals during 1997, strongly suggesting the quality of this lovely wine has been maintained.

hardys ★★★★☆

Reynella Road, Reynella, SA 5161 **region** McLaren Vale
phone (08) 8392 2222 **fax** (08) 8392 2202 **open** 7 days 10–4.30
winemaker Peter Dawson, Stephen Pannell, Tom Newton, Ed Carr **production** NFP **est.** 1853
product range ($5.59–55 R) Starts with Old Castle Rhine Riesling, St Vincent Chablis; then McLaren Vale Hermitage, Classic Dry White; Nottage Hill Riesling, Chardonnay, Cabernet Sauvignon; then the generic Bird series, then Insignia Chardonnay Sauvignon Blanc, and Cabernet Sauvignon Shiraz, followed by Siegersdorf Chardonnay and Rhine Riesling. No Preservative Added Chardonnay and Cabernet Sauvignon are available for allergy sufferers. The Sir James range and the Bankside wines fill in the middle; at the very top Eileen Hardy Chardonnay, Shiraz and Thomas Hardy Cabernet Sauvignon. There is a full range of sparkling wines, superior quality brandies and ports including Australia's finest Vintage Port.
summary Since the 1992 merger of Thomas Hardy and the Berri Renmano group, the business has flourished, and the shareholders have profited greatly. The merged group has confounded expectations by aggressively, and very successfully, pushing the premium end of the business, making a number of acquisitions and investments across the length and breadth of Australia, all aimed at the upper end of the market. A high level of winemaking expertise and commitment has been an essential part of this success. It is basically for these wines that the winery rating is given.

Hardys Eileen Hardy Chardonnay

Prior to the release of the '94 vintage, one might have argued whether or not the wine has a sufficient track record or distinction to justify its rating as a classic, but is a more than usually elegant wine, and some of the early vintages have aged with far greater distinction than most Australian Chardonnays. However, the shift from Padthaway to a Yarra Valley base, coupled with refinements to the winemaking used, has resulted in a great wine. The difficult '95 vintage pushed Eileen Hardy back to a Padthaway, Yarra Valley and Adelaide Hills base. The even better '96 (a multiple trophy winner at the 1997 Royal Adelaide Wine Show, including the Max Schubert Trophy for Best Wine of Show) boasting an even more diverse geographic base, including the Canberra District. It added another trophy to the cabinet with The Regent Wine Trophy for the Best Previous Vintage and Older Premium White Wine at the 1998 Royal Sydney Wine Show.

🍷🍷🍷🍷🍷 **1996** Medium yellow-green; an ultra-sophisticated wine from start to finish, showing enormously skilled use of oak and malolactic fermentation to add texture and character to the peach and citrus fruit. **rating:** 95

➯ **best drinking** 1998 – 2001 **best vintages** '85, '87, '90, '91, '93, '94, '96 **drink with** Fresh Atlantic salmon • $30

Hardys Omni

A curiously named and somewhat curiously packaged non-vintage wine of unspecified varieties and unspecified regions, selling for a song and which almost inevitably attracted little attention from wine-writers and critics until in an unprecedented run it won gold medals in successive capital city wine shows in 1997 – at Brisbane, Melbourne and Adelaide respectively. The frustration of non-vintage sparkling wines is, of course, that one does not know which batch or disgorgement the wine comes from unless – as in this case – Hardy has affixed replicas of the gold medals on the label. One assumes that once the next major blend comes along, the gold medal claim will disappear. Certainly, the wine tasted was a very credible gold medal winner.

🍷🍷🍷🍷 **NV** Bright green-yellow; a clean, smooth melon and citrus bouquet, not showing much complexity of yeast autolysis characters, but bright and attractive. The palate is very crisp and clean in a Blanc de Blanc style; a polar opposite to the Sir James Vintage sparkling wine. **rating:** 87

➯ **best drinking** 1998 – 1999 **best vintages** NA **drink with** Aperitif • $8.90

Hardys Sir James Vintage

In response to Hardys ever-growing wine empire, this top of the range sparkling wine is now sourced almost entirely from the Yarra Valley and Tasmania, and knowing sparkling winemaker Ed Carr's preference for these areas, is likely to remain so in the future. A blend of Pinot Noir, Chardonnay and a little Pinot Meunier, and which spends almost three years on yeast lees. Some strong winemaker inputs are evident, not the least being the apparent adoption of higher than normal fermentation temperatures with what may be unclarified juice. Whatever be the truth, a challenging style.

🍷🍷🍷🍷🍷 **1994** Medium to full yellow-green; an extremely complex bouquet with what I can only describe as wet dog French characters. A powerful, intense and challenging wine, with unusual weight, and again some of those solids fermentation characters evident. Two bottles tasted, with identical notes. **rating:** 90

➯ **best drinking** 1998 – 1999 **best vintages** NA **drink with** Hors d'oeuvres • $21.90

Hardys Eileen Hardy Shiraz

If one includes the 1970 in the range, a wine with a proud history. As is the case with Wynns Michael Hermitage, the reincarnation bears little or no resemblance to the original model, but in common with Michael Hermitage, reflects a determination to produce the best (some would say the biggest) possible wine. A blend of Padthaway and McLaren Vale Shiraz which spends two years in French and American oak, and has been a prolific trophy and gold medal winner in wine shows in recent years.

🍷🍷🍷🍷🍷 **1995** Medium to full purple-red; a rich and full bouquet with masses of ripe black fruits, dark chocolate and some liquorice; the oak is potent, but is justified. A wine which takes no prisoners, but which has fantastic palate flavour, bursting with liquorice, black cherry/berry and spice flavours surrounded by ultra-sophisticated vanilla oak. **rating:** 95

➯ **best drinking** 2005 – 2015 **best vintages** '70, '88, '91, '93, '95 **drink with** Game pie • $54.90

Hardys Thomas Hardy Cabernet Sauvignon

First launched in 1994 when the 1989 vintage was released. Initially a blend of predominantly Coonawarra and McLaren Vale material, it is now entirely sourced from Coonawarra. The wine spends 18 months in a mix of French and American oak, and is given at least two years bottle age prior to release. A wine at the opulent end of the scale, not unlike Wynns John Riddoch in style, and a prolific trophy and gold medal winner.

1994 Medium to full red-purple; a solid, complex bouquet with a range of fruit aromas having nuances of Shiraz, even a touch of liquorice. The palate is rich and voluptuously sweet with high gloss minty berry fruit. The oak has been very well handled, playing a strong but appropriate support role. **rating:** 91

best drinking 1999 – 2006 **best vintages** '89, '90, '91, '92, '94 **drink with** Rich red meat dishes • $54.90

---

hardys (padthaway)

NR

Stonehaven Winery, Riddoch Highway, Padthaway, SA 5271 **region** Padthaway
phone (08) 8765 6140 **fax** (08) 8765 6137 **open** Not
winemaker Tom Newton, Duncan McGillivray, Robert Mann **production** NFP **est.** 1998
product range ($13.99–15.99) Unwooded Chardonnay, Cabernet Sauvignon.
summary The $18 million Stonehaven winery, the largest single new winery to be built in Australia in 20 years, was opened in March 1998. It has a capacity of 10,000 tonnes and will process all of the Hardy intake from the Limestone Coast Zone. A cellar-door and tasting facility will open in 1999.

harewood estate

'Binalong', Scotsdale Road, Denmark, WA 6333 **region** Great Southern
phone (08) 9840 9078 **fax** (08) 9840 9053 **open** By appointment
winemaker John Wade (Contract) **production** 400 **est.** 1988
product range ($28 R) Chardonnay, Pinot Noir.
summary Keith and Margie Graham have established a showpiece vineyard at Binalong. The majority of the grapes are sold to Howard Park and Domaine Chandon, but gradually increasing amounts of wine are being made under the Harewood Estate label.

Harewood Estate Chardonnay

Immaculate viticulture, with a mixture of high-tech trellis systems (Scott Henry, Smart Dyson and Geneva Double Curtain) and varied row orientation pay dividends in this lush vineyard setting. The wine is barrel-fermented and matured in French oak for ten months.

1996 Medium to full yellow-green; a powerful and complex bouquet with malolactic fermentation, barrel fermentation and toasty oak influences woven through melon and peach fruit. The palate has good mouthfeel, with toasty/nutty/creamy flavours offset by well-balanced acidity. **rating:** 89

best drinking 1998 – 2000 **best vintages** NA **drink with** Seafood risotto • $28

---

hartzview wine centre

RSD 1034 Off Cross Road, Gardners Bay, Tas 7112 **region** Southern Tasmania
phone (03) 6295 1623 **open** 7 days 9–5
winemaker Andrew Hood (Contract), Robert Patterson **production** NFP **est.** 1988

product range ($18 CD) Chardonnay, Pinot Noir; also a range of Pig and Whistle Hill fruit wines.

summary A combined wine centre offering wines from a number of local Huon Valley wineries and also newly erected and very comfortable accommodation for six people in a separate, self-contained house. Hartzview table wines (produced from 3 hectares of estate plantings) are much to be preferred to the self-produced Pig and Whistle Hill fruit wines.

haselgrove ★★★★

Foggo Road, McLaren Vale, SA 5171 **region** McLaren Vale

phone (08) 8323 8706 **fax** (08) 8323 8049 **open** Mon-Fri 9–5, weekends 10–5

winemaker Nick Haselgrove **production** 40 000 **est.** 1981

product range ($9.90–40 R) McLaren Vale Pictures Series Sauvignon Blanc, Chardonnay, Chenin Blanc, Frontignac, Grenache Shiraz, Cabernet Merlot Shiraz; Futures Shiraz; premium releases under 'H' Reserve label; Sparkling, Port; lesser priced varietals under Sovereign Series.

summary Haselgrove Wines became a wholly owned subsidiary of the publicly listed Australian Premium Wines Limited in mid-1997. Under Nick Haselgrove's direction, the premium red wines, and in particular the 'H' Reserve range, have gone from strength to strength, the 1996 'H' Reserve Shiraz winning multiple trophies, including Best Wine of Show, at the 1998 Sydney International Wine Competition (otherwise known as the 'Top 100').

Haselgrove 'H' Reserve Shiraz

There is no question this wine is often at the baroque end of the spectrum of Australian red winemaking, a wine for a winter's night and rich food, and not to be taken lightly. The '96 vintage was the top pointed gold medal in the 1996 Shiraz (Firm Finish) Class at the 1997 Liquorland National Wine Show; also winner of three trophies including the Air New Zealand Perpetual Trophy for Best Wine of Show at the 1998 Sydney International Wine Competiton.

🍷🍷🍷🍷🍷 **1996** Strong red-purple; there is beautifully balanced fruit and oak on both bouquet and palate with sweet chocolatey fruit balanced by fine milky vanilla oak and tannins on the palate. Despite all of the depth and lusciousness of the fruit, the wine has finesse to the point of delicacy. **rating:** 95

➾ **best drinking** 2002 – 2010 **best vintages** '91, '94, '96 **drink with** Eye fillet • $35

hawley vineyard NR

Hawley Beach, Hawley, Tas 7307 **region** Northern Tasmania

phone (03) 6428 6221 **fax** (03) 6428 6844 **open** 7 days

winemaker Andrew Pirie (Contract) **production** 1500 **est.** 1988

product range ($18–25 R) Rubicon Chardonnay, Unwooded Chardonnay, Rubicon Pinot Noir.

summary Hawley Vineyard overlooks Hawley Beach, and thence northeast to Bass Strait. It is established on an historic 200-hectare farming property, with Hawley House offering dining and accommodation in a grand style. There are no other vineyards in what is a unique winegrowing region, and few hoteliers-cum-viticulturists as flamboyant as owner Simon Hawley.

Hawley Vineyard Unwooded Chardonnay

Together with most other wine-writers and wine judges in Australia, I shrink at the very mention of unwooded Chardonnay, but every now and then one comes along which suggests the style has legitimacy. This is one such wine.

ΨΨΨΨ **1997** Light green-yellow; crystal clear, albeit light, melon varietal character is followed by a light, lively melon-flavoured palate. Given the terrible vintage, a first-class outcome. **rating:** 85

⇨ **best drinking** 1998 – 1999 **best vintages** NA **drink with** White-fleshed fish • NA

hay shed hill ★★★☆

RSM 398 Harmans Mill Road, Willyabrup, WA 6280 **region** Margaret River
phone (08) 9755 6234 **fax** (08) 9755 6305 **open** Weekends, Mon, Wed and holidays 10–5
winemaker Peter Stanlake **production** 8000 **est.** 1987
product range ($13–28 CD) Sauvignon Blanc, Semillon, Chardonnay, Pitchfork Pink (Rosé), Group 20 Cabernet Sauvignon (light, unwooded), Cabernet Sauvignon, Pinot Noir.
summary A landmark on the Margaret River scene, with a striking new 120-tonne winery, a carefully devised business plan by the Morrison family, energetic marketing, and innovative label design. Wine quality has been a touch inconsistent, but the 'sold-out' sign so often displayed speaks for itself. At their best, tangy and incisive.

Hay Shed Hill Pitchfork Pink

A Rosé made from unspecified varieties, but seemingly including Pinot Noir, which works brilliantly well.

ΨΨΨ **1997** Pale rose; the attractive bouquet is clean, with sweet, gentle strawberry fruit aromas. The palate is well balanced, showing similar fruit-sweet strawberry flavours; excellent acidity gives the wine focus. **rating:** 84

⇨ **best drinking** 1998 – 1999 **best vintages** NA **drink with** Summer salads • $13

hayward's whitehead creek ★★

Lot 18A Hall Lane, Seymour, Vic 3660 **region** Goulburn Valley
phone (03) 5792 3050 **open** Mon-Sat 9–6, Sun 10–6
winemaker Sid Hayward, David Hayward **production** 600 **est.** 1975
product range ($7.50–12.50 CD) Riesling, Shiraz, Cabernet Sauvignon.
summary Produces somewhat rustic wines, but with abundant character. Most of the production from the 4.5 hectares of vineyard is sold to others.

heathcote winery NR

183–185 High Street, Heathcote, Vic 3523 **region** Bendigo
phone (03) 5433 2595 **fax** (03) 5433 3081 **open** 7 days 10–6
winemaker Mark Kelly **production** 5000 **est.** 1982
product range ($19–33.50 CD) Deschamps (Chardonnay Chenin Blanc), Viognier, Seventh Horse Padthaway Chardonnay, Slaughterhouse Paddock Shiraz, Mail Coach Shiraz, Seventh Horse Bendigo Shiraz.
summary Heathcote winery was finally sold in 1997 to a grape-growing syndicate which intends to revitalise and expand the winery. No recent tastings.

heathfield ridge wines NR

Cnr Caves Road & Penola Highway, Naracoorte, SA 5271 **region** Koppamurra
phone (08) 8762 4133 **fax** (08) 8762 4133 **open** Not
winemaker Pat Tocaciu, Neil Dodderidge **production** NA **est.** 1998

product range Planned to comprise Riesling, Sauvignon Blanc, Chardonnay, Shiraz, Merlot and Cabernet Sauvignon.
summary Heathfield Ridge Wines is the major winery in the Naracoorte region. Opened in time for the 1998 vintage, its major function was a contract crush facility, but it offers full winemaking facilities for others and will also release wines under the Heathfield Ridge label.

heemskerk ★★★★

40 Baxters Road, Pipers River, Tas 7252 **region** Northern Tasmania
phone (03) 6382 7122 **fax** (03) 6382 7231 **open** Nov–Apr 10–5
winemaker Fiona West **production** 16 000 **est.** 1974
product range ($18–31 R) Riesling, Semillon Sauvignon Blanc, Chardonnay, Pinot Gris, Botrytis Riesling, Pinot Noir, Cabernet Merlot.
summary In February 1998 the ownership of Heemskerk changed once again, and it is now part of the Pipers Brook Group. It will continue as an important cellar-door site, with the probability of vineyard-linked Chardonnay and Pinot Noir being made. With the sale of the prestige Jansz Méthode Champenoise brand to Yalumba in April 1998, the sparkling wine focus of the group will be firmly placed on the Pipers Brook Méthode Champenoise released mid-1998.

Heemskerk Riesling

Together with pinot noir, riesling is the variety best suited to Tasmania's very cool climates, doing well in most vintages and in most regions.

🍷🍷🍷🍷 **1997** Light straw-yellow; the bouquet is tight and crisp, with lime/apple/citrus aromas running into more herbal/mineral characters. The palate is lively, with citrus, apple and herb flavours; good acidity and length. **rating:** 85

➾ **best drinking** 1998 – 2003 **best vintages** NA **drink with** Scallops • $18

heggies vineyard ★★★★

Heggies Range Road, Eden Valley, SA 5235 **region** Eden Valley
phone (08) 8565 3203 **fax** (08) 8565 3380 **open** Not
winemaker Simon Adams **production** 12 500 **est.** 1971
product range ($15–25 R) Riesling, Viognier, Chardonnay, Botrytis Riesling, Cabernets.
summary Heggies was the second of the high-altitude (570 metres) vineyards established by S Smith & Sons (Yalumba), with plantings on the 120-hectare former grazing property commencing in 1973. The once simple view of Heggies as a better white than red wine producer has become more complicated, with the pendulum swinging backwards and forwards according to vintage.

Heggies Riesling

The wine upon which the Heggies fame, with its ever so distinctive label, was founded. As with Pewsey Vale, hasn't always lived up to its early reputation, but the '95 (on release at the end of 1997) is a very attractive wine.

🍷🍷🍷🍷 **1995** Medium yellow-green; soft, bottle-developed toast, lime and kerosene aromas foreshadow a wine which combines bottled development with delicately toasty lemony fruit on the quite long palate. **rating:** 87

➾ **best drinking** 1998 – 2003 **best vintages** NA **drink with** Seafood salad • $16

helm's ★★★☆

Butt's Road, Murrumbateman, NSW 2582 **region** Canberra District
phone (02) 6227 5536 **fax** (02) 6227 5953 **open** Thur-Mon 10–5
winemaker Ken Helm **production** 5000 **est.** 1973
product range ($12–20 CD) Rhine Riesling Classic Dry, Spätlese Riesling, Late Harvest Riesling, Premium Dry White, Chardonnay (Non Oaked), Cabernet Merlot, Cabernet Sauvignon, Helm (Cabernet blend).
summary Ken Helm is well known as one of the more stormy petrels of the wine industry, and is an energetic promoter of his wines and of the Canberra district generally. His wines have been consistent bronze medal winners, with silvers and the occasional gold dotted here and there.

Helm's The Helm

Initially a blend of Cabernet Sauvignon and Merlot, but since 1994 a blend of Cabernet Sauvignon, Cabernet Franc and Merlot and in that year renamed 'The Helm' although it will only be released under this label if Ken Helm believes the quality justifies it.

🍷🍷🍷🍷 **1996** Medium red-purple; the bouquet is very sweet, with ripe minty, cassis fruit; there is more of that super-ripe fruit on the blackberry and cassis-flavoured palate, which finishes with subtle oak. **rating:** 84

➾ **best drinking** 2000 – 2005 **best vintages** '83, '86, '88, '90, '92, '94, '96 **drink with** Lamb fillets • $20

Helm's Cabernet Merlot

As the name suggests, a blend of Canberra District-sourced Cabernet Sauvignon and Merlot. In 1996 presented a paradoxical contrast with the flagship The Helm, for the latter seemed far riper yet had only 12 degrees alcohol, the Cabernet Merlot, a finer style, had 13 degrees alcohol. One of those tricks of nature.

🍷🍷🍷🍷 **1996** Medium red-purple; the bouquet is clean but more restrained than The Helm, with earthy berry fruit and subtle oak. A stylish wine on the palate, with blackberry, cassis and chocolate flavours, fine tannins and subtle oak. Well made. **rating:** 86

➾ **best drinking** 2000 – 2005 **best vintages** NA **drink with** Calf's liver • $16.50

henke ★★☆

175 Henke Lane, Yarck, Vic 3719 **region** Central Victorian High Country
phone (03) 5797 6277 **fax** (03) 5797 6277 **open** By appointment
winemaker Tim Miller, Caroline Miller **production** 250 **est.** 1974
product range ($11–15 CD) Shiraz, Shiraz Cabernet.
summary Produces tiny quantities of deep-coloured full-flavoured, minty red wines known only to a chosen few. Typically, a range of back vintages up to five years of age are available at cellar door.

henley park wines NR

149 Swan Street, West Swan, WA 6055 **region** Swan District
phone (08) 9296 4328 **fax** (08) 9296 1313 **open** Tues-Sun 10–5
winemaker Claus Petersen, Lisbet Petersen **production** 3500 **est.** 1935
product range ($9.95–15.95 CD) Semillon, Chenin Blanc, Classic White, Muscat Gordo Blanco (late picked), Autumn Harvest (Sauternes-style), Mousse Rosé Brut (Méthode Champenoise), Shiraz, Cabernet Sauvignon, Shiraz Cabernet Merlot, Tawny Port.

summary Henley Park, like so many Swan Valley wineries, was founded by a Yugoslav family, but is now jointly owned by Danish and Malaysian interests, a multicultural mix if ever there was one. Majority owner and winemaker Claus Petersen arrived in 1986, and had his moment of glory in 1990 when Henley Park was the Most Successful Exhibitor at the Mount Barker Wine Show. Much of the production is sold through cellar door (and exported to Denmark and Malaysia).

henschke ★★★★★

Moculta Road, Keyneton, SA 5353 **region** Eden Valley
phone (08) 8564 8223 **fax** (08) 8564 8294 **open** Mon-Fri 9–4.30, Sat 9–12, public holidays 10–3
winemaker Stephen Henschke **production** 40 000 **est.** 1868
product range ($12–150 R) From the Henschke Eden Valley sources, Sauvignon Blanc, Chardonnay, Chenin Blanc, Dry White Frontignac, Joseph Hill Gewurztraminer, Louis Semillon, Tilly's Vineyard, Julius Riesling, Keyneton Estate, Mount Edelstone Cyril Henschke Cabernet Sauvignon, Hill of Grace. From the Lenswood Vineyard in the Adelaide Hills, Green's Hill Riesling, Croft Chardonnay, Giles Pinot Noir, Abbott's Prayer Cabernet Merlot. Also Barossa Ranges Eden Valley Chardonnay.
summary Unchallenged as the best medium-sized red wine producer in Australia, and has gone from strength to strength over the past 14 years or so under the guidance of Stephen and Prue Henschke. The red wines fully capitalise on the very old, low-yielding, high-quality vines, and are superbly made with sensitive but positive use of new small oak; the same skills are evident in the white winemaking. Hill of Grace is second only to Penfolds Grange as Australia's red wine icon.

Henschke Green's Hill Riesling

In the year 1982 the Henschke family acquired a 14-hectare apple orchard at Lenswood, high in the southern end of the Adelaide Hills at an altitude of 550 metres. The first significant vintage was 1989, but production overall is limited. The Green's Hill Riesling, produced from the vineyard block which overlooks the apple orchards operated by the Green family since 1893, is a marvellous example of cool-climate Riesling, intense yet generous. The '95 vintage was the only gold medal winner in the Riesling Class at the 1996 Adelaide Hills Regional Wine Show.

🍷🍷🍷🍷 **1996** Medium yellow-green; a rich bouquet with full lime pastille fruit and a commensurately generous and rich palate with abundant fruit weight, intensity and length, the flavours falling in the same spectrum as those of the bouquet. **rating:** 86

➾ **best drinking** 1998 – 2003 **best vintages** '94, '95 **drink with** Smoked trout pâté • $20.50

Henschke Julius Eden Valley Riesling

In a distinctly different style from the Green's Hill (Adelaide Hills) Riesling, this wine having more concentration and power but arguably less fragrance. Stephen Henschke is not only a great red winemaker. He has also dared to bottle this wine with a Stelvin cap.

🍷🍷🍷🍸 **1997** Light to medium yellow-green; the bouquet is quite fragrant, with lime, citrus and strong spicy notes, the latter almost as if the wine was lightly oaked (it is not, of course). The palate is full, with tropical lime fruit, and on the heavy side. **rating:** 84

➾ **best drinking** 1998 – 2001 **best vintages** NA **drink with** Barramundi • $19.60

Henschke Croft Chardonnay

Another distinguished wine from the cool-climate Lenswood vineyards of Henschke, sitting alongside the Giles Pinot Noir.

🍷🍷🍷🍷 **1996** Medium yellow-green; a quite fragrant bouquet with tangy melon, fig and citrus fruits supported by subtle oak. The flavour builds progressively towards the back of the palate with some evidence of botrytis which does not detract unduly from the wine. **rating:** 87

⇨ **best drinking** 1998 – 2002 **best vintages** NA **drink with** Gravlax • $33.30

Henschke Lenswood Giles Pinot Noir

It seems quite certain that in the years ahead the Adelaide Hills will establish itself as a leading producer of premium Pinot Noir, and that Henschke's Lenswood Vineyard will be in the vanguard. Quite apart from anything else, the Henschkes have established a number of clones of pinot noir, including the new Burgundian clones 114 and 115.

🍷🍷🍷🍷 **1996** Medium purple-red; very ripe, fragrant cherry/strawberry fruit on the bouquet leads into a very ripe palate with some minty notes, too. A warm style, even faintly sweaty, but seems to be typical of the Lenswood region. **rating:** 84

⇨ **best drinking** 1998 – 2001 **best vintages** NA **drink with** Confit of duck • $34.60

Henschke Hill Of Grace

Made entirely from 100-year-old shiraz vines on the Hill of Grace Vineyard, planted in the late 1860s by a Henschke ancestor, Nicholas Stanitzki. Is second only to Penfolds Grange, which it rivals in terms of quality, scarcity and (almost) price. The wine has never been entered in wine shows, nor will it ever be: it has its own standards. Its soaring retail price bears testament to the public esteem in which the wine is rightly held.

🍷🍷🍷🍷🍷 **1993** Medium to full red-purple; the bouquet is essentially fruit-driven, with utterly classic varietal character showing a range of liquorice, earth and black cherry aromas supported by subtle oak. A mouthfilling and luscious wine, with wonderfully rich liquorice and dark chocolate fruit, supported by an echo of vanillin oak. A wine which comes again and again as you taste it. **rating:** 95

⇨ **best drinking** 2000 – 2010 **best vintages** '59, '61, '62, '66, '78, '82, '85, '86, '88, '90, '91, '93 **drink with** Rich casserole dishes • $150

Henschke Mount Edelstone

Made entirely from shiraz grown on the Mount Edelstone Vineyard, planted in the 1920s and acquired by Henschke in 1974, although the wine was first made (and labelled as such) in 1952. A wine of tremendous character and quality. The price is rapidly being pulled upwards by the Hill of Grace, but, here too, the wine quality justifies the price.

🍷🍷🍷🍷🍷 **1995** Medium to full red-purple; a complex bouquet, with fragrant, spice, liquorice, earth and charry oak aromas all intermingling. The palate, too, is multiflavoured, with black cherry, liquorice and charry oak flavours. Fine tannins. **rating:** 93

⇨ **best drinking** 2000 – 2007 **best vintages** '52, '56, '61, '66, '67, '78, '82, '86, '88, '90, '92, '93, '94, '95 **drink with** Beef bourguignon • $52.70

Henschke Keyneton Estate Shiraz Cabernet Malbec

Not, as the label might half suggest, a single vineyard or estate wine in the classic sense of that term, but rather a blend of 70% Shiraz, 25% Cabernet Sauvignon and 5% Malbec grown in the Eden and Barossa Valleys. It is made in the traditional Henschke fashion in open fermenters, and matured in new and used American and French oak for 12 months. It may not be the greatest of the Henschke red wines, but frequently offers the best value for money.

🍷🍷🍷🍷🍷 **1995** Medium to full red-purple; a powerful yet exceptionally smooth bouquet with dark berry and savoury/leafy aromas. The palate has flavours of blackcurrant, plum and mint, showing ripeness and sweetness; subtle oak. **rating:** 91

➪ **best drinking** 2000 – 2007 **best vintages** '82, '84, '86, '88, '90, '92, '93, '94 **drink with** Veal chops • $30.30

Henschke Abbott's Prayer Cabernet Merlot

The evocatively named Abbott's Prayer links the history, religion and pioneers of the Adelaide Hills. Right from the first vintage, this Merlot-dominant blend of Merlot, Cabernet Sauvignon and Cabernet Franc has been of exceptional quality. The '94 carried on the trophy-winning tradition, winning the trophy for Best Red Wine at the 1997 Adelaide Hills Wine Show. Unusually for Henschke, it is matured entirely in French oak.

🍷🍷🍷🍷 **1995** Medium red-purple; fragrant aromas of cedar, spice, earth and leaf are followed by a fine, but relatively light-bodied palate, without the lovely sweet fruit of the best vintages. **rating:** 85

➪ **best drinking** 1999 – 2003 **best vintages** '89, '90, '91, '92, '93, '94 **drink with** Guinea fowl in red wine sauce • $52.70

Henschke Cyril Henschke Cabernet Sauvignon

The 1978 vintage was the first release in 1980, made by Stephen Henschke in memory of his father who had died the previous year. Now a blend of 90% Cabernet Sauvignon, 5% Merlot and 5% Cabernet Franc sourced from the Eden Valley. A prolific trophy and gold medal winner at national wine shows. Undoubtedly one of the three top Henschke wines, and among the best Cabernets in Australia.

🍷🍷🍷🍷 **1995** Medium to full red-purple; the charry oak which is evident in the other Henschke '95 wines, but which seems better-suited there, seems to bite somewhat on both the bouquet and palate of this wine. The palate flavours are of mint, red berry and leaf; again, a wine which seems distinctly off the pace of the best vintages. **rating:** 86

➪ **best drinking** 2001 – 2006 **best vintages** '78, '80, '85, '86, '88, '90, '91, '92, '93, '94 **drink with** Roast lamb • $74.70

henty brook estate NR

Box 49, Dardanup, WA 6236 **region** Geographe
phone (08) 9728 1459 **fax** (08) 9728 1459 **open** Not
winemaker James Pennington (Contract) **production** NA **est.** 1994
product range Semillon, Sauvignon Blanc, Shiraz.
summary One hectare each of shiraz and sauvignon blanc, and half a hectare of semillon were planted in the spring of 1994, and are still coming into bearing. James Pennington is the contract winemaker; the first releases will follow over the next few years.

heritage farm wines NR

RMB 1005 Murray Valley Highway, Cobram, Vic 3655 **region** Goulburn Valley
phone (03) 5872 2376 **open** 7 days 9–5
winemaker Kevin Tyrrell **production** 3400 **est.** 1987

product range ($5–11 CD) Riesling and Chardonnay are the only two varietal releases; there are a considerable number of generic releases and fortified wines on sale at cellar door.

summary Heritage Farm claims to be the only vineyard and orchard in Australia still using horse power, with Clydesdales used for most of the general farm work. The winery and cellar-door area also boasts a large range of restored horse-drawn farm machinery and a bottle collection.

heritage wines ★★★☆

Seppeltsfield Road, Marananga via Tanunda, SA 5352 **region** Barossa Valley
phone (08) 8562 2880 **fax** (08) 8562 2692 **open** 7 days 11–5
winemaker Stephen Hoff **production** 6000 **est.** 1984

product range ($11.50–19 CD) Riesling, Semillon, Chardonnay, Shiraz, Cabernet Franc, Cabernet Malbec, Cabernet Sauvignon, Rosscos Shiraz.

summary A little-known winery which deserves a far wider audience, for Stephen Hoff is apt to produce some startlingly good wines. At various times the Chardonnay, Riesling (from old Clare Valley vines) and Rosscos Shiraz (now the flag-bearer) have all excelled, at other times not.

Heritage Wines Riesling

A wine which, from time to time, excels itself, as it has done in 1996. Produced from old, dry-grown Clare Valley vines.

🍷🍷🍷🍷 **1996** Medium yellow-green; the bouquet has plenty of character, with rich, toast and lime fruit in abundance. In the mouth, attractively complex with toast, lime and honey flavours, finishing with good acidity. Perhaps tastes a little older than it is, but should comfortably see the distance out. **rating:** 87

➾ **best drinking** 1998 – 2002 **best vintages** NA **drink with** Pasta with smoked salmon • $11.50

Heritage Wines Cabernet Sauvignon

Drawn in part from 1 hectare of estate plantings. Conventionally matured in a mix of new and used American oak barrels.

🍷🍷🍷🍷 **1996** Medium to full red-purple; the bouquet is full, ripe and dense with sweet blackcurrant fruit and subtle oak. A high-powered, dense and rich palate follows; there is an echo of the oak which detracts somewhat from the Shiraz of the same vintage (a curious putty character) but the fruit of the Cabernet is so strong it barely matters. **rating:** 88

➾ **best drinking** 2001 – 2006 **best vintages** NA **drink with** Barbecued beef • $15

---

heritage wines of stanthorpe ★★☆

New England Highway, Cottonvale, Qld 4375 **region** Granite Belt
phone (07) 4685 2197 **fax** (07) 4685 2112 **open** 7 days 9–5
winemaker Jim Barnes **production** 4000 **est.** 1992

product range ($10–18 CD) Semillon Chardonnay, Sauvignon Blanc, Classic White (Chardonnay Semillon Sauvignon Blanc), Traminer Riesling, Chardonnay, Light Friendly Red, Shiraz, Cabernet Sauvignon, Fortified and flavoured wines.

summary A tourist-oriented venture, as are many of the Stanthorpe region wineries, established in a painstakingly restored cool-storage shed. The estate plantings comprise chardonnay (2 hectares), merlot (2 hectares), shiraz (1 hectare) and cabernet sauvignon (1 hectare).

hermitage road wines 

Hermitage Road, Pokolbin, NSW 2321 **region** Lower Hunter Valley
phone (02) 9518 9212 **fax** (02) 9518 9212 **open** 7 days 10–5
winemaker Peter Hall **production** 10 000 **est.** 1997
product range ($14–20 R) Varietal Sauvignon Blanc, Chardonnay, Merlot; Reserve Semillon, Chardonnay Shiraz.
summary Hermitage Road is a stand-alone product produced at the Hunter Ridge winery of Brian McGuigan and launched in 1997. Distribution is through restaurants, hotels and fine wine retailers. I have to admit to being very pleasantly surprised by the quality of the wines, some of which are Hunter Valley based, others coming from various parts of southeastern Australia.

Hermitage Road Reserve Semillon

Produced from grapes grown on the Somerset Vineyard in Oakey Creek Road, with a yield of between 2 and 3 tonnes per acre. Cold fermented in stainless steel at 14 degrees for two weeks. The '97 vintage was picked mid-January, prior to the vintage rain.

1997 Medium yellow-green; clean, classic, powerful semillon aromas with a mix of lemon, mineral and herb lead into a palate with considerable length and power, with citrussy undertones. **rating:** 85

best drinking 2002 – 2007 **best vintages** NA **drink with** Flathead fillets • $20

---

herons rise vineyard NR

Saddle Road, Kettering, Tas 7155 **region** Southern Tasmania
phone (03) 6267 4339 **fax** (03) 6267 4245 **open** By appointment
winemaker Andrew Hood **production** 300 **est.** 1984
product range ($12.50–20 CD) Dry White, Pinot Noir.
summary Sue and Gerry White run a small stone country guesthouse in the D'Entrecasteaux Channel area, and basically sell the wines produced from the surrounding 1 hectare of vineyard to those staying at the guesthouse. The postal address for bookings is PO Box 271, Kettering, Tas 7155.

hickinbotham NR

Cnr Wallaces Road and Nepean Highway, Dromana, Vic 3936 **region** Mornington Peninsula
phone (03) 5981 0355 **fax** (03) 5981 0355 **open** 7 days
winemaker Andrew Hickinbotham **production** 6000 **est.** 1981
product range ($15–26 CD) King Valley Riesling, Chardonnay, Classic White, Taminga, Sparkling (Strawberry Kiss and Futures), Pinot Noir, Merlot, Shiraz, Cabernets.
summary After a peripatetic period, and a hiatus in winemaking, Hickinbotham established a permanent vineyard and winery base at Dromana. It now makes only Mornington Peninsula wines, drawing in part on 10 hectares of estate vineyards, and in part on contract-grown fruit. No recent tastings.

highbank NR

Main Penola-Naracoorte Road, Coonawarra, SA 5263 **region** Coonawarra
phone (08) 8736 3311 **open** Holidays and weekends 10–5
winemaker Dennis Vice, Trevor Mast **production** 700 **est.** 1986
product range ($20–25 CD) Chardonnay, Basket Pressed Cabernet Blend.

summary Mount Gambier lecturer in viticulture Dennis Vice makes a tiny quantity of smooth, melon-accented Chardonnay and stylish Coonawarra Cabernet blend of good quality which are sold through local restaurants and cellar door, with limited Melbourne distribution. No recent tastings; much of the fruit from the 4 hectares of vineyard is sold to other producers.

highland heritage estate ★★★☆

Mitchell Highway, Orange, NSW 2800 **region** Orange
phone (02) 6361 3612 **fax** (02) 6361 3613 **open** Mon–Fri 9–3, weekends 9–5
winemaker John Hordern, Rex D'Aquino **production** 3500 **est.** 1984
product range ($10–30 CD) Under the Mount Canobolas label: Chardonnay, Sauvignon Blanc, Pinot Noir; Gosling Creek Chardonnay; and the newly released Wellwood Estate label.
summary The estate plantings have increased from 4 hectares to over 15 hectares, with new plantings in 1995 and 1997 to come into full production by 2001. The tasting facility is unusual: a converted railway carriage overlooking the vineyard.

highway wines NR

Great Northern Highway, Herne Hill, WA 6056 **region** Swan District
phone (08) 9294 4354 **open** Mon–Sat 8.30–6
winemaker Tony Bakranich **production** 4000 **est.** 1954
product range ($5–14.50 CD) Exclusively Fortified wines, of which 20 are available, including six different styles of Sherry, six Muscats, three Ports, and so forth.
summary A survivor of another era, when literally dozens of such wineries plied their business in the Swan Valley. It still enjoys a strong local trade, selling much of its wine in fill-your-own-containers, and 2-litre flagons, with lesser quantities sold by the bottle.

hill of hope NR

Cobcroft Road, Broke, NSW 2330 **region** Lower Hunter Valley
phone (02) 6579 1102 **fax** (02) 6579 1267 **open** 7 days 10–5
winemaker Contract **production** NA **est.** 1996
product range Verdelho, Unwooded Chardonnay, Chardonnay, Blanc de Noir, Cabernet Merlot.
summary The Hill of Hope is the reborn Saxonvale Winery purchased by Michael Hope, a Broke/Fordwich grape grower. It is now a major contract crush facility for numerous small Hunter Valley vineyards. A small amount of wine is made under Hill of Hope's own label.

hill-smith estate

c/o Yalumba Winery, Angaston, SA 5353 **region** Eden Valley
phone (08) 8561 3200 **fax** (08) 8561 3393 **open** Not
winemaker Robert Hill-Smith **production** 6000 **est.** 1973
product range ($16 R) Sauvignon Blanc, Chardonnay.
summary Part of the Yalumba stable, drawing upon its own estate plantings comprising 23 hectares of chardonnay and sauvignon blanc. Over the years, has produced some excellent wines, but quality does seem to vary significantly with vintage, and the winery rating is a compromise between the best and the least.

hillstowe ★★★★

104 Main Road, Hahndorf, SA 5245 **region** Adelaide Hills
phone (08) 8388 1400 **fax** (08) 8388 1411 **open** 7 days 10–5
winemaker Chris Laurie **production** 12 000 **est.** 1980
product range ($14–32 R) A range of vineyard and varietal-designated wines of ascending price and quality, being Buxton McLaren Vale Sauvignon Blanc, Buxton Sauvignon Blanc, Chardonnay, Buxton Shiraz, Buxton Cabernet Merlot; and at the top end Adelaide Hills Udy's Mill Chardonnay, Adelaide Hills Carey Gully Pinot Noir, Yarra Valley Hoddles Pinot Noir.
summary Founded by renowned viticulturist David Paxton and Chris Laurie, but now owned by the latter, and employing the contract-winemaking skills of Martin Shaw, drawing upon vineyard sources in varying regimes of soil and climate of the Adelaide Hills and McLaren Vale respectively, all to great effect. Subtlety and elegance are the keywords here.

Hillstowe Buxton Chardonnay

Produced from Hillstowe's Buxton Vineyard established on alluvial flats in the heart of McLaren Vale, and typically released with two to three years bottle age.

🍷🍷🍷🍷 **1996** Bright yellow-green; the bouquet is clean, with ample buttery/peachy fruit and subtle oak. The rounded palate has less length than the Udy's Mill Chardonnay, but has plenty of honest peachy/buttery flavour, and minimal oak. **rating:** 85

➪ **best drinking** 1998 – 1999 **best vintages** NA **drink with** Gnocchi • $16

Hillstowe Udy's Mill Chardonnay

Produced from 3.2 hectares of chardonnay grown in the Carey Gully subdistrict of the Adelaide Hills, adjacent to McLaren Vale. The climate is distinctly cooler, the grapes harvested later, and clearly reflect the climate. The '92 vintage had spectacular international show success at the 1994 Los Angeles New World International Wine Competition.

🍷🍷🍷🍷 **1996** Medium yellow-green; a quite complex and tangy bouquet with some citrus notes together with cashew and barrel-ferment characters. The palate, likewise, shows tangy citrus/melon/grapefruit flavours running through to a long finish. **rating:** 88

➪ **best drinking** 1999 – 2003 **best vintages** '90, '92, '93, '95, '96 **drink with** Trout or salmon mousse • $28

Hillstowe Buxton Shiraz

The Buxton Vineyard produces both Cabernet Merlot and Shiraz for Hillstowe; in line with the overall profile of McLaren Vale, the Buxton Shiraz is the more reliable wine of the two.

🍷🍷🍷🍷🍷 **1996** Medium to full red-purple; a rich and full bouquet with the promise of luscious dark berry, plum and chocolate fruit is fulfilled on the palate, which shows strong regional fruit varietal character framed with supple, sweet American oak. Delicious. **rating:** 92

➪ **best drinking** 2000 – 2010 **best vintages** '90, '91, '96 **drink with** Steak and kidney pie • $26

---

hjt vineyards NR

Keenan Road, Glenrowan, Vic 3675 **region** Glenrowan
phone (03) 5766 2252 **fax** (03) 5765 3260 **open** Fri, Sat, 10–5 and Sunday during school holidays
winemaker Wendy Tinson **production** 1200 **est.** 1979

product range ($11.50–17.50 CD) A varietal range, with occasional use of bin numbers denoting winemaking approaches, Bin 4 being more delicate, Bin 19 fuller-bodied. Wines include Riesling Bins 4 and 19, Chardonnay, Chenin Blanc Bin 19, Late Picked Riesling, Pinot Noir, Cabernet Pinot, Shiraz, Cabernet Sauvignon, Merlot, Tawny Port.
summary Founded by the late Harry Tinson after he left Baileys after a long and illustrious stewardship, and now run by his daughter Wendy Tinson, with tiny production all sold from the cellar door.

hoffmann's NR

Ingoldby Road, McLaren Flat, SA 5171 **region** McLaren Vale
phone (08) 8383 0232 **fax** (08) 8383 0232 **open** 7 days 10–5
winemaker Nick Holmes (Consultant) **production** 500 **est.** 1996
product range ($12–15 CD) Chardonnay, Shiraz, Cabernet Sauvignon.
summary Peter and Anthea Hoffman have been growing grapes at their property in Ingoldby Road since 1978, and Peter Hoffman has worked at various wineries in McLaren Vale since 1979. Both he and Anthea have undertaken courses at the Regency TAFE Institute in Adelaide, and (in Peter Hoffman's words) 'in 1996 we decided that we knew a little about winemaking and opened a small cellar door'. Only small quantities of wine are made for the Hoffman's label; the balance of the production is sold to Mildara Blass (for the Ingoldby label).

hollick

Riddoch Highway, Coonawarra, SA 5263 **region** Coonawarra
phone (08) 8737 2318 **fax** (08) 8737 2952 **open** 7 days 9–5
winemaker Ian Hollick, Matt Pellew **production** 35 000 **est.** 1983
product range ($12–50 R) A very disciplined array of products with Sauvignon Blanc Semillon, Unoaked Chardonnay and Shiraz Cabernet Malbec at the lower end of the price range; Reserve Chardonnay and Cabernet Sauvignon Merlot in the middle, along with Sparkling Merlot; Ravenswood, the deluxe Cabernet Sauvignon at the top end. Also small range of limited cellar-door releases.
summary Hollick has, if it were possible, added to the reputation of Coonawarra since it released its first wines in the mid-1980s. Winner of many trophies (including the most famous of all, the Jimmy Watson), its wines are well crafted and competitively priced, although sometimes a little on the light side.

Hollick Ravenswood

This is the super-premium wine from Hollick, made entirely from Cabernet Sauvignon. Invariably good, sometimes outstanding. First made in 1988, and without any question, scrupulously selected from the very best material available from the estate vineyards. Hollick Ravenswood is much more concentrated, rich and powerful than the other Hollick reds, and is immaculately made.

1994 Medium to full red-purple; the bouquet is solid and sweet, with chocolatey, blackberry fruit supported by sweet oak. The palate is almost dense, with dark chocolate, blackberry, mulberry and a touch of earth; good tannin structure. **rating:** 90

➾ **best drinking** 1999 – 2005 **best vintages** '88, '90, '91, '93, '94 **drink with** Scotch fillet • $47.35

hollyclare NR

Lot 6 Milbrodale Road, Broke, NSW 2330 **region** Lower Hunter Valley
phone (02) 6579 1193 **fax** (02) 6579 1269 **open** Weekends 10–5
winemaker Tamburlaine (Contract) **production** 1200 **est.** 1987
product range ($11–13.50 CD) Chardonnay, Unoaked Chardonnay, Chardonnay Semillon, Semillon, Shiraz.
summary John Holdsworth established the Hollyclare Vineyard (now totalling 3 hectares of chardonnay, semillon and shiraz) ten years ago, but the Hollyclare label is a relatively new one on the market. While the wines are made under contract at Tamburlaine, Hollyclare has its own dedicated wine tanks and all of the wines are estate-grown.

holm oak ★★★☆

RSD 256 Rowella, West Tamar, Tas 7270 **region** Northern Tasmania
phone (03) 6394 7577 **fax** (03) 6394 7350 **open** 7 days 12–5
winemaker Nick Butler **production** 1800 **est.** 1983
product range ($18.50 R) Pinot Noir Chardonnay (still table wine), Pinot Noir, Cabernet Sauvignon.
summary The Butler family produces tremendously rich and strongly flavoured red wines from the vineyard on the banks of the Tamar River, and which takes its name from the grove of oak trees planted around the turn of the century and originally intended for the making of tennis racquets. Along with Marion's Vineyard, this section of the Tamar Valley may even be too warm for Pinot Noir; certainly it is best suited to Cabernet Sauvignon and Chardonnay.

honeytree estate NR

16 Gillards Road, Pokolbin, NSW 2321 **region** Lower Hunter Valley
phone (02) 4998 7693 **fax** (02) 4998 7693 **open** Fri–Mon 10–5
winemaker Garry Reid, Greg Silkman **production** 2400 **est.** 1970
product range ($16–22 CD) Semillon, Semillon Chardonnay, Clairette (white), Shiraz, Cabernet Sauvignon.
summary The Honeytree Estate vineyard was first planted in 1970, and for a period of time wines were produced under the Honeytree Estate label. It then disappeared, but has since been revived, making a conspicuous return by winning a gold medal and trophy at the 1997 Hunter Valley Boutique Winemakers Show with its 1996 Semillon.

Honeytree Estate Semillon

A classic Hunter Semillon, in large measure reflecting the maturity of the vines, now approaching 30 years of age.

🍷🍷🍷🍷 **1996** Light to medium yellow-green; the bouquet is firm, crisp and clean, with classic youthful herbaceous semillon aromas; the palate likewise delicate, clean and crisp with perfectly balanced lemony fruit and acid. Still a baby. **rating:** 87

⇨ **best drinking** 2001 – 2010 **best vintages** NA **drink with** Thai chicken • $19

hoppers hill vineyards NR

Googodery Road, Cumnock, NSW 2867 **region** Other Wineries of NSW
phone (02) 6367 7270 **open** Weekends 11–5
winemaker Robert Gilmore **production** NFP **est.** 1990

product range ($10–12 CD) Chardonnay, Sauvignon Blanc, Dry White, Cabernet Franc Merlot, Cabernet Sauvignon.

summary The Gilmores planted their vineyard in 1980, using organic growing methods and using no preservatives or filtration in the winery which was established in 1990. Not surprisingly, the wines cannot be judged or assessed against normal standards, but may have appeal in a niche market.

horseshoe vineyard NR

Horseshoe Road, Horseshoe Valley via Denman, NSW 2328 **region** Upper Hunter Valley
phone (02) 6547 3528 **open** Weekends 9–5
winemaker John Hordern **production** NFP **est.** 1986

product range ($13–18 CD) Classic Hunter Semillon, Chardonnay Semillon, Chardonnay, Pinot Noir.

summary Seems to have fallen by the wayside after its wonderful start in 1986, with rich, full-flavoured, barrel-fermented Semillons and Chardonnays. The '87 Semillon was exhibited in the Museum Class at the 1996 Hunter Valley Wine Show and was still drinking beautifully, winning a strong silver medal. Younger vintages do not have the same magic.

hotham valley estate ★★★★

South Wandering Road, Wandering, WA 6308 **region** Other Wineries of WA
phone (08) 9884 1525 **fax** (08) 9884 1079 **open** By appointment
winemaker James Pennington, Garry Baldwin (Consultant) **production** 7000 **est.** 1987

product range ($12–18 CD) Semillon, Chenin Blanc, Classic Dry White, Chardonnay, Cabernets.

summary An impressive newcomer to the scene, situated in a region of its own making, 120 kilometres southeast of Perth. It has a continental climate with cold winters and hot summer days, but cool nights, tempered by the altitude of 350 metres. Some exceptionally good wines have been made by former science teacher and now Charles Sturt University graduate James Pennington, on whose family property Hotham Valley Estate is established, albeit by way of a subdivision with outside investment. A state-of-the-art winery was built in 1993. James Pennington has also created considerable interest with a patented development of oak treatment using sandalwood.

houghton ★★★★★

Dale Road, Middle Swan, WA 6056 **region** Swan District
phone (08) 9274 5100 **fax** (08) 9274 5372 **open** 7 days 10–5
winemaker Paul Lapsley, John Griffiths **production** 300 000 **est.** 1836

product range ($8.99–45 R) At the bottom end come the Wildflower Ridge range; then White Burgundy, Chablis, Frankland River Riesling, Semillon Sauvignon Blanc, Cabernet Sauvignon are the basic wines; next the Crofters range introduced in 1996; at the top end Gold Reserve Verdelho, Chardonnay and Cabernet Sauvignon with occasional special releases of aged Show Reserve wines including White Burgundy, Riesling and Verdelho, always of high quality. Finally, the super-premium Jack Mann (a Cabernet blend) was introduced in July 1997.

summary The five-star rating may seem extreme, but is very deliberate and is in no small measure justified by Houghton White Burgundy, one of Australia's largest selling white wines, almost entirely consumed within days of purchase, but which is superlative with seven or so years bottle age. To borrow a phrase of the late Jack Mann, 'There are no bad wines here'. Paul Lapsley's abundant winemaking skills have brought the Jack Mann red and the Houghton Reserve Shiraz to the very forefront of Australian wine quality.

Houghton Frankland River Riesling

Produced from Houghton's large Frankland River vineyard, and typically has a somewhat unusual passionfruit aroma, which puts it apart from many more conventional Rieslings.

🍷🍷🍷🍷 **1997** Light yellow-green; a crisp, light but fragrant passionfruit-accented bouquet leads into a spotlessly clean, delicate and crisp palate. There isn't a lot of flesh or weight here but I find the filigreed delicacy attractive. **rating:** 86

⇨ **best drinking** 1998 – 2000 **best vintages** NA **drink with** Salad • $10.95

Houghton Show Reserve Riesling

One of the quartet of Show Reserve white wines released in 1997, and the best of an outstanding bunch. Produced from grapes grown on Houghton's Frankland River vineyard, and has amassed four trophies and six gold medals in an extremely distinguished show career.

🍷🍷🍷🍷🍷 **1991** Medium to full yellow-green; the bouquet shows the full expression of mature Riesling, with caressing aromas of honey and lime. The palate is packed with flavour, and then progressing through the honey and lime characters of the bouquet on a lingering finish. **rating:** 94

⇨ **best drinking** 1997 – 2000 **best vintages** NA **drink with** Avocado salad • $11.95

Houghton Crofters Semillon Sauvignon Blanc

The Crofters range of wines was first released in 1996. The name comes from the historic Houghton homestead built in 1863 by Dr John Fergusson and which resembles a Scottish 'crofters' farmhouse. This particular wine is sourced from the Margaret River and Frankland regions; a blend of 50% Semillon and 50% Sauvignon Blanc, with the Semillon component barrel-fermented in new French oak and given three months lees contact.

🍷🍷🍷½ **1997** Light to medium yellow-green; the bouquet is of light to medium intensity, with passionfruit and a touch of gooseberry augmented by light spicy oak. The palate is neither long nor particularly intense, but is clean, with pleasant, nicely balanced fruit and oak flavours. **rating:** 84

⇨ **best drinking** 1998 – 1999 **best vintages** '96 **drink with** Lemon chicken • $15.90

Houghton Jack Mann

Released in July 1997 in honour of the late, great Jack Mann. It is a blend of Cabernet Sauvignon, Malbec and Shiraz primarily sourced from Houghton's Frankland River vineyard, with a lesser component from the Mount Barker Omrah vineyard. It spent two years in a mix of Nevers and Allier French oak; I suspect the cooper was Dargaud & Jaegle. An absolutely superb wine in every respect.

🍷🍷🍷🍷🍷 **1994** Medium to full purple-red; the bouquet and the palate both show marvellously handled, balanced and integrated oak seamlessly woven through the wine. There are aromas of plum and mulberry in the background, but with cedar, vanilla and spice to balance that fruit. It is on the palate that the wine shows its ultimate class, with those fine-grained supple tannins which are almost sweet, or creamy, and which invite mouthful after mouthful. **rating:** 95

⇨ **best drinking** 2000 – 2015 **best vintages** '94 **drink with** Fillet of lamb • $45

Houghton Crofters Cabernet Merlot

A blend of Cabernet Sauvignon and Merlot drawn from the Margaret and Frankland River regions, but with no percentages specified in either instance. The wine is matured for 16 months in a mix of new and one-year-old French oak barriques, and the inaugural release (from the 1994 vintage) won three gold medals, the '95 following in its footsteps with a gold medal at the 1997 Sydney Wine Show.

ΨΨΨΨ **1996** Medium to full red-purple; there is attractive blackberry fruit on the quite intense and complex bouquet also showing lots of sweet oak. Youthful and fresh in the mouth, with cassis and mint fruit together with soft tannins. **rating:** 87

⇨ **best drinking** 2000 – 2004 **best vintages** '94, '95 **drink with** Kangaroo • $21.90

howard park ★★★★★

Lot 377 Scotsdale Road, Denmark, WA 6333 **region** Great Southern
phone (08) 9848 2345 **fax** (08) 9848 2064 **open** 7 days 9–4
winemaker John Wade, Michael Kerrigan **production** 30 000 **est.** 1986
product range ($17–60 R) Madfish Bay Premium Dry White and Red provide low-priced volume; limited quantities of Howard Park Riesling, Chardonnay and Cabernet Merlot.
summary John Wade, one of the most talented winemakers in Western Australia, is poised on the edge of a new venture; he has joined forces with Jeff and Amy Burch to build a winery near Denmark (Mount Shadforth Drive) which will make the Howard Park and Madfish Bay wines, but also act as contract winemaker to a dozen Great Southern vignerons. It will be a singularly important centre of winemaking for the region. The crystal pure Riesling is one of the three best in Australia, the Cabernet Merlot likewise in vintages such as 1994.

Howard Park Riesling

First made in 1986, and in my view the greatest Riesling made in the Great Southern region, itself home of many of Australia's finest examples of the style. It ages superbly, the '86 still with years in front of it.

ΨΨΨΨΨ **1997** Light to medium yellow-green; pristine, lime-accented varietal riesling fruit aromas announce a wine which is on a plane all of its own, immaculately elegant and pure, yet intense. The flavours are predominantly lime, with a hint of pear, the finish crisp but lingering. **rating:** 97

⇨ **best drinking** 2000 – 2010 **best vintages** '86, '87, '88, '91, '93, '94, '95, '96, '97 **drink with** Fresh asparagus, Asian seafood • $22

Howard Park Chardonnay

John Wade long resisted the temptation to make a Chardonnay, arguing that he was not happy to do so until he was assured of grapes of the highest quality. In 1993 he realised that a component of Madfish Bay met his requirements, and the wine was made from a blend of 50% Chardonnay grown in the Denmark area, and 50% at Pemberton. In subsequent vintages the sources have varied according to the quality of the available material.

ΨΨΨΨΨ **1996** Medium yellow-green; a beautifully crafted wine from start to finish, with fine melon/grapefruit aromas backed up by the sophisticated use of high-quality French oak on the bouquet. A fine, long, supple palate with powerful fruit (the wine has 14 degrees alcohol) is similarly surrounded by gently spiced oak. Retasted October '97; retains delicacy, and unquestionably headed for a long life. **rating:** 95

⇨ **best drinking** 1998 – 2004 **best vintages** '93, '94, '95, '96 **drink with** Pan-fried veal • $35

Howard Park Cabernet Merlot

Like the Riesling, first made in 1986. The regional and varietal mix has changed a little over the years, with the Cabernet component ranging from between 70% and 85% and the wine being labelled Cabernet Merlot. Always a great wine, it hit new heights in 1994, placing it in the top half-dozen red wines in the country, slipping in '95.

🍷🍷🍷🍷 **1995** Medium to full red-purple; from this point on I have real problems with the wine. Like the curate's egg, it is great in parts, but not others. The 'others' derive from the degree of what is euphemistically called lift and technically called volatile acidity. There are wonderful dark berry and dark chocolate flavours together with that sweet, cedary oak, but I cannot help but notice the volatility. Others may be less pedantic. **rating:** 89

➾ **best drinking** 1998 – 2003 **best vintages** '86, '88, '89, '90, '92, '93, '94 **drink with** Lamb fillets, mature cheddar • $60

hugh hamilton ★★★☆

Recreation Road, McLaren Vale, SA 5171 **region** McLaren Vale
phone (08) 8323 8689 **fax** (08) 8323 9488 **open** Not
winemaker Hugh Hamilton **production** 6500 **est.** 1992
product range ($12–19 R) Chenin Blanc, Unwooded Chardonnay, Shiraz, Merlot, Cabernet Sauvignon, Sparkling Shiraz.
summary Hugh Hamilton is a member of the famous Hamilton winemaking family, there being an intensely (and well-known) competitive spirit existing between those various members – notably between Richard and Hugh – which can only be good for the consumer.

hugo 

Elliott Road, McLaren Flat, SA 5171 **region** McLaren Vale
phone (08) 8383 0098 **fax** (08) 8383 0446 **open** Sun-Fri 10.30–5, Sat 12–5
winemaker John Hugo **production** 8000 **est.** 1982
product range ($9.50–14.50 CD) Riesling, Sauvignon Blanc, Chardonnay, Unwooded Chardonnay, Shiraz, Cabernet Sauvignon, Port.
summary A winery which came from relative obscurity to prominence in the late 1980s with some lovely ripe, sweet reds which, while strongly American oak influenced, were quite outstanding. Subsequent red releases have continued in the same style, albeit slightly less exciting.

hungerford hill 

McDonalds Road, Pokolbin, NSW 2321 **region** Lower Hunter Valley
phone (02) 4998 7666 **fax** (02) 4998 7682 **open** Mon-Fri 9–4.30, weekends 10–4.30
winemaker Ian Walsh **production** 20 000 **est.** 1967
product range ($7–20 R) Tumbarumba Chardonnay, Tumbarumba Sauvignon Blanc, Cowra Chardonnay, Young Semillon, Hunter Valley Semillon Chardonnay, Show Reserve Chardonnay, Griffith Botrytis Semillon, Cabernet Merlot, Shiraz, Show Reserve Shiraz, Young/Cowra Cabernet Sauvignon.
summary Now purely a brand owned by Southcorp, with the wines being made at Tulloch. However, eye-catching new labels and a new range of regionally sourced wines (all from New South Wales) have substantially elevated the status of the brand on the ever parochial Sydney market and raised wine quality to a significant degree. It should be noted that since 1997 I have had some responsibilities for this brand.

Hungerford Hill Tumbarumba Chardonnay

A new arrival among the dazzling Hungerford Hill labels (and choices) but does fit neatly alongside the highly regarded Tumbarumba Sauvignon Blanc. With vineyards ranging between 580 and 850 metres, high in the Snowy Mountains, this is true cool-country Chardonnay which has happily received subtle oak treatment.

ΥΥΥΥ **1996** Medium yellow-green; delicate, crisp melon and fig fruit is supported by subtle oak on both bouquet and palate. The flavours are in the spectrum one would expect, veering between citrus and melon, and the wine likewise has the length of finish provided by naturally high acidity. **rating:** 88

⇨ **best drinking** 1998 – 2002 **best vintages** NA **drink with** Mussels • $20

hunt's foxhaven estate NR

Canal Rocks Road, Yallingup, WA 6282 **region** Margaret River
phone (08) 9755 2232 **fax** (08) 9255 2249 **open** Weekends, holidays 11–5
winemaker David Hunt **production** 500 **est.** 1978
product range ($12–15 CD) Riesling (dry and sweet), Semillon, Semillon Sauvignon Blanc, Sauvignon Blanc Riesling, Cabernet Sauvignon.
summary Draws upon 4 hectares of vines progressively established, the oldest being 20-year-old riesling. No recent tastings.

hunter ridge NR

Hermitage Road, Pokolbin, NSW 2320 **region** Lower Hunter Valley
phone (02) 4998 7500 **fax** (02) 4998 7211 **open** 7 days 10–5
winemaker Stephen Pannell, Emma Requin **production** NFP **est.** 1996
product range ($12.95 R) Semillon, Verdelho, Chardonnay, Shiraz.
summary Hunter Ridge is effectively a joint venture between BRL Hardy and McGuigan Wines Limited. The grapes come from the vineyards surrounding the Hunter Ridge cellar door and which are owned by McGuigan Wines. The wines are fermented and partially matured in the Hunter Valley, but are finally blended, finished and bottled by BRL Hardy in South Australia.

huntington estate ★★★★☆

Cassilis Road, Mudgee, NSW 2850 **region** Mudgee
phone (02) 6373 3825 **fax** (02) 6373 3730 **open** Mon-Fri 9–5, weekends 10–4
winemaker Susan Roberts **production** 20 000 **est.** 1969
product range ($10–24 CD) Semillon, Semillon Chardonnay, Chardonnay Non Wooded, Rosé, sundry sweet whites; red wines are released under bin numbers (FB = full-bodied, MB = medium-bodied) comprising Shiraz, Cabernet Merlot and Cabernet Sauvignon.
summary The remarkable Roberts family members have a passion for wine which is equalled only by their passion for music, with the Huntington Music Festival a major annual event. The red wines of Huntington Estate are outstanding, and sell for absurdly low prices.

Huntington Estate Shiraz

In very much the same style and quality class as the Cabernet Sauvignon, made from estate-grown grapes and producing wines of great longevity. As the wines age, cherry/berry fruits gradually soften and take on that typically, gently earthy Shiraz character, and the tannins soften at the same rate as the fruit rounds off and develops. Thus the balance of the wine is never threatened, and patience is rewarded.

ΥΥΥΥΥ **1995** Bin FB29. Strong, bright full purple-red; the bouquet is rich and powerful, with strong dark berry and earth fruit, the palate youthful and concentrated, with tightly constructed dark fruit flavours and good acidity. **rating:** 94

⇨ **best drinking** 2000 – 2015 **best vintages** '74, '75, '78, '79, '84, '90, '91, '93, '94, '95 **drink with** Kangaroo fillet • $14

Huntington Estate Special Reserve Shiraz

Small parcels of wine which Susan Roberts considers to be specially ageworthy are held back for release several years after the varietal releases, themselves given more bottle age than most.

🍷🍷🍷🍷🍷 **1993** Bin FB29. Medium to full red-purple; the bouquet is complex and concentrated with rich, dark berry/dark chocolate fruit, just starting to show a touch of softening. The palate is redolent of plum, chocolate and black cherry fruit, with the first sign of the earthy regional characters which will build as the wine slowly ages. **rating:** 95

➯ **best drinking** 1999 – 2013 **best vintages** '93 **drink with** Venison • $24

Huntington Estate Cabernet Sauvignon

As with all of the Huntington Estate wines, made entirely from estate-grown grapes. Yields are low, and the fruit is tremendously powerful and concentrated, producing wines which age slowly but majestically. There is no particular artifice in the making, with American oak playing a minor role.

🍷🍷🍷🍷🍷 **1995** Bin FB30. Medium red-purple; as one would expect, there is pronounced varietal character in an earthy blackberry spectrum; overall of light to medium intensity. The palate, too, shows firm varietal cabernet fruit, with sweet flavours coming through on the mid to back palate before firm tannins stiffen up the finish. Subtle oak. **rating:** 90

➯ **best drinking** 2000 – 2010 **best vintages** '74, '79, '81, '84, '89, '90, '94, '95 **drink with** Grilled rump steak • $14

huntleigh vineyards ★★☆

Tunnecliffes Lane, Heathcote, Vic 3523 **region** Bendigo
phone (03) 5433 2795 **open** 7 days 10–5.30
winemaker Leigh Hunt **production** 425 **est.** 1975
product range ($10–14 CD) Riesling, Traminer, Shiraz, Cabernet Sauvignon; Leckie Shiraz.
summary A retirement hobby, with robust, rather astringent red wines which need time in bottle to lose some of the rough edges. Part of the production from the 5.2 hectares of vines is sold to others.

ibis wines NR

Kearneys Drive, Orange, NSW 2800 **region** Orange
phone (02) 6362 3257 **fax** (02) 6362 3257 **open** Weekends 12–5
winemaker Phil Stevenson **production** 500 **est.** 1988
product range ($14–22 CD) Riesling, Chardonnay, Pinot Noir, Cabernet Sauvignon, Cabernet Franc.
summary Phil Stevenson constructed a small winery in 1995, but his winemaking in fact extends back to 1993. He also acts as winemaker for Habitat. Ibis production comes from 1 hectare of estate plantings, half of which are Cabernet Sauvignon, which is the best of the wines, powerful and concentrated when young, and gaining a vaguely Italianate feel with bottle age. Five vintages of Cabernet Sauvignon ('93 – '97 inclusive) were available at cellar door in early 1998.

idyll vineyard ★★★

265 Ballan Road, Moorabool, Vic 3221 **region** Geelong
phone (03) 5276 1280 **fax** (03) 5276 1537 **open** Tues-Sun, holidays 10–5
winemaker Dr Daryl Sefton **production** 4500 **est.** 1966

product range ($12–18 R) Idyll Blush, Gewurztraminer, Chardonnay, Bone Idyll (Lighter style Shiraz), Shiraz, Cabernet Shiraz; with Sefton Estate as budget-priced second label Dry White and Cabernet Shiraz.
summary A stalwart of the region, producing wines in an individual style (pungent, assertive Traminer, long-vatted reds) which are almost as well known and appreciated overseas as they are in Australia.

inglewood vineyards ★★★

Yarrawa Road, Denman, NSW 2328 **region** Upper Hunter Valley
phone (02) 6547 2556 **fax** (02) 6547 2546 **open** Not
winemaker Simon Gilbert (Contract) **production** 18 000 **est.** 1988
product range ($9–19 R) Broken into three levels: at the bottom the Rivers label Classic Red and White; then under the Two Rivers label Chardonnay, Unwooded Chardonnay, Semillon Sauvignon Blanc, Verdelho, Cabernet Sauvignon; at the top end is Inglewood Show Reserve Chardonnay, Semillon, Verdelho.
summary A very significant addition to the viticultural scene in the Upper Hunter Valley, with almost 170 hectares of vineyards established, involving a total investment of around $7 million. Much of the fruit is sold to Southcorp under long-term contracts, but part is made under contract for the expanding winemaking and marketing operations of Inglewood. The emphasis is on Chardonnay and Semillon, and the wines have been medal winners in the wine show circuit.

ingoldby ★★★★

Kangarilla Road, McLaren Flat, SA 5171 **region** McLaren Vale
phone (08) 8323 8853 **fax** (08) 8323 8550 **open** Mon-Fri 9–5, weekends 11–5
winemaker Phil Reschke **production** 23 600 **est.** 1972
product range ($14 CD) Colombard, Hugo's Hill Riesling, Sauvignon Blanc, Shiraz, Grenache, Cabernet Sauvignon, Meteora Tawny Port.
summary Acquired by Mildara Blass in 1995, apparently for the grapes and grape contracts controlled by Ingoldby. Phil Reschke is making some excellent wines, just as he is for the Andrew Garrett label.

Ingoldby Chardonnay

A very cleverly made wine, sourced entirely from contract-grown fruit in McLaren Vale. It is largely cold fermented in stainless steel, and then transferred to new French and American oak hogsheads at 5° baumé to finish the fermentation. A small proportion of the wine undergoes malolactic fermentation, and the wine is usually bottled six months after vintage. All in all, very clever and effective winemaking, including the use of oak.

🍷🍷🍷🍷🍸 **1997** Medium yellow-green; a harmonious and smooth bouquet with peach, melon and fig fruit of medium to full intensity supported by subtle oak. The palate is richly flavoured with excellent fruit weight and intensity, and that perfectly integrated oak. Has length; exceptional value for money, as was the '96. **rating:** 90

➾ **best drinking** 1998 – 1999 **best vintages** '96, '97 **drink with** Crab with mayonnaise • $14

---

innisfail vineyards NR

Cross Street, Batesford, Vic 3221 **region** Geelong
phone (03) 5276 1258 **fax** (03) 5221 8442 **open** Not
winemaker Ron Griffiths **production** 1800 **est.** 1980

product range ($13–24 ML) Riesling, Chardonnay, Pinot Noir, Cabernet Sauvignon.
summary This 6-hectare vineyard released its first wines in 1988, made in a small but modern winery on-site with a chewy, complex Chardonnay from both 1989 and 1990 attesting to the quality of the vineyard. No recent tastings, however.

iron pot bay wines

West Bay Road, Rowella, Tas 7270 **region** Northern Tasmania
phone (03) 6394 7320 **fax** (03) 6394 7346 **open** By appointment
winemaker Andrew Hood (Contract) **production** 2000 **est.** 1988
product range ($16 CD) Unwooded Chardonnay, Sauvignon Blanc, Pinot Grigio.
summary The Cuthbert family has established an immaculate 4-hectare vineyard, utilising an open Lyre Trellis system and a high density (5000 vines per hectare) planting. The vineyard takes its name from a bay on the nearby Tamar River, and is strongly maritime-influenced, producing delicate but intensely flavoured unwooded white wines.

ironbark ridge vineyard

NR

Middle Road Mail Service 825, Purga, Qld 4306 **region** Other Wineries of Qld
phone (07) 5464 6787 **fax** (07) 3812 1273 **open** By appointment
winemaker Peter Scudamore-Smith MW (Previous) **production** 450 **est.** 1984
product range ($14 ML) Chardonnay.
summary Ipswich is situated on the coastal side of the Great Dividing Range, and the high summer humidity and rainfall will inevitably provide challenges for viticulture here. Peter Scudamore-Smith is no longer involved in the business, its future a little uncertain.

irvine

Roeslers Road, Eden Valley, SA 5235 **region** Eden Valley
phone (08) 8564 1046 **fax** (08) 8564 1046 **open** Not
winemaker James Irvine **production** 7000 **est.** 1980
product range ($16.50–90 R) Under the cheaper Eden Crest label: Unwooded Chardonnay, Pinot Merlot, Merlot Cabernet, Meslier Brut, Pinot Chardonnay Brut; under the premium James Irvine label: Brut Royale, Merlot Brut and (at the top of the tree) Grand Merlot.
summary Industry veteran Jim Irvine, who has successfully guided the destiny of so many South Australian wineries, quietly introduced his own label in 1991, although the vineyard from which the wines are sourced was commenced in 1980, and now comprises 1 hectare of petit meslier, 3 hectares of merlot and 7 hectares of chardonnay. Between one-third and two-thirds of the production is exported each year, principally to the United Kingdom.

James Irvine Grand Merlot

Industry veteran James Irvine has been producing his Grand Merlot for many years now; almost all is sold overseas. Deluxe packaging is matched by deluxe oak handling; the wine spends over three years in oak. Its quality is not in doubt, but one might be hard-pressed to guess what the variety is in a blind tasting.

🍷🍷🍷🍷 **1994** Medium to full red; a scented, fragrant cedary bouquet is followed by a palate in which sweet cedar and vanilla oak and soft, silky tannins produce a seductive wine, with fruit an incidental extra. **rating:** 85

➪ **best drinking** 2000 – 2005 **best vintages** NA **drink with** Smoked lamb • $90

island brook estate NR

Lot 817 Bussell Highway, Metricup, WA 6280 **region** Margaret River
phone (08) 9755 7501 **fax** (08) 9755 7501 **open** 7 days 10–5
winemaker Stuart Pym **production** 700 **est.** 1985
product range ($15 CD) Semillon, Summer Garden (white).
summary Ken and Judy Brook operate a vineyard café offering brunch, lunch, cappuccinos and Devon teas throughout the day, with a most unusual maze (built with rammed earth walls) to occupy children (and perhaps adults). Much of the production from the 8-hectare estate is sold to other makers, with limited quantities of wine made for sale from the restaurant and cellar door.

jackson's hill ★★★

Mount View Road, Mount View, NSW 2321 **region** Lower Hunter Valley
phone (02) 4990 1273 **fax** (02) 4991 3233 **open** Weekends, holidays 9–5
winemaker Mike Winborne **production** 1000 **est.** 1984
product range ($16–18 CD) Semillon, Oak Fermented Semillon, Late Harvest Semillon, Cabernet Franc.
summary One of the newer arrivals on the spectacularly scenic Mount View Road, making tiny quantities of wine sold exclusively through the cellar door, and specialising in Cabernet Franc.

jadran NR

445 Reservoir Road, Orange Grove, WA 6109 **region** Perth Hills
phone (08) 9459 1110 **open** Mon–Sat 10–8, Sun 11–5
winemaker Steve Radojkovich **production** NFP **est.** 1967
product range ($6–12 CD) Riesling, Hermitage, generic red and white table wines, Sparkling, Fortifieds.
summary A quite substantial operation which basically services local clientele, occasionally producing wines of quite surprising quality from a variety of fruit sources.

james estate NR

Mudgee Road, Baerami via Denman, NSW 2333 **region** Upper Hunter Valley
phone (02) 6547 5168 **fax** (02) 6547 5164 **open** Weekends 10–4, Mon–Fri by appointment
winemaker Letitia Cecchini **production** 37 000 **est.** 1971
product range ($7–22 CD) Sylvaner Chardonnay, Semillon, Chardonnay, Limited Released Bin GCC Show Chardonnay, Late Harvest White Hunter, Maria's Bin Shiraz.
summary A very substantial viticultural enterprise with 60 hectares of vineyards equally divided between sylvaner, semillon, chardonnay, shiraz and cabernet sauvignon. Overall quality has been there or thereabouts. Sold in 1997, which – inter alia – led to the name change from Serenella Estate to James Estate although for the time being, at least, the wines are being marketed under the Serenella label. What further changes are in the wind I do not know, but Letitia (Tish) Cecchini remained as winemaker for the 1998 vintage.

jane brook estate ★★★

229 Toodyay Road, Middle Swan, WA 6056 **region** Swan District
phone (08) 9274 1432 **fax** (08) 9274 1211 **open** 7 days 12–5
winemaker Lyndon Crocket, David Atkinson **production** 12 000 **est.** 1972

product range ($14–19 CD) Wood Aged Chenin Blanc, Chardonnay, Sauvignon Blanc, Late Harvest Cabernet Merlot, Shiraz, Elizabeth Jane Méthode Champenoise, Fortifieds.
summary An attractive winery which relies in part on substantial cellar-door trade and in part on varying export markets, with much work having been invested in the Japanese market in recent years. The white wines are usually best, although the quality of the oak isn't always up to the mark.

jardee NR

Old School House, Jardee, WA 6258 **region** Pemberton
phone (08) 9777 1552 **fax** (08) 9777 1552 **open** Not
winemaker Barrie Smith **production** 510 **est.** 1994
product range ($18–22 R) Chardonnay, Pinot Noir.
summary Jardee is a pioneering mill town, the wines are in fact made in tiny quantities from purchased fruit, the operation being a part-time interest for proprietor Steve Miolin.

jasper hill ★★★★★

Drummonds Lane, Heathcote, Vic 3523 **region** Bendigo
phone (03) 5433 2528 **fax** (03) 5433 3143 **open** By appointment
winemaker Ron Laughton **production** 3000 **est.** 1975
product range ($17–66 R) Georgia's Paddock Riesling, Georgia's Paddock Shiraz, Emily's Paddock Shiraz Cabernet Franc.
summary The red wines of Jasper Hill are highly regarded and much sought after, invariably selling out at cellar door and through the mailing list within a short time after release. These are wonderful wines, reflecting the very low yields and the care and attention given to them by Ron Laughton. The oak is not overdone, the fruit flavours showing Central Victoria at its best. Ron Laughton read the last edition of this book, and took pity on me, sending me a precious bottle of each of the 1996 reds and (Murphy's Law) a corked bottle of the 1997 Riesling.

Jasper Hill Georgia's Paddock Shiraz

Georgia's Paddock is by far the larger of the two vineyard blocks, with 9.5 hectares of shiraz and 3 hectares of riesling (the latter of course going to make the varietal wine of that name). The vines are unirrigated, and are normally low-yielding, but yields were reduced even further in 1996 as a result of drought followed by the first frost in 22 years, which destroyed the bottom third of the paddock in December 1995. These calamities to one side, a perfect vintage which produced wines with 14.5 degrees alcohol.

🍷🍷🍷🍷🍷 **1996** Dense red-purple; a powerful, clean bouquet redolent of blackberry, liquorice, briar and earth fruit is followed by an equally powerful palate with ripe black cherry and mint fruit and appropriately strong tannins. Minimal oak influence throughout. Built to live forever.
rating: 94

➾ **best drinking** 2001 – 2011 **best vintages** '90, '91, '93, '95, '96 **drink with** Wild duck • $41

Jasper Hill Emily's Paddock Shiraz Cabernet Franc

Produced from 3 hectares of shiraz and 0.2 hectares of cabernet franc, the latter having an impact on style disproportionate to the area of grapes. Ron Laughton also suggests since 1992 he has endeavoured to move the wine towards a more elegant style, and I think he has succeeded admirably. In 1996, due mainly to low bunch numbers and the impact of the drought, only 100 cases of Emily's Paddock were produced.

▼▼▼▼▽ **1996** Medium to full red-purple; the bouquet is much sweeter than Georgia's Paddock, with more evident spicy vanilla oak. The palate, too, is slightly lighter, with a more supple texture to the mint, berry and leaf fruit flavours, though powerful tannins do come on the finish of the wine. **rating:** 93

⇨ **best drinking** 2000 – 2010 **best vintages** '90, '91, '93, '95, '96 **drink with** Rare eye fillet of beef • $30

jasper valley NR

RMB 880 Croziers Road, Berry, NSW 2535 **region** Shoalhaven
phone (02) 4464 1596 **fax** (02) 4464 1596 **open** 7 days 9.30–5.30
winemaker Contract **production** 1100 **est.** 1976
product range ($4.20–12 CD) White Burgundy, Riesling, Traminer Riesling, Moselle, Summer Red, Cabernet Sauvignon, Port; also non-alcoholic fruit wines.
summary A strongly tourist-oriented winery with most of its wine purchased as cleanskins from other makers. Features about 1 hectare of lawns, barbecue facilities, and sweeping views.

jeanneret wines NR

Jeanneret Road, Sevenhill, SA 5453 **region** Clare Valley
phone (08) 8843 4308 **fax** (08) 8843 4251 **open** 7 days 11–5
winemaker Ben Jeanneret, Denis Jeanneret **production** 3000 **est.** 1992
product range ($12–20 CD) Riesling, Sparkling Grenache, Shiraz, Cabernet Sauvignon.
summary Jeanneret's fully self-contained winery has a most attractive outdoor tasting area and equally attractive picnic facilities situated on the edge of a small lake surrounded by bushland. While it did not open the business until October 1994, its first wine was in fact made in 1992 (Shiraz) and it has already established a loyal following.

jeir creek 

Gooda Creek Road, Murrumbateman, NSW 2582 **region** Canberra District
phone (02) 6227 5999 **fax** (02) 6227 5900 **open** Fri-Sun, holidays 10–5
winemaker Rob Howell **production** 4000 **est.** 1984
product range ($14–18 CD) Riesling, Late Harvest Riesling, Botrytis Semillon Sauvignon Blanc, Semillon Sauvignon Blanc, Sauvignon Blanc, Chardonnay, Pinot Noir, Shiraz, Cabernet Merlot.
summary Rob Howell came to part-time winemaking through a love of drinking fine wine, and is intent on improving both the quality and consistency of his wines. It is now a substantial (and still growing) business, with the vineyard plantings of 8.5 hectares due to be increased to almost 10 hectares in 1998, with additional cabernet sauvignon and shiraz.

jenke vineyards ★★★★

Barossa Valley Way, Rowland Flat, SA 5352 **region** Barossa Valley
phone (08) 8524 4154 **fax** (08) 8524 5044 **open** 7 days 10–4.30
winemaker Kym Jenke **production** 7000 **est.** 1989
product range ($10–22 CD) Semillon, Chardonnay, Late Harvest Riesling, Mourvedre, Merlot, Cabernet Franc, Cabernet Sauvignon, Shiraz.
summary The Jenkes have been vignerons in the Barossa since 1854, and have over 25 hectares of vineyards; a small part of the production is now made and marketed through a

charming restored stone cottage cellar door. The red wines have been particularly impressive, notably the recently introduced Old Vine Mourvedre.

Jenke Shiraz

Jenke regards this wine (and prices it accordingly) as its top red wine. The grapes come from old vines on the banks of Jacobs Creek, which are fermented in old concrete fermenters with traditional heading down boards. It spends 18 months in predominantly new American oak, much of that time on lees. For the record, Kym Jenke rates the '96 as the best yet.

🍷🍷🍷🍷🍷 **1996** Full red-purple; an exceptionally rich, ripe and dense bouquet with full-on blackberry, cherry and vanilla oak runs through to a massive, lusciously ripe juicy berry palate with quite charry American oak coming through on the finish. Needs time for the components to fully marry and soften. **rating:** 90

➾ **best drinking** 2001 – 2011 **best vintages** '90, '91, '96 **drink with** Barbecued rump • $22

Jenke Mourvedre

The revival in the fortunes of Mourvedre (or Mataro, as it used to be called) continues, with increasing amounts being diverted from fortified to table winemaking. As yet, straight varietal examples are few and far between, but d'Arenberg and Jenke in particular are showing just what can be achieved with the variety.

🍷🍷🍷🍷🍷 **1996** Medium to full red-purple; solid, concentrated ripe berry fruit on the bouquet introduces a rich, full-textured palate with abundant dark berry and dark chocolate fruit surrounded by soft tannins. You can really see the old vine influence at work here. **rating:** 90

➾ **best drinking** 1998 – 2006 **best vintages** NA **drink with** Game • $15

jim barry wines ★★★★☆

Main North Road, Clare, SA 5453 **region** Clare Valley

phone (08) 8842 2261 **fax** (08) 8842 3752 **open** Mon-Fri 9–5, weekends, holidays 9–4

winemaker Mark Barry **production** 40 000 **est.** 1959

product range ($10–90 R) Watervale Riesling, Lodge Hill Riesling, Personal Selection Semillon Sauvignon Blanc and Chardonnay, Semillon, Unwooded Chardonnay, Lavendar Hill, Cabernet Shiraz, Personal Selection Cabernet Sauvignon, McCrae Wood Shiraz and Cabernet Malbec, The Armagh (Shiraz).

summary The Armagh and the McCrae Wood range continue to stand out as the very best wines from Jim Barry, exceptionally concentrated and full flavoured. The remainder are seldom less than adequate, but do vary somewhat from one vintage to the next. Has an exceptional viticultural resource base of 160 hectares of mature Clare Valley vineyards.

Jim Barry McCrae Wood Shiraz

Ranks second to The Armagh Shiraz in terms of price, and first released in 1992. As with The Armagh, it is based upon scrupulous fruit selection, and shows the well-handled use of oak. Whereas The Armagh needs decades, this wine only needs ten years.

🍷🍷🍷🍷 **1996** Medium to full red-purple; curious, highly scented mint and fern-like aromas on the bouquet, with all of the above plus five spice on the palate. A wine from left field, but not unattractive. **rating:** 85

➾ **best drinking** 2002 – 2008 **best vintages** '92, '93, '94, '95 **drink with** Jugged hare • $35

Jim Barry The Armagh

First made in 1985 from very old, unirrigated, low-yielding vines. Not produced in 1986, and not exhibited in wine shows until the 1987 vintage was made. Since that time every vintage since the '87 has received at least one gold medal, with numerous trophies bestowed on the '89 and '90 vintages, respectively. Unashamedly a Grange pretender, and succeeding well in its aim.

🍷🍷🍷🍷🍷 **1995** Impenetrable purple; a spotlessly clean yet very concentrated bouquet with ripe blackberry and plum fruit introduces a massively concentrated wine, crammed with black fruits, supplemented by well-balanced tannins and generous but not excessive oak. **rating:** 95

⇨ **best drinking** 2000 – 2015 **best vintages** '89, '90, '91, '92, '93, '95 **drink with** The richest game dish possible • $90

Jim Barry McCrae Wood Cabernet Malbec

The blend of Cabernet and Malbec is a Clare Valley specialty, pioneered by Leasingham in the vinous dawn of time. Malbec flourishes in the Clare Valley as in few parts of Australia, adding a juicy sweetness to the formidable power of Clare Valley Cabernet.

🍷🍷🍷🍷 **1996** Dense red-purple; extremely ripe, lush berry and liquorice fruit intermingles with cedar/sandalwood/spice-accented oak on the bouquet. The palate displays almost riotous fruit with distinct jammy Malbec varietal flavour together with sundry spices; quite potent tannins come on the finish. **rating:** 87

⇨ **best drinking** 2003 – 2010 **best vintages** NA **drink with** Oxtail • $35

---

jindalee wines NR

PO Box 5146, North Geelong, Vic 3215 **region** Geelong
phone (03) 5277 2836 **fax** (03) 5277 2840 **open** Not
winemaker Contract **production** 8000 **est.** 1997
product range ($8–15 CD) Chardonnay, Colombard Chardonnay, Shiraz, Merlot, Cabernet Sauvignon.
summary Jindalee Wines made its debut with the 1997 vintage. It is part of the Littore Group, which currently has 400 hectares of premium wine grapes in wine production and under development in the Riverland. The first wines were contract-made, but it is planned to have a winery constructed by the year 2000, and to expand the product range to include Cabernet Sauvignon, Merlot and Colombard Chardonnay. The first release wines did not rise above their price station.

jingalla ★★★★

RMB 1316 Bolganup Dam Road, Porongurup, WA 6324 **region** Great Southern
phone (08) 9853 1023 **fax** (08) 9853 1023 **open** 7 days 10.30–5
winemaker Brendan Smith (Contract) **production** 3000 **est.** 1979
product range ($11–20 CD) Great Southern White and Red, Riesling, Semillon, Verdelho, Reserve Shiraz, Cabernet Rouge, Cabernet Sauvignon, Late Harvest Semillon, Tawny Port, Liqueur Muscat.
summary Jingalla is a family-run business, owned and run by Geoff and Nita Clarke and Barry and Shelley Coad, the latter the ever-energetic wine marketer of the business. The 8 hectares of hillside vineyards are low-yielding, with the white wines succeeding best. Consistently competent winemaking at Goundrey has resulted in a range of very reliable, positively flavoured wines. While best known for its wooded and unwooded whites, it also produces some lovely red wines.

jinks creek winery NR

Tonimbuk Road, Tonimbuk, Vic 3815 **region** Gippsland
phone (03) 5629 8502 **fax** (03) 5629 8551 **open** By appointment
winemaker Andrew Clarke **production** NA **est.** 1981
product range ($14 CD) Sauvignon Blanc, Chardonnay, Pinot Noir.
summary Jinks Creek Winery is situated between Gembrook and Bunyip, bordering the evocatively named Bunyip State Park. While the winery was not built until 1992, planting of the 2.5-hectare vineyard started back in 1981, and all of the wines are estate-grown. The 'sold out' sign goes up each year.

joadja vineyards ★★★

Joadja Road, Berrima, NSW 2577 **region** Other Wineries of NSW
phone (02) 4878 5236 **fax** (02) 4878 5236 **open** 7 days 10–5
winemaker Kim Moginie **production** 2000 **est.** 1983
product range ($13–21 CD) Classic Dry White, Sauvignon Blanc, Chardonnay, Botrytis Autumn Riesling, Sauternes, Classic Dry Red, Cabernet Malbec, Christopher Tawny Port.
summary The strikingly labelled Joadja Vineyard wines, first made in 1990, are principally drawn from 7 hectares of estate vineyards situated in the cool hills adjacent to Berrima. Both the red and whites have a very unusual and consistent eucalypt/peppermint character which is clearly a product of the climate and (possibly) soil. It makes the wines difficult to assess by conventional standards, but is by no means unpleasant, and Joadja is well worth a visit. The '95 Cabernet Malbec is a pleasant wine, but the '97 Chardonnay is not recommended.

john gehrig wines ★★☆

Oxley-Milawa Road, Oxley, Vic 3678 **region** King Valley
phone (03) 5727 3395 **fax** (03) 5727 3699 **open** 7 days 9–5
winemaker John Gehrig **production** 5600 **est.** 1976
product range ($7–14.50 CD) Oxley Dry White, Riesling, Chenin Blanc, Verdelho, Chardonnay, Sparkling, Pinot Noir, King River Red, Merlot, Cabernet Merlot, Fortifieds.
summary Honest, if seldom exciting, wines; the occasional Chardonnay, Pinot Noir, Merlot and Cabernet Merlot have, however, risen above their station.

jones winery NR

Chiltern Road, Rutherglen, Vic 3685 **region** Rutherglen
phone (02) 6032 9496 **open** Mon-Sat 9–5, weekends, holidays 10–5
winemaker Les Jones **production** NFP **est.** 1864
product range Chablis, Riesling, White Burgundy, Light Red, Dry Red, Fortifieds.
summary An ultra-reclusive and ultra-traditional winery (despite the garish labels) making no-frills wines from 16 hectares of vineyards. Les Jones even regards details of his current wines and prices as 'my business only'. The emphasis is on Port, Sherry and Muscat.

kaesler 

Barossa Valley Way, Nuriootpa, SA 5355 **region** Barossa Valley
phone (08) 8562 2711 **fax** (08) 8562 2788 **open** 7 days 10–5
winemaker Contract **production** 3000 **est.** 1990

product range ($9–30 CD) Prestige Semillon, Cottage Block White, Late Harvest Semillon, Bush Vine Grenache, Old Vine Shiraz, Beerenauslese, Prestige Cuvee, Méthode Champenoise, Old Vine Shiraz, Fortifieds.

summary Toby and Treena Hueppauff purchased Kaesler Farm, with its 12 hectares of vines, in 1985, and since 1990 have had the wines made under contract by others. The winery has an à la carte restaurant offering both indoor and outdoor dining; there is also accommodation.

kaiser stuhl ★★☆

Tanunda Road, Nuriootpa, SA 5355 **region** Barossa Valley
phone (08) 8560 9389 **fax** (08) 8562 1669 **open** Mon–Sat 10–5, Sun 1–5
winemaker Nigel Logos **production** 1.3 million **est.** 1931

product range ($4–12 R) Black Forest, generic whites under bin numbers, Claret Bin 33, Bin 44 Riesling, Bin 55 Moselle, Bin 66 Burgundy, Bin 77 Chablis, Sparkling; also extensive cask and flagon range.

summary Part of the Southcorp Wines empire, but a shadow of its former self, with its once-famous Green Ribbon Riesling and Red Ribbon Shiraz no more. Essentially provides flagon-quality wines in bottles at competitive prices.

kangarilla road vineyard & winery ★★★☆

Kangarilla Road, McLaren Vale, SA 5171 **region** McLaren Vale
phone (08) 8383 0533 **fax** (08) 8383 0044 **open** Mon–Fri 9–5, weekends 11–5
winemaker Kevin O'Brien **production** 10 000 **est.** 1975

product range ($12–18 CD) Chardonnay, Zinfandel, Shiraz, Cabernet.

summary Kangarilla Road Vineyard & Winery was formerly known as Stevens Cambrai. Long-time industry identity Kevin O'Brien and wife Helen purchased the property in July 1997, and are continuing to sell the existing stocks of Cambrai wines, but with the strikingly labelled Kangarilla Road brand to progressively replace it.

Kangarilla Road Zinfandel

Graham Stevens planted zinfandel almost 30 years ago, sometimes releasing it as a straight varietal, but more often blending it with other reds. As the '96 shows, it is not only capable of producing an interesting wine, but a very good one, and once again raises the question why so little zinfandel is grown in Australia.

🍷🍷🍷🍷🍷 **1996** Medium to full red-purple; there are most attractive tobacco and spice edges to the dark berry fruit of the bouquet. The palate is akin to a grenache with balls; emphatic blackberry, tobacco and cigar box flavours running through bright juicy berry fruit. **rating:** 90

⇨ **best drinking** 1998 – 2002 **best vintages** NA **drink with** Spiced Moroccan lamb • $18

kangaroo island vines NR

c/o 413 Payneham Road, Felixstow, SA 5070 **region** Other Wineries of SA
phone (08) 8365 3411 **fax** (08) 8336 2462 **open** Not
winemaker Caj Amadio **production** 600 **est.** 1990

product range ($19–23 ML) Island Sting, Florance Cabernet Merlot, Special Reserve Cabernet Merlot.

summary Kangaroo Island is another venture of Caj and Genny Amadio, with the wines being sold through the Chain of Ponds cellar door. The Amadios have been the focal point of the development of vineyards on Kangaroo Island, producing the wines not only from their own tiny planting of 450 vines on quarter of an acre, but buying grapes from other vignerons on the island. The tiny quantities of wine so far produced strongly support the notion that Kangaroo Island has an excellent climate for Bordeaux-style reds, particularly the excellent Special Reserve Cabernet Merlot.

kangderaar vineyard NR

Melvilles Caves Road, Rheola, Vic 3517 **region** Bendigo
phone (03) 5438 8292 **fax** (03) 5438 8292 **open** Mon-Sat 9–5, Sun 10–5
winemaker James Nealy **production** 500 **est.** 1980
product range ($12–15 CD) Chardonnay, Vintage Reserve Chardonnay, Cabernet Sauvignon.
summary The 4.5-hectare vineyard is situated at Rheola, near the Melville Caves, said to have been the hideout of the bushranger Captain Melville in the 1850s, and surrounded by the Kooyoora State Park. It is owned by James and Christine Nealy.

kara kara vineyard ★★★

Sunraysia Highway via St Arnaud, Vic 3478 **region** Pyrenees
phone (03) 5496 3294 **fax** (03) 5496 3294 **open** Mon-Fri 10.30–6, weekends 9–6
winemaker John Ellis (Contract) **production** 2500 **est.** 1977
product range ($14–19 CD) Fumé Blanc, Chardonnay, Sauvignon Blanc, Chardonnay Semillon, Chardonnay, Semillon, Late Picked Semillon, Shiraz Cabernet.
summary Hungarian-born Steve Zsigmond comes from a long line of vignerons, and sees Kara Kara as the eventual retirement occupation for himself and wife Marlene. The first step has been the decision to have their production contract-made (first by Mitchelton, then John Ellis – previously the grapes were sold) with predictably consistent results over the first few years. Draws upon 9 hectares of estate plantings.

karina vineyard ★★★★

RMB 4055 Harrisons Road, Dromana, Vic 3936 **region** Mornington Peninsula
phone (03) 5981 0137 **fax** (03) 5981 0137 **open** Weekends 11–5, 7 days in January
winemaker Graeme Pinney **production** 1500 **est.** 1984
product range ($14–19 CD) Riesling, Sauvignon Blanc, Chardonnay, Cabernet Merlot, Bald Hill Creek (Cabernet Sauvignon).
summary A typical Mornington Peninsula vineyard, situated in the Dromana/Redhill area on rising, north-facing slopes, just 3 kilometres from the shores of Port Phillip Bay, immaculately tended and with picturesque garden surrounds. Fragrant Riesling and cashew-accented Chardonnay are its best wines.

Karina Riesling

Made from half a hectare of estate plantings employing the neatly trimmed vertical canopy so necessary to obtain fruit ripeness in this cool region. While always elegant and crisp, the wine sometimes lacks depth.

🍷🍷🍷🍷 **1997** Medium yellow-green; a fragrant bouquet with lime and tropical fruit aromas in abundance. The palate is quite delicate, yet reasonably intense, with attractive lime, citrus and passionfruit flavours. **rating:** 87

➾ **best drinking** 1998 – 2002 **best vintages** '94, '97 **drink with** Crab, mussels • $17

Karina Chardonnay

Really impressed with the '94 vintage, which is in true-blue Mornington Peninsula style.

🍷🍷🍷🍷 **1996** Full yellow, reminiscent of New Zealand Chardonnay. The New Zealand connection continues with the strong, complex bouquet with its mix of buttery/cashew and citrus/herbal characters. The palate is also complex, with more of those sweet and sour flavours; there is a slight hole in the mid-palate, followed by firm acidity on the finish. **rating:** 88

⇨ **best drinking** 1998 – 2000 **best vintages** '91, '92, '94, '96, '97 **drink with** Grilled spatchcock • $19

karl seppelt ★★★☆

Ross Dewells Road, Springton, SA 5235 **region** Eden Valley
phone (08) 8568 2378 **fax** (08) 8568 2799 **open** 7 days 10–5
winemaker Karl Seppelt, Petaluma (Contract) **production** 2500 **est.** 1981
product range ($15–22 R) Riesling, Chardonnay, Cabernet Sauvignon, Shiraz, Chardonnay Brut, Sparkling Shiraz, Brut Sauvage, Fino Sherry, Vintage Port, Tawny Port.
summary After experimenting with various label designs and names, Karl Seppelt (former marketing director of Seppelt) has decided to discontinue the brand name Grand Cru (although retaining it as a business name) and henceforth market the wines from his estate vineyards under his own name. The quality is very consistent across the range.

karrivale ★★★★☆

Woodlands Road, Porongurup, WA 6324 **region** Great Southern
phone (08) 9853 1009 **fax** (08) 9853 1129 **open** Wed-Sun 10–5
winemaker Gavin Berry (Contract) **production** 1170 **est.** 1979
product range ($12–18 CD) Riesling, Chardonnay.
summary A tiny Riesling specialist in the wilds of the Porongurups forced to change its name from Narang because Lindemans felt it could be confused with its Nyrang Shiraz brand; truly a strange world. The viticultural skills of owner Campbell McGready and ultra-competent contract winemaking fulfil the promise of this beautifully sited vineyard, and its long-lived Riesling.

karriview ★★★★☆

RMB 913 Roberts Road, Denmark, WA 6333 **region** Great Southern
phone (08) 9840 9381 **fax** (08) 9840 9381 **open** Summer school holidays 7 days 11–4, Feb-Dec Fri-Tues 11–4
winemaker John Wade (Contract) **production** 950 **est.** 1986
product range ($13.50–28 CD) Chardonnay, Late Harvest Riesling, Pinot Noir.
summary One hectare each of immaculately tended pinot noir and chardonnay on ultra-close spacing produce tiny quantities of two wines of remarkable intensity, quality and style. Available only from the winery, but worth the effort. There is some vintage variation; the winery rating is based upon the successes, not the disappointments. Typically, three vintages of each wine are available on sale at any one time; unhappily, I have not tasted the '96 or '97 vintage wines.

katnook estate ★★★★☆

Riddoch Highway, Coonawarra, SA 5263 **region** Coonawarra
phone (08) 8737 2394 **fax** (08) 8737 2397 **open** Mon-Fri 9–4.30, weekends 10–4.30
winemaker Wayne Stehbens **production** 50 000 **est.** 1979

product range ($16–75 R) Under the premium Katnook label: Riesling, Sauvignon Blanc, Chardonnay, Botrytis Riesling, Cabernet Sauvignon, Merlot, Odyssey (super-premium Cabernet) and Chardonnay Brut; under the Riddoch label: Chardonnay, Sauvignon Blanc, Shiraz and Cabernet Shiraz; also Woolshed Chardonnay and Cabernet Shiraz Merlot.

summary Still the largest contract-grape grower and supplier in Coonawarra, selling 60% of its grape production to others. The historic stone woolshed in which the second vintage in Coonawarra (1896) was made and which has served Katnook since 1980 is being restored. Together with the 1997 launch of the flagship Odyssey, points the way for a higher profile for the winemaking side of the venture.

Katnook Estate Riesling

At one point of time there was more riesling planted in Coonawarra than either cabernet sauvignon or shiraz. Times have changed dramatically, but Coonawarra has always been capable of producing first-class Riesling if enough care is taken. It has an elegance seldom achieved in other Australian regions.

🍷🍷🍷🍷 **1996** Glowing yellow-green; the bouquet is very much in the Coonawarra style, elegant and fine, with lemon/citrus aromas and just a hint of toast. The palate is fine and crisp, with an almost silky feel, and a long, lingering finish. **rating:** 87

➭ **best drinking** 1997 – 2005 **best vintages** NA **drink with** Vegetable terrine • $16

Katnook Estate Sauvignon Blanc

One of the signature wines of Katnook Estate, now made from eight remaining hectares of plantings of this variety. A chance tasting of the '82 vintage in late 1994 emphasised how well the wines can age, even if the change in character is quite radical. On balance, best drunk young. The '97 vintage, incidentally, marked the eighteenth release, putting it in the forefront of Australian Sauvignon Blanc in terms of history.

🍷🍷🍷🍷 **1997** Medium yellow-green, of surprising depth; the bouquet is quite rich and full, and a marked departure in style from previous vintages. The palate provides lots of sweet, almost limey, tropical fruit which has presence but which is not particularly varietal. Difficult to know whether it was the warm dry vintage or some change in technique responsible. **rating:** 86

➭ **best drinking** 1998 – 1999 **best vintages** '84, '86, '90, '92, '94, '95, '96 **drink with** Grilled whiting • $25

Katnook Estate Chardonnay

Stands alongside Sauvignon Blanc as Katnook's most consistent wine, always elegant, and always long-lived. Produced from the pick of 18 hectares of mature vineyards.

🍷🍷🍷🍷🍷 **1996** Bright green-yellow; an elegant and stylish bouquet shows attractive melon, white peach and cashew aromas, the palate likewise elegant and restrained, with fine citrus and melon fruit woven through gently nutty barrel-ferment/malolactic ferment characters. **rating:** 90

➭ **best drinking** 1999 – 2006 **best vintages** '84, '86, '90, '92, '94, '96 **drink with** Poached salmon • $30

Katnook Estate Merlot

Produced, as are all of the Katnook Estate wines, from estate-grown grapes. A sophisticated, understated style which will appeal to those with a European bent to their palate.

ΥΥΥΥ **1995** Medium red-purple; cedar/leafy fruit and oak are interwoven on the bouquet, the wine has the authentic feel, flavour and structure of Merlot on the palate, with flavours essentially in the leafy/cedary/woody spectrum. Not a lush wine by any means, but well balanced. **rating:** 84

⇨ **best drinking** 1998 – 2005 **best vintages** NA **drink with** Yearling steak • $35

Katnook Estate Cabernet Sauvignon

Made from the very best selection from 70 hectares of estate vineyards, but over the years has tended to be relatively lean; since 1991 the wine has shown better fruit richness and balance.

ΥΥΥΥ **1996** Medium red-purple; the bouquet is clean, with cassis berry fruit of medium intensity, supported by subtle oak. The palate is finely balanced and modulated, with more cassis berry fruit, fine tannins and subtle, gentle oak. **rating:** 88

⇨ **best drinking** 2001 – 2006 **best vintages** '88, '90, '91, '92, '94 **drink with** Prime rib of beef • $40

Katnook Estate Odyssey Cabernet Sauvignon

The first vintage (1991) was released in February 1997, having been launched at Katnook's centenary celebrations in December of the preceding year. One hundred per cent Cabernet Sauvignon matured in new French oak barriques for 30 months, and then given an additional three years bottle age before release, it is produced in tiny quantities and represents the best Katnook is able to produce.

ΥΥΥΥΥ **1992** Medium to full red-purple; the complex, elegant bouquet shows intense red berry and cedar aromas. A delicious wine on the palate, with red berry/cassis fruit to open, then with fine, dusty tannins running right through to the finish. Food-style. **rating:** 94

⇨ **best drinking** 1998 – 2004 **best vintages** '91, '92 **drink with** Yearling beef • $75

kay bros amery ★★★

Kay Road, McLaren Vale, SA 5171 **region** McLaren Vale
phone (08) 8323 8211 **fax** (08) 8323 9199 **open** Mon-Fri 9–5, weekends and public holidays 12–5
winemaker Colin Kay **production** 6500 **est.** 1890
product range ($15–36 R) Sauvignon Blanc, Late Harvest Frontignac, Chardonnay, Shiraz, Block 6 Shiraz, Grenache, Cabernet Sauvignon; Port Liqueur, Muscat.
summary A traditional winery with a rich history and 13.5 hectares of priceless old vines; while the white wines have been variable, the red wines and fortified wines can be very good. Of particular interest is Block 6 Shiraz, made from 100-year-old vines; both vines and wine are going from strength to strength.

kellermeister ★★★

Barossa Valley Highway, Lyndoch, SA 5351 **region** Barossa Valley
phone (08) 8524 4303 **fax** (08) 8524 4880 **open** 7 days 9–6
winemaker Trevor Jones **production** 7000 **est.** 1970
product range ($12.50–26.50 CD) High Country Riesling, Show Reserve Riesling, Abendlese, Frontignan Spatlese and Auslese, Late Harvest Sylvaner, Cabernet Rosé, Black Sash Shiraz, Cabernet Sauvignon, Cabernet Shiraz, Sparkling and Fortifieds; also the Trevor Jones range (under his own label) of Virgin Chardonnay, Riesling, Cabernet Merlot and Dry Grown Barossa Shiraz.

summary Kellermeister specialises in older vintage wines made in the traditional fashion, an extraordinary array of which are on offer at enticing prices. There is always a range of vintages available; the wines are soft and generous, if very traditional, in style.

kellybrook ★★★☆

Fulford Road, Wonga Park, Vic 3115 **region** Yarra Valley
phone (03) 9722 1304 **fax** (03) 9722 2092 **open** Mon-Sat 9–6, Sun 11–6
winemaker Darren Kelly **production** 3500 **est.** 1960
product range ($13–36 CD) Chardonnay, Riesling, Late Harvest Gewürztraminer, Pinot Noir, Shiraz, Cabernet Merlot, Cabernet Shiraz, Méthode Champenoise, Champagne Cider, Apple Brandy, Liqueur Muscat, Old Vintage Tawny Port.
summary The 8-hectare vineyard is situated at Wonga Park at the entrance to the principal winegrowing areas of the Yarra Valley, replete with picnic area and a full-scale restaurant. As well as table wine, a very competent producer of both cider and apple brandy (in Calvados style).

kennedys keilor valley NR

Lot 3 Overnewton Road, Keilor, Vic 3036 **region** Sunbury
phone (03) 9311 6246 **fax** (03) 9331 6246 **open** By appointment
winemaker Peter Dredge **production** 300 **est.** 1994
product range ($16 CD) Chardonnay.
summary A newly established estate-based Chardonnay specialist, producing its only wine from 1.8 hectares of relatively newly established vineyards.

kevin sobels wines NR

Cnr Broke and Halls Roads, Pokolbin, NSW 2321 **region** Lower Hunter Valley
phone (02) 4998 7766 **fax** (02) 4998 7475 **open** 7 days 10–5
winemaker Kevin Sobels **production** 5000 **est.** 1992
product range ($12–18 CD) Chardonnay, Semillon, Traminer, Pinot Noir.
summary Veteran winemaker Kevin Sobels has found yet another home, drawing upon 8 hectares of vineyards (originally planted by the Ross Jones family) to produce wines sold almost entirely through cellar door and mail order, with limited retail representation. The cellar door offers light meals and picnic and barbecue facilities.

killawarra 

Tanunda Road, Nuriootpa, SA 5355 **region** Barossa Valley
phone (08) 8560 9389 **fax** (08) 8562 1669 **open** See Penfolds
winemaker Ian Shepherd **production** 205 000 **est.** 1975
product range ($8.95–13.95 R) Only Sparkling wines: Non Vintage Brut, Vintage Brut, Brut Cremant, Premier Brut and Reserve Brut; also Non Vintage Sparkling Burgundy.
summary Killawarra is purely a Southcorp brand, without any particular presence in terms of either vineyards or winery, but it is increasingly styled in a mode different from the Seaview or Seppelt wines. As one would expect, the wines are competitively priced, and what is more, regularly sweep all before them in national wine shows.

killerby ★★★☆

Lakes Road, Capel, WA 6230 **region** Geographe
phone 1800 655 722 **fax** 1800 679 578 **open** 7 days 10–5
winemaker Paul Boulden **production** 10 000 **est.** 1973
product range ($15–27 R) Semillon, Chardonnay, Shiraz, Cabernet Sauvignon and budget-priced April Classic White (Traminer Semillon Chardonnay blend) and April Classic Red (Shiraz Pinot Cabernet blend).
summary The members of the Killerby family are long-term residents of the southwest; Ben Killerby is the fourth generation. The 21 hectares of vines were established by Ben's father, the late Dr Barry Killerby, in 1973, and are now fully mature. The Chardonnay, in particular, is highly rated by some critics, but I would like to see a little more succulence and concentration in the wines.

Killerby Cabernet Sauvignon

The Cabernet Sauvignon is the other top performer in the Killerby stable. It is produced from 4 hectares of estate plantings which are now 22 years old, and over the years has accumulated seven trophies and innumerable gold medals. In fact a blend of 95% Cabernet Sauvignon and 5% Cabernet Franc, it is matured in French oak for just under two years.

🍷🍷🍷🍷 **1996** Medium red-purple; the bouquet is extremely herbaceous, with a mix of capsicum, olive and berry fruit, but, as with the Chardonnay, the palate delivers far more. While firm, and with some olive/herbaceous overtones to the core of cassis, fruit, has good length, structure and tannins. **rating:** 86

➯ **best drinking** 2001 – 2007 **best vintages** '87, '89, '92, '93, '94, '96 **drink with** Mature cheddar • $23

---

kings creek vineyard ★★★★

237 Myers Road, Bittern, Vic 3918 **region** Mornington Peninsula
phone (03) 5983 2102 **fax** (03) 5983 2102 **open** Weekends, public holidays 12–5
winemaker Penny Gluyas, Kathleen Quealy **production** 1200 **est.** 1981
product range ($16–28 R) Chardonnay, Pinot Noir, Cabernet Sauvignon.
summary Kings Creek is owned and operated by the Bell, Glover and Perraton families. Planting commenced in 1981, and the vines are now fully mature. Since 1990 the quality of the wines, particularly of the Pinot Noir and Chardonnay, has been beyond reproach, although no tastings since the 1995 vintage.

kingsley ★★★

6 Kingsley Court, Portland, Vic 3305 **region** Far South West Victoria
phone (03) 5523 1864 **open** 7 days 1–4
winemaker Contract **production** 1000 **est.** 1983
product range ($12–14 CD) Riesling, Botrytis Riesling, Chardonnay, Cabernet Sauvignon.
summary Only a small part of the 10 hectares is made into wine under contract, the remainder being sold as grapes. Older vintages are usually available at cellar door. In early 1998, wines spanning the 1994 to 1997 vintages were on sale at low prices.

kingston estate ★★★☆

PO Box 67, Kingston-on-Murray, SA 5331 **region** Riverland
phone (08) 8583 0244 **fax** (08) 8583 0304 **open** Not
winemaker Bill Moularadellis, Rod Chapman **production** 50 000 **est.** 1979

product range ($9.95–16.95 R) Semillon, Semillon Sauvignon Blanc, Chardonnay, Reserve Chardonnay, Shiraz, Reserve Shiraz, Merlot, Reserve Merlot, Reserve Cabernet Merlot, Cabernet Sauvignon, Cuvée Premier.
summary Kingston Estate is a substantial and successful Riverland winery, crushing 10 000 tonnes a year, and exporting 80% of its production. It is only in recent years that it has turned its attention to the domestic market with national distribution. The wines are modestly priced and offer exceptionally good value for money, with some particularly good wines in the Reserve range.

kingtree wines NR

Kingtree Road, Wellington Mills via Dardanup, WA 6326 **region** Geographe
phone (08) 9728 3050 **fax** (08) 9728 3113 **open** 7 days 12–5.30
winemaker Contract **production** 1000 **est.** 1991
product range ($15–18 CD) Riesling, Sauvignon Blanc, Gerrasse White, Cabernet Merlot.
summary Kingtree Wines, with 2.5 hectares of estate plantings, is part of the Kingtree Lodge development, a four and a half star luxury retreat in dense Jarrah forest.

Kingtree Riesling

Produced from half a hectare of estate plantings. Cold fermented and early bottled.
🍷🍷🍷🍷 **1997** Medium yellow-green; the bouquet is clean, of medium intensity with faint tropical fruit and mineral aromas. The tropical/passionfruit/pineapple fruit comes through strongly on the palate, with mid-palate sweetness particularly evident, balanced by a moderately dry finish. Impressive first-up wine. **rating:** 84

➾ **best drinking** 1998 – 2002 **best vintages** NA **drink with** Sugar-cured tuna • $15.50

kinvarra estate NR

RMB 5141, New Norfolk, Tas 7140 **region** Southern Tasmania
phone (03) 6286 1333 **fax** (03) 6286 2026 **open** Not
winemaker Andrew Hood (Table Wine), Greg O'Keefe (Sparkling) **production** 90 **est.** 1990
product range ($13.50–15 ML) Riesling, Pinot Noir.
summary Kinvarra Estate is the part-time occupation of David and Sue Bevan, with their wonderful 1827 homestead depicted on the label. There is only 1 hectare of vines, half riesling and half pinot noir, and most of the crop is sold to Wellington Wines and Fishburn & O'Keefe.

Kinvarra Estate Riesling

Produced, needless to say, in minuscule quantities each year. Unusually, in 1997 the wine was made from cordon cut vines following a frost on April 14, which killed all the leaves.
🍷🍷🍷🍷 **1997** Light to medium yellow-green; the bouquet is light, with pronounced earthy/minerally characters, and the fruit somewhat diminished. The palate is delicate, but does have length, with crisp minerally flavours, finishing with pronounced acidity. **rating:** 84

➾ **best drinking** 1998 – 2001 **best vintages** NA **drink with** Shellfish • $13.50

knappstein wines ★★★★☆

2 Pioneer Avenue, Clare, SA 5453 **region** Clare Valley
phone (08) 8842 2600 **fax** (08) 8842 3831 **open** Mon-Fri 9–5, Sat 11–5, Sun and public holidays 11–4
winemaker Andrew Hardy **production** 40 000 **est.** 1976
product range ($12–21.50 R) Riesling, Gewurztraminer, Fumé Blanc, Chardonnay, Sauvignon Blanc Semillon, Botrytis Riesling, Enterprise Reserve Shiraz, The Franc (Cabernet Franc), Cabernet Merlot, Cabernet Sauvignon.
summary The bell has tolled, and Tim Knappstein (together with wife Annie) are now involved full-time in their Lenswood Vineyard. Petaluma stalwart Andrew Hardy has been placed in charge at Knappstein Wines, and will no doubt place his stamp on the brand. Clever label redesign and a subtle label name change (dropping the word 'Tim') are physical signs of the new order.

Knappstein Riesling

The reputation of the Rieslings of the Clare Valley is as much due to Tim Knappstein as to any other winemaker, past or present. Tim Knappstein himself was the first to say that the quality and style of Riesling is in turn strongly dependent upon the terroir and climate, and that too is true. The combination of man, climate and variety in the outcome produced a classic wine.

▼▼▼▼▽ **1997** Light to medium yellow-green; an attractively rich bouquet with sweet citrus aromas; a marvellously balanced and modulated wine in the mouth, with abundant mid-palate lemony fruit followed by a fine, dry, lingering but not phenolic finish. **rating:** 90

➾ **best drinking** 1998 – 2012 **best vintages** '77, '78, '79, '80, '83, '86, '90, '93, '94, '96, '97 **drink with** Salads of all kinds • $13

Knappstein Sauvignon Blanc Semillon

The result of quite complicated winemaking architecture. Ripe Clare Valley Sauvignon Blanc is barrel-fermented and lees stirred for four months, with a smaller portion tank fermented to provide freshness. The Semillon component is also barrel-fermented, and comes partly from Watervale and partly from the Adelaide Hills.

▼▼▼▼ **1997** Medium yellow-green; soft, gently honeyed, sweet passionfruit aromas on the bouquet are followed by a round, soft, fleshy mouthfilling honey and herb-flavoured palate. The impact of oak on both bouquet and palate is more textural than flavour oriented. **rating:** 89

➾ **best drinking** 1998 – 1999 **best vintages** NA **drink with** Tartare of salmon • NA

Knappstein Cabernet Merlot

A blend of Cabernet Sauvignon (dominant) and Merlot, 75% from the Clare Valley and 25% from the Adelaide Hills.

▼▼▼▼ **1996** Medium red-purple; the bouquet is quite fragrant, with a mix of herbaceous and riper blackberry fruit. Interesting flavours unfold on the palate, running through mint, blackcurrant and mulberry, with a touch of almost saccharine-sweet oak. **rating:** 86

➾ **best drinking** 2000 – 2004 **best vintages** NA **drink with** Roast veal • NA

knight granite hills

Burke and Wills Track, Baynton RSD 391, Kyneton, Vic 3444 **region** Macedon
phone (03) 5423 7264 **fax** (03) 5423 7288 **open** Mon-Sat 10–6, Sun 12–6
winemaker Llew Knight **production** 6000 **est.** 1970

product range ($14–23 R) Riesling, Chardonnay, Pinot Noir, Shiraz, Cabernet Sauvignon; also MICA Unwooded White and Cabernet Sauvignon.
summary Knight Granite Hills was one of the early pacesetters, indeed the first pacesetter, for cool-climate, spicy Shiraz and intense Riesling. Revived marketing in a buoyant market, and the introduction of the lesser-priced MICA range, has resulted in greater activity; plantings remain the same at 9 hectares of mature, low-yielding vineyards.

knowland estate NR

Mount Vincent Road, Running Stream, NSW 2850 **region** Mudgee
phone (02) 6358 8420 **fax** (02) 6358 8423 **open** By appointment
winemaker Peter Knowland **production** 250 **est.** 1990
product range ($12.50–18 CD) Mt Vincent Sauvignon Blanc, Orange Pinot Noir, Mt Vincent Pinot Noir, Wellington Cabernet.
summary The former Mount Vincent Winery which sells much of its grape production from the 3.5 hectares of vineyards to other makers, but which proposes to increase production under its own label.

kominos 

New England Highway, Severnlea, Qld 4352 **region** Granite Belt
phone (07) 4683 4311 **fax** (07) 4683 4291 **open** 7 days 9–5
winemaker Tony Comino **production** 4000 **est.** 1976
product range ($10–13 CD) Riesling, Sauvignon Blanc, Chardonnay, Vin Doux, White Shiraz, Nouveau, Shiraz, Cabernet Merlot, Cabernet Sauvignon.
summary Tony Comino is a dedicated viticulturist and winemaker; and together with his father, battled hard to prevent ACI obtaining a monopoly on glass production in Australia, foreseeing many of the things which have in fact occurred. However, Kominos keeps a very low profile, selling all of its wine through cellar door and mailing list. As well as making a very good Shiraz in 1994, it also produced good Cabernet Sauvignon in both that year and 1993. No recent tastings.

koppamurra 

Joanna via Naracoorte, SA 5271 **region** Koppamurra
phone (08) 8271 4127 **fax** (08) 8271 0726 **open** By appointment
winemaker John Greenshields **production** 2000 **est.** 1973
product range ($7–17.50 ML) Riesling, Autumn Pick Riesling, Botrytis Riesling, Chardonnay, Pinot Meunier, Naracoorte Ranges Dry Red, Cabernet Merlot, Merlot, Cabernet Sauvignon.
summary Which Hollywood actress was it who said 'I don't care what they say about me, as long as they spell my name right'? This might be the motto for Koppamurra, which has become embroiled in a bitter argument over the use of the name Koppamurra for the region in which its vineyards are situated, and which is now an extremely important part of the Limestone Coast Zone. As at February 1998 the question appeared headed to the law courts, with Naracoorte Ranges the temporary (and perhaps permanent) regional name. Regardless of that outcome, Koppamurra is better known than it used to be.

Koppamurra Cabernet Merlot

Made from a varying blend of Cabernet Sauvignon, Cabernet Franc and Merlot, with the Cabernet component ranging between a low of 60% and a high of 88%. Cabernet Merlot has always been the most frequently produced wine in the somewhat unpredictable Koppamurra stable, with wines coming and going, and is invariably a pleasant, if relatively light, wine.

🍷🍷🍷🍷 **1996** Medium red-purple; attractive, sweet cedar, red berry, earth and chocolate aromas to a bouquet of medium intensity are followed by equally attractive fresh, red berry fruit flavours on the palate. Nicely ripened and youthful, with soft, dusty tannins. **rating:** 85

➾ **best drinking** 2001 – 2005 **best vintages** '82, '90, '91, '93, '96 **drink with** Light Italian food • $11.50

Koppamurra Cabernet Sauvignon

While Merlot (and Cabernet Merlot blends) have often produced the best Koppamurra wines, Cabernet Sauvignon outperformed the other varieties in 1996.

🍷🍷🍷🍷 **1996** Medium to full red-purple; solid, dark berry/earthy varietal fruit on the bouquet; the palate is quite luscious, with sweet, intense red berry/cassis fruit, and just the barest touch of oak. **rating:** 86

➾ **best drinking** 2001 – 2006 **best vintages** '90, '91, '96 **drink with** Beef Bordelaise • $17.50

---

kraanwood NR

8 Woodies Place, Richmond, Tas 7025 **region** Southern Tasmania
phone (03) 6260 2540 **open** Not
winemaker Frank van der Kraan, Alan Bird (Consultant) **production** 30 **est.** 1994
product range ($16.20 ML) Schonburger, Montage, Pinot Noir.
summary Frank van der Kraan and wife Barbara established their half-hectare vineyard Kraanwood between 1994 and 1995, with approximately equal plantings of pinot noir, chardonnay and cabernet sauvignon. Frank van der Kraan also manages the 1-hectare Pembroke Vineyard, and procures from it small quantities of Schonberger, Chardonnay, Riesling and Sauvignon Blanc. The Kraanwood wines are made with help from Alan Bird of Palmara.

krondorf ★★★☆

Krondorf Road, Tanunda, SA 5352 **region** Barossa Valley
phone (08) 8563 2145 **fax** (08) 8562 3055 **open** 7 days 9–5
winemaker Nick Walker **production** 30 000 **est.** 1978
product range ($9–18 R) Barossa Valley Riesling, Barossa Valley Chablis, Family Reserve Chardonnay, Semillon, Frontignac Spätlese, Coonawarra Shiraz, Shiraz Cabernet, Family Reserve Cabernet Sauvignon; Show Reserve Chardonnay and Cabernet Sauvignon are top-end wines.
summary Part of the Mildara Blass Group, with a tightly focused and controlled range of wines. The Show Reserve Chardonnay is of particular merit, but all of the wines exhibit the technical gloss and represent the value-for-money expected of one of Australia's foremost wine-producing groups.

Krondorf Semillon

The vast majority of Barossa Valley Semillons are heavy, phenolic wines which seem to be masquerading as detuned Chardonnays. Worst of all is their tendency to develop alarmingly quickly, becoming fat and oily as they do so. The '96 vintage of this wine shows it is possible to avoid the trap.

🍷🍷🍷🍷🍷 **1996** Light to medium yellow-green; the bouquet is still attractive, fresh and lively, with lemony varietal fruit; the tangy palate has excellent length and mouthfeel, the oak barely perceptible. **rating:** 90

➾ **best drinking** 1998 – 2002 **best vintages** '96 **drink with** Avocado salad • $16

Krondorf Family Reserve Cabernet Sauvignon

A new range, and I have to admit to a strong allergic reaction to the concept of Family Reserve being produced by a winery owned by one of the largest brewing companies in the world, Fosters Brewing Group. Brand manager and label quibbles to one side, this is a blend of McLaren Vale, Coonawarra and Barossa Cabernet Sauvignon, part barrel-fermented in French oak and then matured in a mix of French and American. All in all, deserves better than the name it has been given.

🍷🍷🍷🍷 **1995** Medium red; a most attractive bouquet with stylish fruit and French oak neatly balanced and integrated; there is more attractive blackberry fruit on the palate with excellent oak balance and integration. **rating:** 88

➾ **best drinking** 1999 – 2005 **best vintages** NA **drink with** Tongue • $16

kyeema estate ★★★★

PO Box 282, Belconnen, ACT 2616 **region** Canberra District
phone (02) 6254 7536 (ah) **fax** (02) 6254 7536 **open** Not
winemaker Andrew McEwin **production** 700 **est.** 1986
product range ($12–16 ML) Semillon, Chardonnay, Shiraz, Cabernet Merlot.
summary Part-time winemaker, part-time wine critic (with *Winewise* magazine) Andrew McEwin produces wines full of flavour and character; every wine released under the Kyeema Estate label has won a show award of some description.

Kyeema Estate Chardonnay

As with all the Kyeema wines, sourced from vineyards in the Canberra region. The '93 vintage aged gracefully and was a silver medal winner at the 1994 Yass Show, and the second-highest pointed wine at that show.

🍷🍷🍷🍷 **1996** Medium to full yellow-green; the bouquet is full of character, with complex, rich toasty barrel-ferment oak inputs, all of which come through strongly on the palate. There is sufficient melon and peach fruit to sustain those characters, however. **rating:** 87

➾ **best drinking** 1998 – 2000 **best vintages** '88, '89, '91, '92, '93, '96 **drink with** Dim sim • $14

Kyeema Estate Shiraz

A wine of real class, made from grapes sourced from various vineyards in the Canberra region, and which in 1992 and again in 1994 was of outstanding quality. The 1996 vintage won three trophies at the 1997 New South Wales Small Winemakers Wine Show.

🍷🍷🍷🍷🍷 **1996** Medium to full red-purple; the bouquet is solid and dense, with dark berry, liquorice and faintly gamey varietal fruit in abundance. On the palate American oak comes through augmenting the powerful varietal fruit. Rich, full and chewy. **rating:** 90

➾ **best drinking** 2002 – 2008 **best vintages** '87, '88, '89, '90, '92, '94, '96 **drink with** Braised beef • $15

laanecoorie ★★★

Bendigo Road, Betley, Vic 3472 **region** Pyrenees
phone (03) 5468 7260 **fax** (03) 5468 7388 **open** Not
winemaker John Ellis (Contract) **production** 1500 **est.** 1982
product range ($20 R) A single Bordeaux-blend dry red of Cabernet Franc, Cabernet Sauvignon and Merlot in roughly equal proportions.
summary John McQuilten's 7.5-hectare vineyard produces grapes of consistently high quality, and competent contract winemaking by John Ellis at Hanging Rock has done the rest.

ladbroke grove NR

Coonawarra Road, Penola, SA 5277 **region** Coonawarra
phone (08) 8737 2082 **fax** (08) 8762 3236 **open** 7 days 10–4
winemaker Ken Ward **production** 800 **est.** 1982
product range ($8–14 CD) Riesling, Late Picked Riesling, Shiraz, Premium Shiraz.
summary Relaunched with both standard and Premium Shiraz after a hiatus; wine quality has been variable, but it does have 2 hectares of hand-pruned shiraz planted by John Redman in the 1960s upon which to draw.

lake barrington estate ★★★☆

Old Wilmot Road, Sheffield, Tas 7306 **region** Northern Tasmania
phone (03) 6491 1249 **fax** (03) 6434 2892 **open** Weekends 10–5
winemaker Steve Lubiana (Sparkling), Andrew Hood (Table), both contract **production** 1000 **est.** 1988
product range ($14–24 CD) Previously, Riesling, Chardonnay, Pinot Noir, Cabernet Sauvignon; henceforth only sparkling, including Alexandra Méthode Champenoise.
summary Lake Barrington Estate is owned by the vivacious and energetic Maree Taylor, and takes its name from the adjacent Lake Barrington, 30 kilometres south of Devonport, on the northern coast of Tasmania. There are picnic facilities at the vineyard, and, needless to say, the scenery is very beautiful. Future production will be of sparkling wine only, and Maree Taylor is contemplating the sale of the vineyard.

lake breeze wines ★★★★☆

Step Road, Langhorne Creek, SA 5255 **region** Langhorne Creek
phone (08) 8537 3017 **fax** (08) 8537 3267 **open** 7 days 10–5
winemaker Greg Follett **production** 6000 **est.** 1987
product range ($9–25 CD) Chardonnay, White Frontignac, Grenache, Cabernet Sauvignon, Shiraz, Bernoota (Cabernet Shiraz), Tawny Port. The premium Winemakers Selection range was introduced in 1996.
summary The Folletts have been farmers at Langhorne Creek since 1880, grape growers since the 1930s. Since 1987 a small proportion of their grapes has been made into wine, and a cellar-door sales facility was opened in early 1991. The quality of the releases has been exemplary, the new Winemakers Selection red wines particularly striking.

Lake Breeze Winemakers Selection Shiraz

Sold only from cellar door and by mail order, the initial release (of the '96 vintage) scheduled for release in September 1998.

🍷🍷🍷🍷 **1996** Full red-purple; an extremely rich, dense and concentrated bouquet with ultra-ripe black cherry fruit and abundant oak. Improbable though it may seem, the palate actually steps up a notch, and might have been better had it not done so; the ultimate magimix essence of fruit and oak. **rating:** 88

➾ **best drinking** 2006 – 2011 **best vintages** '96 **drink with** Leave it in the cellar • $25

Lake Breeze Cabernet Sauvignon

Originally the flag-bearer, but now supplanted by the Winemakers Selection range. Nonetheless, continues to be an outstanding Cabernet.

🍷🍷🍷🍷🍷 **1996** Medium to full red-purple; a rich, ripe and lush bouquet with dark berry and prune fruit aromas is followed by a very rich, dense and concentrated palate with more of those blackcurrant and prune fruit characters. **rating:** 90

➾ **best drinking** 2001 – 2006 **best vintages** '87, '88, '90, '95, '96 **drink with** Smoked kangaroo fillet • $17

Lake Breeze Winemakers Selection Cabernet Sauvignon

Obviously enough, this is the sister wine to the Winemakers Selection Shiraz. Only 250 cases were made, and, like the Shiraz, it is sold only through cellar door and by mailing list. The inaugural vintage earned the top gold medal in its class at the 1997 McLaren Vale Wine Show.

🍷🍷🍷🍷🍷 **1996** Medium to full red-purple; a complex, full bouquet with sweet berry and mint fruit, and well-balanced oak. The palate is exceptionally rich and round, with luscious, sweet red berry fruit which more than holds its own against the oak. **rating:** 94

➾ **best drinking** 2001 – 2010 **best vintages** '96 **drink with** Rare beef • $25

lake george winery ★★★

Federal Highway, Collector, NSW 2581 **region** Canberra District
phone (02) 4848 0039 **fax** (02) 4848 0039 **open** Not
winemaker Dr Edgar F Riek **production** 500 **est.** 1971
product range ($16.50–32.95 R) Chardonnay, Semillon, Sauternes, Pinot Noir, Cabernet Sauvignon, Merlot, Fortifieds.
summary Dr Edgar Riek is an inquisitive, iconoclastic winemaker who is not content with his role as Godfather and founder of the Canberra district, forever experimenting and innovating. His fortified wines, vintaged in northeastern Victoria but matured at Lake George, are very good. By 1998, however, Edgar Riek was looking for a successor, and threatening to hang up his boots. We shall see.

lake's folly ★★★★★

Broke Road, Pokolbin, NSW 2321 **region** Lower Hunter Valley
phone (02) 4998 7507 **fax** (02) 4998 7322 **open** Mon–Sat 10–4
winemaker Stephen Lake **production** 4000 **est.** 1963
product range ($32 CD) Simplicity itself: Chardonnay and Cabernets (with occasional small releases of Reserve Cabernets).
summary The first of the weekend wineries to produce wines for commercial sale, long revered for its Cabernet Sauvignon and thereafter its Chardonnay. Very properly, terroir and climate produce a distinct regional influence, and thereby a distinctive wine style. Some find this attractive, others are less tolerant.

Lake's Folly Chardonnay

Only 1200 cases a year (with some seasonal variation) are made from estate-grown grapes. The wine is always correct in style, and – unlike the Cabernets – should cause no discussion or argument.

1996 Glowing yellow-green; a complex yet elegant bouquet with multilayered mineral/stone fruit characters, giving a Burgundian tang and grip. A stylish wine in which the winemaker's thumbprints are very evident, yet still retains a core of tight fruit in a highly structured wine with secondary characters giving complexity. Outstanding. **rating:** 94

best drinking 1999 – 2006 **best vintages** '81, '82, '83, '84, '86, '89, '92, '94, '96 **drink with** Sweetbreads • $32

Lake's Folly Cabernets

Like Max Lake himself, never far from controversy; again like Max Lake, full of earthy personality. It is not a wine which can or should be judged by conventional standards; if it were to be so treated, the judgment would not do the wine justice. A slightly varying blend of 65% Cabernet Sauvignon, 15% Petit Verdot, 10% Shiraz and 10% Merlot. Cork taint affecting many older bottles is an unpredictable hazard.

1996 Medium red-purple; a quite austere bouquet with earthy/leathery aromas bordering on the astringent. Loosens up slightly on the palate, which is predominantly driven by austere earthy Cabernet, speaking of the terroir, but with definite hints of violets and mint to provide softer notes. **rating:** 87

best drinking 2000 – 2006 **best vintages** '69, '75, '81, '87, '89, '91, '93, '96 **drink with** Rabbit, hare • $32

---

lalla gully vineyard ★★★☆

Brooks Road, Lalla, Tas 7250 **region** Northern Tasmania
phone (03) 6331 2325 **fax** (03) 6331 2325 **open** By appointment or at Ripples The River Cafe in Launceston
winemaker Andrew Hood (Contract), Kim Seagram **production** 3000 **est.** 1988
product range ($20–25 R) Chardonnay, Sauvignon Blanc, Pinot Noir.
summary Owners Rod and Kim Ascui have established 1 hectare each of pinot noir, chardonnay and sauvignon blanc, producing the first tiny crop in 1992. The beautifully situated vineyard is immaculately tended, and wine quality reflects the care lavished on it.

Lalla Gully Sauvignon Blanc

The immaculately tended Lalla Gully vineyard produced its first Sauvignon Blanc in 1995, making a singularly auspicious debut in a vintage more noted for the generosity of its production than intensity of flavour.

1997 Pale green-yellow; an amazingly pungent and strongly varietal bouquet which explains why some people describe Sauvignon Blanc as smelling like cat's pee; a politer description is grassy/herbal. The palate shows similarly intense grassy/herbaceous flavours which some will love, and some will hate, but there is no questioning its authenticity. **rating:** 84

best drinking 1998 – 1999 **best vintages** NA **drink with** Tasmanian lobster • $20

---

lamont wines

85 Bisdee Road, Millendon, WA 6056 **region** Swan District
phone (08) 9296 4485 **fax** (08) 9296 1663 **open** Wed-Sun 10–4
winemaker Mark Warren **production** 7000 **est.** 1978

product range ($9–16 CD) Riesling, Verdelho, Barrel Fermented Semillon, Chardonnay, Barrel Fermented Chardonnay, WB (White Burgundy), Sweet White, Light Red Cabernet, Cabernet, Shiraz, Merlot; Fortifieds, including Flor Fino, Amontillado and Reserve Sherry (Oloroso style).
summary Corin Lamont is the daughter of the late Jack Mann, and makes her wines in the image of those her father used to make, resplendent in their generosity. Lamont also boasts a superb restaurant, with a gallery for the sale and promotion of local arts.

Lamont Verdelho

Jack Mann used to insist that all grapes, white or red, should be left on the vine 'until the vine is no longer able to nourish them'. Obviously enough, he favoured full-bodied styles; the Lamont Verdelho is exactly as he would have wished it to be, and is an outstanding example of the variety.
🍷🍷🍷🍷 **1997** Light green-yellow; a highly aromatic and wonderfully rich bouquet (boo-key in Mann-speak) with abundant fruit salad aromas is complemented by a rich palate, full of fruit flavour and fruit sweetness, finishing with balancing acidity. **rating:** 86

➪ **best drinking** 1998 – 2000 **best vintages** NA **drink with** Rich pasta • $11

Lamont Barrel Fermented Chardonnay

Jack Mann was big on fruit, but not so much on oak, and in particular, new oak. This wine, however, might well have got through his guard, as the oak has been sensitively handled (much more so than in the Semillon of the same vintage).
🍷🍷🍷🍷 **1997** Medium to full yellow-green; the bouquet is smooth, with ripe melon, fig and peach fruit supported by subtle, slightly charry, oak. The palate is driven by attractive melon, citrus and yellow peach fruit; a touch of oak rounds off the finish. **rating:** 87

➪ **best drinking** 1998 – 1999 **best vintages** NA **drink with** Corn-fed chicken • $16

langmeil winery ★★★☆

Cnr Para and Langmeil Roads, Tanunda, SA 5352 **region** Barossa Valley
phone (08) 8563 2595 **fax** (08) 8563 3622 **open** 7 days 10–5
winemaker Paul Lindner **production** 5000 **est.** 1996
product range ($10.50–25 CD) White Frontignac, Barossa Riesling, Chardonnay, Cabernet Rosé, Shiraz, Barossa Grenache, Selwin's Lot (Cabernet blend), Fortifieds.
summary Vines were first planted at Langmeil in the 1840s, and the first winery on the site, known as Paradale Wines, opened in 1932. In 1996 the Lindner (of St Hallett fame) and Bitter families formed a partnership to acquire and refurbish the winery and its 5-hectare vineyard, planted to shiraz. The quality of the wines is uniformly good.

Langmeil Shiraz

The team at Langmeil describe this wine as 'a classic example of the honest traditional Barossan Shiraz'. No hyperbole here, that is exactly what the wine is.
🍷🍷🍷🍷 **1996** Medium to full red-purple; a rich, ripe and luscious bouquet with abundant black cherry and mint fruit billows into the palate, which delivers the same in spades. Fruit-driven; the barest hint of oak. **rating:** 85

➪ **best drinking** 1998 – 2005 **best vintages** NA **drink with** Kangaroo fillet • $19.50

lark hill ★★★★☆

RMB 281 Gundaroo Road, Bungendore, NSW 2621 **region** Canberra District
phone (02) 6238 1393 **fax** (02) 6238 1393 **open** 7 days 10–5
winemaker Dr David Carpenter, Sue Carpenter **production** 4000 **est.** 1978
product range ($16–24 R) Rhine Riesling, Sauvignon Blanc Semillon, Chardonnay, Late Harvest (dessert wine), Pinot Noir, Cabernet Merlot, The Canberra Fizz Sparkling.
summary The Lark Hill vineyard is situated at an altitude of 860 metres, level with the observation deck on Black Mountain Tower, and offering splendid views of the Lake George Escarpment. Right from the outset, David and Sue Carpenter have made wines of real quality, style and elegance, but achieved extraordinary success at the 1997 Sydney Wine Show, topping two classes (with gold medals in each). At the 1998 Canberra Regional Wine Show, Lark Hill won two trophies, five silver and four bronze medals.

Lark Hill Pinot Noir

A wine which forces me to drink my words, for I have always held the view that the climate of the Canberra district is not suited to Pinot Noir. In 1996, at least, David and Sue Carpenter achieved a minor miracle with this gold medal winner from the 1997 Sydney Wine Show. The '97 vintage, while perhaps not quite in the class of the '96, shows the prior year was no fluke, winning the '97 Pinot Noir Trophy at the 1998 Canberra Regional Wine Show.

1997 Medium to full red-purple; the aromas are fragrant and complex, with positive varietal plummy fruit and well-handled spicy oak. The palate ranges through spice, earth and forest before opening out into the plum flavours promised by the bouquet, the finish still to soften. **rating:** 85

➾ **best drinking** 1998 – 2001 **best vintages** '96, '97 **drink with** Venison • $22

latara NR

Cnr McDonalds and Deaseys Roads, Pokolbin, NSW 2320 **region** Lower Hunter Valley
phone (02) 4998 7320 **open** Sat 9–5, Sun 9–4
winemaker Iain Riggs (Contract) **production** 250 **est.** 1979
product range ($9.50–11 CD) Semillon, Cabernet Sauvignon, Shiraz.
summary The bulk of the grapes produced on the 5-hectare Latara vineyard, which was planted in 1979, are sold to Brokenwood. A small quantity is vinified for Latara and sold under its label. As one would expect, the wines are very competently made, and are of show medal standard.

laurel bank 

130 Black Snake Lane, Granton, Tas 7030 **region** Southern Tasmania
phone (03) 6263 5977 **fax** (03) 6263 3117 **open** By appointment
winemaker Andrew Hood (Contract) **production** 600 **est.** 1987
product range ($17–19.50 R) Sauvignon Blanc, Pinot Noir, Cabernet Merlot.
summary Laurel (hence Laurel Bank) and Kerry planted their 2-hectare vineyard in 1986. They delayed the first release of their wines for some years, and (by virtue of the number of entries they were able to make) won the trophy for Most Successful Exhibitor at the 1995 Royal Hobart Wine Show. Things have settled down since, wine quality is solid and reliable.

Laurel Bank Sauvignon Blanc

Produced from 1 hectare of estate plantings, and raises the question why more Sauvignon Blanc is not grown in Tasmania.

🍷🍷🍷🍷 **1997** Light to medium yellow-green; there is quite potent herbal/grassy Sauvignon Blanc varietal character on the bouquet, which is of good depth. Likewise, the palate has excellent length and bite, with crisp, tangy lemon and herb flavours. An altogether attractive wine. **rating:** 86

➾ **best drinking** 1998 – 1999 **best vintages** NA **drink with** Calamari • $17

lauren brook ★★★☆

Eedle Terrace, Bridgetown, WA 6255 **region** Other Wineries of WA
phone (08) 9761 2676 **fax** (08) 9761 1879 **open** Mon-Fri 11–4, weekends 11–5
winemaker Stephen Bullied **production** 1000 **est.** 1993
product range ($15–22 CD) Riesling, Bridgetown Blend, Late Harvest, Shiraz, Cabernet Sauvignon, Fortissimo.
summary Lauren Brook is established on the banks of the beautiful Blackwood River, and is the only commercial winery in the Bridgetown subregion of Mount Barker. An 80-year-old barn on the property has been renovated to contain a micro-winery and a small gallery. There is 1 hectare of estate chardonnay coming into bearing, supplemented by grapes purchased locally.

Lauren Brook Cabernet Sauvignon

Produced from grapes grown in small local vineyards in the vicinity of Bridgetown, and exhibiting promising varietal character.

🍷🍷🍷🍷 **1996** Bright purple-red; the fruit is clean, of medium intensity, the oak a fraction disjointed on the bouquet. The palate, however, shows good structure and equally good dark berry/cassis varietal character; youthful tannins are on the firm side but should settle down with age. **rating:** 84

➾ **best drinking** 2001 – 2006 **best vintages** NA **drink with** Beef with olives • $20

lavender bay NR

39 Paringa Road, Red Hill South, Vic 3937 **region** Mornington Peninsula
phone (03) 9869 4405 **fax** (03) 9869 4423 **open** Not
winemaker Garry Crittenden (Contract) **production** NA **est.** 1988
product range Chardonnay, Pinot Noir.
summary Marketing consultant Kevin Luscombe established Lavender Bay in 1988 on a spectacular 4-hectare property in Red Hill South. Tiny quantities of the first three vintages were progressively released onto the market in mid-1997, distributed through Flinders Wholesale Wines.

lawson's hill ★★★

Henry Lawson Drive, Eurunderee, Mudgee, NSW 2850 **region** Mudgee
phone (02) 6373 3953 **fax** (02) 6373 3948 **open** 7 days 9.30–5
winemaker Various contract and José Grace **production** 4000 **est.** 1985
product range ($10–20 CD) Chardonnay, Verdelho, Sauvignon Blanc, Riesling, Traminer Riesling, Gewurztraminer, Louisa Rose, Merlot, Cabernet Merlot, Pinot Noir, Dryland Cabernet Sauvignon, Port.
summary Former music director and arranger (for musical acts in Sydney clubs) José Grace and wife June run a strongly tourist-oriented operation situated next-door to the Henry Lawson Memorial, offering a kaleidoscopic array of wines, produced from 8 hectares of vineyard, and made under contract. The red wines are richly representative of the deeply coloured, flavoursome Mudgee-style.

leasingham ★★★★☆

7 Dominic Street, Clare, SA 5453 **region** Clare Valley
phone (08) 8842 2555 **fax** (08) 8842 3293 **open** Mon-Fri 8.30–5.30, weekends 10–4
winemaker Richard Rowe, Rodney Hooper **production** 95 000 **est.** 1893
product range ($12–34 R) Classic Clare Riesling, Shiraz, and Cabernet Sauvignon at the top end; mid-range Bin 7 Riesling, Bin 37 Chardonnay, Bin 42 Semillon Sauvignon Blanc, Bin 56 Cabernet Malbec, Bin 61 Shiraz; finally low-priced Hutt Creek Riesling, Sauvignon Blanc, Shiraz Cabernet.
summary Successive big-company ownerships and various peregrinations in labelling and branding have not resulted in any permanent loss of identity or quality. With a core of high-quality, aged vineyards to draw on, Leasingham is in fact going from strength to strength under BRL Hardy's direction. The Stentorian red wines take no prisoners, compacting densely rich fruit and layer upon layer of oak into every long-lived bottle.

Leasingham Bin 61 Shiraz

A junior brother to the Classic Clare, with less weight and extract, and seemingly relying upon the use of some oak chips as well as barrels. The quality of Clare Valley Shiraz is still very evident, and the wine is exceptionally well-priced. The '94 vintage won three trophies.

🍷🍷🍷🍷 **1996** Medium to full red-purple; a massive wine as ever, but the fruit and oak seem in balance on the bouquet, with ample black cherry/blackberry fruit. The full frontal palate is unashamedly concentrated, with juicy/chewy fruit and oak, but it all works well. **rating:** 89

➾ **best drinking** 2001 – 2010 **best vintages** '88, '90, '91, '93, '94, '96 **drink with** Spiced lamb kebabs • $20.90

Leasingham Classic Clare Shiraz

The best Clare Valley Shiraz available to Leasingham is matured in (real) new American oak barrels, consistently producing a wine of tremendous depth and richness. Whether less would be better depends on one's personal perspective; certainly the wine has had great success in wine shows, none more so than the '94 which won the Jimmy Watson Trophy in 1995.

🍷🍷🍷🍷 **1995** Dense red-purple; the bouquet is quite literally huge, with masses of fruit and masses of blockbuster charry oak; the palate provides the same in spades, simply monumental, with extraordinary amounts of extract and oak. A D9 bulldozer. Retasted January 1998 with identical notes. **rating:** 88

➾ **best drinking** 2004 – 2014 **best vintages** '88, '90, '91, '92, '94, '95 **drink with** Kangaroo, strong red meat, strong cheese • $34

Leasingham Bin 56 Cabernet Malbec

The blend of 85% Cabernet Sauvignon and 15% Malbec has been a Clare Valley specialty for decades; anyone lucky enough to have the '71 Bin 56 or virtually any of Wendouree's Cabernet Malbecs will need no persuasion of the merits of the blend. The '94 vintage won two gold and two silver medals, continuing a consistent record of show success for this wine. The '95 vintage has been particularly successful in the show ring, winning four gold medals.

🍷🍷🍷🍷🍷 (4½) **1995** Full red-purple; a concentrated bouquet with hints of black fruit and dark chocolate aromas supported by abundant but not excessive oak. Voluptuously rich on the palate, with a range of chewy dark fruit and dark chocolate flavours. The wine has good tannin structure, and it is not hard to see why it won four gold medals in the first year of its show life. **rating:** 90

➾ **best drinking** 2000 – 2010 **best vintages** '88, '90, '91, '94, '95 **drink with** Jugged hare • $20.90

---

leconfield ★★★★☆

Penola Road, Coonawarra, SA 5263 **region** Coonawarra
phone (08) 8737 2326 **fax** (08) 8737 2285 **open** 7 days 10–5
winemaker Ralph Fowler **production** 16 000 **est.** 1974
product range ($16–25 R) Riesling, Twelve Rows Commemorative Riesling, Noble Riesling, Chardonnay (Wooded and Unwooded), Merlot, Shiraz, Cabernet.
summary A distinguished estate with a proud, even if relatively short, history. Long renowned for its Cabernet Sauvignon, its repertoire has steadily grown with the emphasis on single varietal wines. The style overall is fruit, rather than oak, driven.

Leconfield Shiraz

A wine which is not produced every vintage, but only in those years in which the fruit is judged to have gained sufficient ripeness and depth. In 1995 the wine won vinous Tattslotto, walking away with a truckload of trophies from the Adelaide Wine Show, including the title of 'Winemaker of the Year' for Ralph Fowler (and a business-class trip around the world for two). The '96 may not be quite in the same class, but is a worthy successor.

🍷🍷🍷🍷🍷 **1996** Medium red-purple; the initial impression is of fresh spice and earth fruit, but complex liquorice characters gradually built in the glass; subtle oak. Similarly, spicy varietal character grew and grew on retasting; an elegant but complex wine in a particular style. **rating:** 90

➪ **best drinking** 2000 – 2004 **best vintages** '88, '90, '91, '94, '95, '96 **drink with** Beef casserole • $22.90

---

leeuwin estate ★★★★★

Stevens Road, Margaret River, WA 6285 **region** Margaret River
phone (08) 9430 4099 **fax** (08) 9430 5687 **open** 7 days 10.30–4.30
winemaker Bob Cartwright **production** 40 000 **est.** 1974
product range ($15–67.45 CD) Art Series Chardonnay, Riesling, Sauvignon Blanc, Pinot Noir, Cabernet Sauvignon; Prelude Classic Dry White, Chardonnay, Pinot Noir, Cabernet Sauvignon are lower-priced alternatives, with a non-vintage Prelude blended white the cheapest wine on the list.
summary Leeuwin Estate's Chardonnay is, in my opinion, Australia's finest example based on the wines of the last 15 years. The Cabernet Sauvignon, too, is an excellent wine with great style and character. Almost inevitably, the other wines in the portfolio are not in the same Olympian class, although the Prelude Chardonnay and Sauvignon Blanc are impressive at their lower price level.

Leeuwin Estate Art Series Sauvignon Blanc

Inevitably, lives in the shade of Leeuwin Estate's Chardonnay, but this is a distinguished wine which once again shows how well Margaret River is suited to Sauvignon Blanc, particularly at the southern end. It is produced on 1.5 hectares of estate plantings; 70% is barrel-fermented in French oak and aged on lees for three months before being blended with the tank-fermented component. None of the oak used is new, and the oak influence is very subtle.

🍷🍷🍷🍷 **1997** Light yellow-green; the bouquet is light and crisp, moderately aromatic, with gentle gooseberry and herb fruit aromas. The palate is clean and fresh, quite delicate, with attractive mouthfeel and finish, but no aggression. **rating:** 85

➪ **best drinking** 1998 – 1999 **best vintages** '95, '97 **drink with** Shellfish • $26.92

Leeuwin Estate Art Series Chardonnay

The core of the Art Series Chardonnay is Block 20 (one of five blocks on the estate) with yields never exceeding 2.5 tonnes to the acre, and frequently less than 2 tonnes. Barrel fermentation in the finest French oak, and prolonged bottle maturation do the rest.

🍷🍷🍷🍷🍷 **1995** Light to medium yellow-green; an exceptionally intense, complex yet fine bouquet with perfectly married nutty barrel-ferment characters running through sweet melon and citrus fruit is followed by an intense, yet elegant palate with melon, cashew, chestnut, citrus and oak spice flavours. Long and penetrating, with excellent acidity, the wine has an indefinite future, however seductive it is now. **rating:** 97

➾ **best drinking** 1999 – 2010 **best vintages** '80, '81, '82, '83, '85, '87, '89, '90, '92, '94, '95 **drink with** Richer veal, chicken dishes • $67.45

Leeuwin Estate Prelude Chardonnay

The second label for Leeuwin Chardonnay, and, as the name indicates, typically released two years before the Art Series wine. Its lower price makes it much more accessible, and it is a wine of considerable quality and character.

🍷🍷🍷🍷 **1996** Glowing yellow-green; the bouquet is intensely fragrant, with pungent grapefruit/melon aromas. The palate has the same intense fruit, with distinct citrussy overtones, and only the barest touch of oak. Not everyone will like this particular fruit character, but I do. **rating:** 89

➾ **best drinking** 1998 – 2003 **best vintages** '95, '96 **drink with** Sashimi • $26.35

Leeuwin Estate Art Series Cabernet Sauvignon

Typically lean and elegant wines which take many years to show their best, making no concessions to the more typical softly fruity Australian commercial red wine styles.

🍷🍷🍷🍷 **1994** Medium red-purple; the bouquet is of medium intensity, with a mix of cedary, earthy and more briary aromas. The palate has attractive texture and flavour, with chocolate, briar and cedar overtones to the red fruits. Almost milky soft tannins run through the length of the palate. **rating:** 86

➾ **best drinking** 1999 – 2006 **best vintages** '79, '86, '87, '89, '90, '92, '93 **drink with** Eye fillet of lamb • $40.20

lefroy brook NR

Glauder Road, Pemberton, WA 6260 **region** Pemberton
phone (08) 9386 8385 **open** Not
winemaker Peter Fimmel (Contract) **production** 350 **est.** 1982
product range ($21.95 R) Chardonnay, Pinot Noir.
summary Owned by Perth residents Pat and Barbara Holt, the former a graduate in biochemistry and microbiology working in medical research, but with a passion for Burgundy. The 1.5 hectares of vines are now both netted and fenced with steel mesh, producing wines which, on tastings to date, are outside the mainstream.

leland estate ★★★★

PO Lenswood, SA 5240 **region** Adelaide Hills
phone (08) 8389 6928 **open** Not
winemaker Robb Cootes **production** 900 **est.** 1986

product range ($18–26 R) Sauvignon Blanc (piercingly pure and fragrant), Pinot Noir, Neudorf Adele (Sparkling).

summary Former Yalumba senior winemaker Robb Cootes, with a Master of Science degree, deliberately opted out of mainstream life when he established Leland Estate, living in a split-level, one-roomed house built from timber salvaged from trees killed in the Ash Wednesday bushfires. The Sauvignon Blanc is usually superb.

lengs & cooter NR

24 Lindsay Terrace, Belair, SA 5042 **region** Warehouse
phone (08) 8278 3998 **fax** (08) 8278 3998 **open** Not
winemaker Contract **production** 2500 **est.** 1993

product range ($13.99–20 ML) Watervale Riesling, Clare Valley Unwooded Semillon, Old Bush Vines Grenache, Clare Valley Old Vines Shiraz, Swinton (Cabernet blend)

summary Carel Lengs and Colin Cooter began making wine as a hobby in the early 1980s. Each had (and has) a full-time occupation outside the wine industry, and it was all strictly for fun. One thing has led to another, and although they still possess neither vineyards or what might truly be described as a winery, the wines have graduated to big boy status, winning gold medals at national wine shows and receiving critical acclaim from writers across Australia. To say the style of the reds is emphatically generous is to damn with faint praise.

Lengs & Cooter Clare Valley Old Vines Shiraz

Produced from grapes grown on four small Clare Valley vineyards matured for 12 months in American oak. A silver medal winner at the 1997 Liquorland National Wine Show.

🍷🍷🍷🍷 **1996** Full red-purple; super sweet black cherry and chocolate fruit constitutes the core of the wine both on the bouquet and palate. There are fine tannins to provide structure and balance, and an attractive hint of mint also appears on the palate. **rating:** 86

➭ **best drinking** 2000 – 2006 **best vintages** '96 **drink with** Rib of beef • $20

Lengs & Cooter Swinton

Swinton takes its name from a property established by the forefathers of the proprietors in 1849 in the Sturt River Gorge of the Coromandel Valley. The property was subdivided in the late 1960s, but a small planting of cabernet sauvignon was established in 1971, and it is this planting, blended with Shiraz and Merlot from Blewitt Springs, which produces Swinton.

🍷🍷🍷🍷½ **1996** Dense red-purple; the bouquet shows massive fruit extract with dark berry/foresty/briary aromas, the palate exhibiting all these flavours together with liquorice and tannins. Truly, a 20-year proposition. **rating:** 90

➭ **best drinking** 2006 – 2016 **best vintages** NA **drink with** Leave it in the cellar • $17.90

---

lenswood vineyards ★★★★★

3 Cyril John Court, Athelstone, SA 5076 **region** Adelaide Hills
phone (08) 8365 3733 **fax** (08) 8365 3766 **open** Not
winemaker Tim Knappstein **production** 5500 **est.** 1981

product range ($23–38 R) Semillon, Sauvignon Blanc, Chardonnay, Pinot Noir, Cabernets.

summary Lenswood Vineyards is now the sole (and full-time) occupation of Tim and Annie Knappstein, Tim Knappstein having retired from the winery which bears his name, and having sold most of the Clare vineyards to Petaluma (along with the wine business). With 25.5 hectares of close-planted, vertically trained vineyards maintained to the exacting standards of Tim Knappstein, the business will undoubtedly add to the reputation of the Adelaide Hills as an ultra-premium area. Complex Chardonnay, intense Sauvignon Blanc and broodingly powerful yet stylish Pinot Noir are trailblazers.

Lenswood Vineyards Semillon

An extension to the Lenswood range of wines, and an impressive addition at that. Three-quarters of the wine is barrel-fermented in a mix of new and one-year-old French oak barriques, and kept on its lees for five months with fortnightly stirring. The balance is stainless steel fermented and kept in steel until blending and bottling.

🍷🍷🍷🍷🍷 **1997** Medium green-yellow; rich, spicy barrel-ferment oak aromas are quite pronounced on the bouquet, but so is the rich fruit. The same dynamics are at work on the palate, with complex, tangy barrel-ferment flavours and lingering fruit on the finish. **rating:** 90

➪ **best drinking** 1999 – 2005 **best vintages** NA **drink with** Pork rillettes • $23

Lenswood Vineyards Sauvignon Blanc

Produced from 7.6 hectares, which is in fact the largest varietal planting at Lenswood Vineyards (22 hectares in all) and which makes a quite superlative wine. The 1997 was the only gold medal winner in its class at the 1997 Adelaide Hills Wine Show, heading a star-studded field.

🍷🍷🍷🍷🍷 **1997** Light green-yellow; attractive, lively passionfruit, herb and gooseberry aromas dance along a fragrant bouquet. It has masses of passionfruit, gooseberry and tropical fruit, with just a touch of herbaceousness lurking underneath to give the wine structure and bite. **rating:** 94

➪ **best drinking** 1998 – 1999 **best vintages** '94, '95, '97 **drink with** Shellfish • $23

Lenswood Vineyards Chardonnay

Produced from 2.2 hectares of estate vineyards planted in 1981 and 1984. Only the best wine is chosen for release under the Lenswood Vineyards label, the remainder being disposed of elsewhere. The few releases to date have been of very high quality.

🍷🍷🍷🍷 **1996** Medium yellow-green; an exceedingly complex wine on both bouquet and palate, with cashew/mealy malolactic fermentation characters to the fore, and likewise fairly pronounced oak. One can see why the malolactic fermentation was employed, as there is quite pronounced acidity on the finish of the wine, which will almost certainly settle down with further time. **rating:** 86

➪ **best drinking** 1999 – 2003 **best vintages** '93, '94, '95 **drink with** Terrine of smoked salmon • $30

Lenswood Vineyards Pinot Noir

Since a stellar debut in 1990, has been quite outstanding, significantly outperforming other producers in the region, and leaving no doubt that the Lenswood area will in time become a most important producer of Pinot Noir. As Tim Knappstein himself observes, the style is fuller, riper and more robust than that of the Yarra Valley. It has found much favour, and the Lenswood Pinots have established themselves as leading examples of the fuller style of Australian Pinot Noir. The '96 won a number of major awards and gold medals in 1997.

🍷🍷🍷🍷🍷 **1996** Incredibly deep, dense red-purple; the bouquet is as concentrated, powerful and as dense as the colour promises, with strong plummy fruit. A wine which takes no prisoners on the palate, again with massively concentrated plummy varietal fruit, and strong tannins to boot. Robert Parker would just love this wine. Gold medal winner 1997 Adelaide Hills Regional Wine Show. **rating:** 90

➭ **best drinking** 2000 – 2005 **best vintages** '91, '93, '94, '95, '96 **drink with** Quail, hare • $38

lenton brae estate NR

Willyabrup Valley, Margaret River, WA 6285 **region** Margaret River
phone (08) 9755 6255 **fax** (08) 9755 6268 **open** 7 days 10–6
winemaker Edward Tomlinson **production** NFP **est.** 1983
product range ($16–21 CD) Chardonnay, Semillon Sauvignon Blanc, Sauvignon Blanc, Late Harvest (dessert wine), Cabernet Sauvignon, Cabernet Merlot.
summary Former architect, town-planner and political wine activist Bruce Tomlinson built a strikingly beautiful winery, but will not stand for criticism of his wines.

leo buring ★★★★

Tanunda Road, Nuriootpa, SA 5355 **region** Barossa Valley
phone (08) 8563 2184 **fax** (08) 8563 2804 **open** Mon-Sat 10–5, Sun 1–5
winemaker Geoff Henriks **production** 18 000 **est.** 1931
product range ($8.30–17 R) A very much simplified range of Clare Valley Riesling, Late Picked Clare Valley Riesling, Clare Valley Chardonnay, Clare Valley Semillon and Barossa/Coonawarra Cabernet Sauvignon, all under the split label introduced in 1996; the Aged Show Releases are now under the Leonay Eden Valley label.
summary Earns its high rating by virtue of being Australia's foremost producer of Rieslings over a 30-year period, with a rich legacy left by former winemaker John Vickery. But it also has the disconcerting habit of bobbing up here and there with very good wines made from other varieties, even if not so consistently.

Leo Buring Leonay Riesling

As part of the 1996 revamp of the Leo Buring range, the old complex bin numbers have been abandoned. The best wines made from the Eden Valley and Clare Valley are held back as show reserve wines, and released with five or more years bottle age under the Leonay label. In a perverse and confusing marketing decision, the label design is identical to the 'split label' commercial release of the current vintage.

🍷🍷🍷🍷🍷 **1992** Watervale. Glowing yellow-green; a rich, soft and toasty bouquet with some citrus in the background and the first signs of varietal kerosene aromas developing. Now full, rich and flavoursome, with smooth lime and toast, seemingly reaching its peak, and will hold it for years to come. **rating:** 92

➭ **best drinking** 1998 – 2005 **best vintages** '70, '72, '75, '77, '79, '90, '91, '92 **drink with** Asparagus and salmon salad • $19.80

Leo Buring Barossa/Coonawarra Cabernet Sauvignon

An approximately equal blend of Barossa Valley and Coonawarra Cabernet Sauvignon matured in a mix of new and two-year-old American oak barrels for 12 months. Has been a consistent medal winner in national wine shows in recent years.

🍷🍷🍷🍷 **1994** Medium to full red-purple; a solid bouquet with plenty of sweet dark berry/blackcurrant/mulberry fruit, with a nice mix of chocolate and berry fruit on the palate. The oak is subtle and well integrated, the tannins balanced. **rating:** 89

➭ **best drinking** 1999 – 2004 **best vintages** '93, '94 **drink with** Rib of beef • $14.95

liebich wein NR

Steingarten Road, Rowland Flat, SA 5352 **region** Barossa Valley
phone (08) 8524 4543 **fax** (08) 8524 4543 **open** Weekends 11–5, Mon-Fri by appointment
winemaker Ron Liebich **production** 600 **est.** 1992
product range ($9–18 CD) Riesling of the Valleys (a blend of Barossa and Clare Valley Riesling), Riesling Traminer, Chardonnay, Cabernet Sauvignon, Bush Vine Grenache, Classic Old Barossa Tawny Port, Benno Port; bulk port constitutes major sales.
summary Liebich Wein is Barossa Deutsch for 'Love I wine'. The Liebich family has been grape growers and winemakers at Rowland Flat since 1919, with Ron 'Darky' Liebich one of the great local characters. He himself commenced making wine in 1969, but it was not until 1992 that together with wife Janet he began selling wine under the Liebich Wein label.

lillydale vineyards ★★★☆

Lot 10, Davross Court, Seville, Vic 3139 **region** Yarra Valley
phone (03) 5964 2016 **fax** (03) 5964 3009 **open** 7 days 11–5
winemaker Jim Brayne **production** NFP **est.** 1976
product range ($14–17 R) Under the Yarra label Sauvignon Blanc, Gewurztraminer, Chardonnay, Pinot Noir, Cabernet Merlot, Yarra Gold.
summary Acquired by McWilliam's Wines in 1994; Alex White has departed, and Max McWilliam is in charge of the business. With a number of other major developments, notably Coonawarra and Barwang, on its plate, McWilliam's has so far adopted a softly, softly approach to Lillydale Vineyards, although a winery restaurant was opened in February 1997.

Lillydale Pinot Noir

An attractive wine very much in the family style, though with (relatively speaking) a little more depth than the white wines.

🍷🍷🍷🍷 **1997** Medium red-purple; the bouquet, initially firm and a little closed, progressively opened up with good plum and cherry varietal fruit. The palate, likewise firm, but with good weight and structure, also has plenty of plummy fruit, finishing with fine tannins. Given two or three years, will soften and gain complexity. **rating:** 86

➪ **best drinking** 1999 – 2002 **best vintages** '95, '96, '97 **drink with** Chinese seafood • $15.95

lillypilly estate ★★★☆

Lillypilly Road, Leeton, NSW 2705 **region** Riverina
phone (02) 6953 4069 **fax** (02) 6953 4980 **open** Mon-Sat 10–5.30, Sun by appointment
winemaker Robert Fiumara **production** 10 000 **est.** 1982
product range ($9.70–21.50 CD) Riesling, Chardonnay, Sauvignon Blanc, Pound Hill Classic Dry White, Tramillon® (Traminer Semillon), Noble Riesling, Noble Traminer, Noble Semillon, Noble Muscat of Alexandria, Red Velvet® (medium sweet red), Cabernet Sauvignon, Shiraz, Vintage Port.
summary Apart from occasional Vintage Ports the best wines by far are the botrytised white wines, with the Noble Muscat of Alexandria unique to the winery; these wines have both style and intensity of flavour, and can age well. The Noble Semillon and Noble Traminer add strings to the bow.

Lillypilly Estate Noble Muscat Of Alexandria

A Lillypilly specialty, and one of the few botrytised Muscats made in the country. Even then, it is only made in exceptional vintages, the only releases to date being from '85, '87, '90, '91 and '96. The wine was a finalist in the 1998 Winewise Small Makers Competition, looking the best of the sweet wines from Lillypilly in the 1996 vintage.

🍷🍷🍷🍷🍷 **1996** Full straw-yellow; both the bouquet and the palate show extraordinarily fragrant and intense muscat aromas, enhanced and enriched by the botrytis, without subverting the essential varietal fruit. Simply delicious. **rating:** 90

➯ **best drinking** 1998 – 2001 **best vintages** '85, '87, '90, '96 **drink with** Tarte Tatin • $16.25

lindemans (coonawarra) ★★★★

Main Penola-Naracoorte Road, Coonawarra, SA 5263 **region** Coonawarra
phone (08) 8736 3205 **fax** (08) 8736 3250 **open** 7 days 10–4
winemaker Phillip John **production** 15 000 **est.** 1908
product range ($36 R) Under the new Coonawarra Vineyard label, Riesling, Sauvignon Blanc; then come the premium red trio of Pyrus (Cabernet blend), Limestone Ridge (Shiraz Cabernet), and St George (Cabernet Sauvignon).
summary Lindemans is clearly the strongest brand other than Penfolds in the Southcorp Group, with some great vineyards and a great history. The Coonawarra vineyards are of ever-increasing importance because of the move towards regional identity in the all-important export markets, which has led to the emergence of a new range of regional/varietal labels. Whether the fullest potential of the vineyards (from a viticultural viewpoint) is being realised is a matter of debate.

Lindemans Limestone Ridge

Arguably the most distinguished of the Coonawarra trio. A variable blend of Shiraz and Cabernet Sauvignon, varying from as much as 80% Shiraz to as little as 55%. The wine is matured in new American oak barrels for 20 months, and is given additional bottle age prior to release.

🍷🍷🍷🍷🍷 **1994** Medium to full red-purple; a powerful, concentrated bouquet with excellent fruit and oak balance and integration; the palate is well balanced and composed, with briar, chocolate and red berry fruit together with generous vanilla oak, finishing with moderate tannins. A typical '94 vintage, not fleshy, but powerful. A prolific gold medal winner in shows. **rating:** 90

➯ **best drinking** 2000 – 2006 **best vintages** '86, '88, '90, '91, '93, '94 **drink with** Beef casserole • $36

Lindemans Pyrus

A label conjured up in the heat of the moment when the 1985 vintage bobbed up with the Jimmy Watson Trophy when Lindemans was least expecting it. It is a blend of Cabernet Sauvignon, Merlot, Malbec and Cabernet Franc; since 1985 the percentage of Cabernet Sauvignon has increased from 35% in the early days to 70%. It has come of age, with the fruit and 18 months new French oak maturation working to great effect.

🍷🍷🍷🍷 **1994** Medium to full red-purple; a complex and rich bouquet with lots of red berry fruit and touches of dark chocolate, the same flavours mark the start of the palate, but then fairly fearsome tannins take over; a very different Pyrus from most vintages. **rating:** 86

➯ **best drinking** 1999 – 2003 **best vintages** '88, '90, '91 **drink with** Entrecôte of beef • $36

lindemans (hunter valley) ★★★★

McDonalds Road, Pokolbin, NSW 2321 **region** Lower Hunter Valley
phone (02) 4998 7684 **fax** (02) 4998 7682 **open** Mon-Fri 9–4.30, weekends and public holidays 10–4.30
winemaker Phillip John, Patrick Auld **production** 16 000 **est.** 1870
product range ($7.50–95 R) Standard wines under annually changing Bin numbers of Semillon, Chablis, White Burgundy, Semillon Chardonnay, Chardonnay, Shiraz Burgundy, Hermitage, deluxe releases under Reserve Bin label, individual vineyard label (e.g. Steven) and revitalised older Classic Release label.
summary I have to declare an interest in Lindemans: not only did I cut my vinous teeth on it, but since 1997 I have had group winemaker responsibility for it within Southcorp. I have long been on record in saying that its crown had slipped somewhat. A major winery upgrade in 1997/98 will help to restore things, as will the renovations to the historic Ben Ean facility.

Lindemans Hunter River Shiraz

This is the 'standard' release, sourced from vineyards in the Pokolbin region, and matured in a mix of one and two-year-old French and American oak barrels for 12 months.

🍷🍷🍷🍷 **1994** Bin 8803. Dark red; the aromas are typically complex, with a mix of plum, sweet leather and earth fruit aromas. The palate is well balanced, with a mix of plummy and more earthy flavours, with those unmistakable tannins of the region, which become positively silky with age. **rating:** 85

➾ **best drinking** 1999 – 2009 **best vintages** '86, '87, '91, '94 **drink with** Marinated beef • $18

Lindemans Hunter River Reserve Shiraz

As with the Semillon, something of a moving feast, albeit less confusing. At the end of 1994 there were two wines on release, 1991 Bin 8203 ($15) and 1988 Reserve Bin 7600 ($19). The 1995 Classic Release was of 1987 Bin 7400, followed by Bin 9200 two years later.

🍷🍷🍷🍷 **1991** Reserve Bin 9200. Medium red-purple; soft, rich and ripe fruit in an earthy/minty/berry spectrum is supported by quite pronounced but not excessive oak. A powerful and rich wine on the palate, with a mix of mint, berry and earth in typical regional style. Finishes with soft tannins. Likely to improve further with age. **rating:** 86

➾ **best drinking** 2000 – 2010 **best vintages** '59, '65, '67, '73, '83, '86, '87, '88, '90, '91 **drink with** Game • $20

---

lindemans (karadoc) ★★★★

Edey Road, Karadoc via Mildura, Vic 3500 **region** Murray Darling and Swan Hill
phone (03) 5051 3333 **fax** (03) 5051 3390 **open** Mon-Sun 10–4.30
winemaker Phillip John (Chief) **production** 10 million **est.** 1974
product range ($7–40 R) Bin 23 Riesling, Bin 65 Chardonnay (one of the largest selling Chardonnay brands in the world), Bin 95 Sauvignon Blanc, Bin 99 Pinot Noir, Bin 50 Shiraz Cabernet, Bin 60 Merlot are the most important in terms of volume; Cawarra range of Colombard Chardonnay, Classic Dry White, Traminer Riesling and Shiraz Cabernet; also Nyrang Semillon and Shiraz. Karadoc also produces the great fortified wines, including the premium Fino, Amontillado and Oloroso Sherries, Old Liqueur Muscat, Tokay and Madeira and fine Tawny Ports.
summary Now the production centre for all of the Lindemans and Leo Buring wines, with the exception of special lines made in the Coonawarra and Hunter wineries. The biggest and

most modern single facility in Australia allowing all-important economies of scale, and the major processing centre for the beverage wine sector (casks, flagons and low-priced bottles) of the Southcorp empire. Its achievement in making several million cases of Bin 65 Chardonnay a year is extraordinary given the quality and consistency of the wines.

Lindemans Bin 65 Chardonnay

A winemaking tour de force, and one of the world's leading brands of Chardonnay. It is sourced from no less than 14 different wine-growing regions across southeastern Australia, and shows no sign of buckling under the ever-increasing production volumes. It has been praised by wine critics around the world, and is the only wine to have ever been rated a 'Best Buy' by the *Wine Spectator* for nine consecutive vintages. The '97 is arguably the best yet under this label, with a string of bronze and silver medals in capital city wine shows and a gold medal in a major overseas competition.

🍷🍷🍷🍷 **1997** Light to medium yellow-green; the bouquet is quite fragrant, with melon and peach fruit and excellently balanced use of a touch of oak. The palate lives up to the bouquet, with similar melon and peach fruit, and an ever so cunning touch of spicy oak, doubtless from the use of innerstaves and chips, but extremely well done. **rating:** 86

➾ **best drinking** 1998 – 1999 **best vintages** NA **drink with** Virtually anything you choose • $9

---

lindemans (padthaway) ★★★★☆

Naracoorte Road, Padthaway, SA 5271 **region** Padthaway
phone (08) 8765 5155 **fax** (08) 8765 5073 **open** Not
winemaker Phillip John **production** 68 000 **est.** 1908
product range ($11–17 R) Sauvignon Blanc, Verdelho, Chardonnay, Pinot Noir, Cabernet Merlot, also Winemakers Reserve Chardonnay and Limestone Coast Chardonnay.
summary Lindemans Padthaway Chardonnay could be said to be the best premium Chardonnay on the market in Australia, with an exceptional capacity to age. Back vintages win gold medals seemingly at will, the performance of the '94 vintage winning the Aged Chardonnay Trophy at the Liquorland National Wine Show in both 1996 and 1997 being quite remarkable.

Lindemans Padthaway Chardonnay

A wine with a long and at times very illustrious history. The style has changed somewhat over the years, starting off as a fruit-driven wine which aged well (winning a major national wine show trophy for mature Chardonnay along the way) then becoming very oaky, but with the '94 vintage returning to its very best, and providing one of the great bargains of 1995, before going on to win the most prestigious Chardonnay trophy in Australia at the Liquorland National Wine Show for two years in succession (1996 and 1997), recalling the feats of Wolf Blass and Cape Mentelle with the Jimmy Watson Trophy in Melbourne. For the record, it is entirely barrel-fermented in a mix of new and one-year-old French (Allier and Troncais) oak, and given extended lees contact.

🍷🍷🍷🍷🍸 **1996** Light to medium yellow-green; much livelier than the '95, with fragrant melon/grapefruit aromas and an attractive touch of spicy French oak. There are similarly lively tangy/melon/citrus/white peach fruit flavours, which invest the wine with length on the palate; well-handled oak rounds off an excellent commercial wine. Retasted October and November '97 with similar notes. **rating:** 92

➾ **best drinking** 1998 – 2002 **best vintages** '84, '85, '90, '94, '96 **drink with** Chinese prawns with cashew nuts • $17

---

lirralirra estate ★★★

Paynes Road, Lilydale, Vic 3140 **region** Yarra Valley
phone (03) 9735 0224 **fax** (03) 9735 0224 **open** Weekends and holidays 10–6, Jan 7 days
winemaker Alan Smith **production** 400 **est.** 1981
product range ($14–20 CD) Semillon, Wooded Semillon, Semillon Sauvignon Blanc, Sauvignon Blanc, Pinot Noir, Yarra Valley Cabernets.
summary Off the beaten track, and one of the lesser-known Yarra Valley wineries; owner Alan Smith originally intended to make a Sauternes-style wine from Semillon, Sauvignon Blanc and Muscadelle, but has found the conditions do not favour the development of botrytis, and is hence producing dry red and white wines.

Lirralirra Semillon Sauvignon Blanc

Lirralirra follows a variable roster with its Semillon and Sauvignon Blanc, in some vintages presenting both as straight varietals, in other vintages releasing a blend. Doubtless the very low yields in 1997 precipitated the decision to make this wine in that vintage.

🍷🍷🍷🍷 **1997** Medium yellow-green; a quite potent bouquet with a clean mix of lemony and minerally aromas is followed by a palate with good intensity and weight to the lemon and herb flavours. Well-balanced acidity, and a wine which could age with grace. **rating:** 85

➾ **best drinking** 1998 – 2003 **best vintages** NA **drink with** Lobster bisque • $15

Lirralirra Pinot Noir

Like so many Yarra Valley producers, Lirralirra produced a striking Pinot Noir in the low-yielding 1996 vintage, the tiny berries producing wines of unusually strong flavour and colour.

🍷🍷🍷🍷 **1996** Amazingly deep purple-red; a clean, potent, powerful mint and cherry bouquet is replicated on the strongly flavoured palate. A wine which will appeal more to some than to others, scoring on the strength of its muscle rather than its finesse or varietal definition. **rating:** 86

➾ **best drinking** 1999 – 2005 **best vintages** NA **drink with** Smoked quail • $16

little river wines ★★

Cnr West Swan and Forest Roads, Henley Brook, WA 6055 **region** Swan District
phone (08) 9296 4462 **fax** (08) 9296 1022 **open** 7 days 10–5
winemaker Bruno de Tastes **production** 3000 **est.** 1934
product range ($10–18 CD) Chenin Blanc, Sauvignon Blanc, Chardonnay, Cabernet Sauvignon, Shiraz, Florial Rosé, Méthode Champenoise, Vin Doux Late Harvest, Noble Classic.
summary Following several quick changes of ownership (and of consultant winemakers) the former Glenalwyn has gone through a period of change. It now has as its winemaker the eponymously named Count Bruno de Tastes. Three wines entered in the 1995 Mount Barker Wine Show all showed bitter, astringent characters.

little's winery ★★☆

Lot 3 Palmers Lane, Pokolbin, NSW 2321 **region** Lower Hunter Valley
phone (02) 4998 7626 **fax** (02) 4998 7867 **open** 7 days 10–4.30
winemaker Ian Little **production** 6000 **est.** 1984
product range ($12–18 CD) Chardonnay, Semillon, Gewurztraminer, Late Harvest Semillon, Pinot Noir Blanc de Noir, Shiraz, Cabernet Sauvignon, Vintage Port.
summary A successful cellar-door operation with friendly service and friendly wines: aromatic, fresh and sometimes slightly sweet white wines and light, inoffensive red wines.

lochvie wines NR

28 Lavender Park Road, Eltham, Vic 3095 **region** Yarra Valley
phone (03) 9439 9444 **open** Weekends 9.30–5.30, weekdays by appointment
winemaker John Lewis **production** NFP **est.** 1985
product range ($10 CD) Cabernet Merlot.
summary A tiny home winery producing a single 65%/35% Cabernet Merlot blend. Since 1993 the grapes have been sold to others, and no further wines made, but the '90 to '92 wines are available at cellar door.

long gully estate ★★★

Long Gully Road, Healesville, Vic 3777 **region** Yarra Valley
phone (03) 9807 4246 **fax** (03) 9807 2213 **open** Weekends, holidays 11–5
winemaker Peter Florance **production** 30 000 **est.** 1982
product range ($8.30–29 CD) Riesling, Chardonnay, Semillon, Sauvignon Blanc, Merlot, Irmas Cabernets, Pinot Noir, Shiraz; Limited Edition Reserve Chardonnay and Cabernet.
summary Long Gully Estate is one of the larger (but by no means largest) of the Yarra Valley producers which has successfully established a number of export markets over recent years. Wine quality is consistent rather than exhilarating; it is able to offer a range of wines with two to three years bottle age. Recent vineyard extensions underline the commercial success of Long Gully.

Long Gully Sauvignon Blanc

Yarra Ridge leapt out of the blocks and into the public consciousness with its first Sauvignon Blanc from the Yarra Valley. Subsequent releases have broadened their geographic base, and the wine has lost some of its impact. The Long Gully turns back the clock, as it were. Stainless steel fermented, without the intrusion of oak or residual sugar.

🍷🍷🍷🍸 **1997** Light to medium green-yellow; a quite fragrant bouquet with a mix of gooseberry and more herbal aromas leads into a positively flavoured herb and gooseberry palate of medium weight, and a pleasantly soft finish. **rating:** 84

➪ **best drinking** 1998 – 1999 **best vintages** NA **drink with** Calamari • $11.30

longleat ★★★

Old Weir Road, Murchison, Vic 3610 **region** Goulburn Valley
phone (03) 5826 2294 **fax** (03) 5826 2510 **open** 7 days 10–5
winemaker Alister Purbrick (Consultant) **production** 1500 **est.** 1975
product range ($10.50–17 CD) Riesling, Sauvignon Blanc, Chardonnay, Shiraz, Cabernet Sauvignon, Liqueur Muscat, Sparkling.
summary Longleat has long had a working relationship with Chateau Tahbilk, which makes the Longleat wines under contract, and buys significant quantities of grapes surplus to Longleat's requirements. The wines are always honest and full-flavoured.

longview creek vineyard NR

150 Palmer Road, Sunbury, Vic 3429 **region** Sunbury
phone (03) 9744 1050 **fax** (03) 9744 1050 **open** 7 days 11–5
winemaker David Hodgson **production** 750 **est.** 1988
product range ($14–20 CD) Chardonnay, Chenin Blanc, Pinot Noir, Cabernet Sauvignon.

summary A relatively new arrival in the Sunbury subdistrict of the Macedon region, owned by Ron and Joan Parker. A total of 3.3 hectares of chardonnay, pinot noir and chenin blanc are in production with an additional 2 hectares of shiraz coming into bearing.

lovey's estate NR

1548 Melba Highway, Yarra Glen, Vic 3775 **region** Yarra Valley
phone (03) 5965 2444 **fax** (03) 5965 2460 **open** Wed-Sun 12–5
winemaker Tarrawarra (Contract) **production** 1200 **est.** 1989
product range ($15–24.50 CD) Sauvignon Blanc, Chardonnay, Muscadelle, Pinot Noir, Shiraz, Cabernet Sauvignon.
summary Lovey's Estate is part of a restaurant and accommodation complex situated prominently on the Melba Highway, just on the far side of Yarra Glen. The majority of the production from the 11-hectare vineyard is sold; part is made under contract at Tarrawarra, and was previously sold as Mount Hope.

lowe family wines ★★★

9 Paterson Road, Bolwarra, NSW 2320 **region** Mudgee
phone (02) 4930 0233 **fax** (02) 4930 0233 **open** Not
winemaker David Lowe, Jane Wilson **production** 4000 **est.** 1987
product range ($11.40 CD) Semillon, Peacock Hill Chardonnay, Lawless Chardonnay, Peacock Hill Shiraz.
summary Former Rothbury winemaker David Lowe and Jane Wilson make the Lowe Family Wines at the Oakvale Winery, drawing upon a little over 10 hectares of family-owned vineyards in Mudgee, supplemented by purchases from Orange and the Hunter Valley.

lyre bird hill ★★★

Inverloch Road, Koonwarra, Vic 3954 **region** Gippsland
phone (03) 5664 3204 **fax** (03) 5664 3206 **open** Weekends, holidays 10–5
winemaker Owen Schmidt **production** 750 **est.** 1986
product range ($11–20 CD) Riesling, Traminer, Chardonnay (wooded and unwooded), Pinot Noir, Pinot Noir Cellar Reserve, Cabernet Sauvignon, Shiraz, Phantasy (sparkling).
summary Former Melbourne professionals Owen and Robyn Schmidt make small quantities of estate-grown wine (the vineyard is 2.4 hectares in size), offering accommodation for three couples (RACV four-star rating) in their newly built spacious house. Shiraz has been the most successful wine to date, although the Pinot Noir has pronounced varietal character in a sappy/tomato vine style which will appeal to some. The Cabernet Sauvignon is also a pleasant, well-made wine.

madew wines NR

Westering, Federal Highway, Lake George, NSW 2581 **region** Canberra District
phone (02) 4848 0026 **open** Weekends, public holidays 11–5
winemaker David Madew **production** 2500 **est.** 1984
product range ($13–20 CD) Riesling, Reserve Riesling, Semillon, Chardonnay, Phoenix (Botrytis Chardonnay), Dry Red, Merlot, Cabernets.
summary Madew Wines bowed to the urban pressure of Queanbeyan, and purchased the Westering Vineyard from Captain G P Hood some years ago. Plantings there have now increased to 9.5 hectares, with 1 hectare each of shiraz and pinot gris coming into bearing.

maglieri ★★★★☆

Douglas Gully Road, McLaren Flat, SA 5171 **region** McLaren Vale
phone (08) 8383 0177 **fax** (08) 8383 0136 **open** Mon-Sat 9–4, Sun 12–4
winemaker John Loxton **production** 110 000 **est.** 1972
product range ($4.50–25 CD) While still billing itself as the 'House of Lambrusco', and still producing a range of Italian-derived styles for specialty markets within Australia, is increasingly known for the quality of its varietal table wines, spearheaded by Semillon, Cabernet Sauvignon and Shiraz, the last released in two guises: as a simple varietal, and the top-end Steve Maglieri. Typically several vintages available at any one time.
summary One of the better-kept secrets among the wine cognoscenti, but not among the many customers who drink thousands of cases of white and red Lambrusco every year, an example of niche marketing at its profitable best. Its dry red wines are invariably generously proportioned and full of character, the Shiraz particularly so – and of the highest quality. It is for these wines that the winery rating is given.

main ridge estate ★★★★

Lot 48 William Road, Red Hill, Vic 3937 **region** Mornington Peninsula
phone (03) 5989 2686 **fax** (03) 5931 0000 **open** Mon-Fri 12–4, weekends 12–5
winemaker Nat White **production** 1100 **est.** 1975
product range ($22–35 CD) Chardonnay, Pinot Noir, Half Acre Pinot Noir, Cabernet Merlot.
summary Nat White gives meticulous attention to every aspect of his viticulture and winemaking, doing annual battle with one of the coolest sites on the Peninsula. The same attention to detail extends to the winery and the winemaking.

Main Ridge Chardonnay

Since 1991 Nat White has moved away from conventional Australian techniques to a far more French-influenced regimen, using barrel fermentation, malolactic fermentation and lees contact. As is inevitably the case in the Mornington Peninsula, style and quality reflect vintage variations, with the warmer, drier years tending to produce the best wines.

🍷🍷🍷🍷 **1996** Full yellow; a very complex and rich bouquet with a mix of nutmeg, cinnamon, yellow peach and cashew variously deriving from fruit, oak and malolactic fermentation introduce a high-flavoured wine with a similar range of characters and flavours on the palate. Finishes with good acidity. **rating:** 89

➯ **best drinking** 1998 – 2000 **best vintages** '91, '92, '94, '96, '97 **drink with** Sweetbreads • $33

Main Ridge Half Acre Pinot Noir

The cold-climate Main Ridge vineyard does peculiar things to Pinot Noir, sometimes producing wines with spicy pepper characteristics which makes them look for all the world like light-bodied Shiraz. In other years the flavours are more towards the stalky/tobacco end; never does the wine become jammy or heavy.

🍷🍷🍷🍷 (3½) **1996** Medium red-purple; while there is the hallmark leafy/spicy/slippery/earthy fruit aromas, they are less extreme than in some years. The palate is not luscious, but has quite good length, with tight earthy/sappy/foresty/tobacco leaf nuances. Unequivocally cool-climate Pinot Noir. **rating:** 84

➯ **best drinking** 1998 – 1999 **best vintages** NA **drink with** Grilled salmon • $27

---

mair's coalville ★★★

Moe South Road, Moe South, Vic 3825 **region** Gippsland
phone (03) 5127 4229 **fax** (03) 5127 2148 **open** By appointment
winemaker Dr Stewart Mair **production** 250 **est.** 1985
product range ($15 ML) A single wine, predominantly Cabernet Sauvignon with a little Cabernet Franc, Malbec and Merlot, labelled Coalville Red.
summary Dr Stewart Mair has fashioned a remarkably consistent wine from his small vineyard, on the lean side perhaps, but with the elegance which comes from very cool-grown fruit.

majella ★★★★

Lynn Road, Coonawarra, SA 5263 **region** Coonawarra
phone (08) 8736 3055 **fax** (08) 8736 3057 **open** By appointment
winemaker Brian Lynn, Bruce Gregory **production** 2000 **est.** 1969
product range ($16–24 CD) Shiraz, Cabernet Sauvignon, Sparkling Shiraz.
summary Majella is one of the more important contract grape growers in Coonawarra, with 47.5 hectares of vineyard, principally shiraz and cabernet sauvignon, and with a little riesling and merlot, in production and now fully mature. Common gossip has it that part finds its way into the Wynns John Riddoch Cabernet Sauvignon and Michael Shiraz, or their equivalent within the Southcorp Group. Production under the Majella label is increasing as long-term supply contracts expire.

Majella Cabernet Sauvignon

The '93 vintage was the first Cabernet to be released from Majella, produced from the House Block. Aged in French oak hogsheads for two years, and deservedly accumulated five gold medals. Not surprisingly, the '95 is a lesser wine.

🍷🍷🍷🍷 **1995** Medium red-purple; the bouquet is of light to medium intensity, with sweet berry fruit and gentle vanilla oak. Attractive, softly sweet cassis fruit on the palate is again supported by well-handled oak. Won't be particularly long-lived, but its softness and approachability are a very good outcome for a vintage which produced many tough wines. **rating:** 84

➾ **best drinking** 1999 – 2004 **best vintages** '94 **drink with** Rack of lamb • $20

malcolm creek ★★★

Bonython Road, Kersbrook, SA 5231 **region** Adelaide Hills
phone (08) 8389 3235 **fax** (08) 8389 3235 **open** Weekends, public holidays 11–5
winemaker Reg Tolley **production** 500 **est.** 1982
product range ($15 R) Chardonnay, Cabernet Sauvignon.
summary Following the sale of Tolleys to Mildara Blass, Reg Tolley doubled the plantings of Malcolm Creek to a total of 2 hectares. Even in retirement, it remains very much a hobby for Reg Tolley.

mann NR

105 Memorial Avenue, Baskerville, WA 6056 **region** Swan District
phone (08) 9296 4348 **fax** (08) 9296 4348 **open** Weekends 10–5 and by appointment
winemaker Dorham Mann **production** 500 **est.** 1988
product range ($15 CD) Méthode Champenoise.

summary Industry veteran Dorham Mann has established a one-wine label for what must be Australia's most unusual wine: a dry, only faintly pink, sparkling wine made exclusively from cabernet sauvignon grown on the 2.4-hectare estate surrounding the cellar door. Dorham Mann explains, 'our family has made and enjoyed the style for more than 30 years, although just in a private capacity until recently'.

manning park NR

Cnr Olivers and Chalk Hill Roads, McLaren Vale, SA 5171 **region** McLaren Vale
phone (08) 8323 8209 **fax** (08) 8323 9474 **open** 7 days 10–5
winemaker Warren Randall **production** 5000 **est.** 1979
product range ($11–20 CD) Great White (Sauvignon Blanc/Semillon), Colombard, Chenin Blanc, Savage Grenache, Native Cabernet, Wild Shiraz, Stormy Shiraz (Sparkling Burgundy), Tawny Port.
summary Once a low-key operation focusing primarily on fortified wines, has been revived by former Seppelt and Andrew Garrett wunderkind Warren Randall, now offering a range of exclusively McLaren Vale-sourced table wines. A barbecue and paved garden area are available for the use of cellar-door visitors.

marienberg ★★☆

2 Chalk Hill Road, McLaren Vale, SA 5171 **region** McLaren Vale
phone (08) 8323 9666 **fax** (08) 8323 9600 **open** 7 days 10–5
winemaker Grant Burge (Contract) **production** 35 000 **est.** 1966
product range ($8–17 R) Riesling, Semillon Sauvignon Blanc, Semillon Chardonnay, Chardonnay, Nicolle Méthode Champenoise, Shiraz, Cabernet Sauvignon, Tawny Port.
summary The Marienberg brand was purchased by the Hill group of companies in late 1991 following the retirement of Ursula Pridham. Releases under the new regime have been honest, if unashamedly commercial, wines.

mariners rest NR

Jamakarri Farm, Roberts Road, Denmark, WA 6333 **region** Great Southern
phone (08) 9840 9324 **fax** (08) 9840 9324 **open** 7 days 11–5
winemaker Ron Cocking, Peter Cocking **production** 450 **est.** 1996
product range ($13.50–19 R) Chardonnay, Autumn Gold, Autumn Red, Southern Red, Pinot Noir.
summary Mariners Rest is the reincarnation of the now defunct Golden Rise winery. A new 2.5-hectare vineyard was planted in the spring of 1997, and in the meantime some excellent wines from the Golden Rise days are being marketed under the Mariners Rest label.

marion's vineyard 

Foreshore Drive, Deviot, Tas 7275 **region** Northern Tasmania
phone (03) 6394 7434 **fax** (03) 6394 7434 **open** 7 days 10–5
winemaker Mark Semmens, Marion Semmens **production** 2400 **est.** 1980
product range ($15–23 ML) Chardonnay, Müller Thurgau, Pinot Noir, Cabernet Sauvignon.
summary The irrepressible Mark Semmens and indefatigable wife Marion have one of the most beautifully situated vineyards and wineries in Australia on the banks of the Tamar River. As well as an outdoor restaurant and accommodation, there is a jetty and a stage – indeed, life is a stage for Mark Semmens.

maritime estate NR

Tucks Road, Red Hill, Vic 3937 **region** Mornington Peninsula
phone (03) 9848 2926 **fax** (03) 9882 8325 **open** Weekends and public holidays 11–5
winemaker T'Gallant (Contract) **production** 1000 **est.** 1988
product range ($17–24 CD) Unwooded Chardonnay, Chardonnay, Cabernet Sauvignon.
summary John and Linda Ruljancich have enjoyed great success since their first vintage in 1994, due in part to skilled contract winemaking, but also to the situation of their vineyard looking across the hills and valleys of the Red Hill region. As from 1998 a Pinot Noir is likely to be added to the roster in the wake of grafting over part of the original plantings of cabernet sauvignon.

markwood estate NR

Morris Lane, Markwood, Vic 3678 **region** King Valley
phone (03) 5727 0361 **fax** (03) 5727 0361 **open** 7 days 9–5
winemaker Rick Morris **production** 900 **est.** 1971
product range ($15–21 CD) Rhine Riesling, Chardonnay, Cabernet Sauvignon, Shiraz, Muscat, Tokay, Port.
summary A member of the famous Morris family, Rick Morris shuns publicity, and relies almost exclusively on cellar-door sales for what is a small output. Of a range of table and fortified wines tasted in February 1997, the Old Tawny Port (a cross between Port and Muscat, showing more of the character of the latter than the former) and a White Port (seemingly made from Muscadelle) were the best. Agglomerate corks may present a threat for prolonged cellaring, however.

marribrook 

Rocky Gully Road, Frankland, WA 6396 **region** Great Southern
phone (08) 9457 7885 **fax** (08) 9457 7885 **open** Not
winemaker Gavin Berry (Contract) **production** 1200 **est.** 1990
product range ($13–16 CD) Unwooded Chardonnay, Botanica Chardonnay, Marsanne, Cabernet Sauvignon, Cabernet Malbec.
summary The Brooks family purchased the former Marron View 5.6-hectare vineyard from Kim Hart in 1994, and renamed the venture Marribrook Wines. Those wines are now made by Gavin Berry at Plantagenet, having been made at Alkoomi up to 1994. An interesting wine on the roster is Western Australia's only Marsanne, although it has to be said that the wine in the bottle is perhaps less interesting than the label.

Marribrook Cabernet Malbec

A blend of equal portions of Cabernet Sauvignon and Malbec, which might have done with a touch more time in oak and more handling in the winery, but which attests to the capacity of the region to produce excellent Malbec.

1995 Medium purple-red; the bouquet is youthful and slightly unformed, but with plenty of clean, fresh fruit. Sweet juicy Malbec flavours, with some more chocolatey notes helps provide an unexpectedly sweet and soft palate, finishing with soft tannins. **rating:** 84

best drinking 1999 – 2004 **best vintages** NA **drink with** Rib of beef • $16

marsh estate 

Deasey Road, Pokolbin, NSW 2321 **region** Lower Hunter Valley
phone (02) 4998 7587 **fax** (02) 4998 7884 **open** Mon-Fri 10–4.30, weekends 10–5
winemaker Peter Marsh **production** 4000 **est.** 1971

product range ($16–21 CD) High Hill Semillon, Semillon, Semillon Chardonnay, Chardonnay (oaked and unoaked), Traminer, Semillon Sauternes, Shiraz (Private Bin, Vat S and Vat R), Cabernet Merlot, Champagne Brut, Semillon Sauternes, Andre IV Vintage Port.
summary Through sheer consistency, value-for-money and hard work, the Marsh family (who purchased the former Quentin Estate in 1978) has built up a sufficiently loyal cellar-door and mailing list clientele to allow all of the considerable production to be sold direct. Wine style is always direct, with oak playing a minimal role, and prolonged cellaring paying handsome dividends.

marybrook vineyards NR

Vasse-Yallingup Road, Vasse, WA 6280 **region** Margaret River
phone (08) 9755 1143 **fax** (08) 9755 1112 **open** Fri-Mon 10–5, 7 days 10–5 school holidays
winemaker Willespie (Contract) **production** 1500 **est.** 1986
product range ($12–20 CD) Semillon, Chardonnay, Verdelho, Nectosia (sweet), Cabernet Sauvignon, Temptation (sweet red).
summary Owned by Tony Ward, the 5-hectare Marybrook vineyards have come progressively into bearing, and production has increased significantly. No recent tastings.

massoni main creek ★★★★

Mornington-Flinders Road, Red Hill, Vic 3937 **region** Mornington Peninsula
phone (03) 5989 2352 **fax** (03) 5989 2014 **open** By appointment
winemaker Ian Home **production** 2000 **est.** 1984
product range ($32–37 R) Red Hill Chardonnay, Red Hill Pinot Noir, Ian Home Lectus Cuvée.
summary In June 1995 Ian Home (best known as the founder of Yellowglen) acquired the remaining 50% of Massoni from former Melbourne restaurateur Leon Massoni. Ian and Sue Home now own and run the business, and soon marked the change with the release of the first sparkling wine. Production of Chardonnay and Pinot Noir will, however, continue.

Red Hill Massoni Main Creek Chardonnay

Produced from 1.5 hectares of estate plantings, and made using the full gamut of barrel fermentation, malolactic fermentation and lees contact. In many ways the most striking example of Mornington Peninsula Chardonnay, with tremendous character, body and richness.
🍷🍷🍷🍷 **1996** Medium to full yellow-green; a solidly rich and ripe bouquet with strong melon and peach fruit, together with subtle oak; the malolactic influence is restrained. On the palate there is more of the same, with solidly ripe fig and melon fruit, even more powerful than that of the bouquet. The oak is subtle; well-made wine. **rating:** 88

⇨ **best drinking** 1997 – 2001 **best vintages** '89, '90, '92, '93, '94, '96, '97 **drink with** Veal, pork • $32

Red Hill Massoni Main Creek Pinot Noir

The mirror image of the Chardonnay, always rich, full-bodied and opulent, where so many of the Mornington wines – Pinot and Chardonnay alike – tend to be prettier and more elegant.
🍷🍷🍷🍷 **1996** Bright but light red-purple; the aromas are fragrant and intense, with plum fruit touched with spice and subtle oak. The palate is very lively, with sappy/spicy/plummy fruit flavours; the only possible criticism is that the acid is a little brisk. **rating:** 88

⇨ **best drinking** 1997 – 1999 **best vintages** '91, '92, '93, '94, '96, '97 **drink with** Breast of duck • $37

matilda's meadow ★★★☆

Eladon Brook Estate, RMB 654 Hamilton Road, Denmark, WA 6333 **region** Great Southern
phone (08) 9848 1951 **fax** (08) 9848 1957 **open** Wed-Mon 10–4
winemaker Brenden Smith **production** 1500 **est.** 1990
product range ($12.50–23.50 CD) Riesling, Late Picked Riesling, Unwooded Chardonnay, Semillon Chardonnay, Autumn Amethyst (light red), Pinot Noir, Cabernet Sauvignon Cabernet Franc.
summary Former hotelier Don Turnbull and oil-industry executive Pamela Meldrum have quickly established a thriving business at Matilda's Meadow, based on 6 hectares of estate plantings, and with a restaurant offering morning and afternoon teas and lunches every day.

maxwell wines ★★★★

Olivers Road, McLaren Vale, SA 5171 **region** McLaren Vale
phone (08) 8323 8200 **fax** (08) 8323 8900 **open** 7 days 10–5
winemaker Mark Maxwell **production** 6000 **est.** 1979
product range ($10–30 R) Under the Maxwell Wines brand, Semillon, Sauvignon Blanc, Chardonnay, Cabernet Merlot, Reserve Shiraz; Ellen Street Shiraz and Lime Cave Cabernet Sauvignon; and excellent Honey Mead, Spiced Mead and Liqueur Mead.
summary Maxwell Wines has come a long way since opening for business using an amazing array of Heath Robinson equipment in cramped surroundings. A state-of-the-art and infinitely larger winery was built on a new site in time for the 1997 vintage, appropriate for a brand which has produced some excellent white and red wines in recent years.

Maxwell Semillon

As with all Maxwell wines, sourced primarily from grapes grown on Maxwell's own vineyards. A full-flavoured style, which neither needs nor is given any oak input, and should age very well. A wine which hit a new height in 1995, coming first in its class at the annual Winewise Small Makers Competition in February 1996. The '97 marks a return to the form shown by the '95.

🍷🍷🍷🍷🍸 **1997** Medium yellow-green; the bouquet is clean, with good depth and varietal character in a lemony mould. A very well-made wine on the palate, with plenty of depth to the fruit, yet avoiding over-extraction or phenolics, the absence of oak a plus. Exceptional value at the price. **rating:** 90

➾ **best drinking** 1998 – 2001 **best vintages** '86, '88, '91, '92, '94, '95, '97 **drink with** Char-grilled octopus • $10

Maxwell Sauvignon Blanc

Part of a suite of white wines from Maxwell which rely on varietal character and depth of flavour rather than artifice in the winery, and underlining the fact that McLaren Vale has always been a superior area for the growing and making of Sauvignon Blanc.

🍷🍷🍷🍸 **1997** Light to medium green-yellow; a clean, firm bouquet of medium intensity although a little subdued. The palate is crisp and clean with a mix of mineral and herbaceous flavours, all one could expect at the price. **rating:** 84

➾ **best drinking** 1998 – 1999 **best vintages** NA **drink with** Crab or shellfish • $11

Maxwell Reserve Shiraz

Maxwell produces two Shiraz-based wines, Ellen Street and (in smaller volume) the Reserve. On occasions the Reserve has seemed over-extracted and over-oaked, but most certainly not in 1995.

🍷🍷🍷🍷🍷 **1995** Medium to full red-purple; a rich and concentrated bouquet with complex liquorice, briar and black fruit aromas. A sophisticated wine on the palate with excellent black cherry and liquorice varietal fruit supported by subtle but powerful tannins and forceful but convincing use of American oak. **rating:** 90

➡ **best drinking** 2000 – 2015 **best vintages** NA **drink with** Char-grilled rump • $30

Maxwell Lime Cave Cabernet Sauvignon

The prestige Cabernet from Maxwell, the '96 vintage being the runner-up in the Cabernet Class at the 1998 Winewise Small Makers Competition.

🍷🍷🍷🍷🍷 **1996** Medium to full red-purple; the bouquet is dense, with masses of ripe blackberry/blackcurrant fruit, the palate showing similarly abundant sweet blackberry, blackcurrant and chocolate fruit supported by persistent tannins and nicely judged oak. **rating:** 93

➡ **best drinking** 2001 – 2010 **best vintages** NA **drink with** Rare rump steak • $14

mcalister vineyards NR

Golden Beach Road, Longford, Vic 3851 **region** Gippsland
phone (03) 5149 7229 **fax** (03) 5149 7229 **open** By appointment
winemaker Peter Edwards **production** 550 **est.** 1975
product range A single wine, The McAlister, a blend of Cabernet Sauvignon, Cabernet Franc and Merlot.
summary The McAlister Vineyards actively shun publicity or exposure which, on the basis of prior tastings, is a pity.

mcguigan brothers ★★★

PO Box 31, Cessnock, NSW 2335 **region** Lower Hunter Valley
phone (02) 4998 7400 **fax** (02) 4998 7401 **open** 7 days 10–5
winemaker Brian McGuigan **production** 400 000 **est.** 1992
product range ($9.50–25 R) The wines are sold in three price brackets: at the bottom, Harvest Range Semillon Chardonnay, Night Harvest Graves, Autumn Harvest Traminer Riesling, Black Shiraz; then the Bin range 2000 Hermitage, 3000 Merlot, 4000 Cabernet Sauvignon, 6000 Verdelho, 7000 Chardonnay; finally Shareholder Reserve Chardonnay, Cabernet Merlot, Sauternes; also Personal Reserve recently added to the range.
summary A public-listed company which is the ultimate expression of McGuigan's marketing drive and vision, on a par with that of Wolf Blass in his heyday. Highly successful in its chosen niche market, notwithstanding garish labels. Has been particularly active in export markets, notably the United States, and recently in China. Wine quality seems less important than marketing magic.

mcivor creek NR

Costerfield Road, Heathcote, Vic 3523 **region** Bendigo
phone (03) 5433 3000 **fax** (03) 5433 2609 **open** 7 days 10–5.30
winemaker Peter Turley **production** 5000 **est.** 1973
product range ($8.95–14.95 CD) Riesling, Auslese Riesling, Shiraz, Cabernet Shiraz, Old Tawny Port.
summary The beautifully situated McIvor Creek winery is well worth a visit, and does offer wines in diverse styles of which the red wines are the most regional. Peter Turley has 5 hectares of cabernet sauvignon together with 2.5 hectares of cabernet franc and merlot and supplements his intake with grapes from other growers. No recent tastings.

mclarens on the lake ★★☆

Kangarilla Road, McLaren Vale, SA 5171 **region** McLaren Vale
phone (08) 8323 8911 **fax** (08) 8323 9010 **open** Mon-Fri 10–6, weekends 9–5
winemaker Andrew Garrett **production** NA **est.** 1981
product range ($10–13 R) Colombard Semillon Chardonnay, Brut Cuvee, Grenache Shiraz, Cabernet Shiraz.
summary The indestructible Andrew Garrett is building yet another wine empire, starting with McLarens on the Lake, hitherto a cellar-door and mail order operation only, but now moving into the broader retail and restaurant markets. With grapes sourced primarily from the Riverland regions, quality is modest, but then so are the prices. Garrett will move up-market with forthcoming wines from the Yarra Valley under the Yarra Glen label and from the Adelaide Hills under the Springwood Park label.

mcmanus NR

Rogers Road, Yenda, NSW 2681 **region** Riverina
phone (02) 6968 1064 **open** 7 days 9–5
winemaker Dr David McManus **production** 500 **est.** 1972
product range ($4–8 CD) Chardonnay, Chardonnay Semillon, Malbec, Merlot, Shiraz, Pinot Malbec Shiraz; many named after family members.
summary An extremely idiosyncratic winery run by Griffith GP Dr David McManus, his sister and other family members. Natural winemaking methods lead to considerable variation in quality, but the prices are from another era, some of the vintages likewise.

mcwilliam's ★★★★

Winery Road, Hanwood, NSW 2680 **region** Riverina
phone (02) 6963 0001 **fax** (02) 6963 0002 **open** Mon-Sat 9–5
winemaker Jim Brayne **production** NFP **est.** 1877
product range ($6–40 R) A disciplined and easy-to-follow product range (all varietally identified) commencing with Hillside casks; Inheritance Range; Hanwood; Charles King; JJ McWilliams (first released 1996), finally Limited Release Hunter Valley Chardonnay, Eden Valley Riesling and JJ McWilliam Riverina Botrytis Semillon. Also superb fortified wines including MCW11 Liqueur Muscat and 10-Year-Old Hanwood Tawny Port heading a much larger range of Sherries which still form an important part of the business.
summary Some of the best wines to emanate from the Hanwood winery are from other regions, notably the Barwang Vineyard at Hilltops in New South Wales, Coonawarra and Eden Valley; on the other side of the coin as it were, the critical mass of the business continues to come from the Murrumbidgee Irrigation Area, which provides the bulk of the rapidly growing export business of the company. The rating is a compromise between the best and the least of the wide range.

mcwilliam's mount pleasant ★★★★★

Marrowbone Road, Pokolbin, NSW 2321 **region** Lower Hunter Valley
phone (02) 4998 7505 **fax** (02) 4998 7761 **open** 7 days 10–4.30
winemaker Phillip Ryan **production** NFP **est.** 1880
product range ($10–40 R) Much simplified and rationalised over the past year. The base range now comprises Mount Pleasant Elizabeth, Philip, Late Harvest Dessert Wine, Chardonnay and Verdelho; then individual vineyard wines, Rosehill Shiraz, Old Paddock & Old Hill Shiraz, Lovedale Semillon (previously known as Anne), then Maurice O'Shea Chardonnay and Shiraz; finally Museum releases of Elizabeth.

summary McWilliam's Elizabeth and the glorious Lovedale Semillon are now the only mature Hunter Semillons generally commercially available, and are undervalued and underpriced treasures, with a consistently superb show record. The three individual vineyard wines, together with the Maurice O'Shea memorial wines, add to the lustre of this proud name.

McWilliam's Mount Pleasant Elizabeth

A wine with an exceptional pedigree and deserved reputation for consistency, yet chronically underpriced and hence underrated (or the reverse, I am not sure which). Changes to the packaging, notably the bottle shape, and the hand of McWilliam's chief executive Kevin McLintock may well see the wine gradually being repositioned in the market to assume its rightful place. Even without this, an undoubted classic, having won 13 trophies and 129 gold medals since 1981.

🍷🍷🍷🍷🍷 **1993** Glowing yellow-green; the bouquet shows intense varietal character, with a mix of herbaceous and more honeyed fruit, together with hints of toast starting to develop. The palate is quite outstanding, with a lovely combination of honey and herbs; delicious mouthfeel and excellent structure. The best since 1987. **rating:** 95

⇨ **best drinking** 1998 – 2008 **best vintages** '75, '81, '82, '83, '86, '89, '90, '91, '93 **drink with** Rich seafood • $13.50

McWilliam's Mount Pleasant O'Shea Chardonnay

This is the flagship Chardonnay from the Hunter Valley, sitting alongside the O'Shea Shiraz. Only limited quantities are made, and indeed is not necessarily produced every vintage.

🍷🍷🍷🍷 **1995** Medium yellow-green; a clean and smooth bouquet with soft peach/melon fruit and subtle oak leads on to a quite rich and full-bodied palate with peachy fruit; good length and subtle oak throughout. **rating:** 85

⇨ **best drinking** 1998 – 1999 **best vintages** NA **drink with** Roast pork • $27

McWilliam's Mount Pleasant O'Shea (OP & OH) Shiraz

OP & OH is the sort of obscure designation which so delighted Maurice O'Shea. The letters in fact stand for Old Paddock and Old Hill, planted respectively, in 1880 and 1920, and which provide the bulk of the grapes which go into this distinguished wine. To confuse matters a little, since 1987 it has been sold as O'Shea Hermitage, in honour of Maurice O'Shea, in outstanding vintage years. So sometimes you will see it sold as O'Shea, sometimes as OP & OH.

🍷🍷🍷🍷 **1995** OP & OH. Medium red-purple; the aromas are quite potent, ranging through earth, sweet leather and spice. The palate opens with earthy cherry fruit of medium weight, but does toughen up ever so slightly on the finish. Will presumably soften with age. **rating:** 88

⇨ **best drinking** 2000 – 2010 **best vintages** '65, '66, '67, '79, '85, '87, '90, '91, '94, '95 **drink with** Roast veal • $19.95

McWilliam's Mount Pleasant Rosehill Shiraz

The Rosehill Vineyard shares a hill of terra rossa soil bisected in the middle by the Broke Road, with Lake's Folly on the opposite side to Rosehill. Over the years it has produced many great wines (the '59 is particularly memorable) and, it must be said, a few disappointments too. The '96, happily, is in the mould of the '59.

🍷🍷🍷🍷🍷 **1996** Medium to full red-purple; excellent weight and extract, with strong black cherry and earth varietal fruit, together with touches of spice and liquorice. The palate is almost deceptively light after the bouquet, but has the structure and inner core to sustain it for decades. Fine tannins are a feature. **rating:** 90

➾ **best drinking** 2001 – 2011 **best vintages** '59, '65, '66, '67, '75, '95, '96 **drink with** Marinated spatchcock • $19.95

McWilliam's Mount Pleasant Merlot

Produced from grapes grown by McWilliam's long-serving winemaker Phillip Ryan. As with all Hunter Valley reds, does show vintage variation, but was a major success in 1996.

🍷🍷🍷🍷 **1996** Medium red-purple; a relatively light but fragrant cedary, leafy, berry bouquet is followed by a wine which has excellent feel and balance in the mouth. There is a mix of leafy and sweeter berry fruit, with sensitively handled oak and soft tannins on the finish. As a Merlot should be. **rating:** 88

➾ **best drinking** 1998 – 2003 **best vintages** '96 **drink with** Rabbit • NA

meadowbank wines

'Meadowbank', Glenora, Derwent Valley, Tas 7410 **region** Southern Tasmania
phone (03) 6286 1269 **fax** (03) 6286 1133 **open** 7 days 11–5
winemaker Greg O'Keefe (previous) **production** 3000 **est.** 1974
product range ($17–24 CD) Riesling, Chardonnay, Grace Elizabeth Chardonnay, Pinot Noir, Cabernet Sauvignon.
summary Now an important part of the Ellis family business on what was once (but no more) a large grazing property on the banks of the Derwent. Increased plantings are being established under contract to BRL Hardy.

Meadowbank Riesling

Produced from just under 1 hectare of estate-grown riesling, which constituted the first plantings at Meadowbank, and which were initially sold to Hickinbotham Winemakers (in the late 1970s), transported across Bass Strait in styrene containers.

🍷🍷🍷🍷 **1997** Light to medium yellow-green; a highly floral, scented bouquet with a wonderful mix of apple blossom, cinnamon and spice aromas. Those same Gewurztraminer-like spicy characters come through on a palate with distinct Germanic characters, and a blossom-like delicacy. **rating:** 89

➾ **best drinking** 1998 – 2003 **best vintages** NA **drink with** Asparagus • $17

Meadowbank Grace Elizabeth Chardonnay

A small quantity of the grapes harvested from the 4 hectares of estate plantings is set aside for the Grace Elizabeth Chardonnay. It is barrel-fermented in new French (Dargaud & Jaegle) oak, taken through malolactic fermentation, and left on lees for nine months. A distinguished wine. The 1995 vintage (in unbottled form but drawn from the final blend immediately prior to bottling) was awarded the Chairman's Trophy at the 1996 Tasmanian Wines Show. The '97 was a silver medal winner at the 1998 Tasmanian Wines Show.

🍷🍷🍷🍷 **1997** Medium yellow-green; a complex bouquet with some malolactic fermentation influences and slightly malty/hessiany oak which likewise comes through on the palate. However, the wine has above-average richness and weight, with just a hint of mandarin botrytis which actually adds to the character, rather than detracting from it. **rating:** 87

➾ **best drinking** 1998 – 1999 **best vintages** '93, '95, '97 **drink with** Fresh Tasmanian salmon • $24

meerea park ★★★★

2 Denton Close, Windella via Maitland, NSW 2321 **region** Upper Hunter Valley
phone (02) 4930 7332 **fax** (02) 4930 7906 **open** At The Boutique Wine Centre, Broke Road, Pokolbin
winemaker Rhys Eather **production** 10 500 **est.** 1991
product range ($15–38 ML) Sauvignon Blanc Semillon, Lindsay Hill Verdelho, Unoaked Chardonnay, Chardonnay, Alexander Munro Chardonnay, Cabernet Merlot, Cabernet Sauvignon.
summary An interesting operation, selling its substantial production primarily through The Boutique Wine Centre, Broke Road, Pokolbin and by mailing list. All of the wines are produced from grapes purchased from growers, primarily in the Broke/Fordwich region, but also from as far afield as McLaren Vale, the Barossa Valley, Mudgee and Orange. It is the brainchild of Rhys Eather, great-grandson of Alexander Munro, a leading vigneron in the middle of the nineteenth century, and who makes the wine in Simon Gilbert's contract winery at Muswellbrook.

Meerea Park Cabernet Merlot

Released under the Art label, and a blend of 70% Cabernet Sauvignon and 30% Merlot grown in the Hunter Valley, Mudgee and Orange regions. The wine is given two weeks post-fermentation maceration, and matured in a mix of new and used American oak barrels. Won a gold, three silver and two bronze medals in capital city wine shows in 1997.

🍷🍷🍷🍷 **1996** Medium red-purple; the bouquet is clean and smooth, with gently sweet ripe berry fruit of medium intensity. The palate, likewise of medium weight, is well balanced and composed, with a mix of berry, mint, leaf and earth flavours. The oak influence is subtle throughout. **rating:** 87

➪ **best drinking** 1999 – 2003 **best vintages** NA **drink with** Washed rind cheese • NA

merrebee estate NR

Lot 3339 St Werburghs Road, Mount Barker, WA 6234 **region** Great Southern
phone (08) 9851 2424 **fax** (08) 9851 2425 **open** Weekends and public holidays 10–4 and by appointment
winemaker Contract **production** 400 **est.** 1985
product range ($13–19 CD) Riesling, Chardonnay, Shiraz.
summary The 3.5-hectare Merrebee Estate vineyards were established in 1985, and the first wines released from the 1995 and 1996 vintages.

merricks estate ★★★☆

Thompsons Lane, Merricks, Vic 3916 **region** Mornington Peninsula
phone (03) 5989 8416 **fax** (03) 9627 4035 **open** First weekend of each month 12–5
winemaker Alex White **production** 1750 **est.** 1977
product range ($20–25 CD) Chardonnay, Shiraz, Cabernet Sauvignon, Pinot Noir.
summary Melbourne solicitor George Kefford, together with wife Jacquie, runs Merricks Estate as a weekend and holiday enterprise as a relief from professional practice. Right from the outset it has produced very distinctive, spicy, cool-climate Shiraz which has accumulated an impressive array of show trophies and gold medals.

merrivale wines ★★★☆

Olivers Road, McLaren Vale, SA 5171 **region** McLaren Vale
phone (08) 8323 9196 **fax** (08) 8323 9746 **open** 7 days 11–5
winemaker Pam Dunsford **production** 7000 **est.** 1971
product range ($12–20 CD) Semillon Chardonnay, Cabernet Malbec Shiraz; Tapestry Riesling, Chardonnay, Spätlese Muscat of Alexandria, Shiraz, Cabernet Sauvignon, Tawny Port; Brian Light Reserve Shiraz; Tawny Port.
summary After a relatively brief period of ownership by Brian Light and family, was then acquired by Chapel Hill in 1997, but will strive to keep its identity separate from Chapel Hill.

middlebrook NR

Sand Road, McLaren Vale, SA 5171 **region** McLaren Vale
phone (08) 8383 0600 **fax** (08) 8383 0557 **open** Mon-Fri 9–5, weekends 10–5
winemaker Walter (Bill) Clappis **production** 5000 **est.** 1947
product range ($14–20 CD) In the course of redevelopment, with a top-end range under the Walter Clappis label, and a mid-range under the Middlebrook label.
summary Middlebrook has been acquired and is being redeveloped by industry veteran Bill Clappis after his former winery, Ingoldby, was acquired by Mildara Blass. The Middlebrook winery and restaurant are currently under renovation, and will be reopened in the second-half of 1998 with an appropriate fanfare of trumpets.

middleton estate NR

Flagstaff Hill Road, Middleton, SA 5213 **region** McLaren Vale
phone (08) 8555 4136 **fax** (08) 8555 4108 **open** Fri-Sun 11–5
winemaker Nigel Catt **production** 3000 **est.** 1979
product range ($9–16 CD) Riesling, Sauvignon Blanc, Semillon Sauvignon Blanc, Cabernet Hermitage.
summary Nigel Catt has demonstrated his winemaking skills at Andrew Garrett and elsewhere, so wine quality should be good; despite its decade of production, I have never seen or tasted its wines. A winery restaurant helps the business turnover.

mildara (coonawarra) ★★★★

Penola-Naracoorte Road, Coonawarra, SA 5263 **region** Coonawarra
phone (08) 8736 3380 **fax** (08) 8736 3307 **open** Mon-Fri 9–4.30, weekends 10–4
winemaker Gavin Hogg **production** 400 000 **est.** 1955
product range ($10–40 R) The volume is driven by Jamiesons Run Red and Jamiesons Run Chardonnay, then comes Robertson's Well Chardonnay (in fact a blend of Yarra Valley and King Valley fruit) and Cabernet Sauvignon and Flanagan's Ridge Cabernet Sauvignon. Jamiesons Run has been 'brand-extended' with the introduction of a smartly packaged Reserve, but Alexanders remains the top-end wine for the time being.
summary The quality jewel in the crown of the Fosters Brewing Group's Mildara Blass wine empire, but a jewel which has always been put to industrial use, with the emphasis on volume brands such as Jamiesons Run, Robertson's Well and so forth. For all that, it has to be said the quality of Jamiesons Run has been zealously protected, notwithstanding the growth in volume of its production (and the 1998 introduction of Jamiesons Run Reserve).

Mildara Jamiesons Run Reserve Red

Given Mildara's penchant for creating new labels, the brand extension of Jamiesons Run into a Reserve Red comes as something of a surprise, but then Ray King has pulled many rabbits from the hat in his time as chief executive. The wine comes in its own branded, embossed bottle, and there is no doubt the first vintage ('95) is significantly better than the standard release of that year.

🍷🍷🍷🍷🍷 **1995** Medium to full red-purple; the bouquet is clean, of medium intensity, with dark berry, earth, subtle oak and a degree of lift. The palate is smooth and round, with sweet cassis/raspberry fruit, and judiciously balanced tannin and oak inputs. **rating:** 90

➾ **best drinking** 2000 – 2007 **best vintages** NA **drink with** Porterhouse steak • $39

Mildara Jamiesons Run Coonawarra Red

A blend of Cabernet Sauvignon, Shiraz, Merlot and Cabernet Franc, the last two in lesser quantities, entirely sourced from Mildara's extensive Coonawarra vineyards. Has enjoyed extraordinary show success over the years, and held its quality, notwithstanding vast increases in volume.

🍷🍷🍷🍷🍷 **1996** Strong red-purple; a fragrant, potent mix of berry, leaf, spice and earth aromas lead into a wine of excellent weight and structure, right back to the best. Sweet red cherry, mint and blackberry flavours run through the palate; subtle oak. **rating:** 90

➾ **best drinking** 2000 – 2005 **best vintages** '86, '88, '90, '91, '94, '96 **drink with** Mediterranean, Italian cuisine • $15

mildara (murray darling) ★★★

Wentworth Road, Merbein, Vic 3505 **region** Murray Darling and Swan Hill
phone (03) 5025 2303 **fax** (03) 5025 3300 **open** Mon–Fri 9–5, weekends 10–4
winemaker Steve Guy **production** 2.4 million **est.** 1888
product range ($8–10 R) Church Hill Chardonnay, Fumé Blanc, Cabernet Merlot; Jimmy Watson Chardonnay and Cabernet Sauvignon; also makes fine Sherries (Chestnut Teal, George and Supreme) and superb Pot Still Brandy.
summary A somewhat antiquated Merbein facility remains the overall group production centre following its acquisition of Wolf Blass, although all of its premium wines are sourced from and made at Coonawarra.

millers samphire NR

Watts Gully Road, Cnr Robertson Road, Kersbrook, SA 5231 **region** Adelaide Hills
phone (08) 8389 3183 **open** 7 days 9–6 by appointment
winemaker Tom Miller **production** 150 **est.** 1982
product range ($10 CD) Riesling.
summary Next after Scarp Valley, the smallest winery in Australia offering wine for sale; pottery also helps. Tom Miller has one of the more interesting and diverse CVs, with an early interest in matters alcoholic leading to the premature but happy death of a laboratory rat at Adelaide University and his enforced switch from biochemistry to mechanical engineering. The Riesling is a high-flavoured wine with crushed herb and lime aromas and flavours.

millinup estate NR

RMB 1280 Porongurup Road, Porongurup, WA 6324 **region** Great Southern
phone (08) 9853 1105 **fax** (08) 9853 1105 **open** Weekends 10–5
winemaker Gavin Berry (Contract) **production** 220 **est.** 1989

product range ($12–16 CD) Twin Peaks Riesling, Late Harvest Riesling, Cabernet Sauvignon Franc Merlot.

summary The Millinup Estate vineyard was planted in 1978, when it was called Point Creek. Owners Peter and Lesley Thorn purchased it in 1989, renaming it and having the limited production (from half a hectare each of riesling and merlot, supplemented by purchased cabernet sauvignon) vinified at Plantagenet.

minimbah NR

Minimbah House, Whittingham, NSW 2330 **region** Upper Hunter Valley

phone (02) 6572 4028 **fax** (02) 6572 1513 **open** Not

winemaker Simon Gilbert (Contract) **production** NA **est.** 1996

product range Chardonnay, Shiraz.

summary 4 hectares of chardonnay and 1 hectare of shiraz were planted in 1996, and the first vintage, to be made by Simon Gilbert, is expected in 1999.

minot vineyard NR

PO Box 683, Margaret River, WA 6285 **region** Margaret River

phone (08) 9757 3579 **fax** (08) 9757 2361 **open** Not

winemaker Andrew Forsell (Contract) **production** 220 **est.** 1600

product range ($10–15 ML) Semillon Sauvignon Blanc, Cabernet Sauvignon.

summary Minot, which takes its name from a small Chateau in the Loire Valley in France, is the husband and wife venture of the Miles family, producing just two wines from the 4-hectare plantings of semillon, sauvignon blanc and cabernet sauvignon. Both wines won silver medals at the 1997 Mount Barker Wine Show.

mintaro wines NR

Leasingham Road, Mintaro, SA 5415 **region** Clare Valley

phone (08) 8843 9046 **fax** (08) 8843 9050 **open** 7 days 9–5

winemaker Peter Houldsworth **production** 4000 **est.** 1984

product range ($9–20 CD) Dry Riesling, Late Picked Riesling, Shiraz, Shiraz Cabernet Franc Cabernet Sauvignon, Cabernet Sauvignon Cabernet Franc.

summary Has produced some very good Riesling over the years, developing well in bottle. The red wines are formidable, massive in body and extract, built for the long haul.

miramar ★★★★

Henry Lawson Drive, Mudgee, NSW 2850 **region** Mudgee

phone (02) 6373 3874 **fax** (02) 6373 3854 **open** 7 days 9–5

winemaker Ian MacRae **production** 8000 **est.** 1977

product range ($10–30 CD) Semillon, Chardonnay, Fumé Blanc, Riesling, Eurunderee Rosé, Cabernet Sauvignon, Shiraz, Encore (Sparkling).

summary Industry veteran Ian MacRae has demonstrated his skill with every type of wine over the decades, ranging through Rosé to Chardonnay to full-bodied reds. All have shone under the Miramar label at one time or another, although the Ides of March are pointing more to the red than the white wines these days.

Miramar Shiraz

Another slow-developing wine made from estate-grown grapes, moving progressively earthy, cedary characters as it ages. The oak contribution is typically subtle.

🍷🍷🍷🍷 **1996** Medium to full red-purple; the bouquet is clean, full and smooth with nicely balanced black cherry and sweet vanilla oak. There is similarly attractive cherry and mint fruit on the entry of the wine into the mouth, although the finish is fractionally hard; lots of flavour **rating:** 85

➯ **best drinking** 2001 – 2011 **best vintages** '86, '90, '94, '95 **drink with** Braised oxtail, or better still, the ox • $15

miranda ★★★☆

57 Jondaryan Avenue, Griffith, NSW 2680 **region** Riverina
phone (02) 6962 4033 **fax** (02) 6962 6944 **open** 7 days 9–5
winemaker Doug Wilson **production** 1.5 million **est.** 1939
product range ($4.95–23.95 R) Top of the range is Show Reserve Chardonnay, Old Vine Shiraz, Shiraz Cabernet; Golden Botrytis; followed by the High Country series (from the King Valley) of Riesling, Chardonnay, Merlot, Shiraz and Cabernet; Mirool Creek Dry White, Chardonnay and Cabernet Shiraz; Somerton Riesling Traminer, Semillon Chardonnay and Shiraz Cabernet; also lower priced Christy's Land and assorted varietals, generics, sparkling and ports.
summary Miranda Wines continues its aggressive and successful growth strategy, having opened a new winery in the King Valley in 1998, and previously expanded winemaking operations into the Barossa Valley. A veritable cascade of wines now appear under the various brand names, the majority representing good value for money.

Miranda Golden Botrytis

Introduced in 1993, and the only Semillon Riesling blend so far marketed in Australia. The '93 was a blend of 65% Semillon and 35% Riesling; in 1994 the percentages swapped around to 53% Riesling and 47% Semillon, the Riesling coming from the King Valley and the Semillon from Griffith. Both the '93 and '94 wines were of great quality, and prolific gold medal winners in wine shows. Since 1993 has been of outstanding quality, the '96 and '97 vintages providing the two gold medals in Class 38 at the 1997 Royal Adelaide Wine Show.

🍷🍷🍷🍷🍷 **1997** Deep, bright yellow; an incredibly rich and intense wine with complex cumquat and lime aromas and flavours, balanced by powerful acidity on the finish. **rating:** 94

➯ **best drinking** 1998 – 2001 **best vintages** '93, '94, '96, '97 **drink with** Fruit ice-cream, sweet pastries • $15.95

Miranda Botrytis Semillon

Produced from heavily botrytised semillon grapes grown in the Riverina region, and a prolific show medal winner.

🍷🍷🍷🍷 **1997** Glowing yellow-green; a very ripe, almost raisiny bouquet with honeyed toffee cumquat aromas moving into a more tangy grapefruit marmalade palate, which is lively and fresh, with pronounced acidity on a long finish. **rating:** 85

➯ **best drinking** 1998 – 2001 **best vintages** NA **drink with** Pecan pie • NA

miranda rovalley estate ★★★☆

Barossa Highway, Rowland Flat, SA 5352 **region** Barossa Valley
phone (08) 8524 4537 **fax** (08) 8524 4066 **open** 7 days 9–4.30
winemaker David Norman **production** NA **est.** 1919
product range ($9–25 CD) Premium Late Harvest Riesling; the Grey Series of Riesling, Semillon, Sauvignon Blanc, Chardonnay, Shiraz, Bush Vine Grenache and Cabernet Sauvignon; followed by Show Reserve range of Chardonnay, Old Vine Shiraz and Shiraz Cabernet.
summary Increasingly absorbed into the Miranda Wine Group since its acquisition, drawing on grapes produced both in the Barossa Valley and throughout other parts of southeast Australia. The accent is on value for money, with consistent show success underlining the quality.

mistletoe wines NR

Lot 1 Hermitage Road, Pokolbin, NSW 2335 **region** Lower Hunter Valley
phone (02) 4998 7770 **fax** (02) 4998 7792 **open** Mon-Fri 10–6 or by appointment
winemaker Jon Reynolds (Contract) **production** 2000 **est.** 1967
product range ($15.50–17 R) Semillon, Barrel Fermented Chardonnay, Shiraz.
summary Mistletoe Wines, owned by Ken and Gwen Sloan, can trace its history back to 1909, when a substantial vineyard was planted on what was then called Mistletoe Farm. The Mistletoe Farm brand made a brief appearance in the late 1970s, but disappeared, and has now been revived under the Mistletoe Wines label by the Sloans, with contract-winemaking by Jon Reynolds. The Shiraz is the best of the wines, with pleasant, straightforward varietal character, the white wines adequate. The wines won a number of medals in wine shows in 1997 and are available both at the McGuigan Bros cellar door and at the old Hungerford Hill Village site on the corner of McDonalds and Broke Roads.

mitchell ★★★★☆

Hughes Park Road, Sevenhill via Clare, SA 5453 **region** Clare Valley
phone (08) 8843 4258 **fax** (08) 8843 4340 **open** 7 days 10–4
winemaker Andrew Mitchell **production** 20 000 **est.** 1975
product range ($14–21 CD) Watervale Riesling, Peppertree Vineyard Shiraz, The Growers Semillon, The Growers Grenache, Cabernet Sauvignon, Sparkling Peppertree.
summary For long one of the stalwarts of the Clare Valley, producing long-lived Rieslings and Cabernet Sauvignons in classic regional style, but having extended the range with very creditable Semillon and Shiraz. A lovely old stone apple shed provides the cellar door and upper section of the compact winery.

Mitchell Watervale Riesling

First made in 1977 and produced from the estate vineyards in the Watervale region. This is a classic Clare Riesling which, as the classic tasting shows, ages magnificently for up to 15 years in good vintages.

YYYY **1997** Medium yellow-green; a rich, full and toasty bouquet, one of the big '97 Clare Valley styles. A big, generously flavoured palate. **rating:** 85

➾ **best drinking** 2002 – 2007 **best vintages** '78, '84, '90, '92, '93, '94, '95 **drink with** Grilled fish • $14

Mitchell The Growers Semillon

Introduced in 1996 and replaced the former Barrel Fermented Semillon. As with its predecessor, an each-way drinking style, good when young, but even better with some age. The grapes are grown by the Pulford, Haig and Howard families, and the wine is invested with a touch of Sauvignon Blanc and just a touch of French oak.

🍷🍷🍷🍷 **1997** Glowing medium yellow-green; a clean, rich and full bouquet, tangy yet sweet, with subtle oak is followed by a lively wine on the palate, showing excellent tangy, mouthfilling fruit and again just the faintest touch of oak. **rating:** 85

➾ **best drinking** 1998 – 2002 **best vintages** NA **drink with** Sugar-cured tuna • $15

Mitchell Peppertree Vineyard Shiraz

Like the Semillon, first made in 1984, and which takes its name from the old peppertree which grows in the shiraz vineyard at Watervale. The wine is aged for 18 months in small French and American oak; in some years it shows minty characters, in other years more spice and cherry.

🍷🍷🍷🍷 **1996** Medium to full red-purple; there are solid, dark berry and chocolate fruit aromas supported by subtle but sweet oak on the bouquet. The palate is at once elegant yet strongly flavoured with red berry, mint, touches of spice, soft tannins and subtle oak. **rating:** 89

➾ **best drinking** 2001 – 2006 **best vintages** '84, '86, '87, '94, '95, '96 **drink with** Devilled kidneys • $21

Mitchell Cabernet Sauvignon

First made in 1976; from then to 1983 fashioned entirely from Cabernet Sauvignon, but between then and 1985 first Cabernet Franc and then Merlot were added, now contributing 5–15% of the finished wine, which is aged in a mix of new and older French oak.

🍷🍷🍷🍷 **1995** Medium to full red-purple; a solid and full bouquet with ripe earthy blackberry fruit runs into a palate of medium weight which starts with good cassis berry fruit, although it seems to fall away slightly on the mid to back palate. **rating:** 85

➾ **best drinking** 2000 – 2007 **best vintages** '78, '80, '84, '86, '90, '92, '94 **drink with** Roast lamb • $21

mitchelton ★★★★☆

Mitchellstown via Nagambie, Vic 3608 **region** Goulburn Valley
phone (03) 5794 2710 **fax** (03) 5794 2615 **open** 7 days 9–5
winemaker Don Lewis **production** 200 000 **est.** 1974

product range ($9–35 CD) Top-of-the-range Print Label Red, then come Reserve Chardonnay, Cabernet Sauvignon, Marsanne; next Mitchelton III wines, White (Marsanne, Grenache, Viognier), Red (Shiraz, Grenache, Mourvedre); Chinaman's Bridge Merlot, Blackwood Park Riesling. Preece Chardonnay, Sauvignon Blanc, Merlot and Cabernet Sauvignon are volume sellers; Goulburn Valley Shiraz introduced in 1996. Finally, intermittent aged classic releases.

summary Acquired by Petaluma in 1994, having already put the runs on the board in no uncertain fashion with a gifted team of Stephen Shelmerdine and winemaker Don Lewis. Boasts an impressive array of wines across a broad spectrum of style and price, but each carefully aimed at a market niche.

Mitchelton Blackwood Park Riesling

Over the past few years Blackwood Park has laid claim to being the best commercial Riesling in Australia, even though its origins go back to 1978 under different labels. Since that time various vintages have won eight trophies, 51 gold, 66 silver and 102 bronze medals, with the '94 and '95 vintages adding to both the trophy and gold medal records.

🍷🍷🍷🍷 **1997** Medium to full yellow-green; rich, forward and full tropical/passionfruit aromas introduce a ripe fleshy wine with more of that tropical/pineapple fruit of the bouquet. Flavoursome, quick-developing style. **rating:** 85

⇨ **best drinking** 1998 – 2000 **best vintages** '85, '90, '91, '92, '94, '95 **drink with** Sashimi • $12.95

Mitchelton Goulburn Valley Marsanne

Mitchelton adopts precisely the opposite approach to Chateau Tahbilk by seeking to invest its Marsanne with complexity from the word go. For many years the approach was to give the wine substantial oak, but the approach is now more subtle. The Marsanne is barrel-fermented, and also has 15% Viognier and Roussane included.

🍷🍷🍷🍷 **1996** Medium yellow-green; the bouquet is complex with attractive fruit and spicy oak. A wine with lots of character on the palate, with well-handled oak adding a dimension, likewise the Viognier and Roussane components. Not overblown, nor a heavyweight, and may well repay medium-term cellaring. **rating:** 88

⇨ **best drinking** 1998 – 2003 **best vintages** NA **drink with** Creamy pasta • $14.95

Mitchelton Goulburn Valley Shiraz

Yet another new label from Mitchelton, using a blend of 85% Shiraz and 15% Grenache and Mourvedre. I suspect this has replaced the former Mitchelton III Red.

🍷🍷🍷🍷 **1995** Medium purple-red; a high-toned bouquet with a mix of juicy berry aromas and a quite pronounced overlay of mint. The palate is complex and interesting; the grenache seems to have made a major contribution to what are quite complex fruit flavours, again with a strong strand of Central Victorian mint coming through. **rating:** 85

⇨ **best drinking** 1998 – 2002 **best vintages** NA **drink with** Braised duck • $15.95

Mitchelton Print Label Red

In 1981 Mitchelton conceived the idea of staging a Print Exhibition and making an annual purchase of the best print in the exhibition for subsequent use as the label of the best red wine of the vintage. Both the '90 and '91 vintages were outstanding, the former winning the Jimmy Watson Trophy. Having started life as a Cabernet Sauvignon, Shiraz has ruled the roost for most recent vintages. However, the best wine of the 1994 vintage was a Cabernet Sauvignon, but with 1995 the wine will revert to Shiraz. For the record, only 400 cases were made of the Cabernet.

🍷🍷🍷🍷 **1994** Medium to full red-purple; the bouquet is intense to the point of being strident, with minty aromas typical of Central Victoria. The palate is powerful and concentrated, with a mix of mint, cassis and raspberry flavours, supported by powerful tannins. Others will rate the wine even more highly; I would simply like a little less mint. **rating:** 85

⇨ **best drinking** 2000 – 2010 **best vintages** '81, '82, '90, '91, '92 **drink with** Marinated venison • $23.95

---

molly morgan vineyard NR

Talga Road, Lovedale, NSW 2321 **region** Lower Hunter Valley
phone (02) 4930 7695 **fax** (02) 9235 1876 **open** Weekends, public holidays 10–5
winemaker Geoffrey Broadfield **production** 1400 **est.** 1984
product range ($12–18 CD) Non-Wooded Semillon, Barrel Fermented Semillon, Joe's Block Semillon, Chardonnay, Shiraz.
summary The weekend retreat of Sydney barrister Geoff Petty; much of the production from the 10-hectare plantings of semillon, chardonnay, shiraz and riesling is sold elsewhere. Tastings over the years have always shown rich, well-flavoured wines. No recent tastings; however the 1997 Joe's Block Semillon was rated Top 1997 Hunter Semillon by *Winestate* magazine and the '96 Chardonnay won a bronze medal at the 1997 Hunter Valley Wine Show.

monbulk winery ★★☆

Macclesfield Road, Monbulk, Vic 3793 **region** Yarra Valley
phone (03) 9756 6965 **fax** (03) 9756 6965 **open** Weekends and public holidays 12–5, or by appointment
winemaker Paul Jabornik **production** 1000 **est.** 1984
product range ($10–15 CD) Chardonnay, Riesling, Pinot Noir, Cabernet Sauvignon, Shiraz; also Kiwifruit wines.
summary Originally concentrated on Kiwifruit wines, but now extending to table wines; the very cool Monbulk subregion should be capable of producing wines of distinctive style, but the table wines are (unfortunately) not of the same standard as the Kiwifruit wines, which are quite delicious.

monichino wines ★★☆

1820 Berrys Road, Katunga, Vic 3640 **region** Goulburn Valley
phone (03) 5864 6452 **fax** (03) 5864 6538 **open** Mon–Sat 9–5, Sun 10–5
winemaker Carlo Monichino, Terry Monichino **production** 14 000 **est.** 1962
product range ($8–22 CD) Riesling, Semillon Sauvignon Blanc Sauvignon Blanc (Stratbogie) Semillon Sauvignon Blanc, Botrytis Semillon, Orange Muscat, Lexia, Rose Petals Spätlese, Shiraz, Merlot, Malbec, Cabernet Franc, Cabernet Sauvignon; various Ports and fortifieds; bulk sales also available.
summary A winery which has quietly made some clean, fresh wines in which the fruit character is carefully preserved.

montara 

Chalambar Road, Ararat, Vic 3377 **region** Grampians
phone (03) 5352 3868 **fax** (03) 5352 4968 **open** Mon–Sat 9.30–5, Sun 12–4
winemaker Mike McRae **production** NFP **est.** 1970
product range ($10–18 CD) Chardonnay, Riesling, Ondenc, Chasselas, Pinot Noir, Shiraz, Cabernet Sauvignon, Port; second label is 'M' range of Riesling, Ondenc and Pinot Noir Shiraz.
summary Achieved considerable attention for its Pinot Noirs during the 1980s, but other regions (and other makers) have come along since. Recent tastings across the board show wines of serviceable quality, particularly the spicy, juicy 'M' Pinot Shiraz and a spicy, liquorice-accented Shiraz.

montrose ★★★☆

Henry Lawson Drive, Mudgee, NSW 2850 **region** Mudgee
phone (02) 6373 3853 **fax** (02) 6373 3795 **open** Mon–Fri 9–4, weekends 10–4
winemaker Robert Paul **production** 50 000 **est.** 1974
product range ($8.95–25 R) Poet's Corner Semillon Sauvignon Blanc Chardonnay, Unwooded Chardonnay and Shiraz Cabernet Sauvignon Cabernet Franc are at the inexpensive end; premium varietals are Chardonnay, Barbera, Sangiovese, Black Shiraz and Cabernet Sauvignon.
summary A small piece of the Orlando/Wyndham empire, acting partly as a grape and bulk wine source for that empire, and partly as a quality producer in its own right, making typically full-flavoured whites and deep-coloured reds. Poet's Corner always provides excellent value for money.

Montrose Barbera

Montrose was established by Italian-born engineers Carlo Salteri and Franco Belgiorno-Nettis (of Transfield Corporation), who in turn hired Italian winemaker Carlo Corino as winemaker. Inevitably, Italian grape varieties were planted and were briefly made, but disappeared from the scene for over a decade (although the plantings were not removed). The Italian craze has led to their reappearance, and not before time. I preferred the '96 Barbera to the '96 Sangiovese.

🍷🍷🍷🍷 **1996** Medium purple-red; the bouquet is clean and fresh with red cherry and plum fruit, tinged with earth; the palate is firm, as befits the variety, with plummy/briary fruit, supple tannins and good length and structure. **rating:** 85

➯ **best drinking** 2000 – 2005 **best vintages** NA **drink with** Bistecca fiorentina • $25

---

moondah brook ★★★★

c/o Houghton, Dale Road, Middle Swan, WA 6056 **region** Swan District
phone (08) 9274 5372 **fax** (08) 9274 5372 **open** Not
winemaker Paul Lapsley **production** 90 000 **est.** 1968
product range ($12.95–17.90 R) Chardonnay, Chenin Blanc, Verdelho, Sauvignon Blanc, Shiraz, Cabernet Sauvignon; also occasional Show Reserve releases of Chenin Blanc and Verdelho.
summary Part of the Houghton Wine Group which has its own special character as it draws part of its fruit from the large Gingin vineyard, 70 kilometres north of the Swan Valley, and part from the Margaret River and Great Southern. In recent times it has excelled even its own reputation for reliability with some quite lovely wines, in particular honeyed, aged Chenin Blanc and finely structured Cabernet Sauvignon.

Moondah Brook Shiraz

The back label is equivocal about the regional sources used to make this wine, but it is a fair bet they extend south. Whatever be the answer, a wine which shows the customary Moondah Brook flair.

🍷🍷🍷🍷 **1996** Medium red-purple; the bouquet unfolds chocolate and earth initially, then hints of leather followed by touches of spice; on the palate, chocolatey flavours come to the fore, supported by pleasant berry notes and utterly appropriate oak. **rating:** 85

➯ **best drinking** 1999 – 2004 **best vintages** NA **drink with** Spiced lamb • $17.90

---

moonshine valley winery NR

374 Mons Road, Forest Glen, Buderim, Qld 4556 **region** Other Wineries of Qld
phone (07) 5445 1198 **fax** (07) 5445 1799 **open** 7 days 10–5
winemaker Frederick Houweling **production** 1700 **est.** 1985
product range ($10.40–32.95 CD) A kaleidoscopic array of basically fruit-based wines including Le Dry (Mulberries and Blueberries, oak-matured), Moonlight White (West Indian Limes), Sunshine Nouveau (locally grown Jaboticabas), Old Buderim Ginger (fortified base with Honey and Ginger added), Strawberry Wine, Exporto (Mulberry and Blueberry-based Port Wine).
summary Frederick Houweling brings a European background to his making of these fruit-based wines. The winery is situated on a large property among natural lakes and forest, and also offers a restaurant, cafeteria, and souvenir shop.

moorebank vineyard NR

Palmers Lane, Pokolbin, NSW 2320 **region** Lower Hunter Valley
phone (02) 4998 7610 **fax** (02) 4998 7367 **open** Fri–Mon 10–5 or by appointment
winemaker Iain Riggs (Contract) **production** 1500 **est.** 1977
product range ($17.50–24.50 CD) Chardonnay, Summar Semillon, Gewurztraminer, Merlot, now sold in the narrow 500-ml Italian glass bottle known as Bellissima.
summary Ian Burgess and Debra Moore own a mature 5.5-hectare vineyard with a small cellar-door operation offering immaculately packaged wines in avant-garde style. The peachy Chardonnay has been a bronze medal winner at Hunter Valley Wine Shows.

moorilla estate ★★★★☆

655 Main Road, Berriedale, Tas 7011 **region** Southern Tasmania
phone (03) 6249 2949 **fax** (03) 6249 4093 **open** 7 days 10–5
winemaker Alain Rousseau **production** 9000 **est.** 1958
product range ($19–32 R) Riesling, Chardonnay, Gewurztraminer, Pinot Noir, Reserve Pinot Noir, Winter Collection Cabernet Merlot, Cabernet Sauvignon, Vintage Brut.
summary Moorilla Estate is an icon in the Tasmanian wine industry. The financial problems which led to the disappearance of the founding Alcorso family have saddened many, and even under its present syndicated ownership, some believe the future is far from certain, if only because of the sheer real estate value of the superb site on the Derwent River. The Rieslings, Chardonnays and Gewurztraminers are invariably stylish and elegant wines.

Moorilla Estate Riesling

In my view, consistently the best of the Moorilla Estate wines, reaching a high point in 1994, but with a long track record of excellence. Produced from 1.5 hectares of estate vineyards. In addition, the occasional releases of Botrytised Riesling (by mailing list and through cellar door), are sensational. The 1994 won the trophy for Best Museum Wine in the 1998 Tasmanian Wines Show.
🍷🍷🍷🍷 **1997** Light to medium yellow-green; a clean, smooth bouquet with sweet, gentle lime aromas and a similarly clean, pleasant, soft and well-balanced palate with lime and lemon fruit flavours. Reflects the difference in Southern and Northern Tasmanian Riesling in 1997. **rating:** 85

⇒ **best drinking** 1998 – 2004 **best vintages** '81, '82, '90, '91, '93, '94, '95 **drink with** Asparagus • $19.50

Moorilla Estate Chardonnay

A complex wine which is, as one would expect, very much in cool-climate style. It is produced from 2.5 hectares of immaculately trained estate vineyards, and given what might loosely be called 'the full treatment' in the winery. Sometimes, as in 1993, botrytis makes an impact on the wine. The '95 won the trophy for Best Wine of Show at the 1997 Tasmanian Wines Show, bettering the trophy (Best White Wine) won by the '94 the previous year.

1996 Medium to full yellow-green; the aromas are smooth, with a mix of citrus, lime and stone fruit; subtle oak. Similar flavours run through the long palate, which terminates with typically brisk Tasmanian acid. **rating:** 85

⇨ **best drinking** 1998 – 2001 **best vintages** '81, '82, '90, '91, '92, '94, '95 **drink with** Tasmanian salmon • $24

Moorilla Estate Reserve Pinot Noir

So far as I am aware, a recent introduction into the Moorilla Estate range, and on the evidence of the '96 vintage, significantly superior to the varietal (or standard) release.

1996 Medium to full red, with just a touch of purple. The clean but intense bouquet has strong varietal fruit, the palate depth, weight and considerable lusciousness to the solid plummy fruit. Some earthy foresty secondary characters are starting to build, too. **rating:** 85

⇨ **best drinking** 1998 – 2001 **best vintages** NA **drink with** Breast of squab • $30

mooroodoc estate

Derril Road, Mooroodoc, Vic 3936 **region** Mornington Peninsula
phone (03) 9696 4130 **fax** (03) 9696 2841 **open** First weekend each month 12–5
winemaker Dr Richard McIntyre **production** 3000 **est.** 1983
product range ($25–32 R) Chardonnay, Pinot Noir, Cabernet Sauvignon.
summary Dr Richard McIntyre regularly produces one of the richest and most complex Chardonnays in the region, with grapefruit/peach fruit set against sumptuous spicy oak, and that hallmark soft nutty/creamy/regional texture.

morning cloud wines NR

15 Ocean View Avenue, Red Hill South, Vic 3937 **region** Mornington Peninsula
phone (03) 5989 2762 **fax** (03) 5989 2700 **open** By appointment
winemaker Ken Lang (Contract), Lindsay McCall (Contract) **production** 500 **est.** 1983
product range ($17–20 R) Chardonnay, Cabernet Sauvignon.
summary Morning Cloud Wines (previously Cloud Valley) is a joint venture between Kathy and Bill Allen and Peter and Judy Maxwell. Each family has its own vineyard at Red Hill South, and the grapes are pooled and the wine made under contract at Stonier's Winery. The Cabernet Sauvignon tends to be very leafy in Chinon-style; the Chardonnay, medium-bodied crisp and citrus-tinged.

morningside wines NR

RMB 3002 Middle Tea Tree Road, Tea Tree, Tas 7017 **region** Southern Tasmania
phone (03) 6268 1748 **open** Not
winemaker Peter Bosworth **production** 300 **est.** 1980
product range ($11–16 ML) Riesling, Pinot Noir, Cabernet Sauvignon.
summary The name 'Morningside' was given to the old property on which the vineyard stands because it gets the morning sun first. The property on the other side of the valley was

known as 'Eveningside', and, consistently with the observation of the early settlers, the Morningside grapes achieve full maturity with good colour and varietal flavour. Production is as yet tiny, but will increase as the 1.5-hectare vineyard matures.

mornington vineyards estate ★★★☆

Moorooduc Road, Mornington, Vic 3931 **region** Mornington Peninsula
phone (03) 5974 2097 **fax** (03) 5974 2097 **open** Weekends, public holidays and 7 days in January
winemaker Vincent Gere, Kim Hart **production** 2000 **est.** 1989
product range ($18–25 CD) Chardonnay, Sauvignon Blanc, Pinot Noir, Shiraz.
summary As with so many Mornington Peninsula vineyards, a high degree of viticultural expertise, care and attention, coupled with skilled contract-winemaking has paid dividends. In cool, wet vintages such as 1996, however, the vineyard does struggle to achieve full fruit ripeness.

morris 

Mia Mia Road, Rutherglen, Vic 3685 **region** Rutherglen
phone (02) 6026 7303 **fax** (02) 6026 7445 **open** Mon-Sat 9–5, Sun 10–5
winemaker David Morris **production** NFP **est.** 1859
product range ($11.95–41.95 R) A limited range of table wines sparingly distributed, the most important of which is the red wine Durif, and also Shiraz; then fortified wines comprising Mick Morris Old Tawny Port, Liqueur Tokay, Old Premium Liqueur Tokay, Mick Morris Muscat, Old Premium Liqueur Muscat, Mick Morris Commemorative Liqueur Muscat; Old Premium Liqueur Muscat at the top end of the range; tiny quantities of Show Reserve are released from time to time, mainly ex-winery.
summary One of the greatest of the fortified winemakers, some would say the greatest. If you wish to test that view, try the Old Premium Muscat and Old Premium Tokay, which are absolute bargains given their age and quality and which give rise to the winery rating. The table wines are dependable, the white wines all being made by owner Orlando.

Morris Durif

Durif is an exceedingly obscure variety closely related to another grape of similar ilk, peloursin. It may or may not be the same as California's petite syrah; if it is not, Australia is the only country in the world producing wines from it. It is as much for its rarity and for its individuality as its ultimate quality that it is included as a classic in my *Classic Wines of Australia* book.

1996 Full red-purple; ripe prune, liquorice, hay and straw aromas announce a potently ripe wine on the palate with masses of prune and blackberry flavour. There is no oak influence, not excessively tannic. **rating:** 86

➾ **best drinking** 2000 – 2010 **best vintages** '70, '72, '74, '80, '83, '86, '88, '90, '92, '94, '96 **drink with** Biltong • $19.95

Morris Liqueur Tokay

Made from the muscadelle grape, used as a minor component in Sauternes, but nowhere else in the world used to make fortified dessert wines. In this version, which contains a greater percentage of younger material (two to four years old) than the premium labels, the accent is thrown firmly onto the very distinctive varietal character of muscadelle.

🍷🍷🍷🍷🍷 **NV** Light to medium golden-brown; a fragrant bouquet with fresh tea-leaf varietal aroma. There is masses of flavour on the palate, yet the wine is quite fresh with archetypal cold tea and butterscotch flavours, with the mid-palate sweetness followed by a cleansing, crisp finish. **rating:** 90

➾ **best drinking** 1998 – 2008 **best vintages** NA **drink with** Either aperitif or at the end of the meal • $15.95

Morris Liqueur Muscat

As with the Tokay in the same range, the accent is thrown onto the varietal character of Muscat, otherwise known as Brown Frontignac. The style differs from that of Baileys, which tends to be sweet and in some ways more complex, but with less clarity of varietal character. Which of the two one prefers is very much a matter of personal taste.

🍷🍷🍷🍷🍷 **NV** Light to medium red-brown; clearly articulated, lively, raisiny muscat varietal aromas. In the mouth you can literally taste the grapes, as if one were chewing on an explosively rich raisin; great length, and perfect balance. **rating:** 91

➾ **best drinking** 1998 – 2008 **best vintages** NA **drink with** Aperitif or digestif • $13.95

Morris Old Premium Liqueur Muscat

Here the component of old material is much greater than in the less-expensive standard Liqueur range. The blending of young, middle-aged and very old wines lies at the heart of the style, with a tiny percentage of 30 and 40-year-old wood-aged material having a disproportionate impact on the blend.

🍷🍷🍷🍷🍷 **NV** Medium to full tawny, with a hint of olive on the rim. A rich bouquet with complex caramel, toffee and coffee aromas intermingling with the raisins. The palate shows more of the raisiny varietal fruit, although the complexity of the bouquet does repeat itself. A great example of blending. **rating:** 95

➾ **best drinking** 1998 – 2008 **best vintages** NA **drink with** Coffee, petits fours • $41.95

moss brothers ★★☆

Caves Road, Willyabrup, WA 6280 **region** Margaret River
phone (08) 9755 6270 **fax** (08) 9755 6298 **open** 7 days 9–5.30
winemaker Jane Moss, David Moss **production** 8000 **est.** 1984
product range ($15–35 R) Semillon, Sauvignon Blanc, Unwooded Chardonnay, Barrel Fermented Chardonnay, Sauvignon Blanc, Cabernet Merlot, Cellar Door Red, Moses Rock Red (the last two unusual blends, Moses Rock including Merlot, Pinot Noir, Grenache, and Cabernet Franc).
summary Established by long-term viticulturist Jeff Moss and his family, notably sons Peter and David and Roseworthy graduate daughter Jane. A 100-tonne rammed-earth winery was constructed in 1992, and draws upon both estate-grown and purchased grapes. Wine quality is, quite frankly, disappointing, particularly by the standards of Margaret River.

moss wood ★★★★★

Metricup Road, Willyabrup, WA 6280 **region** Margaret River
phone (08) 9755 6266 **fax** (08) 9755 6303 **open** By appointment
winemaker Keith Mugford **production** 5000 **est.** 1969
product range ($20–40 R) Semillon, Wood Matured Semillon, Chardonnay, Cabernet Sauvignon, Pinot Noir.

summary Widely regarded as one of the best wineries in the region, capable of producing glorious Semillon (the best outside the Hunter Valley) in both oaked and unoaked forms, unctuous Chardonnay and elegant, gently herbaceous, superfine Cabernet Sauvignon which lives for many years.

Moss Wood Semillon

As with all the Moss Wood wines, entirely estate-grown and produced from 1.35 hectares of fully mature vines (the first vintage was 1977). Produced in both unoaked and oaked versions, both superb and age-worthy.

1997 Medium to full yellow-green; voluminous aromas, rich, full and complex introduce a full-bodied, multiflavoured wine with tropical fruit flavours. **rating:** 90

➪ **best drinking** 1998 – 2004 **best vintages** '81, '82, '83, '84, '86, '87, '92, '94, '95, '97 **drink with** Crab, lobster • $21

Moss Wood Cabernet Sauvignon

First made in 1973, and has established itself as one of the classic wine styles not only of the Margaret River, but of Australia. The wines have a distinctive suppleness and softness which sets them apart from other Margaret River Cabernets, and which Dr John Gladstones firmly attributes to the particular terroir of the vineyard.

1995 Medium to full purple-red; a smooth gently sweet-textured bouquet with that very special character of Moss Wood, a particular softness which is quite unique. The palate is in precisely the same mould, with soft, luscious mouthfilling blackcurrant and dark chocolate fruit flavours with perfectly integrated and balanced sweet oak. The tannins, likewise, are extraordinarily supple and fine. **rating:** 96

➪ **best drinking** 2000 – 2015 **best vintages** '77, '80, '86, '87, '90, '91, '93, '94, '95 **drink with** Beef with olives • $32

---

mount alexander vineyard ★★

Calder Highway, North Harcourt, Vic 3453 **region** Bendigo
phone (03) 5474 2262 **fax** (03) 5474 2553 **open** 7 days 10–5.30
winemaker Keith Walkden **production** 6000 **est.** 1984
product range ($10–14 CD) A wide range of various table wines, sparkling, fortifieds, meads and liqueurs.
summary A substantial operation with large vineyards with 12 hectares of vineyards planted to all the right varieties. It is several years since I have tasted the wines, but I have no reason to suppose they have changed much.

mount anakie wines

Staughton Vale Road, Anakie, Vic 3221 **region** Geelong
phone (03) 5284 1452 **fax** (03) 5284 1405 **open** Tues–Sun 11–6
winemaker Otto Zambelli **production** 6000 **est.** 1968
product range ($10–18 R) Biancone, Riesling, Semillon, Chardonnay, Dolcetto, Shiraz, Cabernet Franc, Cabernet Sauvignon.
summary Also known as Zambelli Estate, and once produced some excellent wines (under its various ownerships and winemakers), all distinguished by their depth and intensity of flavour. No recent tastings; prior to that, the wines tasted were but a shadow of their former quality. The level of activity seems relatively low; the current price list was issued in 1995, and spans the 1992 to 1995 vintages.

mount avoca vineyard ★★★☆

Moates Lane, Avoca, Vic 3467 **region** Pyrenees
phone (03) 5465 3282 **fax** (03) 5465 3544 **open** Mon-Fri 9–5, weekends 10–5
winemaker John Barry, Matthew Barry **production** 11 000 **est.** 1970
product range ($14.20–50 R) Classic Dry White, Sauvignon Blanc, Chardonnay, Autumn White, Shiraz, Cabernets.
summary A substantial winery which has for long been one of the stalwarts of the Pyrenees region, and steadily growing, with 25 hectares of vineyards. Slightly flinty white wines and robust reds are the order of the day.

Mount Avoca Chardonnay

A very well-made wine, with fermentation commenced in stainless steel and transferred at 4° baumé to new medium toast oak hogsheads. Fifteen per cent is taken through malolactic fermentation, and the wine kept on lees (with stirring) for just over four months.

 **1996** Light to medium yellow-green; a clean, smooth bouquet of light to medium intensity with melon, cashew and subtle oak aromas intermingling. The palate is spotlessly clean, with good length and intensity, well balanced and fresh; creamy melon flavours hold the wine in good stead. **rating:** 90

➯ **best drinking** 1998 – 2003 **best vintages** NA **drink with** Corn-fed chicken • $20.60

mount beckworth ★★★☆

RMB 915 Learmonth Road, Tourello via Ballarat, Vic 3363 **region** Ballarat
phone (03) 5343 4207 **fax** (03) 5343 4207 **open** Weekends 10–6 and by appointment
winemaker Simon Clayfield (Consultant), Paul Lesock **production** 630 **est.** 1984
product range ($12–16 CD) Chardonnay, Pinot Noir, Shiraz, Cabernets, Malbec Mac.
summary The 4-hectare Mount Beckworth vineyard was planted between 1984 and 1985, but it was not until 1995 that the full range of wines under the Mount Beckworth label appeared. Until that time much of the production was sold to Seppelt Great Western for sparkling wine use. It is owned and managed by Paul Lesock, who studied viticulture at Charles Sturt University, and his wife Jane, and the wines are made at Best's. The wines reflect the very cool climate.

Mount Beckworth Pinot Noir

Produced from 1.2 hectares of estate plantings. The '96 is an impressive wine, winning well-deserved silver medals at the 1997 Ballarat and Hobart Wine Shows.

 **1996** Medium to full red-purple; a solid bouquet with a mix of dark fruit, plum and foresty notes, but not the slightest bit green. The palate is very substantial with dark plum, almost into blackberry; while powerful, not abrasive. **rating:** 84

➯ **best drinking** 1999 – 2003 **best vintages** NA **drink with** Venison ragout • $16

mount duneed ★★☆

Feehan's Road, Mount Duneed, Vic 3216 **region** Geelong
phone (03) 5264 1281 **fax** (03) 5264 1281 **open** Public holidays and weekends 11–5 or by appointment
winemaker Ken Campbell, John Darling **production** 1000 **est.** 1970
product range ($10–18 CD) Semillon, Sauvignon Blanc, Riesling, Botrytis Semillon, Malbec, Cabernet Malbec, Cabernet Sauvignon.

summary Rather idiosyncratic wines are the order of the day, some of which can develop surprisingly well in bottle; the Botrytis Noble Rot Semillon has, from time to time, been of very high quality. A significant part of the production from the 7.5 hectares of vineyards is sold to others.

mount gisborne wines NR

5 Waterson Road, Gisborne, Vic 3437 **region** Macedon
phone (03) 5428 2834 **fax** (03) 5428 2834 **open** By appointment
winemaker Stuart Anderson **production** 1200 **est.** 1987
product range ($10–24 CD) Chardonnay, Dessert Chardonnay, Pinot Noir, Pinot Noir Limited Release.
summary Mount Gisborne Wines is very much a weekend and holiday occupation for proprietor David Ell, who makes the wines from the 6-hectare vineyard under the watchful and skilled eye of industry veteran Stuart Anderson, now living in semi-retirement high in the Macedon Hills.

mount helen ★★★★

Strathbogie Ranges (vineyard only), Vic 3666 **region** Central Victorian High Country
open Not
winemaker Toni Stockhausen **production** 5000 **est.** 1978
product range ($22 R) Chardonnay, Cabernet Merlot.
summary Owned by Mildara Blass; a small portion of the production from the large Mount Helen vineyard is used to make two premium wines, Chardonnay and Cabernet Merlot, both released with bottle age. The quality of the rich, dense Cabernet Merlot has been consistently good; smart new packaging also helps the image.

Mount Helen Cabernet Merlot

This wine formed part of the re-launch of the Mount Helen label in early 1995, and it is easy to see why it was selected for this purpose. An estate-grown wine, now reaching the peak of its development. The outstanding '91 has been followed by a good '94 and an even better '96, winning the trophy for Best Cabernet at the 1997 Victorian Wine Show.

🍷🍷🍷🍷🍷 **1996** Medium to full red-purple; smooth and rich blackcurrant fruit aromas, with touches of vanilla and caramel, lead into a full-bodied but smooth palate. Here cassis/redcurrant fruit is supported by soft tannins and ever so slightly hessiany oak. **rating:** 90

➾ **best drinking** 2000 – 2005 **best vintages** '91, '94, '96 **drink with** Yearling beef • $22

mount horrocks ★★★★

The Old Railway Station, Curling Street, Auburn, SA 5451 **region** Clare Valley
phone (08) 8849 2243 **fax** (08) 8849 2243 **open** Weekends and public holidays 11–5
winemaker Stephanie Toole **production** 5500 **est.** 1982
product range ($13.50–25.50 R) Watervale Riesling, Unwooded Chardonnay, Semiilon, Semillon Sauvignon Blanc, Cordon Cut Riesling, Cabernet Merlot.
summary Mount Horrocks has well and truly established its own identity in recent years, aided by positive marketing and, equally importantly, wine quality which has resulted in both show success and critical acclaim.

Mount Horrocks Watervale Riesling

Mount Horrocks was originally the wine-production end of the Ackland Brothers' extensive vineyard holdings. The two have now effectively been split, and Mount Horrocks is dependent on contract-grown grapes through the Watervale region. Sourced from two growers in the Watervale subdistrict of the Clare Valley who continue to both hand-prune and hand-pick their vines.

🍷🍷🍷🍷🍷 **1997** Medium yellow-green; a riotous bouquet with powerful fruit and some degree of faintly medicinal lift. The palate has masses and masses of flavour, flooding the mouth with sweet citrussy fruit, yet remaining well balanced. Trophy winner at the 1997 Clare Valley Wine Show, and has drawn hyperbolic praise from various critics. **rating:** 90

➪ **best drinking** 1999 – 2005 **best vintages** '86, '87, '90, '93, '94, '97 **drink with** Fresh seafood • $14.50

Mount Horrocks Semillon

I suspect this wine replaces the former Semillon Sauvignon Blanc. Certainly, it is made in a similar fashion, fermented and then matured in French oak barriques for six months on yeast lees. An outstanding success in 1997.

🍷🍷🍷🍷🍷 **1997** Medium yellow-green; the bouquet is complex, but the fruit has soaked up the oak, and one suspects that only a fraction of it was new. On the palate, a tangy and stylish wine, with the extremely successful use of oak adding greatly to the texture without taking away the fruit. **rating:** 90

➪ **best drinking** 1998 – 2005 **best vintages** NA **drink with** Pan-fried fish • $15.50

mount hurtle ★★★☆

291 Pimpala Road, Woodcroft, SA 5162 **region** McLaren Vale
phone (08) 8381 6877 **fax** (08) 8322 2244 **open** Mon-Fri 10–5, Sun 12–5
winemaker Geoff Merrill, Goe DiFabio **production** 50 000 **est.** 1897
product range ($9.99–12 R) Sauvignon Blanc Semillon, Grenache Shiraz, Grenache Rosé. The cheekily named Who Cares White (66% Chenin Blanc, 34% Sauvignon Blanc) and Who Cares Red (90% Grenache, 10% Shiraz) were introduced in 1996.
summary The current release wines reflect the joint ownership of Mount Hurtle by Geoff Merrill and Chateau Tahbilk. The fruit sources for all of the wines have diversified considerably, and the volume increased significantly in consequence. The result is wines of consistent quality which are competitively priced.

mount ida ★★★★

Northern Highway, (vineyard only) Heathcote, Vic 3253 **region** Bendigo
open At Tisdall
winemaker Toni Stockhausen **production** 3000 **est.** 1978
product range ($25 R) Shiraz.
summary Established by the famous artist Leonard French and Dr James Munro, but purchased by Tisdall after the 1987 bushfires and thereafter by Mildara Blass when it acquired Tisdall. Up to the time of the fires, wonderfully smooth, rich red wines with almost voluptuous sweet, minty fruit were the hallmark. After a brief period during which the name was used as a simple brand (with various wines released) has returned to a single estate-grown wine, sharing similar packaging with Mount Helen.

Mount Ida Shiraz

A single-vineyard wine produced from an estate established by noted Australian artist Leonard French, but which was acquired by Tisdall in the 1980s. Produced in limited quantities, but well worth the search. Smart new packaging, bringing it into line with the Mount Helen releases, was introduced in 1997. In that year the '96 vintage won four gold medals.

🍷🍷🍷🍷 **1996** Dense red-purple; the bouquet is full and rich, with abundant dark berry fruit, although the oak is a tad assertive. A big, concentrated, splashy oaky show style on the palate; while there is plenty of fruit, a little less oak might have made an even better wine. **rating:** 87

➭ **best drinking** 2001 – 2010 **best vintages** NA **drink with** Australian parmesan • $25

mount langi ghiran vineyards ★★★★★

Warrak Road, Buangor, Vic 3375 **region** Grampians
phone (03) 5354 3207 **fax** (03) 5354 3277 **open** Mon-Fri 9–5, weekends 12–5
winemaker Trevor Mast, Andrew McLoughney **production** 20 000 **est.** 1969
product range ($14–42 R) Chardonnay, Riesling, Pinot Grigio; under Langi label Shiraz and Cabernet Merlot; Billi Bill Creek Shiraz Cabernet.
summary A maker of outstanding cool-climate peppery Shiraz, crammed with flavour and vinosity, and very good Cabernet Sauvignon. The Shiraz points the way for cool-climate examples of the variety, for weight, texture and fruit richness all accompany the vibrant pepper-spice aroma and flavour.

Langi Shiraz

One of the top half-dozen Shirazes in Australia. The site climate of the Mount Langi Ghiran vineyards produces wines which have tremendous depth and complexity: there are pepper and spice notes, but there are also all of the lush ripe fruit flavours running from cherry to liquorice which a top Rhône Valley maker would immediately recognise and appreciate.

🍷🍷🍷🍷🍷 **1996** Medium to full red-purple; a classic Langi bouquet with Rhône-like game, spice and liquorice aromas of medium intensity; subtle oak. An absolutely delicious wine on the palate, with all of the foregoing flavours, smooth and supple, with soft tannins on the finish. Not a heavyweight, but it doesn't need to be. **rating:** 94

➭ **best drinking** 2000 – 2006 **best vintages** '86, '88, '90, '92, '93, '94, '96 **drink with** Kangaroo, venison • $19.80

mount macedon NR

Bawden Road, Mount Macedon, Vic 3441 **region** Macedon
phone (03) 5427 2735 **fax** (03) 5427 1071 **open** 7 days 10–6
winemaker Peter Dredge **production** 1500 **est.** 1989
product range ($15–20 CD) Chardonnay, Unwooded Chardonnay, Macedon Ranges Chardonnay, Winemaker's Reserve Chardonnay, Pink Reflections, Pinot Noir, Macedon Ranges Pinot Noir, Hay Hill Shiraz.
summary Don and Pam Ludbey have established a substantial operation at Mount Macedon drawing upon two separate vineyards, Mount Macedon and Hay Hill. In all, they have 12.5 hectares under vine, and also operate a restaurant during the weekend. The '96 Chardonnay and Pinot Noir lacked the necessary fruit ripeness.

mount mary ★★★★★

Coldstream West Road, Lilydale, Vic 3140 **region** Yarra Valley
phone (03) 9739 1761 **fax** (03) 9739 0137 **open** Not
winemaker Dr John Middleton, Mario Marson, Peter Draper **production** 3500 **est.** 1971
product range ($33–58 ML) Chardonnay, Triolet (Sauvignon Blanc, Semillon, Muscadelle), Pinot Noir, Cabernets Quintet (Bordeaux-blend).
summary Superbly refined, elegant and intense Cabernets, and usually outstanding and long-lived Pinot Noirs, fully justify Mount Mary's exalted reputation. The Triolet blend is very good, more recent vintages of Chardonnay likewise. However, John Middleton does not believe in wine critics, and, least of all myself, so no (official) tastings.

mount prior vineyard ★★★

Cnr River Road and Popes Lane, Rutherglen, Vic 3685 **region** Rutherglen
phone (02) 6026 5591 **fax** (02) 6026 7456 **open** 7 days 10–5
winemaker Anthony Lacy **production** 15 000 **est.** 1860
product range ($11–23 CD) Chardonnay, Chenin Blanc, Classic Ibis White, Semillon Chardonnay, Late Picked Riesling, Noble Gold, Classic Ibis Dry Red, Cabernet Merlot, Shiraz, Durif, Sparkling Shiraz/Durif, Brut Cuvée, Port, Muscat, Tokay.
summary A full-scale tourist facility, with yet more in the pipeline. Full accommodation packages at the historic Mount Prior House, a restaurant operating weekends under the direction of Trish Hennessy, with four consecutive *Age Good Food Guide* awards to its credit, picnic and barbecue facilities, and a California-style gift shop. The wines are basically sold through cellar door and an active mailing list. No current tastings, but four of the wines came top in their category in the 1997 Winestate North East Victorian Regional Tasting, which is a considerable achievement.

mount tamborine winery NR

32 Hartley Road, Mount Tamborine, Qld 4272 **region** Other Wineries of Qld
phone (07) 5545 3506 **fax** (07) 5545 3506 **open** 7 days 10–4
winemaker Craig Robinson **production** 4000 **est.** 1993
product range ($9–43 ML) Sauvignon Blanc Chardonnay, Cedar Creek Chardonnay, Merlot Emily Cuvee De Rouge, Cedar Creek Blanc De Blanc, Black Shiraz, Cabernet Merlot Shiraz, Mountain Muscat, Bush Turkey (Port).
summary Mount Tamborine Winery draws upon 3 hectares of estate plantings adjacent to the winery, 30 hectares in Stanthorpe, and also purchases wine from the King Valley, Cowra and the Riverland to produce a wide range of wine styles. The Chardonnay and Merlot have both had success in Queensland wine shows and competitions, and the wines are sold both locally and exported to South-East Asia.

mount view estate ★★★

Mount View Road, Mount View, NSW 2325 **region** Lower Hunter Valley
phone (02) 4990 3307 **fax** (02) 4991 1289 **open** Mon–Fri 10–4, weekends, holidays 9–5
winemaker Keith Tulloch **production** 3000 **est.** 1971
product range ($16–20 CD) Verdelho, Chardonnay, Verdelho Chardonnay, Shiraz, Cabernet Sauvignon, Cabernet Port, Shiraz, Liqueur Verdelho, Trophy Muscat.
summary Some new oak would help the table wines immeasurably; the range of fortified wines is distinctly better. The fortified and late-harvest styles were largely responsible for Mount

View winning four trophies, six gold medals and three silver medals at the Hunter Valley Small Winemakers Show between 1991 and 1993. Postscript: a large number of wines arrived too late for this edition.

mount vincent mead NR

Common Road, Mudgee, NSW 2850 **region** Mudgee
phone (02) 6372 3184 **fax** (02) 6372 3184 **open** Mon-Sat 10–5, Sun 10–4
winemaker Jane Nevell **production** 2000 **est.** 1972
product range ($3–32 CD) Does make a Shiraz and a Liqueur Muscat, but is essentially a meadery, with White Box Honey Wine, Napunyah Dry Mead, White Box Dry Mead, Napunyah Medium Sweet, Stringy Bark Sweet, Thistle Sweet Metheglin and Stringy Bark Liqueur Mead. Each of these is vintage dated.
summary Forget the table wines, and concentrate on the meads, which can be absolutely outstanding, dramatically reflecting the impact of the different plants from which the bees have collected their honey.

mount william winery NR

Mount William Road, Tantaraboo, Vic 3764 **region** Macedon
phone (03) 5429 1595 **fax** (03) 5429 1998 **open** 7 days 11–5
winemaker Murray Cousins, Michael Cope-Williams (Contract) **production** 1000 **est.** 1987
product range ($15–23 CD) Chardonnay Semillon, Chardonnay, Pinot Noir, Cabernet Franc, Louis Clare Sparkling Red.
summary Adrienne and Murray Cousins established 6 hectares of vineyards between 1987 and 1992, planted to pinot noir, cabernet franc, semillon and chardonnay. The wines are made under contract (Cope-Williams), and are sold through a stone tasting room cellar-door facility which was completed in 1992, and also through a number of fine wine retailers around Melbourne.

mountadam 

High Eden Road, High Eden Ridge, SA 5235 **region** Eden Valley
phone (08) 8564 1101 **fax** (08) 8361 3400 **open** 7 days 11–4
winemaker Adam Wynn **production** 12 000 **est.** 1972
product range ($12–35 R) Under the premium Mountadam label, Riesling, Chardonnay, Pinot Noir, The Red (50% Merlot, 50% Cabernet), Merlot, Cabernet Sauvignon, Pinot Chardonnay Brut; under the David Wynn label Riesling, Sauvignon Blanc, Chardonnay, Pinot Noir, Shiraz, Patriarch Shiraz, Cabernet Sauvignon; under organically grown Eden Ridge label, Sauvignon Blanc, Cabernet Sauvignon; also Ratafia Riesling and Chardonnay.
summary One of the leading small wineries, founded by David Wynn and run by winemaker son Adam Wynn, initially offering only the Mountadam range at relatively high prices. The subsequent development of the three ranges of wines has been very successful, judged both by the winemaking and wine-marketing viewpoint.

Mountadam Chardonnay

The Mountadam Chardonnay accounts for around 70% of the total 10 000-case production under the Mountadam label. It is 100% estate-grown from low-yielding, high-altitude vineyards, the resulting fruit concentration fully expressing itself in the wine. Although Adam Wynn says that the changes in winemaking since 1984 have essentially been limited to finetuning, there is no doubt that there has been a sea change in the end product since 1989.

🍷🍷🍷🍷 **1996** Medium yellow-green; the bouquet is complex, with cashew and melon aromas supported by subtle oak, but gives relatively little indication of the 14.5 degrees alcohol which manifests itself on the palate. The flavours are in the creamy cashew nut spectrum, but the wine is in a sense at unresolved war with itself, and you cannot help but wonder whether the level of alcohol was part of the design of the wine or not. **rating:** 89

➩ **best drinking** 1998 – 2002 **best vintages** '86, '89, '90, '91, '92, '93, '94 **drink with** Salmon terrine • $32

Mountadam Pinot Chardonnay Brut

An elegantly packaged wine employing the ancient dumbbell bottle shape found with some of the oldest French Champagnes. I have not always taken to previous vintages, but the '92 is a delicious wine. Made from 80% Pinot Noir and barrel-fermented, it spends five years on lees, and no attempt is made to remove the colour of the Pinot Noir.

🍷🍷🍷🍷 **1992** Rose pink; the bouquet is clean, with no excess aldehydes, exhibiting a mix of strawberry, vanilla and spice. The attractively fine but well-flavoured palate is strawberry-accented, with nuances of spice and citrus, and an appropriately long finish. **rating:** 88

➩ **best drinking** 1998 – 1999 **best vintages** NA **drink with** Sunlight • $34

Mountadam Cabernet Sauvignon

As with all of the wines under the premium Mountadam label, estate-grown, and made from vines which are now over 20 years old.

🍷🍷🍷🍷 **1994** Medium red-purple; the bottle development has seen the emergence of secondary fruit aromas in an earthy/chocolatey spectrum, with subtle oak in support. There is a pleasant mix of berry, leaf, mint and chocolate flavours on a restrained and stylish palate. **rating:** 84

➩ **best drinking** 1999 – 2008 **best vintages** '90, '91, '94 **drink with** Lamb cutlets • $32

mountain creek wines NR

Mountain Creek Road, Moonambel, Vic 3478 **region** Pyrenees
phone (03) 5467 2230 **fax** (03) 5467 2230 **open** Weekends, holidays 10–7
winemaker Contract **production** 500 **est.** 1973
product range ($10–16 CD) Sauvignon Blanc, Sparkling Passion, Cabernet Shiraz, Frontignac, Muscat.
summary Brian Cherry acquired the Mountain Creek Vineyard in 1975 and has extended it to a total of 13 hectares. The first wine was made in 1987, all or part of the grapes before and in some years since then sold to other Pyrenees wineries. The wine is made under contract, and shows all of the substance and weight for which the district is renowned.

mountford ★★★

Bamess Road, West Pemberton, WA 6260 **region** Pemberton
phone (08) 9776 1439 **fax** (08) 9776 1439 **open** Fri–Sun 10–4
winemaker Andrew Mountford **production** 5000 **est.** 1987
product range ($16–25.50 CD) Sauvignon Blanc, Chardonnay, Blanc de Noir, Pinot Noir, Merlot Cabernet Sauvignon.
summary English-born and trained, winemaker Andrew Mountford and his wife Sue migrated to Australia in 1983, first endeavouring to set up a winery at Mudgee, and thereafter moving to Pemberton with far greater success. Their strikingly packaged wines

(complete with beeswax and paper seals) have been well-received on eastern Australian markets, being produced from 6 hectares of permanently netted, dry-grown vineyards.

mountilford NR

Mount Vincent Road, Ilford, NSW 2850 **region** Mudgee
phone (02) 6358 8544 **fax** (02) 6358 8544 **open** 7 days 10–4
winemaker Don Cumming **production** NFP **est.** 1985
product range ($8–16 CD) Rhine Riesling, Gewurztraminer, Chardonnay, Late Picked Chardonnay, Sylvaner, Cabernet Shiraz, Pinot Shiraz, Sir Alexander Port.
summary Surprisingly large cellar-door operation which has grown significantly over the past few years. I have not, however, had the opportunity of tasting the wines.

mountview wines ★★★☆

Mount Stirling Road, Glen Aplin, Qld 4381 **region** Granite Belt
phone (07) 4683 4316 **open** Wed-Sat 9–5, Sun 10–4
winemaker David Price **production** 1000 **est.** 1990
product range ($10–20 CD) Semillon, Chardonnay Royal (sparkling), Bianco (sweet white), Cerise (light red), Shiraz, Cabernet Merlot.
summary David and Linda Price are refugees from the Sydney rat-race operating a small, neat, red cedar farm-style winery. Their Shirazes have been winners at the Courier-Mail Queensland Wine Awards (for Best Red Wine) and the Australian Small Winemakers Show (for Best Queensland Shiraz).

mudgee wines NR

Henry Lawson Drive, Mudgee, NSW 2850 **region** Mudgee
phone (02) 6372 2258 **open** Thur-Mon 10–5, holidays 7 days
winemaker Jennifer Meek **production** 1000 **est.** 1963
product range ($9–15 CD) Chardonnay, Gewurztraminer, Crouchen, Riesling, Rosé, Shiraz, Pinot Noir, Cabernet Sauvignon.
summary All of the wines are naturally fermented with wild yeasts and made without the addition of any chemicals or substances including sulphur dioxide, a very demanding route, particularly with white wines. For some consumers, any shortcoming in quality will be quite acceptable.

murray robson wines NR

'Bellona' Old North Road, Rothbury, NSW 2335 **region** Lower Hunter Valley
phone (02) 4938 3577 **fax** (02) 4938 3577 **open** 7 days 10–5
winemaker Murray Robson **production** 3000 **est.** 1993
product range ($18–24 CD) Traminer, Semillon, Chardonnay, Shiraz, Merlot Cabernet, Cabernet Sauvignon.
summary Like a phoenix from the ashes, Murray Robson Wines rises once again, having reopened in its new location in February 1997. Four hectares of estate plantings are supplemented by grapes purchased from other growers in the valley; the initial releases from 1996 were all produced in tiny quantities of 150 cases or less, produced and packaged with the irrepressible flair of Murray Robson and using the same label which appeared back in the early 1970s, each one hand-signed – as ever – by Murray Robson.

murrindindi ★★★★

Cummins Lane, Murrindindi, Vic 3717 **region** Central Victorian High Country
phone (03) 5797 8217 **fax** (03) 5797 8422 **open** Not
winemaker Alan Cuthbertson, Hugh Cuthbertson **production** 1500 **est.** 1979
product range ($18.95 R) Chardonnay, Cabernets Merlot.
summary Situated in an unequivocally cool climate which means that special care has to be taken with the viticulture to produce ripe fruit flavours. In more recent vintages, Murrindindi has succeeded handsomely in so doing.

Murrindindi Chardonnay

The original plantings of 2.5 hectares of chardonnay have been dramatically extended in the mid-1990s with an additional 12 hectares, attesting to the suitability of the climate for this variety. Both in 1993 and 1995 the grapes reached 13° baumé, notwithstanding vintage conditions which in southern Victoria were far from ideal.

🍷🍷🍷🍷 **1996** Medium yellow-green; a complex bouquet showing both barrel-ferment and malolactic-ferment influences on attractive cashew and fig fruit. The palate shows similar flavours, with cashew almost into tobacco, characters, yet subtle and harmonious; good balance and flavour. **rating:** 88

➾ **best drinking** 1998 – 2001 **best vintages** '84, '90, '91, '92, '93, '96 **drink with** Mussels • $22

murrumbateman winery NR

Barton Highway, Murrumbateman, NSW 2582 **region** Canberra District
phone (02) 6227 5584 **open** 7 days 10–5
winemaker Duncan Leslie **production** 1000 **est.** 1972
product range Riesling, Sauvignon Blanc, Chardonnay, Shiraz, Cabernet Sauvignon.
summary Revived after a change of ownership, the Murrumbateman Winery draws upon 2.3 hectares of vineyards, and also incorporates an à la carte restaurant, function room, together with picnic and barbecue areas.

narkoojee ★★★☆

1110 Francis Road, Glengarry, Vic 3854 **region** Gippsland
phone (03) 5192 4257 **fax** (03) 5192 4257 **open** By appointment
winemaker Harry Friend **production** 600 **est.** 1981
product range ($19.50–28 CD) Chardonnay, Cabernets Merlot, The Athelstan Merlot.
summary Narkoojee Vineyard is within easy reach of the old goldmining town of Walhalla, and looks out over the Strzelecki Ranges. The wines are produced from 2.5 hectares of estate vineyards. Harry Friend was an amateur winemaker of note before turning to commercial winemaking with Narkoojee, his skills showing through with all the wines.

nashdale wines NR

Borenore Lane, Nashdale, NSW 2800 **region** Orange
phone (02) 6365 2463 **fax** (02) 6361 4495 **open** Weekends 2–6
winemaker Mark Davidson (Contract) **production** 1000 **est.** 1990
product range ($10–25 CD) Riesling, Sauvignon Blanc, Chardonnay, Pinot Noir, Cabernet Sauvignon.

summary Orange solicitor Edward Fardell commenced establishing the 10-hectare Nashdale Vineyard in 1990. At an elevation of 1000 metres, it offers panoramic views of Mount Canobolas and the Lidster Valley, with a restaurant-café open on weekends.

nepenthe vineyards ★★★★☆

Vickers Road, Lenswood, SA 5240 **region** Adelaide Hills
phone (08) 8389 8218 **fax** (08) 8389 8140 **open** By appointment
winemaker Peter Leske **production** 10 000 **est.** 1994
product range Semillon, Sauvignon Blanc, Unwooded Chardonnay, Chardonnay, Pinto Noir, Zinfandel, Cabernet Merlot.
summary The Tweddell family established 25 hectares of close-planted vineyards at Lenswood between 1994 and 1997. In late 1996 it obtained the second licence to build a winery in the Adelaide Hills, Petaluma being the only other successful applicant back in 1978. A 500-tonne winery has been constructed, with Peter Leske in charge of winemaking. The initial releases establish Nepenthe as one of the most exciting new wineries in Australia.

Nepenthe Vineyards Semillon

Like the Nepenthe Chardonnay, shows the skilled use of high-quality French oak.
🍷🍷🍷🍷🍷 **1997** Light to medium green-yellow; the fruit, with intriguing hints of gooseberry, is surrounded with well-balanced and integrated spicy oak. The palate is highly sophisticated, with passionfruit overtones to the fruit threaded through delicately spicy oak. Utterly seductive. **rating:** 93

⇨ **best drinking** 1998 – 2002 **best vintages** NA **drink with** Sautéed veal • $22

Nepenthe Vineyards Chardonnay

Takes its grapes from 5 hectares of estate plantings. Expansive but skilled use of high-quality French oak and utilisation of all the winemaking techniques for Chardonnay has had the desired result.
🍷🍷🍷🍷🍷 **1997** Medium yellow-green; the aromas ripple through melon and citrus to cashew and toast, with the oak influence subtle throughout. The palate is quite elegant and tight, with the sensitive use of barrel-ferment characters giving a mix of creamy cashew characters to the core of melon fruit. **rating:** 90

⇨ **best drinking** 1999 – 2003 **best vintages** NA **drink with** Chinese steamed fish • $27

newstead winery NR

Tivey Street, Newstead, Vic 3462 **region** Bendigo
phone (03) 5476 2733 **fax** (03) 5476 2536 **open** By appointment
winemaker Ron Snep, Cliff Stubbs **production** 900 **est.** 1994
product range ($15–16 CD) Welshmans Reef Semillon, Barrel Fermented Semillon, Unwooded Chardonnay, Cabernet Sauvignon; Burnt Acre Riesling, Shiraz.
summary Newstead Winery is established in the old Newstead Butter Factory, drawing upon two distinct vineyards at Welshman's Reef (near Maldon) and Burnt Acre Vineyard at Marong, west of Bendigo. Vineyard designations are used for each of the wines.

nicholson river ★★★★

Liddells Road, Nicholson, Vic 3882 **region** Gippsland
phone (03) 5156 8241 **fax** (03) 5156 8433 **open** 7 days 10–4
winemaker Ken Eckersley **production** 1500 **est.** 1978
product range ($15–45 CD) Gippsland White (Semillon Riesling Chardonnay), Semillon, Cuvée, Gippsland Red (Pinot Shiraz), Montview Cabernet Merlot, Tawny Port. The Chardonnays come in four levels: at the bottom Gippsland, then Montview, then Montview Special, and finally Nicholson River.
summary The fierce commitment to quality in the face of the temperamental Gippsland climate and frustratingly small production has been handsomely repaid by some stupendous Chardonnays, mostly sold through cellar door, and a little is exported. Ken Eckersley does not refer to his Chardonnays as white wines, but as gold wines, and lists them accordingly in his newsletter.

Nicholson River Semillon

A blend of 90% Semillon and 10% Sauvignon Blanc, made in a style almost unique to Ken Eckersley.

🍷🍷🍷🍷 **1996** Deep yellow, quite amazing for a relatively young wine. The bouquet is striking with a dry herb underlay to lemony fruit. The palate is massive, almost impossibly full flavoured, and difficult to judge by conventional standards. **rating:** 84

➾ **best drinking** 1998 – 1999 **best vintages** NA **drink with** Grilled eggplant • $19.80

noon winery NR

Rifle Range Road, McLaren Vale, SA 5171 **region** McLaren Vale
phone (08) 8323 8290 **fax** (08) 8323 8290 **open** 7 days 10–5
winemaker Drew Noon **production** 2500 **est.** 1976
product range ($12.50–23 CD) One Night (Rosé), Twelve Bells, The Reles, Grenache Shiraz, Reserve Cabernet Sauvignon, Solaire Reserve Grenache, Chalice (Vintage Port).
summary Drew Noon has returned to McLaren Vale and purchased Noon's from his parents, having spent many years as a consultant oenologist and viticulturist in Victoria, thereafter as winemaker at Cassegrain. Some spectacular and unusual wines have followed, such as the 16.8 degrees alcohol Solaire Grenache, styled like an Italian Amarone.

Noon Grenache Shiraz

A conventionally made wine which relies upon the proposition that McLaren Vale produces the best Grenache Shiraz blends in Australia. Once you have a conjunction of climate, soil and variety such as this, the winemaker's task becomes very much more simple.

🍷🍷🍷🍷 **1996** Medium red-purple; a clean, rich bouquet with attractive juicy blackberry fruit flows into a rich, ripe and concentrated palate with a touch of mint to go with the other juicy fruit flavours, and soft milky/vanilla oak in support. **rating:** 87

➾ **best drinking** 1999 – 2003 **best vintages** NA **drink with** Beef in red wine • $15

Noon Solaire Reserve Grenache

Surely one of the most extraordinary table wines made in Australia. It has achieved 16.8 degrees alcohol without fortification, a technical feat in itself, and spent 18 months on yeast lees, like Italian Amarone Recioto. As rare and as exotic as they come.

ΥΥΥΥ **1996** Medium to full red-purple; the ripe and concentrated juicy berry bouquet gives little hint of the almost unbelievably rich, concentrated and amazingly sweet palate. That sweetness is fruit and alcohol, and not unfermented sugar. **rating:** 88

➾ **best drinking** 2000 – 2015 **best vintages** NA **drink with** You tell me • $23

Noon Reserve Cabernet Sauvignon

Another blockbuster, although not as awe-inspiring as the Reserve Grenache. Drew Noon has followed in the footsteps of his father in one respect, at least, neither fining nor filtering this wine, and (again in Noon tradition) allowing it to reach 14.5 degrees alcohol.

ΥΥΥΥ **1996** Medium to full red-purple; a concentrated briary/earthy bouquet with some blackberry fruit poking through. The ultra-concentrated palate is redolent of rich blackberry/blackcurrant fruit before moving into a fairly rough-cut finish. A full-on macho style. **rating:** 86

➾ **best drinking** 2001 – 2011 **best vintages** NA **drink with** Rich game • $18

Noon Chalice

Made from old bush vine Grenache, packaged in one of those fashionable straight-sided bottles which seem to have more to do with olive oil than wine, and a major, albeit very pleasant, surprise. Described in small print as a vintage port style, it is exactly that – or to be more precise, reminiscent of a Portuguese (as opposed to Australian) Vintage Port.

ΥΥΥΥ **1996** Full red-purple; a clean, balanced bouquet with berry and chocolate fruit aromas laced with subtle spirit. The palate is extremely well balanced, with a range of spicy, nutmeg and berry flavours with fine, soft Brandy spirit. The wine is neither aggressive nor too sweet, and is one of those relatively rare Australian Vintage Ports which I could contemplate drinking with enjoyment while it is young. **rating:** 89

➾ **best drinking** 1998 – 2003 **best vintages** NA **drink with** Cake • $18

normans ★★★☆

Grant's Gully Road, Clarendon, SA 5157 **region** McLaren Vale

phone (08) 8383 6138 **fax** (08) 8383 6089 **open** Mon-Fri 10–5, weekends and public holidays 11–5

winemaker Roger Harbord, Peter Fraser **production** 1.1 million **est.** 1853

product range ($3.95–35 R) A spread of wines starting with the Riverland-sourced Lone Gum range of Chardonnay and Shiraz Cabernet and Jesse's Blend Colombard Chenin Riesling and Shiraz Grenache Ruby Cabernet introduced in 1996; Chandlers Hill Chardonnay Semillon, Chenin Blanc, Fumé Blanc and Shiraz; Conquest and Pinot Noir Brut; then the White Label series of Bin number-identified Chardonnay, Verdelho, Merlot, Pinot Noir and Shiraz; and at the top of the scale Chais Clarendon Chardonnay, Shiraz and Cabernet Sauvignon.

summary In late 1994 Normans raised $6 million in new share capital, joining the lists of Australian Associated Stock Exchanges. The issue reflected the success Normans has enjoyed in recent years in establishing its brand both in domestic and export markets. The quality of the Chais Clarendon range is exemplary.

Normans Chais Clarendon Chardonnay

A brand extension has seen Chais Clarendon extend its fiefdom to Padthaway. This has been to good effect.

🍷🍷🍷🍷 **1996** Medium to full yellow-green; the bouquet is quite fragrant and aromatic with a mix of grapefruit and canned fruit aromas. There is lots of ripe melon and grapefruit on the palate with attractive mouthfeel and balance. Judicious oak handling throughout. **rating:** 85

⇨ **best drinking** 1998 – 2001 **best vintages** NA **drink with** Fricassee of veal • $24

Normans Chais Clarendon Shiraz

Although the Chais Clarendon label is strictly a brand, the majority of the grapes for the wines under the label does come from the Clarendon district at the southern end of the Adelaide Hills. Normans has a 6.6-hectare vineyard here which produces fruit of high quality.

⇨ **best drinking** 1999 – 2004 **best vintages** '82, '86, '90, '91, '92, '94, '95 **drink with** Shoulder of lamb • $35

Normans Old Vine Shiraz

How old are old vines? There is in fact no legal definition, nor any common practice or understanding of the term, except to say that the usage in France is even more elastic and questionable than it is in Australia. In the case of this wine, Normans say the vines are between 26 and 42 years old, a statement made about both the '95 and '96 vintages, which also suggests the vines' eternal youth.

🍷🍷🍷🍷 **1996** Medium to full red-purple; the bouquet is quite rich with dark berry and chocolate aromas with nicely judged oak in support. The palate provides attractive cherry, plum and chocolate fruit flavours of medium weight; gentle oak. Motors along on its 14 degrees alcohol. **rating:** 84

⇨ **best drinking** 1999 – 2004 **best vintages** NA **drink with** Victorian parmesan cheese • $14.50

notley gorge ★★★☆

Loop Road, Glengarry, Tas 7275 (vineyard only) **region** Northern Tasmania
phone (03) 6396 1166 **fax** (03) 6396 1200 **open** By appointment
winemaker Andrew Hood (Contract) **production** 3200 **est.** 1983
product range ($16–20 R) Sauvignon Blanc, Chardonnay, Tamar Dry White, Pinot Noir, Glengarry Cabernet Sauvignon, Cabernet Merlot (light red).
summary Dr Michael Beamish has assembled a substantial viticultural enterprise by Tasmanian standards, acquiring the Glengarry Vineyard established by Gavin Scott in 1980 and the Notley Gorge Vineyard which marine engineer Doug Bowen established in 1983. Mike Beamish has spent considerable money in revitalising both vineyards and was rewarded with a triumphant 1997 Tasmanian Wines Show, winning the majority of the trophies on offer.

Notley Gorge Cabernet Merlot

Produced from 0.6 hectares of 15-year-old cabernet sauvignon vines on the Glengarry Vineyard, together with a dash of merlot (from elsewhere). Matured for ten months in a mix of new and used French oak, and made for the first time by Andrew Hood in 1995. It resulted in what must be one of the best Cabernets ever to come from Tasmania, proving beyond a shadow of doubt that the Tamar Valley can produce gloriously ripe fruit flavours. Mike Beamish must be regretting his decision to remove a significant portion of the cabernet sauvignon vines which were on Glengarry when he purchased it, although clearly the best vines remain. Winner of the Best Full Bodied Red at the 1997 Tasmanian Wines Show, and came within an eyelash of repeating that success at the 1998 show, where it won another gold medal.

🍷🍷🍷🍷🍷 **1995** Full purple-red; a rich, almost voluptuously ripe and concentrated bouquet with delicious blackcurrant and mulberry fruit leads on to a palate as rich and as mouthfilling as any cool-climate mainland Cabernet. Soft but persistent tannins add authority and structure and, together with that lovely ripe fruit, will guarantee a long life. Retasted February 1998; seems to have, if anything, gained fruit sweetness and weight. **rating:** 93

➾ **best drinking** 1999 – 2005 **best vintages** '95 **drink with** Grass-fed scotch fillet • $19.50

nuggetty ranges winery NR

Maldon-Shelbourne Road, Nuggetty, Vic 3463 **region** Bendigo
phone (03) 5475 1347 **fax** (03) 5475 1647 **open** Not
winemaker Greg Dedman **production** NA **est.** 1993
product range ($20–28 ML) Semillon, Shiraz, Cabernet Sauvignon.
summary Draws upon 5 hectares of estate plantings, with mailing list sales commencing in 1998 and cellar door planned to open in 1999.

oakridge estate ★★★★

864 Maroondah Highway, Coldstream, Vic 3770 **region** Yarra Valley
phone (03) 9739 1920 **fax** (03) 9739 1923 **open** 7 days 10–5
winemaker Michael Zitzlaff **production** 8000 **est.** 1982
product range ($12–90 R) Riesling, Chardonnay, Cabernet Merlot; Reserve Chardonnay, Merlot and Cabernet Sauvignon.
summary The 1997 capital raising by Oakridge Vineyards Limited was successful, and a new winery was built and officially opened on 31 January 1998. Production of the Oakridge Estate wines is projected to increase in leaps and bounds during the remainder of this decade and into the first few years of the next millennium.

Oakridge Chardonnay

A solid wine, not in the class of the Reserve, but then why should it be. Barrel-fermented in a mix of French and American oak, and given the usual winemaking treatment for quality Chardonnay.

🍷🍷🍷🍷 **1996** Medium to full yellow-green; both bottle development and barrel-ferment characters make their mark on a rich, complex and tangy bouquet after which the short palate comes as a minor disappointment. Certainly there is full peach and citrus fruit there on entry, but the finish is somewhat abrupt. **rating:** 84

➾ **best drinking** 1998 – 1999 **best vintages** NA **drink with** Sweet and sour pork • $18

Oakridge Estate Reserve Merlot

A wine which has attracted a great deal of attention, partly because of its excellent show record, and partly because of its daunting price. Some have criticised that price, but I am far from convinced that criticism is justified. For the record, was produced from mature vines which yielded one tonne per hectare, and has been given Rolls Royce oak treatment.

🍷🍷🍷🍷🍷 **1995** Medium to full red; the bouquet is at once complex and classy, with berry, leaf and mint varietal fruit having that haunting medicinal character of top-class Merlot; suave, cedary oak adds yet another dimension. The palate has great richness and texture; despite all of its fruit and all of its oak, retains suppleness. **rating:** 94

➾ **best drinking** 1999 – 2009 **best vintages** NA **drink with** Aged eye fillet • $90

Oakridge Reserve Cabernet Sauvignon

The Oakridge Cabernet Sauvignons have been reliable, those with the Reserve tag particularly so.

YYYY **1995** Medium to full purple-red; the bouquet is youthful, and not particularly complex, but does have attractive, fresh earthy/berry varietal fruit. The palate has slightly more structure and form than the bouquet suggests, with well-ripened cassis fruit, hints of olive and subtle oak. **rating:** 87

⇨ **best drinking** 1999 – 2005 **best vintages** '88, '90, '91, '94, '95 **drink with** Yarra Valley venison • $35

oakvale ★★★

Broke Road, Pokolbin, NSW 2321 **region** Lower Hunter Valley
phone (02) 4998 7520 **fax** (02) 4998 7747 **open** 7 days 10–5
winemaker Barry Shields **production** 5000 **est.** 1893
product range ($16–25 CD) Peach Tree Semillon, Selections Chardonnay (unwooded), Peach Tree Unwooded Chardonnay, Frontignac, Peppercorn Shiraz, Cabernet Merlot and a handful of fortified wines.
summary Former Sydney solicitor Barry Shields seems content with the change in his lifestyle as he presides over the historic Oakvale winery which he purchased from the Elliott family over a decade ago. The emphasis is on Semillon, Chardonnay and a blend of the two in both oaked and unoaked versions, most of which are offered with three to five years bottle age, with deep-yellow colour and rich, sometimes heavy, buttery/nutty flavours.

old barn NR

Langmeil Road, Tanunda, SA 5352 **region** Barossa Valley
phone (08) 8563 0111 **open** Mon-Fri 9–5, weekends 10–5
winemaker Trevor Jones **production** 2200 **est.** 1990
product range ($6–13 CD) Riesling, Semillon, Traminer Riesling, Fumé Blanc, Old Fashioned Hock, Barossa Dry Red, Cabernet Shiraz, Light Sweet Red, and a range of other sweet and fortified wines.
summary Owned by a partnership of Barry and Elizabeth Chinner and Janet Hatch, with an honorary establishment date of 1861, being the date of construction of the old stone barn from which the wines are exclusively sold. The wines are made by Trevor Jones, also winemaker at Kellermeister and Glenara, and are available only from cellar door, where back vintages are available.

old caves NR

New England Highway, Stanthorpe, Qld 4380 **region** Granite Belt
phone (07) 4681 1494 **fax** (07) 4681 2722 **open** Mon-Sat 9–5, Sun 10–5
winemaker David Zanatta **production** 2200 **est.** 1980
product range ($7.50–13.50 CD) Chardonnay, Classic Dry White, Light Red, Shiraz, Cabernet Sauvignon and a range of generic wines in both bottle and flagon, including fortifieds.
summary Has a strictly local, relatively uncritical and evidently loyal clientele.

old kent river ★★★☆

Turpin Road, Rocky Gully, WA 6397 **region** Great Southern
phone (08) 9855 1589 **fax** (08) 9855 1589 **open** By appointment
winemaker Alkoomi (Contract), Michael Staniford **production** 2000 **est.** 1985

product range ($12–22 CD) Chardonnay, Sauvignon Blanc, Pinot Noir, Shiraz, Diamontina (Sparkling).

summary Mark and Debbie Noack have done it tough all of their relatively young lives, but have earned respect from their neighbours and from eastern Australian producers, such as Domaine Chandon, now buying over 80% of the 50 tonnes of grapes they produce each year on their sheep property. 'Grapes', they say, 'saved us from bankruptcy.'

olive farm ★★★

77 Great Eastern Highway, South Guildford, WA 6055 **region** Swan District
phone (08) 9277 2989 **fax** (08) 9279 4372 **open** Mon-Tues and Thurs-Fri 10–5, weekends 11–3
winemaker Ian Yurisich **production** 4000 **est.** 1829
product range ($12.90–24.50 CD) Verdelho, Chenin Blanc, Classic White, Chardonnay, Gewurztraminer, Sauterne Style, Pinot Noir, Cabernet Sauvignon, Cabernet Shiraz Merlot, Sherry, Port, Sparkling.
summary The oldest winery in Australia in use today, and arguably the least communicative. The ultra-low profile tends to disguise the fact that wine quality is by and large good. The wines come from 12 hectares of estate plantings of 11 different varieties.

oliverhill NR

Seaview Road, McLaren Vale, SA 5171 **region** McLaren Vale
phone (08) 8323 8922 **open** 7 days 10–5
winemaker Stuart Miller **production** 1300 **est.** 1973
product range ($5–11 CD) Great Outdoors White and Red, Chardonnay, Shiraz Cabernet, Port, Muscat.
summary Oliverhill has changed hands, but otherwise continues an operation aimed almost entirely at the local tourist trade.

olssens of watervale NR

Government Road, Watervale, SA 5452 **region** Clare Valley
phone (08) 8843 0065 **fax** (08) 8843 0065 **open** 7 days 11–5 or by appointment
winemaker Andrew Mitchell (Contract) **production** 1000 **est.** 1994
product range ($12–15 CD) Riesling, Semillon, Cabernet Sauvignon Cabernet Franc Merlot.
summary Kevin and Helen Olssen first visited the Clare Valley in December 1986. Within two weeks they and their family had decided to sell their Adelaide home, and purchase a property in a small, isolated valley 3 kilometres north of the township of Watervale. Between 1987 and 1993 production from the 5-hectare vineyard was sold to other makers, but during 1993 the decision was taken to produce wine under the Olssen label. Rich, full-flavoured and deeply coloured Semillon, and powerful Cabernet Sauvignon Cabernet Franc Merlot are the best of the releases.

orani vineyard NR

Arthur Highway, Sorrel, Tas 7172 **region** Southern Tasmania
phone (03) 6225 0330 **fax** (03) 6225 0330 **open** Weekends and public holidays 9.30–6.30
winemaker Various contract **production** NA **est.** 1986
product range Riesling, Chardonnay, Pinot Noir.

summary The first commercial release from Orani was of a 1992 Pinot Noir, with Chardonnay and Riesling following in the years thereafter. The solidly constructed '96 Orani Pinot Noir, with abundant plum and mint fruit, is the best yet, well deserving of its bronze medal at the 1998 Tasmanian Wines Show.

orlando ★★★★☆

Barossa Valley Way, Rowland Flat, SA 5352 **region** Barossa Valley
phone (08) 8521 3111 **fax** (08) 8521 3100 **open** Mon-Fri 10–5, weekends 10–4
winemaker Phil Laffer **production** NFP **est.** 1847
product range ($8.95–49.95 R) The table wines are sold in four ranges: first the national and international best-selling Jacobs Creek Semillon Sauvignon Blanc, Chardonnay, Riesling, Shiraz Cabernet and Grenache Shiraz and special Limited Releases; then the Gramps range of Chardonnay, Botrytis Semillon, Grenache, Cabernet Merlot; next the Saint range, St Helga Eden Valley Riesling, St Hilary Padthaway Chardonnay, St Hugo Coonawarra Cabernet Sauvignon; finally the premium range of Steingarten Riesling, Jacaranda Ridge Cabernet Sauvignon and Lawsons Padthaway Shiraz. Also Russet Ridge Coonawarra Chardonnay and Cabernet Shiraz Merlot off to one side; sparkling wines under the Trilogy and Carrington labels.
summary Jacobs Creek is one of the largest-selling brands in the world, and is almost exclusively responsible for driving the fortunes of this French (Pernod Ricard) owned company. The super-premium wines in the range continue to improve; Orlando had conspicuous trophy success at the 1997 National Wine Show.

Orlando Jacobs Creek Riesling

Jacobs Creek is one of the marketing miracles of the modern world, with more than one million cases a year sold in the United Kingdom market alone. It has been brand-extended from its original Shiraz Cabernet Malbec base to a range of four, also including Riesling, Chardonnay and Semillon Chardonnay. Notwithstanding the very large volume in which the Jacobs Creek Riesling is made, recent vintages have been consistent gold medal winners in national wine shows, competing against far more expensive (and more prestigious) wines. The '97 is yet another success for an extraordinarily successful label, winning The Wine Society Trophy for Best Commercial Dry White at the 1997 National Wine Show.

🍷🍷🍷🍷 **1997** Light to medium yellow-green; an aromatic bouquet with attractive, soft lime/tropical aromas and a very well-constructed palate, delivering all one could possibly expect in a wine made in this volume and sold at this price. **rating:** 89

➾ **best drinking** 1998 – 1999 **best vintages** NA **drink with** Salads, seafood • $8.95

Orlando St Helga Eden Valley Riesling

Produced from grapes grown on Orlando's St Helga Vineyard in the Eden Valley and first made in 1980. That initial release was not put onto the market until it was four years old, and was initially priced as a premium product. It is now conventionally marketed in the year of production, and in real terms the price has come down significantly.

🍷🍷🍷🍷🍷 **1996** Light to medium green-yellow; at the end of 1997 starting to show the classic bottle development that it promised as a young wine, and will improve even more from here. Ultra-classic lime, toast and kerosene aromas and flavours on a perfectly structured and balanced palate. An extremely distinguished wine at the price, and deservedly a top gold medal winner at the 1997 Liquorland National Wine Show. **rating:** 92

➾ **best drinking** 1998 – 2001 **best vintages** '90, '92, '94, '96 **drink with** Asian cuisine • $12.95

Orlando Jacobs Creek Limited Release Chardonnay

Produced entirely from Padthaway-grown grapes with an ultra-careful process of selection. The partially clarified juice was barrel-fermented in new French oak barriques and given prolonged lees contact. The 1996, which may prove to be a one-off bottling, commenced its gold medal and trophy-winning career at the Adelaide Wine Show in 1996, winning the Bert Bear Memorial Trophy at the 1997 Royal Sydney Wine Show, and winning multiple trophies at the 1997 Liquorland National Wine Show including trophies for Best Dry White Table Wine of Show and Best White Table Wine of Show.

🍷🍷🍷🍷🍷 **1996** Medium to full yellow-green; an exceedingly complex bouquet with powerful white peach fruit and positively handled but well-integrated French oak. Equally complex and rich on the palate, with white peach and nectarine flavours, hints of cashew and the oak under restraint. **rating:** 95

➾ **best drinking** 1998 – 2002 **best vintages** NA **drink with** Volute of chicken • NA

Orlando St Hilary Padthaway Chardonnay

A wine which has surged into prominence in recent years, based on premium Padthaway fruit. The '96 vintage won gold medals as far afield as the 1997 Asia Pacific Wine Challenge, the Concours Mondiale in Brussels and the International Wine Challenge in London.

🍷🍷🍷🍷🍷 **1996** Glowing yellow-green; a cavalcade of fruit aromas running through grapefruit, melon and nectarine are supported by excellent French oak barrel-fermentation characters. A marvellously balanced and constructed wine on the palate with lingering but not heavy melon and nectarine fruit, and more of that sophisticated oak. **rating:** 94

➾ **best drinking** 1998 – 2003 **best vintages** '96 **drink with** Veal • $14.95

Orlando Lawson's Padthaway Shiraz

Named after a nineteenth-century pioneer surveyor, Robert Lawson. It is matured for two years in new Nevers oak hogsheads, with further bottle maturation before release. This expansive oak input made its mark on the wine: the regular shower of gold and silver medals that descend on the wine shows that many judges did not regard the input as excessive. I have to admit that the vintages of the 1990s seem to me to be getting better and better, particularly so far as the oak regime is concerned.

🍷🍷🍷🍷🍸 **1994** Strong red-purple; a rich, concentrated and powerful bouquet with plum, cherry and mint fruit; well-balanced subtle oak. The palate is still firm and youthful, with dark chocolate, mint and cherry fruit. Loaded with development potential. **rating:** 90

➾ **best drinking** 2000 – 2010 **best vintages** '88, '90, '91, '93, '94 **drink with** Beef stroganoff • $49.95

Orlando Jacobs Creek Limited Release Shiraz Cabernet

A super-premium blend of Shiraz from the Barossa Valley and Cabernet Sauvignon from Coonawarra, the Shiraz being matured in new American oak hogsheads for 12 months and the Cabernet Sauvignon in new French oak for 16 months. The components were then blended, the finished blend then being matured for a further eight months in a new series of French oak hogsheads – the so-called double oak technique.

🍷🍷🍷🍷🍷 **1994** Medium to full red-purple; notwithstanding the elaborate oak treatment, a very elegant wine, beautifully built and structured, with intense black cherry and blackberry fruit running through to soft tannins on the finish. **rating:** 95

➾ **best drinking** 1999 – 2005 **best vintages** NA **drink with** Beef spare ribs • NA

Orlando Jacaranda Ridge Cabernet Sauvignon

A Coonawarra Cabernet Sauvignon which has been the red wine flagship for Orlando, sitting alongside Lawson's Shiraz. As with Lawson's, the American oak treatment has seemed rather heavy-handed, but good things are happening at Orlando, and recent vintages are much improved.

YYYY **1994** Full red-purple; the bouquet is rich, with lots of vanilla oak in typical Orlando-style, but there is plenty of earthy black fruit character there in support. A chewy palate with blackberry, chocolate and oaky flavours interwoven in a complex structure. **rating:** 88

➭ **best drinking** 1999 – 2006 **best vintages** '86, '88, '90, '94 **drink with** Grilled beef • $49.95

Orlando St Hugo Cabernet Sauvignon

When first released around 1980, a benchmark, but which seemed to lose its way in a competitive field. Once again, resurgent, and a particularly good outcome for 1994.

YYYY **1994** Medium red-purple; a smooth and moderately intense bouquet has pleasantly ripe and sweet blackcurrant and chocolate fruit leading the way; the palate shows similarly attractive chocolate and blackberry fruit, with well-balanced oak in a support role. The structure, too, is well above average. **rating:** 86

➭ **best drinking** 1999 – 2004 **best vintages** '86, '88, '90, '91, '92, '94 **drink with** Mixed grill • $28.95

orlando (padthaway) NR

c/o Barossa Valley Way, Rowland Flat, SA 5352 **region** Padthaway
phone (08) 8521 3111 **fax** (08) 8521 3100 **open** Not
winemaker Phil Laffer **production** NFP **est.** NA
product range ($14.95–49.95 R) St Hilary Padthaway Chardonnay, Jacobs Creek Limited Release Chardonnay, Lawsons Padthaway Shiraz.
summary While Padthaway serves the same purpose for Orlando as it does for the other major companies in the region by providing good-quality wine for cross-regional blends, it also produces three of Orlando's most distinguished wines. The first to appear was Lawson's Shiraz; St Hilary Chardonnay is a more recent arrival, the special Jacob's Creek Limited Release Chardonnay even more noteworthy. Other than its large vineyard, Orlando has no physical presence in Padthaway, but its Padthaway wines are sold at Padthaway Estate (and, of course, through retail shops).

osborns harwood vineyard ★★★☆

RMB 5935 Ellerina Road, Merricks North, Vic 3926 **region** Mornington Peninsula
phone (03) 5989 7417 **fax** (03) 5989 7510 **open** By appointment
winemaker Richard McIntyre (Consultant) **production** 850 **est.** 1988
product range ($20–23 CD) Chardonnay, Pinot Noir, Cabernet Merlot.
summary Frank and Pamela Osborn are now Mornington Peninsula veterans, having purchased the vineyard land in Ellerina Road in 1988, and (with help from son Guy) planted the vineyard over the following four years. The first release of wines in 1997 offered six vintages each of Chardonnay and Pinot Noir and five vintages of Cabernet Sauvignon, quite a debut. Many of these wines were available in only tiny quantities, however, for much of the production from the Harwood vineyard of 5.5 hectares is sold to other makers in the region.

padthaway estate ★★★☆

Keith-Naracoorte Road, Padthaway, SA 5271 **region** Padthaway
phone (08) 8765 5039 **fax** (08) 8765 5097 **open** 7 days 10–4.30
winemaker Nigel Catt **production** 6000 **est.** 1980
product range ($15–20 R) Eliza Pinot Chardonnay Cuvée, Eliza Pinot Noir Brut, Eliza Sparkling Burgundy, Eliza Chardonnay (wooded and unwooded).
summary The only functioning winery in Padthaway, set in the superb grounds of the Estate in a large and gracious old stone woolshed; the homestead is in the Relais et Chateaux mould, offering luxurious accommodation and fine food. Sparkling wines are the specialty of the Estate. Padthaway Estate also acts as a tasting centre for other Padthaway-region wines.

palmara ★★★☆

1314 Richmond Road, Richmond, Tas 7025 **region** Southern Tasmania
phone (03) 6260 2462 **open** Weekends winter 1–4, summer 12–6
winemaker Allan Bird, Andrew Hood (Contract) **production** 260 **est.** 1985
product range ($15–23 CD) Chardonnay, Semillon Ehrenfeltzer, Montage Blend, Exotica (Siegerrebe), Pinot Noir, Cabernet Sauvignon.
summary Allan Bird has the Palmara wines made for him by Andrew Hood, all in tiny quantities. The Pinot Noir has performed consistently well since 1990. The Exotica Siegerrebe blend is unchallenged as Australia's most exotic and unusual wine, with amazing jujube/lanolin aromas and flavours.

palmer wines ★★★★

Caves Road, Willyabrup, WA 6280 **region** Margaret River
phone (08) 9797 1881 **fax** (08) 9797 0534 **open** By appointment
winemaker Eddie Price, Amberley Estate (Contract) **production** 5000 **est.** 1977
product range ($15–19.50 R) Sauvignon Blanc, Semillon, Classic White, Chardonnay, Merlot, Cabernet Sauvignon.
summary Stephen and Helen Palmer planted their first hectare of vines way back in 1977, but a series of events (including a cyclone and grasshopper plagues) caused them to lose interest and instead turn to thoroughbred horses. But, with encouragement from Dr Michael Peterkin of Pierro, and after a gap of almost ten years, they again turned to viticulture, and now have 15 hectares planted to the classic varieties. The Merlot is especially good.

pankhurst NR

Old Woodgrove, Woodgrove Road, Hall, NSW 2618 **region** Canberra District
phone (02) 6230 2592 **fax** (02) 6230 2592 **open** Sundays and by appointment
winemaker Sue Carpenter (Contract) **production** 1500 **est.** 1986
product range ($13–15 ML) Chardonnay, Semillon, Semillon Sauvignon Blanc, Pinot Noir, Cabernet Merlot.
summary Agricultural scientist and consultant Allan Pankhurst and wife Christine (with a degree in pharmaceutical science) have established a 3-hectare, split canopy vineyard. Tastings of the first wines produced showed considerable promise; there have been no recent tastings other than a casual encounter with an impressive Pinot Noir. In recent years Pankhurst has shared success with Lark Hill in the production of surprisingly good Pinot Noir – surprising given the climatic limitations. Says Christine Pankhurst 'the result of good viticulture here and great winemaking at Lark Hill', and she may well be right.

panorama ★★★

RSD 297 Lower Wattle Grove, Cradoc, Tas 7109 **region** Southern Tasmania
phone (03) 6266 3409 **fax** (03) 6266 3409 **open** 6 days 10–5
winemaker Steve Ferencz, Michael Vishaeki **production** 250 **est.** 1974
product range ($10–22 CD) Chardonnay, Sauvignon Blanc, Pinot Noir, Cabernet Sauvignon.
summary The quality of the underlying fruit, particularly with the red wines, is not in doubt, which have great colour and startling richness of flavour in favoured vintages.

paracombe wines ★★★★

Main Road, Paracombe, SA 5132 **region** Adelaide Hills
phone (08) 8380 5058 **fax** (03) 8380 5488 **open** Not
winemaker Paul Drogemuller (Overseeing Contract) **production** 1500 **est.** 1983
product range ($18–22 R) Chardonnay, Sauvignon Blanc, Pinot Noir, Cabernet Franc, Shiraz Cabernet, Pinot Chardonnay Méthode Champenoise, Sparkling Shiraz.
summary The Drogemuller family have established 6 hectares of vineyards at Paracombe, reviving a famous name in South Australian wine history. The wines are in fact contract-made at Petaluma, and are sold by mail order and through retailers in South Australia. It has had particular success with its Sauvignon Blanc (1997 Adelaide Wine Show trophy) but all of the wines in the range are worth chasing. A substantial portion of the production from the 13 hectares of estate plantings is sold to others.

Paracombe Sauvignon Blanc

In 1995, and again in 1996, Paracombe's best wine was its Sauvignon Blanc, made in a simple unoaked-style but totally delicious. The 1997 triumphantly reiterated the point by winning the Sauvignon Blanc Trophy at the 1997 Royal Adelaide Wine Show.

🍷🍷🍷🍷🍷(half) **1997** Light yellow-green; the bouquet is of light to medium intensity with a delicate mix of passionfruit and gooseberry aromas. The palate, likewise, veers from crisper, herbal notes to riper tropical fruit flavours. Crisp, clean and bright. **rating:** 91

➾ **best drinking** 1998 – 1999 **best vintages** '95, '96, '97 **drink with** Trout mousse • $18

Paracombe Shiraz Cabernet

A blend of estate-grown Shiraz and Cabernet Sauvignon, which spends two years in a mix of French and American oak. Exceedingly youthful, it barely shows the long time it has spent in wood.

🍷🍷🍷🍷 **1995** Full red-purple; there is a range of mint, plum, spice and liquorice aromas running through sweet fruit on both the bouquet and palate. The palate runs in the liquorice, plum and berry spectrum, with good length, and has particularly sweet tannins. **rating:** 88

➾ **best drinking** 1998 – 2006 **best vintages** NA **drink with** Roast lamb • $18

Paracombe Cabernet Franc

One of the few varietal Cabernet Francs being made in Australia, the others of note coming from Knappstein and Chatsfield. A silver medal winner at the 1997 Adelaide Hills Wine Show.

🍷🍷🍷(half) **1996** Medium purple-red; the sweet minty fruit aromas of the bouquet are repeated more or less precisely on the palate, which is ripe, with minty/berry flavours and a nicely judged touch of oak. **rating:** 84

➾ **best drinking** 1998 – 2002 **best vintages** NA **drink with** Pastrami • $18

paradise enough NR

Stewarts Road, Kongwak, Vic 3951 **region** Gippsland
phone (03) 5657 4241 **fax** (03) 5657 4229 **open** Sun, public holidays 12–5
winemaker John Bell, Sue Armstrong **production** 600 **est.** 1987
product range ($13–25 CD) Chardonnay, Reserve Chardonnay, Pinot Noir, Cabernet Merlot, Pinot Chardonnay.
summary Phillip Jones of Bass Phillip persuaded John Bell and Sue Armstrong to establish their small vineyard on a substantial dairy and beef cattle property.

paringa estate ★★★★★

44 Paringa Road, Red Hill South, Vic 3937 **region** Mornington Peninsula
phone (03) 5989 2669 **fax** (03) 5989 2669 **open** Mon, Wed-Fri 12–5, weekends, public holidays 11–5
winemaker Lindsay McCall **production** 2000 **est.** 1985
product range ($20–28.95 R) Chardonnay, Pinot Noir, Shiraz, Cabernet Sauvignon.
summary No longer a rising star, but a star shining more brightly in the Mornington Peninsula firmament than any other. As recent vintages have emphasised, the Mornington Peninsula region is very sensitive to growing season conditions, with problems in 1995 and 1996, but having a wonderful year in 1997, and the promise of doing so in 1998. Paringa shines most brightly in the warmer years. A restaurant under construction was due to be completed by mid-1998.

parker coonawarra estate ★★★★

Penola Road, Coonawarra, SA 5263 **region** Coonawarra
phone (02) 9357 3376 **fax** (02) 9358 1517 **open** Not
winemaker Chris Cameron **production** 4000 **est.** 1985
product range ($25–65 R) Cabernet Sauvignon under two labels, Parker Coonawarra Estate First Growth and Parker Coonawarra Estate Terra Rossa.
summary Parker Coonawarra Estate is now a 50/50 joint venture between founder John Parker and family and James Fairfax. It is by this mechanism that Pepper Tree in the Hunter Valley (controlled by James Fairfax) has its Coonawarra stake. It has also led to the highly regarded wines being made by Pepper Tree winemaker Chris Cameron, albeit using the Balnaves winery in Coonawarra to do so. A maturation cellar and cellar-door sales facility in Coonawarra is planned to be functional by early 1999.

Parker Coonawarra Estate First Growth Cabernet Sauvignon

Notwithstanding the very pretentious label, this wine is always far superior to the second Cabernet, and an excellent example of super-premium Coonawarra Cabernet. After the hiatus in production, and the change in winemaking teams, the '96 rejoins the field with even more style and certainly more elegance than its predecessors. More sensitive oak handling is particularly commendable.

🍷🍷🍷🍷🍷 **1996** Medium to full red-purple; ripe cassis/blackberry fruit with most attractive cedary oak in a support role is followed by an elegant yet flavoursome palate which shows pristine cassis/blackberry fruit, fine tannins and well-balanced and integrated oak. **rating:** 92

➯ **best drinking** 2002 – 2012 **best vintages** '88, '90, '91, '96 **drink with** Prime rib of beef • $60

passing clouds ★★★★

RMB 440 Kurting Road, Kingower, Vic 3517 **region** Bendigo
phone (03) 5438 8257 **fax** (03) 5438 8246 **open** 7 days 12–5 by appointment
winemaker Graeme Leith, Greg Bennett **production** 4000 **est.** 1974
product range ($17–30 CD) Red wine specialist; principal wines include Pinot Noir, Grenache, Shiraz, Shiraz Cabernet, Graeme's Blend (Shiraz Cabernet), Angel Blend (Cabernet), Merlot Cabernet Franc; also Onidne (Sparkling Shiraz Cabernet); Chardonnay and Sauvignon Blanc from the Goulburn Valley.
summary Graeme Leith is one of the great personalities of the industry, with a superb sense of humour, and makes lovely regional reds, with cassis, berry and mint fruit. His smiling, bearded face has adorned the front cover of many of the Victorian Tourist Bureau's excellent tourist publications over the past few years. The cellar in which he is seen dispensing wine is not his, incidentally; it is that of Chateau Tahbilk.

paternoster ★★★

17 Paternoster Road, Emerald, Vic 3782 **region** Yarra Valley
phone (03) 5968 3197 **open** Weekends 10.30–5.30
winemaker Philip Hession **production** 600 **est.** 1985
product range ($12–30 CD) Semillon, Chardonnay, Pinot Noir, Shiraz, Cabernets, Vintage Port.
summary The densely planted, non-irrigated vines (at a density of 5000 vines to the hectare) cascade down a steep hillside at Emerald in one of the coolest parts of the Yarra Valley. Pinot Noir is the specialty of the winery, producing intensely flavoured wines with a strong eucalypt mint overlay reminiscent of the wines of Delatite.

patrick creek vineyard NR

Springfield Park, North Down, Tas 7307 **region** Northern Tasmania
phone (03) 6424 6979 **fax** (03) 6424 6380 **open** By appointment
winemaker Andrew Hood (Contract) **production** 350 **est.** 1990
product range ($15 CD) Semillon, Chardonnay, Classic Dry White, Pinot Noir.
summary Patrick Creek Vineyard came into being in 1990 when Pat and Kay Walker established high-density plantings of chardonnay, pinot noir, semillon and sauvignon blanc in a 1-hectare vineyard. Patrick Creek produced a commendably sturdy Pinot Noir in 1996 which won a bronze medal at the 1997 Tasmanian Wines Show, repeating the dose with its '97 Pinot Noir at the 1998 Tasmanian Wines Show.

patritti wines ★★☆

13–23 Clacton Road, Dover Gardens, SA 5048 **region** Other Wineries of SA
phone (08) 8296 8261 **fax** (08) 8296 5088 **open** Mon-Sat 9–6
winemaker G Patritti, J Patritti **production** 65 000 **est.** 1926
product range ($4.50–8 CD) A kaleidoscopic array of table, sparkling, fortified and flavoured wines (and spirits) offered in bottle and flagon. The table wines are sold under the Blewitt Springs Estate, Patritti and Billabong Wines brands.
summary A traditional, family-owned business offering wines at modest prices, but with impressive vineyard holdings of 40 hectares in Blewitt Springs and another 40 hectares at Aldinga.

pattersons ★★★★

St Werburghs Road, Mount Barker, WA 6234 **region** Great Southern
phone (08) 9851 2063 **fax** (08) 9851 2063 **open** Sun-Wed 10–5
winemaker Plantagenet (Contract) **production** 1500 **est.** 1982
product range ($15–24 CD) Chardonnay, Unwooded Chardonnay, Pinot Noir, Shiraz, Sparkling Shiraz.
summary Schoolteachers Sue and Arthur Patterson have grown chardonnay and pinot noir and grazed cattle as a weekend relaxation for a decade. The cellar door is in a recently completed and very beautiful rammed-earth house, and a number of vintages are on sale at any one time. Good Chardonnay and Shiraz have been complemented by the occasional spectacular Pinot Noir.

Pattersons Chardonnay

Planting of the vineyard commenced in the early 1980s, and the first Chardonnay was made in 1986. It is consistently the best of the Pattersons wines, developing very well with age into a rich, full-blown style. Typically released with two years bottle age, the unwooded version in the year of its making.

🍷🍷🍷🍷 **1995** Medium straw-yellow; the bouquet shows quite pronounced spicy/charry oak which is also quite evident on the very ripe fruit of the palate. Here the flavours run through peach to more nutty/mealy characters, attesting to the 14 degrees alcohol. **rating:** 85

➾ **best drinking** 1998 – 2001 **best vintages** '88, '90, '91, '92, '93, '94 **drink with** Roast pork • $19

paul conti ★★★☆

529 Wanneroo Road, Woodvale, WA 6026 **region** Swan District
phone (08) 9409 9160 **fax** (08) 9309 1634 **open** Mon-Sat 9.30–5.30, Sun by appointment
winemaker Paul Conti, Jason Conti **production** 7000 **est.** 1948
product range ($9–16 CD) Chenin Blanc, Sauvignon Blanc, Chardonnay, Carabooda Chardonnay, Late Harvest Muscat, Grenache, Marigíniup Shiraz, Cabernet Sauvingon, White Port, Reserve Port.
summary In 1968 Paul Conti succeeded his father in the business the latter had established in 1948, and since assuming responsibility has quietly gone about making some outstanding wines, doing much to help pioneer the Mount Barker region, even though most of the wines are made from grapes grown on the southwest coastal plains around Perth. However, it has to be said this one-time leader of the field has been caught by the pack.

Paul Conti Carabooda Chardonnay

Paul Conti developed the Carabooda Vineyard in the early 1980s, selecting the site for its unique sand over limestone soil, and close proximity to the Indian Ocean which provides cool coastal sea breezes. The 1994 vintage of the wine was a gold medal winner at the Mount Barker Wine Show, narrowly missing out on several major trophies.

🍷🍷🍷🍷 **1997** Light to medium yellow-green; a subtle and smooth bouquet with melon and cashew aromas is followed by a gentle, smooth palate, again showing melon and touches of cashew. Sensitive oak handling throughout. **rating:** 85

➾ **best drinking** 1998 – 1999 **best vintages** '89, '90, '91, '92, '94, '97 **drink with** King prawns • $16

paul osicka ★★★★

Majors Creek Vineyard at Graytown, Vic 3608 **region** Bendigo
phone (03) 5794 9235 **fax** (03) 5794 9288 **open** Mon-Sat 10–5, Sun 12–5
winemaker Paul Osicka **production** NFP **est.** 1955
product range ($14–18 CD) Chardonnay, Riesling, Cabernet Sauvignon, Shiraz.
summary A low-profile producer but reliable, particularly when it comes to its smooth but rich Shiraz.

Paul Osicka Shiraz

Estate-grown from vines which are up to 40 years old, and almost always the pick of the Osicka wines.

🍷🍷🍷🍷🍷 **1996** Medium to full red-purple; the bouquet is clean and ripe, with rich, intense black cherry and blackberry fruit. The palate provides precisely the same sweet fruit flavours in restrained abundance; fine but persistent tannins run throughout. **rating:** 90

➭ **best drinking** 2000 – 2010 **best vintages** NA **drink with** Kangaroo fillet • $19

paulett ★★★★

Polish Hill Road, Polish Hill River, SA 5453 **region** Clare Valley
phone (08) 8843 4328 **fax** (08) 8843 4202 **open** 7 days 10–5
winemaker Neil Paulett **production** 14 000 **est.** 1983
product range ($13–19 CD) Riesling, Late Harvest Riesling, Shiraz, Cabernet Merlot, Trillians (Sparkling).
summary The completion of the winery and cellar-door sales facility in 1992 marked the end of a development project which began back in 1982 when Neil and Alison Paulett purchased a 47-hectare property with a small patch of old vines and a house in a grove of trees (which were almost immediately burnt by the 1983 bushfires). The beautifully situated winery is one of the features of the scenic Polish Hill River region, as is its Riesling and its Cabernet Merlot.

pearson vineyards NR

Main North Road, Penwortham, SA 5453 **region** Clare Valley
phone (08) 8843 4234 **fax** (08) 8843 4141 **open** Mon-Fri 11–5, weekends 10–5
winemaker Jim Pearson **production** 600 **est.** 1993
product range ($12–16 CD) Riesling, Late Picked Riesling, Cabernet Franc, Cabernet Sauvignon.
summary Jim Pearson makes the Pearson Vineyard wines at Mintaro Cellars. The 1.5-hectare estate vineyards surround the beautiful little stone house which acts as a cellar door and which appears on the cover of my book *The Wines, The History, The Vignerons of the Clare Valley*.

peel estate ★★★★

Fletcher Road, Baldivis, WA 6171 **region** South West Coast
phone (08) 9524 1221 **fax** (08) 9524 1625 **open** 7 days 10–5
winemaker Will Nairn **production** 8000 **est.** 1974
product range ($12.50–29.50 R) Chardonnay, Wood Matured Chenin Blanc, Medium Dry Chenin Blanc, Unwooded Chardonnay, Classic White, Verdelho, Shiraz, Zinfandel, Cabernet Sauvignon.
summary The winery rating is given for its Shiraz, a wine of considerable finesse and with a remarkably consistent track record. Every year Will Nairn holds a Great Shiraz tasting for

six-year-old Australian Shirazes, and pits Peel Estate (in a blind tasting attended by 60 or so people) against Australia's best. It is never disgraced. The white wines are workmanlike, the wood-matured Chenin Blanc another winery specialty, although not achieving the excellence of the Shiraz. At five years of age it will typically show well, with black cherry and chocolate flavours, a strong dash of American oak, and surprising youth.

peerick vineyard NR

Wild Dog Track, Moonambel, Vic 3478; postal 48 Alfred Street, Kew, Vic 3101 **region** Pyrenees
phone (03) 9817 1611 **fax** (03) 9817 1611 **open** Not
winemaker Contract **production** 1500 **est.** 1990
product range ($18–26 R) Sauvignon Blanc, Cabernet Sauvignon.
summary Peerick is the venture of Melbourne lawyer Chris Jessup and wife Meryl. They have established a Joseph's coat vineyard with cabernet sauvignon, shiraz, cabernet franc, malbec, merlot, sauvignon blanc, semillon and viognier crammed into the 4.27 hectares of vines. So far only a Sauvignon Blanc and a Cabernet Sauvignon have been released, but – not surprisingly – more wines are planned for the future.

pendarves estate 

110 Old North Road, Belford, NSW 2335 **region** Lower Hunter Valley
phone (02) 6574 7222 **fax** (02) 9970 6152 **open** Weekends 11–5, Mon–Fri by appointment
winemaker Greg Silkman (Contract) **production** 6000 **est.** 1986
product range ($16–20 CD) An unusual portfolio of Verdelho, Sauvignon Blanc, Semillon, Chardonnay, Pinot Noir, Chambourcin, Shiraz, Merlot Malbec Cabernet.
summary The perpetual-motion general practitioner and founder of the Australian Medical Friends of Wine, Dr Philip Norrie, is a born communicator and marketer, as well as a wine historian of note. He also happens to be a passionate advocate of the virtues of Verdelho, inspired in part by the high regard held for that variety by vignerons around the turn of the century.

Pendarves Estate Chardonnay

While not looking good at the 1997 Hunter Valley Wine Show (prior to bottling), scored well at the 1998 Winewise Small Makers Competition, at once showing, yet rising above, the effects of the difficult, rain-affected vintage.

1997 Light to medium yellow-green; the bouquet is powerful, with slightly herbaceous overtones to the tangy fruit. The palate has intensity and power, although admittedly in the green spectrum. Long finish; subtle oak. **rating:** 84

⇨ **best drinking** 1998 – 2002 **best vintages** NA **drink with** Sautéed prawns • $18

penfolds ★★★★★

Tanunda Road, Nuriootpa, SA 5355 **region** Barossa Valley
phone (08) 8560 9389 **fax** (08) 8562 2494 **open** Mon–Fri 9–5, Sat 10–5, Sun 1–5
winemaker John Duval **production** 1.1 million **est.** 1844
product range ($9–250 R) Kalimna Bin 28 Shiraz, 128 Coonawarra Shiraz, 389 Cabernet Shiraz, 407 Cabernet Sauvignon, 707 Cabernet Sauvignon and Special Show Bin reds. Brands include Minchinbury Sparkling; Rawson's Retreat Semillon Chardonnay and Cabernet Shiraz; Penfolds The Valleys Chardonnay, Old Vine Barossa Valley Semillon and Old Vine Barossa Valley Shiraz Grenache Mourvedre; Koonunga Hill Shiraz Cabernet, Semillon Sauvignon Blanc and Chardonnay; Magill Estate; Clare Estate and Clare Estate Chardonnay; St Henri Cabernet

Shiraz; Yattarna Chardonnay, Grange. Also various export-only labels. Finally, Grandfather Port and Great Grandfather Port.

summary Senior among the 17 wine companies or stand-alone brands in Southcorp Wines, and undoubtedly one of the top wine companies in the world in terms of quality, product range and exports. The consistency of the quality of the red wines and their value for money can only be described as breathtaking. In 1998 it released its long-awaited super-premium white wine, Yattarna Chardonnay, intended to sit alongside Grange, Australia's greatest red wine. It is also increasingly giving a regional identity to its fighting varietal brands.

Penfolds Trial Bin Adelaide Hills Semillon

This wine was developed as part of Penfolds' on-going search for a long-lived white wine to sit alongside Grange. It demonstrates that the Penfolds team was, at least toying with the idea of using semillon as the base.

🍷🍷🍷🍷🍷 **1995** Medium yellow-green; the bouquet is complex, of medium to full intensity, with subtle oak surrounding fruit showing a mix of herbaceous and riper aromas and flavours, gently honeyed, and with a hint of melon. The wine has good mouthfeel and weight, abundant flavour, yet is not the least bit phenolic. **rating:** 90

➭ **best drinking** 1998 – 2003 **best vintages** NA **drink with** Rich seafood or veal • $27

Penfolds Reserve Bin Chardonnay

Keeping up with the twists and turns of Penfolds development of a super-premium white wine to sit alongside Grange is not easy. Between 1992 and 1997 more than 12 experimental wines have been made by Penfolds, some commercially released, some not. In November 1997 there was a one-off release of Bin 94A, an extraordinarily complex wine produced from 90% Chardonnay and 10% Sauvignon Blanc grown in the Adelaide Hills (52%), Eden Valley (24%), Tumbarumba (21%) and Macedon (3%). It was totally barrel-fermented in French oak (72% new) and matured on lees in those barrels for ten months, with 90% of the wine undergoing malolactic fermentation. A tasting note seems almost superfluous.

🍷🍷🍷🍷🍷 **1994** Bin 94A. Glowing yellow-green; the bouquet is driven by extremely rich, complex and tangy fruit which has largely swallowed up the oak. That oak becomes a little more evident on the palate which is as full flavoured and complex as virtually any Australian Chardonnay could expect to be. **rating:** 94

➭ **best drinking** 1998 – 2003 **best vintages** '94 **drink with** Smoked chicken • $42

Penfolds Trial Bin Adelaide Hills Chardonnay

This wine marks an important step down the road for Penfolds in its quest for a super-premium white wine to sit, if not quite alongside Grange, at the top of the white wine tree. Penfolds is seeking a wine of complexity and longevity; there may be some way to go yet, but this wine represents real progress.

🍷🍷🍷🍷🍷 **1995** Medium to full yellow-green; a powerful bouquet, tangy and stylish, with well-balanced and integrated oak. The palate is likewise powerful and concentrated, with ripe melon and fig fruit woven through toasty/spicy French oak. **rating:** 91

➭ **best drinking** 1998 – 2002 **best vintages** NA **drink with** Loin of pork • $30

Penfolds Yattarna Chardonnay

In April 1998 the long-awaited 'White Grange' was finally released, its name putting to rest forever the idea that there could possibly be a brand extension of what is, and always will be, a unique wine. A blend of 50% Adelaide Hills and 50% McLaren Vale Chardonnay, given Rolls

Royce treatment from start to finish, including a full malolactic fermentation, it should disappoint no one. In 1997 it won numerous trophies at the Royal Sydney Wine Show, including the prestigious Tucker Seabrook Trophy for best wine (white or red) in the Australian show system in the preceding 12 months.

🍷🍷🍷🍷🍷 **1995** Glowing yellow-green; while the bouquet is undoubtedly complex and powerful, it has a subtlety and a smoothness which takes it separate and apart from all of the Trial and Reserve Bin whites previously released by Penfolds. The bouquet and palate have melon, fig, citrus and apple aromas and flavours with perfectly integrated and balanced oak. The word 'seamless' was invented for wines such as this. **rating:** 96

➯ **best drinking** 1998 – 2005 **best vintages** '95 **drink with** Richer white meat dishes of all kinds • $75

Penfolds Grange

Australia's greatest red wine, with a turbulent early history chronicled in Huon Hooke's book entitled *Max Schubert: Winemaker* (1994). What can be said in a few words? The bare bones are: first made 1955; sourced from low-yielding, old shiraz vines (and up to 15% Cabernet Sauvignon) chiefly from the Barossa but also from the Clare Valley and McLaren Vale. Fermentation finished in and matured in new American oak. The 1990 was rated the 'Number One Wine in the World' by the all-powerful *Wine Spectator* in December 1995.

🍷🍷🍷🍷🍷 **1993** Medium to full red-purple; voluminous blackberry, liquorice, black cherry and chocolate fruit aromas completely integrated with sweet vanillin oak on the bouquet; has a texture and structure all of its own, not monolithic, yet meltingly smooth. Maintains the great tradition. **rating:** 94

➯ **best drinking** 2005 – 2025 **best vintages** '52, '53, '55, '62, '66, '67, '71, '76, '78, '80, '85, '86, '90, '91, '92 **drink with** Rich game dishes • $250

Penfolds Kalimna Bin 28 Shiraz

A multi-region blend sourced from the Barossa and Clare Valleys, McLaren Vale and Langhorne Creek regions. There is a good argument to be made that it should be Bin 28, rather than Bin 389, which is 'Poor Man's Grange'. The emphasis is on the same lush fruit; the oak used is second- and third-use American barrels handed down through the Grange and Bin 389 programmes.

🍷🍷🍷🍷🍷 (4.5) **1995** Medium to full red-purple; the bouquet is smooth and clean, with a mix of dark chocolate and berry fruit of medium to full intensity; oak in restraint. The palate is rich and full, with dark berry fruit and layers of texture and structure; subtle oak. 1995 was far from a poor vintage for Shiraz. **rating:** 91

➯ **best drinking** 2000 – 2010 **best vintages** '64, '66, '71, '80, '81, '83, '86, '90, '91, '94, '95 **drink with** Lamb or beef casserole • $17

Penfolds Bin 389 Cabernet Shiraz

First made in 1960, and promptly dubbed 'Poor Man's Grange'. A blend of 50% to 60% Cabernet Sauvignon and 40% to 50% Shiraz from the Barossa Valley, Coonawarra, Padthaway, McLaren Vale, Langhorne Creek and the Clare Valley. Matured in a mixture of new (20%) and older American oak barrels.

🍷🍷🍷🍷🍷 (4.5) **1995** Medium to full red-purple; the bouquet is rich, with berry, chocolate and some vanilla oak inputs. The palate has abundant flavour with chocolate and dark berry fruit flavours woven through with soft, lingering tannins. **rating:** 92

➯ **best drinking** 2000 – 2015 **best vintages** '66, '70, '71, '86, '90, '93, '94 **drink with** Double lamb loin chops • $24

Penfolds St Henri Cabernet Shiraz

Born of the vigorous rivalry between and radically different winemaking philosophies of Max Schubert and John Davoren. With the exception of emphasis on the highest-quality grape sources, Grange and St Henri are polar opposites. This traditional wine is made from Barossa, Clare and Eden Valleys, McLaren Vale, and Langhorne Creek Shiraz; and Cabernet Sauvignon from Coonawarra and the Barossa Valley. Oak influence is minimal.

1994 Medium purple-red; the bouquet is quite powerful, with a mix of dark berry and more minty characters; the palate has that racy character of the '94 vintage, with blackberry, black cherry and mint fruit, and a long finish. **rating:** 90

best drinking 1999 – 2009 **best vintages** '66, '67, '76, '82, '85, '88, '90, '91, '93, '94 **drink with** Steak and kidney pie • $33

Penfolds Bin 407 Cabernet Sauvignon

A relatively recent introduction to the Penfolds range, first made in 1990 from a blend of McLaren Vale, Padthaway, Coonawarra, Barossa and Clare Valleys Cabernet Sauvignon. Matured in a mix of 30% new oak (American and French) and 70% hand-me-downs from Bin 707. Initially conceived as a lower-priced wine, the sheer quality of Bin 407 and its already illustrious show record led to its higher price when released.

1995 Medium purple-red; the bouquet is clean and soft with red berry/cassis fruit supported by relatively restrained oak. The palate has good length and structure, with ripe cassis/berry fruit, a touch of mint, relatively soft tannins and well-integrated oak. No doubt strengthened by the decision not to make any Bin 707 or John Riddoch in 1995. **rating:** 90

best drinking 2000 – 2010 **best vintages** '90, '91, '92, '93, '94 **drink with** Venison, kangaroo fillet • $22

Penfolds Grandfather Port

First released in the 1960s; made from Barossa Valley Shiraz and Mourvedre which is oak-matured in old barrels for decades, and which is finally blended from selection of very old and much younger material. Penfolds has always kept a tight rein on production, thus preserving the all-important old material which forms the base of the wine.

NV Medium to full tawny-red; exceedingly complex, with strong barrel-aged rancio characters and attractively earthy spirit. A long and richly flavoured wine, with the cleansing, drying finish which is so essential to the style. **rating:** 90

best drinking 1997 – 2007 **best vintages** NA **drink with** Coffee • $79.95

Penfolds Great Grandfather Port

First released in 1994 to celebrate the 150th birthday of Penfolds. In a neat marketing gimmick, 1994 bottles were blended and bottled, utilising the very oldest and best stocks, dating back to the early years of the twentieth century. The concentration and power of the wine is reminiscent of the very old Seppelt Liqueur Tawny Ports.

NV Deep tawny with an olive-green rim; both the bouquet and palate are extraordinarily concentrated and rich, very much into the liqueur style of Port which is unique to Australia. Shows the Brandy spirit which was used in the fortifying process, and which adds yet extra complexity. **rating:** 95

best drinking 1997 – 2007 **best vintages** NA **drink with** Coffee • $150

---

penley estate ★★★★☆

McLeans Road, Coonawarra, SA 5263 **region** Coonawarra
phone (08) 8231 2400 **fax** (08) 8231 0589 **open** By appointment
winemaker Kym Tolley **production** 20 000 **est.** 1988
product range ($18–50 R) Chardonnay, Hyland Shiraz, Shiraz Cabernet, Cabernet Sauvignon, Phoenix Cabernet Sauvignon, Pinot Noir Chardonnay.
summary Owner winemaker Kym Tolley describes himself as a fifth-generation winemaker, the family tree involving both the Penfolds and the Tolleys. He worked 17 years in the industry before establishing Penley Estate and has made every post a winner since, producing a succession of rich, complex, full-bodied red wines and stylish Chardonnays. Now ranks as one of the best wineries in Coonawarra, drawing upon 81 precious hectares of estate plantings.

Penley Estate Chardonnay

No region of origin claim is made on the front label, and the back label is equivocal as to its origin, contenting itself with saying that the wine is made from grapes grown on selected vineyard sites. Part, presumably, comes from the 5 hectares of Coonawarra chardonnay owned by Penley Estate. The wine is barrel-fermented, and 20% is taken through malolactic fermentation.

🍷🍷🍷🍷 **1996** Medium yellow-green; a restrained bouquet with subtle fruit and oak providing an interplay between mineral, nectarine and cashew aromas. The palate is in similar restrained style, with nutty cashew flavours from the partial malolactic fermentation providing much of the flavour. Overall, harmonious. **rating:** 86

⇨ **best drinking** 1998 – 2001 **best vintages** NA **drink with** Yakitori chicken • $20

Penley Estate Shiraz Cabernet

A blend of 50% Shiraz and 50% Cabernet Sauvignon, sourced from Coonawarra (65%), the balance from McLaren Vale (25%) and Barossa Valley (10%). Matured for two years in a mix of 75% American and 25% French (Troncais) oak. Like the Cabernet Sauvignon, a prolific medal winner.

🍷🍷🍷🍷 **1995** Medium red-purple; the bouquet is clean, of medium to full intensity, with earthy blackberry fruit and subtle oak. Sweet cassis berry flavours come through strongly on the forepalate before moving through to a firmer finish. Nicely judged oak. **rating:** 86

⇨ **best drinking** 2000 – 2004 **best vintages** '88, '90, '91, '92, '94 **drink with** Soft ripened cheese • $23

Penley Estate Cabernet Sauvignon

Made from the pick of 38 hectares of estate-grown Cabernet Sauvignon, matured in a cleverly handled mix of American and French oak. Over the years, various vintages of the wine have won a quite extraordinary number of trophies and gold medals.

🍷🍷🍷🍷 **1995** Medium red-purple; an unexpectedly rich and sweet bouquet with blackcurrant and blackberry fruit is followed by a supple palate with red berry, blackcurrant and bitter chocolate flavours supported by perfectly balanced oak and tannins. An exceptionally good outcome for a difficult Coonawarra vintage. **rating:** 88

⇨ **best drinking** 1999 – 2005 **best vintages** '89, '90, '91, '92, '94 **drink with** Rare beef • $48

---

pennyweight winery NR

Pennyweight Lane, Beechworth, Vic 3747 **region** Ovens Valley
phone (03) 5728 1747 **fax** (03) 5728 1704 **open** Thur–Tues 10–5
winemaker Stephen Newton Morris **production** 1000 **est.** 1982
product range ($11–27 CD) A fortified specialist, but also producing limited table wines including Trebbiano Riesling and Shiraz; the primary focus is on Fino and Amontillado Sherries, a range of Ports from Old Tawny to Ruby, Vintage Port, White Port and Muscat.
summary Pennyweight was established by Stephen Morris, great-grandson of G F Morris, founder of Morris Wines. The 3 hectares of vines are not irrigated, and are moving towards organic certification. The business is run by Stephen, together with his wife Elizabeth assisted by their three sons; Elizabeth Morris says, 'It's a perfect world' suggesting Pennyweight is more than happy with its lot in life.

penwortham wine cellars NR

Government Road, Penwortham, SA 5453 **region** Clare Valley
phone (08) 8843 4345 **open** Sat 10–5, Sun, holidays 10–4
winemaker Richard Hughes **production** 1500 **est.** 1985
product range ($13–16 CD) Riesling, Cabernet Sauvignon, Shiraz.
summary A relatively new arrival on the Clare Valley scene; a '95 unwooded Shiraz tasted in 1996 was fearsomely strong and tannic.

pepper tree ★★★★

Halls Road, Pokolbin, NSW 2321 **region** Lower Hunter Valley
phone (02) 4998 7539 **fax** (02) 4998 7746 **open** 7 days 9–5
winemaker Chris Cameron, Chris Archer **production** 40 000 **est.** 1993
product range ($10–60 CD) Sundial White and Red; Chardonnay, Shiraz, Cabernet Franc; Reserve range of Semillon, Chardonnay, Verdelho, Traminer, Malbec, Coonawarra Merlot and Cabernet Sauvignon.
summary The Pepper Tree winery is situated in the complex which also contains The Convent guesthouse and Roberts Restaurant. The company which now owns Pepper Tree is headed by Chris Cameron, chief winemaker since 1991. It made a decisive move in 1996, formalising the acquisition of a major interest in the Parker (Coonawarra) Estate vineyards, having purchased some of the fruit from those vineyards in 1995. The acquisition will see a further expansion in production and in the range of wines available. Quality, too, has seen a significant lift, particularly with the trophy-winning Chardonnay and Merlot.

Pepper Tree Chardonnay

The first fruits of the link with Parker (Coonawarra) Estate, and presumably setting a pattern for future releases. Blends of Hunter and Coonawarra red wines stretch back to the 1950s (notably the famous 1958 Mildara Hunter Coonawarra) but this is the first Hunter Coonawarra Chardonnay blend I have encountered. The '96 in fact marks the extension of the blend into three regions.

🍷🍷🍷🍷🍸 **1996** Medium to full yellow-green; a rich, buttery ripe bouquet leads into a smooth tropical/yellow peach-flavoured palate, supported by subtle oak. **rating:** 90

➾ **best drinking** 1998 – 2001 **best vintages** NA **drink with** Brains • $18

Pepper Tree Reserve Coonawarra Merlot
Has rapidly become the flag-bearer for Pepper Tree, which has not hesitated to compare it (in formal comparative tastings) with the great Merlots of the world, including Chateau Petrus. Certainly hit a high spot with the much-bemedalled '96 vintage, adding to its tally with the top gold medal in the Merlot class at the 1998 Royal Sydney Wine Show.

🍷🍷🍷🍷🍷 **1996** Medium red-purple; a scented, aromatic bouquet with sweet French oak neatly woven through the fruit. That sophisticated oak handling is very evident on the palate, which has extremely good texture, structure and mouthfeel; there is berry and mint varietal fruit, but it is the silky feel which is the major attraction. **rating:** 93

➾ **best drinking** 1999 – 2006 **best vintages** NA **drink with** Smoked lamb • $60

peppers creek NR

Broke Road, Pokolbin, NSW 2321 **region** Lower Hunter Valley
phone (02) 4998 7532 **fax** (02) 4998 7531 **open** Wed-Sun 10–5
winemaker Peter Ireland **production** 700 **est.** 1987
product range ($12–25 CD) Enzo Bianco, Enzo Rosé, Unwooded Chardonnay, Chardonnay, Enzo Rosso, Merlot, Yacht Squadron Port.
summary A combined winery and antique shop which sells all its wine through the cellar door, and runs the Cafe Enzo. The red wines previously tasted were clean and full flavoured, the Merlot coming from the 1 hectare of estate vineyards. No recent tastings.

pertaringa ★★★★

Cnr Hunt and Rifle Range Roads, McLaren Vale, SA 5171 **region** McLaren Vale
phone (08) 8383 8125 **fax** (08) 8383 7766 **open** Not
winemaker Geoff Hardy, Ben Riggs **production** 1200 **est.** 1980
product range ($14–30 R) Under the Pertaringa label Semillon, Sauvignon Blanc, Shiraz and Cabernet Sauvignon; under the Geoff Hardy label Kuitpo Shiraz and Cabernet.
summary The Pertaringa and Geoff Hardy labels are made from a small percentage of the grapes grown by leading viticulturists Geoff Hardy and Ian Leask. The Pertaringa vineyard of 24 hectares was acquired in 1980 and rejuvenated; establishment of the ultra-cool Kuitpo vineyard in the Adelaide Hills began in 1987 and now supplies leading makers such as Southcorp, Petaluma and Shaw & Smith.

petaluma ★★★★★

Spring Gully Road, Piccadilly, SA 5151 **region** Adelaide Hills
phone (08) 8339 4122 **fax** (08) 8339 5253 **open** See Bridgewater Mill
winemaker Brian Croser **production** 30 000 **est.** 1976
product range ($19–44 R) Riesling, Chardonnay, Coonawarra (Cabernet Blend), Croser (Sparkling); Second label Sharefarmers White and Red. Bridgewater Mill is another second label – see separate entry.
summary The Petaluma empire continues to flourish now taking in both Knappstein Wines and Mitchelton. While running a public-listed group, Brian Croser has never compromised his fierce commitment to quality, and doubtless never will. The Riesling is almost monotonously good; the Chardonnay is the big mover, going from strength to strength; the Merlot another marvellously succulent wine to buy without hesitation.

Petaluma Riesling

A 100% estate-produced wine from Petaluma's Hanlins Hill Vineyard in the Clare Valley, one of the classic Australian Riesling regions. The wine is made with iron discipline, and is a crystal-pure reflection of the interaction of climate, soil and variety. As the notes indicate, it ages with grace.

YYYYY **1997** Light to medium yellow-green; the bouquet is quintessential, classic Clare, firm and with a mix of mineral, toast and lime aromas. The powerfully structured palate runs through the same mineral/toast, spice and lime flavours, the palate bone-dry and clean. Regarded by Brian Croser as one of the great vintages for Petaluma. **rating:** 94

⇨ **best drinking** 1999 – 2009 **best vintages** '80, '85, '86, '88, '90, '92, '93, '94, '95, '97 **drink with** Sashimi • $19

Petaluma Chardonnay

One of the more elegant and refined Australian Chardonnays which has, however, radically changed its geographic base since it was first made in 1977, starting in Cowra then moving to Coonawarra, then partly to the Clare Valley, and ultimately (since 1990) being made from Piccadilly Valley grapes. The style of the wine has been refined over the period, but has remained remarkably consistent given the quite radically changing regional base.

YYYYY **1996** Spotlessly clean, it ripples with a marvellous array of fruit aromas and flavours ranging from stony-minerally through citrus-grapefruit to tropical, yet retains exceptional finesse and elegance. **rating:** 96

⇨ **best drinking** 1999 – 2006 **best vintages** '87, '90, '91, '92, '95, '96 **drink with** Slow-roasted Tasmanian salmon • $36

Petaluma Merlot

Two vintages are typically available at any one time, one on indent for physical delivery 12 months hence, and one representing the balance of the previous year's indent offering sold through normal commercial channels. An interesting way to go, with a substantial cost saving between the indent and normal release wine (the indent price being $30 per bottle). Both the '94 and '95 are at the top end of Australian red winemaking, without definitively answering the question concerning the taste of Merlot.

YYYYY **1994** Medium red-purple; a thrusting bouquet with fragrant, almost medicinal, notes running through to red berry and earth. A powerhouse in the mouth, which takes Merlot to another dimension, with inimitable slightly medicinal flavours. **rating:** 95

YYYYY **1995** Strong red-purple; a spotlessly clean bouquet with fruit and oak seamlessly interwoven in a display of berry, cedar and more earthy notes leads on to a palate with a mix of red berry, earth and leaf flavours, perhaps as indicative of Merlot as any example from Australia. The wine has excellent structure and weight, with classy oak-handling throughout. **rating:** 94

⇨ **best drinking** 2000 – 2005 **best vintages** '94, '95, '96 **drink with** Veal • $44

Petaluma Coonawarra

A logical counterpart to the Chardonnay in the sense that it is far more elegant and refined than the more typical South Australian (and in particular, Coonawarra) Cabernet. Its regional base has remained the same since 1979, but the varietal composition has changed significantly, moving from Shiraz and Cabernet in '79 through to a Cabernet-dominant blend with around 15% Merlot. As with the Chardonnay, the more recent vintages are best.

🍷🍷🍷🍷🍷 **1995** Strong red-purple; spotlessly clean, ripe blackberry/blackcurrant aromas of medium to full intensity are followed by a stylish palate, with particularly soft, almost creamy, tannins, with hints of cedar and chocolate. **rating:** 95

➯ **best drinking** 2000 – 2008 **best vintages** '79, '86, '88, '90, '91, '92, '95 **drink with** Saddle of lamb • $42

peter lehmann ★★★☆

Para Road, Tanunda, SA 5352 **region** Barossa Valley

phone (08) 8563 2500 **fax** (08) 8563 3402 **open** Mon-Fri 9.30–5, weekends, holidays 10.30–4.30

winemaker Peter Lehmann, Andrew Wigan, Peter Scholz, Leonie Lange **production** 200 000 **est.** 1979

product range ($9–150 R) Eden Valley Riesling, Barossa Semillon, Barossa Chenin Blanc, Semillon Chardonnay, Chardonnay, Clancy's Classic Dry White, Botrytis Riesling, Noble Semillon, Grenache, Seven Surveys Dry Red, Barossa Shiraz, Barossa Cabernet Sauvignon, Clancy's Red, and Bin AD2015 Vintage Port. Premium wines are Reserve Riesling, Reserve Chardonnay, Mentor, Stonewell Shiraz.

summary Public listing on the Stock Exchange has not altered the essential nature of the company, resolutely and single-mindedly focused on Peter Lehmann's beloved Barossa Valley. Some of the top-of-the-range wines are seriously good, the base range reliable rather than inspiring.

Peter Lehmann Stonewell Shiraz

The wine is made solely from low-yielding old vineyards of the Stonewell, Ebenezer and Moppa subdistricts of the Barossa Valley. The fermentation is finished in new American oak, in which it is then matured for two years prior to bottling. It is then given three years bottle age before release. The wine has a supremely illustrious show record, with many major trophies to its credit.

🍷🍷🍷🍷🍷 **1993** Medium to full red-purple; the bouquet is rich and complex with abundant ripe fruit and lots of vanilla oak. The same play occurs on the palate, with rich, ripe cherry and raspberry fruit laden with sweet vanilla oak, and finishing with soft, chewy tannins. **rating:** 90

➯ **best drinking** 1999 – 2003 **best vintages** '80, '89, '91, '92, '93, '94 **drink with** Kangaroo fillet • $45

Peter Lehmann Clancy's Red

A blend of Barossa-grown Shiraz, Cabernet Sauvignon, Cabernet Franc and Merlot, spiced with the American oak which is so much part of the Peter Lehmann style. Right from the outset, an unqualified success in the marketplace simply because it represents such good value for money, and because it is ready to drink when released.

🍷🍷🍷🍷 **1996** Medium to full red-purple; the bouquet is exactly as one would expect it to be, full and scented with dark berry fruits surrounded by solid American oak. The palate is a mix of high-toned juicy minty berry fruit and vanillin oak. Works very well. **rating:** 85

➯ **best drinking** 1999 – 2004 **best vintages** '91, '92, '94, '96 **drink with** Pasta with tomato or meat sauce • $12.50

Peter Lehmann Mentor

This wine is based predominantly on Cabernet Sauvignon, blended in varying proportions with Malbec, Merlot and Shiraz which fluctuate from year to year. Fermentation is finished in barrel and then matured for a further two and a half years in French and American oak hogsheads prior to bottling. Incidentally, Mentor is the new label for what was previously styled 'Cellar Collection Cabernet Blend'.

1994 Dense red-purple; an extremely ripe and rich bouquet with cassis, chocolate and mint fruit aromas and pleasantly subdued American oak heralds a quite excellent wine on the palate, with lots of character and ripe fruit flavours, lingering tannins and subtle oak. **rating:** 90

best drinking 1999 – 2006 **best vintages** '80, '89, '91, '93, '94 **drink with** Spiced beef • $23

Peter Lehmann Bin AD2015 Vintage Port

Produced from old, low-yielding shiraz vines grown in the Koonunga Hill district of the Barossa Valley. Imitation being the sincerest form of flattery, many years ago Peter Lehmann set out to essentially duplicate the Hardy Reynella style of Vintage Port, and has done so with verve.

1994 Medium to full purple-red; the bouquet is fragrant, indeed pungent, with penetrating earthy blackberry fruit and overtones of citrus and lantana. The palate is extremely well balanced, with chocolate, earth and berry fruit, substantial but not aggressive tannins, and a relatively dry finish – the best feature of a good wine. **rating:** 90

best drinking 2005 – 2015 **best vintages** NA **drink with** Friends • NA

peter rumball wines NR

PO Box 195, Glen Osmond, SA 5067 **region** Warehouse
phone (08) 8332 2761 **fax** (08) 8364 0188 **open** Not
winemaker Peter Rumball **production** 5000 **est.** 1988
product range ($12.90–49.90 R) Sparkling Shiraz, Vintage Pinot Noir Chardonnay Brut, The Pink.
summary Peter Rumball has been making and selling sparkling wine for as long as I can remember, but has led a somewhat peripatetic life, starting in the Clare Valley but now operating what I can only describe as a 'warehouse winery' operation, with neither vineyards nor winery of his own. The grapes are purchased and the wines made at various places under the supervision of Peter Rumball. His particular specialty has always been Sparkling Shiraz, and was so long before it became flavour of the month.

peterson house NR

Cnr Broke and Branxton Roads, Cessnock, NSW 2321 **region** Lower Hunter Valley
phone (02) 4998 7841 **fax** (02) 4998 7880 **open** 7 days 9–5
winemaker Gary Reed **production** 2000 **est.** 1994
product range ($14–25 CD) Chardonnay, Sparkling.
summary Prominently and provocatively situated on the corner of Broke and Branxton Roads, as one enters the main vineyard and winery district in the Lower Hunter Valley. It is an extension of the Peterson family empire, and no doubt very deliberately aimed at the tourist. While the dreaded word 'Champagne' has been retained in the business name, the wine labels now simply say Peterson House, which is a big step in the right direction.

petersons ★★★☆

Mount View Road, Mount View, NSW 2325 **region** Lower Hunter Valley
phone (02) 4990 1704 **fax** (02) 4991 1344 **open** Mon-Sat 9–5, Sun 10–5
winemaker Gary Reed **production** 10 500 **est.** 1971
product range ($12.50–28 CD) Semillon, Chardonnay, Pinot Noir, Shiraz, Cabernet Sauvignon, Sauternes, Vintage Port, Sparkling; Back Block is premium red wine label for rich, full-flavoured Shiraz and Cabernet Sauvignon.
summary After a period in the doldrums, Petersons seems to be resurgent, although there has been no change in the team. Certainly it retains a high reputation in the marketplace, sustained by wines such as the splendidly rich and concentrated Back Block dry reds.

pewsey vale ★★★☆

Brownes Road, Pewsey Vale, SA (vineyard only) **region** Eden Valley
phone (08) 8561 3200 **open** At Yalumba
winemaker Louisa Rose **production** 30 000 **est.** 1961
product range ($10–15 R) Riesling, Botrytis Riesling, Sauvignon Blanc, Cabernet Sauvignon.
summary Pewsey Vale was a famous vineyard established in 1847 by Joseph Gilbert, and it was appropriate that when S Smith & Son (Yalumba) began the renaissance of the high Adelaide Hills plantings in 1961, they should do so by purchasing Pewsey Vale and establishing 59 hectares of riesling and cabernet sauvignon. Once famous for its Riesling, recent vintages have not been inspiring, tending to be somewhat dilute and unfocused.

pfeiffer ★★★

Distillery Road, Wahgunyah, Vic 3687 **region** Rutherglen
phone (02) 6033 2805 **fax** (02) 6033 3158 **open** Mon-Sat 9–5, Sun 11–4
winemaker Christopher Pfeiffer **production** 12 000 **est.** 1984
product range ($9.90–20 CD) Riesling, Auslese Tokay, Chardonnay Semillon, Chardonnay, Spätlese Frontignac, Ensemble (light Rosé-style), Pinot Noir, Shiraz, Shiraz Cabernet, Cabernet Sauvignon, Vintage Port, Old Distillery Tawny, Old Distillery Liqueur Gold (Tokay).
summary Ex-Lindeman fortified winemaker Chris Pfeiffer occupies one of the historic wineries (built 1880) which abound in northeast Victoria, and which is worth a visit on this score alone. The fortified wines are good, and the table wines have improved considerably over recent vintages, drawing upon 21 hectares of estate plantings. The winery offers barbecue facilities, children's playground, gourmet picnic hampers, and dinners (by arrangement).

phillip island vineyard ★★★★

Berrys Beach Road, Phillip Island, Vic **region** Gippsland
phone (03) 5956 8465 **fax** (03) 5956 8465 **open** 7 days 11–7 (Nov-March) 11–5 (April-Oct)
winemaker David Lance **production** 1500 **est.** 1993
product range ($14–24 CD) Sea Spray (Sparkling), Sauvignon Blanc, Cape Woolamai (Semillon Sauvignon Blanc), Summerland (Chardonnay), Newhaven (Riesling Traminer), The Pinnacles (Botrytis Riesling), The Nobbies (Pinot Noir), Berry's Beach (Cabernet Sauvignon), Western Port.
summary A separate operation of Diamond Valley Vineyards, now coming into full flower.The year 1997 marked the first substantial vintage from the spectacular Phillip Island Vineyard, totally enclosed in the permanent silon net which acts both as a windbreak and protection against birds. In the meantime a range of specially made and labelled wines produced from Yarra Valley, Gippsland and Phillip Island wines are available, some of which had

outstanding show success in 1997. Definitely not a tourist trap cellar door but a serious producer of excellent wine.

Phillip Island Sauvignon Blanc

Only 100 half-bottles of this wine were made in 1996, the first from Phillip Island. The '97 moved into commercial production scale, and promptly won two trophies (including Best White Wine) at the 1997 Lilydale Wine Show.

🍷🍷🍷🍷🍷 **1997** Light to medium yellow-green; a clean and fresh bouquet of light to medium intensity, with delicate passionfruit aromas; the palate is similarly fresh, delicate and well balanced, simply lacking the fruit intensity of top-end New Zealand Sauvignon Blancs. **rating:** 90

⇨ **best drinking** 1998 – 1999 **best vintages** '97 **drink with** Fresh crab • $24

Phillip Island Vineyard The Nobbies Pinot Noir

A blend of Gippsland and Yarra Valley grapes and produced for sale only at the Phillip Island Vineyard cellar door. Won two trophies at the 1997 Victorian Wine Show, Best Pinot Noir and Best Wine of Show.

🍷🍷🍷🍷🍷 **1996** Medium red-purple; the clean, generous bouquet is followed by a supple, smooth palate with very flavoursome plum and dark berry fruit. A wine which will have broad appeal thanks to that rich fruit. **rating:** 90

⇨ **best drinking** 1998 – 2001 **best vintages** NA **drink with** Smoked quail • $22

piano gully ★★☆

Piano Gully Road, Manjimup, WA 6258 **region** Pemberton
phone (08) 9772 3583 **fax** (08) 9771 2886 **open** Weekends, public holidays 10–5
winemaker Haydon White **production** 450 **est.** 1987
product range ($12–15 CD) Chardonnay, Pinot Noir, Cabernet Sauvignon, Concerto.
summary The 4-hectare vineyard was established in 1987 on rich Karri loam, 10 kilometres south of Manjimup, with the first wine made from the 1991 vintage. Wine quality to date has failed to impress.

pibbin NR

Greenhill Road, Balhannah, SA 5242 **region** Adelaide Hills
phone (08) 8388 4794 **fax** (08) 8398 0015 **open** Weekends 11–5.30
winemaker Roger Salkeld **production** 1200 **est.** 1991
product range ($18–21CD) Pinot Noir, White Pinot, Sparkling Pinot.
summary The 2.5-hectare Pibbin vineyard, near Verdun, is managed on organic principles; owners Roger and Lindy Salkeld explain that the name 'Pibbin' is a corruption of a negro-spiritual word for Heaven, adding that while the wines may not have achieved that lofty status yet, the vineyard has. Pibbin has made a name for itself for producing massive, dense Pinot Noir in a style radically different from that of the rest of the Adelaide Hills.

picardy NR

Cnr Vasse Highway and Eastbrook Road, Manjimup, WA 6260 **region** Pemberton
phone (08) 9779 0036 **fax** (08) 9776 0036 **open** By appointment
winemaker Bill Pannell, Dan Pannell **production** 1000 **est.** 1993
product range ($28–30 CD) Chardonnay, Pinot Noir, Shiraz, Merlot Cabernet.

summary Picardy is owned by Dr Bill Pannell and his wife Sandra, who were the founders of Moss Wood winery in the Margaret River region (in 1969). Picardy reflects Bill Pannell's view that the Pemberton area will prove to be one of the best regions in Australia for Pinot Noir and Chardonnay, but it is perhaps significant that the wines to be released include a Shiraz, and a Bordeaux-blend of 50% Merlot, 25% Cabernet Franc and 25% Cabernet Sauvignon. Time will tell whether Pemberton has more Burgundy, Rhône or Bordeaux in its veins.

Picardy Pinot Noir

A wine which will only serve to intensify the debate over the suitability of the Pemberton area for Pinot Noir, as it provides support for those who say it is. An impressive first vintage.

🍷🍷🍷🍷 **1996** Medium red; a complex bouquet with stemmy/leafy/briary/foresty aromas leads on to a palate which shows plenty of forest floor and leafy characters, but which has good length and undeniable varietal character. **rating:** 85

➾ **best drinking** 1998 – 1999 **best vintages** NA **drink with** Braised pheasant • NA

piccadilly fields NR

185 Piccadilly Road, Piccadilly, SA 5151 **region** Adelaide Hills
phone (08) 8272 2239 **fax** (08) 8232 5395 **open** Not
winemaker Sam Virgara **production** 3000 **est.** 1989
product range ($17.95 ML) Chardonnay, Merlot Cabernet Franc Cabernet Sauvignon.
summary Piccadilly Fields draws upon a very substantial vineyard, with much of the production being sold to Petaluma. The plantings include 10 hectares of pinot meunier, 8 hectares of pinot noir, 5 hectares each of chardonnay, merlot and sauvignon blanc, 2 hectares of cabernet franc and 1 hectare of cabernet sauvignon.

Piccadilly Fields Chardonnay

Always made in a very delicate style, typified by the '96 which won a gold medal at the 1997 Royal Adelaide Wine Show.

🍷🍷🍷🍷 **1996** Light yellow-green; the bouquet is clean, of light to medium intensity, with very subtle oak. An extremely delicate and crisp palate, Chablis-like, and not exhibiting the intense varietal fruit we are used to in Australia. For all that, very well crafted. **rating:** 87

➾ **best drinking** 1998 – 2003 **best vintages** NA **drink with** Shellfish • NA

pierro ★★★★☆

Caves Road, Willyabrup via Cowaramup, WA 6284 **region** Margaret River
phone (08) 9755 6220 **fax** (08) 9755 6308 **open** 7 days 10–5
winemaker Dr Michael Peterkin **production** 5000 **est.** 1979
product range ($23–44.70 R) Chardonnay, LTC Semillon Sauvignon Blanc, Pinot Noir, Cabernets.
summary Dr Michael Peterkin is another of the legion of Margaret River medical practitioners who, for good measure, married into the Cullen family. Pierro is renowned for its stylish white wines, which often exhibit tremendous complexity. The Chardonnay can be monumental in its weight and complexity.

Pierro Semillon Sauvignon Blanc

Made from relatively low-yielding estate-grown grapes, and originally marketed under the 'Les Trois Cuvées' label, now abbreviated to LTC, which (coincidentally) can also stand for 'a little touch of Chardonnay'. The wine tastes as if it may have been wholly or partially barrel-fermented, though no mention of this is made on the label.

🍷🍷🍷🍷 **1997** Light green-yellow; a delicate but multifaceted bouquet including a touch of spice suggesting the Chardonnay component may have been barrel-fermented. The palate is complex, and richer and fuller than the bouquet suggests, with pronounced fruit sweetness on the mid-palate and attractive echoes of oak. **rating:** 90

⇨ **best drinking** 1998 – 2000 **best vintages** '87, '89, '90, '94, '95, '97 **drink with** Veal cutlets • $22.80

Pierro Chardonnay

One of the most distinguished of a band of striking wines from the Margaret River region and which achieved great acclaim during the second half of the 1980s. The style is invariably complex, concentrated and powerful, with the emphasis on secondary rather than primary fruit characters.

🍷🍷🍷🍷🍷 **1996** Medium to full yellow-green; a smooth and rounded, yet complex bouquet with a seamless marriage of fruit and oak. The palate is similarly perfectly modulated and rounded, with the sweet fig and melon fruit woven through with creamy/nutty/toasty inputs from barrel-fermentation and malolactic-fermentation influences. The alcohol does catch you ever so slightly on the finish, not surprising at 14.5°. **rating:** 94

⇨ **best drinking** 1998 – 2003 **best vintages** '86, '87, '89, '90, '92, '94, '95, '96 **drink with** Seafood pasta • $44.70

Pierro Cabernets

A challenging, high-quality blend of the five red varieties of Bordeaux: Cabernet Sauvignon, Cabernet Franc, Merlot, Petit Verdot and Malbec. A serious wine made in serious style.

🍷🍷🍷🍷 **1995** Medium red-purple; a powerful, potent bouquet with distinctive regional gravelly overtones. A similarly powerful palate, with the same depth and forceful tannins which marked the '94. **rating:** 84

⇨ **best drinking** 2005 – 2010 **best vintages** NA **drink with** Boned leg of lamb • $44.70

piesse brook NR

226 Aldersyde Road, Bickley, WA 6076 **region** Perth Hills

phone (08) 9293 3309 **fax** (08) 9443 2839 **open** Sat 1–5, Sun, public holidays 10–5 and by appointment

winemaker Di Bray, Ray Boyanich (Michael Davies Consultant) **production** 1000 **est.** 1974

product range ($10–18 CD) Chardonnay, Shiraz, Merlot, Cabernet Sauvignon, Cabernet Merlot, Cabernet Shiraz, Cabernova (early-drinking style).

summary Surprisingly good red wines made in tiny quantities, and which have received consistent accolades over the years. The first Chardonnay was made in 1993; a trophy-winning Shiraz was produced in 1995. Now has 4 hectares of chardonnay, shiraz, merlot and cabernet sauvignon under vine.

pieter van gent ★★★

Black Springs Road, Mudgee, NSW 2850 **region** Mudgee

phone (02) 6373 3807 **fax** (02) 6373 3910 **open** Mon-Sat 9–5, Sun 11–4

winemaker Pieter van Gent, Philip van Gent **production** 10 000 **est.** 1978

product range ($9.50–16.90 CD) The only dry wines are the Chardonnay, Müller Thurgau, and Cabernet Sauvignon; the Frontignac, Rivaner, Angelic White and Sundance Soft Red all have varying degrees of sweetness; fortified wines are the specialty including Pipeclay Port, Mudgee White Port, Cornelius Port, Mudgee Oloroso, Pipeclay Muscat, Mudgee Liqueur Frontignac, Pipeclay Vermouth.
summary Many years ago, Pieter van Gent worked for Lindemans, before joining Craigmoor, then moving to his own winery in 1979 where he and his family have forged a strong reputation and following for his fortified wines in particular, although the range extends far wider. The wines are seldom seen outside cellar door.

pikes ★★★★

Polish Hill River Road, Sevenhill, SA 5453 **region** Clare Valley
phone (08) 8843 4370 **fax** (08) 8843 4353 **open** 7 days 10–4
winemaker Neil Pike **production** 24 000 **est.** 1984
product range ($13–40 R) Riesling, Reserve Riesling, Sauvignon Blanc, Chardonnay, Shiraz, Reserve Shiraz, Cabernet Sauvignon.
summary Owned by the Pike brothers, one of whom (Andrew) is the senior viticulturist with Southcorp, the other (Neil) a former winemaker at Mitchells. Pikes now has its own winery, with Neil Pike presiding. Generously constructed and flavoured wines are the order of the day.

Pikes Reserve Riesling

The first commercial release of this wine was in May 1998, but it made a pre-release appearance at the Riesling Masterclasses conducted around Australia by Pikes' distributor, Negociants Australia. Thoroughly deserves its Reserve status.

🍷🍷🍷🍷🍷 **1997** Light green-yellow; flowery apple blossom/apple cake aromas with some mineral undertones, even a hint of kerosene (desirable, that is) on the bouquet lead into a classically firm, dry, low phenolic-level palate. Built to stay. **rating:** 90

➾ **best drinking** 2002 – 2007 **best vintages** '97 **drink with** Salmon roulade • $20

pinelli NR

18 Bennett Street, Caversham, WA 6055 **region** Swan District
phone (08) 9279 6818 **fax** (08) 9377 4259 **open** 7 days 10–6
winemaker Robert Pinelli **production** 7000 **est.** 1979
product range ($5–16 CD) Limited table wine range centred on Chenin Blanc, Chardonnay, Shiraz and Cabernet Sauvignon, and an extensive range of fortified wines including Cabernet-based Vintage Port. The wines have won a number of medals at the Perth Show in recent years.
summary Dominic Pinelli and son Robert – the latter a Roseworthy Agricultural College graduate – sell 75% of their production in flagons, but are seeking to place more emphasis on bottled-wine sales in the wake of recent show successes with Chenin Blanc.

pipers brook vineyard ★★★★☆

Bridport Road, Pipers Brook, Tas 7254 **region** Northern Tasmania
phone (03) 6382 7197 **fax** (03) 6382 7226 **open** Mon-Fri 10–4, weekends 11–5 Nov-Apr
winemaker Andrew Pirie **production** 30 000 **est.** 1974
product range ($16–49 CD) The wine is released in two tiers: Pipers Brook Chardonnay, Riesling, Pinot Gris, Gewurztraminer, Opimian, Pellion (Pinot Noir), Méthode Champenoise; and second label Ninth Island Chardonnay, Riesling, Chardonnay, Straits Dry White, Rosé, Tamar Cabernets, Pinot Noir.

summary If all goes to plan, the much-expanded Pipers Brook group, with Pipers Brook Vineyard as the jewel in the crown, will have joined the Lists of the Stock Exchanges by the time of publication. The group, comprising Pipers Brook, Heemskerk and Rochecombe, will account for 35% of the Tasmanian wine industry. Fastidious viticulture and winemaking, immaculate packaging and enterprising marketing constitute a potent and effective blend.

Pipers Brook Riesling

First made in 1979. The 3 hectares of riesling at the home Pipers Brook Vineyard are situated on the favourable north- and northeast-facing aspects, and are now approaching 20 years of age. The wine is excellent, and invariably develops well with prolonged cellaring.

🍷🍷🍷🍷 **1997** Light yellow-green; a crisp, aromatic bouquet with a mix of herb, lime blossom and orange peel aromas is followed by a pungent palate with green lime flavours and high acidity. Aggressive now, but should mellow with time. **rating:** 87

➯ **best drinking** 1999 – 2005 **best vintages** '82, '91, '92, '93, '94 **drink with** Lemon chicken salad • $21.10

Pipers Brook Ninth Island Chardonnay

Ninth Island is the new name for the previous Tasmania Wine Company second label, which suffered from obvious problems of anonymity. Ninth Island derives its name from the Bass Strait island which lies just off the coast of northern Tasmania adjacent to the Pipers Brook region. The wine is made from both estate and contract-grown grapes, and is unwooded.

🍷🍷🍷🍷 **1997** Light to medium green-yellow; a crisp, clean bouquet with a mix of mineral, herb and mint aromas. A refreshing, cool-grown style, with lively, zesty lemony overtones to the crisp fruit on the palate. **rating:** 86

➯ **best drinking** 1998 – 2001 **best vintages** '92, '93, '94, '96, '97 **drink with** Crab, shellfish • $17.80

Pipers Brook Pellion

First made in 1981 (a bucketful of remarkable wine) but changed its name to Pellion only in 1992. Pellion was an artist on one of the very early voyages of discovery to Tasmania, hence the name; notwithstanding the absence of any varietal claim on the label, the wine is in fact 100% Pinot Noir. Winemaker Andrew Pirie says, 'the expression of this grape in the red soils and climate of the region is so individual that we do not think we should be constrained by names which lead to preconceived ideas as to the taste of the wine'.

🍷🍷🍷🍷 **1996** Medium red-purple; there are a range of aromas, with a mix of tobacco leaf, stem, forest floor, spice and cherry which lead into a penetrating, sappy/stemmy/foresty palate. Acidity lengthens the finish; at the far end of the style spectrum. **rating:** 84

➯ **best drinking** 1998 – 1999 **best vintages** '81, '85, '91, '92, '94 **drink with** Ripe King Island brie • $26.30

pirramimma ★★★★

Johnston Road, McLaren Vale, SA 5171 **region** McLaren Vale
phone (08) 8323 8205 **fax** (08) 8323 9224 **open** Mon-Fri 9–5, Sat 10–5, Sun, public holidays 12–4
winemaker Geoff Johnston **production** 18 000 **est.** 1892

product range ($11–21.50 R) Stock's Hill Semillon Chardonnay, Adelaide Hills Semillon, Sauvignon Blanc Semillon, Chardonnay, Stock's Hill Shiraz, Petit Verdot, Hillsview Cabernet Merlot, Cabernet Sauvignon, Ports.

summary An operation with large vineyard holdings of very high quality, and a winery which devotes much of its considerable capacity to contract-processing of fruit for others. In terms of the brand, has been a consistent under-performer during the 1990s. The marketing of the brand does scant justice to the very considerable resources available to it, notably its gold medal Petit Verdot and fine elegant Chardonnay.

Pirramimma Chardonnay

Pirramimma now has over 66 hectares of chardonnay in production, much of it contracted to major Australian wine producers. That produced under the Pirramimma label relies primarily on its fruit, with minimal oak influence – a style which in today's market is proving increasingly popular. An absolute bargain at the price; the '94 was excellent, the '95 (a gold medal winner at the 1997 Royal Adelaide Wine Show) every bit as good.

🍷🍷🍷🍷🍸 **1995** Medium yellow-green; the bouquet is fruit-driven with tangy citrus and melon aromas, the palate with more of those sweet melon flavours, and a faint touch of cashew; all in all, a wine with a lot of fruit character. **rating:** 90

➾ **best drinking** 1998 – 2003 **best vintages** '94, '95 **drink with** Calamari • $14

Pirramimma Petit Verdot

Petit verdot is the least known of the principal Bordeaux red varieties, and is of declining importance there, partly because of difficulties with cropping, and partly because it ripens very late in the season. There is no problem with ripening in McLaren Vale (or in most regions of Australia, for that matter) but it is even rarer here than in Bordeaux. Amazing, but in a sense typically for Pirramimma, it planted petit verdot way back in 1983, and is the source for a number of other makers in the region. To my knowledge, this is the only varietal Petit Verdot commercially marketed in Australia. The '95 won a well-deserved gold medal at the 1997 Royal Adelaide Wine Show.

🍷🍷🍷🍷🍷 **1995** Medium red-purple; the bouquet is clean and fragrant with subtle oak, with hints of cedar and tobacco. The palate is firm and fine, with dark berry fruits, and a touch of regional chocolate. The outstanding feature of the wine is its structure built around fine, long tannins. **rating:** 94

➾ **best drinking** 2000 – 2008 **best vintages** NA **drink with** Grilled lamb chops • $21.50

plantagenet ★★★★☆

Albany Highway, Mount Barker, WA 6324 **region** Great Southern

phone (08) 9851 2150 **fax** (08) 9851 1839 **open** Mon-Fri 9–5, weekends 10–4

winemaker Gavin Berry, Gordon Parker **production** 35 000 **est.** 1974

product range ($11–45 CD) Riesling, Omrah Sauvignon Blanc, Omrah Chardonnay (unoaked), Mount Barker Chardonnay, Fronti, Fine White, Fine Red, Pinot Noir, Shiraz, Henry II, Cabernet Sauvignon, Mount Barker Brut.

summary The senior winery in the Mount Barker region which is making superb wines across the full spectrum of variety and style – highly aromatic Riesling, tangy citrus-tinged Chardonnay, glorious Rhône-style Shiraz, ultra-stylish Cabernet Sauvignon and an occasional inspiring Pinot Noir.

Plantagenet Riesling

Draws upon 6.2 hectares of estate vineyards, all of which are now fully mature, and which (along with a similar amount of Cabernet Sauvignon) constitute the major estate plantings. First made in 1975, one of the flagships not only for Plantagenet but for the region as a whole. The 1995 was the top-pointed gold medal at the 1995 Mount Barker Wine Show.

🍷🍷🍷🍷 **1997** Light straw-green; a fresh, floral passionfruit and citrus bouquet is followed by a wine with abundant lime and passionfruit flavour, yet which retains elegance. Distinct regional style which you either like or dislike. **rating:** 86

➾ **best drinking** 2000 – 2007 **best vintages** '81, '83, '86, '92, '94, '95, '96 **drink with** Most Asian dishes • $14.50

Plantagenet Henry II

First made in 1993 from a blend of Merlot, Shiraz and Cabernet Sauvignon grown on the Bouverie Vineyard (estate-owned) which was planted in 1968. Matured for 18 months in predominantly new French oak barriques.

🍷🍷🍷🍷🍷 **1993** Medium to full red; a supremely elegant mix of sweet fruit and fine, gently cedary oak introduce a wine which is absolutely evocative of a ripe Bordeaux. Excellent fine-grained tannins run throughout a mix of red berry and cedar flavours, giving the wine unusually silky texture. **rating:** 93

➾ **best drinking** 1998 – 2008 **best vintages** NA **drink with** Tea-smoked lamb • $45

Plantagenet Cabernet Sauvignon

First made in 1974 (in fact at Sandalford in the Swan Valley) and has established itself as one of the West Australian classics over the intervening years. While primarily based upon estate-grown Cabernet Sauvignon, Malbec, Cabernet Franc and Merlot have all contributed to the wine over the last decade, with the core of the wine coming from the Plantagenet Bouverie Vineyard at Denbarker. The '94 was the gold medal winner at the 1996 Perth/Sheraton Wine Show.

🍷🍷🍷🍷 **1995** Medium purple-red; there is quite pronounced vanillin oak on the bouquet, with soft chocolatey/earthy fruit to follow. However, on the palate, sweet cassis and currant fruit is more evident than the bouquet suggests, finishing with delicate tannins and cedary oak. **rating:** 89

➾ **best drinking** 2000 – 2005 **best vintages** '81, '83, '85, '86, '90, '91, '94 **drink with** Rack of lamb • $26.50

platt's ★★☆

Mudgee Road, Gulgong, NSW 2852 **region** Mudgee
phone (02) 6374 1700 **fax** (02) 6372 1055 **open** 7 days 9–5
winemaker Barry Platt **production** 4000 **est.** 1983
product range ($9–12 CD) Chardonnay, Semillon, Gewurztraminer, Cabernet Sauvignon.
summary Inconsistent and often rather unhappy use of oak prevents many of the wines realising their potential.

plunkett ★★★★

Lambing Gully Road, Avenell, Vic 3664 **region** Central Victorian High Country
phone (03) 5796 2150 **fax** (03) 5796 2147 **open** 7 days 11–5
winemaker Sam Plunkett **production** 10 000 **est.** 1980
product range ($14–20 CD) The top-of-the-range wines are released under the Strathbogie Range label (Cabernet Merlot and Chardonnay); standard wines under the

Blackwood Ridge brand of Riesling, Gewurztraminer, Unwooded Chardonnay, Sauvignon Blanc Semillon, and Shiraz.
summary The Plunkett family first planted grapes way back in 1968, establishing 3 acres with 25 experimental varieties. Commercial plantings commenced in 1980, with 100 hectares now under vine. While holding a vigneron's licence since 1985, the Plunketts did not commence serious marketing of the wines until 1992, and have since produced an impressive array of wines.

pokolbin estate ★★☆

McDonalds Road, Pokolbin, NSW 2321 **region** Lower Hunter Valley
phone (02) 4998 7524 **fax** (02) 4998 7765 **open** 7 days 10–6
winemaker Contract **production** 3500 **est.** 1980
product range ($15–40 CD) Semillon, Riesling, Pokolbin Horse Coaches Verdelho, Unwooded Chardonnay, Show Reserve Chardonnay, Pinot Noir, Shiraz Merlot, Shiraz; Port.
summary An unusual outlet, offering its own-label wines made under contract by Trevor Drayton, together with the wines of Lake's Folly, Peacock Hill and Pothana, and with cheap varietal 'cleanskins'. Wine quality under the Pokolbin Estate label is very modest, although the 1997 Hunter Riesling (perversely, true Riesling, not Semillon) won a silver medal and was the top-pointed wine in its class at the 1997 Hunter Valley Wine Show.

poole's rock ★★★☆

Lot 41 Wollombi Road, Broke, NSW 2330 **region** Lower Hunter Valley
phone (02) 6579 1251 **fax** (02) 6579 1277 **open** Not
winemaker Philip Ryan (Contract) **production** 3800 **est.** 1988
product range ($20–24 R) Chardonnay.
summary Sydney merchant banker David Clarke has had a long involvement with the wine industry, ranging from his chairmanship of the Royal Sydney Wine Show Committee to partnership with Sydney retailer Andrew Simon in Wollombi Brook, through to directorship of McGuigan Brothers Limited. The 5-hectare Poole's Rock vineyard, planted purely to chardonnay, is his personal venture.

poplar bend NR

RMB 8655 Main Creek Road, Main Ridge, Vic 3928 **region** Mornington Peninsula
phone (03) 5989 6046 **fax** (03) 5989 6460 **open** Weekends and public holidays 10–5, also by appointment
winemaker David Briggs **production** 350 **est.** 1988
product range ($16–28 ML) Pineau Chloe, Cabernet Chloe, Sparkling Chloe, Pinot Noir, Cellar Reserve Pinot Noir, Cabernet Shiraz.
summary Poplar Bend was the child of Melbourne journalist, author and raconteur Keith Dunstan and wife Marie, who moved into full-scale retirement in 1997, selling Poplar Bend to David Briggs. The changes are few; the label still depicts Chloe in all her glory, which could be calculated to send the worthy inhabitants of the Bureau of Alcohol, Tobacco and Firearms (of the United States) into a state of cataleptic shock.

port phillip estate ★★★★

261 Red Hill Road, Red Hill, Vic 3937 **region** Mornington Peninsula
phone (03) 5989 2708 **fax** (03) 5989 2891 **open** Weekends and public holidays 12–5
winemaker Lindsay McCall (Contract) **production** 2500 **est.** 1987
product range ($20–28 R) Sauvignon Blanc, Chardonnay, Pinot Noir, Reserve Pinot Noir.

summary Established by leading Melbourne QC Jeffrey Sher, who, having briefly flirted with the idea of selling Port Phillip, has decided to continue – not surprising, given the quality of the wines. Lindsay McCall proves his success at Paringa Estate is no fluke; the Port Phillip wines are also excellent.

Port Phillip Estate Chardonnay

Produced from a little over 1 hectare of chardonnay planted in 1988. High natural acidity often forces Mornington Peninsula winemakers to rely on the malolactic fermentation to a considerable degree, and not always to the benefit of the wines. One of the attractions of this wine is that the malolactic characters are not overdone. The '96 is the best yet, apparently reflecting low yield.

🍷🍷🍷🍷🍸 **1996** Medium yellow-green; a wine with abundant character throughout, commencing with stylish fruit supported by strong toasty oak on the bouquet, and a quite striking palate: while having strong toasty/oaky characters, there is lovely melon and cashew fruit and equally good acidity on the finish. While big, doesn't cloy. **rating:** 93

⇨ **best drinking** 1998 – 2000 **best vintages** NA **drink with** Lobster, shellfish • $20

port stephens wines NR

69 Nelson Bay Road, Bobs Farm, NSW 2316 **region** Other Wineries of NSW
phone (02) 4982 6411 **fax** (02) 4982 6411 **open** 7 days 10–5
winemaker Wilderness Estate (Contract) **production** 3500 **est.** 1984
product range ($10–19.50 CD) Chardonnay, Tri-Blend, Tomaree White, Late Harvest, Golden Sands, Shiraz, Cabernet Merlot, Cabernet Sauvignon, Sparkling and Fortifieds.
summary Planting of the quite substantial Port Stephens Wines vineyard began in 1984, and there are now 4 hectares of vines in production. The wines are made under contract by John Baruzzi at Wilderness Estate in the Hunter Valley, but are sold through an attractive, dedicated cellar-door sales outlet on site.

portree ★★★☆

Powells Track via Mount William Road, Lancefield, Vic 3455 **region** Macedon
phone (03) 5429 1422 **fax** (03) 5429 2205 **open** Weekends and public holidays at 6 High Street, Lancefield 11–5
winemaker Ken Murchison **production** 1200 **est.** 1983
product range ($14–20 ML) Chardonnay, Greenstone, Damask (Cabernet Franc Rosé), Quarry Red (Cabernet Franc Merlot).
summary Owner Ken Murchison selected his 4-hectare Macedon vineyard after studying viticulture at Charles Sturt University and being strongly influenced by Dr Andrew Pirie's doctoral thesis. All of the wines show distinct cool-climate characteristics, the Quarry Red having distinct similarities to the wines of Chinon in the Loire Valley.

pothana NR

Carramar, Belford, NSW 2335 **region** Lower Hunter Valley
phone (02) 6574 7164 **fax** (02) 6574 7209 **open** By appointment
winemaker David Hook **production** 2000 **est.** 1984
product range Chardonnay, Semillon, Pinot Noir.
summary Principally sold through Pokolbin Estate and by mailing list; the Chardonnay is a soft, buttery/toasty wine in mainstream Hunter Valley-style.

preston peak NR

Old Wallangarra Road, Wyberba via Ballandean, Qld 4382 **region** Granite Belt
phone (07) 4639 1265 **fax** (07) 4638 1195 **open** At Wyberba Vineyard
winemaker Philippa Hambleton (Contract) **production** 3000 **est.** 1994
product range ($14–15 ML) Sauvignon Blanc, Semillon Chardonnay, Sauvignon Blanc Semillon, Shiraz, Cabernets.
summary The spectacular growth plans of dentist owners Ashley Smith and Kym Thumpkin have seemingly slowed to a more realistic level, although production has doubled over the past year. Winemaking continues at Wyberba, with the proposed winery at Toowoomba on hold.

primo estate ★★★★★

Old Port Wakefield Road, Virginia, SA 5120 **region** Adelaide Plains
phone (08) 8380 9442 **fax** (08) 8380 9696 **open** June-Sept Mon-Fri 9–5, Sat, holidays 10–4.30
winemaker Joseph Grilli, Peter Godden **production** 17 000 **est.** 1979
product range ($12–95 R) Colombard, La Magia Botrytis Riesling, Shiraz, Cabernet Merlot, Adelaide Shiraz, Joseph Moda Amarone Cabernet Merlot, Joseph Sparkling Red.
summary Roseworthy dux Joe Grilli has risen way above the constraints of the hot Adelaide Plains to produce an innovative and always excellent range of wines. The biennial release of the Joseph Sparkling Red (in its tall Italian glass bottle) is eagerly awaited, the wine immediately selling out. However, the core lies with the zingy, fresh Colombard, the velvet-smooth Adelaide Shiraz and the distinguished, complex Joseph Cabernet Merlot.

Primo Estate Colombard

Joe Grilli has always been able to conjure something quite magical from the 4.5 hectares of estate plantings of colombard. The variety is known for its capacity to hold its natural acidity in hot climates (and the Adelaide Plains are hot) but no one else seems to be able to invest the wine with the fruit freshness and crispness – almost Sauvignon Blanc-like – achieved by Joe Grilli.

🍷🍷🍷🍷 **1997** Light to medium green-yellow; the bouquet has that extra edge of vinosity which Primo Estate so often achieves; the citrus-accented palate is lively, fresh and crisp, again showing something extra on the mid-palate, before finishing pleasantly dry. **rating:** 88

➯ **best drinking** 1998 – 1999 **best vintages** NA **drink with** Oysters, shellfish • $12

Primo Estate Adelaide Shiraz

As the name suggests, produced primarily from the 2.6 hectares of 21-year-old estate plantings at the home vineyard on the Adelaide Plains. Out of this hot and unforgiving environment, Joe Grilli has fashioned a remarkably good wine, utilising open fermenters and ageing in a mix of new and older American, French and German oak puncheons.

🍷🍷🍷🍷🍸 **1995** Medium red-purple; there are quite complex aromas with spicy/leafy Shiraz offset by sweet oak. The smoothness and sophistication of the wine becomes immediately apparent on the marvellous palate, with gentle, soft mouthfilling fruit showing touches of chocolate together with the red berry fruit, surrounded by sweetly soft oak and finishing with perfectly judged tannins. **rating:** 93

➯ **best drinking** 1998 – 2003 **best vintages** '90, '92, '93, '94, '95 **drink with** Pizza • $17

Primo Estate Joseph Moda Amarone Cabernet Merlot

Although the front label does not make reference to it, the back label says 'moda amarone' – a modest claim which has brought the wrath of the Italians down on the head of Joe Grilli, and his promise to desist from using it. The wine does in fact use the amarone methods of partially drying the red grapes before fermentation. The blend varies between Coonawarra and McLaren Vale according to the vintage.

🍷🍷🍷🍷🍷 **1995** Medium to full red-purple; as always, superbly crafted, with a seamless marriage between fruit and cedary oak. The palate is concentrated with cassis/blackcurrant fruit supported by fine-grained but obvious tannins throughout. A wine which magically combines finesse with power. **rating:** 95

➯ **best drinking** 1998 – 2008 **best vintages** '81, '84, '86, '90, '91, '93, '94, '95 **drink with** Bistecca Fiorentina • $35

prince albert ★★★★

100 Lemins Road, Waurn Ponds, Vic 3221 **region** Geelong
phone (03) 5241 8091 **fax** (03) 5241 8091 **open** By appointment
winemaker Bruce Hyett **production** 500 **est.** 1975
product range ($28 R) Pinot Noir.
summary Australia's true Pinot Noir specialist (it has only ever made the one wine) which also made much of the early running with the variety: the wines always show good varietal character, and have rebounded after a dull patch in the second half of the 1980s.

providence vineyards NR

236 Lalla Road, Lalla, Tas 7267 **region** Northern Tasmania
phone (03) 6395 1290 **fax** (03) 6395 1290 **open** 7 days 10–5
winemaker Andrew Hood (Contract) **production** 1100 **est.** 1956
product range ($16–20 CD) Semillon, Chardonnay, Pinot Noir; in exceptional years may be released under the Miguet label.
summary Providence incorporates the pioneer vineyard of Frenchman Jean Miguet, now owned by the Bryce family which purchased it in 1980. The original 1.3-hectare vineyard has been expanded to a little over 3 hectares, as well as grafting over unsuitable grenache and cabernet (left from the original plantings) to chardonnay and pinot noir and semillon. Miguet in fact called the vineyard 'La Provence', reminding him of the part of France from whence he came, but after 40 years the French authorities forced a name change to Providence.

Providence Pinot Noir

The '96 was an exceptional achievement for a difficult vintage in Tasmania.

🍷🍷🍷🍷 **1996** Medium red-purple, still bright; the bouquet shows excellent varietal character with solid plummy/foresty fruit, and there is more of the same on the powerful palate. Plummy/foresty flavours are there in abundance; the texture is, perhaps, fractionally hard. **rating:** 85

➯ **best drinking** 1998 – 2002 **best vintages** NA **drink with** Tasmanian venison • $20

punters corner ★★★★

Cnr Riddoch Highway and Racecourse Road, Coonawarra, SA 5263 **region** Coonawarra
phone (08) 8737 2007 **fax** (08) 8737 2007 **open** 7 days 10–5
winemaker Balnaves (Contract) **production** 7000 **est.** 1988

product range ($12–19 ML) Riesling, Chardonnay, Shiraz, Cabernet Merlot, Cabernet Sauvignon.

summary The quaintly named Punters Corner started off life in 1975 as James Haselgrove, but in 1992 was acquired by a group of investors who quite evidently had few delusions about the uncertainties of viticulture and winemaking, even in a district as distinguished as Coonawarra. The arrival of Peter Bissell as winemaker at Balnaves has paid immediate dividends, with some quite excellent reds from 1996 and Chardonnay from 1997 the result. Sophisticated packaging and label design adds to the appeal of the wines.

Punters Corner Chardonnay

Produced from grapes grown on Punters Corner Victoria and Albert Block (more commonly known as the V & A Block) in the centre of Coonawarra. The wine is cold-settled, and then fermented in 100% new Seguin Moreau American oak hogsheads.

🍷🍷🍷🍷 **1997** Glowing yellow-green; relatively light melon and citrus fruit intermingles with gently toasty vanilla oak on the bouquet. The palate is fresh and lively, driven by melon, nectarine and citrus fruit which has literally gobbled up the oak in which it was fermented and matured. **rating:** 88

⇨ **best drinking** 1998 – 2001 **best vintages** NA **drink with** Honey prawns • $14

Punters Corner Shiraz

Sourced from both the Victoria and Albert Block and the Punters Corner Cellardoor Block, and employing sophisticated winemaking techniques. The V & A component is fermented on skins for four days, followed by barrel fermentation in new American oak, while the Cellardoor component is given extended post-fermentation maceration.

🍷🍷🍷🍷 **1996** Medium purple-red; clean, fresh cherry, spice and mint fruit aromas come through on a palate led by cherry, mint, leaf and spice flavours, finishing with soft vanillin American oak, and even softer tannins. Seductive. **rating:** 87

⇨ **best drinking** 1999 – 2003 **best vintages** NA **drink with** Mushroom risotto • $18

Punters Corner Cabernet Sauvignon

The sourcing and making of this wine is similar to the Shiraz. Part, coming from the V & A vineyard, is barrel-fermented; most comes from low-yielding old vines on the high-bank red soil on the Cellardoor Block, which is given extended maceration.

🍷🍷🍷🍷 **1996** Medium red-purple; the bouquet is spotlessly clean, with gentle red berry and cassis fruit aromas with a nice but gentle touch of oak. The palate has attractive cassis and redcurrant fruit with supple tannins; harmonious oak; adroit winemaking. **rating:** 88

⇨ **best drinking** 2000 – 2005 **best vintages** NA **drink with** Yearling beef • $16

Punters Corner Cabernet Sauvignon

While the label is a relatively new one, the vineyard is not, having been established over 25 years ago in the heart of the terra rossa region of Coonawarra.

🍷🍷🍷🍷 **1994** Medium red-purple; the bouquet has fragrant and lifted briary/earthy/leafy aromas, typical of 1994, but also reminiscent of Bordeaux. The palate has a lightness to it which suggests the inclusion of Merlot or Cabernet Franc, but the wine is in fact pure Cabernet Sauvignon. Almost delicate, it has a silky texture and a low tannin finish. **rating:** 88

⇨ **best drinking** 1998 – 2003 **best vintages** NA **drink with** Yearling veal • $16

queen adelaide ★★

Sturt Highway, Waikerie, SA 5330 **region** Barossa Valley
phone (08) 8541 2588 **fax** (08) 8541 3877 **open** Not
winemaker Nigel Logos **production** 550 000 **est.** 1858
product range ($6–8 R) A revamped product range with White Burgundy, Chablis and Claret phased out and in their place Semillon Sauvignon Blanc, Chenin Blanc and Ruby Cabernet/Cabernet Sauvignon added to the range which includes Queen Adelaide Chardonnay; Riesling and Pinot Noir complete the range.
summary The famous brand established by Woodley Wines, and some years ago subsumed into the Seppelt and now Penfolds Wine Group. It is a pure brand, without any particular home, either in terms of winemaking or fruit sources, but is hugely successful; Queen Adelaide Chardonnay is and has for some time been the largest selling bottled white wine in Australia. However, the use of agglomerate corks precludes assessment of the true quality of the wines, because of the near-certainty of lesser or greater degrees of cork taint. The move to synthetic corks cannot come too soon; all the wines tasted in January 1998 show agglomerate cork taint to a lesser or greater degree.

quelltaler ★★★★

Main North Road, Watervale, SA 5452 **region** Clare Valley
phone (08) 8843 0003 **fax** (08) 8843 0096 **open** Mon-Fri 9–5, weekends 12–4
winemaker David O'Leary **production** 50 000 **est.** 1856
product range ($12–20 CD) Annie's Lane Riesling, Semillon, Chardonnay, Shiraz and Cabernet Merlot; Polish Hill River Vineyard Riesling, Carlsfield Vineyard Riesling, Prospect Vineyard Riesling.
summary The wheel has turned full circle, and after some regrettable decisions to progressively change the name of Quelltaler to Eaglehawk Estate and Black Opal, this great legacy of the nineteenth century once again proudly bears the Quelltaler name. The Eaglehawk brand continues, but is made at Wolf Blass in the Barossa Valley, and has a southeastern Australia origin; Black Opal is made, but only for export; Quelltaler as a brand name is, at least for the time being, in suspense; and the Clare Valley portfolio made at Quelltaler is sold under the Annie's Lane label. The name comes from Annie Weyman, a turn-of-the-century local identity.

Annie's Lane Riesling

Produced from a blend of Watervale and Polish Hill-grown grapes. Notwithstanding the emergence of three Quelltaler single vineyard Rieslings from the '97 vintage, Annie's Lane Riesling was good enough to gain the top gold medal in Class 1 at the 1997 Royal Adelaide Wine Show.

🍷🍷🍷🍷🍷 **1997** Medium to full yellow-green; a solid, rich bouquet with a mix of lime, pastille and a hint of spice. The palate is powerful, with some toasty characters which will grow with age; a well judged touch of sugar on the finish.
rating: 90

➾ **best drinking** 1998 – 2003 **best vintages** '96, '97 **drink with** Asparagus • $13

Carlsfield Vineyard Riesling

Carlsfield Vineyard was planted in 1935 on a sweeping hillside of red loam over limestone. The vineyard is situated just to the southeast of the Quelltaler winery at an elevation of 470 metres. The Riesling is the celebration Geisenheim clone.

🍷🍷🍷🍷🍷 **1997** Light to medium yellow-green; the bouquet is quite rich with lime and tropical fruit aromas, almost into peach. The rich palate is balanced by good acidity and held together by excellent structure; while unashamedly generous, it is not phenolic. **rating:** 92

➯ **best drinking** 1999 – 2006 **best vintages** NA **drink with** Eggplant terrine • $15

Polish Hill River Vineyard Riesling

The vineyard was planted in 1979 (by Wolf Blass) on a site of clay loam over the classic Polish Hill River slate. It matures several weeks later than the Watervale vineyards, and in classic Polish Hill River style, produces a tight, more restrained wine which has the capacity to age wonderfully.

🍷🍷🍷🍷🍷 **1997** Light to medium yellow-green; a complex bouquet with sweet lime, mineral and hints of honey all intermingling leads into a long and intense palate with toasty/mineral undertones to lime fruit; very well structured, and a died-in-the-wool stayer. **rating:** 92

➯ **best drinking** 2000 – 2010 **best vintages** NA **drink with** Grilled sardines • $15

Prospect Vineyard Riesling

The Prospect Vineyard is situated across the road from the Quelltaler winery on similar red soil over limestone to that of Carlsfield. At a slightly lower elevation, it is the earliest-ripening of the three vineyards.

🍷🍷🍷🍷🍷 **1997** Light to medium yellow-green; a classically restrained, almost delicate, lime and toast bouquet, and a very pure wine on the palate, intense, yet not the least bit heavy. Herb and fine lime/lemon fruit is followed by a dry, crisp finish. **rating:** 91

➯ **best drinking** 1999 – 2009 **best vintages** NA **drink with** Fresh asparagus • $15

Annie's Lane Shiraz

Comes from predominantly old vines on both the Annie's Lane Vineyard in Polish Hill as well as from contract growers throughout the Clare Valley. Fermented in small 4-tonne open fermenters, and matured in a mix of French and American oak hogsheads for 20 months. As with all the Annie's Lane wines, a consistent show winner, and a testimonial to the skills of winemaker David O'Leary.

🍷🍷🍷🍷 **1996** Medium to full red-purple; smooth, rich dark berry and dark chocolate fruit is balanced by oak on the bouquet; a big, rich cherry-ripe and mint style on the palate, with soft tannins and unintrusive oak. **rating:** 85

➯ **best drinking** 2000 – 2006 **best vintages** '94 **drink with** Pepper steak • $15

Annie's Lane Cabernet Merlot

A blend of 85% Cabernet Sauvignon and 15% Merlot, the Cabernet Sauvignon coming in part from Annie's Lane Vineyard in Polish Hill and from other Clare Valley growers, the Merlot component from the Quelltaler Estate vineyard. Fermented in small 4-tonne open fermenters, then matured in French oak (20% new) for a period of 15 months.

🍷🍷🍷🍷 **1996** Medium to full red-purple; the bouquet is inky, almost murky, loaded with blackcurrant/cassis and vanillin oak. The palate is similarly youthful and dense, with strong mint, heaps of blackcurrant, lots of oak and appropriate tannins. Just give it time. **rating:** 87

➯ **best drinking** 2003 – 2013 **best vintages** '94, '95 **drink with** Illabo spring lamb • $15

raleigh winery NR

Queen Street, Raleigh, NSW 2454 **region** Other Wineries of NSW
phone (02) 6655 4388 **fax** (02) 6655 4265 **open** 7 days 10–5
winemaker Lavinia Dingle **production** 1600 **est.** 1982
product range ($13 CD) Semillon Chardonnay, Traminer Riesling, Rouge (Rosé), Shiraz Cabernet Merlot, Port.
summary Raleigh Winery lays claim to being Australia's most easterly vineyard. The vineyard was initiated in 1982, and purchased by Lavinia and Neil Dingle in 1989, with the wine produced in part from 1 hectare of vines planted to no less than six varieties. The wines have won bronze medals at the Griffith Wine Show.

ravenswood lane vineyard NR

Ravenswood Lane, Hahndorf, SA 5245 **region** Adelaide Hills
phone (08) 8388 1250 **open** Not
winemaker Hardys (Contract) **production** 1000 **est.** 1993
product range ($20–40 ML) The Gathering Sauvignon Blanc, Chardonnay, Reunion Shiraz.
summary With a sales and marketing background, John and Helen Edwards opted for a major lifestyle change when they established the first of 13 hectares of vineyards in 1993. Most of the production is sold to Hardys, which makes a small quantity of high-quality wines for sale under the Ravenswood Lane Label.

Ravenswood Lane Chardonnay

Complex winemaking techniques and what is obviously a very promising vineyard have produced a spectacular first wine, one of only two gold medals in the strong Chardonnay Class at the 1997 Adelaide Hills Wine Show.

🍷🍷🍷🍷🍷 **1997** Light to medium yellow-green; a stylish bouquet with strong toasty oak and nutty malolactic fermentation influences are largely mirrored on the palate, where barrel fermentation and malolactic fermentation both make a very strong statement. **rating:** 93

➪ **best drinking** 1998 – 2000 **best vintages** NA **drink with** Wiener schnitzel • $40

Ravenswood Lane Reunion Shiraz

A striking first-up red, with the Hardy winemaking stamp firmly on it, but also with some fruit characters reminiscent of the extreme southern end of the Napa Valley around a little town called Coombsville. The aroma and flavour is quite unique, and I have only encountered it once or twice before.

🍷🍷🍷🍷 **1996** Strong red-purple; powerful fruit on the bouquet is supported by strong charry toasty oak. The vibrant, youthful and juicy palate has lantana-like overtones, running into exotic oriental fruits. Unconventional but very interesting. **rating:** 87

➪ **best drinking** 2000 – 2005 **best vintages** NA **drink with** Highly spiced red meat • $40

ray-monde NR

250 Dalrymple Road, Sunbury, Vic 3429 **region** Sunbury
phone (03) 5428 2657 **fax** (03) 5428 3390 **open** Sundays or by appointment
winemaker John Lakey **production** 770 **est.** 1988
product range ($25 CD) Pinot Noir.

summary The Lakey family has established a little under 4 hectares of pinot noir on their 230-hectare grazing property at an altitude of 400 metres. Initially the grapes were sold to Domaine Chandon, but in 1994 son John Lakey (who had gained experience at Tarrawarra, Rochford, Virgin Hills, Coonawarra plus a vintage in Burgundy) commenced making the wine – and very competently.

Ray-Monde Pinot Noir

Made using what John Lakey describes as 'low technology', with open fermenters, hand-plunging, and ageing in French oak, part new, most first and second use.

🍷🍷🍷🍷 **1996** Medium red-purple; the bouquet is fragrant, with some slippery, almost citrussy overtones to the plum, berry and mint aromas of the bouquet. The palate has distinctive style and feel, lively and tingling, with plum, cherry and mint flavours. Just made it over the edge of ripeness. **rating:** 85

⇨ **best drinking** 1998 – 2001 **best vintages** NA **drink with** Grilled Tasmanian salmon • $24.80

---

reads ★★

Evans Lane, Oxley, Vic 3678 **region** King Valley
phone (03) 5727 3386 **fax** (03) 5727 3559 **open** Mon-Sat 9–5, Sun 10–6
winemaker Kenneth Read **production** 1900 **est.** 1972
product range ($7.50–13 CD) Riesling, Chardonnay, Sauvignon Blanc, Crouchen, Cabernet Shiraz, Cabernet Sauvignon, Port.
summary Limited tastings have not impressed, but there may be a jewel lurking somewhere, such as the medal-winning though long-gone 1990 Sauvignon Blanc.

red hill estate ★★★☆

53 Redhill-Shoreham Road, Red Hill South, Vic 3937 **region** Mornington Peninsula
phone (03) 5989 2838 **fax** (03) 5989 2855 **open** 7 days 11–5
winemaker Jenny Bright **production** 6000 **est.** 1989
product range ($18–28 R) Particular emphasis on Méthode Champenoise, but also producing Waterholes Creek Bass Blend (Unwooded Chardonnay and Sauvignon Blanc), Chardonnay, Waterholes Creek Muscat, Pinot Noir, Waterholes Creek Cabernet, Cabernet Sauvignon and Merlot, with Muscat (from Rutherglen material) available cellar door only.
summary Sir Peter Derham and family completed the construction of an on-site winery in time for the 1993 vintage, ending a period in which the wines were made at various wineries under contract arrangements. The 8-hectare vineyard is one of the larger plantings on the Mornington Peninsula, and the newly opened tasting room and restaurant have a superb view across the vineyard to Westernport Bay and Phillip Island.

redbank winery ★★★★

Sunraysia Highway, Redbank, Vic 3467 **region** Pyrenees
phone (03) 5467 7255 **fax** (03) 5467 7248 **open** Mon-Sat 9–5, Sun 10–5
winemaker Neill Robb **production** 58 000 **est.** 1973
product range ($9.90–66 CD) The range centres on a series of evocatively named red wines, with Sally's Paddock the flagship, followed by Cabernet Sauvignon and Cabernet Franc; then Hard Hill Cabernet Sauvignon, Fighting Flat Shiraz and Spud Gully Pinot; and various specialties available cellar door. Long Paddock Shiraz, Long Paddock Chardonnay and Emily Brut are cheaper, larger-volume second labels.

summary Neill Robb makes very concentrated wines, full of character; the levels of volatile acidity can sometimes be intrusive, but are probably of more concern to technical tasters than to the general public. Sally's Paddock is the star, a single vineyard block with an esoteric mix of Cabernet, Shiraz and Malbec and which over the years has produced many great wines.

redgate ★★★☆

Boodjidup Road, Margaret River, WA 6285 **region** Margaret River
phone (08) 9757 6488 **fax** (08) 9757 6308 **open** 7 days 10–5
winemaker Andrew Forsell **production** 8000 **est.** 1977
product range ($14–26 CD) Classic Semillon OFS Semillon, Sauvignon Blanc, Sauvignon Blanc Reserve, Chenin, Late Harvest Riesling, Cabernet Sauvignon, Pinot Noir Méthode Champenoise, Port.
summary Twenty hectares of vineyard provide the base for one of the larger wineries of the Margaret River region which probably has a lower profile than it deserves.

redman ★★★

Riccoch Highway, Coonawarra, SA 5253 **region** Coonawarra
phone (08) 8736 3331 **fax** (08) 8736 3013 **open** Mon-Fri 9–5, weekends 10–4
winemaker Bruce Redman, Malcolm Redman **production** 18 000 **est.** 1966
product range ($13–25 R) Shiraz (formerly labelled as Claret), Cabernet Merlot (the first new wine in 26 years), Cabernet Sauvignon.
summary After a prolonged period of mediocrity, the Redman wines are showing distinct signs of improvement, partly through the introduction of modest amounts of new oak, even if principally American. It would be nice to say the wines now reflect the full potential of the vineyard, but there is still some way to go.

Redman Cabernet Merlot

Introduced into the Redman range in the early 1990s, and since that time has been one of the few bright lights in the Redman stable. The '95 continues the good form of preceding years, notwithstanding the difficulties Coonawarra presented that year.

🍷🍷🍷🍷 **1995** Medium red-purple; the bouquet is clean, quite intense, with sweet red berry and earth fruit supported by a nice touch of charry oak. The palate too shows lots of sweet redcurrant, raspberry and minty fruit with soft tannins and nicely judged charry vanilla oak. **rating:** 85

➪ **best drinking** 1999 – 2005 **best vintages** '93, '94 **drink with** Shoulder of lamb • $25

reg drayton wines ★★★☆

Cnr Pokolbin Mountain Road and McDonalds Road, Pokolbin, NSW 2321 **region** Lower Hunter Valley
phone (02) 4998 7523 **fax** (02) 4998 7523 **open** Fri-Mon and public holidays 10–5
winemaker Tyrrell's (Contract) **production** 3000 **est.** 1989
product range ($15–25 CD) Lambkin Semillon, Pokolbin Hills Chardonnay, Pokolbin Hills Chardonnay Semillon, Pokolbin Hills Shiraz Cabernet, Port.
summary Reg and Pam Drayton were among the victims of the Seaview/Lord Howe Island air crash in October 1984, having established Reg Drayton Wines after selling their interest in the long-established Drayton Family Winery. Their daughter Robyn (a fifth-generation Drayton, and billed as the Hunter's first female vigneron) and husband Craig continue the business, which draws chiefly upon the Pokolbin Hills Estate, but also takes fruit from the historic Lambkin Estate vineyard. The wines are made for them at Tyrrell's.

Reg Drayton Lambkin Semillon

By far the greatest part of Drayton's Lambkin Estate is planted to semillon, with over 11 hectares under vine on the basically sandy alluvial soils so well suited to the variety. Unsurprisingly, this is Reg Drayton's best white wine.

YYYY **1997** Medium yellow-green; the bouquet is clean and smooth, with a mix of lemon/mineral and some sweeter notes of moderate intensity. A solidly structured wine, with good depth and length, and which will develop nicely over the medium term. **rating:** 86

➯ **best drinking** 2000 – 2007 **best vintages** NA **drink with** Salmon roulade • $17

Reg Drayton Pokolbin Hills Chardonnay

While the Pokolbin Hills Estate was first planted in 1970 (with 8.4 hectares of semillon) the chardonnay was not planted until 1988, when 1.8 hectares were established. Like the Chardonnay Semillon, a medal winner in every vintage since 1993, the first vintage of the wine.

YYYY **1997** Medium yellow-green; complex tangy melon and citrus fruit with well-handled oak on the bouquet; the palate shows more of the same, with attractive tangy fruit, and an ever so gently charry oak tang to the finish. **rating:** 89

➯ **best drinking** 1998 – 1999 **best vintages** NA **drink with** Ravioli • $17

reilly's cottage NR

Cnr Hill and Burra Streets, Mintaro, SA 5415 **region** Clare Valley
phone (08) 8843 9013 **fax** (08) 8337 4111 **open** 7 days 10–5
winemaker Justin Ardill **production** 4000 **est.** 1994
product range ($12.50–25 CD) Watervale Riesling, Late Picked Riesling, Sparkling Grenache, Old Bushvine Grenache, Clare Valley Shiraz, Dry Land Shiraz, Cabernet Sauvignon, Port.
summary Justin and Julie Ardill are the newest arrivals in the Clare Valley, with just a handful of vintages under their belt. An unusual sideline of Reilly's Cottage is the production of an Extra Virgin Olive Oil; unusual in that it is made from wild olives found in the Mintaro district of the Clare Valley.

reilly's creek ★★★

226A Lower White Hills Road, Relbia, Tas 7258 **region** Northern Tasmania
phone (03) 6391 8974 **open** Not
winemaker Andrew Hood (Contract) **production** 100 **est.** 1995
product range ($16 ML) Riesling, Pinot Noir.
summary Reilly's Creek is the label for Relbia Vineyards, which sells most of its grapes to contract winemaker Andrew Hood. Small quantities are made for it by Hood and, as one would expect, are of good quality.

renmano 

Sturt Highway, Renmark, SA 5341 **region** Riverland
phone (08) 8586 6771 **fax** (08) 8586 5939 **open** Mon–Sat 9–5
winemaker Frank Neuman, Glenn James, Tony Angle **production** 1.6 million **est.** 1914
product range ($9.95 R) Chairman's Selection Chardonnay; River Breeze is a second label.
summary Part of the BRL Hardy group. A radical change in winemaking technique and philosophy in 1996 has wrought miracles with the Chairman's Selection Chardonnay, now the only premium wine under the Renmano label.

reynell ★★★★☆

Reynella Road, Reynella, SA 5161 **region** McLaren Vale
phone (08) 8392 2222 **fax** (08) 8392 2202 **open** 7 days 10–4.30
winemaker Stephen Pannell (Red), Tom Newton (White) **production** NFP **est.** 1838
product range ($36.90 R) Basket Pressed Shiraz, Basket Pressed Merlot, Basket Pressed Cabernet Sauvignon.

summary Reynell is the name under which all future wines from the historic Reynella winery (once called Chateau Reynella) will be released. What is more, the range of wines has been compressed, and taken into the super-premium category with the initial release in July 1997 of three multi award-winning wines, all effectively Show Reserve releases.

Reynell Basket Pressed Shiraz

The initial release of this wine (the '94) had won seven gold medals prior to its release, and is the type of wine which will continue to amass gold medals so long as it is exhibited in wine shows. Hugely powerful and concentrated, it was matured in American oak for 24 months. Initially that oak is married well with the wine but does gradually build-up on retasting, and ultimately threatens the balance of the wine. Those more tolerant of the flavour of American oak will find no problem with it, however.

🍷🍷🍷🍷 **1994** Full purple-red; the bouquet is complex and distinguished, at once powerful yet elegant, with vanilla oak to the fore, but spice, earth and boot-polish varietal fruit are there in strong support. The palate initially shows many of the same characteristics, but the oak becomes steadily more aggressive as the wine sits in the glass and is retasted. **rating:** 88

➪ **best drinking** 2000 – 2010 **best vintages** '94 **drink with** Barbecued rump steak • $36.90

Reynell Basket Pressed Merlot

This wine will not be produced every year (none was in fact made in 1995) but the quality of the inaugural 1994 vintage was such that it demanded to be kept as a single varietal wine. It was matured in a mix of new and one-year-old French oak barriques for two years and possesses a depth and richness of flavour seldom encountered in Australian Merlots. Only 1500 cases were made.

🍷🍷🍷🍷🍷 **1994** Full red-purple; there is an extraordinary array of aromas on the bouquet, running through leather, leaf, spice and earth, with vaguely medicinal overtones. No less impressive is the structure and texture on the palate, with almost tangy, lingering tannins providing grip without ferocity. Upholstered by lushly sweet fruit. **rating:** 94

➪ **best drinking** 1998 – 2006 **best vintages** '94 **drink with** Baked ox kidney • $36.90

Reynell Basket Pressed Cabernet Sauvignon

After a formidable, indeed intimidating, '94 comes a much more approachable '95; like the '94, given prolonged oak ageing.

🍷🍷🍷🍷🍷 **1995** Full red-purple; an excellent, unforced bouquet with very good varietal character and subtle oak; on the palate there is a touch of mint to go along with the cassis berry fruit, soft oak and supple tannins. **rating:** 93

➪ **best drinking** 2000 – 2008 **best vintages** '94, '95 **drink with** Leave it in the cellar • $36.90

---

reynolds yarraman ★★★★

Yarraman Road, Wybong, NSW 2333 **region** Upper Hunter Valley
phone (02) 6547 8127 **fax** (02) 6547 8013 **open** Mon-Sat 10–4, Sun, public holidays 11–4
winemaker Jon Reynolds **production** 12 000 **est.** 1967
product range ($15–21 CD) From the Hunter Valley: Semillon, Chardonnay, Shiraz; from Orange: Chardonnay, Cabernet Sauvignon; Cabernet Merlot is a blend from both the Hunter Valley and Orange.
summary With the Orange region steadily assuming greater importance for Reynolds Yarraman, wine quality (and consistency) likewise continues to increase, although the Semillons will of course remain Hunter Valley-sourced. The skills of Jon Reynolds as a winemaker have never been in doubt, and as the size and maturity of the Orange vineyards grow, it seems certain that even better wines will appear in the future.

Reynolds Yarraman Hunter Valley Semillon

Made entirely from estate-grown grapes from the Yarraman Vineyard picked at a relatively high baumé (for Semillon) of 12.5 degrees, tank fermented and given extended lees contact.
🍷🍷🍷🍸 **1997** Medium to full yellow-green; a rich, full and complex bouquet marked by some tropical honeyed fruit is reflected in a rich, powerful full-on palate, utterly unexpected from the '97 vintage. Perhaps a fraction thick, but ... **rating:** 84

➾ **best drinking** 1998 – 1999 **best vintages** '91, '92, '96 **drink with** Mussels • $15

Reynolds Yarraman Orange Chardonnay

The two most distinguished wines in the Reynolds portfolio now come not from the Upper Hunter but from Orange, whence Jon Reynolds has sourced increasing amounts of fruit over the recent years. This is in fact the first 100% Orange district wine made by Jon Reynolds; barrel-fermented in French oak, with the full range of malolactic fermentation and lees contact. It comes from the Bloodwood and Bantry Grove vineyards.
🍷🍷🍷🍸 **1996** Medium yellow-green; restrained peach and melon, with mineral hints and subtle oak aromas are followed by a lively wine with a pleasant array of melon, citrus and peach flavours. Once again, the oak is subtle. **rating:** 84

➾ **best drinking** 1998 – 2000 **best vintages** NA **drink with** Sautéed veal • $19

Reynolds Yarraman Shiraz

A powerful, concentrated and strongly structured wine which really defies much of the reputation of the Upper Hunter Valley. Reynolds is consistently producing Shiraz with good concentration and flavour.
🍷🍷🍷🍸 **1996** Medium red; the clean and smooth bouquet of dark chocolate and earth is of moderate intensity. The palate is quite substantial, well composed, with attractive cedar/vanilla oak together with cherry, chocolate and earthy fruit. **rating:** 83

➾ **best drinking** 1999 – 2004 **best vintages** '94, '96 **drink with** Barbecued beef • $18

Reynolds Yarraman Orange Cabernet Sauvignon

Make no mistake about it, Orange is a cool region. This means site selection for the later-ripening varieties is important, and also that vintage conditions will be of greater than usual importance. Not everything went right in 1995, but it certainly did in 1996.

1996 Medium red-purple; the bouquet is distinctly riper than the '95, with attractive sweet cassis fruit which comes through on the equally attractive palate. Cassis, cedar and fine but lingering tannins all go to make an elegant, delicious wine. **rating:** 90

⇨ **best drinking** 2000 – 2005 **best vintages** '96 **drink with** Beef stroganoff • $21

ribbon vale estate ★★★☆

Lot 5 Caves Road, Willyabrup via Cowaramup, WA 6284 **region** Margaret River
phone (08) 9755 6272 **fax** (08) 9755 6337 **open** Weekends, holidays 10–5
winemaker Mike Davies **production** 4000 **est.** 1977
product range ($15–17 CD) Semillon, Semillon Sauvignon Blanc, Sauvignon Blanc, Cabernet Merlot, Merlot, Cabernet Sauvignon.
summary When in form, Ribbon Vale Estate makes crisp, herbaceous Semillon and Sauvignon Blanc (and blends), ideal seafood wines, and austere, very firm Cabernets, all in mainstream regional-style.

Ribbon Vale Sauvignon Blanc

Unoaked, but picked ripe from vines which are 15 years old.

1997 Dull straw colour; unexpectedly, the bouquet has lots of character with rich gooseberry/tropical varietal aroma. The palate, too, has abundant, soft tropical/gooseberry fruit, softening slightly on the finish. Would have received higher points were it not for the colour; the other '97 whites from Ribbon Vale suffer even more from this problem. **rating:** 86

⇨ **best drinking** 1998 – 1999 **best vintages** NA **drink with** Avocado and seafood salad • NA

Ribbon Vale Cabernet Sauvignon

Made from 100% Cabernet Sauvignon; a Cabernet Merlot is also made. Like the Sauvignon Blanc, produced from fully mature, low-yielding vines.

1995 Medium to full red-purple; the bouquet is quite ripe, with sweet, clean chocolatey/berry fruit and soft oak. The palate is powerful but well balanced, with blackberry, chocolate and earthy fruit. **rating:** 85

⇨ **best drinking** 2000 – 2005 **best vintages** NA **drink with** Ragout of beef • NA

richard hamilton

Willunga Vineyards, Main Road, Willunga, SA 5172 **region** McLaren Vale
phone (08) 8556 2288 **fax** (08) 8556 2868 **open** 7 days 10–5
winemaker Ralph Fowler **production** 28 000 **est.** 1972
product range ($12–45 R) Synergy Dry White, Natural Chardonnay, Chenin Semillon, Cabernet Merlot; Richard Hamilton Chenin Blanc, Muscat Blanc, McLaren Vale Shiraz, Hut Block Cabernet Sauvignon, Merlot; Hamilton Ewell Reserve Marion Vineyard Grenache Shiraz, Reserve Merlot, Old Vines Shiraz; Burtons Vineyard Old Bush Vine Grenache Shiraz is premium release.
summary The quality and character of the Richard Hamilton wines have grown in leaps and bounds over the past five years or so, no doubt due to the skills of winemaker Ralph Fowler and support from owner Dr Richard Hamilton. The wines are boldly styled, full of flavour and character.

Richard Hamilton Hamilton Ewell Reserve Old Vines Shiraz

As the name suggests, the wine is made from vines dating back more than a century, located at the southern fringe of McLaren Vale. First made in 1990, with a minor label change in 1996 through the addition of the word 'Reserve'. A wine which varies in weight and style according to the vintage, but is seldom less than very good.

🍷🍷🍷🍷🍷 **1996** Strong purple-red; the bouquet is complex, with ripe earthy, berry fruits supported by positive oak. An enormously powerful, rich and concentrated wine on the palate, with briary/dark berry fruit and formidable tannins. **rating:** 91

⇨ **best drinking** 2002 – 2010 **best vintages** '90, '91, '92, '93, '96 **drink with** Casserole of venison • $29.95

Richard Hamilton McLaren Vale Shiraz

Introduced in 1996 to sit underneath the Hamilton Ewell Reserve Old Vines Shiraz.

🍷🍷🍷🍷 **1996** Vivid purple-red; concentrated juicy berry fruit on the bouquet leads into a lusciously ripe palate with blackberry and black cherry flavours supported by subtle oak and slightly furry tannins on the finish. **rating:** 87

⇨ **best drinking** 2000 – 2005 **best vintages** NA **drink with** Devilled kidneys • $17.95

Richard Hamilton Hut Block Cabernet Sauvignon

The original vines of the Hut Block were planted by Richard Hamilton's father, Burton Hamilton, in 1947.

🍷🍷🍷🍷 **1996** Medium purple-red; strong berry and earth fruit drives the bouquet, and similarly concentrated rich and juicy berry fruit dominates the palate. Seems slightly underworked. **rating:** 84

⇨ **best drinking** 1998 – 2003 **best vintages** '86, '90, '91, '93 **drink with** Beef Provençale • $17.95

richfield vineyard NR

Bruxner Highway, Tenterfield, NSW 2372 **region** Other Wineries of NSW
phone (02) 6737 5588 **fax** (02) 6737 5598 **open** Not
winemaker Contract **production** NA **est.** 1997
product range Chardonnay, Shiraz, Merlot, Cabernet Sauvignon, with the first release unlikely before the end of the decade.
summary Richfield Vineyard points to the tyranny of State boundaries. Established at the instigation of Denis Parsons of Bald Mountain vineyards in the Granite Belt [of Queensland], Richfield is little more than 30 kilometres south of Bald Mountain vineyards as the crow flies. A little over 11 hectares were planted in 1997, with plans to at least double those plantings in 1998. All of the indications are that the Tenterfield–Granite Belt area will become a very significant cross-border wine growing region.

richmond grove ★★★★

Para Road, Tanunda, SA 5352 **region** Barossa Valley
phone (08) 8563 2184 **fax** (08) 8563 2804 **open** Mon–Fri 10–5, weekends 10–4
winemaker John Vickery **production** NFP **est.** 1977

product range ($8.95–12.95 R) Eden Valley Traminer Riesling, Watervale Riesling, Barossa Riesling, Oak Matured Chablis, Cowra Chardonnay, Cowra Verdelho, French Cask Chardonnay, Hunter Valley Classic Dry White, Marlborough Sauvignon Blanc, Barossa Shiraz, Cabernet Merlot.
summary Richmond Grove now has two homes, including one in the Barossa Valley, where John Vickery presides. It is owned by Orlando Wyndham, and draws its grapes from diverse sources. The Richmond Grove Barossa Valley and Watervale Rieslings made by John Vickery represent the best value for money (for Riesling) year in, year out. If these were the only wines produced by Richmond Grove, it would have five-star rating.

Richmond Grove Barossa Riesling

A twin to the Watervale Riesling, likewise made by John Vickery, and a supremely honest wine offering plenty of flavour from a young age. The '97 and '95 vintages respectively provided a unique double in winning the only two gold medals in Class 30 at the 1997 Royal Adelaide Wine Show.

🍷🍷🍷🍷🍷 **1996** Medium yellow-green; spotlessly clean, with the first signs of honey developing, but with good concentration. A seductive palate with ripe lime, citrus and honey fruit flavours, and excellent mouthfeel. Showing none of the flatness expected from Riesling in transition. **rating:** 94

⇨ **best drinking** 1998 – 2010 **best vintages** '94, '95, '96, '97 **drink with** Pasta, white meat dishes • $12.95

Richmond Grove Watervale Riesling

With John Vickery's vast experience and impeccable contacts, it is not surprising that Richmond Grove Rieslings should be as exceptionally good as they are.

🍷🍷🍷🍷🍷 **1997** Light to medium yellow-green; a spotlessly clean and powerful bouquet with predominantly citrus/lime fruit, and just a hint of tropical sweetness. The palate unfolds progressively, with a steely core around which pristine varietal fruit flavours are folded. Has all the indications of becoming a great classic. **rating:** 94

⇨ **best drinking** 1998 – 2017 **best vintages** '94, '96, '97 **drink with** Asparagus with hollandaise sauce • $12.95

---

rimfire vineyards ★★★☆

Bismarck Street, MacLagan, Qld 4352 **region** Other Wineries of Qld
phone (07) 4692 1129 **fax** (07) 4692 1260 **open** 7 days 10–5
winemaker Bruce Humphery-Smith (Consultant), Tony Connellan **production** 5000
est. 1991
product range ($9–16 CD) Verdelho, Semillon Chardonnay, Chardonnay, Colombard, Homestead Classic White, Pioneer White, Shiraz, Colonial Cabernet, Light Fruity Red; Fortifieds.
summary The Connellan family (parents Margaret and Tony and children Michelle, Peter and Louise) began planting the 6-hectare Rimfire Vineyards in 1991 as a means of diversification of their very large (1500-hectare) cattle stud in the foothills of the Bunya Mountains, 45 minutes drive northeast of Toowoomba. Rimfire has had one success after another in Queensland wine shows, and on this yardstick has to be regarded as the best producer in Queensland.

Rimfire Chardonnay

Estate-grown, and, barrel-fermented in new French oak, this wine has led the way for Rimfire since its debut in 1996, winning the Courier-Mail/Sheraton Wine Award for Best Queensland

Dry White Wine, and moving to even greater heights with the 1997, which won the first-ever gold medal for a Queensland wine in the Australian Small Winemakers Show.

1997 Medium yellow-green; fine, melon and fig fruit on the bouquet is supported by just a touch of oak, less assertively so than the '96 was. The palate, too, is elegant and fine, with melon, citrus and fig fruit, good length and attractively subtle oak. **rating:** 90

⇨ **best drinking** 1998 – 1999 **best vintages** '96, '97 **drink with** Rack of veal • $13

rivendell 

Lot 328 Wildwood Road, Yallingup, WA 6282 **region** Margaret River
phone (08) 9755 2235 **fax** (08) 9755 2295 **open** 7 days 10–5
winemaker Mike Davies, Jan Davies (Contract) **production** 2750 **est.** 1987
product range ($12.50–14.50 CD) Semillon Sauvignon Blanc, Honeysuckle Late Harvest Semillon, Verdelho, Shiraz Cabernet.

summary With 13.5 hectares of vineyards coming into bearing, production for Rivendell will increase significantly over the coming years. The cellar-door sales facility is in a garden-setting complete with restaurant. An unusual sideline is the sale of 50 types of preserves, jams and chutneys. No recent tastings.

Rivendell Verdelho

Verdelho was the first wine released, and has consistently shown good varietal character and flavour.

1997 Medium to full yellow-green; the bouquet is quite striking, with complex, ripe fruit salad aromas but the palate, while clean and well balanced, lacks the exotic characters of the bouquet. A worthy wine, nonetheless. **rating:** 84

⇨ **best drinking** 1998 – 1999 **best vintages** NA **drink with** Parma ham with figs • $12.50

riverbank estate NR

126 Hamersley Road, Caversham, WA 6055 **region** Swan District
phone (08) 9377 1805 **fax** (08) 9377 2168 **open** Weekends and public holidays 10–5
winemaker Robert James Bond **production** 3500 **est.** 1993
product range ($12–16 CD) Semillon, Verdelho, Chenin, Chardonnay, Cabernet.

summary Robert Bond, a graduate of Charles Sturt University and Swan Valley viticulturist for 20 years, established RiverBank Estate in 1993. He draws upon 11 hectares of estate plantings, and, in his words, 'the wines are unashamedly full-bodied, produced from ripe grapes in what is recognised as a hot grape growing region'.

riverina wines 

Farm 1305 Hillston Road, Tharbogang via Griffith, NSW 2680 **region** Riverina
phone (02) 6962 4122 **fax** (02) 6962 4628 **open** 7 days 9–5.30
winemaker Sam Trimboli **production** 150 000 **est.** 1969
product range ($4.50–12 CD) An extensive range of varietal wines under the Ballingal Estate Cooper County, Ridgewood and Warburn Estate labels, the former being slightly higher priced, each including Chardonnay, Semillon, Semillon Chardonnay, Shiraz, Cabernet Sauvignon and Cabernet Merlot, with a few additions under the Ballingal Estate label. There is also a range of sparkling wines and fortifieds in both bottle and cask.

summary One of the large producers of the region drawing upon 1100 hectares of estate plantings. While much of the wine is sold in bulk to other producers, selected parcels of the best of the grapes are made into table wines with quite spectacular success. At the 1997 National Wine Show, Riverina Wines won an astonishing six gold medals, topping no less than four classes, and – on one view of the matter, anyway – being unlucky not to win more than one trophy. The medals were spread across the full range of wine from Semillon to Merlot to Cabernet Sauvignon.

Riverina Ballingal Semillon

In an almost embarrassing display, another wine to top its class (4.5 points clear of the next nearest wine, as was the case for the Semillon Chardonnay) at the 1997 Liquorland National Wine Show.

🍷🍷🍷🍷 **1997** Medium to full yellow-green; a complex, powerful and already quite developed bouquet with subtle oak supporting the fruit. There is plenty of ripe varietal flavour in a lemony spectrum balanced by a hint of sweetness which may come from fruit or a well-judged flick of residual sugar. Best now. **rating:** 89

➯ **best drinking** 1998 – 1999 **best vintages** NA **drink with** Pasta marinara • $10

Riverina Ridgewood Semillon Chardonnay

Part of the Riverina Wines juggernaut at the 1997 Liquorland National Wine Show, winning the only gold medal in (the relatively small) Class 6.

🍷🍷🍷🍷½ **1997** Extremely sophisticated winemaking evident, with a seamless marriage of fruit and oak in a wine with considerable power and length. Was 4.5 points clear of the next highest pointed wine in the class. **rating:** 90

➯ **best drinking** 1998 – 1999 **best vintages** NA **drink with** Roast chicken • $10

Riverina Ballingal Estate Premium Selection Chardonnay

Produced from estate-grown grapes, and yet another gold medal winner for Riverina Wines at the 1997 Liquorland National Wine Show. What is more, it was the second highest pointed wine in the largest class in the show, 120 of the country's best 1996 Chardonnays.

🍷🍷🍷🍷🍷 **1996** Medium yellow-green; a complex and exceptionally intensely flavoured wine, particularly given its origins. Powerful fruit is supported by nutty, smoky bacon oak on a long, lingering finish. **rating:** 94

➯ **best drinking** 1998 – 1999 **best vintages** NA **drink with** Fricassee of veal • $10

Riverina Ridgewood Cabernet Sauvignon

Another outstanding wine from estate-grown grapes which well and truly challenges the view that the Riverina region cannot produce first class red wines. Top gold medal in the Commercial Dry Red Firm Finish Class at the 1997 Liquorland National Wine Show.

🍷🍷🍷🍷½ **1996** Youthful purple; excellent cassis and earth Cabernet varietal aromas supported by subtle oak on the bouquet. A well-balanced wine on the palate with a mix of cassis, mint and earthy fruit flavours, supported by firm but not aggressive tannins. **rating:** 92

➯ **best drinking** 1999 – 2003 **best vintages** NA **drink with** Yearling beef • $12

Riverina Warburn Estate Cabernet Sauvignon
Produced from low-yielding grapes grown in the Riverina region, predominantly from vineyards owned by Riverina Wines. The second highest pointed gold medal in an extremely distinguished class of 1996 Cabernet Sauvignons at the 1997 Liquorland National Wine Show.
YYYYY **1996** Full red-purple; the bouquet shows first class varietal character with a mix of cassis and more earthy notes. The palate is youthful but unforced, and has the balance to develop well. For how long is the question much more difficult to answer. **rating:** 94

⇨ **best drinking** 1999 – 2003 **best vintages** NA **drink with** Loin of lamb • $10

robinsons family vineyards ★★★

Curtins Road, Ballandean, Qld 4382 **region** Granite Belt
phone (07) 4684 1216 **fax** (07) 4639 2718 **open** 7 days 9–5
winemaker Rod MacPherson, Philippa Hambledon **production** 2000 **est.** 1969
product range ($10–18.50 CD) Sauvignon Blanc Semillon, Chardonnay, Lyra Dry White, Traminer, Late Harvest Traminer, Shiraz, Shiraz Cabernet, Cabernet Sauvignon, Sparkling.
summary The conjunction of a picture of a hibiscus and 'cool climate' in prominent typeface on the labels is a strange one, but then that has always been the nature of Robinsons Family Vineyards. The red wines can be very good, particularly when not overly extracted and tannic.

Robinsons Family Cabernet Sauvignon
In 1995, at least, distinctly the best of the Robinson reds, well balanced and with good fruit ripeness.
YYYY **1995** Medium to full red-purple; the bouquet is quite sweet overall, partly driven by well-handled vanilla oak, with attractive red berry fruit, with touches of mint and chocolate, coming up on the palate. The tannins are well balanced, the oak subtle. **rating:** 85

⇨ **best drinking** 2000 – 2007 **best vintages** NA **drink with** Roast beef • NA

robinvale ★★☆

Sea Lake Road, Robinvale, Vic 3549 **region** Murray Darling and Swan Hill
phone (03) 5026 3955 **fax** (03) 5026 1123 **open** Mon-Fri 9–6, Sun 1–6
winemaker Bill Caracatsanoudis **production** 3000 **est.** 1976
product range ($2.50–18 CD) A kaleidoscopic array of wines including five preservative-free wines, white wines which run from Retsina through to Auslese Muscat Hamburg, Dry Marsanne, red wines which encompass Lambrusco, Scarlet Bliss, Cabernet Sauvignon/Franc, Kokkineli, Fruity Rosé; and fortified wines ranging from Mavrodaphne to Cream Marsala, with a few Vintage Ports thrown in for good measure.
summary Robinvale claims to be the only winery in Australia to be fully accredited with the Biodynamic Agricultural Association of Australia. Most, but not all, of the wines are produced from organically-grown grapes, with certain of the wines made preservative-free.

rochecombe vineyard NR

Baxter's Road, Pipers River, Tas 7252 **region** Northern Tasmania
phone (03) 6382 7122 **fax** (03) 6382 7231 **open** 7 days 10–5
winemaker Fiona West **production** 14 000 **est.** 1985
product range ($18–24.95 R) Riesling, Chardonnay, Sauvignon Blanc, Pinot Noir, Cabernet Sauvignon Cabernet Franc Merlot, RV (sparkling).

summary Rochecombe, complete with its much-expanded and state-of-the-art winery, became part of the Pipers Brook Group in February 1998. With its excellent location and restaurant, it will continue to be a significant attraction, but the future of the brand is obscure, particularly given the former owner Joe Chromy of the JAC Group has retained ownership of the Rochecombe RV Méthode Champenoise and Fluyt brands.

Rochecombe Riesling

One of surprisingly few Rieslings to be grown in northern Tasmania, and which stands well apart from mainland Riesling in its style.

1996 Light green-yellow; a fragrant mix of herb, thyme and spice aromas are strikingly different; the palate is similarly herbaceous, appealing in a Germanic fashion. A crisp, clean low phenolic finish is a logical conclusion. **rating:** 88

best drinking 1999 – 2006 **best vintages** NA **drink with** Caesar salad • $18

Rochecombe RV Sparkling

Produced predominantly from Pinot Noir, with selected parcels of Chardonnay also, we are told. Reflects the sparkling wine expertise within the Heemskerk/Jansz/Rochecombe Group. (Will go to a separate winery entry in future editions.)

1995 Medium straw-yellow; a fine, crisp bouquet with mineral, bread and biscuit aromas is followed by a lively palate with citrus, lemon and apple fruit running through a lingering finish; has considerable finesse. **rating:** 85

best drinking 1998 – 1999 **best vintages** NA **drink with** Tasmanian seafood • $24.95

rochford

Romsey Park, Rochford, Vic 3442 **region** Macedon
phone (03) 5429 1428 **fax** (03) 5429 1066 **open** By appointment
winemaker David Creed **production** 2500 **est.** 1983
product range ($19–32 R) Chardonnay, Pinot Noir, Cabernet Sauvignon; Romsey Park is second label.

summary In February 1998 Helmut Konecsny and Yvonne Lodoco-Konecsny acquired Rochford. David Creed continues as winemaker, and it is the Konecsnys' intention to leave wine style unchanged with the emphasis on Chardonnay and Pinot Noir, and gradually increase production.

Rochford Chardonnay

Sourced from a number of vineyards in the Macedon Ranges. The full range of Chardonnay winemaking techniques is applied to the wine.

1996 Medium yellow-green; there are strong toasty malolactic fermentation aromas overlying a more minerally, citrussy base. A well-made wine on the palate, with delicate slightly grassy/herbal characters together with citrus and melon fruit; crisp, high-acid finish. **rating:** 84

best drinking 1999 – 2003 **best vintages** NA **drink with** Baked ham • $27

Rochford Pinot Noir

Pinot has consistently been the outstanding wine from Rochford, typically exhibiting both complexity and richness of flavour, and helping establish the reputation of the Macedon region as yet another area suited to this fickle variety.

🍷🍷🍷🍷🍷 **1996** Medium red; a very potent bouquet with cherry and plum fruit complexed by stemmy tones. The palate is powerful; forest and stem characters are woven through the intense dark berry fruit on a long finish. **rating:** 92

➪ **best drinking** 1998 – 2002 **best vintages** '91, '92, '93, '95, '96 **drink with** Breast of squab • $32

rockford ★★★★

Krondorf Road, Tanunda, SA 5352 **region** Barossa Valley
phone (08) 8563 2720 **fax** (08) 8563 3787 **open** Mon-Sat 11–5
winemaker Robert O'Callaghan, Chris Ringland **production** 15 000 **est.** 1984
product range ($9.50–40 CD) Eden Valley Riesling, Local Growers Semillon, Alicante Bouchet, White Frontignac, Basket Press Shiraz, Sparkling Black Shiraz, Dry Country Grenache, Cabernet Sauvignon, Tawny Port.
summary The wines are sold through Adelaide retailers only (and cellar door), and are unknown to most eastern Australian wine-drinkers, which is a great pity, for these are some of the most individual, spectacularly flavoured wines made in the Barossa today, with an emphasis on old low-yielding dry-land vineyards.

Rockford Black Shiraz

This, quite simply, is a great sparkling Shiraz, inspired by the Sparkling Burgundies of Colin Preece at Great Western, and made using fundamentally the same techniques. The base wine is matured in large old wood for three years before being tiraged, and then left on lees for a year before disgorgement and further cellaring prior to release. This particular bottle was part of the September '96 disgorgement. Almost impossible to procure; sold only through Adelaide retailers and by mailing list and cellar door, and sells out almost overnight with a limit of six bottles per customer. The unique personality of Robert O'Callaghan comes rocketing through the newsletter, which at the end of the day is probably the best way of getting hold of these scarce wines.

🍷🍷🍷🍷🍷 **NV** Dark red, but with some brick hues evident. There is an attractive mix of spice and earth aromas on the bouquet, but the palate is something else, with that fine, faintly spicy, faintly earthy taste of mature Shiraz of the old Great Western style. It is neither heavy nor sweet, and has tremendous balance and length. **rating:** 94

➪ **best drinking** 1998 – 2020 **best vintages** NA **drink with** Needs no accompaniment • $37

romavilla NR

Northern Road, Roma, Qld 4455 **region** Other Wineries of Qld
phone (07) 4622 1822 **fax** (07) 4622 1822 **open** Mon-Fri 8–5, Sat 9–12, 2–4
winemaker David Wall **production** 2500 **est.** 1863
product range ($11–35 CD) An extensive range of varietal and generic table wines and fortified wine styles including Madeira and Tawny Port are on sale at the winery; the Very Old Tawny Port is made from a blend of material ranging in age from ten to 25 years.
summary An amazing, historic relic, seemingly untouched since its nineteenth-century heyday, producing ordinary table wines but still providing some extraordinary fortifieds, including a truly stylish Madeira, made from Riesling and Syrian (the latter variety originating in Persia).

rosabrook estate ★★★

Rosa Brook Road, Margaret River, WA 6285 **region** Margaret River
phone (08) 9757 2286 **fax** (08) 9757 3634 **open** Thurs-Sun 11–4 summer
winemaker Dan Pannell, Simon Keall **production** 5000 **est.** 1980
product range ($12–17 CD) Semillon, Semillon Sauvignon Blanc, Chardonnay, Autumn Harvest Riesling, Botrytis Riesling, Cabernet Merlot.
summary The 7-hectare Rosabrook Estate vineyards have been established progressively since 1980, with no less than nine varieties planted. The cellar-door facility is housed in what was Margaret River's first commercial abattoir, built in the early 1930s, with a new winery constructed in 1993. No recent tastings.

rosemount estate (hunter valley) ★★★★★

Rosemount Road, Denman, NSW 2328 **region** Upper Hunter Valley
phone (02) 6549 6400 **fax** (02) 6549 6499 **open** Mon-Sat 10–4; Sun summer 10–4, winter 12–4
winemaker Philip Shaw **production** 700 000 **est.** 1969
product range ($8.99–45 R) A very large range of wines which in almost all instances are varietally identified, sometimes with the conjunction of vineyards at the top end of the range, and which in the case of the lower-priced volume varietals increasingly come from all parts of southeast Australia. Names and label designs change regularly but the emphasis remains on the classic varietals. Roxburgh Chardonnay is the white flag-bearer; Chardonnay, Shiraz, Mountain Blue Shiraz Cabernet and Cabernet Sauvignon under the standard labels consistently excellent at the price. In 1997 a Yarra Valley Chardonnay was added to the regional range, which also encompasses Coonawarra, Orange and Mudgee.
summary Rosemount Estate has achieved a miraculous balancing act over the past years maintaining – indeed increasing – wine quality while presiding over an ever-expanding empire and ever-increasing production. The wines are consistently of excellent value; all have real character and individuality; not a few are startlingly good.

Rosemount Estate Hunter Valley Semillon

Notwithstanding Rosemount's domicile in the Upper Hunter, this is one of the few commercial wines produced by Rosemount which has a Hunter Valley appellation. That, of course, is no accident, and simply reflects the fact that there is a true synergy between the region and the variety. Just for the record, this wine won two gold medals in the year of its making.

🍷🍷🍷🍷 **1996** Light green-yellow; a crisp, clean bouquet of light to medium intensity with utterly correct toasty/grassy varietal character. A fresh and lively wine on the palate, crisp and clean, and eschewing the use of either oak or residual sugar to pump it up. **rating:** 86

➾ **best drinking** 1998 – 2003 **best vintages** '96 **drink with** Mussels • $15.50

Rosemount Estate Show Reserve Semillon

Rosemount's Show Reserve label means what it says: this really is a carefully selected wine of well-above-average quality, sourced from Rosemount's best vineyards in the Hunter Valley.

🍷🍷🍷🍷🍸 **1995** Medium yellow-green; the bouquet is starting to develop classic honey and toast aromas, yet retains fruit smoothness. A most attractive wine on the palate, with considerable length, again retaining lively, tangy lemony fruit flavours. Excellent each-way proposition. **rating:** 93

➾ **best drinking** 1998 – 2004 **best vintages** NA **drink with** Breast of turkey • $24.50

Rosemount Estate Reserve Chardonnay

Sourced from Rosemount's Giants Creek and Roxburgh vineyards in the Upper Hunter, and made with all the skill and flair one expects from Rosemount. A variety of juice handling and settling techniques are employed, and the wine spends eleven months on lees in 50% French Allier barriques and 50% American barrels. The malolactic fermentation occurs naturally, and proceeds to completion.

🍷🍷🍷🍷 **1996** Glowing yellow-green; the aromas are complex, with peachy fruit of medium to full intensity married with gently spicy oak on the bouquet. An expertly crafted wine, showing the skilled use of smoky/spicy oak; the finish is long, even if a fraction on the warm side. **rating:** 89

➾ **best drinking** 1997 – 1999 **best vintages** NA **drink with** Pan-fried veal • NA

Rosemount Estate Rose Label Orange Chardonnay

The vineyard was planted in 1989 at an elevation of 900 metres. The planting density is high, and a high-wall vertical trellis is used. The wine undergoes barrel fermentation and usually undergoes 100% malolactic fermentation. Both the '95 and '96 vintages won gold medals at the 1997 Liquorland National Wine Show, an outstanding achievement.

🍷🍷🍷🍷🍷 **1996** Light to medium yellow-green; an elegant wine, proclaiming its cool-grown origins with crisp, almost herbaceous fruit, gently nutty malolactic fermentation influence, and subtle oak on a long finish. Veers towards Chablis in style. **rating:** 91

➾ **best drinking** 1998 – 2003 **best vintages** '92, '95, '96 **drink with** Oyster soup • NA

Rosemount Estate Roxburgh Chardonnay

Since 1983 the flagship of Rosemount Estate and, at least in some quarters, regarded as the premier Australian white. Throughout the 1980s the style was quite controversial but has become more conventional in the 1990s as more emphasis has been placed on fresh fruit. It is a single-vineyard wine, most of the fruit coming from two 3.5-hectare blocks at the top of the Roxburgh Vineyard planted on limestone-impregnated terra rossa soil. I am left to ponder whether time has passed the style by.

🍷🍷🍷🍷🍷 **1995** Full yellow; the bouquet has voluminous ripe peach fruit and lots of toasty, charry barrel-ferment oak. The palate is mouthfilling, with ripe peachy/buttery fruit, and again that slice of toasty oak. Made in a tried and true fashion, and also reflecting its terroir. **rating:** 90

➾ **best drinking** 1998 – 1999 **best vintages** '86, '87, '89, '91, '92, '93, '95 **drink with** Veal, pork • $45

Rosemount Estate Diamond Label Shiraz

A wine which has been largely responsible for the phenomenal success of Rosemount Estate in the United States, winning consistently high points from the world's most influential wine magazine, *The Wine Spectator*. While Rosemount has never made any secret of the fact that it does subtly alter the balance of the wines according to the market of destination, the quality of this wine throughout the 1990s has been extraordinarily consistent and extraordinarily good. Like the Cabernet Sauvignon, drawn principally from McLaren Vale, Langhorne Creek and Mudgee; is aged in American oak for ten months prior to bottling.

🍷🍷🍷🍷🍷 **1996** Medium to full red-purple; the bouquet is solid, clean and rich with a mix of black cherry and blackberry fruit. The palate is round and mouthfilling, with most attractive sweet black cherry and blackberry fruit, finished off with soft tannins and subtle oak. They don't come much better than this at the price. **rating:** 92

➾ **best drinking** 1999 – 2004 **best vintages** '88, '90, '91, '92, '94, '96 **drink with** Lamb shanks • $15.50

Rosemount Estate Mountain Blue Shiraz Cabernet

The first regional release by Rosemount from Mudgee, but doubtless not the last. The Rosemount jigsaw puzzle continues to spread across the premium wine-growing regions of Australia, but without any compromise on quality, as evidenced by the trophy and seven gold medals which this wine has won. The '95 is a blend of 90% Shiraz and 10% Cabernet Sauvignon, much of the Shiraz coming from the 40-year-old shiraz planted on the Mountain Blue vineyard, and which yielded only half a tonne to the acre. Matured in a mix of French and American oak for 18 months, 100% new.

🍷🍷🍷🍷🍷 **1995** Strong red-purple; exceptionally rich and ripe aromas with luscious blackberry, blackcurrant and spice introduce a lusciously ripe blackberry/currant flavoured palate. The fruit has swallowed up all that new oak, and the acid and tannin balance has been judged to perfection. **rating:** 95

➯ **best drinking** 2000 – 2010 **best vintages** NA **drink with** Barbecued beef • $45

Rosemount Estate Diamond Label Cabernet Sauvignon

Since the 1993 vintage of this wine, Rosemount has achieved a level of excellence hitherto only consistently achieved by its Shiraz. The regional base varies a little from year to year, but is principally drawn from McLaren Vale and Langhorne Creek in South Australia and Mudgee in New South Wales. The wine is fermented warm, given five to seven days extended maceration, and then aged for 12 months in one-year-old and older French and American barriques.

🍷🍷🍷🍷 **1996** Medium purple-red; sweet and clean dark berry fruit is supported by subtle oak on the bouquet; a solidly flavoured wine with blackberry/blackcurrant fruit, harmoniously sweet. Outstanding at its price point. **rating:** 90

➯ **best drinking** 1998 – 2001 **best vintages** '86, '88, '90, '92, '93, '94, '96 **drink with** Rare sirloin steak • $15.50

rosemount estate (mclaren vale) ★★★★★

Ingoldby Road, McLaren Vale, SA 5171 **region** McLaren Vale
phone (08) 8383 0001 **fax** (08) 8383 0456 **open** Mon-Fri 10–5, weekends 11–5
winemaker Charles Whish **production** 100 000 **est.** 1888
product range ($20–47.50 CD) Balmoral Syrah, Show Reserve Shiraz, GSM (Grenache Shiraz Mourvedre blend), Traditional (Cabernet blend).
summary The specialist red wine arm of Rosemount Estate, responsible for its prestigious Balmoral Syrah, Show Reserve Shiraz and GSM.

Rosemount Estate Balmoral Syrah

The name comes from the 1852 Hunter Valley homestead of the Oatley family, founders of the Rosemount Estate. Tastings of all the wines so far released ('89 to '94) have shown an incredible consistency of style, with the 100-year-old vines at Rosemount's Ryecroft Vineyard in McLaren Vale at the heart of the wine. Less than 2000 cases are made each year, 50% being exported to the United States. The '95 won three trophies at the 1997 Liquorland National Wine Show including the Len Evans Trophy for Best Table Wine of Show.

🍷🍷🍷🍷🍷 **1995** Deep red-purple; an extremely powerful, concentrated and rich bouquet leads into an opulently layered palate with a range of black cherry and blackberry fruit, ample tannins and lush oak in support. **rating:** 95

➯ **best drinking** 2005 – 2015 **best vintages** '86, '87, '88, '89, '91, '93, '95 **drink with** Char-grilled rump • $47.50

Rosemount Estate GSM

Grenache (typically 50%), Shiraz (typically 40%) and Mourvedre (typically 10%) grapes are selected from old, low-yielding vines drawn from vineyards across McLaren Vale, and are separately fermented in a mix of traditional open fermenters and vinomatics (rotary fermenters). The wines are matured for 18 months in a mix of new and used American oak, and a final blend decision taken shortly prior to bottling, the blend components varying slightly according to the outcome of vintage. Both the '94 and '95 wines add lustre to the cornucopia of Rhône-style wines from McLaren Vale. The '95 received the Chairman's Trophy at the 1998 Sydney International Wine Competition.

 **1995** Medium to full red-purple; the wine follows very closely in the track and style of the '94, with a powerful and complex briary/woodsy bouquet leading on to a palate full of character and with complex flavour components avoiding the jammy/berry/confection notes that overripe grenache can provide. Retasted end 1997, fulfilling all its early promise. **rating:** 94

➯ **best drinking** 2000 – 2008 **best vintages** '94, '95 **drink with** Beef with olives • $20

rosewhite vineyards NR

Happy Valley Road, Rosewhite via Myrtleford, Vic 3737 **region** Ovens Valley
phone (03) 5752 1077 **open** Weekends and public holidays 10–5, 7 days January
winemaker Joan Mullett **production** 300 **est.** 1983
product range ($10 CD) Traminer, Chardonnay, Pinot Noir, Shiraz, Cabernet Sauvignon, Tawny Port.
summary After a career with the Victorian Department of Agriculture, agricultural scientists Ron and Joan Mullett began the establishment of Rosewhite in 1983, and have since established a little over 2 hectares of vineyards at an altitude of 300 metres.

rossetto ★★☆

Farm 576 Rossetto Road, Beelbangera, NSW 2686 **region** Riverina
phone (02) 6963 5214 **fax** (02) 6963 5542 **open** Mon-Sat 8.30–5.30
winemaker Eddy Rossi **production** 450 000 **est.** 1930
product range ($5.50–20 R) Three ranges, the commercial Wattle Glen series ($5.50), the Rossetto premium varietals ($9-$16) and the Promenade Range, introduced in August 1997 of Riverina Chardonnay, Watervale Riesling and Riverina Cabernet Merlot ($12.50-$20).
summary Another family-owned and run Riverina winery endeavouring to lift the profile of its wines, although not having the same spectacular success as Riverina Wines.

rothbury estate ★★★★☆

Broke Road, Pokolbin, NSW 2321 **region** Lower Hunter Valley
phone (02) 4998 7555 **fax** (02) 4998 7870 **open** 7 days 9.30–4.30
winemaker Adam Eggins **production** 200 000 **est.** 1968
product range ($9–25 R) At the top comes the Individual Vineyard range of Hunter Valley Semillon, Chardonnay and Shiraz; next the Hunter Valley range of varietals; and finally varietals from Mudgee and Cowra.
summary Rothbury celebrated its 30th birthday in 1998, albeit not quite in the fashion that founder and previous chief executive Len Evans would have wished. After a protracted and at times bitter takeover battle, it became part of the Fosters/Mildara empire in 1996, but is still a much-visited landmark in the Hunter Valley.

Rothbury Estate Brokenback Semillon

One of three wines at the top of the quality tree for Rothbury, and, fittingly in my view, the best of the three (the other two being Chardonnay and Shiraz respectively). It seems almost superfluous to say it is made in the traditional fashion, cold-fermented in stainless steel and early bottled.

🍷🍷🍷🍷🍷 **1997** Light to medium yellow-green; the bouquet is powerful, yet smooth, with lemony/herbaceous varietal fruit. The palate has good balance and style, showing citrus and lemon fruit, well-judged acidity and no characters from the wet vintage. **rating:** 90

⇨ **best drinking** 2000 – 2005 **best vintages** NA **drink with** Sushi • $18

Rothbury Estate Hunter Valley Semillon

Has appeared under various guises since the first experimental vintage in 1971 (first full commercial 1972). Winemakers have come and gone; labels have changed, recently with increasing rapidity; and, inevitably, quality has wandered all over the place, at times great, at times not. The '97, from a difficult vintage, suggests there is hope for the wine yet.

🍷🍷🍷🍷 **1997** Medium yellow-green; the bouquet is clean, showing attractive lemony citrus aromas to the clearly accented varietal fruit. The palate, like the bouquet, is of medium intensity and weight, but does have good feel on the tongue and grip and power on the finish. **rating:** 86

⇨ **best drinking** 2000 – 2007 **best vintages** '72, '73, '74, '75, '76, '79, '84, '89, '93, '94, '96, '97 **drink with** Smoked eel • $14

Rothbury Estate Brokenback Shiraz

Vintaged in the pre-Mildara Blass days, but selected and finished after the takeover. An attractive wine.

🍷🍷🍷🍷 **1995** Medium to full red-purple; the bouquet is solid, with a mix of plum and earth fruit, the palate is of medium weight with more of those regional earthy flavours, some plum and soft tannins. Will gain complexity as it ages. **rating:** 84

⇨ **best drinking** 2000 – 2005 **best vintages** NA **drink with** Shepherd's pie • $24

rotherhythe ★★★★☆

Hendersons Lane, Gravelly Beach, Exeter, Tas 7251 **region** Northern Tasmania
phone (03) 6394 4869 **open** By appointment
winemaker Meadowbank (Contract) **production** 1600 **est.** 1976
product range ($16–20 CD) Chardonnay, Pinot Noir, Cabernet Sauvignon, Pinot Chardonnay.

summary At the 1996 Tasmanian Wines Show Rotherhythe swept all before it, winning trophies for Most Successful Exhibitor, Best Light to Medium Bodied Red Wine, Best Full Bodied Red Wine and Best Wine of Show. Ironically, two days later, Dr Steven Hyde sold the vineyard, although he has retained all of the existing wine stocks and will remain involved in the winemaking for some time to come. In both 1997 and again in 1998 Rotherhythe was awarded the trophy for Most Successful Exhibitor at the Tasmanian Wines Show.

rouge homme ★★★☆

Riddoch Highway, Coonawarra, SA 5263 **region** Coonawarra
phone (08) 8736 3205 **fax** (08) 8736 3250 **open** 7 days 10–4
winemaker Paul Gordon **production** 45 000 **est.** 1954

product range ($10–20 R) Richardson's White Block (Chardonnay), Pinot Noir, Shiraz Cabernet, Richardson's Red Block, Cabernet Sauvignon.
summary From time to time I have described Rouge Homme as the warrior brand of the Lindeman Group Coonawarra operations. In recent times it has proved a formidable warrior, most surprisingly with its Pinot Noir, but also with its Richardson's Red Block.

Rouge Homme Chardonnay

Given the full winemaking treatment, barrel-fermented then matured on yeast lees in new and one-year-old French oak barriques and hogsheads for seven months, with partial malolactic fermentation. Has been a consistent show medal winner in recent times.

🍷🍷🍷🍷 **1996** Light to medium green-yellow; pleasant melon-accented fruit with fairly assertive oak on the bouquet, and a repeat on the palate with smooth melon fruit at the centre, surrounded by assertive oak. The two components will marry with bottle age. **rating:** 86

➾ **best drinking** 1999 – 2003 **best vintages** '94, '96, '97 **drink with** Richly sauced white meat dishes • $20

Rouge Homme Richardson's Red Block

Named after one of Coonawarra's pioneer viticulturists, and the first of the Rouge Homme red wines to incorporate Malbec and Merlot together with Cabernet Sauvignon in the manner of a junior brother to Lindemans Pyrus. A Bordeaux-blend of Cabernet Sauvignon, Merlot, Malbec and Cabernet Franc; partial barrel fermentation is followed by maturation in new and used French and American oak for 12 months. The '93 won the Jimmy Watson Trophy at the Melbourne Wine Show in 1994, and the '94 has slowly come out of a fairly lean and austere shell since first released.

🍷🍷🍷🍷 **1994** Medium red-purple; the bouquet is firm, with distinctly earthy/briary notes. The palate follows down the same track, with much of the character of a Bordeaux red from a good but not great vintage. **rating:** 87

➾ **best drinking** 1998 – 2001 **best vintages** NA **drink with** Lamb shanks • $20

ruker wines NR

Barton Highway, Dickson, ACT 2602 **region** Canberra District
phone (02) 6230 2310 **fax** (02) 6230 2818 **open** Weekends, public holidays 10–5
winemaker Richard Ruker **production** 500 **est.** 1991
product range ($15 CD) Riesling, Gewurztraminer.
summary Barbara and Richard Ruker, with the assistance of eldest daughter Niki, planted 2 hectares of riesling and traminer in 1984. The cellar door-cum-winery is a farmshed, subsequently converted to an office and then to its present function of winery and restaurant; it is finished with heavy wooden beams salvaged from a railway bridge near Tarago and clad with the remains of an old slab hut, while the tables are made from huge red and yellow box trees cut down when the vineyard was planted.

rumbalara ★★☆

Fletcher Road, Fletcher, Qld 4381 **region** Granite Belt
phone (07) 4684 1206 **fax** (07) 4683 4335 **open** 7 days 9–5
winemaker Bob Gray **production** 3000 **est.** 1974
product range ($6.50–14.50 CD) Barrel Fermented Semillon, Granitegolde, Light Shiraz, Cabernet Sauvignon, Pinot Noir, Cabernet Shiraz and a range of fortified wines, Cider and Vermouth.

summary Has produced some of the Granite Belt's finest, honeyed Semillon and silky, red berry Cabernet Sauvignon, but quality does vary, and has recently disappointed. The winery incorporates a spacious restaurant, and there are also barbecue and picnic facilities.

ryland river NR

RMB 8945 Main Creek Road, Main Ridge, Vic 3928 **region** Mornington Peninsula
phone (03) 5989 6098 **fax** (03) 9899 0184 **open** Weekends and public holidays 10–5 or by appointment
winemaker John W Bray **production** 2000 **est.** 1986
product range ($14–36 CD) Semillon Sauvignon Blanc, Chardonnay, Cabernet Sauvignon, Jack's Delight Tawny Port and Muscat.
summary John Bray has been operating Ryland River at Main Ridge on the Mornington Peninsula for a number of years, but not without a degree of controversy over the distinction between Ryland River wines produced from Mornington Peninsula grapes and those produced from grapes purchased from other regions. The distinction has not always been clear, it would seem.

rymill ★★★☆

The Riddoch Run Vineyards, Coonawarra, SA 5263 **region** Coonawarra
phone (08) 8736 5001 **fax** (08) 8736 5040 **open** 7 days 10–5
winemaker John Innes **production** 50 000 **est.** 1970
product range ($12.50–47 R) Sauvignon Blanc, Chardonnay, March Traminer, June Traminer, Shiraz, Merlot Cabernets, Cabernet Sauvignon and Coonawarra Brut.
summary The Rymills are descendants of John Riddoch, and have long owned some of the finest Coonawarra soil upon which they have grown grapes since 1970. Peter Rymill has made a small amount of Cabernet Sauvignon since 1987, and has now plunged headlong into commercial production, with winemaker John Innes presiding over the striking winery portrayed on the label.

Rymill Coonawarra Brut

A blend of Pinot Noir and Chardonnay, which spends two years on yeast lees prior to disgorgement.

YYYY **1995** Light straw-yellow, with good mousse; the bouquet is clean, and pleasantly fruity, with citrus peach aromas. The nicely balanced palate is fresh, with citrus and apple flavours, good length and good mouthfeel. **rating:** 87

⇨ **best drinking** 1998 – 2000 **best vintages** NA **drink with** Aperitif • $23

Rymill June Traminer

As the name of the wine implies, an ultra-late harvest style picked in June. It would seem that botrytis plays only a minor role in achieving the end result, with dehydration doing much of the work. A rare style in Australia, and no doubt with a limited market, but a particularly good example, nonetheless.

YYYY **1997** Medium to full yellow, with just a touch of green; the palate is rich and full with tropical apricot and cumquat aromas initially dominant, but with some Traminer spice appearing as the wine breathes. There is a similar melange of flavours on the palate, again with the varietal spice coming through at the end. Has a potent 13.5% alcohol with 124 grams of residual sugar. **rating:** 86

➾ **best drinking** 1998 – 2001 **best vintages** NA **drink with** Asian food • $12.50

Rymill Shiraz

Produced entirely from estate-grown grapes, and matured in a mix of new and used French and American oak barrels.

🍷🍷🍷🍷 **1995** Medium to full red-purple; a youthful bouquet with exuberant black cherry, liquorice and earth varietal fruit aromas is followed by a bright and powerful palate packed with varietal character in a similar liquorice, cherry and spice spectrum; a somewhat angular finish needs to soften. **rating:** 87

➾ **best drinking** 1999 – 2005 **best vintages** '90, '91, '92, '95 **drink with** Stuffed eggplant • $19.50

---

s kidman wines

Riddoch Highway, Coonawarra, SA 5263 **region** Coonawarra
phone (08) 8736 5071 **fax** (08) 8736 5070 **open** 7 days 9–5
winemaker John Innes **production** 5400 **est.** 1984
product range ($10–16 CD) Riesling, Sauvignon Blanc, Cabernet Sauvignon, Shiraz.
summary One of the district pioneers, with an estate vineyard which is now fully mature. I am not certain why wine quality is not better.

saddlers creek

Marrowbone Road, Pokolbin, NSW 2321 **region** Lower Hunter Valley
phone (02) 4991 1770 **fax** (02) 4991 1778 **open** 7 days 9–5
winemaker Craig Brown-Thomas **production** 8000 **est.** 1989
product range ($16–25 CD) Marrowbone Chardonnay, Traminer Riesling, Semillon Chardonnay, Semillon Sauvignon Blanc, Fumé Blanc, Hermitage, Cabernet Merlot, Bluegrass Cabernet Sauvignon.
summary Made an impressive entrance to the district with consistently full-flavoured and rich wines. No recent tastings.

salisbury estate

Campbell Avenue, Irymple, Vic 3498 **region** Murray Darling and Swan Hill
phone (03) 5024 6800 **fax** (03) 5024 6605 **open** Mon-Sat 10–4.30
winemaker Bob Shields, David Martin **production** 385 000 **est.** 1977
product range ($5–13 R) Top-end wines under the Milburn Park label are Chardonnay and Cabernet Sauvignon and under the Salisbury Estate label Show Reserve Chardonnay and Show Reserve Cabernet Sauvignon. Then comes the standard Salisbury Estate range of Rhine Riesling, Chardonnay Semillon, Sauvignon Blanc Semillon, Chardonnay, Cabernet Sauvignon, Cabernet Merlot; the Castle Crossing range is even cheaper, consisting of Fumé Blanc, Colombard Chardonnay, Spätlese Rhine Riesling, Chenin Blanc, Chambourcin, Shiraz Malbec Mourvedre, Claret; Acacia Ridge non-vintage generics bring up the rear, with two wines in the Tennyson Vineyard off to one side.
summary Salisbury Estate, Milburn Park and Castle Crossing are three of the principal brands of Australian Premium Wines Limited, a public company which moved onto the lists of the

Australian Stock Exchange in 1998, having acquired the 157-hectare Kasbah Vineyard near Loxton and a 40-hectare property at Koppamurra in South Australia (both in 1995) and Haselgrove Wines (in mid-1997). Also produces 4.9 million litres of bulk wine.

salitage ★★★★

Vasse Highway, Pemberton, WA 6260 **region** Pemberton
phone (08) 9776 1771 **fax** (08) 9776 1772 **open** 7 days 10–4
winemaker Patrick Coutts, Ross Pammelt **production** 15 000 **est.** 1989
product range ($16–32 R) Chardonnay, Unwooded Chardonnay, Sauvignon Blanc, Treehouse Chardonnay Verdelho, Pinot Noir, Cabernet Merlot.
summary Salitage is the showpiece of Pemberton. If it had failed to live up to expectations, it is a fair bet the same fate would have befallen the whole of the Pemberton region. The quality and style of Salitage has varied substantially, presumably in response to vintage conditions and yields. It still remains the key producer in the Pemberton region, but the variability is a little unsettling.

Salitage Unwooded Chardonnay

The opulent use of oak in what might loosely be called the 'normal' Salitage Chardonnay serves to highlight the difference between the two wines, with quality of the underlying fruit very evident from this wine. Unwooded Chardonnays work when the fruit quality is there, and don't when it is not. This one does work.

🍷🍷🍷🍷 **1997** Medium yellow-green; fragrant grapefruit and melon varietal fruit aromas leap from the glass; the palate shows relatively light but most attractive cool-grown melon/grapefruit flavours. Well balanced, but at its best now. **rating:** 86

⇨ **best drinking** 1998 – 1999 **best vintages** '97 **drink with** Vegetarian dishes • $18

Salitage Cabernet Merlot

Yet another wine from Pemberton to make its debut after Pinot and Chardonnay, and similarly to suggest it may after all be the Cabernet family to which the region is best suited. Certainly possesses the strength and fruit flavour lacking from some of the other wines. For the record, it is a blend of Cabernet Sauvignon, Cabernet Franc, Malbec and Petit Verdot.

🍷🍷🍷🍷🍸 **1995** Dense red-purple; a rich, dense chocolatey dark berry bouquet leads on to an amazingly rich, ripe and concentrated wine on the palate with abundant tannins running through on the mid to back palate. **rating:** 90

⇨ **best drinking** 2000 – 2007 **best vintages** NA **drink with** Venison • $32

saltram ★★★☆

Angaston Road, Angaston, SA 5353 **region** Barossa Valley
phone (08) 8564 3355 **fax** (08) 8564 3384 **open** 7 days 10–5
winemaker Nigel Dolan **production** 200 000 **est.** 1859
product range ($10–30 R) At the top is No. 1 Shiraz; then Mamre Brook, now 100% Barossa and comprising Chardonnay, Shiraz and Cabernet Sauvignon; Metala Black Label and White Label; and the Saltram Classic range sourced from southeast Australia.
summary Following its absorption into the Mildara Blass Group, a certain amount of brand repositioning has taken place, but on coherent lines. The wines being produced are strikingly rich and full-flavoured. The product range has been tightened up, with the focus being placed on Mamre Brook, No. 1 Shiraz and the Metala labels.

Saltram Metala Black Label Shiraz

The Metala label, originally that of Stonyfell (itself long-since subsumed into Saltram) has a great history, and in its (conventional) white background form was one of the most famous in the 1960s and '70s. Its strong calligraphic design still evokes potent memories for old-timers such as myself. The Black Label variant came into being when the oldest part of the Metala vineyards reached their centenary, and has been continued with limited production from the now more than 100-year-old vines.

🍷🍷🍷🍷 **1996** Medium to full red-purple; the voluminous bouquet is full of ripe, very slightly jammy berry fruit, the palate providing similar amounts of mouth-coating, almost essencey, berry fruit, and subtle oak. A wine which will probably live off this unusual sweetness and richness of the fruit for decades. **rating:** 85

➾ **best drinking** 2001 – 2011 **best vintages** NA **drink with** Stewed venison • NA

sand hills vineyard ★★☆

Sandhills Road, Forbes, NSW 2871 **region** Other Wineries of NSW

phone (02) 6852 1437 **fax** (02) 6852 4401 **open** Mon-Sat 9–5, Sun 12–5

winemaker Various contract **production** 500 **est.** 1920

product range ($10–15 CD) Classic Dry White, Chardonnay, Shiraz, Shiraz Cabernet, Tawny Port.

summary Having purchased Sand Hills from long-term owner Jacques Genet, the Saleh family have replanted the vineyard to appropriate varieties, with over 3 hectares of premium varieties having been established between 1989 and 1995. Winemaking duties are split between John Saleh at Sand Hills (Pinot Noir and fortifieds), Charles Sturt University (Cabernet Shiraz) and Jill Lindsay of Woodonga Hill (white wines).

sandalford ★★★☆

West Swan Road, Caversham, WA 6055 **region** Swan District

phone (08) 9274 5922 **fax** (08) 9274 2154 **open** 7 days 10–5

winemaker Bill Crappsley, Andrew Spencer-Wright **production** 90 000 **est.** 1840

product range ($12–35 R) At the bottom end under the Caversham label Chenin Verdelho, Late Harvest Cabernet Shiraz; then the 1840 Collection of Semillon Sauvignon Blanc, Chardonnay and Cabernet Merlot; under the premium range Margaret River Mount Barker Riesling, Margaret River Verdelho, Mount Barker Margaret River Chardonnay, Mount Barker Margaret River Shiraz, Mount Barker Margaret River Cabernet Sauvignon; also excellent fortifieds, notably Sandalera.

summary The arrival of Bill Crappsley as winemaker coupled with the refurbishment of the winery, has heralded major changes at Sandalford. Wine quality has improved year by year, with Chenin Blanc and Chardonnay leading the way, but not alone. The quality of the labelling and packaging has also taken a giant leap forwards.

Sandalford Margaret River Mount Barker Riesling

The 1996 was the first 100% Mount Barker Riesling released by Sandalford since 1992. Sandalford felt the quality of the wine was outstanding, and I can but agree, although it is in the family of Mount Barker Rieslings with highly floral characteristics which take it outside the mainstream.

🍷🍷🍷🍷🍸 **1996** Light to medium yellow-green; a super-fragrant bouquet with striking passionfruit/lime aromas, and an array of flavours on the palate from passionfruit to nettle. Long finish to a strikingly different wine. **rating:** 90

➾ **best drinking** 1998 – 2000 **best vintages** '92, '96 **drink with** Sashimi • $13.95

Sandalford Margaret River Mount Barker Shiraz

First appeared on the scene with the '93 vintage, and has improved each year since.

🍷🍷🍷🍷🍷 **1995** Medium to full red-purple; the bouquet is solid and rich, with dark berry and mint fruit aromas. The palate is equivalently rich, with abundant sweet juicy fruit in a blackberry/mulberry/plum spectrum; the oak handling is subtle throughout. **rating:** 91

➾ **best drinking** 2000 – 2008 **best vintages** '94, '95 **drink with** Lamb chops • $19.95

Sandalford Caversham Cabernet Shiraz

A blend of Swan Valley-sourced Cabernet and Shiraz.

🍷🍷🍷🍷 **1996** Medium to full red-purple; a solid bouquet, with blackberry fruit aromas leads into a strongly flavoured palate with abundant, ripe sweet berry fruits and soft tannins. **rating:** 84

➾ **best drinking** 1999 – 2004 **best vintages** NA **drink with** Rich stews • $11.95

sandalyn wilderness estate NR

Wilderness Road, Rothbury, NSW 2321 **region** Lower Hunter Valley
phone (02) 4930 7611 **fax** (02) 4930 7611 **open** 7 days 10–5
winemaker Gary Reed (Contract) **production** 3500 **est.** 1988
product range ($14–20 CD) Semillon, Verdelho, Chardonnay, Pinot Noir.
summary Sandra and Lindsay Whaling preside over the picturesque cellar-door building of Sandalyn on the evocatively named Wilderness Road, where you will find a one-hole golf range and views to the Wattagan, Brokenback and Molly Morgan ranges. The estate has 6.5 hectares of vineyards, with contract-making by Hunter Valley veteran Alasdair Sutherland.

sandstone ★★★

CMB Carbunup River, WA 6280 **region** Margaret River
phone (08) 9755 6271 **fax** (08) 9755 6292 **open** Not
winemaker Mike Davies, Jan Davies **production** 750 **est.** 1988
product range ($18–22 R) Semillon, Cabernet Sauvignon.
summary The family operation of consultant-winemakers Mike and Jan Davies, who also operate very successful mobile bottling plants. The wines are made at Ribbonvale, where the Davies work as consultants and contract-winemakers for others.

scarborough ★★★★

Gillards Road, Pokolbin, NSW 2321 **region** Lower Hunter Valley
phone (02) 4998 7563 **fax** (02) 4998 7786 **open** 7 days 9–5
winemaker Ian Scarborough **production** 10 000 **est.** 1985
product range ($19.50–20 CD) A Chardonnay specialist, making token quantities of Pinot Noir.
summary Ian Scarborough put his white winemaking skills beyond doubt during his years as a consultant, and his exceptionally complex and stylish Chardonnay is no disappointment. Vintage conditions permitting, Ian Scarborough makes two styles: a rich, traditional buttery White Burgundy version for the Australian market (exemplified by the 1995 with its mustard-gold label) and a lighter, more elegant Chablis-style (under a blue-silver label) for the export market.

scarp valley NR

6 Robertson Road, Gooseberry Hill, WA 6076 **region** Perth Hills
phone (08) 9454 5748 **open** Not
winemaker Peter Fimmel (Contract) **production** 25 **est.** 1978
product range ($15 ML) Hermitage.
summary Owner Robert Duncan presides over what has to be the smallest producer in Australia, with one-quarter acre of shiraz producing a single cask of wine each year if the birds do not get the grapes first. Recently introduced netting should help alleviate that problem, but on the evidence of the '95 vintage, a new barrel is urgently needed.

scarpantoni estate ★★★☆

Scarpantoni Drive, McLaren Flat, SA 5171 **region** McLaren Vale
phone (08) 8383 0186 **fax** (08) 8383 0490 **open** Mon-Fri 10–5, weekends 11–5
winemaker Michael Scarpantoni, Filippo Scarpantoni **production** 25 000 **est.** 1979
product range ($8–25 CD) Sauvignon Blanc, Unwooded Chardonnay, Chardonnay, Fleurieu Brut, Gamay, Fiori, School Block (Cabernet Shiraz Merlot), Block 3 Shiraz, Cabernet Sauvignon, Botrytis Riesling, Tawny Port, Vintage Port.
summary While an erratic producer at times, and not helped by the earlier use of agglomerate corks, has made some excellent wines in recent years which – if repeated – would earn the winery an even higher rating.

Scarpantoni Estate Block 3 Shiraz

Yet another McLaren Vale Shiraz to score high points on my judging sheet in the 1997 Great Australian Shiraz Challenge.

 **1996** Medium purple-red; powerful earthy berry fruit is cradled by vanilla oak on the bouquet, heralding an enormously flavoursome and rich wine on the palate, with a sensual mix of chocolate, red berry and sweet vanilla oak. **rating:** 90

➪ **best drinking** 1999 – 2009 **best vintages** NA **drink with** Seared kangaroo fillet • $15

schmidts tarchalice NR

Research Road, Vine Vale via Tanunda, SA 5352 **region** Barossa Valley
phone (08) 8563 3005 **fax** (08) 8563 0667 **open** Mon-Sat 10–5, Sun 12–5
winemaker Christopher Schmidt **production** 1500 **est.** 1984
product range ($8.50–19.75 CD) Barossa Riesling, Eden Valley Riesling, Barossa Chardonnay, Barossa Semillon, Auslese Riesling, Shiraz Cabernet/Cabernet Franc, four different Ports and Old Liqueur Frontignac.
summary Typically has a range of fully mature wines at low prices available at cellar door.

scotchmans hill ★★★★

190 Scotchmans Road, Drysdale, Vic 3222 **region** Geelong
phone (03) 5251 3176 **fax** (03) 5253 1743 **open** 7 days 10.30–4.30
winemaker Robin Brockett **production** 14 000 **est.** 1982
product range ($18.50–19.95 R) Riesling, Sauvignon Blanc, Chardonnay, Pinot Noir, Cabernet Merlot; Spray Farm is the second label.
summary In fact situated on the Bellarine Peninsula, southeast of Geelong, with a very well-equipped winery and first class vineyards. It is a consistent performer with its Pinot Noir, and has a strong following in both Melbourne and Sydney for its well-priced, well-

made wines. The second label of Spray Farm takes its name from a National Trust property with panoramic views of Port Phillip Bay and Melbourne, which has also been planted to vines by the Brown family.

scotts brook NR

Scotts Brook Road, Boyup Brook, WA 6244 **region** Other Wineries of WA
phone (08) 9765 3014 **fax** (08) 9765 3015 **open** Weekends, school holidays 10–5 or by appointment
winemaker Aquila Estate (Contract) **production** 1000 **est.** 1987
product range ($12–19 CD) Riesling, Autumn Harvest White, Chardonnay, Cabernet Sauvignon.
summary The Scotts Brook winery at Boyup Brook (equidistant between the Margaret River and Great Southern regions) has been developed by local schoolteachers Brian Walker and wife Kerry – hence the opening hours during school holidays. There are 17.5 hectares of vineyards, but the majority of the production is sold to other winemakers, with limited quantities being made by contract.

seaview ★★★★☆

Chaffey's Road, McLaren Vale, SA 5171 **region** McLaren Vale
phone (08) 8323 8250 **fax** (08) 8323 9308 **open** Mon-Fri 9–4.30, Sat 11–5, Sun 11–4
winemaker Steve Chapman **production** 500 000 **est.** 1850
product range ($10–31 R) Increasingly tied to McLaren Vale, with only the Riesling and the sparkling wines using fruit from outside the region. Riesling, Chardonnay, Semillon Sauvignon Blanc, Verdelho, Shiraz, Grenache and Cabernet Sauvignon make up the basic range. Recently introduced super-luxury Edwards & Chaffey range of Chardonnay, Shiraz, Cabernet Sauvignon and Pinot Noir Chardonnay, the latter replacing Edmond Mazure.
summary A maker of table wines which are frequently absurdly underpriced and perhaps suffer in consequence and, of course, of some of the country's best-known sparkling wines, which have gone from strength to strength over recent years. Moreover, the addition of the super-premium Edwards & Chaffey range has done much to change perceptions and lift the profile of the brand.

Seaview Verdelho

Produced from Verdelho predominantly grown at one of the few verdelho vineyards in McLaren Vale, with a small component of Padthaway material. Unoaked and early-bottled. The '96 produced one of the major surprises of the 1997 Liquorland National Wine Show, topping Class 22.

🍷🍷🍷🍷 **1996** Light to medium straw-green; intense, tangy citrussy passionfruit aromas and fruit flavours mark a wine with unusual length and persistence of flavour. **rating:** 89

➾ **best drinking** 1998 – 1999 **best vintages** NA **drink with** Light Asian dishes • $10

Seaview Chardonnay

Made entirely from McLaren Vale Chardonnay. Part was barrel-fermented in French oak, and part of the wine was matured on yeast lees for three months and underwent malolactic fermentation prior to blending. Making techniques like this are truly remarkable for a wine made in such volumes and priced around $10–11.

🍷🍷🍷🍷🍸 **1997** Medium yellow-green; a complex, tangy and stylish bouquet with grapefruit/melon fruit and no hint of the use of oak chips. The palate has exceptional intensity of fruit flavour with some ripe fig flavours coming through together with the grapefruit and melon. Good length, subtle oak. Yet another outstanding achievement for a $10 wine. **rating:** 90

➾ **best drinking** 1998 – 1999 **best vintages** '90, '92, '93, '96, '97 **drink with** Pan-fried veal • $11

Seaview Edwards & Chaffey Chardonnay

The super-premium Edwards & Chaffey range, introduced in the early 1990s, honours the founders of Seaview, F H Edwards and W B Chaffey. The Chardonnay is 100% barrel-fermented in a mix of new, one and two-year-old French oak barriques, and undergoes malolactic fermentation. Since 1994 it has been unfiltered, a fact prominently displayed on the label. The '94, '95 and '96 wines were prolific gold medal (and trophy) winners; each year seems to bring more refinement to the style.

🍷🍷🍷🍷🍷 **1996** Medium yellow-green; a complex bouquet with the full array of winemaking techniques coming through to best advantage: nutty malolactic fermentation influences, good fruit weight and well-balanced and integrated oak. The palate is in distinctive style with full-on barrel-ferment and malolactic-fermentation influences, but rich fruit there to support those winemaking inputs. **rating:** 94

➾ **best drinking** 1998 – 2002 **best vintages** '95, '96 **drink with** Breast of turkey • $24

Seaview Edwards & Chaffey Pinot Chardonnay

The premium sparkling wine from Seaview, first made in 1991. The '93 vintage is a blend of 72% Pinot Noir and 28% Chardonnay, sourced predominantly from the Adelaide Hills and Yarra Valley. The wine spends three years on yeast lees, and during 1996 and 1997 won two trophies and five gold medals in less than 12 months between 1996 and 1997.

🍷🍷🍷🍷🍷 **1993** Strong yellow-green, with persistent fine bead; an extremely complex bouquet with toasty autolysis characters, almost charry yet not rough, is followed by an intense and still tight palate. Citrussy flavours run through a long finish with neatly balanced acidity. **rating:** 94

➾ **best drinking** 1998 – 1999 **best vintages** '93 **drink with** Salmon roulade • $22

Seaview Shiraz

Introduced in 1992 as part of the repositioning and refocusing of the Seaview range. Prior to 1992 there was a Shiraz Cabernet which was sourced from many South Australian regions. This wine effectively replaces it, and is a distinct improvement.

🍷🍷🍷🍷 **1996** Medium red-purple; well-ripened red cherry and red berry fruit aromas of medium intensity are supported by subtle oak. The palate has good flavour and weight, with more of those ripe berry flavours together with some minty notes. Impeccable value.
rating: 87

➾ **best drinking** 1999 – 2004 **best vintages** NA **drink with** Lamb shashlik • $13

seldom seen vineyard NR

Craigmoor Road, Mudgee, NSW 2850 **region** Mudgee
phone (02) 6372 4482 **fax** (02) 6372 1055 **open** 7 days 9.30–5
winemaker Barry Platt **production** 5000 **est.** 1987
product range ($11–16 CD) Semillon (wooded and unwooded), Chardonnay Semillon, Chardonnay, Traminer.
summary A substantial grape grower (with 18 hectares of vineyards) which reserves a proportion of its crop for making and release under its own label. No recent tastings.

seppelt ★★★★★

Seppeltsfield via Nuriootpa, SA 5355 **region** Barossa Valley
phone (08) 8568 6200 **fax** (08) 8562 8333 **open** Mon-Fri 9–5, Sat 10.30–4.30, Sun 11–4
winemaker James Godfrey, Jonathan Ketley **production** NFP **est.** 1851
product range ($8–3000 R) The great wines of Seppeltsfield are first and foremost Para Liqueur Port, Show Tawny Port DP90, Seppeltsfield Fino Sherry and Dorrien Cabernet Sauvignon. The other wines in the Seppelt portfolio are handled at Great Western. The 100 Year Old Para Liqueur Port is the $3000 a bottle jewel in the crown.
summary A multi-million-dollar expansion and renovation programme has seen the historic Seppeltsfield winery become the production centre for the Seppelt wines, adding another dimension to what was already the most historic and beautiful major winery in Australia. It is now home to some of the unique fortified wines in the world, nurtured and protected by the passionate James Godfrey.

Seppelt Show Reserve DP63 Muscat

I have now finally come to terms with the olive oil bottles used to package this great wine, and find on looking through my tasting notes that I accorded it the highest points of any wine in wine shows I judged in 1997, when I gave it 19.5 (perilously close to 100 points on the 100-point scale) at the 1997 Sydney Wine Show. Yet, on a side-by-side basis, I'm not too sure that I don't prefer the Tokay.

🍷🍷🍷🍷🍷 **NV** Deep mahogany brown, with an olive green rim; an exceptionally concentrated and infinitely complex wine in which very old material is interwoven with fresher, intensely raisined fruit. Plum pudding, Christmas cake, caramel and toffee all in a glass together. **rating:** 98

⇨ **best drinking** 1998 – 1999 **best vintages** NA **drink with** Dried fruits • NA

Seppelt Show Fino Sherry Bin DP117

Made from Barossa-grown Palomino and matured in a traditional flor Sherry solera system of small casks. The wine remains under a flor yeast for a minimum of seven years before the long process of final blending takes place. A prolific trophy and gold medal winner at Australian shows. The reduction to 15.5 degrees as the minimum legal level of alcohol has allowed James Godfrey to further refine and lighten the style, making it (if it were possible) better than ever.

🍷🍷🍷🍷🍷 **NV** Light straw-yellow; penetrating floor aromas which almost defy description, having a penetrating mineral and nutty aroma. The flavour is almost tingling in its dryness, and now has the combination of delicacy and pungency of the top Spanish Finos and Manzanillas. **rating:** 95

⇨ **best drinking** 1998 – 1999 **best vintages** NA **drink with** Consommé • $19

Seppelt Show Tawny Port Bin DP90

DP90 has an average age of 21 years, blended from the reserve stocks of very old Tawny Port made from Barossa Valley Shiraz and Grenache, with a little Cabernet Sauvignon. Between 1968 and 1991 alone DP90 won 30 trophies and 106 gold medals at Australian wine shows, making it the most-awarded wine of any style. It is intermittently released in limited quantities.

🍷🍷🍷🍷🍷 **NV** Light golden-tawny; the bouquet is incredibly penetrating and fine, with intense rancio and an underlay of caramel and spice. The palate is relatively light-bodied, yet piercingly intense, with sweet faintly raisiny fruit on the mid-palate, finishing with cleansing acidity. **rating:** 94

⇨ **best drinking** 1998 – 2008 **best vintages** NA **drink with** The ultimate winter aperitif • $76

Seppelt 100 Year Old Para Liqueur Port

Every year since 1986 Seppelt has made a tiny release of 100 Year Old Para Liqueur Port, kept in cask for a century and not diluted or maintained by a solera system of topping up. In other words, it is a true vintage wine. Made from Barossa Shiraz and Grenache, the analysis of the 1894 vintage tells just how much it has concentrated with age: 16.25° baumé, 25.5% alcohol and 10.8 grams per litre of acid, with a pH of 3.68. The baumé and acid levels have more than doubled over the years as the wine has become incredibly concentrated.

🍷🍷🍷🍷🍷 **1897** Dark olive-brown, tinged with green, and pours like viscous oil; the bouquet leaps out of the glass, with cascades of aroma; plum pudding, toffee and the works lifted by the touch of volatility one always encounters. The tiniest sip is overwhelming, drawing saliva from every corner of the mouth; incredibly concentrated and essencey. **rating:** 94

➡ **best drinking** 1997 – 2017 **best vintages** 1886, 1887, 1890, 1892, 1894, 1897 **drink with** The finest quality double expresso coffee • $3000

---

seppelt great western ★★★★★

Moyston Road, Great Western, Vic 3377 **region** Grampians
phone (03) 5361 2239 **fax** (03) 5361 2200 **open** 7 days 10–5
winemaker Ian McKenzie (Chief) **production** NFP **est.** 1865
product range ($5.95–51 R) Méthode Champenoise comprising (from the bottom up) Brut Reserve, Imperial Reserve, Rosé Reserve, Grande Reserve, Sunday Creek Pinot Noir Chardonnay, Fleur de Lys, Harpers Range, Rhymney Sparkling Sauvignon Blanc, Original Sparkling Shiraz and Salinger; table wines include Moyston Unoaked Chardonnay and Cabernet Shiraz; Sheoak Riesling; Terrain Series Chardonnay and Cabernet Sauvignon; Eden Valley Botrytis Gewurztraminer, Corella Ridge Chardonnay, Harpers Range Cabernet Sauvignon, Chalambar Shiraz, Sunday Creek Pinot Noir, Drumborg Riesling, Partalunga Vineyard Chardonnay, Great Western Shiraz, Dorrien Cabernet Sauvignon and Drumborg Cabernet Sauvignon. Great Western Hermitage and Show Reserve Sparkling Burgundy are the flag-bearers alongside Salinger.
summary Australia's best-known producer of sparkling wine, always immaculate in its given price range, but also producing excellent Great Western-sourced table wines, especially long-lived Shiraz and Australia's best Sparkling Shirazes. Now the production centre for many Southcorp Group brands, with a vast new bottling plant and attendant warehouse facilities.

Seppelt Great Western Sheoak Riesling

First released in 1994, and made entirely from Great Western Riesling. Chronically under-appreciated and underpriced in the market, and deserves far more recognition. A gold and silver medal winner at national wine shows in 1996 and 1997.

🍷🍷🍷🍷🍷(4.5) **1996** Light to medium green-yellow; a wonderful mix of citrus, lime and more tropical notes on the bouquet, but the palate showing the tightness and restraint which will guarantee the wine a long life. The barest hint of residual sugar does no more than flesh out the finish. **rating:** 90

➡ **best drinking** 1998 – 2004 **best vintages** '96 **drink with** Asian cuisine • NA

Seppelt Great Western Corella Ridge Chardonnay

First made in 1991, utilising grapes grown in premium cool-climate Victorian regions, and 100% barrel-fermented in new and one-year-old French oak barriques. Matured on its yeast lees for nine months. In 1996 the grapes came from Great Western, Strathbogie Ranges and Drumborg. A much underrated and under-appreciated wine.

🍷🍷🍷🍷 **1996** Medium yellow-green; obvious barrel-ferment oak inputs do not swamp the fruit on the bouquet, and on the palate tangy melon and citrus varietal flavours drive the wine through to a long finish with fine acid. Here the oak input is very much in restraint. **rating:** 87

⇨ **best drinking** 1998 – 2003 **best vintages** NA **drink with** Fish mornay • $14

Seppelt Great Western Partalunga Chardonnay

The Partalunga Vineyard in the Adelaide Hills region of South Australia was planted in 1982, but the on-again, off-again marketing of the various Seppelt wines has not done the quality of the fruit (or the resulting wines) any justice at all. At one time the label was headed for extinction, being saved at the last moment by winning a series of important trophies. On the other hand, one cannot quarrel with the decision to only release the wine in exceptional vintages; thus there was not Partalunga Chardonnay in either 1994 or 1995. For the record, the wine is totally barrel-fermented in a mix of new and used French oak barriques.

🍷🍷🍷🍷🍷 **1996** Glowing yellow-green; melon, fig and cashew are woven through subtle oak on a bouquet which is deceptively sweet, for the palate is a marvellously understated, elegant style with melon/mineral fruit and subtle oak. A most beautifully balanced and constructed wine. **rating:** 92

⇨ **best drinking** 1998 – 2003 **best vintages** NA **drink with** Lobster • $22

Seppelt Great Western Show Sparkling Burgundy

Made from old vine Shiraz grown at Seppelt Great Western, matured in large oak casks for one year before tiraging, and then on yeast lees for nine to ten years before disgorgement. Always an exceptionally complex wine, which will live for decades, as the classic wine notes demonstrate.

🍷🍷🍷🍷🍷 **1986** Medium to full red; a complex mix spice, plum, game and earth claim the varietal origin of the wine. A marvellously balanced palate with spice, liquorice, game and earth flavours, with a dash of dark chocolate thrown in for good measure, and most impressively of all, without undue sweetness. Winner of 16 gold medals. **rating:** 95

⇨ **best drinking** 1997 – 2017 **best vintages** '44, '46, '54, '61, '64, '67, '84, '85, '86, '87, '90, '91 **drink with** Borscht • $51

Seppelt Great Western Original Sparkling Shiraz

After a mercifully brief (and quite disastrous) flirtation with the Harpers Range label, the 'commercial' Sparkling Shiraz from Seppelt has regained its primary brand label, for good measure being given the not-so-original 'Original Sparkling Shiraz' label. Brand management carping to one side, this wine streaks the commercial Sparkling Burgundy field, an exceptional bargain at the price. A blend of Padthaway, Barossa and Coonawarra Shiraz, it spent 16 months in large oak before being tiraged, and then spent 18 months on yeast lees.

🍷🍷🍷🍷🍷 **1993** Medium to full red-purple; strong earthy varietal fruit, with hints of liquorice are followed by liquorice, earth and berry fruit flavours on the palate. Do not be the least bit hesitant to cellar this wine for a long time. **rating:** 90

⇨ **best drinking** 2000 – 2007 **best vintages** NA **drink with** Pâté and game • $16.95

Seppelt Great Western Sunday Creek Pinot Noir

The Sunday Creek name comes from Western Victoria, where the creek in question flows near the Seppelt Drumborg Vineyard. As with all of the Sunday Creek releases, Drumborg produces almost all of the limited production of this underrated wine. The '96 has been a prolific trophy and gold medal winner at national wine shows throughout 1997, often upstaging far more expensive (and better known) Pinots. Just when wholesale and retail supplies were exhausted, the '96 won two trophies at the 1998 Royal Sydney Wine Show, for Best Pinot Noir and Best Red Wine Not Exceeding $15 Retail.

🍷🍷🍷🍷🍷 **1996** Medium purple-red; the wine has a great bouquet, with complex yet soft cherry and plum fruit, characters which also drive the supple plummy palate. Has swallowed up the new French oak in which it was matured. **rating:** 94

➾ **best drinking** 1998 – 2001 **best vintages** '94, '96 **drink with** Quail or duck • $15

Seppelt Great Western Chalambar Shiraz

Anyone with Chalambar Shiraz made between 1953 and 1963 in their cellar will have one of Australia's great red wines, still drinking superbly if the cork has held. From 1963 onwards, following the retirement of Colin Preece, it was all downhill, with sporadic releases of vastly inferior quality, label changes and general brand neglect. However, the 1990s has seen a significant return to form with the '94 deservedly winning three trophies at the 1996 Royal Sydney Wine Show and the '96 doing even better at Adelaide and Canberra in 1997. It is sourced from Great Western, Ovens Valley, Geelong and Bendigo and spends 17 months in a mix of predominantly new American and French oak barrels.

🍷🍷🍷🍷🍷 **1996** Strong red-purple; a wine which shows exceptional varietal character throughout, with a marvellous amalgam of liquorice, game and spice on the bouquet, mixed with touches of sweet cherry and mint on the palate. A wine with excellent vinosity and a soft finish. **rating:** 94

➾ **best drinking** 2000 – 2010 **best vintages** '53–'63, '91, '93, '94, '95, '96 **drink with** Braised game dishes • $16

serventy ★★☆

Valley Home Vineyard, Rocky Road, Forest Grove via Margaret River, WA 6286 **region** Margaret River

phone (08) 9757 7534 **fax** (08) 9757 7534 **open** Fri–Sun, holidays 10–4

winemaker Peter Serventy **production** 1500 **est.** 1984

product range ($15 CD) Chardonnay, Pinot Noir, Shiraz.

summary Peter Serventy is nephew of the famous naturalist Vincent Serventy and son of ornithologist Dominic Serventy. It is hardly surprising, then, that Serventy should practise strict organic viticulture, using neither herbicides nor pesticides. The wines, too, are made with a minimum of sulphur dioxide, added late in the piece and never exceeding 30 parts per million.

sevenhill cellars ★★★★

College Road, Sevenhill via Clare, SA 5453 **region** Clare Valley

phone (08) 8843 4222 **fax** (08) 8843 4382 **open** Mon–Fri 8.30–4.30, Sat, public holidays 9–4

winemaker Brother John May, John Monten **production** 20 000 **est.** 1851

product range ($12–20 CD) St Aloysius (Chenin Blanc, Chardonnay, Verdelho blend), Semillon, Riesling, College White, Traminer Frontignac, St Ignatius (Cabernet Sauvignon, Malbec, Franc and Merlot blend), Shiraz, Cabernet Sauvignon, Fortifieds, Sacramental Wine.

summary One of the historical treasures of Australia; the oft-photographed stone wine cellars are the oldest in the Clare Valley, and winemaking is still carried out under the direction of the Jesuitical Manresea Society and in particular, Brother John May. Quality is very good, particularly that of the powerful Shiraz, all the wines reflecting the estate-grown grapes from old vines.

Sevenhill Cellars Riesling

Produced from a fraction under 3 hectares of old-vine, estate-grown Riesling, and more often than not very good.

🍷🍷🍷🍷🍷 **1997** Light to medium yellow-green; a very fragrant bouquet, with lots of attractive lime juice aromas introduces a wine bursting with lime and passionfruit on the mid-palate before moving on to a crisp, dry finish. **rating:** 92

⇨ **best drinking** 1998 – 2007 **best vintages** '87, '89, '91, '92, '94, '97 **drink with** Antipasto • $12

Sevenhill Cellars Shiraz

With 11.4 hectares, shiraz is the dominant variety among the 56 hectares of Sevenhill's vineyard holdings. With the resurgence in interest in Shiraz, it is a great asset, particularly given the age of the vines. The '93 vintage was a magnificent wine, with extraordinary spice and liquorice varietal character, reflecting the cool vintage. The subsequent vintages are awesome in their power, but really needed more work to bring out the best in them.

🍷🍷🍷🍷 **1996** Strong purple-red; rich, ripe, potent juicy berry fruit in typical slightly callow style. The palate is ripe and concentrated, loaded with blackberry and cherry fruit. As with the preceding vintages, needs time in bottle. **rating:** 86

⇨ **best drinking** 2001 – 2010 **best vintages** '89, '91, '93, '94, '95 **drink with** Barbecued beef • $16

Sevenhill Cellars St Ignatius

A blend of Cabernet Sauvignon, Malbec, Cabernet Franc and Merlot, all of which are estate-grown. The policy has always been to pick the grapes very ripe, thus producing a densely coloured and massively flavoured wine which really needs much time to soften and mature. The '96 topped its class at the 1997 Liquorland National Wine Show.

🍷🍷🍷🍷 **1996** Deep red-purple; like all of the Sevenhill wines, very powerful and concentrated, with pronounced mint characters on both bouquet and palate – a tad too exaggerated for my personal taste, though the judges thought otherwise. **rating:** 89

⇨ **best drinking** 2002 – 2008 **best vintages** '80, '87, '89, '91, '92, '96 **drink with** Strong cheese or red meat • $18

---

severn brae estate NR

Lot 2 Back Creek Road (Mount Tully Road), Severnlea, Qld 4352 **region** Granite Belt
phone (07) 4683 5292 **fax** (07) 3391 3821 **open** Weekends 9–5 or by appointment
winemaker Bruce Humphery-Smith **production** 300 **est.** 1990
product range ($14–16 ML) Chardonnay, Shiraz, Liqueur Muscat.

summary Patrick and Bruce Humphery-Smith have established 5.5 hectares of chardonnay with relatively close spacing and trained on a high two-tier trellis. Winery and cellar-door facilities were completed in time for the 1995 vintage. Prior to that time, the Chardonnay was made at Sundown Valley winery.

seville estate ★★★★☆

Linwood Road, Seville, Vic 3139 **region** Yarra Valley
phone (03) 5964 4556 **fax** (03) 5964 3585 **open** Not
winemaker Iain Riggs **production** 7000 **est.** 1970
product range ($18–45 ML) Chardonnay, Chardonnay Sauvignon Blanc, Pinot Noir, Shiraz, Cabernet Sauvignon.

summary In February 1997 a controlling interest in Seville Estate was acquired by Brokenwood (of the Hunter Valley), and interests associated with Brokenwood. I was one of the founding partners of Brokenwood, and the acquisition meant that the wheel had turned full circle. This apart, Seville Estate will add significantly to the top-end of the Brokenwood portfolio, without in any way competing with the existing styles.

Seville Estate Shiraz

Consistently the best of the Seville Estate wines but little known outside a select circle simply because production is so limited. It is matured in a mixture of French and American oak, but it is the fruit which really drives the wine.

🍷🍷🍷🍷 **1996** Excellent purple-red colour; the bouquet is clean, with black cherry, earth and spice in abundance; the palate shows a similar range of cherry, spice and earthy fruit, supported by subtle oak and moderate tannins. In retrospect, the rating may be a little on the harsh side. **rating:** 85

➾ **best drinking** 2000 – 2003 **best vintages** '88, '90, '91, '92, '93, '94 **drink with** Pot-au-feu • $45

Seville Estate Cabernet Sauvignon

Brokenwood did not time its acquisition of a controlling interest in Seville Estate as well it might, running into the problem vintages (unusual vintage rainfall) of 1995 and 1996, a problem which was particularly severe for the late-ripening varieties. This makes the achievement with the '95 Cabernet Sauvignon all the more meritorious, perhaps emphasising once again what a marvellous grape the thick-skinned cabernet sauvignon is in adverse conditions.

🍷🍷🍷🍷 **1995** Medium red-purple; the bouquet is clean, of medium intensity with perfectly ripened red fruit Cabernet aromas, and no herbal green overtones. A most attractive, unforced style on the palate with soft red fruits, subtle oak and fine tannins. **rating:** 88

➾ **best drinking** 2000 – 2008 **best vintages** NA **drink with** Rack of veal • $35

shantell ★★★★

1974 Melba Highway, Dixons Creek, Vic 3775 **region** Yarra Valley
phone (03) 5965 2264 **fax** (03) 5965 2331 **open** Thurs-Mon 10.30–5
winemaker Shan Shanmugam, Turid Shanmugam **production** 1200 **est.** 1980
product range ($14–20 CD) Semillon, Chardonnay, Pinot Noir, Cabernet Sauvignon.
summary The substantial and now fully mature Shantell vineyards provide the winery with a high-quality fruit source; part is sold to other Yarra Valley makers, the remainder vinified at Shantell. In January 1998 Shantell opened a new cellar door situated at 1974 Melba Highway, 50 metres along a service road from the highway proper. Chardonnay, Semillon and Cabernet Sauvignon are its benchmark wines, sturdily reliable.

Shantell Semillon

There is not a great deal of semillon grown in the Yarra Valley, but what there is produces some attractive wines. In most vintages, as one would expect, the wine has a distinctly herbaceous feel akin to Sauvignon Blanc, but enough intensity not to require oak. The Shantell wine is made in this fashion from half a hectare of estate grapes.

🍷🍷🍷🍷 **1997** Light to medium yellow-green; the bouquet is firm, with clearly defined varietal fruit in a herbaceous, lemon/mineral spectrum. The palate has good flavour and structure, offering plenty now, but with even more to come with age. **rating:** 87

➾ **best drinking** 1999 – 2004 **best vintages** '88, '90, '91, '92, '93, '97 **drink with** Abalone • $14

Shantell Chardonnay

The Shantell vineyard has been producing high-quality chardonnay grapes for well over a decade producing elegant fruit-driven wines which age with grace.

1996 Light to medium yellow-green; the bouquet is very light, but has typical Yarra melon fruit, and barely perceptible oak. The palate has similarly clearly defined citrus, melon and lemon fruit with good length and acidity. **rating:** 84

best drinking 1998 – 2004 **best vintages** '90, '92, '94 **drink with** Yarra Valley smoked trout • $18

Shantell Cabernet Sauvignon

Shantell has produced consistently good Cabernet Sauvignon during the 1990s, inevitably reflecting vintage variation but always showing ripe fruit flavours.

1995 Strong, bright red-purple; the bouquet is ripe, with attractive cassis fruit to the fore. The palate shows similarly ripe berry flavours, with a hint of mint, sweet tannins and a flick of oak. **rating:** 87

best drinking 2000 – 2005 **best vintages** '90, '91, '92, '93, '95 **drink with** Shoulder of lamb • $20

sharmans

Glenbothy, RSD 175 Glenwood Road, Relbia, Tas 7258 **region** Northern Tasmania
phone (03) 6343 0773 **fax** (03) 6343 0773 **open** By appointment
winemaker Andrew Hood (Contract) **production** 300 **est.** 1987
product range ($14.50–16.50 ML) Riesling, Sauvignon Blanc, Chardonnay, Pinot Noir.
summary Mike Sharman has very probably pioneered one of the most promising wine regions of Tasmania, not far south of Launceston but with a distinctly warmer climate than (say) Pipers Brook. Ideal north-facing slopes are home to a vineyard now approaching 3 hectares, most still to come into bearing. The few wines produced in sufficient quantity to be sold promise much for the future.

shaw & smith

PO Box 172, Stirling, SA 5152 **region** Adelaide Hills
phone (08) 8370 9911 **fax** (08) 8370 9339 **open** Not
winemaker Martin Shaw **production** 18 000 **est.** 1989
product range ($18–25 R) Sauvignon Blanc, Unoaked Chardonnay, Reserve Chardonnay.
summary Has progressively moved from a contract grape growing base to estate production, with the development of a 40-hectare vineyard at Woodside in the Adelaide Hills. Wine quality has been exemplary throughout, and the wines have wide international distribution.

Shaw & Smith Sauvignon Blanc

The first vintages were produced on grapes grown on Geoff Hardy's Range Vineyard at Kuitpo in the Adelaide Hills; the '96 contained 20% from Shaw & Smith's new Woodside Vineyard in the Hills, and in 1997 half the wine came from that source.

1997 Light green-yellow; a light, fresh tangy bouquet which is crisp, with muted herbaceous/asparagus aroma. The palate is spotlessly clean and utterly correct, again more in the herbaceous end of the spectrum than the tropical. **rating:** 88

best drinking 1998 – 1999 **best vintages** '92, '93, '95 **drink with** Grilled whiting • $18

Shaw & Smith Unoaked Chardonnay

First made in 1993, and part of the modern trend away from oaky, high-alcohol Chardonnays. The fruit is sourced primarily from the Adelaide Hills.

🍷🍷🍷🍷 **1997** Light to medium yellow-green; the bouquet is complex, with more substance than most unoaked Chardonnays, almost giving an illusion of oak. The palate, too, has some presence and grip to the citrus and melon fruit; developing well. **rating:** 85

⇨ **best drinking** 1998 – 1999 **best vintages** NA **drink with** Delicate seafood • $18

Shaw & Smith Reserve Chardonnay

First made in 1992 and undoubtedly merits the Reserve designation. Using fruit from Geoff Hardy's vineyard, winemaker Martin Shaw applies the full gamut of Burgundian techniques of barrel fermentation, extended time on yeast lees and partial malolactic fermentation, using only finest French oak. A mini vertical tasting in January 1997 of all four vintages then released underlined how well these wines mature in bottle.

🍷🍷🍷🍷🍷 **1996** Medium yellow-green; a smooth, fruit-driven bouquet with ripe melon and fig fruit interwoven with subtle oak and malolactic fermentation influences. The palate is similarly fine and elegant, quite tight and citrussy, finishing with crisp acid. Very well balanced, and will be long-lived. **rating:** 94

⇨ **best drinking** 1999 – 2006 **best vintages** '92, '94, '95, '96 **drink with** Baked schnapper • $25

shottesbrooke ★★★☆

Bagshaws Road, McLaren Flat, SA 5171 **region** McLaren Vale

phone (08) 8383 0002 **fax** (08) 8383 0222 **open** Mon-Fri 10–4.30, weekends and public holidays 11–5

winemaker Nick Holmes **production** 8000 **est.** 1984

product range ($13.50–16.50 CD) Fleurieu Sauvignon Blanc, Chardonnay, Eliza Shiraz, Merlot, Cabernet Merlot Malbec.

summary Now the full-time business of former Ryecroft winemaker Nick Holmes, made from grapes grown on his vineyard at Myoponga, at their best showing clear berry fruit, subtle oak and a touch of elegance. A compact, handsome new winery was erected prior to the 1997 vintage.

Shottesbrooke Eliza Shiraz

A premium label introduced with the 1995 vintage, and named in honour of Eliza Harris, the daughter of Edward Harris who purchased the land upon which Shottesbrooke now stands from the Crown in 1847. Five hundred cases only of the wine are made.

🍷🍷🍷🍷 **1995** Medium red-purple; a clean, fresh bouquet with red berry and mint fruit which progressively unfolded in the glass. Smooth cherry, plum and mint fruit is woven through attractive oak on the palate; harmonious and long, though by no means a heavyweight. **rating:** 87

⇨ **best drinking** 1999 – 2005 **best vintages** NA **drink with** Grilled calf's liver • $14

silvan winery NR

Lilydale-Silvan Road, Silvan, Vic 3795 **region** Yarra Valley

phone (03) 9737 9392 **open** Weekends, public holidays 11–6

winemaker John Vigliaroni **production** 500 **est.** 1993

product range ($8 CD) Chardonnay, Pinot Noir, Cabernet, Cabernet Shiraz Merlot, Merlot.
summary One of the newest and smallest of the Yarra Valley wineries; tastings are held in the Vigliaronis' spacious Italian villa.

simon hackett ★★★

PO Box 166, Walkerville, SA 5081 **region** Warehouse
phone (08) 8232 4305 **fax** (08) 8223 3714 **open** Not
winemaker Simon Hackett **production** 14 000 **est.** 1981
product range ($12–28 R) Barossa Valley Semillon, Barossa Valley Chardonnay, McLaren Vale Anthony's Reserve Shiraz, McLaren Vale Old Vine Grenache, McLaren Vale Foggo Road Cabernet Sauvignon.
summary Simon Hackett runs a very interesting operation, owning neither vineyards nor winery, but purchasing grapes and then making the wines at various establishments on a lend-lease basis. With considerable industry experience, he is thus able to produce a solid range of wines at competitive prices. The red wines are distinctly better than the whites.

sinclair wines NR

Graphite Road, Glenoran, WA 6258 **region** Pemberton
phone (08) 9421 1399 **fax** (08) 9421 1191 **open** By appointment
winemaker Brenden Smith **production** 1000 **est.** 1993
product range ($16–20 CD) Sauvignon Blanc, Chardonnay, Merlot, Cabernet Sauvignon.
summary Sinclair Wines is the child of Darelle Sinclair, a science teacher, wine educator and graduate viticulturist from Charles Sturt University, and John Healy, a lawyer, jazz musician and graduand wine marketing student of Adelaide University, Roseworthy Campus. Five hectares of estate plantings are coming into production, with the first wines being released in August 1998.

skillogalee ★★★★

Off Hughes Park Road, Sevenhill via Clare, SA 5453 **region** Clare Valley
phone (08) 8843 4311 **fax** (08) 8843 4343 **open** 7 days 10–5
winemaker Dave Palmer **production** 7000 **est.** 1970
product range ($14–25 R) Riesling, Late Picked Riesling, Gewurztraminer, Chardonnay, Shiraz, The Cabernets, Fortifieds.
summary David and Diana Palmer purchased the small hillside stone winery from the George family at the end of the 1980s, and have capitalised to the full on the exceptional fruit quality of the Skillogalee vineyards. The winery also has a well-patronised lunchtime restaurant. All of the wines are generous and full-flavoured, particularly the reds.

Skillogalee Riesling

The principal wine of Skillogalee, produced from 8 hectares of estate grapes which wind up and down the steep hills of the Skilly Valley, and which are now fully mature. The style is consistently at the fuller end of the Clare Valley spectrum, honest, generous and relatively quick-maturing.

🍷🍷🍷🍷 **1997** Medium yellow-green; the bouquet is rich, with solid lime fruit supported by a mineral/herb substrate. The palate is powerful, with that extra intensity, structure and grip virtually unique to Clare Riesling; citrus/lime flavours. **rating:** 86

➾ **best drinking** 2000 – 2005 **best vintages** '80, '84, '87, '90, '92, '97 **drink with** Quiche Lorraine • $14

Skillogalee Shiraz

The hillside vineyards of Skillogalee, now over 20 years old, should by rights produce very concentrated and powerful red wines. The '95 vintage of this wine shows all of the power and concentration one expects. The '96 is a multiple gold medal winner (Rutherglen and Brisbane).

🍷🍷🍷🍷 **1996** Medium to full red-purple; a ripe, sweet bouquet with powerful minty berry fruit is followed by an extremely sweet and ripe palate with mint and black cherry fruit. **rating:** 85

➾ **best drinking** 2001 – 2006 **best vintages** NA **drink with** Rich game • $24.50

Skillogalee The Cabernets

Predominantly Cabernet Sauvignon, with a small percentage of estate-grown Cabernet Franc and Malbec making up the blend. The style is relatively light-bodied, often with distinctly minty overtones, balanced by a touch of American oak. The '96 has won three gold medals (Perth, Rutherglen and Brisbane).

🍷🍷🍷🍷🍷 **1996** Medium to full red-purple; the bouquet balances abundant ripe earthy/cassis cabernet fruit with ample vanillin oak, predominantly American. The palate, while having plenty of extract and richness, is not overblown; the tannins are supple and soft, and the oak flavours well balanced and integrated. **rating:** 90

➾ **best drinking** 2001 – 2006 **best vintages** '84, '87, '90, '93, '96 **drink with** Yearling steak • $24.50

smithbrook ★★★☆

Smith Brook Road, Middlesex via Manjimup, WA 6258 **region** Pemberton
phone (08) 9772 3557 **fax** (08) 9772 3579 **open** By appointment
winemaker Matt Steel **production** 14 000 **est.** 1988
product range ($22.50–28 R) Chardonnay, Merlot, Cabernet Merlot.
summary Smithbrook is a major player in the Pemberton region with 60 hectares of vines in production. It was acquired by Petaluma in 1997, but will continue its role as a contract grower for other companies, as well as supplying Petaluma's needs and making relatively small amounts of wine under its own label. Perhaps the most significant change has been the removal of Pinot Noir from the current range of products, and the introduction of Merlot.

Smithbrook Chardonnay

Produced from 23 hectares of estate vineyards. Quality has varied somewhat over the years, no doubt in part reflecting vintage conditions.

🍷🍷🍷🍷 **1996** Medium yellow-green; there are ripe, tropical canned fruit aromas on the bouquet; the wine is quite rich on the mid-palate in particular, with soft peachy/buttery fruit, and minimal oak input. **rating:** 85

➾ **best drinking** 1998 – 1999 **best vintages** '92, '94, '96 **drink with** Scampi, marron • $22.50

Smithbrook Merlot

A debut release from 1995, which lends strong support to the view held by some that the Pemberton/Warren region is in fact better suited to the Bordeaux varieties than the Burgundian. Aged in 100% new French oak barriques, the wine won a series of gold medals following its first show in August 1997.

🍷🍷🍷🍷🍷 **1995** Medium to full red-purple; the bouquet is smooth, with gently sweet/ripe fruit and cleverly balanced and integrated oak. There is a mix of sweet fruit, cedar and faintly chocolatey undertones on the palate; the major feature of the wine is its silky mouthfeel and structure. **rating:** 90

⇨ **best drinking** 1998 – 2005 **best vintages** NA **drink with** Milk-fed veal • $28

snowy river winery NR

Rockwell Road, Berridale, NSW 2628 **region** Other Wineries of NSW
phone (02) 6456 5041 **fax** (02) 6456 5005 **open** 7 days 10–5
winemaker Geoff Carter **production** 2500 **est.** 1984
product range ($10–20 CD) Riesling, Semillon, Sauvignon Blanc, Semillon Chardonnay, Müller Thurgau Sylvaner, Sieger Rebe [sic], Trocken Beeren Auslese [sic], Cabernet Sauvignon, Port.
summary Claims the only Eiswein to have been made in Australia, picked on 8 June 1990 after a frost of – 8 degrees Celsius. Also makes a Trocken Beeren Auslese [sic] picked mid-May from the vineyard situated on the banks of the Snowy River, one hour from Mount Kosciuszko. One suspects many of the wines are purchased from other makers.

somerset hill wines NR

891 McLeod Road, Denmark, WA 6333 **region** Great Southern
phone (08) 9840 9388 **open** By appointment
winemaker Brenden Smith (Contract) **production** NA **est.** 1995
product range Sauvignon Blanc, Pinot Noir.
summary Graham Lipson commenced planting 9 hectares of pinot noir, chardonnay, semillon and sauvignon blanc in 1995, and plans to open for cellar-door sales in newly built but rustic-style stone building in late 1998. The full name of the venture is Somerset Hills Wines and Lavender, and lavender crafts will also be on sale.

sorrenberg ★★★

Alma Road, Beechworth, Vic 3747 **region** Ovens Valley
phone (03) 5728 2278 **fax** (03) 5728 2278 **open** Mon-Fri by appointment, weekends 1–5
winemaker Barry Morey **production** 1200 **est.** 1986
product range ($18–22 CD) Sauvignon Blanc Semillon, Chardonnay, Gamay, Cabernet Merlot Franc.
summary Barry and Jan Morey made their first wines in 1989 from the 2.5-hectare vineyard situated on the outskirts of Beechworth. Wine quality has steadily improved since the early days.

spring vale vineyards ★★★☆

Spring Vale, Swansea, Tas 7190 **region** Southern Tasmania
phone (03) 6257 8208 **fax** (03) 6257 8598 **open** Weekends, holidays 10–5
winemaker Andrew Hood (Contract) **production** 1500 **est.** 1986
product range ($22.50–25 CD) Chardonnay, Pinot Noir.
summary Rodney Lyne has progressively established 1.2 hectares of pinot noir and 0.8 hectares of chardonnay in the uniquely favoured climate of Tasmania's east coast, and has produced wonderfully rich and generous Pinot Noir well worth the search. Half a hectare each of gewurztraminer and pinot gris are still coming into production, lifting total plantings to 3 hectares.

st francis NR

Bridge Street, Old Reynella, SA 5161 **region** McLaren Vale
phone (08) 8381 1925 **fax** (08) 8322 6655 **open** Mon–Fri 9–5, weekends 10–5
winemaker Various Contract **production** 12 000 **est.** 1869
product range ($7–22 CD/ML) Riesling, Classic Dry White, Chardonnay, Sauvignon Blanc, Botrytis Riesling, Grenache, Cabernet Merlot, Cabernet Shiraz Merlot, Sparkling and Fortifieds including Old Mr Boston Collectors Port. Substantial business in cleanskins for corporate use and functions, and also miniatures.
summary A full-blown tourist facility and convention centre with a thriving cellar-door sales facility and an active mail sales business offering wines purchased from other makers. No recent tastings.

st gregory's NR

Bringalbert South Road, Bringalbert South via Apsley, Vic 3319 **region** Far South West Victoria
phone (03) 5586 5225 **open** By appointment
winemaker Gregory Flynn **production** NFP **est.** 1983
product range ($14 ML) Port.
summary Unique Port-only operation selling its limited production direct to enthusiasts (by mail list).

st hallett ★★★★☆

St Hallett's Road, Tanunda, SA 5352 **region** Barossa Valley
phone (08) 8563 2319 **fax** (08) 8563 2901 **open** 7 days 10–4
winemaker Stuart Blackwell, Cathy Spratt **production** 65 000 **est.** 1944
product range ($10.95–39.95 R) Poacher's Blend (White), Eden Valley Riesling, Semillon Sauvignon Blanc, Semillon Select, Chardonnay, Gamekeeper's Reserve (Red), Faith Shiraz, Blackwell Shiraz, Cabernet Merlot, Old Block Shiraz.
summary Nothing succeeds like success, and St Hallett continues to grow, significantly expanding the range of its Shiraz-based wines, but also coming up with wines such as the multiple gold medal and trophy winning 1997 Eden Valley Riesling. One has to say that some of the wines (even Old Block Shiraz) don't seem to have quite the intensity (or is it excitement?) they once had. Elegant and smooth, yes, but with a certain sameness about the wines.

St Hallett Eden Valley Riesling

A wine which burst from the ruck in 1997, winning a trophy at the 1997 Barossa Valley Wine Show, and then going on to win a gold medal in Class 1 at the 1997 Liquorland National Wine Show. Eden Valley Riesling at its best.

🍷🍷🍷🍷☐ **1997** Light to medium yellow-green; a classic, dry minerally, toasty bouquet leads into a similarly classically constructed, reserved and long-flavoured palate. A wine which will mature magnificently in bottle. **rating:** 91

➾ **best drinking** 2002 – 2007 **best vintages** NA **drink with** Crab • $17.95

St Hallett Semillon Sauvignon Blanc

Fits in above Poacher's Blend, but, like it and Gamekeeper's Reserve, aimed fairly and squarely at the café and brasserie market. Unwooded, of course.

🍷🍷🍷🍷 **1997** Light to medium yellow-green; a clean, fresh, light herbal bouquet and a fresh, lively tangy palate, with good length, all attest to early bottling (and early consumption). **rating:** 84

➾ **best drinking** 1998 – 1999 **best vintages** NA **drink with** Fish and chips • $13.95

St Hallett Blackwell Shiraz

Blackwell Shiraz, named after long-term winemaker Stuart Blackwell, fits in between Faith Shiraz and Old Block. On the evidence of the '95, it is in fact far closer to Old Block than to Faith, and had better keep its distance.

🍷🍷🍷🍷 **1995** Medium red-purple; a smooth bouquet with touches of chocolate and earth surrounded by obvious but well-balanced and integrated vanillin oak; the palate has an extra dimension, with plum, cherry and chocolate fruit, again supported by nicely judged oak. Finishes with soft tannins. **rating:** 88

➾ **best drinking** 2000 – 2005 **best vintages** NA **drink with** Lamb shanks • $28.95

St Hallett Old Block Shiraz

A wine which has propelled St Hallett into international stardom, and which is responsible for the overall winery rating. Made from 60 to 100-year-old dry-grown Barossa vines, with the addition of new American oak making its impact since 1988.

🍷🍷🍷🍷🍷 **1995** Medium red-purple; a clean, smooth bouquet of medium intensity with cherry and vanilla aromas interwoven announces an ultra-smooth palate with a mix of dark plum and black cherry fruit supported by soft vanilla oak and fine tannins. An understatement, rather than an overstatement. **rating:** 90

➾ **best drinking** 1999 – 2009 **best vintages** '80, '84, '87, '88, '90, '91, '93, '94 **drink with** Kangaroo, game • $39.95

st huberts ★★★★

Maroondah Highway, Coldstream, Vic 3770 **region** Yarra Valley
phone (03) 9739 1118 **fax** (03) 9739 1015 **open** Mon-Fri 9–5, weekends 10.30–5.30
winemaker Adam Marks **production** 20 000 **est.** 1966
product range ($19–30 R) Chardonnay, Pinot Noir, Cabernet Sauvignon, Cabernet Merlot; under the second label Rowan Sauvignon Blanc, Chardonnay, Shiraz, Pinot Noir, Cabernet Merlot.
summary The changes have come thick and fast at St Huberts, which is now part of the Mildara Blass (Rothbury Estate) Group. It has produced some quite lovely wines, notably Chardonnay and Cabernet Sauvignon. Plans are afoot for the rebuilding of the ornate nineteenth-century winery on its original (recently repurchased) site.

St Huberts Pinot Noir

St Huberts Pinot Noir has always lived in the shadow of its far superior Chardonnay and Cabernet Sauvignon. How much this has been due to vineyard resources, and how much to winemaking technique, is open to question. However, the '96 vintage (followed by the '97) cannot be ignored, even if I am no great admirer of the Leviathan-style of the '96 (which, incidentally, won the silver medal at the 1997 Concours des Vins du Victoria).

🍷🍷🍷🍷 **1997** Medium to full red-purple; a solid, very ripe, slightly gamey bouquet with plummy fruit, followed by an even more powerful palate, with abundant ripe fruit, and considerable complexity. **rating:** 85

➾ **best drinking** 2000 – 2003 **best vintages** '96, '97 **drink with** Strong red meat dishes • $19

St Huberts Cabernet Merlot

One can but wonder how St Huberts attains such sweetness in difficult vintages. It is perfectly legal to incorporate 15% of wine from (say) Baileys at Glenrowan, and maybe this is the answer. However that may be, what is most important is the end result, which is impressive.

🍷🍷🍷🍷 **1996** Medium red-purple; the aromas are predominantly in the spicy/leafy spectrum, but there is some attractive cassis fruit there, if not quite of the same impressive quality as the Cabernet of the same vintage. The palate, however, shows much more of that cassis blackcurrant fruit, and is richer than the bouquet suggests. Fine, supple tannins and subtle oak round off an impressive achievement for a difficult vintage for the late-ripening varieties. **rating:** 86

➯ **best drinking** 1999 – 2004 **best vintages** NA **drink with** Lamb kebabs • $19

St Huberts Cabernet Sauvignon

Almost 50% of the 20 hectares of estate plantings at St Huberts are cabernet sauvignon, some of it original plantings, and more grafted over from other varieties. The '77 St Huberts Cabernet caused a sensation at the time, both for its quality and its then astronomically high price of $17 a bottle. Clever winemaking continues to produce rich, smooth wines.

🍷🍷🍷🍷 **1996** Medium to full purple-red; there is a mix of ripe cassis fruit and cedary oak on the smooth bouquet; the palate provides more of that sweet cassis-accented fruit, finishing with soft tannins. An exceptional achievement for the vintage. **rating:** 89

➯ **best drinking** 2000 – 2006 **best vintages** '77, '88, '90, '91, '92, '96 **drink with** Rich casserole dishes • $19

st leonards ★★★☆

Wahgunyah, Vic 3687 **region** Rutherglen
phone (02) 6033 1004 **fax** (02) 6033 3636 **open** Mon-Sat 9–5, Sun 10–4
winemaker Terry Barnett **production** 8000 **est.** 1860
product range ($8.90–25 CD) Carlyle Chardonnay, Wahgunyah Shiraz, Carlyle Cabernet Sauvignon.
summary An old favourite, relaunched in late 1997 with a range of three premium wines cleverly marketed through a singularly attractive cellar door and bistro at the historic winery on the banks of the Murray.

st mary's NR

V & A Lane, via Coonawarra, SA 5277 **region** Other Wineries of SA
phone (08) 8736 6070 **fax** (08) 8736 6045 **open** 7 days 10–4
winemaker Barry Mulligan **production** 4000 **est.** 1986
product range ($12–20 CD) Riesling, Chardonnay, Shiraz, House Block Cabernet Sauvignon.
summary Established by the Mulligan and Hooper families in 1986, but with Tyrrell's Vineyards purchasing the Hooper interest in the vineyards (though not the brand name St Mary's) in 1995. The winemaking operation continues as a separate entity, now wholly owned by the Mulligans.

st matthias NR

113 Rosevears Drive, Rosevears, Tas 7277 **region** Northern Tasmania
phone (03) 6330 1700 **fax** (03) 6330 1975 **open** 7 days 10–5
winemaker Alain Rousseau **production** 4000 **est.** 1983

product range ($13–21 CD) Riesling, Chardonnay, Pinot Noir, Cabernet Sauvignon Merlot, Brut, Cuvee Printemps Dry White, Cuvee Printemps Dry Red.

summary Acquired by Moorilla Estate in 1995 and, after a quiet period, now fully back in business. The wines are made at Moorilla Estate by Alain Rousseau, but are sold through the cellar door (along with those of Moorilla itself).

St Matthias Riesling

Yet another wine to show the use of substantial residual sugar to balance the high acidity of Northern Tasmanian Riesling in the 1997 vintage. Topped its class at the 1998 Tasmanian Wines Show, just edging out the Sterling Heights, although neither wine was awarded a gold medal.

🍷🍷🍷🍷 **1997** Medium yellow-green; the bouquet is smooth, with lime, citrus and passionfruit aromas, the palate having good weight and length, running through soft lime and lemon fruit, building towards the finish with some cleverly controlled sweetness. **rating:** 87

➾ **best drinking** 1998 – 2004 **best vintages** NA **drink with** Chinese pork with ginger • $15.95

st peter's winery NR

Whitton Stock Route, Yenda, NSW 2681 **region** Riverina
phone (018) 421 000 **fax** (02) 4285 3180 **open** Not
winemaker Wilton Estate (Contract) **production** 250 tonnes **est.** 1978

product range ($7.99–18.99 CD) A wide variety of wines under the Edenhope, St Peter's and Sydney labels.

summary St Peter's Winery is not only the physical home of the perhaps better-known Wilton Estate (as tenant) but also produces three ranges of wine for itself, Edenhope being conventionally distributed through the wholesale/retail chain, and St Peter's and Sydney sold direct ex-winery to selected outlets. Managing Director Stephen Chatterton's other claim to fame is as a fanatical fly-fisher and fly-tyer which necessarily means he is made of the right stuff.

stanley brothers ★★☆

Barossa Valley Way, Tanunda, SA 5352 **region** Barossa Valley
phone (08) 8563 3375 **fax** (08) 8563 3758 **open** 7 days 9–5
winemaker Lindsay Stanley **production** 7000 **est.** 1994

product range ($9–19 CD) Sylvaner, Full Sister Semillon, Chardonnay (Unwooded), John Hancock Shiraz, Cabernet Sauvignon, Thoroughbred Cabernet, Cabernet Shiraz, Late Harvest Sylvaner; Sparkling; Fortifieds.

summary Former Anglesey winemaker and industry veteran Lindsay Stanley established his own business in the Barossa Valley when he purchased (and renamed) the former Kroemer Estate in late 1994. As one would expect, the wines are competently made, including vintages from 1991 to 1994 made elsewhere by Lindsay Stanley. Twenty-one hectares of estate plantings have provided virtually all of the grapes for the business.

stanton & killeen wines ★★★★

Jacks Road, Murray Valley Highway, Rutherglen, Vic 3685 **region** Rutherglen
phone (02) 6032 9457 **fax** (02) 6032 8018 **open** Mon–Sat 9–5, Sun 10–5
winemaker Chris Killeen **production** 20 000 **est.** 1875

product range ($10–37.50 CD) A red wine and fortified wine specialist, though offering Chardonnay, Riesling, White Frontignac and Dry White as well as Cabernet Sauvignon, Shiraz, Durif, Old Tawny Port, Old Rum Port, Vintage Port, Liqueur Port, Liqueur Tokay, Liqueur Muscat and top-of-the-range Special Old Liqueur Muscat.
summary A traditional maker of smooth, rich reds, some very good Vintage Ports, and attractive, fruity Muscats and Tokays.

Stanton & Killeen Durif

A rare grape variety brought to northeast Victoria around the turn of the century, and which may or may not be the same as California's petite syrah. Wherever grown, it makes a massively dense and potent wine, characteristics enhanced by the climate of northeast Victoria, to which it is ideally suited.

🍷🍷🍷🍷 **1995** Medium to full red-purple; the bouquet runs through dark berry fruit with touches of both liquorice and chocolate, rich and intense. The palate is attractive, with sweet but not heavy or extractive dark chocolate and blackberry fruit supported by a hint of vanilla oak. Despite its size, has balance and style. **rating:** 87

➾ **best drinking** 2000 – 2010 **best vintages** NA **drink with** Game • $20

Stanton & Killeen Vintage Port

A blend of Shiraz, Touriga and Durif, principally drawn from 75-year-old vines. Has been a prolific medal and trophy winner; the '92 vintage, released in 1998, won trophies for the Best Port at the Rutherglen Show in the year it was made and again in 1997, and has won 11 gold medals.

🍷🍷🍷🍷🍷 **1992** Dense red-purple; the bouquet has lovely spicy, dark forest fruits with fine Brandy spirit woven through. The palate is powerful and complex, with tannins running right through bitter chocolate, earth and spice flavours; well balanced, and not excessively sweet. **rating:** 94

➾ **best drinking** 2002 – 2012 **best vintages** NA **drink with** Nuts • $18

stefano lubiana ★★★★

60 Rowbottoms Road, Granton, Tas 7030 **region** Southern Tasmania
phone (03) 6263 7457 **fax** (03) 6263 7430 **open** Fri-Mon 10–3 or by appointment
winemaker Steve Lubiana **production** 2000 **est.** 1990
product range ($16–25 CD) Riesling, Chardonnay, Pinot Noir, Primavera Pinot, NV Brut.
summary Steve Lubiana has moved from one extreme to the other, having run Lubiana Wines at Moorook in the South Australian Riverland for many years before moving to the Tamar Valley region of Tasmania to set up a substantial winery which acts as both contract-maker and maker for its own label wines, and which was also known as Granton Vineyard. He has progressively grown his contract-making business, and in particular the sparkling wine side. For the past three years, has made the trophy-winning sparkling wine at the Tasmanian Wines Show, first for Barrington Estate and (in 1998) for Elsewhere Vineyard. The estate-produced Stefano Lubiano wines come from 5.5 hectares of beautifully located vineyards sloping down to the Derwent River.

Stefano Lubiana Riesling

Produced from riesling grown on the estate on the banks of the Derwent River; the 1996 was the top-pointed wine in the 1997 Tasmanian Wines Show, simply because it was better balanced and less acidic than the other wines in the class.

ΥΥΥΥ **1997** Medium yellow-green; a clean and quite smooth bouquet, with herb, lime and mineral aromas is followed by a delicate and crisp palate with fresh herb and lime flavours, perhaps a little lacking in intensity. **rating:** 85

⇨ **best drinking** 1998 – 2001 **best vintages** NA **drink with** Marinated scallops • $16

steins ★★★

Pipeclay Lane, Mudgee, NSW 2850 **region** Mudgee
phone (02) 6373 3991 **fax** (02) 6373 3709 **open** 7 days 10–4
winemaker Robert Stein, Greg Barnes **production** 6000 **est.** 1976
product range ($10–18 CD) Semillon, Semillon Riesling, Traminer, Chardonnay, Late Harvest Riesling, Rosé, Mt Buckaroo Dry Red, Shiraz, Cabernet Sauvignon and a range of Muscats and Ports.
summary The sweeping panorama from the winery is its own reward for cellar-door visitors. Wine quality, too, has been very good from time to time, particularly the Shiraz. Rather indifferent, hard green oak does not help the wooded white wines.

Steins Chardonnay

An extremely good wine which deservedly won a gold medal at the 1996 Australian Small Makers Wine Show, and I must say came as a considerable – albeit pleasant – surprise.

ΥΥΥΥ **1995** Medium yellow-green; the bouquet is stylish, with attractive barrel-ferment characters surrounding tangy melon/grapefruit characters. A wine with real verve on the palate, tangy, long and intense. **rating:** 88

⇨ **best drinking** 1997 – 2000 **best vintages** NA **drink with** Rack of veal • $14

Steins Late Harvest Riesling (375 ml)

I know little of the background of this wine, except to say that it is an unusual style for Mudgee, and has almost certainly been made from grapes unaffected by botrytis. However, it succeeds admirably.

ΥΥΥY **1996** Light to medium yellow-green; the bouquet is clean, with quite intense lime fruit aromas, the palate similarly well balanced, clean and flavoursome, with richly sweet lime fruit balanced by appropriate acidity. **rating:** 84

⇨ **best drinking** 1998 – 2000 **best vintages** NA **drink with** Prosciutto and melon • $10

stephen john wines ★★★

PO Box 345, Watervale, SA 5452 **region** Clare Valley
phone (08) 8843 0105 **fax** (08) 8843 0105 **open** By appointment
winemaker Stephen John **production** 2500 **est.** 1994
product range ($10–17.50 CD) Watervale Riesling, Watervale Pedro Ximinez, Watervale Shiraz, Shiraz Cabernet Sauvignon.
summary The John family is one of the best-known names in the Barossa Valley, with branches running Australia's best cooperage (AP John & Sons) and providing the chief winemaker of Lindemans (Philip John) and the former chief winemaker of Quelltaler (Stephen John). Stephen and Rita John have now formed their own family business in the Clare Valley, based on a 6-hectare vineyard overlooking the town of Watervale, supplemented by modest intake from a few local growers. The cellar-door sales area is housed in an 80-year-old stable which has been renovated, and is full of rustic charm.

Stephen John Watervale Shiraz

Said to have been matured in 'imported oak casks' for 18 months, although the provenance of the oak is not disclosed.

🍷🍷🍷🍷 **1996** Medium to full red-purple; solid, dark berry fruit on the bouquet is replicated by concentrated black cherry, faintly minty fruit flavours on the palate. Pleasant oak and moderate tannins provide balance and structure. **rating:** 85

➾ **best drinking** 2001 – 2006 **best vintages** NA **drink with** Marinated beef • $15

Stephen John Cabernet Sauvignon

Stephen John's strength, these days, lies emphatically with the red wines, rather than the white. As with the Shiraz, fruit, rather than oak, drives the wine.

🍷🍷🍷🍷 **1996** Medium to full red-purple; a strong, dense blackberry, cassis and chocolate bouquet is followed by a smooth but flavoursome palate neither extractive nor tannic. Despite its approachability now, will age well. **rating:** 86

➾ **best drinking** 2000 – 2008 **best vintages** NA **drink with** Braised beef • NA

sterling heights ★★★☆

Faulkners Road, Winkleigh, Tas 7275 **region** Northern Tasmania
phone (03) 6396 3214 **fax** (03) 6396 3214 **open** By appointment
winemaker Moorilla Estate (Contract) **production** 400 **est.** 1988
product range ($11–16 CD) Riesling, Chardonnay, Breton Rose, Pinot Noir.
summary With just over 1.5 hectares of vines, Sterling Heights will always be a small fish in a small pond. However, the early releases had considerable success in wine shows, and the quality is all one could expect.

Sterling Heights Riesling

Yet another Riesling from the 1997 vintage to show some unconventional but nonetheless attractive flavours, with the decision taken to retain considerable sweetness in the wine. Scored strongly at the 1998 Tasmanian Wines Show.

🍷🍷🍷🍷 **1997** Medium yellow-green; a potent spice and herb bouquet is followed by an exceptionally powerful palate with lots of extract, flavour and abundant fruit on the mid to back palate, augmented by significant residual sugar. **rating:** 88

➾ **best drinking** 1998 – 2002 **best vintages** NA **drink with** Pork with ginger • $16

stone ridge ★★★

Limberlost Road, Glen Aplin, Qld 4381 **region** Granite Belt
phone (07) 4683 4211 **open** 7 days 10–5
winemaker Jim Lawrie, Anne Kennedy **production** 1450 **est.** 1981
product range ($10–40 CD) Under the Stone Ridge label Semillon, Chardonnay, Shiraz, Cabernet Malbec; under the Mount Sterling label Dry Red Shiraz.
summary Spicy Shiraz is the specialty of the doll's house-sized winery, but the portfolio has progressively expanded over recent years to include two whites and the only Stanthorpe region Cabernet Malbec (and occasionally a straight varietal Malbec). No recent tastings.

stoney vineyard NR

Campania, Tas 7026 **region** Southern Tasmania
phone (03) 6260 4174 **fax** (03) 6260 4390 **open** By appointment
winemaker Peter Althaus **production** 3500 **est.** 1973
product range ($20–45 CD) Domaine A is the top label with Cabernet Sauvignon and Pinot Noir; second label is Stoney Vineyard with Aurora (wood-matured Sylvaner), Sauvignon Blanc, Pinot Noir, Cabernet Sauvignon.
summary The striking black label of the premium Stoney Vineyard wine, dominated by the single, multicoloured 'A', signified the change of ownership from George Park to Swiss businessman Peter Althaus. The NR rating for the winery is given in deference to Peter Althaus, who has no faith whatsoever in Australian wine judges or critics, and profoundly disagrees with their ratings.

stonier's 

362 Frankston-Flinders Road, Merricks, Vic 3916 **region** Mornington Peninsula
phone (03) 5989 8300 **fax** (03) 5989 8709 **open** 7 days 12–5
winemaker Tod Dexter **production** 18 000 **est.** 1978
product range ($18–35 CD) Chardonnay, Pinot Noir and Cabernet under the Stonier's and Stonier's Reserve labels.
summary Looked at across the range, Stonier's is now the pre-eminent winery in the Mornington Peninsula; its standing is in turn based more or less equally on its Chardonnay and Pinot Noir under the Reserve label. A sizeable operation which also undertakes significant amounts of contract-winemaking.

Stonier's Reserve Chardonnay

Produced from 3.5 hectares of estate-grown grapes, and made using the full gamut of Burgundian techniques including barrel fermentation, lees contact and malolactic fermentation. The wines are exceptionally complex and stylish; the '93 was selected for Qantas First Class service, won a number of gold medals at national wine shows, and two trophies at the 1994 Ballarat Wine Show, including the trophy for Best Wine of Show (the first time it had been awarded to a white wine). The '94, '95 and '96 wines are of similar quality (and style).

1996 Medium yellow-green; exceptionally well-balanced and integrated fruit, oak and malolactic-fermentation inputs weave a subtle yet complex bouquet which retains attractive melon and fig fruit. There is more elegance and harmony on the palate with melon and cashew flavours supported by nicely judged oak. Top-class making. **rating:** 95

⇨ **best drinking** 1998 – 2002 **best vintages** '86, '88, '91, '93, '94, '95, '96 **drink with** Milk-fed veal • $35

Stonier's Pinot Noir

Like the Chardonnay, the volume brand for Stonier's, derived from 10 hectares of estate plantings. The winemaking skills of Tod Dexter are very much apparent; he is totally at ease in dealing with cool-climate Chardonnay and Pinot Noir, and has managed to clearly define the line between the varietal and Reserve ranges.

1997 Medium to full red-purple; the bouquet is full of ripe, sweet plummy fruit, as is the palate. Still in its primary phase, but has both the fruit and tannin to develop marvellously well. Underlines the outstanding vintage; the Reserve Pinot Noir should be exceptional. **rating:** 88

⇨ **best drinking** 1998 – 2002 **best vintages** '92, '94, '95, '97 **drink with** Game of any kind • $18

Stonier's Reserve Pinot Noir

If it were possible, the Reserve Pinot Noir has an even more distinguished track record than the Reserve Chardonnay. The 1992 vintage was nominated as the Best Pinot Noir in the 1994/95 Penguin *Good Australian Wine Guide*, by Huon Hooke and Mark Shield, while the 1993 vintage won two major trophies at the 1994 Royal Adelaide Wine Show, including the trophy for Best Varietal Dry Red Table Wine – Any Variety. The wine is exceedingly complex and stylish. None was made in 1996.

🍷🍷🍷🍷🍷 **1995** Medium red-purple; quite pronounced spicy oak introduces a light but stylish bouquet with hints of strawberry and violets. The palate is delicate but refined, with good mouthfeel, balance and structure; the sweet, spicy French oak has been very well handled. Retasted October 1997 and has developed beautifully, with strong Burgundian characteristics. **rating:** 95

➾ **best drinking** 1997 – 1998 **best vintages** '90, '91, '92, '93, '94, '95, '97 **drink with** Coq au vin • $35

strathêrne vale estate NR

Campbell Street, Caballing, WA 6312 **region** Other Wineries of WA
phone (08) 9881 2148 **fax** (08) 9881 3129 **open** Not
winemaker James Pennington (Contract) **production** 600 **est.** 1980
product range A single red wine made from a blend of Cabernet Sauvignon, Zinfandel, Merlot and Shiraz.
summary Stratherne Vale Estate stretches the viticultural map of Australia yet further. It is situated near Narrogin, which is north of the Great Southern region and south of the most generous extension of the Darling Ranges. The closest viticultural region of note is at Wandering, to the northeast.

strathkellar NR

Murray Valley Highway, Cobram, Vic 3644 **region** Goulburn Valley
phone (03) 5873 5274 **fax** (03) 5873 5270 **open** 7 days 10–6
winemaker Chateau Tahbilk (Contract) **production** 2500 **est.** 1990
product range ($9–15 CD) Chenin Blanc, Chardonnay, Late Picked Chenin Blanc, Shiraz, Muscat, Tokay, Putters Port.
summary There are 5.5 hectares of estate vineyards, planted to chenin blanc, chardonnay and shiraz, that provide the grapes, with contract winemaking by Chateau Tahbilk.

stringy brae NR

Sawmill Road, Sevenhill, SA 5453 **region** Clare Valley
phone (08) 8843 4313 **fax** (08) 8843 4313 **open** Weekends and public holidays 10–5
winemaker Contract (Mitchell) **production** 1200 **est.** 1991
product range ($11.50–17.50 CD) Riesling, Shiraz, Cabernet Sauvignon.
summary Donald and Sally Willson have established 5 hectares of vineyards which since the 1996 vintage have produced all the grapes for their wines. (Previously grapes from Langhorne Creek were used.)

Stringy Brae Shiraz

Not surprisingly, the '96 won a gold medal at the Clare Valley Regional Wine Show, and is comprehensively the best wine yet from Stringy Brae.

ŸŸŸŸ **1996** Medium red-purple; a potent bouquet with excellent dark liquorice, leather and boot polish varietal aromas is followed by a richly flavoured palate with abundant dark cherry and dark berry fruit, finishing with supple tannins. The oak is in restraint throughout. **rating:** 88

➯ **best drinking** 2003 – 2010 **best vintages** NA **drink with** Venison • $17.50

Stringy Brae Cabernet Sauvignon

Now produced entirely from 1.6 hectares of estate-grown Cabernet.

ŸŸŸŸ **1996** Dark purple-red; the bouquet is powerful and complex with a range of briary/earthy/dark berry fruit aromas. The wine is quite sweet and succulent on the mid-palate, with dark chocolate and berry fruit before finishing with slightly hard tannins which will (hopefully) soften with age. **rating:** 85

➯ **best drinking** 2001 – 2006 **best vintages** NA **drink with** Chump chops • NA

stumpy gully ★★★☆

1247 Stumpy Gully Road, Moorooduc, Vic 3933 **region** Mornington Peninsula
phone (03) 5978 8429 **fax** (03) 5978 8429 **open** First weekend of each month 12–5
winemaker Frank Zantvoort, Wendy Zantvoort **production** 1500 **est.** 1988
product range ($15–18 CD) Sauvignon Blanc, Marsanne, Pinot Grigio, Pinot Noir, Merlot Cabernet.
summary Frank and Wendy Zantvoort have progressively established 9 hectares of vineyard planted to chardonnay, marsanne, sauvignon blanc, pinot noir, cabernet sauvignon and merlot, electing to sell 80% of the production to local winemakers, and vinifying the remainder, with impressive results.

summerfield ★★★★

Main Road, Moonambel, Vic 3478 **region** Pyrenees
phone (03) 5467 2264 **fax** (03) 5467 2380 **open** 7 days 9–6
winemaker Ian Summerfield, Mark Summerfield **production** 2300 **est.** 1979
product range ($15–22 CD) Sauvignon Blanc Chardonnay, Trebbiano, Shiraz, Cabernet Shiraz, Cabernet Sauvignon.
summary A specialist red wine producer, the particular forte of which is Shiraz. The wines since 1988 have been consistently excellent, luscious and full-bodied and fruit-driven but with a slice of vanilin oak to top them off.

Summerfield Shiraz

Produced from 3.56 hectares of estate plantings, and now just a single release without differentiation of what was previously a varietal Shiraz (regionally sourced) and an estate-grown wine styled 'Estate'. Incidentally, Summerfield has moved straight from the '94 to the '96 vintage.

ŸŸŸŸ **1996** Dark red-purple; the bouquet is redolent of potent gamey blackberry, spice and plum varietal fruit; spicy characters come charging through the dark cherry and plum flavours on the palate, and the oak influence is subtle throughout. **rating:** 87

➯ **best drinking** 2000 – 2006 **best vintages** '88, '90, '91, '92, '93, '94, '96 **drink with** Lamb in filo pastry • $19.95

sutherland ★★☆

Deasey's Road, Pokolbin, NSW 2321 **region** Lower Hunter Valley
phone (02) 4998 7650 **fax** (02) 4998 7603 **open** 6 days 10–4.30
winemaker Neil Sutherland, Nicholas Sutherland **production** 7000 **est.** 1979
product range ($15–40 CD) Chardonnay, Chenin Blanc, Chenin Cremant, Shiraz, Cabernet Shiraz, Cabernet Sauvignon.
summary With substantial and now fully mature vineyards to draw upon, Sutherland is a more or less consistent producer of generous, mainstream Hunter whites and reds, albeit with a high level of phenolic extraction.

sutherland smith wines NR

Cnr Falkners Road and Murray Valley Highway, Rutherglen, Vic 3685 **region** Rutherglen
phone (03) 6032 8177 **fax** (03) 6032 8177 **open** Weekends 10–5 or by appointment
winemaker George Sutherland Smith **production** 1000 **est.** 1993
product range ($10.90–16.50 CD) Riesling, Josephine (Riesling Traminer), Chardonnay, Merlot, Cabernet Shiraz, Port.
summary George Sutherland Smith, for decades managing director and winemaker at All Saints, has opened up his own small business at Rutherglen, making wine in the refurbished Emu Plains winery, originally constructed in the 1950s. He draws upon fruit grown in a leased vineyard at Glenrowan and also from grapes grown in the King Valley.

t'gallant ★★★★☆

Mornington Road, Red Hill, Vic 3937 **region** Mornington Peninsula
phone (03) 5989 6565 **fax** (03) 5989 6577 **open** 7 days 11–5
winemaker Kathleen Quealy, Kevin McCarthy **production** 10 000 **est.** 1990
product range ($15–35 R) An ever-changing list of names (and avant-garde label designs) but with Unwooded Chardonnay and Pinot Gris at the centre. Labels include Chardonnay, Lot 2 Chardonnay, Flag Pinot Grigio, Tribute Pinot Gris, Celia's White Pinot, Holystone, Cyrano Pinot Noir, and a range of wines under the Lyncroft label.
summary Husband and wife consultant-winemakers Kathleen Quealy and Kevin McCarthy are starting to carve out an important niche market for the T'Gallant label, noted for its innovative label designs and names. The acquisition of a 15-hectare property, and the planting of 10 hectares of pinot gris gives the business a firm geographic base, as well as providing increased resources for its signature wine.

T'Gallant Flag Pinot Grigio

Yet another name and label change which keeps even the most dedicated T'Gallant sailors on their toes. The key is the use of the name 'Pinot Grigio' (the Italian version) as opposed to Pinot Gris (the French). The Pinot Grigio is always lighter, crisper and less opulent than the Pinot Gris.

YYYY **1997** Light green-yellow; a quite aromatic and sweet bouquet with hints of white peach suggests a role-reversal for the two wines, but the palate proves otherwise, being lighter than the Tribute, fresh and crisp, with a bone-dry finish. **rating:** 88

⇒ **best drinking** 1998 – 1999 **best vintages** NA **drink with** Smoked salmon • $19

T'Gallant Tribute Pinot Gris

An extraordinarily powerful and complex wine at its best, sometimes nearing 15 degrees alcohol. The grapes come from the vineyard of Madeleine and Patrick McCabe. The Tribute, incidentally, is to the distinguished viticulturist and consultant Max Loader.

🍷🍷🍷🍷🍷 **1997** Light green-yellow; a clean, firm tangy bouquet with echoes of fruit spice; the bouquet is firm and tangy, with the usually high alcohol not overly obvious, although there is that extra dimension of flesh compared to the Flag Pinot Grigio. **rating:** 94

⇨ **best drinking** 1998 – 2002 **best vintages** '94, '95, '97 **drink with** Gravlax • $28

T'Gallant Lyncroft Pinot Noir

The 5-hectare Lyncroft vineyard is owned by Geoff Slade and partner Anita Ziermer, but is managed by T'Gallant and, of course, the wines are made by T'Gallant as part of the so-called Partnership Services.

🍷🍷🍷🍷🍷 **1995** Light to medium red, with just a touch of purple; a stylish and fragrant bouquet with an amazing array of aromas spanning oriental spices, tobacco, plums and violets. The palate is as long and as classy as the bouquet promises, lingering and tangy, in true Burgundian-style. **rating:** 94

⇨ **best drinking** 1997 – 1999 **best vintages** NA **drink with** Spiced quail • NA

tait wines NR

Yaldara Drive, Lyndoch, SA 5351 **region** Barossa Valley
phone (08) 8524 5000 **fax** (08) 8524 5220 **open** Weekends 10–5 also by appointment
winemaker Contract **production** 1000 **est.** 1994
product range ($12–17 CD) Chardonnay, Bush Vine Grenache, Shiraz, Cabernet Sauvignon.
summary The Tait family has been involved in the wine industry in the Barossa for over 100 years, making not wine, but barrels. Their recent venture into winemaking has been extremely successful, with four of the five wines on release in early 1998 having won either a silver or gold medal.

Tait Chardonnay

A voluptuous, early-developing Barossa-style which stood out at the 1998 Winewise Small Makers Competition. It is hand-picked at around 14° baumé, crushed and drained overnight and barrel-fermented for three to four weeks before being transferred to tank and bottled in August.

🍷🍷🍷🍷 **1997** Medium to full yellow-green; a complex, rich and powerful bouquet with tangy fruit and spicy nutmeg oak. The palate is powerful and rich, with masses of peach and nectarine fruit flavour; there is a viscosity to the mouthfeel, and a long finish. **rating:** 90

⇨ **best drinking** 1998 – 1999 **best vintages** NA **drink with** Roast chicken • $14

talijancich ★★☆

26 Hyem Road, Herne Hill, WA 6056 **region** Swan District
phone (08) 9296 4289 **fax** (08) 9296 1762 **open** Sun-Fri 11–5
winemaker James Talijancich **production** 5000 **est.** 1932
product range ($15–85 CD) Verdelho, Semillon, Grenache, Shiraz, Ruby Port, Julian James White Liqueur, Julian James Red Liqueur, Old Liqueur Muscat.
summary A fortified wine specialist also producing a small range of table wines. Still has stocks of Old Liqueur Muscat.

tallara NR

Cassilis Road, Mudgee, NSW 2850 **region** Mudgee
phone (02) 6372 2408 **fax** (02) 6372 6924 **open** Not
winemaker Simon Gilbert (Contract) **production** 1800 **est.** 1973
product range ($15 ML) Chardonnay, Cabernet Sauvignon.
summary Tallara's large, 54-hectare vineyard, was first established in 1973 by KPMG Peat Marwick partner Rick Turner. Only a fraction of the production has ever been made into wine, currently by Simon Gilbert. It is sold principally through a mailing list, with a little local distribution.

taltarni 

Taltarni Road, Moonambel, Vic 3478 **region** Pyrenees
phone (03) 5467 2218 **fax** (03) 5467 2306 **open** 7 days 10–5
winemaker Dominique Portet, Greg Gallagher, Shane Clohesy **production** 65 000 **est.** 1972
product range ($10–75 R) Fumé Blanc, Sauvignon Blanc, Blanc des Pyrenees, Reserve Red des Pyrenees, Merlot Cabernet, Shiraz, Cabernet Sauvignon, Merlot; Sparkling Blanc de Blanc Tete de Cuvée, Cuvée Brut, Brut Tache, Clover Hill.
summary Taltarni seems to have backed off the high levels of tannin and extract evident in the older vintage wines, which ought really to be a step in the right direction, but (perversely) seems to have robbed the red wines of some of their (formidable) character. A rock and a hard place, it seems.

Taltarni Sauvignon Blanc

Made in an uncomplicated and direct style, and in good years (such as 1996) produces a very attractive wine. In the warmer vintages it seems to lose varietal definition. The 1996 won a major trophy in an international competition in the United States, while the '97 is an even better wine.

▼▼▼▼▽ **1997** Light green-yellow; excellent varietal character on the bouquet with gooseberry and herbal aromas of medium intensity. A well-balanced palate showing good varietal character throughout building with a nice touch of tropical gooseberry flavour towards the finish. **rating:** 90

⇨ **best drinking** 1998 – 1999 **best vintages** '96, '97 **drink with** Calamari • $15

talunga NR

Adelaide to Mannum Road, (PO Box 134) Gumeracha, SA 5233 **region** Adelaide Hills
phone (08) 8389 1222 **open** Wed-Sun and public holidays 11–5
winemaker Contract **production** NA **est.** 1994
product range Sauvignon Blanc.
summary A relatively new venture of the di Cesare and Scaffidi families, making an auspicious debut with the 1997 Sauvignon Blanc showing well at the Adelaide Hills Wine Show of that year.

Talunga Sauvignon Blanc

Estate-grown, rich and full; stainless steel fermented.

▼▼▼▽ **1997** Medium yellow-green; ripe gooseberry/tropical aromas of medium to full intensity build further on a full-blown tropical/gooseberry palate. Good length. **rating:** 84

⇨ **best drinking** 1998 – 1999 **best vintages** NA **drink with** Mussels • NA

tamburlaine ★★★☆

McDonalds Road, Pokolbin, NSW 2321 **region** Lower Hunter Valley
phone (02) 4998 7570 **fax** (02) 4998 7763 **open** 7 days 9.30–5
winemaker Mark Davidson **production** 20 000 **est.** 1966
product range ($14–20 CD) Semillon, Verdelho, Sauvignon Blanc, 3 Parishes Chardonnay, The Chapel Reserve Chardonnay, Botrytis Semillon, Cabernet Merlot Malbec, The Chapel Reserve Red.
summary A thriving business which, not withstanding its substantial production, sells over 90% of its wine through cellar door and by mailing list (with an active tasting club members' cellar programme offering wines which are held and matured at Tamburlaine). Unashamedly and deliberately focused on the tourist trade.

Tamburlaine The Chapel Reserve Chardonnay

As the name suggests, the top-of-the-range Chardonnay release from Tamburlaine. Whether this much American oak is a good thing with Chardonnay is a matter of personal opinion.

🍷🍷🍷🍷 **1997** Full yellow-green, already advanced for its age. The bouquet opens with pungent, potent American oak which tends to initially swamp the fruit, but it fights back on a potent peach and vanilla palate, finishing with zingy acid. Whatever else, not short on flavour or character. **rating:** 84

➭ **best drinking** 1998 – 1999 **best vintages** NA **drink with** Pork chops • $20

tanglewood downs NR

Bulldog Creek Road, Merricks North, Vic 3926 **region** Mornington Peninsula
phone (03) 5974 3325 **fax** (03) 5974 4170 **open** Sun-Mon 12–5
winemaker Ken Bilham **production** 1000 **est.** 1984
product range ($15–18 CD) Riesling, Chardonnay, Pinot Noir, Cabernet.
summary One of the smaller and lower-profile wineries on the Mornington Peninsula, with Ken Bilham quietly doing his own thing on 2.5 hectares of estate plantings. Winery lunches and dinners are available by arrangement.

tantemaggie NR

Kemp Road, Pemberton, WA 6260 **region** Pemberton
phone (08) 9776 1164 **fax** (08) 9776 1164 **open** Weekends 9–5
winemaker Contract **production** 110 **est.** 1987
product range ($21 CD) Cabernet Sauvignon.
summary Tantemaggie was established by the Pottinger family with the help of a bequest from a deceased aunt named Maggie. It is part of a mixed farming operation, and by far the greatest part of the 20 hectares is under long-term contract to Houghton. The bulk of the plantings are cabernet sauvignon and verdelho, the former producing the light-bodied style favoured by the Pottingers.

tarrawarra estate ★★★★☆

Healesville Road, Yarra Glen, Vic 3775 **region** Yarra Valley
phone (03) 5962 3311 **fax** (03) 5962 3887 **open** Mon-Fri 10–5
winemaker Clare Hatton **production** 15 000 **est.** 1983
product range ($17.50–36 R) Chardonnay and Pinot Noir each released under the Tarrawarra Estate and second label Tunnel Hill.

summary Slowly evolving Chardonnay of great structure and complexity is the winery specialty; robust Pinot Noir also needs time and evolves impressively if given it. The second label Tunnel Hill wines are more accessible when young, and better value for those who do not wish to wait for the Tarrawarra wines to evolve.

Tarrawarra Chardonnay

Produced from 11.5 hectares of estate-grown grapes in a state-of-the-art winery using a complex range of viticultural and winemaking techniques including multiple picking of the grapes at different maturity levels, barrel fermentation of partly clarified juice, lees contact and malolactic fermentation. The style is always very complex with much of the emphasis placed on structure and texture, the resulting style being quite different from most other wines of the Yarra Valley.

🍷🍷🍷🍷 **1996** Medium to full yellow-green; an exceedingly complex bouquet with many winemaker inputs on top of quite powerful melon/fig fruit. There are abundant nutty/cashew and fig flavours on the palate, although there is a slightly burnt edge which appears every now and then on both bouquet and palate. **rating:** 89

➾ **best drinking** 1999 – 2004 **best vintages** '87, '88, '90, '92, '93, '94 **drink with** Pheasant, turkey • $32

Tarrawarra Pinot Noir

Produced from 6.5 hectares of estate plantings of several different clones. As with the Chardonnay, much attention is paid to style and structure: the grapes are picked when very ripe, and the winemaking techniques are designed to gain maximum extraction of colour and flavour from the grapes. The wines are often awkward when young, powerfully impressive with age and have won a significant number of trophies in Australian wine shows in recent years.

🍷🍷🍷🍷🍷 **1996** Medium to full red-purple; a robust and complex bouquet with plum, spice and touches of tobacco leads into a palate as powerful and as complex as the label and the vintage would suggest. Just lacks a fraction of fresh mid-palate fruit, but a very good wine nonetheless. **rating:** 90

➾ **best drinking** 1999 – 2004 **best vintages** '88, '90, '91, '92, '94, '95, '96 **drink with** Squab • $36

Tarrawarra Tunnel Hill Pinot Noir

The second label is not simply a selection of those barrels of Tarrawarra Pinot which have been less successful, but at least part of the wine is deliberately made in a different fashion right from the outset, placing less emphasis on structure, more on fruit and using less new oak. Quite deliberately designed to make a simpler style.

🍷🍷🍷🍷 **1996** Light to medium red; by the standards of Tarrawarra, a relatively light, fresh and simple bouquet, but perhaps none the worse for that, with attractive varietal cherry fruit. The palate is very good, fruit-driven, but with some real style, and a mix of cherry and more sappy flavours. An excellent entry point for those not familiar with Pinot Noir. **rating:** 87

➾ **best drinking** 1998 – 2000 **best vintages** '91, '92, '94, '96, '97 **drink with** Poached Tasmanian salmon • $17.50

tarwin ridge NR

Wintles Road, Leongatha South, Vic 3953 **region** Gippsland
phone (03) 5664 3211 **fax** (03) 5664 3211 **open** Weekends and holidays 10–5
winemaker Brian Anstee **production** 700 **est.** 1983

product range ($16–27 CD) Sauvignon Blanc, White Merlot, Pinot Noir, Pinot Noir Premium, Cabernet Merlot.
summary For the time being Brian Anstee is making his wines at Nicholson River under the gaze of fellow social worker Ken Eckersley; the wines come from 2 hectares of estate pinot and half a hectare each of cabernet and sauvignon blanc.

tatachilla ★★★★

151 Main Road, McLaren Vale, SA 5171 **region** McLaren Vale
phone (08) 8323 8656 **fax** (08) 8323 9096 **open** Mon-Sat 10–5, public holidays 11–5
winemaker Michael Fragos, Justin McNamee, Daryl Groom (Consultant) **production** 100 000 **est.** 1901
product range ($11–25 CD) Clarendon Vineyard Riesling, Late Harvest Riesling, Sauvignon Blanc, Chardonnay, Growers (Chenin Blanc Semillon Sauvignon Blanc), Bluestone Brut, Sparkling Malbec, Merlot, Foundation Shiraz, Keystone (Grenache Shiraz), Cabernet Sauvignon, Partners (Cabernet Sauvignon Shiraz), Tawny Port.
summary Tatachilla was reborn in 1995, but with an at-times tumultuous history going back to 1901. For most of the time between 1901 and 1961 the winery was owned by Penfolds, but was closed in that year before being re-opened in 1965 as the Southern Vales Co-operative. In the late 1980s it was purchased and renamed The Vales, but did not flourish, and in 1993 was purchased by local grower Vic Zerella and former Kaiser Stuhl chief executive Keith Smith. After extensive renovations, the winery was officially re-opened in 1995, and has won a number of tourist awards and accolades. The star turns are Keystone (Grenache Shiraz) and Foundation Shiraz, bursting with vibrant fruit.

Tatachilla Foundation Shiraz

Foundation Shiraz is Tatachilla's flag-bearer, taking its name from the foundation stone of the winery which was laid in place in 1901 by founder Cyril Pridmore. Open fermentation, using a mixture of heading down boards and plunging is followed by partial barrel fermentation, before the wine is matured in a mix of predominantly American (70% new) oak for 18 months. The '95 was the top gold medal winner in Class 30 (Shiraz, soft finish '95 and older) at the 1997 National Wine Show; also winner of the Fesq Dorado Trophy for Best Medium Bodied Dry Red at the 1998 Sydney International Wine Competition.

🍷🍷🍷🍷🍷 **1995** Medium to full red-purple; potent red and black cherry fruit aromas are interwoven through obvious vanillin American oak on the bouquet. The voluptuous palate, with its glossy cherry and blackberry fruit, once again surrounded by sweet vanillin oak, is an enormously impressive example of a top show style. Masses of flavour, but not over-extracted, and should develop exceptionally well. **rating:** 94

⇨ **best drinking** 2000 – 2010 **best vintages** '95 **drink with** Kangaroo fillet • $25

Tatachilla Clarendon Vineyard Merlot

1995 was the first vintage under this label, produced from grapes grown at an altitude of 215 metres above the floor of McLaren Vale. The wine is made in open fermenters, pressed before dryness, and matured in a mix of predominantly French (80%) and American oak, half-new and half-used. A particularly good Merlot.

🍷🍷🍷🍷🍷 (4½) **1996** Deep red-purple; both bouquet and palate show excellent varietal definition with fresh earthy berry fruit. The structure of the wine is particularly pleasing, with fine tannins and subtle oak. **rating:** 92

⇨ **best drinking** 1999 – 2004 **best vintages** NA **drink with** Rack of veal • $20

Tatachilla Partners Cabernet Sauvignon Shiraz

The inaugural release (1996) of Partners won a gold medal at the 1997 International Wine Challenge in London, an auspicious start. But this blend of Cabernet Sauvignon and Shiraz, sourced from the relatively unfashionable South Australian Riverland and Adelaide Plains areas hit even greater heights with the '97 release, winning a gold medal at the Liquorland National Wine Show in Canberra in November 1997, before receiving the Arthur Kelman Trophy at the 1998 Royal Sydney Wine Show.

🍷🍷🍷🍷🍷 **1997** Strong purple; a vibrant and intense wine, tending firm throughout both bouquet and palate, but neither excessively extractive nor astringent. Very clever winemaking, but one cannot help wonder whether an extra few months in barrel might not have produced an even-better wine. **rating:** 91

⇨ **best drinking** 2000 – 2005 **best vintages** '97 **drink with** Marinated beef • $13.50

taylors ★★★

Taylors Road, Auburn, SA 5451 **region** Clare Valley
phone (08) 8849 2008 **fax** (08) 8849 2240 **open** 7 days 10–5
winemaker Susan Mickan, Kelvin Budarick **production** 250 000 **est.** 1972
product range ($7.45–14.50 R) The premium range consists of Chardonnay, Clare Riesling, White Clare, Promised Land Unwooded Chardonnay, Pinot Noir, Shiraz and Cabernet Sauvignon; the lower-priced Clare Valley range consists of Riesling, Dry White, Sweet White and Dry Red.
summary Taylors continues to flourish and expand, with yet further extensions to its vineyards. Now totalling 501 hectares, by far the largest holding in Clare Valley. There have also been substantial changes on the winemaking front, both in terms of the winemaking team and in terms of the wine style, the latter moving to fresher, earlier release wines. Change always brings a measure of pain, but I wonder whether Taylors has not gone from one extreme to the other.

Taylors Clare Riesling

In the midst of the debate over the use of the word 'Rhine' in connection with Riesling, Taylors throws in a further confusion. Clare Riesling was the name incorrectly given to a second-rate variety called Crouchen; this wine is in fact made from Riesling, and the incorrect labelling borders on the bizarre. The wine itself is good.

🍷🍷🍷🍷 **1997** Light to medium yellow-green; the bouquet is crisp, with spice, mineral, lime and toast aromas. Lime fruit comes to the fore on a light to medium-weight palate, which is well balanced and has good mouthfeel. Somewhere in the centre of the extremes of Clare Valley-style from the '97 vintage. **rating:** 85

⇨ **best drinking** 1999 – 2004 **best vintages** '82, '87, '92, '93, '94, '96 **drink with** Avocado • $10.50

temple bruer ★★★☆

Milang Road, Strathalbyn, SA 5255 **region** Langhorne Creek
phone (08) 8537 0203 **fax** (08) 8537 0131 **open** Tues-Sun 10–4.30
winemaker David Bruer **production** 11 000 **est.** 1980
product range ($12.20–22.05 R) Riesling, Verdelho, Botrytis Riesling, Cornucopia Grenache, Cabernet Merlot, Shiraz Malbec.
summary Always known for its eclectic range of wines, Temple Bruer (which also carries on a substantial business as a vine propagation nursery) has seen a sharp lift in wine quality. Clean, modern, redesigned labels add to the appeal of a stimulatingly different range of red wines.

terrace vale ★★★

Deasey's Lane, Pokolbin, NSW 2321 **region** Lower Hunter Valley
phone (02) 4998 7517 **fax** (02) 4998 7814 **open** 7 days 9–5
winemaker Alain Leprince **production** 10 000 **est.** 1971
product range ($10–17.50 CD) Semillon, Chardonnay, Semillon Chardonnay, Gewurztraminer, Elizabeth Sauvignon Blanc, Fine Hunter White, Pinot Noir, Shiraz, Fine Hunter Red, Cabernet Sauvignon, Sparkling.
summary Long-established but relatively low-profile winery heavily dependent on its cellar-door and local (including Newcastle) trade. Smart new packaging has lifted the presentation, and, as always, there are one or two very good wines among the portfolio.

thalgara estate NR

De Beyers Road, Pokolbin, NSW 2321 **region** Lower Hunter Valley
phone (02) 4998 7717 **fax** (02) 4998 7774 **open** 7 days 10–5
winemaker Steve Lamb **production** 3000 **est.** 1985
product range ($15–30 CD) Chardonnay, Show Reserve Chardonnay, Semillon Chardonnay, Shiraz, Show Reserve Shiraz, Shiraz Cabernet.
summary A low-profile winery but given to surprising show success, never more so than at the 1997 Hunter Valley Wine Show when it won the Doug Seabrook Memorial Trophy for Best Dry Red of Show with its 1995 Show Reserve Shiraz.

the gurdies NR

St Helier Road, The Gurdies, Vic 3984 **region** Gippsland
phone (03) 5997 6208 **fax** (03) 5997 6511 **open** 7 days 10–5
winemaker Peter Kozik **production** 1000 **est.** 1991
product range ($15–18 R) Riesling, Pinot Noir, Shiraz, Cabernet Sauvignon.
summary The only winery in the southwest Gippsland region, established on the slopes of The Gurdies hills overlooking Westernport Bay and French Island. Plantings of the 3.5-hectare vineyard commenced in 1981, but no fruit was harvested until 1991 owing to bird attack. A winery has been partially completed, and it is intended to increase the vineyards to 25 hectares and ultimately build a restaurant on-site.

the minya winery NR

Minya Lane, Connewarre, Vic 3227 **region** Geelong
phone (03) 5264 1397 **open** Public holidays and by appointment
winemaker Susan Dans **production** 1330 **est.** 1974
product range ($10.50–15.50 CD) Gewurztraminer, Chardonnay, Grenache, Cabernet Shiraz Merlot.
summary Geoff Dans first planted vines in 1974 on his family's dairy farm, followed by further plantings in 1982 and 1988. I have not tasted any of the wines.

the silos estate NR

Princes Highway, Jaspers Brush, NSW 2535 **region** Shoalhaven
phone (02) 4448 6082 **fax** (02) 4448 6246 **open** Wed-Mon 10–5
winemaker Gaynor Sims, Kate Khoury **production** 1000 **est.** 1985
product range ($11–14 CD) Traminer Riesling, Classic Dry White, Semillon, Chardonnay, Chardonnay Sauvignon Blanc, Wileys Creek Brut, Shiraz Cabernet, Tawny Port, Liqueur Muscat.

summary Since 1995, Gaynor Sims and Kate Khoury, together with viticulturist Jovica Zecevic, have worked hard to improve the quality of the wine, starting with the 5 hectares of estate vineyards but also in the winery. The winery continues to rely on the tourist trade, however, and the wines do not appear in normal retail channels.

the warren vineyard NR

Conte Road, Pemberton, WA 6260 **region** Pemberton
phone (08) 9776 1115 **fax** (08) 9776 1115 **open** Weekends and holidays 10–5, weekdays by appointment
winemaker Andrew Forsell **production** 600 **est.** 1985
product range ($13–16 CD) Chardonnay, Riesling, Merlot, Cabernet Merlot, Cabernet Blanc, Vintage Port.
summary The 1.4-hectare vineyard was established in 1985, and is one of the smallest in the Pemberton region, coming to public notice when its 1991 Cabernet Sauvignon won the award for the Best Red Table Wine from the Pemberton Region at the 1992 SGIO Western Australia Winemakers Exhibition. The wine in question showed very cool-growing conditions, being a little leafy and astringent, but with pleasant overall flavour.

the willows 

Light Pass Road, Light Pass, Barossa Valley, SA 5355 **region** Barossa Valley
phone (08) 8562 1080 **fax** (08) 8562 3447 **open** 7 days 10.30–4.30
winemaker Peter Scholz, Michael Scholz **production** 3500 **est.** 1989
product range ($9–14 R) Riesling, Semillon, Pinot Noir, Shiraz, Cabernet Sauvignon.
summary The Scholz family has been grape growers for generations. Current generation winemakers Peter and Michael Scholz could not resist the temptation to make smooth, well-balanced and flavoursome wines under their own label. These are all marketed with some years bottle age.

thistle hill 

McDonalds Road, Mudgee, NSW 2850 **region** Mudgee
phone (02) 6373 3546 **fax** (02) 6373 3540 **open** Thurs-Mon 10–4
winemaker David Robertson **production** 2500 **est.** 1976
product range ($11–19 CD) Riesling, Semillon, Chardonnay, Pinot Noir, Merlot, Zinfandel, Cabernet Sauvignon.
summary David and Leslie Robertson produce supremely honest wines, always full of flavour and appropriately reflecting the climate and terroir. Some may be a little short on finesse, but never on character. Chardonnay and Cabernet Sauvignon lead the way, and age well.

thomas NR

23–24 Crowd Road, Gelorup, WA 6230 **region** Geographe
phone (08) 9795 7925 **open** By appointment
winemaker Gill Thomas **production** 600 **est.** 1976
product range ($4.50–25 CD) Pinot Noir, Cabernet Sauvignon.
summary I have not tasted the elegant wines of Bunbury pharmacist Gill Thomas for several years; they are only sold to a local clientele.

thornhill/the berry farm NR

Bessel Road, Rosa Glen, WA 6285 **region** Margaret River
phone (08) 9757 5054 **fax** (08) 9757 5116 **open** 7 days 10–4.30
winemaker Eion Lindsay **production** NFP **est.** 1990
product range ($11.50–25 CD) Under the Thornhill label Classic Dry Semillon, Sauvignon Blanc, Cabernet Sauvignon, Tickled Pink (Sparkling Cabernet Sauvignon), Still Tickled Pink (Light Cabernet Sauvignon). Under The Berry Farm label a range of fruit-based wines including Sparkling Strawberry and Plum Port.
summary Although I have not enjoyed the Thornhill table wines, the fruit wines under The Berry Farm label are extraordinarily good. The sparkling strawberry wine has intense strawberry flavour; the plum port likewise, carrying its 16% alcohol with remarkable ease.

tilba valley NR

Glen Eden Vineyard, Corunna Lake via Tilba, NSW 2546 **region** Other Wineries of NSW
phone (02) 4473 7308 **open** Mon-Sat 10–5, Sun 11–5
winemaker Barry Field **production** 1400 **est.** 1978
product range ($10–14 CD) Traminer Riesling, Semillon, Chardonnay, Cabernet Hermitage.
summary A strongly tourist-oriented operation, serving a ploughman's lunch daily from noon to 2 pm. Has 5 hectares of estate vineyards; no recent tastings.

tim adams ★★★★

Warenda Road, Clare, SA 5453 **region** Clare Valley
phone (08) 8842 2429 **fax** (08) 8842 3550 **open** Mon-Fri 10.30–5, weekends 11–5
winemaker Tim Adams **production** 15 000 **est.** 1986
product range ($11.50–45 CD) Riesling, Semillon, Botrytis Semillon, Shiraz, Aberfeldy Shiraz, Cabernet.
summary Tim and Pam Adams have built a first class business since Tim Adams left his position as winemaker at Leasingham in 1985. Nine local growers provide the grapes for the enterprise, which has consistently produced wines of exceptional depth of flavour, and which also makes significant quantities of wine under contract for others in the district.

Tim Adams Riesling

Tim Adams is an immensely experienced winemaker, and now a veteran of the Clare Valley. Since establishing his own label, his forté has been full-bodied wooded whites and reds, but this wine shows that his skills most certainly extend to Riesling – where he started off many years ago at Leasingham.

🍷🍷🍷🍷 **1997** Light to medium yellow-green; a reserved, crisp minerally bouquet, unequivocally on the lighter side of the schizophrenic Clare vintage of '97. A tightly constructed palate, powerful but not lush, with mineral, toast and lime flavours; should age well. **rating:** 85

➾ **best drinking** 2000 – 2005 **best vintages** NA **drink with** Seafood salad • $11.50

Tim Adams Semillon

It is made to develop early, with substantial oak input (75% American, 25% French) and what appears to be skin contact used prior to fermentation. The wine is barrel-fermented and spends five months in oak.

🍷🍷🍷🍷 **1996** Medium to full yellow-green; the bouquet is typically full-bodied, but has swallowed up the oak. The palate has plenty of flavour and depth, and, against all the odds, it is neither phenolic nor excessively oaky. Finishes with good acidity. **rating:** 85

➭ **best drinking** 1998 – 2002 **best vintages** '89, '90, '92, '94, '95, '96 **drink with** Rich white meat dishes • $13.50

Tim Adams Shiraz

Produced from 4 hectares of shiraz owned by the Adams and Crawley families.

🍷🍷🍷🍷 **1996** Medium red-purple; the bouquet is concentrated, with briar and liquorice fruit; the palate is likewise concentrated, but not heavy, with mulberry, plum and a touch of liquorice. Does lighten off slightly on the finish, which may be no bad thing. **rating:** 88

➭ **best drinking** 2000 – 2006 **best vintages** '86, '88, '90, '92, '93, '96 **drink with** Spit roast lamb • $16

tim gramp ★★★☆

Mintaro Road, Watervale, SA 5452 **region** Clare Valley
phone (08) 8431 3338 **fax** (08) 8431 3229 **open** Weekends and holidays 10.30–4.30
winemaker Tim Gramp **production** 4000 **est.** 1990
product range ($11–25 R) Watervale Riesling, McLaren Vale Shiraz, McLaren Vale Grenache, Watervale Cabernet Sauvignon.
summary Tim Gramp runs an operation very similar to that of Simon Hackett, owning neither vineyards nor a winery, but simply purchasing grapes and making the wines in leased facilities – and succeeding handsomely in so doing.

Tim Gramp Watervale Riesling

With the underlying philosophy of matching variety and region, it is not surprising Tim Gramp's Riesling comes from Watervale in the Clare Valley. Made in a bold, full-frontal style.

🍷🍷🍷🍷 **1997** Medium to full yellow-green; a bouquet which falls on the full side of the Clare watershed, with a powerfully structured palate of lemon/citrus and mineral flavours, with a dry finish. **rating:** 84

➭ **best drinking** 1998 – 2002 **best vintages** NA **drink with** Bouillabaisse • $12

Tim Gramp McLaren Vale Shiraz

The inaugural 1991 Shiraz won a trophy, six gold and two silver medals, including a gold medal at the 1993 Intervin International Wine Show in New York. The wine is made in a full-throated, full-blooded style, using low-yielding dry-grown grapes and lots of American oak, and works to perfection. The wine is sourced from Willunga (in McLaren Vale) and spends 14 months in oak.

🍷🍷🍷🍷 **1996** Full red-purple; a powerful, dense bouquet with dark fruits and hints of bitter chocolate leads logically into a rich, dark chocolate and black cherry-flavoured palate with soft but persistent tannins woven throughout. Subtle oak. **rating:** 89

➭ **best drinking** 2000 – 2008 **best vintages** '91, '92, '94, '96 **drink with** Barbecued, marinated steak • $25

tingle-wood ★★★★★

region Great Southern
Glenrowan Road, Denmark, WA 6333 **region** Great Southern
phone (08) 9840 9218 **open** 7 days 9–5
winemaker Brenden Smith (Contract) **production** 1000 **est.** 1976
product range ($16–20 CD) Yellow Tingle (Riesling), Late Harvest Yellow Tingle, Red Tingle (Cabernet Shiraz), Ruby Tingle (Port-style).
summary An intermittent producer of Riesling of extraordinary quality, although birds and other disasters do intervene and prevent production in some years.

tinlins NR

Kangarilla Road, McLaren Flat, SA 5171 **region** McLaren Vale
phone (08) 8323 8649 **fax** (08) 8323 9747 **open** 7 days 9–5
winemaker Warren Randall **production** 30 000 **est.** 1977
product range ($1.50–3.40 CD) Generic table, fortified and flavoured wines sold for $1.50 for table wines and $3.40 for fortified wines.
summary A very interesting operation, run by former Seppelt sparkling winemaker Warren Randall, drawing upon 100 hectares of estate vineyards which specialises in bulk-wine sales to the major Australian wine companies. A small proportion of the production is sold direct through the cellar door at mouthwateringly low prices to customers who provide their own containers and purchase by the litre. McLaren Vale's only bulk-wine specialist.

tinonee vineyard NR

Milbrodale Road, Broke, NSW 2330 **region** Lower Hunter Valley
phone (02) 6579 1308 **fax** (02) 6579 1146 **open** Weekends 10–5
winemaker Simon Gilbert (Contract) **production** 1200 **est.** 1997
product range ($18 R) Chardonnay, Merlot, Shiraz.
summary Ian Craig has established 14 hectares of vineyards on a mix of red volcanic and river flat soils at Broke. Part are in production, and the remainder will come into bearing by the end of the decade, ultimately producing 5000 cases of wine per year.

tipperary hill estate NR

Alma-Bowendale Road, Alma via Maryborough, Vic 3465 **region** Bendigo
phone (03) 5461 3312 **fax** (03) 5461 3312 **open** Weekends 10–5, or by appointment
winemaker Paul Flowers **production** 250 **est.** 1986
product range ($15–25 CD) Shiraz, Pinot Noir, Cabernets.
summary All of the wine is sold through the cellar door and on-site restaurant, open on Sundays. Says Paul Flowers, production depends 'on the frost, wind and birds', which perhaps explains why this is very much a part-time venture. Situated 7 kilometres west of the city of Maryborough, Tipperary Hill Estate is the only winery operating in the Central Goldfields Shire. Winemaker Paul Flowers built the rough-cut pine winery and the bluestone residential cottage next-door with the help of friends. Together with wife Margaret he also operates a restaurant.

tizzana NR

518 Tizzana Road, Ebenezer, NSW 2756 **region** Other Wineries of NSW
phone (02) 4579 1150 **fax** (02) 4579 1216 **open** Weekends, holidays 12–6
winemaker Peter Auld **production** 200 **est.** 1887

product range ($5.50–16.50 CD) Estate-grown and made Shiraz, Cabernet Sauvignon, Port; cleanskin wines under Tizzana Selection label.

summary The only estate wines tasted (several years ago) were not good, but the historic stone winery is most certainly worth a visit, and a wide selection of Tizzana Selection wines from other makers gives a broad choice.

tollana ★★★★

Tanunda Road, Nuriootpa, SA 5355 **region** Barossa Valley

phone (08) 8560 9389 **fax** (08) 8562 2494 **open** Mon-Sat 10–5, Sun 1–5

winemaker Neville Falkenberg **production** 25 000 **est.** 1888

product range ($10–21 R) Riesling, Chardonnay, Sauvignon Blanc, Semillon, Botrytis Riesling, Hermitage, Show Reserve Shiraz, Cabernet Sauvignon Bin TR222, all Eden Valley-sourced with the exception of the Botrytis Riesling.

summary As the Southcorp Wine Group moves to establish regional identity for its wines, Tollana is emphasising its Eden Valley base. The white wines, made in a full-bodied, high-flavoured, relatively quick-maturing style, the red wines with a pleasing combination of power and elegance.

Tollana Riesling

For the better part of two decades, the Tollana Riesling has been one of Australia's better-kept secrets, particularly under its prior ownerships. It ages well, and has not infrequently collected trophies at national wine shows as a mature wine. Invariably released with several years bottle age.

🍷🍷🍷🍷 **1995** Brilliant, glowing yellow-green; the bouquet is soft but quite rich with pleasant bottle-developed toasty aromas. The palate seems fully developed, with lots of soft honey and toast flavours, finishing with soft acid. Will no doubt surprise by hanging in there indefinitely.

rating: 85

➯ **best drinking** 1998 – 2003 **best vintages** '86, '87, '90, '92, '93 **drink with** Seafood salad • $8

Tollana Show Reserve Shiraz

Only three vintages of this wine have been so far released: '91, '93 and '95. The policy is that it will only be released in exceptional years and with an appropriate record of success in wine shows. The wine is held for extra bottle maturation prior to release; thus the '93 was released in November 1996, with a show record of one trophy, three gold, three silver and five bronze medals.

🍷🍷🍷🍷 **1995** Full red-purple; much more concentrated than the varietal Shiraz Bin TR16, with abundant black cherry and blackberry fruit. The palate likewise offers another dimension of flavour and concentration, with dark cherry, plum and berry fruit leading the way, and well-balanced oak. **rating:** 89

➯ **best drinking** 2000 – 2005 **best vintages** '91, '93, '95 **drink with** Roast beef • $21

toorak estate NR

Toorak Road, Leeton, NSW 2705 **region** Riverina

phone (02) 6953 2333 **fax** (02) 6953 4454 **open** Mon-Sat 9–5

winemaker Frank Bruno, Robert Bruno **production** 80 000 **est.** 1965

product range ($6–15 CD) Rhine Riesling, Traminer Riesling, Colombard, Sauvignon Blanc, Semillon Riesling, Semillon, Chardonnay, Autumn Harvest, Lambrusco Red and White, Leeton Shiraz, Shiraz Cabernet, Cabernet Sauvignon, Sparkling, Fortifieds.

summary A traditional, long-established Riverina producer with a strong Italian-based clientele around Australia. Production has been increasing significantly, utilising 50 hectares of estate plantings and grapes purchased from other growers.

torresan estate NR

Manning Road, Flagstaff Hill, SA 5159 **region** McLaren Vale
phone (08) 8270 2500 **fax** (08) 8270 3848 **open** Mon–Sat 8–5
winemaker Michael Torresan, John Torresan **production** 13 000 **est.** 1972
product range ($6–13 CD) Riesling, Semillon, Cabernet Shiraz, Cabernet Sauvignon, Fortifieds.
summary A substantial cellar-door trade and local clientele account for most sales of mature but uninspiring wines.

treen ridge estate NR

Parker Road, Pemberton, WA 6260 **region** Pemberton
phone (08) 9776 1131 **fax** (08) 9776 1176 **open** Not
winemaker Andrew Mountford, Donnelly River Wines (Contract) **production** NFP **est.** 1992
product range ($NFP) Riesling, Sauvignon Blanc, Shiraz, Cabernet Sauvignon.
summary As the details indicate, the venture is in its infancy, with the first wine sales in 1997. Plans are for the cellar door to open by 1 July 1998, with bed and breakfast accommodation under construction. Draws upon 2 hectares of vines.

treeton estate ★★★

North Treeton Road, Cowaramup, WA 6284 **region** Margaret River
phone (08) 9755 5481 **fax** (08) 9755 5051 **open** 7 days 10–6
winemaker David McGowan **production** 3000 **est.** 1984
product range ($15–17 R) Chardonnay, Riesling, Estate White, Petit Rouge, Shiraz, Liqueur Muscat.
summary David McGowan and wife Corinne purchased the 30-hectare property upon which Treeton Estate is established in 1982, beginning to plant the vines two years later. He has done just about everything in his life, and in the early years was working in Perth, which led to various setbacks for the vineyard. The wines are light and fresh, sometimes rather too much so.

trentham estate ★★★☆

Sturt Highway, Trentham Cliffs, NSW 2738 **region** Murray Darling and Swan Hill
phone (03) 5024 8888 **fax** (03) 5024 8800 **open** Mon–Fri 8.30–5, weekends 9.30–5
winemaker Anthony Murphy, Shane Kerr **production** 30 000 **est.** 1988
product range ($8.50–14 R) Riesling, Sauvignon Blanc, Colombard Chardonnay, Chardonnay, Noble Taminga, Pinot Noir, Merlot, Grenache Shiraz, Shiraz, Burke & Wills Tawny Port; Tresoli White and Red, Falling Leaf Autumn White and Red.
summary Remarkably consistent tasting notes across all wine styles from all vintages since 1989 attest to the expertise of ex-Mildara winemaker Tony Murphy, now making the Trentham wines from his family vineyards. Indeed, Trentham seems to be going from strength to strength with each succeeding vintage, exemplified by the Tresoli White and Red wines. The winery restaurant is also recommended.

Trentham Estate Shiraz
Quite simply, a testament to Tony Murphy's winemaking skills, with far more character and weight than one normally associates with Riverland red wines.

🍷🍷🍷🍷 **1996** Medium to full red; the bouquet is rich, with blackberry, briar and liquorice varietal fruit, moving more to cherry, blackberry and mint on the palate. Gentle oak and soft tannins round off a pleasing wine. **rating:** 84

➾ **best drinking** 1999 – 2003 **best vintages** NA **drink with** Pizza • NA

tuck's ridge ★★★☆

37 Red Hill-Shoreham Road, Red Hill South, Vic 3937 **region** Mornington Peninsula
phone (03) 5989 8660 **fax** (03) 5989 8579 **open** 7 days 12–5
winemaker Daniel Greene **production** 12 000 **est.** 1988
product range ($16–32 R) Semillon, Riesling, Chardonnay, Pinot Noir, Cabernet Sauvignon Merlot, Vues Méthode Champenoise.
summary After an initial burst of frenetic activity following its launch in July 1993, Tuck's Ridge has slowed down a little. Nonetheless, plantings have been increased to a little over 25 hectares, making it one of the largest vineyards in production on the Mornington Peninsula.

tulloch ★★★

'Glen Elgin', De Beyers Road, Pokolbin, NSW 2321 **region** Lower Hunter Valley
phone (02) 4998 7580 **fax** (02) 4998 7682 **open** Mon-Fri 9–4.30, weekends 10–4.30
winemaker Patrick Auld **production** 35 000 **est.** 1895
product range ($11.20–13.80 R) Unoaked Chardonnay, Classic Hunter White, Semillon Chardonnay, Verdelho, Justina (Fruity White), Classic Rich Red, Cabernets, Hector of Glen Elgin (Hermitage), Fortifieds.
summary A once-great name and reputation which suffered enormously under multiple ownership changes, with a loss of identity and direction. In production terms at least, it has found its feet, for it is now the centre of winemaking activities in the Hunter Valley for the Lindeman, Tulloch and Hungerford Hill brands, the last suckling at the breast of the Verdelho, and doing very nicely. Once again, a disclosure of interest, as for Lindemans and Hungerford Hill.

tumbarumba wine cellars NR

Sunnyside, Albury Close, Tumbarumba, NSW 2653 **region** Tumbarumba
phone (02) 6948 3055 **fax** (02) 6948 3055 **open** Weekends and public holidays, or by appointment
winemaker Charles Sturt University (Contract) **production** 600 **est.** 1990
product range ($15–25) Chardonnay, Pinot Noir and Pinot Chardonnay sparkling wines under the Black Range label, with further individual labels likely for the future.
summary Tumbarumba Cellars has taken over the former George Martins Winery (itself established in 1990) to provide an outlet for wines made from Tumbarumba region grapes. It is essentially a co-operative venture, involving local growers and businessmen, and with modest aspirations to growth.

tumbarumba wine estates NR

Maragle Valley via Tumbarumba, NSW 2653 **region** Tumbarumba
phone (02) 6948 4457 **fax** (02) 6948 4457 **open** Not
winemaker Charles Sturt University (Contract) **production** **est.** 1995
product range Chardonnay, Pinot Chardonnay Sparkling.
summary Having established his vineyards progressively since 1982, Frank Minutello decided to seek to add value (and interest) to the enterprise by having a small proportion of his production vinified at Charles Sturt University, commencing with the 1995 vintage. The wines are sold by mail order and from The Elms Restaurant in Tumbarumba.

turkey flat ★★★★☆

Bethany Road, Tanunda, SA 5352 **region** Barossa Valley
phone (08) 8563 2851 **fax** (08) 8563 3610 **open** 7 days 11–5
winemaker Peter Schulz **production** 7000 **est.** 1990
product range ($11–21 CD) Semillon, Rosé, Grenache Noir, Shiraz, Cabernet Sauvignon.
summary The establishment date of Turkey Flat is given as 1990, but it might equally well have been 1870 (or thereabouts) when the Schulz family purchased the Turkey Flat vineyard, or 1847 when the vineyard was first planted to the very shiraz which still grows today. In addition there are 6 hectares of very old grenache, and 3 hectares of much younger semillon and cabernet sauvignon. A significant part of the output is sold to some of the best-known Barossa Valley makers, not the least being Charles Melton, St Hallett, and Rockford.

Turkey Flat Rosé

A delicious wine, made from a blend of 80% Grenache, 10% Cabernet Sauvignon and 10% Shiraz. The addition of the Cabernet Sauvignon and Shiraz components in fact takes the wine from a conventional Rosé-style towards a light-bodied dry red, an elusive goal for most winemakers.

🍷🍷🍷🍷 **1997** Vivid fuschia pink; as you would expect, the bouquet is clean and fresh, with a mix of vibrant cherry and more herbal notes. The palate is fresh, with the crisp young fruit neatly balanced by a touch of sweetness on the finish. **rating:** 85

➾ **best drinking** 1998 – 1999 **best vintages** NA **drink with** Nothing or anything • $11

Turkey Flat Shiraz

Based upon a precious patch of 145-year-old vines at the heart of the Turkey Flat Vineyard. It was made at Rockford by Chris Ringland, and has had the Adelaide wine press in a paroxysm of delight since it was released.

🍷🍷🍷🍷 **1995** Medium to full red-purple; a ripe and rich bouquet is full of sweet fruit, although there are some slightly blurry characters lurking in the background. On the palate ripe blackberry and blackcurrant fruit is to the fore, although again there is an echo of that character on the bouquet. May simply have been a poor cork. **rating:** 88

➾ **best drinking** 2000 – 2005 **best vintages** '90, '92, '93, '94 **drink with** Smoked kangaroo • $21

---

turramurra estate NR

RMB 4327 Wallaces Road, Dromana Vic 3926 **region** Mornington Peninsula
phone (03) 5987 1146 **fax** (03) 5987 1286 **open** By appointment
winemaker David Leslie **production** 750 **est.** 1989

product range ($20–25) Sauvignon Blanc, Chardonnay, Pinot Noir, Shiraz, Cabernet Sauvignon.
summary Dr David Leslie gave up his job as a medical practitioner after completing the Bachelor of Applied Science (Wine Science) at Charles Sturt University to concentrate on developing the family's 10-hectare estate at Dromana. Wife Paula is the vigneron.

twelve acres 

Nagambie-Rushworth Road, Bailieston, Vic 3608 **region** Goulburn Valley
phone (03) 5794 2020 **fax** (03) 5794 2020 **open** Thurs-Mon 10–6, July weekends only
winemaker Peter Prygodicz, Jana Prygodicz **production** 700 **est.** 1994
product range ($13–16 CD) Shiraz, Merlot, Cabernet Sauvignon.
summary The charmingly named Twelve Acres is a red wine specialist, with Peter and Jana Prygodicz making the wines on-site in a tiny winery. The wines could benefit from renewal of the oak in which they are matured, for they are all quite astringent.

twin bays NR

Lot 1 Martin Road, Yankalilla, SA 5203 **region** Other Wineries of SA
phone (08) 8267 2844 **fax** (08) 8239 0877 **open** Weekends and holidays
winemaker Bruno Georgio, Alan Dyson **production** 2000 **est.** 1989
product range ($9–19 CD) Riesling, Light Red, Wild Grenache, Shiraz, Cabernet Sauvignon, Fortifieds.
summary Twin Bays operates the first winery in the Yankalilla district, one hour's drive south of Adelaide on the Fleurieu Peninsula. Two hectares of estate plantings have been established, but until these and future plantings come into bearing, the wines are made by district veterans Alan Dyson and Bruno Georgio from grapes purchased from McLaren Vale. Production is planned to ultimately increase to 4000 cases by 1999; both the '95 and '96 Shiraz won medals at the Royal Hobart Wine Show.

twin valley estate NR

Hoffnungsthal Road, Lyndoch, SA 5351 **region** Barossa Valley
phone (08) 8524 4584 **fax** (08) 8524 4978 **open** 7 days 10–5
winemaker Fernando Martin **production** 2000 **est.** 1990
product range ($8.90–15 CD) Traminer, Frontignac Spätlese, Eden Valley Rhine, Chardonnay, Cabernet Sauvignon Franc, Classic Burgundy, Pinot Cabernet, White Port, Martin's Mead.
summary While Fernando Martin has always had his sights set firmly on the tourist trade, the Twin Valley Estate wines are more than acceptable, the spicy, limey Frontignac Spätlese being a particularly good example of its kind.

tyrrell's ★★★★★

Broke Road, Pokolbin, NSW 2321 **region** Lower Hunter Valley
phone (02) 4998 7509 **fax** (02) 4998 7723 **open** Mon-Sat 8–5
winemaker Andrew Spinaze **production** 600 000 **est.** 1858
product range ($7–35 R) At the bottom end the large-volume Long Flat White and Red; next in price is Old Winery Chardonnay, Semillon, Chardonnay Semillon, Semillon Sauvignon Blanc, Riesling, Pinot Noir, Shiraz, Cabernet Merlot; next a range of individual vineyard wines including Shee-Oak Chardonnay, Stevens Semillon, Lost Block Semillon, Brookdale Semillon,

Fordwich Verdelho, Brokenback Shiraz, Stevens Shiraz; at the very top Vat 1 Semillon, Vat 6 Pinot Noir, Vat 9 Shiraz, Vat 47 Chardonnay.

summary A quite extraordinary family winery which has grown up from an insignificant base in 1960 to become one of the most influential mid-sized companies, successfully competing with wines running all the way from cheap, volume-driven Long Flat White up to the super-premium Vat 47 Chardonnay, which is one of Australia's best. There is a similar range of price and style with the red wines, and in recent years Tyrrell's has simply never faltered within the parameters of price and style.

Tyrrell's Vat 1 Semillon

One of the great, classic Hunter Valley Semillons, produced from unirrigated vines which, because of their superior soils, do in fact yield well. Released as a young wine through the Tyrrell's mailing list and cellar door, but re-released through the retail trade at various intervals according to the vintage. Vat 1 Semillons have won 12 trophies, 87 gold, 72 silver and 99 bronze medals since 1964.

🍷🍷🍷🍷🍷 **1993** Full, glowing yellow-green; a complex bouquet, toasty with hints of spice; a supple and delicate array of flavours on the palate which are starting to sing. Between the time it was first tasted in 1995 and late 1997 had developed out of all recognition, and will go on from here. **rating:** 95

➪ **best drinking** 1998 – 2008 **best vintages** '75, '76, '77, '86, '87, '89, '90, '92, '93, '94
drink with Pan-fried veal • $18.50

undercliff NR

Yango Creek Road, Wollombi, NSW 2325 **region** Lower Hunter Valley
phone (02) 4998 3322 **fax** (02) 4998 3322 **open** Weekends 10–4 or by appointment
winemaker James Luxton, Janet Luxton **production** 1000 **est.** 1990
product range ($12–18 CD) Semillon, Shiraz, Sparkling Shiraz.

summary A combined winery and studio owned and run by James and Janet Luxton situated at Wollombi, on the edge of the Hunter Valley. Janet Luxton is the artist, having studied etching and printing at the Jerusalem Print Workshop, and James Luxton is the printer. The wines, produced from 2.5 hectares of estate vineyards, have won a number of awards in recent years at the Hunter Valley Wine Show and the Hunter Valley Small Winemakers Show.

van de scheur NR

O'Connors Lane, Pokolbin, NSW 2321 **region** Lower Hunter Valley
phone (02) 4998 7789 **fax** (02) 4998 7789 **open** Weekends 10–5
winemaker Kees Van De Scheur **production** 1500 **est.** 1995
product range ($16.50 CD) Semillon, Chardonnay, Shiraz.

summary Kees Van De Scheur is a Hunter Valley veteran, having spent the last 25 years in the Hunter Valley, first with the Robson Vineyard, and then Briar Ridge, before leaving in November 1993 to establish his own winery and label. He has purchased part of the historic Ingleside property, established by vigneron Frederick Ingle in 1872. After a hiatus of 60 years, vines have returned, with an initial planting of a little over 1 hectare (semillon, chardonnay and shiraz), increasing to 4 hectares by 1997. In the meantime, grapes purchased within the Hunter Valley provide the base for the Van De Scheur Wines.

vasse felix ★★★★★

Caves Road, Willyabrup, WA 6280 **region** Margaret River
phone (08) 9755 5242 **fax** (08) 9755 5425 **open** 7 days 10–5.30
winemaker Clive Otto, Will Shields **production** 40 000 **est.** 1967
product range ($12–48 R) Classic Dry White, Flinders Bay Semillon Sauvignon Blanc, Theatre White and Red, Forest Hill Riesling, Semillon, Chardonnay, Noble Riesling, Classic Dry Red, Shiraz, Flinders Bay Cabernet Sauvignon, Sparkling Brut, Heytesbury.

summary The 1999 vintage will see Vasse Felix wines produced in a brand-new 2000-tonne winery situated 200 metres to the west of the current facility; the old winery will be dedicated entirely to the restaurant and tasting rooms. A new 140-hectare vineyard at Jindong in the north of the Margaret River will supply a large part of the increased fruit intake.

Vasse Felix Semillon

Drawn primarily from 4 hectares of estate plantings. A very richly structured wine with an unusual depth of flavour, enhanced by 100% barrel fermentation in mainly new French oak, and five months in barrel thereafter.

🍷🍷🍷🍷🍸 **1997** Medium to full yellow-green; sophisticated spicy/charry oak leads the bouquet into a very rich palate, which carries the oak very well, for there are masses of lemon and tropical fruit flavours. Despite all this flavour, not heavy, and has good balance and length. **rating:** 90

➾ **best drinking** 1998 – 2001 **best vintages** '92, '93, '95, '96 **drink with** Coquilles St Jacques • $22.50

Vasse Felix Reserve Chardonnay

Yet another distinguished string to the Vasse Felix bow, and likewise the Chardonnay bow of Margaret River.

🍷🍷🍷🍷🍷 **1996** Medium to full yellow-green; in strong Margaret River-style with potent tangy/melon fruit and positive but not overdone spicy/clove oak. A perfectly balanced wine in the mouth, with sumptuous and ripe nectarine/peach fruit, yet not excessively heavy. Swallows up the high-quality oak. **rating:** 96

➾ **best drinking** 1998 – 2002 **best vintages** NA **drink with** Roast pork • $35

Vasse Felix Shiraz

Draws upon a little under 7 hectares of estate plantings, and over the years has produced some outstanding wines. The 1983 vintage, tasted in 1993 was wonderfully complex, rich and full with a touch of Rhône Valley gaminess. Since 1991 the quality of the wine has been outstanding, and it has enjoyed extraordinary success in wine shows, the 1996 winning trophies for Best Shiraz and Best Varietal Dry Red Table Wine (Any Variety) at the 1997 Royal Adelaide Wine Show.

🍷🍷🍷🍷🍸 **1996** Medium to full red-purple; a rich and complex bouquet with abundantly lush and ripe fruit, though lots of oak influence evident. A wine with lots of flavour and character in a no-holds-barred show style; blackberry fruit is touched by spice and surrounded by vanillin oak. **rating:** 92

➾ **best drinking** 2003 – 2013 **best vintages** '83, '85, '88, '90, '91, '92, '94, '96 **drink with** Rich casseroles • $33

Vasse Felix Heytesbury

Heytesbury is the flagship red of Vasse Felix, taking its name from Heytesbury Holdings, the company led by Janet Holmes à Court since the death of her husband, and which owns Vasse Felix. A blend of Cabernet Sauvignon, Cabernet Franc and Malbec which has been generously oaked.

🍷🍷🍷🍷 **1996** Strong red-purple; the bouquet is scented and aromatic with a potent mix of leaf, spice and mint, together with oak. The palate is potent and youthful with high-toned, slightly edgy fruit, and not showing the same lusciously ripe characters of the '95. **rating:** 86

➾ **best drinking** 2001 – 2011 **best vintages** NA **drink with** Beef Bordelaise • $48

veritas ★★★

94 Langmeil Road, Tanunda, SA 5352 **region** Barossa Valley
phone (08) 8563 2330 **open** Mon-Fri 9–5, weekends 11–5
winemaker Rolf Binder **production** 7500 **est.** 1955
product range ($10–14 CD) Riesling, Semillon Sauvignon Blanc, Tramino, Leanyka, Cabernet Franc Merlot, Cabernet Sauvignon, Shiraz Cabernet, Bikaver Bull's Blood, Heysen Vineyard Shiraz, Fortifieds.
summary The Hungarian influence is obvious in the naming of some of the wines, but Australian technology is paramount in shaping the generally very good quality. Rolf Binder seeks no publicity for the wines outside South Australia.

vicarys ★★☆

Northern Road, Luddenham, NSW 2745 **region** Other Wineries of NSW
phone (02) 4773 4161 **fax** (02) 4773 4411 **open** Mon-Fri 9–5, weekends 11.30–5.30
winemaker Chris Niccol **production** 2500 **est.** 1923
product range ($6.70–12 CD) Chardonnay, Semillon, Riesling, Gewurztraminer, Fumé Blanc, Cabernet Sauvignon, Shiraz Cabernet Merlot, Sparkling, Fortifieds.
summary Vicarys justifiably claims to be the Sydney region's oldest continuously operating winery, having been established in a very attractive, large, stone shearing shed built around 1890. Most of the wines come from other parts of Australia, but the winery does draw upon 1 hectare of estate traminer and 3 hectares of chardonnay for those wines, and has produced some good wines of all styles over the years.

villa primavera NR

Mornington-Flinders Road, Red Hill, Vic 3937 **region** Mornington Peninsula
phone (03) 5989 2129 **open** Weekends, public holidays 10–5, January 7 days 10–5
winemaker Peter Cumming **production** 400 **est.** 1984
product range ($20–30 CD) Chardonnay, Cabernets, Méthode Champenoise.
summary A most unusual operation, which is in reality a family Italian-style restaurant at which the wine is principally sold and served, and which offers something totally different on the Mornington Peninsula. A consistent winner of tourism and food awards, it is praised by all who go there, particularly for the concerts staged throughout January each year.

vintina estate NR

1282 Nepean Highway, Mt Eliza, Vic 3930 **region** Mornington Peninsula
phone (03) 9787 8166 **fax** (03) 9775 2035 **open** 7 days 9–5
winemaker Jim Filippone, Kevin McCarthy (Consultant) **production** 400 **est.** 1985

product range ($12–14 CD) Chardonnay, Semillon, Pinot Gris, Pinot Noir, Cabernet Sauvignon.
summary The initial releases of Vintina (the only wines tasted to date), were mediocre. With competent contract-winemaking, improvement can be expected. However, no recent tastings.

violet cane vineyard NR

13 Wallace Court, Glen Aplin, Qld 4381 **region** Granite Belt
phone (018) 987 276 **open** Not
winemaker Adam Chapman **production** 85 **est.** 1994
product range ($22 ML) Semillon, Merlot, Sparkling.
summary The intriguingly named Violet Cane Vineyard, and no less startlingly labelled wine, is the tiny personal business of Ballandean winemaker Adam Chapman, who manages to fit in three winemaking lives: one at Ballandean, one for Violet Cane, and the last as a Flying Winemaker travelling to Europe each Australian spring. It is perhaps fitting that Adam Chapman should have married Elle Sigurdardottir in her native Iceland in June 1998.

virage

13B Georgette Road, Gracetown, WA 6284 **region** Margaret River
phone (08) 9755 5318 **fax** (08) 9755 5318 **open** Not
winemaker Bernard Abbott **production** 1000 **est.** 1990
product range ($13–20 R) Sauvignon Blanc, Semillon Chardonnay, Traminer Riesling, Cabernet Shiraz Zinfandel, Cabernet Merlot.
summary Former Vasse Felix winemaker Bernard Abbott, together with wife Pascale, acquired (under long-term lease) the former government research station vineyard at Bramley Estate in 1990. Bernard Abbott makes the wines at a local Margaret River winery, and sells them by mailing list and direct to retailer and restaurants in Perth, Melbourne and Sydney.

virgin hills

Salisbury Road, Lauriston West via Kyneton, Vic 3444 **region** Macedon
phone (03) 5423 9169 **fax** (03) 5423 9324 **open** By appointment
winemaker Martin Williams **production** 3500 **est.** 1968
product range ($35 R) A single Cabernet Sauvignon Shiraz Merlot Blend called Virgin Hills; occasional limited Reserve release.
summary The Macedon region is not normally a kind host to the cabernet sauvignon family nor shiraz, but in the warmer vintages in particular, Virgin Hills produces one of Australia's great red wines. Very quietly, it has moved to sulphur-free red winemaking, adding yet a further dimension of interest to this fascinating winery.

Virgin Hills

An entirely estate-grown blend (in descending order) of Cabernet Sauvignon, Shiraz, Merlot, Malbec and occasionally a touch of Pinot Noir. Not only are the grapes organically grown, but since 1988 the wine has been made without the use of added sulphur dioxide. It is a brave move which makes world's best preservative-free red; only time will tell how these wines age over a decade. The '95 is a blend of 59% Cabernet Sauvignon, 33% Shiraz, 4% Malbec and 4% Merlot; the grapes were picked between 13 April and 5 June, surely the longest period for any single estate anywhere in the world.

🍷🍷🍷🍷🍷 **1995** Medium to full red-purple; the bouquet is fragrant, of moderate intensity, with cedar, cigar box, leaf and spice aromas. The palate is fine and elegant, with leaf, mint and spice flavours underlying the red cherry/berry fruit; fine-grained tannins on a delicate but long finish. **rating:** 90

⇨ **best drinking** 1998 – 2005 **best vintages** '74, '75, '76, '80, '82, '85, '88, '90, '91, '92, '95 **drink with** Duck • $35

voyager estate ★★★★☆

Lot 1 Stevens Road, Margaret River, WA 6285 **region** Margaret River
phone (08) 9385 3133 **fax** (08) 9383 4029 **open** 7 days 10–4
winemaker Stuart Pym **production** 22 000 **est.** 1978
product range ($14–25 R) Chenin Blanc, Classic White, Semillon, Chardonnay, Cabernet Merlot.
summary Formerly Freycinet Estate, renamed after its purchase (in May 1991) from Western Australian viticulturist Peter Gherardi. Much money has been spent on the property by new owner, the mining magnate Michael Wright, although the winery itself remains in strictly utilitarian form. The wines are rich and opulent, particularly the white wines.

Voyager Estate Semillon

Produced from 7.5 hectares of estate plantings, and right from the outset has proved itself a very distinguished wine. Partial barrel fermentation in a mix of French and American oak has been skilfully employed to add a dimension to the wine, but without taking away from the varietal fruit character. Good in 1995, and even better in 1996.

🍷🍷🍷🍷🍷 **1996** Light green-yellow; an intense, pungent herbal/grassy bouquet in the best Margaret River style leads on to a palate full of character and flavour, with spicy oak appearing only on the finish. Good acidity stops the wine from cloying. **rating:** 91

⇨ **best drinking** 1999 – 2006 **best vintages** '95, '96 **drink with** Chicken • $20.44

Voyager Estate Chardonnay

In the majority of vintages Voyager Estate produces a Chardonnay of complexity, style and verve typical of the Margaret River at its very best.

🍷🍷🍷🍷🍷 **1996** Medium yellow-green; by Margaret River standards, relatively subtle and elegant, with seductive melon and fig fruit interwoven with smooth oak. An excellent wine on the palate with an admirable touch of restraint, achieving that elegance without sacrificing flavour or length. **rating:** 95

⇨ **best drinking** 1998 – 2003 **best vintages** '92, '93, '95, '96 **drink with** Braised pork neck • $23.60

wa de lock ★★★

Stratford Road, Maffra, Vic **region** Gippsland
phone (03) 5147 3244 **fax** (03) 5147 3132 **open** Thur-Tues 10–5
winemaker Graeme Little **production** 1500 **est.** 1987
product range ($13.95–16.95 R) Chameleon White Pinot, Chardonnay, Reserve Chardonnay, Sauvignon Blanc, Noble Sauvignon Blanc, Pinot Noir, Cabernet Merlot.
summary The initial plantings of pinot noir, cabernet sauvignon and sauvignon blanc in 1987 have been progressively expanded, with chardonnay being added, and 6.7 hectares now under vine. Grape intake has been supplemented by purchases of riesling, merlot and cabernet franc

grown at Maffra. The quality of the wines has improved steadily as Graeme Little's handling of oak has become more assured, and the range of wines has increased.

Wa De Lock Noble Sauvignon Blanc

Necessity was very probably the mother of the invention of this wine, prompted by the cool and wet 1996 vintage. The wine is in fact only lightly botrytis-affected, and is an interesting example of a rare wine style in this country. The '97, even better than the '96, suggests Graeme Little is onto something.

🍷🍷🍷🍷 **1997** Brilliant green-yellow; herbaceous, varietal sauvignon blanc comes through strongly on the bouquet. The palate is clean and fresh, with honey and herb flavours of spätlese sweetness. Pristinely clean throughout, and very well made. **rating:** 85

➾ **best drinking** 1998 – 2001 **best vintages** '96, '97 **drink with** Prosciutto and melon • $16.95

wandering brook estate NR

PO Box 32, Wandering, WA 6308 **region** Other Wineries of WA
phone (08) 9884 1064 **fax** (08) 9884 1064 **open** Weekends 9.30–6
winemaker Steve Radikovich **production** 2000 **est.** 1989
product range ($10–14.95 CD) Verdelho, Chardonnay, Unwooded Chardonnay, Soft Red and White, Cabernet Sauvignon, Sparkling Verdelho, Port.
summary Laurie and Margaret White have planted 10 hectares of vines on their 130-year-old family property in a move to diversify. Up to 1994 the wines were made at Goundrey, since 1994 at the nearby Hotham Valley. Renamed Wandering Brook Estate late 1994; up till then known as Redhill Estate.

wandin valley estate ★★★★

Wilderness Road, Rothbury, NSW 2321 **region** Lower Hunter Valley
phone (02) 4930 7313 **fax** (02) 4930 7814 **open** 7 days 10–5
winemaker Geoff Broadfield **production** 8000 **est.** 1973
product range ($13–22 R) Pavilion Range Dry White, Classic White and Dry Red; Estate Range of Semillon, Chardonnay, Cabernet Sauvignon, Shiraz, Ruby Cabernet and Muscat; top of the range WVE Cabernet Brut Champagne, Reserve Chardonnay, Bridie's Shiraz and Reserve Cabernet Sauvignon.
summary The former Millstone vineyard now owned by the producer of Australian television's classic 'A Country Practice' who has acquired the services of Allanmere winemaker Geoff Broadfield. Rapidly developing Chardonnays have been the focal point of Wandin Valley's considerable show success. The estate also boasts a Cope Williams-type village cricket oval and extensive cottage accommodation.

Wandin Valley WVE Reserve Chardonnay

The Reserve Chardonnay was introduced with effect from the 1994 vintage, and was a gold medal winner at the 1994 Australian National Wine Show in Canberra. Part of the wine is barrel-fermented in a mix of French and American oak barriques, and part is fermented in stainless steel. The two portions are then blended, although the American oak (as ever) does tend to dominate proceedings.

🍷🍷🍷🍷 **1997** Glowing yellow-green; voluminous charry/toasty American barrel-ferment oak on the bouquet, and clove/spice charry oak is likewise very evident on the palate. However, all of this oak has been well handled and integrated, and there is fruit lurking there in support. Will have enormous appeal to those who like oaky styles. **rating:** 87

➾ **best drinking** 1998 – 1999 **best vintages** '94, '97 **drink with** Barbecued spatchcock • $22

Wandin Valley Estate Bridie's Shiraz

Whether James and Phillipa Daverne's granddaughter came first, I am not sure, but I suspect the wine was named in her honour. Whatever be the answer, a most attractive wine.

🍷🍷🍷🍷 **1996** Medium red-purple; a spotlessly clean bouquet of medium intensity, with cherry, vanilla and plum aromas leads into a wine which is ever so slightly on the oaky side, but has nice flavour and balance, with hints of spice, black cherry and plum. **rating:** 86

➾ **best drinking** 2000 – 2006 **best vintages** NA **drink with** Moroccan lamb • $22

Wandin Valley Estate WVE Reserve Cabernet Sauvignon

Like the Reserve Chardonnay, made in restricted quantities, typically 500 cases. A consistent show medal winner, but the '96 is absolutely the best wine to come from Wandin Valley since 1991.

🍷🍷🍷🍷🍷 **1996** Medium to full red-purple; abundant, lush, ripe cassis blackcurrant fruit is supported by pleasant oak on the bouquet. There is more of the same rich, ripe voluptuously textured sweet cassis fruit on the palate, with sweet vanillin oak in perfect harmony. **rating:** 91

➾ **best drinking** 2000 – 2006 **best vintages** '91, '96 **drink with** Braised duck • $22

waninga ★★★★

Hughes Park Road, Sevenhill via Clare, SA 5453 **region** Clare Valley
phone (08) 8843 4395 **fax** (08) 8843 4395 **open** 7 days 10–5
winemaker Tim Adams, Jeffrey Grosset (Contract) **production** 1500 **est.** 1989
product range ($30 CD) Skilly Hills Riesling, Late Picked Riesling, Chenin Blanc, Chardonnay, Shiraz, Reserve Shiraz, Cabernet Sauvignon, Port.
summary The large vineyards owned by Waninga were established in 1974, but it was not until 1989 that a portion of the grapes was withheld from sale and vinified for the owners. Since that time, Waninga has produced some quite lovely wines, having wisely opted for very competent contract-winemaking. At any one time, a number of different vintages of several of the wines are available from cellar door.

Waninga Shiraz

Mature vines and the Tim Adams winemaking stamp produce an excellent Clare Valley-style. The '96 came first in the Shiraz Class in the 1998 Winewise Small Makers Competition.

🍷🍷🍷🍷🍷 **1996** Medium to full red-purple; red berry and mint varietal fruit on both bouquet and palate is supported by positive, but by no means excessive, American oak. Well balanced, with soft tannins. **rating:** 90

➾ **best drinking** 2000 – 2006 **best vintages** '89, '91, '96 **drink with** Steak and kidney pie • $16

wansbrough wines NR

Richards Road, Ferguson, WA 6236 **region** Geographe
phone (08) 9728 3091 **fax** (08) 9728 3091 **open** Weekends 10–5
winemaker Willespie Wines (Contract) **production** 250 **est.** 1986
product range ($12–18 CD) Riesling, Semillon, Sauvignon Blanc, Constantia (late-picked Semillon), Shiraz Cabernet, Port.
summary Situated east of Dardanup in the picturesque Ferguson Valley, Wansbrough enjoys views of the distant Geographe Bay and the nearer state forest, with the Bibblemun Track running along its northern and eastern borders. To taste the wine you need either to order by mail or visit the Wansbrough restaurant on weekends.

wantirna estate NR

Bushy Park Lane, Wantirna South, Vic 3152 **region** Yarra Valley
phone (03) 9801 2367 **fax** (03) 9887 0225 **open** By appointment
winemaker Reg Egan, Maryann Egan **production** 1000 **est.** 1963
product range ($30 CD) Isabella Chardonnay, Lily Pinot Noir, Cabernet Merlot.
summary Situated well within the boundaries of the Melbourne metropolitan area Wantirna Estate is part of a nature reserve. The only retail outlet for the wine is Richmond Hill Cellars; all the remainder is sold through mail order, to selected restaurants and to a few overseas customers. In deference to Reg Egan's very firmly held views on the subject, neither the winery nor the wines are rated.

Wantirna Estate Isabella Chardonnay

Produced from 1.3 hectares of estate plantings. The grapes are picked at maximum ripeness, whole-bunch pressed, and barrel-fermented in a mix of 50% new and 50% second-use barriques from central France, and left on lees until the following March, when the wine is racked, fined and bottled.

1996 Light to medium yellow-green; the bouquet is soft, with discreet melon and fig fruit, and hints of cashew. The palate shows some green apple and mineral notes alongside the melon and fig of the bouquet; neither rich nor luscious. **rating:** NR

➾ **best drinking** 1998 – 2002 **best vintages** '91, '92, '93, '94 **drink with** Pan-fried trout in black butter • $30

Wantirna Estate Lily Pinot Noir

A new label for a wine which has been made for almost 20 years at Wantirna Estate, adorned with a Michael Leunig drawing, as far removed from the original Wantirna Estate label as the earth is from the sun. The wine is just great.

1996 Medium red-purple; the bouquet is quite ripe, with foresty/gamey overtones to the plummy fruit. A similar range of flavours come through on the relatively firm palate, finishing with life-sustaining tannin. **rating:** NR

➾ **best drinking** 1999 – 2003 **best vintages** '91, '92, '94, '96 **drink with** Peking duck • $25

wards gateway ★★☆

Barossa Valley Highway, Lyndoch, SA 5351 **region** Barossa Valley
phone (08) 8524 4138 **open** 7 days 9–5.30
winemaker Ray Ward (plus contract winemakers) **production** 5000 **est.** 1979

product range ($7.50–9 CD) Riesling, Chablis, Frontignac, Fumé Blanc, Shiraz, Cabernet Sauvignon, Port.
summary The very old vines surrounding the winery produce the best wines, which are made without frills or new oak and sold without ostentation.

warrabilla NR

Murray Valley Highway, Rutherglen, Vic 3685 **region** Rutherglen
phone (02) 6032 9461 **fax** (02) 6032 9461 **open** 7 days 10–5
winemaker Andrew Sutherland-Smith **production** 2000 **est.** 1986
product range ($12–18 ML) King Valley Riesling, Chardonnay, Brimin Series Cabernet Shiraz, Glenrowan Cabernet Sauvignon, Shiraz, Vintage Port.
summary Former All Saints winemaker Andrew Sutherland-Smith has leased a small winery at Corowa to make the Warrabilla wines from a vineyard developed by himself and Carol Smith in the Indigo Valley.

warramate 

27 Maddens Lane, Gruyere, Vic 3770 **region** Yarra Valley
phone (03) 5964 9219 **fax** (03) 5964 9219 **open** Weekends 10–6, Mon-Fri by appointment
winemaker Jack Church, David Church **production** 800 **est.** 1970
product range ($16–22 CD) Riesling, Shiraz, Cabernet Sauvignon.
summary Wine quality has been variable in recent years; it would seem that the oak in some of the older barrels questionable. At their best, reflect the distinguished site on which the vineyard sits.

Warramate Cabernet Sauvignon

Produced from 0.8 of a hectare of cabernet sauvignon, with a little merlot included in the plantings. Like the Shiraz, the vines are not irrigated, and are consequently low-yielding.
1995 Medium red-purple; the bouquet is clean, with pleasant earthy/berry cabernet fruit of medium intensity. The palate is particularly attractive, with cassis/redcurrant fruit and barely perceptible oak. Much the best of the currently available Warramate wines. **rating:** 85

best drinking 1999 – 2004 **best vintages** '88, '95 **drink with** Mature cheddar • $22

warrenmang vineyard 

Mountain Creek Road, Moonambel, Vic 3478 **region** Pyrenees
phone (03) 5467 2233 **fax** (03) 5467 2309 **open** 7 days 9–5
winemaker Simon Clayfield **production** 8450 **est.** 1974
product range ($10–24.95 CD) Bazzani Chardonnay Chenin Blanc, Estate Chardonnay, Late Harvest Traminer, Bazzani Cabernet Shiraz Dolcetto, Estate Shiraz, Grand Pyrenees (Cabernet-blend), Vintage Port.
summary Warrenmang is now the focus of a superb accommodation and restaurant complex created by former restaurateur Luigi Bazzani and wife Athalie, which is in much demand as a conference centre as well as for weekend tourism. The striking black Bazzani label is gradually overtaking the Warrenmang label in importance, and is responsible for the growth in the volume of production. It is partially sourced from contract-growers; the estate wines are, as their name suggests, estate-grown.

Warrenmang Grand Pyrenees

A blend of predominantly Cabernet Sauvignon, but also including Merlot, Cabernet Franc and Shiraz; estate-produced, and has always been on the big, if not huge, side, but which has now come under control.

1995 Full red-purple; dense, dark briary berry fruit aromas and a touch of cedar mark a powerful bouquet. The palate is powerful, dense and still tight and tannic, but is clean, and will progressively open up and soften with age. **rating:** 84

best drinking 2002 – 2007 **best vintages** NA **drink with** Aged rump • $25

water wheel

Bridgewater-on-Loddon, Bridgewater, Vic 3516 **region** Bendigo
phone (03) 5437 3060 **fax** (03) 5437 3082 **open** Mon-Sat 9–5, Sun 12–5
winemaker Peter Cumming, Bill Trevaskis **production** 27 000 **est.** 1972
product range ($8–14 R) Chardonnay, Riesling, Sauvignon Blanc, Pinot Noir, Shiraz, Cabernet Sauvignon; grapes from other districts under premium Wing Fields label.
summary Peter Cumming gained great respect as a winemaker during his four-year stint with Hickinbotham Winemakers, and his 1989 purchase of Water Wheel was greeted with enthusiasm by followers of his wines. Recent releases have been of consistent quality and modest price.

Water Wheel Shiraz

The Shiraz is always presented in a way which encourages early consumption, for the wines are never tannic or extractive, and put the emphasis on fresh fruit. However, in vintages such as 1995 and 1996 there is the substance for medium-term cellaring.

1996 Medium to full red; ripe earthy varietal shiraz and well judged vanillin oak on the bouquet are followed by a strongly flavoured black cherry and plum palate. Plenty of texture and structure, and nice oak handling all contribute to a good wine. **rating:** 88

best drinking 1999 – 2004 **best vintages** '94, '96 **drink with** Cold meats • $12

watson

NR

75 Monbulk-Seville Road, Wandin East, Vic 3139 **region** Yarra Valley
phone (03) 5964 3059 **fax** (03) 5964 3059 **open** Weekends and public holidays 11–5
winemaker Oakridge (Contract) **production** 700 **est.** 1986
product range ($13–16.50 CD) Chardonnay, Cabernet Sauvignon.
summary Production from the 4-hectare vineyard has been sold to other makers in some years, and in others part has been contract-made for owner Geoffrey Watson. It has made a somewhat uncertain entry onto the marketplace.

waybourne

NR

60 Lemins Road, Waurn Ponds, Vic 3221 **region** Geelong
phone (03) 5241 8477 **fax** (03) 5241 8477 **open** By appointment
winemaker Various Consultant/Contract **production** 400 **est.** 1980
product range ($8–12 ML) Rhine Riesling, Frontignac, Pinot Gris, Cabernet Sauvignon.
summary Owned by Tony and Kay Volpato, who have relied upon external consultants to assist with the winemaking. No recent tastings.

wayne thomas wines NR

26 Kangarilla Road, McLaren Vale, SA 5171 **region** Warehouse
phone (08) 8323 9737 **fax** (08) 8323 9737 **open** Not
winemaker Wayne Thomas **production** 4000 **est.** 1994
product range ($16–45 ML) Sauvignon Blanc, Chardonnay, Shiraz.
summary Wayne Thomas is a McLaren Vale veteran, having commenced his winemaking career in 1961, working for Stonyfell, Ryecroft and Saltram before establishing Fern Hill with his wife Pat in 1975. When they sold Fern Hill in April 1994 they started again, launching the Wayne Thomas Wines label, using contract-grown grapes sourced from throughout McLaren Vale.

wellington ★★★★☆

Cnr Richmond and Denholms Roads, Cambridge, Tas 7170 **region** Southern Tasmania
phone (03) 6248 5844 **fax** (03) 6243 0226 **open** By appointment
winemaker Andrew Hood **production** 2000 **est.** 1990
product range ($16–20 ML) Riesling, Sweet Riesling, Chardonnay, Pinot Noir.
summary Consultant-winemaker Andrew Hood (ex-Charles Sturt University) and wife Jenny have constructed a state-of-the-art winery on land leased from the University of Tasmania. The 2000-case production of Wellington is dwarfed by the 4500 cases contract-made for others, but the wines are always flawlessly crafted, particularly the Chardonnay.

Wellington Riesling

Another wine from the Wellington stable to repay cellaring, and, as with the other wines, immaculately made. Sourced not from southern Tasmania, but from a vineyard at Relbia, on the outskirts of Launceston. The '97 is a most interesting wine, which has distinct overtones of Alsace, and which I tasted in several shows, with similar notes, but a very different points outcome – perhaps not surprising given the characters.

🍷🍷🍷🍷🍷 **1997** Medium yellow-green; the bouquet is rich, with Alsatian-like phenolics, showing a mix of lime, herb and mineral. The palate lives up to the bouquet, powerful, and well outside traditional Australian mainstream style. It would seem this character came from the unseasonable 1997 vintage, rather than any winemaking tricks. Has considerable length. **rating:** 90

⇨ **best drinking** 1998 – 2003 **best vintages** NA **drink with** Sautéed prawns • $16.60

Wellington Chardonnay

Andrew Hood is nothing if not economical in his back label description of this wine as 'a dry, lightly wooded wine made from fruit grown mainly in northern Tasmania'. The '95 has matured superbly, winning a gold medal at the 1997 Tasmanian Wines Show, the very personification of elegance. The '97 followed suit at the 1998 Tasmanian Wines Show. The '92, tasted socially (in February 1998) is as fresh as a daisy, with years in front of it yet.

🍷🍷🍷🍷🍷 **1997** Light to medium yellow-green; a wine which has true elegance from start to finish, and which is driven largely, though not entirely, by its mix of citrus, melon and faintly herbal fruit. Immaculately balanced, and literally caresses the mouth. **rating:** 94

⇨ **best drinking** 1998 – 2003 **best vintages** '92, '95, '96, '97 **drink with** Gravlax • $16.60

Wellington Iced Riesling

Produced using freeze concentration of the unfermented juice in a stainless steel tank. Water freezes first, and is removed in solid form, lifting the sugar, acidity (and flavour) of the remaining juice which is then conventionally cold-fermented. Awarded the trophy for Best Unwooded Table Wine (Dry or Sweet) at the 1998 Tasmanian Wines Show.

🍷🍷🍷🍷🍷 **1997** Bright, light green-yellow; both aromatic and flavoursome, with a beguiling mix of lime and white peach flavours, spotlessly clean and well balanced with pleasantly soft acidity. **rating:** 91

➾ **best drinking** 1998 – 2001 **best vintages** '97 **drink with** Poached peaches • NA

wendouree ★★★★★

Wendouree Road, Clare, SA 5453 **region** Clare Valley
phone (08) 8842 2896 **open** By appointment
winemaker Tony Brady **production** 2500 **est.** 1895
product range ($26–30 ML) Shiraz Malbec, Shiraz Mataro, Cabernet Malbec, Cabernet Sauvignon, Muscat of Alexandria.

summary The iron fist in a velvet glove best describes these extraordinary wines. They are fashioned with passion and yet precision from the very old vineyard with its unique terroir by Tony and Lita Brady, who rightly see themselves as custodians of a priceless treasure. The 100-year-old stone winery is virtually unchanged from the day it was built; this is in every sense a treasure beyond price.

Wendouree Shiraz

One hundred per cent estate-grown from vines of varying ages, but none immature. A varying percentage of the wine is declassified each year. Five hundred cases made.

🍷🍷🍷🍷🍷 **1996** Medium to full purple-red; the bouquet is highly scented, with pungent earth and mint aromas. Black cherry flavours progressively appeared through the powerful, earthy and tightly knit palate; awesome tannins. **rating:** 94

➾ **best drinking** 2003 – 2013 **best vintages** NA **drink with** Aged beef • $26

Wendouree Shiraz Malbec

A blend of 80% Shiraz and 20% Malbec, with the same rigid fruit selection from old vines which is invariable Wendouree practice. Two hundred and fifty cases made.

🍷🍷🍷🍷🍷 **1996** Medium to full purple-red; the bouquet is similar to that of the Shiraz, but with slightly softer dark berry fruit blending into that faintly jammy character of Malbec. On the palate the rich, juicy Malbec contribution is quite evident, yet the predominant structure is provided by the Shiraz. **rating:** 95

➾ **best drinking** 2006 – 2016 **best vintages** NA **drink with** Aged beef • $30

Wendouree Shiraz Mataro

A blend of 80% Shiraz and 20% Mourvedre (Tony Brady, ever the traditionalist, clings doggedly to the Mataro dialectic name) a time-honoured blend with a history stretching back well over 100 years in South Australia, and very nearly that long at Wendouree. 500 cases made.

🍷🍷🍷🍷🍷 **1996** Medium to full purple-red; the bouquet is stylish, with berry, earthy, mint and leaf aromas, the palate again showing some minty notes and an exceptionally long finish – supported, needless to say, by abundant tannins. **rating:** 93

➾ **best drinking** 2003 – 2013 **best vintages** NA **drink with** Aged beef • $26

Wendouree Cabernet Malbec

This is but one of five wines produced in most vintages from the estate. Each one is entitled to be classed as a classic wine, each one a monument to the terroir and to the Bradys' passionate defence of it. The 1995 was the centenary release, incidentally. Five hundred cases made.

ΥΥΥΥΥ **1996** Medium to full red-purple; a stupendously concentrated and powerful bouquet, bursting with ripe blackberry fruit; the palate is opulently rich, ripe and round, with the Malbec influence very evident. Luscious and mouthfilling. **rating:** 95

⇨ **best drinking** 2006 – 2016 **best vintages** '83, '86, '89, '90, '91, '92, '94, '95, '96 **drink with** Leave it in the cellar for a decade • $26

Wendouree Cabernet Sauvignon

Classic old-vine Clare Cabernet, unforced by oak, and probably needing longer than all of the other Wendouree wines to reveal its true character. Two hundred and fifty cases made.

ΥΥΥΥΥ **1996** Medium red-purple; a pungent, scented bouquet with a mix of herbaceous, cassis and earth aromas; the potent, herbal palate has undertones of mint, olive and cassis; all fairly angular and hard at this juncture, but will undoubtedly soften and flower with age. **rating:** 92

⇨ **best drinking** 2006 – 2016 **best vintages** NA **drink with** Aged beef • $30

west cape howe wines NR

PO Box 548, Denmark, WA 6333 **region** Great Southern
phone (08) 9848 2959 **fax** (08) 9848 2903 **open** Not
winemaker Brenden Smith **production** 300 **est.** 1997
product range ($18–22 R) Sauvignon Blanc, Shiraz.
summary Brenden Smith was senior winemaker at Goundrey Wines for many years, and has branched into business on his own with a contract-winemaking facility for growers throughout the Great Southern region. The 1998 vintage will see West Cape Howe wines crush 250 tonnes for 11 different producers; a tiny amount of wine will be made under the West Cape Howe label.

west end ★★★

1283 Brayne Road, Griffith, NSW 2680 **region** Riverina
phone (02) 6964 1506 **fax** (02) 6962 1673 **open** Mon-Fri 9–4.30
winemaker William Calabria, James Cecato **production** 25 000 **est.** 1945
product range ($5.90–19.95 CD) Spumante, Port and Outback range are lower-priced wines, followed by Richland range of Semillon Chardonnay, Chardonnay, Shiraz, Merlot, Cabernet Merlot and Cabernet Sauvignon; then 3 Bridges range of Chardonnay, Golden Mist Botrytis, Semillon and Cabernet Sauvignon.
summary Along with a number of Riverina producers, West End is making a concerted move to lift both the quality and the packaging of its wines, spearheaded by the 3 Bridges range which has an impressive array of gold medals to its credit since being first released in April 1997.

westfield ★★★☆

Cnr Memorial Avenue and Great Northern Highway, Baskerville, WA 6056 **region** Swan District
phone (08) 9296 4356 **fax** (08) 9296 4356 **open** 7 days 10–5.30
winemaker John Kosovich **production** 11 000 **est.** 1922

product range ($12–36 CD) Verdelho, Sauvignon Blanc, Unwooded Chardonnay, Chardonnay, Bronze Wine Chardonnay, Chenin Blanc, Semillon, Riesling, Verdelho, Bronze Wine Verdelho, Merlot, Shiraz, Cabernet Sauvignon, Vintage Port, Liqueur Muscat, Sparkling.
summary Consistent producer of a surprisingly elegant and complex Chardonnay; the other wines are more variable, but from time to time has made attractive Verdelho and excellent Cabernet Sauvignon. John Kosovich is a perfectionist, and I look forward to the release of his Pemberton wines from his recently established vineyard in that area.

wetherall NR

Naracoorte Road, Coonawarra, SA 5263 **region** Coonawarra
phone (08) 8737 2104 **fax** (08) 8737 2105 **open** 7 days 9.30–5
winemaker Michael Wetherall **production** 2000 **est.** 1991
product range ($14.50–18 CD) Chardonnay, Cabernet Sauvignon, Shiraz.
summary The Wetherall family has been growing grapes in Coonawarra for more than 30 years, and Michael Wetherall (a Roseworthy graduate), has been responsible for overseeing wine production since Wetherall extended its operations into winemaking in 1991. Most of the grapes are still sold; no recent tastings.

wharncliffe NR

Summerleas Road, Kingston, Tas 7050 **region** Southern Tasmania
phone (03) 6229 7147 **fax** (03) 6229 2298 **open** Not
winemaker Andrew Hood (Contract) **production** 32 **est.** 1990
product range ($20 ML) Chardonnay.
summary With total plantings of 0.75 hectare, Wharncliffe could not exist without the type of contract-winemaking service offered by Andrew Hood, which would be a pity, because the vineyard is beautifully situated on the doorstep of Mount Wellington, the Huon Valley and the Channel regions of southern Tasmania.

whisson lake NR

PO Box 91, Uraidla, SA 5142 **region** Adelaide Hills
phone (08) 8390 1303 **fax** (08) 8390 3822 **open** By appointment
winemaker Roman Bratasiuk (Contract) **production** 300 **est.** 1985
product range ($25–35 CD) Pinot Noir.
summary Mark Whisson is primarily a grape grower, with 4.5 hectares of close-planted, steep-sloped north-facing vineyard. A small quantity of the production is made for the Whisson Lake label by Roman Bratasiuk, best known as the owner/winemaker of Clarendon Hills.

whitehorse wines NR

4 Reid Park Road, Mount Clear, Vic 3350 **region** Ballarat
phone (03) 5330 1719 **fax** (03) 5330 1288 **open** Weekends 11–5
winemaker Noel Myers **production** 900 **est.** 1981
product range ($10–18 CD) Riesling, Riesling Müller Thurgau, Chardonnay, Pinot Noir, Cabernet Shiraz.
summary The Myers family has moved from grape growing to winemaking, utilising the attractive site on its sloping hillside south of Ballarat. Four hectares of vines are in production, with pinot noir and chardonnay the principal varieties.

wignalls wines ★★★★

Chester Pass Road (Highway 1), Albany, WA 6330 **region** Great Southern
phone (08) 9841 2848 **fax** (08) 9841 9003 **open** 7 days 12–4
winemaker Bill Wignall **production** 5000 **est.** 1982
product range ($12–32 R) Chardonnay, Sauvignon Blanc, Late Harvest Frontignac, Pinot Noir, Reserve Pinot Noir, Cabernet Sauvignon, Tawny Port, White Port.
summary A noted producer of Pinot Noir which has extended the map for the variety in Australia. The Pinots have tremendous style and flair, but do age fairly quickly. The white wines are elegant, and show the cool climate to good advantage. A new winery was constructed and opened for the 1998 vintage.

Wignalls Pinot Noir

An enigmatic wine, even by the standards of the perversely unpredictable Pinot Noir variety. By and large, has tended to look excellent when young but to develop with disconcerting rapidity, sometimes problematically. Note also there are tiny quantities of a Reserve Pinot released from time to time.

🍷🍷🍷🍸 **1996** Medium red; the bouquet is light but quite stylish with a mix of cedary/tobacco/stemmy aromas, and shows no signs of volatility. The palate has good feel and structure, although the sweet oak is unusual. As with all the Wignall Pinots, quite advanced for its vintage. **rating:** 84

➾ **best drinking** 1998 – 1999 **best vintages** '85, '86, '88, '91, '93, '95 **drink with** Seared Tasmanian salmon • $24

wild dog NR

South Road, Warragul, Vic 3820 **region** Gippsland
phone (03) 5623 1117 **fax** (03) 5623 6402 **open** 7 days 10–5
winemaker John Farrington **production** 1200 **est.** 1982
product range ($12–18 CD) Riesling, Chardonnay, Rosé, Shiraz, Darling Dog Shiraz Grenache.
summary An aptly named winery, which produces somewhat rustic wines; even the Farringtons say that the Shiraz comes 'with a bite', also pointing out that there is minimal handling, fining and filtration. Be warned.

wild duck creek estate NR

Spring Flat Road, Heathcote, Vic 3523 **region** Bendigo
phone (03) 5433 3133 **fax** (03) 5433 3133 **open** By appointment
winemaker David Anderson **production** 500 **est.** 1980
product range ($15–25 CD) Springflat Shiraz, Alan's Cabernets, The Blend, Duck Muck (which rivals Demondrille's Purgatory in the contest for the worst wine name).
summary The first release of Wild Duck Creek Estate from the 1991 vintage marks the end of 12 years of effort by David and Diana Anderson, who commenced planting the 4.5-hectare vineyard in 1980, made their first tiny quantities of wine in 1986, the first commercial quantities of wine in 1991, and built their winery and cellar-door facility in 1993. The 1996 Shiraz was the public choice as the Best Red Wine at the 1997 Victorian Winemakers Exhibition.

wilderness estate NR

Branxton Road, Pokolbin, NSW 2321 **region** Lower Hunter Valley
phone (02) 4998 7755 **fax** (02) 4998 7750 **open** 7 days 9–5
winemaker John Baruzzi, Josef Lesnik **production** 20 000 **est.** 1986
product range ($12–15 CD) The premium varietal range of Unwooded Chardonnay, Reserve Chardonnay, Unwooded Semillon, Individual Block Semillon, Shiraz, Cabernet Merlot and Merlot is under the Wilderness Estate label; the second Black Creek label encompasses a similar range of lower-priced varietals.
summary Long-term Wyndham Estate winemaker John Baruzzi has formed a 50–50 joint venture with Joe Lesnik, resulting in the former Lesnik Family Winery now renamed Wilderness Estate. The Lesnik label will be phased out, with all wines from the '95 vintage and onwards being released either under the Wilderness Estate label or under the Black Creek label.

wildwood ★★★

St John's Lane, Wildwood, Bulla, Vic 3428 **region** Sunbury
phone (03) 9307 1118 **fax** (03) 9331 1590 **open** 7 days 10–6
winemaker Dr Wayne Stott, Peter Dredge **production** 2000 **est.** 1983
product range ($20–25 CD) Chardonnay, Viognier, Cabernets, Merlot Cabernet Franc, Pinot Noir, Shiraz.
summary Wildwood is situated just 4 kilometres past Melbourne airport. The vineyard and cellar door are situated at an altitude of 130 metres in the Oaklands Valley, which provides unexpected views back to Port Phillip Bay and the Melbourne skyline. Plastic surgeon Wayne Stott has taken what is very much a part-time activity rather more seriously than most by undertaking (and completing) the Wine Science degree at Charles Sturt University.

Wildwood Pinot Noir

The progress of Pinot Noir in both Sunbury and the Macedon Ranges reminds me strongly of its first decade or so in Tasmania: in theory the climate was perfect, but with the odd exception, Pinot simply failed to live up to expectations. Then, all of a sudden, the variety (and its makers) started to feel at home. So it may prove in Sunbury; this wine certainly suggests so.

🍷🍷🍷🍷 **1996** Medium red-purple; the bouquet is clean, with good varietal character, driven by rich and full plummy fruit. The palate has more of that ripe, sweet, plummy fruit; good balance and mouthfeel to the plum and cherry fruit; barely any input from oak. Has developed well between 1997 and 1998. **rating:** 85

➪ **best drinking** 1997 – 2000 **best vintages** NA **drink with** Duck breast • $20

---

will taylor wines NR

1 Simpson Parade, Goodwood, SA 5034 **region** Warehouse
phone (08) 8271 6122 **fax** (08) 8271 6122 **open** Not
winemaker Various contract **production** NA **est.** 1997
product range ($20 R) Clare Valley Riesling, Adelaide Hills Sauvignon Blanc.
summary Will Taylor is a partner in the leading Adelaide law firm Finlaysons specialising in wine law. Together with Suzanne Taylor, he has established a classic negociant wine business, having wines contract-made to his specification from premium South Australian regions, commencing with a Clare Valley Riesling and an Adelaide Hills Sauvignon Blanc.

Will Taylor Adelaide Hills Sauvignon Blanc

Once again, we know a great deal about the wine which was picked on 11 April 1997 from a vineyard at 340 metres established on sandstone over rich red clay, receiving a rainfall of 1000 mm and having a heat degree day summation of 1270. Eight per cent of the wine was fermented in new French barriques, the rest in stainless steel, and the wine was bottled 8 September 1997.

🍷🍷🍷🍷 **1997** Medium green-yellow; the bouquet is quite full with a mix of gooseberry and nectarine, and the oak imperceptible. A pleasant well-balanced palate with pleasant limey/gooseberry fruit; dips a little on the mid-palate, but does have length. **rating:** 85

➾ **best drinking** 1998 – 1999 **best vintages** NA **drink with** Oysters • $20

willespie ★★★☆

Harmans Mill Road, Willyabrup via Cowaramup, WA 6284 **region** Margaret River
phone (08) 9755 6248 **fax** (08) 9755 6210 **open** 7 days 10.30–5
winemaker Michael Lemmes **production** 4000 **est.** 1976
product range ($15–35 R) Sauvignon Blanc, Semillon Sauvignon Blanc, Verdelho, Riesling, Cabernet Sauvignon, Merlot; Harmans Mill White and Harmans Mill Red are cheaper second-label wines.
summary Willespie has produced many attractive white wines over the years, typically in brisk, herbaceous Margaret River-style. All are fruit rather than oak driven; the newer Merlot also shows promise. The wines have had such success that the Squance family (which founded and owns Willespie) have announced plans to substantially increase winery capacity, drawing upon an additional 25 hectares of estate vineyards in the course of establishment.

Willespie Cabernet Sauvignon

As with all the Willespie wines, estate-grown, produced from 4 hectares of plantings. Made in the austere end of the Margaret River spectrum, but certainly very typical.

🍷🍷🍷🍷 **1994** Medium to full red-purple; the bouquet is clean, with quite powerful blackberry and earth varietal fruit; subtle oak. The powerful and slightly austere palate has blackberry, earth and chocolate flavours on the mid-palate before moving through to a cedary/briary finish supported by quite persistent tannins. **rating:** 85

➾ **best drinking** 2000 – 2007 **best vintages** NA **drink with** Butterfly leg of lamb • $25

williams rest NR

Lot 195 Albany Highway, Mount Barker, WA 6324 **region** Great Southern
phone (08) 9367 3277 **fax** (08) 9367 3328 **open** Not
winemaker Contract **production** NA **est.** 1972
product range Granite Flats White and Red.
summary A long-established vineyard, planted way back in 1972, which is now part of the Selwyn Wine Group. The vineyard is named after Benjamin Williams, an eight-year-old boy who was accidentally killed by a mail coach in 1890, hence the name Williams Rest.

willow bend

Lyndoch Valley Road, Lyndoch, SA 5351; PO Box 107, Lyndoch, SA 5351 **region** Barossa Valley
phone (08) 8524 4169 **fax** (08) 8524 4169 **open** Not
winemaker Wayne Dutschke **production** 1500 **est.** 1990

product range ($14–15 R) Chardonnay, Shiraz, Shiraz Merlot Cabernet, Shiraz Cabernet Merlot.

summary Wayne Dutschke has had ten years of winemaking experience with major wine companies in South Australia, Victoria and New South Wales, but has returned to South Australia to join his uncle, Ken Semmler, a leading grape grower in the Barossa Valley and now in the Adelaide Hills. No recent tastings, simply because Willow Bend sells out of wine in less than six months each year. Next release August 1998.

willow creek ★★★☆

166 Balnarring Road, Merricks North, Vic 3926 **region** Mornington Peninsula
phone (03) 5989 7448 **fax** (03) 5989 7584 **open** 7 days 10–5
winemaker Simon Black **production** 8000 **est.** 1989
product range ($16–25 CD) Unoaked Chardonnay, Tulum Chardonnay, Pinot Noir, Cabernet Sauvignon, Sparkling Cuvee.

summary Yet another significant entrant in the fast-expanding Mornington Peninsula area, with 15 hectares of vines planted to cabernet sauvignon, chardonnay and pinot noir. The cellar-door sales area boasts picnic areas, barbecue facilities, trout fishing and bocce; lunches are served every day, and dinners by appointment. Expansion of the cellar door was completed by January 1998, with a winery constructed for the 1998 vintage.

wilson vineyard ★★★★

Polish Hill River, Sevenhill via Clare, SA 5453 **region** Clare Valley
phone (08) 8843 4310 **open** Weekends 10–4 May-Oct
winemaker John Wilson **production** 5000 **est.** 1974
product range ($12–28 CD) Gallery Series Riesling, Cabernet Sauvignon, Hippocrene Sparkling Burgundy, Chardonnay, Zinfandel, Liqueur Gewurztraminer.

summary Dr John Wilson is a tireless ambassador for the Clare Valley and for wine (and its beneficial effect on health) in general. His wines are made using techniques and philosophies garnered early in his wine career, and can occasionally be idiosyncratic, but in recent years have been most impressive.

Wilson Gallery Series Riesling

John Wilson has always made powerful Riesling from his Polish Hill River vineyards, almost invariably at the upper end of the Clare Valley hierarchy. A bottle of 1991 tasted in January 1997 was magnificent, a great Riesling at the height of its power and complexity. The '96 and '97 will go down the same path; Wilson builds Rieslings of unusual concentration and flavour.

 **1997** Light green-yellow; a powerful wine with lots of spicy lime fruit aromas, and similarly abundant flavours, particularly on the mid-palate. **rating:** 93

➯ **best drinking** 1999 – 2005 **best vintages** '85, '90, '91, '92, '94, '96, '97 **drink with** Japanese cuisine • $16

wilton estate ★★★

Whitton Stock Route, Yenda, NSW 2681 **region** Riverina
phone (02) 6968 1303 **fax** (02) 6968 1328 **open** Mon-Fri 9–5
winemaker Ralph Graham **production** 250 000 **est.** 1977
product range ($7.95–17.95 CD) Chardonnay Reserve, Botrytis Semillon, NV Brut, Shiraz Cabernet, Cabernet Merlot; also wines under Hidden Valley and Yenda Vineyards labels.

summary Wilton Estate draws grapes and wine from various parts of southern Australia and New South Wales for its dry table wines, but having outstanding success with its Botrytis Semillon from locally grown fruit. It shares the winemaking facilities at St Peters.

windowrie estate NR

Windowrie, Canowindra, NSW 2804 **region** Cowra
phone (02) 6344 3234 **fax** (02) 6344 3227 **open** 7 days 10–6
winemaker Rodney Hooper, Iain Riggs **production** 2500 **est.** 1988
product range ($10–19 CD) Chardonnay, Sauvignon Blanc, Pinot Noir, Cabernet Sauvignon.
summary Windowrie Estate was established in 1988 on a substantial grazing property at Canowindra, 30 kilometres north of Cowra, and in the same viticultural region. Most of the grapes from the substantial vineyard are sold to other makers, with small quantities being made for the Windowrie Estate label, the Chardonnays enjoying show success.

windy ridge vineyard NR

Foster-Fish Creek Road, Foster, Vic 3960 **region** Gippsland
phone (03) 5682 2035 **open** Holiday weekends – Sat 10–5, Sun 1–5
winemaker Graeme Wilson **production** 300 **est.** 1978
product range ($15–25 CD) Pinot Noir, Cabernet Sauvignon, Vintage Port, Georgia's Liqueur Pinot Noir, Graeme's Late Bottled Vintage Port.
summary The Windy Ridge Vineyard was planted between 1978 and 1986, with the first vintage not taking place until 1988. Winemaker Graeme Wilson favours prolonged maturation, part in stainless steel and part in oak, before bottling his wines, typically giving the Pinot Noir two and a half years and the Cabernet four years before bottling. Robin Bradley accorded the 1995 Pinot Noir (released Easter 1998) five stars.

winewood NR

Sundown Road, Ballandean, Qld 4382 **region** Granite Belt
phone (07) 4684 1187 **fax** (07) 4684 1187 **open** Weekends, public holidays 9–5
winemaker Ian Davis **production** 1000 **est.** 1984
product range ($12–15 CD) Chardonnay, Chardonnay Marsanne, Shiraz Marsanne, MacKenzies Run (Cabernet blend), Muscat.
summary A weekend and holiday activity for schoolteacher Ian Davis and town-planner wife Jeanette; the tiny winery is a model of neatness and precision planning. The use of Marsanne with Chardonnay and Semillon shows an interesting change in direction.

winstead ★★★★☆

Lot 7 Winstead Road, Bagdad, Tas 7030 **region** Southern Tasmania
phone (03) 6268 6417 **fax** (03) 6268 6417 **open** Wed-Sun 11–5
winemaker Andrew Hood (Contract) **production** 400 **est.** 1989
product range ($14.50–17.50 CD) Riesling, Pinot Noir.
summary The good news about Winstead is the outstanding quality of its extremely generous and rich Pinot Noirs, rivalling those of Freycinet for the abundance of their fruit flavour without any sacrifice of varietal character. The bad news is that production is so limited, with only half a hectare each of riesling and pinot noir being tended by fly-fishing devotee Neil Snare and wife Julieanne.

Winstead Pinot Noir

Like the Riesling, produced from a little over half a hectare of estate plantings. Going from strength to strength as the vines mature, with a now consistently produced depth and richness of flavour not far removed from that of Freycinet. Very much a Pinot to watch (and buy); it is just a pity there is not more of it.

🍷🍷🍷🍷🍷 **1997** Medium red-purple; a powerful bouquet with spice and ripe plum and black cherry fruit, supported by abundant oak. The palate is flavoursome and rich, reminiscent in some ways of the Lenswood Vineyards Pinot Noirs. Tasted at the very start of its life, with great potential. **rating:** 90

⇨ **best drinking** 1999 – 2003 **best vintages** '95, '96, '97 **drink with** Saddle of hare • $17.50

winters vineyard NR

Clarke Road, O.B. Flat via Mount Gambier, SA 5290 **region** Mount Gambier

phone (08) 8726 8255 **fax** (08) 8726 8255 **open** 7 days 10–5

winemaker Bruce Gregory **production** 500 **est.** 1988

product range ($10–14 CD) Chardonnay, Cabernet Sauvignon.

summary Former restaurateurs Martin and Merrilee Winter have established 8 hectares of vineyards 6 kilometres south of Mount Gambier and about 60 kilometres south of Coonawarra proper. The wines are contract-made, with an ultimate production target of 2500 cases. Light, leafy but pleasant Cabernet Sauvignon shows the cool climate, but is well made with a nice touch of cedary vanillin oak.

wirilda creek ★★★☆

32 McMurtrie Road, McLaren Vale, SA 5171 **region** McLaren Vale

phone (08) 8323 9688 **fax** (08) 8323 9688 **open** 7 days 10–5

winemaker Kerry Flanagan **production** 2000 **est.** 1993

product range ($11–22 CD) Oak Matured Semillon, Sauvignon Blanc, Trinity – The Blend (Cabernet Malbec Shiraz), Cabernet Merlot, Shiraz, Rare Shiraz, Rare Liqueur, Port.

summary Wirilda Creek may be one of the newer arrivals in McLaren Vale, but it offers the lot: wine, lunch every day (Pickers Platters reflecting local produce) and accommodation (four rooms opening on to a private garden courtyard). Co-owner Kerry Flanagan (with partner Karen Shertock) has had great experience in the wine and hospitality industries: a Roseworthy graduate (1980) he has inter alia worked at Penfolds, Coriole and Wirra Wirra, and also owned the famous Old Salopian Inn for a period of time. The red wines are the best bet, the white wines a less safe haven.

wirra wirra ★★★★☆

McMurtie Road, McLaren Vale, SA 5171 **region** McLaren Vale

phone (08) 8323 8414 **fax** (08) 8323 8596 **open** Mon-Sat 10–5, Sun 11–5

winemaker Benjamin Riggs **production** 63 000 **est.** 1969

product range ($13–28 R) The Cousins (Sparkling), Hand Picked Riesling, Late Picked Riesling, Semillon Sauvignon Blanc, Scrubby Rise Semillon, Sauvignon Blanc, Scrubby Rise Semillon Sauvignon Blanc Chardonnay, Chardonnay, Wood Matured Semillon Sauvignon Blanc, The Angelus Cabernet Sauvignon, Pinot Noir, Church Block (Cabernet Shiraz Merlot), RSW Shiraz, Original Blend (Grenache Shiraz), Fortifieds.

summary Long-respected for the consistency of its white wines, Wirra Wirra has now established an equally formidable reputation for its reds. Right across the board, the wines are of exemplary character, quality and style, The Angelus Cabernet Sauvignon and RSW Shiraz battling with each other for supremacy. Long may the battle continue.

Wirra Wirra Hand Picked Riesling

When, well over a decade ago, Wirra Wirra incorporated the words 'Hand Picked' into its Riesling label, it was regarded as another example of owner Greg Trott's notorious sense of humour. In the intervening years it has come to represent a statement of individuality for one of the region's better Rieslings (all things being relative). Typically, a blend of 80% McLaren Vale and 20% Clare Valley material.

🍷🍷🍷🍸 **1997** Light to medium yellow-green; the bouquet is quite fragrant, with passionfruit and citrus aromas, the palate similarly showing more life, flavour and delicacy than most McLaren Vale Rieslings; the floral blossom notes are quite reminiscent of Coonawarra Riesling. **rating:** 84

➭ **best drinking** 1999 – 2003 **best vintages** '82, '89, '91, '92, '94, '96, '97 **drink with** South Australian whiting • $12.50

Wirra Wirra Sauvignon Blanc

One of the pioneers of quality Sauvignon Blanc in McLaren Vale. Wine quality is never less than good, excelling in the cooler vintages. Draws principally upon 3.5 hectares of estate plantings.

🍷🍷🍷🍷 **1997** Medium yellow-green; there is an attractive mix of tropical and gooseberry fruit aromas on the bouquet, supported on the palate by some minerally characters which aid the structure. Fine and long flavoured. **rating:** 87

➭ **best drinking** 1998 – 1999 **best vintages** '91, '92, '94, '96, '97 **drink with** Blue swimmer crab • $14

Wirra Wirra Chardonnay

Eight hectares of estate vineyards provide the core of what is always a stylish wine, rising to great heights in years such as 1991. The full range of modern Chardonnay winemaking techniques is applied, with as much focus on structure and complexity as on fruit, producing a wine which ages very well.

🍷🍷🍷🍷🍸 **1996** Medium yellow-green; the bouquet is smooth in that typically restrained, understated style of Wirra Wirra, the palate in similar mode. Beautifully balanced, with fig, melon and nutty/cashew characters on a long finish. Subtle oak. **rating:** 90

➭ **best drinking** 1998 – 2003 **best vintages** '82, '89, '91, '92, '94, '96 **drink with** Wiener schnitzel • $18

Wirra Wirra RSW Shiraz

RSW Shiraz is named after Robert Strangways Wigley, who founded Wirra Wirra in 1894. While The Angelus has brought much recognition to Wirra Wirra, it is arguable that, viewed over 1994 and 1995, RSW Shiraz is its best wine. In both vintages it is a beautifully elegant, constructed and structured wine, showing a particular sensitive use of French (80%) and American (20%) oak.

🍷🍷🍷🍷🍷 **1995** Medium red-purple; ripe but not heavy fruit in the dark plum/black cherry spectrum with evident but perfectly integrated and balanced oak on the bouquet. The palate is beautifully balanced, with a fine array of dark berry fruits, finishing with fine, silky tannins.

Seduction in a red wine glass which invites you to have the second, the third, and the fourth glass. Retasted several times towards the end of 1997; the wine gets better and better. **rating:** 97

➯ **best drinking** 2000 – 2010 **best vintages** '94, '95 **drink with** Smoked beef • $25

Wirra Wirra Original Blend Grenache Shiraz

The first red wine produced by cousins Greg and Roger Trott in 1972 was a blend of Grenache and Shiraz grown on one of Greg Trott's vineyards which became known as the Church Block. In time that vineyard was replanted to cabernet and merlot (retaining some shiraz) and it was not until 1992 that another Grenache appeared under the Wirra Wirra label, bearing the name 'Original Blend'. Now a blend of approximately two-thirds Grenache and one-third Shiraz, it has become an important part of the Wirra Wirra stable. The '96 was a gold medal winner at the 1997 Royal Adelaide Wine Show.

🍷🍷🍷🍷🍸 **1996** Bright red-purple; an ultra-fragrant bouquet with wonderful Grenache varietal character coming through, supported by the Shiraz. There are spicy berry aromas and flavours throughout, yet the wine is not the least bit jammy. Simply delicious. **rating:** 92

➯ **best drinking** 1998 – 2001 **best vintages** '95 **drink with** Kangaroo tail stew • $16

wise wines NR

Lot 4 Meelup Road, Dunsborough, WA 6281 **region** Margaret River
phone (08) 9756 8098 **fax** (08) 9755 3979 **open** 7 days 10.30–4.30
winemaker Mark Ravenscroft (previous) **production** 8000 **est.** 1986
product range ($12.50–20 CD) Sauvignon Blanc Semillon, Aquercus Chardonnay (Unwooded), Chardonnay, Late Harvest (Chenin Blanc, Semillon, Muscat), Pinot Noir, Classic Soft Red, Shiraz Merlot, Cabernet Sauvignon, Tawny Port.
summary Wise Wines is an amalgam of Geographe Estate, Eagle Bay Estate and the Newlands Vineyard at Donnybrook. The head of the syndicate is former medical practitioner and stock market entrepreneur extraordinaire Ron Wise, who has always been a wine connoisseur, and now has the economic means to indulge himself to the full. Wise Wines also offers a spectacular outdoor restaurant overlooking Geographe Bay. No recent tastings, nor information.

wolf blass ★★★★

Bilyara Vineyards, Sturt Highway, Nuriootpa, SA 5355 **region** Barossa Valley
phone (08) 8562 1955 **fax** (08) 8562 2156 **open** Mon-Fri 9.15–4.30, weekends 10–4.30
winemaker John Glaetzer (Red), Wendy Stuckey (White) **production** 1 million **est.** 1966
product range ($10.95–100 R) White wines under White, Yellow, Green and Gold labels, with emphasis on Riesling and blended Classic Dry White; red wines under Red, Yellow, Brown, Grey and Black labels with emphasis on Cabernet Sauvignon, Shiraz and blends of these. Also sparkling and fortified wines. The Eaglehawk now roosts here too.
summary Although merged with Mildara and now under the giant umbrella of the Fosters Brewing Group, the brands (as expected) have been left largely intact, and – so far at least – the style of the wines has changed little. The red wines continue to be very oaky and to my palate, at least, increasingly old-fashioned. The white wines (made by Wendy Stuckey) are particularly impressive, none more so than the Gold Label Riesling.

Wolf Blass Gold Label Riesling

Produced from Wolf Blass's only significant vineyard holdings in the Clare Valley. It is significantly more fruit-driven than enzyme-driven (the latter being the case with the Yellow Label Riesling). Has been a prolific medal and trophy winner in national wine shows over the past four or five years, the '96 topping the Premium Dry White Table Wine class at the 1997 Sydney Wine Show, the '97 sweeping all before it in wine shows in the second half of 1997, seemingly winning trophies at will.

1997 Light green-yellow; an utterly beguiling bouquet, crisp and clean, with floral, lime fruit and just a hint of toast. On the palate combines delicacy with power; the lime/citrus fruit has a nice cut which freshens the long, clean, relatively dry finish. **rating:** 95

⇨ **best drinking** 1998 – 2000 **best vintages** '90, '92, '95, '96, '97 **drink with** Salad Niçoise • $13

wood park NR

RMB 1139, Milawa, Vic 3678 **region** King Valley
phone (03) 5727 3367 **fax** (03) 5727 3682 **open** By appointment
winemaker John Stokes **production** NA **est.** 1989
product range ($15–17 CD) Meadow Creek Chardonnay, Shiraz, Shiraz Cabernet, Cabernet Sauvignon.
summary The first vines were planted at Wood Park in 1989 by John Stokes as part of a diversification programme for his property at Bibinwarrah in the hills of the Lower King Valley to the east of Milawa. The bulk of the 8-hectare production is sold to Brown Brothers, with a further 8 hectares of vineyard being established for Southcorp. In an unusual twist, Stokes acquires his chardonnay from cousin John Leviny, one of the King Valley pioneers with his vineyard at Meadow Creek. To complicate matters further, all four vintages of Chardonnay ('95 to '98) were made by Rick Kinzbrunner. 1995 Cabernet Shiraz won a silver medal at the Victorian Wines Show in 1996, the '96 and '97 Shiraz following suit in 1997.

woodend winery NR

82 Mahoneys Road, Woodend, Vic 3442 **region** Macedon
phone (03) 5427 2183 **fax** (03) 5427 4007 **open** Weekends from October 1998
winemaker Keith Brian (Contract) **production** 300 **est.** 1995
product range Chardonnay, Pinot Noir.
summary Also known as Bluestone Bridge Wines, the Woodend Winery draws upon 2.5 hectares of estate plantings dating back to 1983. In the intervening time, the grapes were sold to others, but the wine is now being contract-made for it. It will be opening for cellar-door sales on weekends as from 30 October 1998, the weekend of the Macedon Ranges Budburst Festival.

woodlands

Cnr Caves and Metricup Roads, Willyabrup via Cowaramup, WA 6284 **region** Margaret River
phone (08) 9755 6226 **fax** (08) 9321 6385 **open** Weekends by appointment
winemaker David Watson, Dorham Mann (Consultant) **production** 1000 **est.** 1973
product range ($20–30 CD) Chardonnay, Pinot Noir, James Cabernet, Emily Cabernets.
summary Burst on the scene with some superlative Cabernet Sauvignons early on, but did not manage to maintain the momentum; and indeed made no red wine in 1988, 1989 or 1991. The 1992 red wines marked a return to form, but no recent tastings.

woodonga hill NR

Cowra Road, Young, NSW 2594 **region** Hilltops
phone (02) 6382 2972 **fax** (02) 6382 2972 **open** 7 days 9–5
winemaker Jill Lindsay **production** 4000 **est.** 1986
product range ($12.50–21 CD) Dry Rhine Riesling, Sauvignon, Chardonnay, Botrytis Semillon, Auslese Gewurztraminer, Meunier, Shiraz, Vintage Port, Cherry Liqueur Port.
summary Early problems with white wine quality appear to have been surmounted. The majority of the wines on release in 1998 have won bronze or silver medals at regional wine shows in New South Wales and Canberra, and Jill Lindsay is also a successful contract winemaker for other small producers.

woodstock ★★★★

Douglas Gully Road, McLaren Flat, SA 5171 **region** McLaren Vale
phone (08) 8383 0156 **fax** (08) 8383 0437 **open** Mon-Fri 9–5, weekends, holidays 12–5
winemaker Scott Collett **production** 12 000 **est.** 1974
product range ($8–29 R) Riesling, Semillon, Chardonnay, Semillon Sauvignon Blanc, Botrytis Sweet White, Grenache, Cabernet Sauvignon, Shiraz, Vintage Port, Tawny Port and Muscat. The Stocks Shiraz is a recently introduced flagship; the Douglas Gully range is a cheaper, second label.
summary One of the stalwarts of McLaren Vale, producing archetypal, invariably reliable, full-bodied red wines and showing versatility with spectacular botrytis sweet whites and high-quality (14-year-old) Tawny Port. Also offers a totally charming reception-cum-restaurant which understandably does a roaring trade with wedding receptions.

Woodstock Shiraz

Produced from 5.3 hectares of estate plantings, and one of the most reliable – and most typical – examples of McLaren Vale Shiraz. It relies almost entirely on its rich fruit; oak would simply be a distraction.

🍷🍷🍷🍷 **1995** Very good purple-red; a clean bouquet of medium to full intensity with aromas of chocolate, briar and earth supported by subtle oak. The palate delivers precisely what the bouquet promises, a solid, rich traditional ultra-chocolatey McLaren Vale red wine. **rating:** 85

➯ **best drinking** 1999 – 2005 **best vintages** '82, '84, '91, '92, '93, '94 **drink with** Steak in black bean sauce • $15

Woodstock The Stocks Shiraz

First made in the 1991 vintage, and released in late 1994. It is made from century-old (99-year-old, to be precise) vines, and matured in new American oak hogsheads. The '94 vintage continues the line: very ripe, concentrated fruit with expansive use of new American oak. Made in what is now a recognised style, but certainly for oak lovers.

🍷🍷🍷🍷 **1995** Medium to full red-purple; a smooth and harmonious bouquet with rich chocolate and berry fruit woven through vanilla oak. The elegant palate provides all of the flavours promised by the bouquet together with a touch of mint. I particularly like the judicious oak handling. **rating:** 87

➯ **best drinking** 2000 – 2005 **best vintages** '91, '94, '95 **drink with** Barbecued steak • $25

---

woody nook ★★★★

Metricup Road, Busselton, WA 6280 **region** Margaret River
phone (08) 9755 7547 **fax** (08) 9755 7547 **open** 7 days 10–4.30
winemaker Neil Gallagher **production** 3000 **est.** 1982
product range ($14–17 CD) Chenin Blanc, Sauvignon Blanc, Classic Dry White, Late Picked Chenin Blanc, Late Harvest Semillon, Merlot, Cabernet Sauvignon; Gallagher's Choice Cabernet Sauvignon is top of the range.
summary This improbably named and not terribly fashionable winery has produced some truly excellent wines in recent years, with its Classic Dry White and Cabernet Sauvignon both starring at the 1998 Winewise Small Makers Competition – having put in a similar performance at prior Winewise competitions, and likewise at the Mount Barker Wine Show.

Woody Nook Classic Dry White

Once again, the perhaps unfashionable and little known (in the eastern States at least) Woody Nook has come up with a quite lovely white wine, a blend of Semillon, Sauvignon Blanc and Chenin Blanc.
🍷🍷🍷🍷🍷 **1997** Light green-yellow; the bouquet is light and crisp, with a mix of herbaceous and gooseberry aromas, reminiscent of New Zealand. The palate is fresh, lively and crisp, with most attractive Semillon Sauvignon Blanc flavours. Well balanced and approachable right now. **rating:** 90

⇨ **best drinking** 1998 – 1990 **best vintages** '95, '97 **drink with** Rich seafood pasta • $16

Woody Nook Gallagher's Choice Cabernet Sauvignon

As the name suggests, the pick of the vintage, and winemaker Neil Gallagher certainly got it right in 1993, for this wine is far superior to the standard Cabernet Sauvignon of the same year. The '95 was placed first in the Cabernet Class at the 1998 Winewise Small Makers Competition.
🍷🍷🍷🍷🍷 **1995** Medium to full red-purple; the bouquet is complex and powerful with a mix of earthy cabernet and cedary oak. A well-balanced palate of medium weight with cassis, leaf and cedar flavours running through a long finish. **rating:** 92

⇨ **best drinking** 1999 – 2005 **best vintages** '95 **drink with** Herbed rack of lamb • $15

wrights NR

Harmans South Road, Cowaramup, WA 6284 **region** Margaret River
phone (08) 9755 5314 **fax** (08) 9755 5459 **open** 7 days 10–4.30
winemaker Henry Wright **production** 2500 **est.** 1973
product range ($12–25 CD) Premium Estate (Semillon Riesling), Semillon, Hermitage, Henry Wright's Chardonnay White Port.
summary Continues to go about its business and selling its wines locally.

wyanga park ★★

Baades Road, Lakes Entrance, Vic 3909 **region** Gippsland
phone (03) 5155 1508 **fax** (03) 5155 1443 **open** 7 days 9–5
winemaker Andrew Smith **production** 5000 **est.** 1970
product range ($9.50–16 CD) Riesling Traminer, Colombard, Chardonnay, Rosé, Boobialla (medium sweet white), Shiraz, Shiraz Cabernet Sauvignon, Fortifieds.

summary Offers a broad range of wines of diverse provenance directed at the tourist trade; the Cabernet Sauvignon is the only 100% estate-grown wine. Winery cruises up the north arm of the Gippsland Lake to Wyanga Park are scheduled four days a week throughout the entire year.

wyldcroft estates NR

98 Stanleys Road, Red Hill South, Vic 3937 **region** Mornington Peninsula
phone (03) 5989 2646 **fax** (03) 5989 2646 **open** Weekends and public holidays 10–5
winemaker Kevin McCarthy (Contract) **production** 800 **est.** 1987
product range ($18–21 CD) Chardonnay, Unwooded Chardonnay, Pinot Noir, Cabernet Sauvignon.
summary Richard Condon and Sharon Stone commenced planting Wyldcroft Estates in 1987, extending the plantings in 1993 and 1996 to the present total of just under 3 hectares, constructing a mudbrick winery and cellar door in 1995.

wyndham estate ★★★

Dalwood Road, Dalwood, NSW 2335 **region** Lower Hunter Valley
phone (02) 4938 3444 **fax** (02) 4938 3422 **open** Mon-Fri 9.30–5, weekends 10–4
winemaker Philip Laffer **production** NFP **est.** 1828
product range ($6.95–30 R) In ascending order: Bin TR2 Classic White and Classic Red; Chablis Superior Semillon Sauvignon Blanc, Bin 777 Semillon Chardonnay; Bin 222 Chardonnay, Bin 111 Verdelho, Bin 333 Pinot Noir, Bin 555 Shiraz; Oak Cask Chardonnay, Bin 444 Cabernet Sauvignon, Bin 888 Cabernet Merlot; Show Reserve Semillon and Shiraz.
summary An absolutely reliable producer of keenly priced mid-range table wines which are smoothly and precisely aimed at those who enjoy wine but don't wish to become over-involved in its mystery and intrigue. Every now and then it comes up with a wine of surprising quality, although there does seem to be some variation between different batch bottlings.

Wyndham Estate Show Reserve Semillon

Due for release in October 1998.
🍷🍷🍷🍷 **1995** Medium to full yellow-green; the bouquet is smooth, of medium intensity, with gently honeyed fruit. The palate is similarly pleasant and smooth, with a mix of honey, mineral and faintly herbaceous flavours. **rating:** 85

➪ **best drinking** 2000 – 2003 **best vintages** NA **drink with** Roast chicken • $25

wynns coonawarra estate ★★★★★

Memorial Drive, Coonawarra, SA 5263 **region** Coonawarra
phone (08) 8736 3266 **fax** (08) 8736 3202 **open** 7 days 10–4
winemaker Peter Douglas **production** 220 000 **est.** 1891
product range ($8–53 R) Riesling, Chardonnay, Shiraz, Cabernet Shiraz Merlot, Black Label Cabernet Sauvignon, Michael Shiraz, John Riddoch Cabernet Sauvignon; also Ovens Valley Shiraz (not sourced from Coonawarra).
summary The large-scale production has in no way prevented Wynns from producing excellent wines covering the full price spectrum from the bargain basement Riesling and Shiraz through to the deluxe John Riddoch Cabernet Sauvignon and the more-recently introduced Michael Shiraz. Even with recent price increases, Wynns offers extraordinary value for money.

Wynns Coonawarra Estate Riesling

Arguably the best value Riesling in the country – a label revamp has slightly lifted the cachet of the wine, however much I personally disapprove of the new label. Extensive vertical tastings of the wines show that the better vintages can live for 20 years or more, becoming great classics in the course of so doing.

🍷🍷🍷🍷 **1997** Light to medium yellow-green; the bouquet is fragrant, with quite pungent herb and lime aromas, the palate likewise with plenty happening; lime and herb flavours, crisp acid and good length. **rating:** 85

⇨ **best drinking** 1998 – 2004 **best vintages** '90, '91, '93, '95, '96 **drink with** Tiger prawns • $15

Wynns Coonawarra Estate Chardonnay

A wine which has evolved dramatically over the years. 1985 was the first vintage to utilise barrel fermentation; in 1992 winemaking was moved back to Coonawarra from McLaren Vale, and French oak was introduced (previously German and American was used). By 1995 only French oak was being employed, and in 1996 the barrel size had started to change from puncheon to barrique, with tight-grained French oak. All of these changes have progressively tightened and refined a wine which deserves greater recognition from critics and consumers – it has, in fact, done very well in wine shows in recent years.

🍷🍷🍷🍷 **1997** Medium yellow-green; a sophisticated bouquet, at once subtle yet complex, with melon and cashew barrel-ferment and malolactic-ferment influences all at work. The fruit comes through on the palate, carrying on to the finish, with citrus and melon flavours. Not a heavyweight, but has considerable style. **rating:** 88

⇨ **best drinking** 1998 – 2001 **best vintages** '92, '93, '94, '96, '97 **drink with** Fillet of pork • $11

Wynns Coonawarra Estate Shiraz

Estate means what it says; this is 100% estate-grown Coonawarra Shiraz, a wine which vies with Penfolds Koonunga Hill dry red for the title of best-value red wine in Australia. A vertical tasting in March 1997 climaxed with the magnificent '53, '54 and '55 vintages. While the new generation wines may not last for 40 years, those made in the 1990s are the best since the 1950s, and the recommended drinking range should be regarded as strictly nominal. Well-corked and well-cellared, the wines have almost indefinite life.

🍷🍷🍷🍷🍷 **1996** Strong purple-red; an exceptionally smooth and intense bouquet, with abundant rich and sweet dark cherry and plum fruit swells into a round, mouth-filling palate, showing more of the same fruit flavours tinged with spice and subtle oak, closing with soft tannins. **rating:** 90

⇨ **best drinking** 2000 – 2010 **best vintages** '54, '55, '62, '65, '70, '85, '86, '89, '90, '91, '92, '93 **drink with** Spiced lamb • $12

Wynns Coonawarra Estate Michael Shiraz

First made in the outstanding Coonawarra vintage of 1990, to stand alongside the John Riddoch Cabernet Sauvignon. It takes its name from the most famous of all of the Wynns wines, the glorious 1955 Michael Hermitage, which still rates as one of the top half-dozen wines made in Australia since the Second World War. A prolific trophy and gold medal winner, every bit as powerful as the Riddoch. No '95 was made or released.

🍷🍷🍷🍷🍷 **1994** Dense purple-red; extremely rich, ripe and concentrated mulberry and spice fruit is supported by toasty vanillin oak. The palate is every bit as concentrated and chewy as the bouquet suggests it will be, with abundant spicy berry fruit and even more abundant oak. Retasted October 1997 and developing exceptionally well, losing brashness and gaining elegance. **rating:** 95

➯ **best drinking** 2004 – 2024 **best vintages** '90, '91, '93, '94 **drink with** Leave it in the cellar • $53

Wynns Coonawarra Estate Black Label Cabernet Sauvignon

Given the volume in which this wine is made (said to be over 40 000 cases) it has to be the most important Cabernet in Australia, a powerful testament to the synergy between Coonawarra and Cabernet Sauvignon. Another dyed-in-the-wool classic with a magnificent history.

🍷🍷🍷🍷🍷 **1995** Medium to full red-purple; there is a classic mix of cassis, olive/herb and earth on the strong bouquet, with just a hint of oak. The palate is complex, with strong varietal character (olive and cassis) and exhibiting quite pronounced tannins which build on the second half of the palate. Gentle oak throughout. **rating:** 91

➯ **best drinking** 2000 – 2015 **best vintages** '53, '57, '58, '62, '82, '86, '88, '90, '91, '94, '95 **drink with** Roast beef • $20

---

xanadu wines ★★★★

Terry Road, Margaret River, WA 6285 **region** Margaret River
phone (08) 9757 2581 **fax** (08) 9757 3389 **open** 7 days 10–5
winemaker Jürg Muggli **production** 16 000 **est.** 1977
product range ($13.50–165 R) Semillon, Chenin Blanc, Chardonnay, Unwooded Chardonnay, Secession (Semillon Sauvignon Blanc Chenin Blanc), Semillon, Late Harvest Riesling, Featherwhite (Rosé), Hesperos Shiraz, Merlot, Cabernet Franc, Cabernet Sauvignon, Cabernet Reserve.
summary Samuel Taylor Coleridge would thoroughly approve of the labels on the Xanadu wines, and one imagines would be equally pleased with wine quality – quality which can be excitingly variable, but is more often good than not.

Xanadu Semillon

Yet another wine from Margaret River which emphasises first what a great region for the variety the Margaret River is, and secondly, how different the style is from that of the Hunter River, and in particular, how well the wine lends itself to sophisticated handling techniques (including the use of oak). This wine is whole-bunch pressed, is taken through a full malolactic fermentation, and then barrel-aged – techniques one normally associates with Chardonnay. Yet it is in no sense overworked or overblown. Produced from 20-year-old vines.

🍷🍷🍷🍷🍷 **1997** Medium yellow-green; extremely complex, powerful, herbaceous fruit is complexed by clever use of tangy oak. The palate is rich, complex and mouthfilling, with all of the winemaking influences evident, yet harmonious. Excellent wine. **rating:** 90

➯ **best drinking** 1998 – 2003 **best vintages** NA **drink with** Richer fish dishes • $20

Xanadu Cabernet Sauvignon

Extraordinary packaging has been a feature of the Xanadu wines in recent years, but the label of the '92 Cabernet Sauvignon is an absolutely outstanding piece of graphic design. The wine itself, released under both a standard and Reserve label, is in the typical Margaret River-style, edged with astringency and needing time. The Reserve can be outstanding.

🍷🍷🍷🍷🍸 **1995** Medium red-purple; a fragrant bouquet with earthy varietal fruit woven through cedary oak heralds a beautifully made wine with most attractive fruit showing perfectly ripened cabernet flavours. The palate is long and fine, with excellent tannin and acid balance. **rating:** 90

⇨ **best drinking** 1999 – 2007 **best vintages** '83, '84, '86, '90, '91, '93, '95 **drink with** Strong, aged cheddar • $24.50

yaldara ★★★

Gomersal Road, Lyndoch, SA 5351 **region** Barossa Valley
phone (08) 8524 4200 **fax** (08) 8524 4678 **open** 7 days 9–5
winemaker Robert Thumm, Jim Irvine **production** 650 000 **est.** 1947
product range ($4–90 R) A kaleidoscopic array of wines under (in ascending order) the Ducks Flat, Lyndoch Valley, Acacia Hill, Lakewood, Julians, and the recently released super-premium The Farms labels. The Lakewood range is the largest, covering all major wine styles and varietals. There is also a substantial range of sparkling, non-alcoholic and fortified wines.
summary A winery whose activities have ebbed and flowed over the years, and which one suspects has focused a lot of attention on price-conscious sectors of the export market. Quality is there, or thereabouts.

yalumba ★★★★☆

Eden Valley Road, Angaston, SA 5353 **region** Barossa Valley
phone (08) 8561 3200 **fax** (08) 8561 3393 **open** Mon-Fri 8.30–5, Sat 10–5, Sun 12–5
winemaker Simon Adams **production** 55 000 **est.** 1849
product range ($7–50 R) Under the Yalumba label (in ascending order) Oxford Landing range, Galway Hermitage, and Christobels Dry White, Family Selection range, The Menzies Cabernet Sauvignon, The Signature Collection and Octavius Shiraz. Separate brand identities for Hill-Smith Estate, Pewsey Vale and Heggies, with strong emphasis on key varietals Riesling, Chardonnay, Semillon and Cabernet Sauvignon. Angas Brut is a leader in the sparkling wine market, with Yalumba D at the top end of the quality tree.
summary Family-owned and run by Robert Hill-Smith; much of its prosperity in the late 1980s and early 1990s turned on the great success of Angas Brut in export markets, but the company has always had a commitment to quality and shown great vision in its selection of vineyard sites and brands. In particular, it has always been a serious player at the top end of full-bodied (and full-blooded) Australian reds.

Yalumba Barossa Semillon

Made in uncompromising Barossa-style from fruit grown by the Hahn, Rozenzweig, Koch, Grossman and Johns families. The inaugural release won a gold medal at the 1997 Barossa Valley Wine Show, underlining how typical (and Teutonic) the style is, although it was also selected in the Top 100 1998 Sydney International Wine Competition.

🍷🍷🍷🍷 **1997** Medium to full yellow-green; the bouquet is powerful and concentrated with lemon-butter aromas which come through on the generously flavoured palate; incipient honey notes augur well for medium-term cellaring. **rating:** 85

⇨ **best drinking** 1998 – 2002 **best vintages** NA **drink with** Smoked chicken • $14.95

Yalumba Reserve Viognier

Yalumba was the first winery in South Australia (and the second in Australia, the first being Elgee Park in the Mornington Peninsula) to commercially grow and make Viognier. Planted in the East Barossa Ranges, it is perhaps a mark of the long learning curve through which Yalumba has gone that this is the first occasion on which a wine entry has appeared in the *Wine Companion*. That learning curve has finally led to the conclusion that viognier has to be allowed to ripen way beyond the normal point, with flavour changes occurring well after sugar accumulation has ceased – a unique characteristic.

YYYY **1996** Medium to full yellow; some real pastille fruit varietal character to a richly floral/apricot-accented bouquet; the palate has the distinctive feel of the Northern Rhône to it, with pronounced dried apricot nuances. No doubting this is a very different variety. **rating:** 88

➯ **best drinking** 1998 – 2000 **best vintages** '96 **drink with** Peach-fed pork • $20

Yalumba D

Deliberately and consistently made at the fuller end of the Australian sparkling wine spectrum. Always a complex, rich, mouthfilling-style, although the levels of aldehyde in older vintages were somewhat controversial. Typically a blend of Pinot Noir from Eden Valley, Coonawarra, Adelaide Hills; Chardonnay from Coonawarra and Eden Valley; and Pinot Meunier from Eden Valley.

YYYY **1995** Light straw-yellow; the bouquet is very restrained, with crisp apple and pear aromas predominant; some creamy autolysis evident. The palate is likewise fresh, with pronounced green apple flavours, and a crisp, fine, long finish. **rating:** 86

➯ **best drinking** 1998 – 1999 **best vintages** '90, '91, '93, '95 **drink with** Richer seafood dishes • $30

Yalumba Barossa Shiraz

Part of a new range of Yalumba wines released in 1997. Predominantly Barossa Valley fruit, with a lesser component from the Eden Valley. Won The Wine Society trophy for Best Dry Red Table Wine, Large Commercial Classes at the 1997 Liquorland National Wine Show.

YYYY **1995** Medium red-purple; a soft, easy wine, with spice and plum fruit aromas supported by quite positive vanillin American oak. The palate shows more of the same, finishing with soft tannins, and with the oak input an integral part of the style. **rating:** 89

➯ **best drinking** 1998 – 2002 **best vintages** NA **drink with** Rare beef fillet • $14.95

Yalumba Octavius Shiraz

Octavius is the super-premium Yalumba red. The first vintage was 1988 (Coonawarra Cabernet) but the two subsequent vintages have been of old Barossa Shiraz, and this is where the future of the wine will lie. The distinguishing feature of the wine is its opulent oak treatment: it is matured in barrels made at Yalumba's own cooperage from American oak from Missouri which was seasoned for eight years before being made into barrels. More is not always best, but in this instance it is. Incidentally, the barrels are unusually small (octaves) which increases the impact of the oak.

YYYYY **1993** Medium to full red-purple; a complex, concentrated bouquet with abundant dark, plummy fruit aromas, and surprisingly restrained oak. Plum, dark berry and dark chocolate flavours on the fore and mid-palate are then supported by persistent tannins and generous vanillin oak. Retasted October 1997 with near identical notes. Deliciously, voluptuously ripe with creamy vanilla oak and soft tannins. **rating:** 94

➯ **best drinking** 2000 – 2010 **best vintages** '88, '90, '92, '93 **drink with** The biggest steak imaginable • $50

Yalumba Bush Vine Grenache

Produced from old (70-year) low-yielding bush vines on the Anderson, Burgermeister, Habermann and Waechter families.

🍷🍷🍷🍷 **1996** Medium red-purple; a full, glossy/juicy berry fruit bouquet runs into a no-holds-barred jammy/berry varietal fruit palate. Does show slightly hot alcohol on the finish (14.5°) but this is all pretty much in mainstream style. **rating:** 84

⇒ **best drinking** 1998 – 2002 **best vintages** NA **drink with** Moroccan curry • $14.95

Yalumba Signature Cabernet Shiraz

An Australian Classic, dating back to 1962, but deriving from Sir Robert Menzies' declaration at a lunch in Adelaide that the '61 Special Vintage Galway Claret was 'the finest Australian wine I have ever tasted'. A blend of 65% Coonawarra Cabernet Sauvignon and 35% old-vine Barossa Shiraz, it spends 24 months in American oak prior to bottling, but never seems to be overwhelmed by it. The '93 was the top gold medal in its class at the 1997 Royal Adelaide Wine Show.

🍷🍷🍷🍷 **1994** Peter Graugh. Strong red; an excellently rich and complex bouquet with blackberry, chocolate and earth supported by harmonious and sweet oak, and a substantial, chewy palate with an identical range of flavours. Will reach a peak somewhere over the next four or five years, but will hold that peak almost indefinitely. **rating:** 88

⇒ **best drinking** 2000 – 2010 **best vintages** '62, '66, '75, '81, '85, '88, '90, '91, '92, '93 **drink with** Rare roast beef • $30

Yalumba The Menzies Cabernet Sauvignon

Introduced almost 30 years after Sir Robert Menzies made his famous remark about Yalumba's 'Claret' which led to the Signature Range. Nonetheless, the connection was there, and the name was given to Yalumba's Coonawarra Cabernet Sauvignon when first introduced to the market.

🍷🍷🍷🍷 **1995** Bright red-purple; the bouquet has sweet cassis fruit of medium intensity backed by some pleasant cedary oak, the palate likewise turning around smooth, sweet fruit rather than structure or power. **rating:** 84

⇒ **best drinking** 1998 – 1999 **best vintages** '90, '91, '94 **drink with** Rack of lamb • $20

yanwirra ★★★

Redman Road, Denmark, WA 6333 **region** Great Southern
phone (08) 9386 3577 **fax** (08) 9386 3578 **open** Not
winemaker John Wade (Contract) **production** 400 **est.** 1989
product range ($10–20 CD) Riesling, Sauvignon Blanc, Semillon Sauvignon Blanc, Cabernet Merlot.
summary Perth anaesthetist Ian McGlew and wife Liz have a liquorice allsorts 4-hectare vineyard, with contract-winemaking by John Wade. The white wines are particularly modestly priced, being sold by word of mouth and mail order.

yarra burn ★★★★

Settlement Road, Yarra Junction, Vic 3797 **region** Yarra Valley
phone (03) 5967 1428 **fax** (03) 5967 1146 **open** 7 days 10–5
winemaker Tom Newton, Ed Carr, Stephen Pannell **production** 4500 **est.** 1975
product range ($14.50–42 R) Sauvignon Blanc Semillon, Chardonnay, Pinot Noir, Shiraz, Cabernet Sauvignon, Sparkling Pinot, Chardonnay Pinot; Bastard Hill Chardonnay, Bastard Hill Pinot Noir.

summary Acquired by BRL Hardy in 1995, and destined to become the headquarters of Hardy's very substantial Yarra Valley operations, the latter centring on the 1000-tonne production from its Hoddles Creek vineyards. The new brand direction is slowly taking shape, though not helped by the very difficult 1995 and 1996 Yarra Valley vintages.

Yarra Burn Sauvignon Blanc Semillon

Since 1995, a well-put-together blend of Yarra Valley and King Valley fruit; comparisons with the Sauvignon Blanc of Yarra Ridge are inevitable, and Yarra Burn comes off best in that comparison.

YYYY **1997** Light yellow-green; a highly fragrant and aromatic bouquet with attractive passionfruit aromas leads into a lively, fresh, tangy passionfruit and gooseberry-accented palate, finishing with crisp acidity. **rating:** 85

⇒ **best drinking** 1998 – 1999 **best vintages** NA **drink with** Light seafood • $15.90

yarra edge ★★★☆

PO Box 390, Yarra Glen, Vic 3775 **region** Yarra Valley
phone (03) 9730 1107 **fax** (03) 9739 0135 **open** At Yering Station
winemaker Tom Carson, Darren Rathbone **production** 2000 **est.** 1984
product range ($27 CD) Chardonnay, Cabernets.
summary Now leased to Yering Station, which makes the wines but continues to use the Yarra Edge brand for grapes from this estate. Tom Carson, the Yering Station winemaker, was briefly winemaker/manager at Yarra Edge, and knows the property intimately, so the rich style can be expected to continue.

Yarra Edge Chardonnay

Made entirely from estate-grown fruit, and in years such as '92, '93, '94 and '96 provided a very rich, concentrated wine.

YYYY **1996** Medium to full yellow-green; the bouquet is tangy and complex, with some bottle-developed characters already evident, and concentrated melon aromas. The palate is rich and mouthfilling, almost syrupy, with peachy/buttery fruit in typical Yarra Edge-style. **rating:** 85

⇒ **best drinking** 1998 – 2002 **best vintages** '92, '93, '95 **drink with** Smoked salmon pasta • $27

yarra ridge ★★★★

Glenview Road, Yarra Glen, Vic 3755 **region** Yarra Valley
phone (03) 9730 1022 **fax** (03) 9730 1131 **open** Mon–Fri 10–5, weekends, holidays 10–5.30
winemaker Rob Dolan **production** 60 000 **est.** 1983
product range ($18–40 R) Chardonnay, Sauvignon Blanc, Botrytis Semillon, Pinot Noir, Reserve Pinot Noir, Merlot, Shiraz, Cabernet Sauvignon.
summary Now under the sole ownership and control of Mildara Blass, but with the ever-affable Rob Dolan continuing to work winemaking and production miracles at a winery which is strained to its limits. Recent vineyard plantings in the Yarra Valley, and continued purchasing of Yarra Valley grapes, means that the majority of the wines will continue to be Yarra Valley sourced. Sometimes it is not easy to tell which are, and which aren't, even if one has a master's degree in label-reading and interpretation.

Yarra Ridge Pinot Noir

Anchored in the Yarra Valley, and with a Reserve Pinot Noir recently added to the range, albeit in small quantities. One of the lesser lights in the Yarra Ridge stable, but always a pleasant wine. The '96 vintage received the trophy for Best Varietal Pinot Noir at the 1997 Royal Sydney Wine Show; in my view the '97 is an even better wine.

🍷🍷🍷🍷🍷 **1997** Medium to full red; a ripe, rich, plummy/gamey bouquet with lots of stuffing in typical '97 style is followed by a powerful, stylish, multiflavoured palate. Here, plum, berry, spice and forest all intermingle, supported by very clever oak handling. **rating:** 93

➾ **best drinking** 1998 – 2002 **best vintages** '91, '92, '93, '96 **drink with** Poultry • $19

Yarra Ridge Reserve Pinot Noir

A genuine reserve wine, made in limited quantities and built from the time the grapes are picked. Hit new heights of opulence in the 1996 vintage, although the style (and the degree of oak) is bound to polarise opinions. The high rating is given as much for the bouquet (which is spectacular) as for the palate. I have to say there appears to have been significant variation in the '96 wine, and in particular the amount and type of oak.

🍷🍷🍷🍷🍷 **1996** Dark red; the bouquet is complex, powerful, aristocratically rich and full, showing the unbridled use of oak with very strong, powerful fruit. The fore-palate is exceptionally complex and rich; the sting comes in the tail, when oak phenolics seem to build up and unbalance the wine a little, even in the presence of food. It will be fascinating to see how the wine develops. Top gold medal winner at both the Royal Adelaide and National Wine Shows in November 1997. **rating:** 93

➾ **best drinking** 1998 – 2002 **best vintages** '94, '96 **drink with** Game, jugged hare • $38.95

---

yarra valley hills ★★★★☆

Delaneys Road, Warranwood, Vic 3134 **region** Yarra Valley
phone (03) 5962 4173 **fax** (03) 5962 4059 **open** Weekends, public holidays 11–5
winemaker Martin Williams (Consultant) **production** 15 000 **est.** 1989
product range ($16–27 CD) Warranwood Riesling, Log Creek Sauvignon Blanc, Kiah Yallambee Chardonnay, Log Creek Pinot Noir, Log Creek Cabernet Sauvignon.
summary Former schoolteacher Terry Hill has built-up a very successful empire in a short period of time through leasing two substantial vineyards and principally acting as a grape supplier to others, with a small proportion of the grapes being contract-made by a range of Yarra Valley winemakers. No 1997 vintage tastings.

yarra yarra ★★★★☆

239 Hunts Lane, Steels Creek, Vic 3775 **region** Yarra Valley
phone (03) 5965 2380 **fax** (03) 9830 4180 **open** Not
winemaker Ian Maclean **production** NFP **est.** 1979
product range ($23.50–35 ML) Semillon Sauvignon Blanc, Merlot, Cabernets.
summary Notwithstanding its tiny production, the wines of Yarra Yarra have found their way onto a veritable whos who listing of Melbourne's best restaurants. This has rightly encouraged Ian Maclean to increase the estate plantings from 2 hectares to over 6 hectares during the 1996 and 1997 seasons. The demand for the wines will only be intensified by the quality of the current releases.

Yarra Yarra Semillon Sauvignon Blanc

A blend of 70% Semillon, fermented and aged for 15 months in 30% new, the remainder in older, French oak barriques. A number of different yeasts including wild yeasts are used and the wine is left on lees and stirred regularly.

🍷🍷🍷🍷 **1996** Medium yellow-green; the bouquet shows an attractive blend of gooseberry fruit and spicy oak, harmonious and balanced. The palate has abundant tangy, fresh fruit offset by nutmeg oak. Heaps of flavour, but not aggressive. **rating:** 88

➪ **best drinking** 1997 – 2001 **best vintages** NA **drink with** Weiner schnitzel • $25

Yarra Yarra Cabernets

Produced from 4 hectares of cabernet sauvignon, cabernet franc and merlot grown on a north-facing slope, and which are not irrigated. The final wine (a blend of 80% Cabernet and 13% Cabernet Franc and 7% Merlot) reflects the low-yielding vines, and is not released every year. Basket-pressed, and incorporating the pressings fraction. Aged for two years in 40% new French oak barriques.

🍷🍷🍷🍷🍷 **1995** Medium red-purple; the bouquet is clean and smooth, with sweet cassis/blackberry fruit and just a trace of oak. The palate is silky smooth and most attractive, with cassis fruit which follows on precisely from the bouquet; a great outcome for the vintage. **rating:** 90

➪ **best drinking** 2000 – 2005 **best vintages** '84, '86, '89, '90, '92, '95 **drink with** Osso buco • $30

yarra yering ★★★★★

Briarty Road, Coldstream, Vic 3770 **region** Yarra Valley
phone (03) 5964 9267 **fax** (03) 5964 9239 **open** Sat, public holidays 10–5, Sun 12–5
winemaker Bailey Carrodus **production** 6000 **est.** 1969
product range ($30–100 CD) Dry White No 1 (Sauvignon Blanc Semillon), Chardonnay, Pinot Noir, Dry Red No 1 (Bordeaux-blend), Dry Red No 2 (Rhône-blend), Merlot (tiny quantities at $100 a bottle), Underhill Shiraz, Portsorts.
summary Dr Bailey Carrodus makes extremely powerful, occasionally idiosyncratic wines from his 25-year-old, low-yielding unirrigated vineyards. Both red and white wines have an exceptional depth of flavour and richness, although my preference for what I believe to be his great red wines is well known.

Yarra Yering Underhill Shiraz

Made entirely from the former Prigorje Vineyard, which adjoins that of Yarra Yering and is now, indeed, part of the Yarra Yering estate – and has been so for some years. Here, too, the vines are old, low-yielding and unirrigated.

🍷🍷🍷🍷 **1996** Medium red-purple; the bouquet shows a mix of spice, berry, leaf and cherry fruit, the oak evident but restrained. The palate has a light texture, with cherry and spice fruit, and will build complexity, and quite possibly weight, as it ages. As with all the Yarra Yering '96 wines, tasted within weeks of bottling. **rating:** 88

➪ **best drinking** 2000 – 2006 **best vintages** '91, '92, '93 **drink with** Kraft Victorian parmesan • $23

Yarra Yering Dry Red No 2

Predominantly Shiraz, with a little Viognier and a few scraps of other things from time to time. Entirely estate-grown, of course, and produced from vines which are now over 25 years old.

🍷🍷🍷🍷🍸 **1996** Medium purple-red; the bouquet is redolent of glossy minty/cherry shiraz varietal fruit, the palate with abundant ripe fruit, balanced by a hint of leaf and briar, but, interestingly, no spice. Lingering acidity on the finish. **rating:** 92

➾ **best drinking** 2001 – 2011 **best vintages** '80, '81, '86, '89, '90, '91, '92, '93, '96 **drink with** Beef bourguignon • $23

Yarra Yering Dry Red No 1

Predominantly Cabernet Sauvignon, with small quantities of Merlot, Cabernet Franc and Malbec, and a tiny contribution of Petit Verdot. Entirely estate-grown from low-yielding, unirrigated vines, and matured in high-quality new French oak.

🍷🍷🍷🍷🍷 **1996** Medium to full red-purple; the bouquet is ripe and full, with strong Cabernet varietal aromas; cassis and earth. The palate is powerful and well structured, with potent blackberry and cassis fruit, the oak immaculately balanced and integrated. **rating:** 94

➾ **best drinking** 2001 – 2011 **best vintages** '80, '81, '86, '89, '90, '91, '93, '94, '96 **drink with** Roast leg of lamb • $23

Yarra Yering Portsorts

Only Bailey Carrodus could come up with a name such as this for the first micro (but official) release of his vintage port, made from the classic Portuguese varieties planted on a single, dedicated vineyard immediately abutting his original plantings. When I first came to the Yarra Valley and planted Coldstream Hills in 1985, Bailey suggested to me I should plant the port varieties. I thought he was joking. Now I know he was not.

🍷🍷🍷🍷🍷 **1996** Deep, dense purple; the bouquet is pungent and intense with pepper, spice and blackberry aromas and classy spirit. The palate is intense and long, with a perfectly amazing finish, which seems to go on forever. **rating:** 94

➾ **best drinking** 2000 – 2020 **best vintages** NA **drink with** As many friends as possible • NA

yarrabank ★★★★☆

42 Melba Highway, Yarra Glen, Vic 3775 **region** Yarra Valley
phone (03) 9730 2188 **fax** (03) 9730 2189 **open** 7 days 10–5
winemaker Claude Thibaut, Tom Carson, Darren Rathbone **production** 2000 **est.** 1993
product range ($30 R) Thibaut & Gillet Cuvée Brut, Cuvée Rosée
summary The 1997 vintage saw the opening of the majestic new winery established as part of a joint venture between the French Champagne House Devaux and Yering Station, and which adds another major dimension to the Yarra Valley. Until 1997 the Yarrabank Cuvée Brut was made under Claude Thibaut's direction at Domaine Chandon, but henceforth the entire operation will be conducted at Yarrabank. Four hectares of dedicated 'estate' vineyards have been established at Yering Station; the balance of the intake comes from other growers in the Yarra Valley and southern Victoria. Wine quality has been quite outstanding.

Yarrabank Brut Cuvée

The first release of Yarrabank is a blend of 50% Pinot Noir and 50% Chardonnay, half of each variety coming, respectively, from the Yarra Valley and Mornington Peninsula. It spent three years on yeast lees prior to disgorgement. The rating of the '93 previously appearing was erroneous; it should have been five glasses (or 94 points).

🍷🍷🍷🍷🍷 **1994** Light yellow-green; a spotless bouquet, with quite intense lime/citrus aromas and some bready autolysis characters in the background. An exemplary palate, intense and lively, with crisp citrus and apple flavours; long, faintly creamy finish. Gets better every time I taste it (which is very frequently). **rating:** 94

➾ **best drinking** 1998 – 1999 **best vintages** '93, '94 **drink with** Aperitif, shellfish • $30

Yarrabank Cuvée Rosée

Made almost entirely from Pinot Noir (80%), with a small component of the '93 Cuvée blended prior to tiraging. The wine spent four years on lees prior to disgorgement. The curious spelling of Rosée is unique to Yarrabank.

🍷🍷🍷🍷🍷 **1993** Pale salmon onion skin; the bouquet is clean and crisp, with a mix of faintly nutty/strawberry aromas. The palate has excellent feel and texture, with delicate strawberry and spice flavours, and none of those meaty/Bonox characters which predominantly Pinot-based sparkling wines can sometimes acquire. **rating:** 92

➾ **best drinking** 1998 – 1999 **best vintages** NA **drink with** Poached salmon • NA

yass valley wines NR

9 Crisps Lane, Murrumbateman, NSW 2582 **region** Canberra District

phone (02) 6227 5592 **fax** (02) 6227 5592 **open** Weekends, public holidays 11–5 or by appointment

winemaker Michael Withers **production** 800 **est.** 1979

product range ($9–14 CD) Riesling, Traminer, Chardonnay, Chardonnay Semillon, Shiraz, Cabernet Sauvignon.

summary Michael Withers and Anne Hillier purchased Yass Valley in January 1991, and have subsequently rehabilitated the existing run-down vineyards and extended the plantings. Mick Withers is a chemist by profession and has completed a Wine Science degree at Charles Sturt University; Anne is a registered psychologist and has completed a Viticulture diploma at Charles Sturt.

yellowglen ★★★★

Whites Road, Smythesdale, Vic 3551 **region** Ballarat

phone (03) 5342 8617 **fax** (03) 5333 7102 **open** 7 days 10–5

winemaker Nick Walker **production** 400 000 **est.** 1975

product range ($10–25 R) Brut Cremant, Brut Pinot Chardonnay, Brut Rosé, Cuvée Victoria, Vintage Pinot Chardonnay, Y, Yellow.

summary Just as the overall quality of Australian sparkling wine has improved out of all recognition over the past five or so years, so has that of Yellowglen. Initially the quality lift was apparent at the top end of the range, but now extends right to the non-vintage commercial releases.

yering grange vineyard NR

14 McIntyre Lane, Coldstream, Vic 3770 **region** Yarra Valley

phone (03) 9739 1172 **fax** (03) 9739 1172 **open** By appointment

winemaker John Ellis (Contract) **production** 300 **est.** 1989

product range ($15 CD) Cabernet Sauvignon.

summary Yering Grange has 2 hectares of cabernet sauvignon under vine, part being sold and part made under the Yering Grange label by John Ellis at Hanging Rock. The tiny production is sold through a mailing list.

yering station ★★★★

Melba Highway, Yering, Vic 3770 **region** Yarra Valley
phone (03) 9730 1107 **fax** (03) 9739 0135 **open** Thur-Sun 10–5
winemaker Tom Carson, Darren Rathbone **production** 8000 **est.** 1988
product range ($19.50 CD) Chardonnay, Touché Chardonnay, Unwooded Chardonnay, Botrytis Semillon, Pinot Noir, Cabernet Merlot.

summary The historic Yering Station (or at least the portion of the property on which the cellar-door sales and vineyard are established) was purchased by the Rathbone family in January 1996, and is now the site of a joint venture with the French Champagne House Devaux. A spectacular and very large winery has been erected which handles the Yarrabank sparkling wines, and the Yering Station and Yarra Edge table wines. It is certain to become one of the focal points of the Yarra Valley, particularly with the historic Yering Homestead next door. Here, luxury accommodation and the finest dining in the Yarra Valley is available.

Yering Station Pinot Noir

Like the Chardonnay, taken to bottle by Tom Carson, who also had considerable input into the fermentation of the wine. Partial barrel fermentation in a small percentage of new oak adds to the complexity of the wine, and 1996 was, of course, a very good vintage for Pinot Noir in the Yarra Valley.

🍷🍷🍷🍷 **1997** Medium red-purple; a quite powerful bouquet with a mix of earth, plum and spice, and hints of carbonic maceration is followed by a solid/plummy/cherry palate, still showing primary fruit flavours. Has time to go. **rating:** 85

⇨ **best drinking** 1999 – 2003 **best vintages** '91, '94, '96, '97 **drink with** Smoked quail • $17.50

yeringberg ★★★★★

Maroondah Highway, Coldstream, Vic 3770 **region** Yarra Valley
phone (03) 9739 1453 **fax** (03) 9739 0048 **open** By appointment
winemaker Guill de Pury **production** 1200 **est.** 1863
product range ($29–35 CD) Chardonnay, Yeringberg White (Marsanne/Roussanne), Pinot Noir, Yeringberg Red (Cabernet-blend).

summary Makes wines for the next millennium from the low-yielding vines re-established on the heart of what was one of the most famous (and infinitely larger) vineyards of the nineteenth century. In the riper years, the red wines have a velvety generosity of flavour which is rarely encountered, yet never lose varietal character, while the Yeringberg White takes students of history back to Yeringberg's fame in the nineteenth century.

Yeringberg Marsanne/Roussanne

In fact simply labelled 'Yeringberg' (as is the dry red) in the tradition of the nineteenth-century label, which is faithfully reproduced. The wine is predominantly Marsanne, with just a touch of Roussanne, and in 1994 achieved a level of flavour and richness which one imagines the great wines of the nineteenth century possessed.

🍷🍷🍷🍷🍷 **1997** Light green-yellow; a spotlessly clean but fragrant and tangy bouquet has citrus characters akin to that of sauvignon blanc. The palate has considerable presence, with attractive, ripe pear and lemon flavours. Long finish; carries the 14 degrees alcohol with ease. **rating:** 90

➾ **best drinking** 1990 – 2009 **best vintages** '94, '97 **drink with** Snowy Mountains trout • $29

Yeringberg Chardonnay

Produced from the half-hectare of estate plantings, and made in necessarily very limited quantities. This restricts its opportunity for show entries, but it has been a consistent trophy and gold medal winner at the Lilydale Wine Show.

🍷🍷🍷🍷🍷 **1997** Brilliant green-yellow; clean and smooth, with melon, fig and subtle oak aromas of medium intensity. The palate is elegant, but long, with as-yet delicate melon and white peach fruit; certain to develop well. **rating:** 90

➾ **best drinking** 2000 – 2005 **best vintages** '88, '90, '91, '92, '93, '94, '97 **drink with** Sweetbreads • $29

Yeringberg Dry Red

Produced from an estate-grown blend of Cabernet Sauvignon, Merlot, Cabernet Franc and Malbec (with Cabernet Sauvignon dominant, and the other components in descending order as listed). The vineyard is established on the precise site of the great nineteenth-century plantings, albeit but a fraction of the size of those vineyards, enjoying a prime north-facing slope.

🍷🍷🍷🍷 **1996** Medium red; the bouquet is distinctly herbaceous, with leafy/earthy fruit, but the palate has surprisingly good mouthfeel, smooth and gentle with savoury red berry, leaf and mint flavours. **rating:** 85

➾ **best drinking** 2000 – 2006 **best vintages** '85, '86, '88, '90, '91, '93, '94 **drink with** Yarra Valley venison • $35

yungarra estate NR

Yungarra Drive, Dunsborough, WA 6281 **region** Margaret River
phone (08) 9755 2153 **fax** (08) 9755 2310 **open** 7 days 10–5
winemaker Erland Happ (Contract) **production** 1450 **est.** 1988
product range ($10.50–12 CD) Semillon, Sauvignon Blanc, Quartet (Semillon, Sauvignon Blanc, Chenin Blanc, Verdelho), Chenin Blanc Verdelho, Pink Opal (sweet red table wine made from Cabernet and Merlot), Springtime (sweet Sauvignon Blanc, Verdelho), Cabernet Sauvignon, Cabernet Merlot, Royale.
summary Yungarra Estate is a combined tourist lodge and cellar-door facility set on a 40-hectare property overlooking Geographe Bay. The 9-hectare vineyard was first planted in 1988, producing its first wines in 1992, contract-made by Erland Happ. Cellar-door sales commenced in 1993, and there are five bed and breakfast cottages on the Yungarra Estate property.

zappacosta estate NR

Farm 161 Hanwood Road, Hanwood, NSW 2680 **region** Riverina
phone (02) 6963 0278 **fax** (02) 6963 0278 **open** By appointment
winemaker Judy Zappacosta, Dino Zappacosta **production** 22 000 **est.** 1996
product range ($12 CD) Riesling, Semillon, Dry White, Shiraz.
summary Zappacosta Estate, briefly known as Hanwood Village Wines, is a relatively new business, with the first release from the 1996 vintage.

zarephath wines NR

Moorialup Road, East Porongurup, WA 6324 **region** Great Southern
phone (08) 9853 1152 **fax** (08) 9841 8124 **open** 7 days 9–4
winemaker Brenden Smith **production** 300 **est.** 1994
product range ($15–20 CD) Riesling, Chardonnay, Pinot Noir, Shiraz, Cabernet Sauvignon.
summary The Zarephath vineyard is owned and operated by Brothers and Sisters of The Christ Circle, a Benedictine community. They say the most outstanding feature of the location is the feeling of peace and tranquillity which permeates the site, something I can well believe on the basis of numerous visits to the Porongurups.

zema estate

Riddoch Highway, Coonawarra, SA 5263 **region** Coonawarra
phone (08) 8736 3219 **fax** (08) 8736 3280 **open** 7 days 9–5
winemaker Matt Zema, Nick Zema **production** 10 000 **est.** 1982
product range ($19 CD) Shiraz, Cabernet Sauvignon, Cluny (Cabernet-blend).
summary Zema is one of the last outposts of hand-pruning and hand-picking in Coonawarra, the various members of the Zema family tending a 40-hectare vineyard progressively planted between 1982 and 1994 in the heart of Coonawarra's terra rossa soil. Winemaking practices are straightforward; if ever there was an example of great wines being made in the vineyard, this is it.

Zema Estate Shiraz

So far as I know, the only dryland, hand-pruned and hand-picked vineyard in Coonawarra. This very conservative approach to viticulture has paid big dividends, with outstanding wines produced consistently over the past 15 years. Matured for 16 months in a mix of French and American oak, mostly used.

1996 Medium to full red-purple; the intense bouquet is clean, with powerful black cherry and earth shiraz varietal character; the palate smooth, rich and mouthfilling, running through black cherry, earth, a touch of chocolate and the barest hint of oak. Overall, has a deliciously silky feel. **rating:** 91

best drinking 2000 – 2006 **best vintages** '84, '86, '88, '92, '94, '96 **drink with** Bistecca Fiorentina • $19

Zema Estate Cluny

First made in 1993. An estate-grown blend of Cabernet Sauvignon (65%), Merlot (25%) and the remainder Cabernet Franc and Malbec. The '96 is the best to this point of time.

1996 Full red-purple; the sweet, ripe cherry and blackcurrant bouquet introduces a quite complex wine on the palate with mint and berry flavours, supple tannins and a long finish. **rating:** 87

best drinking 2000 – 2005 **best vintages** '96 **drink with** Braised lamb • $19

Zema Estate Cabernet Sauvignon

Just as is the case with the Shiraz, produced from dryland, hand-pruned, hand-picked vines. A 100% Cabernet Sauvignon wine, matured in small French and American wood, but with the fruit – rather than the oak – driving the wine.

ΥΥΥΥΥ **1996** Tremendous depth to the colour; the bouquet is powerful and intense, with blackberry and blackcurrant fruit, the palate luscious yet not jammy; here blackberry and cassis fruit ripples through a sweet mid-palate closing with fine tannins and subtle oak. **rating:** 94

➾ **best drinking** 2002 – 2008 **best vintages** '84, '86, '88, '92, '93, '96 **drink with** Barbecued lamb • $19

zuber estate NR

Northern Highway, Heathcote, Vic 3523 **region** Bendigo
phone (03) 5433 2142 **open** 7 days 9–6
winemaker A Zuber **production** 450 **est.** 1971
product range ($10–12 CD) Chardonnay, Pinot Noir, Shiraz, Cabernet Sauvignon.
summary A somewhat erratic winery which is capable of producing the style of Shiraz for which Bendigo is famous, but does not always do so. No recent tastings.

new zealand

wineries and wines

wine regions of new zealand

key to regions

1 Northland and Matakana
2 Auckland Area
3 Waiheke Island
4 Waikato and Bay of Plenty
5 Gisborne/Poverty Bay
6 Hawke's Bay
7 Wairarapa/Martinborough
8 Nelson
9 Marlborough
10 Canterbury
11 Otago

akarangi NR

River Road, Havelock North, Hawke's Bay **region** Hawke's Bay
phone (06) 877 8228 **fax** (06) 877 7947 **open** Weekends, public holidays and summer 9–5
winemaker Morton Osborne **production** 780 **est.** 1988
product range ($9.90–15 CD) Sauvignon Blanc, Müller Thurgau, Chenin Blanc, Chardonnay, Cabernet Sauvignon.
summary Former contract grape growers now making and selling tiny quantities cellar door and through one or two local shops. Morton and Vivien Osborne have 5 hectares of vineyards, and operate the cellar-door sales through a century-old Presbyterian church moved onto the property.

alexander vineyard NR

Dublin Street Extension, Martinborough (PO Box 87) **region** Wairarapa
phone (06) 306 9389 **open** Not
winemaker Kingsley Alexander, Deborah Alexander **production** 650 **est.** 1991
product range ($26.50 CD) Bordeaux-blend.
summary The Alexanders share with Benfield & Delamere the conviction that Martinborough is best-suited to the Bordeaux varieties of cabernet sauvignon, cabernet franc and merlot which they have planted on a high-density, low-trellis, guyot-pruned configuration. The first small vintage was in 1994; an on-site winery was built for the 1996 vintage.

allan scott wines ★★★★

Jacksons Road, RD3, Blenheim **region** Marlborough
phone (03) 572 9054 **fax** (03) 572 9053 **open** 7 days 9.30–4.30
winemaker Paddy Borthwick **production** 30 000 **est.** 1990
product range ($15–20 R) Marlborough Sauvignon Blanc, Marlborough Riesling, Autumn Riesling, Chardonnay.
summary The collapse of Vintech in 1995 accelerated former Corbans' chief viticulturist Allan Scott's plans for his own winery and full-time winemaker (previously the wines were contract-made at Vintech). Thus from 1996 a winery joined the attractive cellar-door sales and restaurant open seven days a week from noon to 4 pm, utilising 63 hectares of estate vineyards. Wine quality is all one could ask for.

Allan Scott Marlborough Riesling

Drawn from about 8 hectares of estate plantings. Both the 1992 and the 1993 vintages were outstanding wines, the former winning a gold medal at the Air New Zealand Wine Show, the latter a gold medal at the 1994 Sydney International Wine Competition. The '97 is in the same class.

🍷🍷🍷🍷🍷 **1997** Light to medium yellow-green; the bouquet has attractive lime and toast fruit, with plenty of style. The palate is flavoursome with fresh lemony/lime juice fruit; good length and equally good balance. **rating:** 90

⇨ **best drinking** 1998 – 2002 **best vintages** '92, '93, '97 **drink with** Fresh asparagus • $19.95

Allan Scott Marlborough Sauvignon Blanc

Given normal vintage conditions this is a classic example of Marlborough Sauvignon Blanc, reflecting the viticultural skills and experience of Allan Scott and the maturity of the estate vineyards.

ΥΥΥΥ **1997** Light yellow-green; the bouquet is clean, but light and lacking the intensity of the best wines of the vintage; the palate, similarly, is clean, crisp and fresh, with just a touch of passionfruit and gentle acid on the finish. Easy drinking. **rating:** 85

⇨ **best drinking** 1998 – 1999 **best vintages** '92, '94, '97 **drink with** Sugar-cured tuna • $16.95

alpha domus NR

1829 Maraekakaho Road, RD1, Bridge Pa, Hastings **region** Hawke's Bay
phone (06) 879 6752 **fax** (06) 879 6952 **open** Nov–Apr weekends 10–4, Christmas to end Jan, 7 days 10–4
winemaker Evert Nijzink **production** 6500 **est.** 1996
product range ($10–40 R) Chardonnay, Semillon, Semillon Sauvignon Blanc, Sauvignon Blanc, Noble Selection, Rosé, Pinot Noir, Cabernet Merlot, Cabernet Merlot Malbec.
summary An estate-based operation drawing upon 20 hectares of vineyards and poised to grow to 14 000 cases. The five members of the Ham family run the business, with the seemingly obligatory plans for a winery café in the pipeline. The wines have made a major impact in New Zealand since their launch.

arahura vineyard NR

Ness Valley Road, Clevedon **region** Auckland and South Auckland
phone (09) 292 8749 **fax** (09) 292 8749 **open** 10–4 summer
winemaker Ken Mason, Tim Mason **production** 300 **est.** 1991
product range Clevedon Merlot, Merlot Cabernet.
summary Retired judge Ken Mason and wife Dianne are following in the footsteps of Tony Molloy QC by venturing into a new viticultural area and specialising in a single Bordeaux-style red (the plantings also include a little cabernet franc and merlot). A micro-winery was built in 1997 to handle the production from the 2 hectares of vineyards. If the Masons are as successful as Tony Molloy (of St Nesbit) they will have done well.

ashwell vineyards NR

Kitchener Street, Martinborough **region** Wairarapa
phone (04) 472 0519 **fax** (04) 389 8748 **open** Not
winemaker John Phipps **production** 250 **est.** 1989
product range ($17–25 ML) Sauvignon Blanc, Rosé, Pinot Noir, Cabernet Merlot.
summary Vivienne and John Phipps planted 2 hectares of vines in 1989, only to suffer severe frost damage in 1991. Undaunted, they doubled plantings in 1994, and are looking forward to the release of their first Pinot Noir (from 1997) in 1998. The vineyard, incidentally, takes its name from John Phipps' grandfather's village in Hertfordshire, England.

Ashwell Vineyards Sauvignon Blanc

Produced from 1 hectare of estate plantings, and made in a ripe, lush style.

ΥΥΥΥ **1997** Medium yellow-green; rich, ripe tropical gooseberry fruit aromas are repeated on similarly ripe, slightly soft, gooseberry-accented palate. **rating:** 84

⇨ **best drinking** 1998 – 1999 **best vintages** NA **drink with** Prawns with ginger • $17.50

askerne NR

267 Te Mata-Magateretere Road, Havelock North **region** Hawke's Bay
phone (06) 877 6085 **fax** (06) 877 2089 **open** Weekends 10.30–4.30, summer 7 days 10–5
winemaker Jenny Dobson, Sorrelle Pearson **production** 1000 **est.** 1993
product range ($15.50–24 CD) Riesling, Semillon, Semillon Sauvignon Blanc, Sauvignon Blanc, Chardonnay.
summary Askerne is the venture of John Loughlin, son of Dr John Loughlin of Waimarama Estate, who has named his vineyard after the Yorkshire town which was his wife's birthplace. The wines are made at Waimarama.

Askerne Sauvignon Blanc

Made with the clear intention of obtaining every ounce of fruit aroma and flavour, and succeeding in so doing, even if at the expense of some slow ferment characters.

ΥΥΥΥ **1997** Light straw-yellow; a voluminous, highly charged bouquet with lots of passionfruit, and slightly sweaty overtones. The palate, too, is flavoursome in the extreme, with gooseberry and passionfruit, cloying fractionally on the finish. **rating:** 85

➩ **best drinking** 1998 – 1999 **best vintages** NA **drink with** Crab mornay • $15.50

ata rangi ★★★★★

Puruatanga Road, Martinborough **region** Wairarapa
phone (06) 306 9570 **fax** (06) 306 9523 **open** 7 days 11–5 Sept-Mar
winemaker Clive Paton, Oliver Masters **production** 6000 **est.** 1980
product range ($16–35 CD) Craighall Chardonnay, Petrie Chardonnay, Dalnagairn Chardonnay (Hawke's Bay), Summer Rosé, Pinot Noir, Celebre (Cabernet, Syrah, Merlot blend).
summary Consistently ranks among the best wineries in New Zealand, let alone Martinborough. Both the Pinot Noir and Celebre are remarkable for their depth of colour and sweetness of fruit, showing the impact of full physiological ripeness. A splendid new winery was commissioned for the 1996 vintage, handling the grapes from the 19 hectares of estate plantings as well as the grapes purchased from other regions.

Ata Rangi Craighall Chardonnay

Phyll Pattie was the Chardonnay maker and her stated aim was to produce a food style, with the emphasis on complexity and structure. New oak barriques are used, with barrel fermentation, partial malolactic fermentation and lees maturation. Pattie succeeded admirably in her aim; Oliver Masters will no doubt keep the style intact. The 1996 was a gold medal winner at the 1997 Air New Zealand Wine Awards.

ΥΥΥΥ **1996** Medium to full yellow-green; a rich toasty oaky bouquet leads logically into an extremely rich and complex wine on the palate, with pronounced malolactic fermentation influences, and even more new oak – just a little too much for my taste. **rating:** 85

➩ **best drinking** 1998 – 2000 **best vintages** '92, '94 **drink with** Smoked chicken • $30

Ata Rangi Pinot Noir

Made in a very different style from the other consistently great Pinot Noir from the Wairarapa, that of Martinborough Vineyard. Ata Rangi is bigger, richer and more fleshy; that of Martinborough tighter and perhaps more elegant. There should not be a question of choice between the two styles: both should be in your cellar.

🍷🍷🍷🍷🍷 **1996** Medium to full red-purple; a reversion to the concentration of the '94 and preceding vintages, awesome in the depth of its fruit. Plum, black cherry and spice run through both the bouquet and the palate, which finishes with just the right amount of tannins to sustain the wine as it matures and develops more foresty/gamey characters. **rating:** 95

➯ **best drinking** 1998 – 2004 **best vintages** '86, '88, '89, '90, '91, '92, '93, '94, '96 **drink with** New Zealand venison • $30

babich ★★★★

Babich Road, Henderson **region** Henderson
phone (09) 833 7859 **fax** (09) 833 9929 **open** Mon-Fri 9–5, Sat 9–6, Sun 11–5
winemaker Neil Culley **production** 80 000 **est.** 1916
product range ($10.95–30 R) The Patriarch Chardonnay, Cabernet Sauvignon; Irongate Chardonnay, Cabernet Merlot; Mara Estate Chardonnay, Sauvignon, Merlot, Cabernet Sauvignon, Syrah; also varietal/regional wines such as Marlborough Sauvignon Blanc, East Coast Chardonnay.
summary Continues to uphold the reputation it gained in the 1960s, but has moved with the times in radically changing its fruit sources and wine styles. Particularly given the volume of production, quality is admirably consistent, with the expanded Mara Estate range leading the way, and strong support from Irongate Chardonnay.

Babich Marlborough Sauvignon Blanc

At the opposite end of the spectrum to Babich's opulent Mara Estate Sauvignon (from Hawke's Bay). This Marlborough version is made in the traditional, no-frills approach, but succeeds brilliantly thanks to the quality of the fruit. Has won a number of gold medals at New Zealand wine shows, and it is not hard to see why.

🍷🍷🍷🍷 **1997** Light yellow-green; light, crisp and more in the herbal than riper end of the spectrum; on the palate there is an attractive mix of herbal and riper, gooseberry-accented, fruit. Crisp, clean, non-phenolic finish. **rating:** 89

➯ **best drinking** 1998 – 1999 **best vintages** '91, '92, '94, '96, '97 **drink with** Sautéed prawns • $14

Babich Irongate Chardonnay

Produced from relatively low-yielding vineyards on the shingle soils to the west of Hastings, and rated as a classic by both Bob Campbell and Michael Cooper. The wine receives the full winemaking treatment, being barrel-fermented and held on lees for nine months, with evident malolactic fermentation.

🍷🍷🍷🍷🍸 **1996** Light to medium yellow-green; there is quite prominent toasty barrel-ferment oak on the bouquet, but the oak stops short of being aggressive or out of balance, and on the palate there is abundant melon and cashew fruit, well balanced with above-average length. A genuinely stylish wine of international quality. **rating:** 90

➯ **best drinking** 1998 – 2000 **best vintages** NA **drink with** Boned spatchcock • $26

Babich Mara Estate Chardonnay

The wine comes from the Fern Hill subregion of Hawke's Bay, and is barrel-fermented and matured in French oak (25% new) for eight months, being given the usual lees contact and malolactic-fermentation handling.

🍷🍷🍷🍷 **1996** Light to medium yellow-green; a clean bouquet of medium intensity with cashew nut malolactic-fermentation characters on moderately subdued fruit. The palate has much more style and fruit, with melon, citrus and cashew flavours on a long, ever so slightly edgy, finish. **rating:** 85

➯ **best drinking** 1998 – 1999 **best vintages** NA **drink with** Avocado salad • $17

bazzard estate NR

Awa Road, RD1, Kumeu **region** Kumeu and Huapai
phone (09) 412 8486 **fax** (09) 412 8486 **open** By appointment
winemaker Sarah Hennessy **production** 500 **est.** 1991
product range ($18–28 CD) Chardonnay, Merlot, Pinot Noir, Huapai Reserve Pinot Noir.
summary Charles Bazzard, a former Buckinghamshire solicitor (and transient waterfront worker), together with his wife Kay, has developed an organically grown vineyard in the Awa Valley. Pinot Noir is the current specialty with chardonnay and cabernet merlot planted and earmarked for future releases. Various tastings of the Pinot Noirs in 1997 and 1998 simply confirmed that Auckland is several hundred kilometres too far north to produce Pinot Noir with varietal character.

benfield & delamere NR

Cambridge Road, Martinborough **region** Wairarapa
phone (06) 306 9926 **fax** (06) 306 9926 **open** By appointment
winemaker Bill Benfield, Sue Delamere **production** 350 **est.** 1987
product range ($35–38 ML) 'Martinborough', a single Cabernet Sauvignon Merlot Cabernet Franc blend. A second label is in the offing.
summary Wellington architect Bill Benfield and partner librarian Sue Delamere have single-mindedly set about recreating Bordeaux, with an ultra-high density, very low-trellised vineyard and utilising 'conservative' techniques of the kind favoured by the Bordelaise. All of the tiny production is sold by mailing list.

bentwood wines NR

Akaroa Highway, Tai Tapu, Canterbury **region** Canterbury
phone (03) 329 6191 **fax** (03) 329 6192 **open** By appointment
winemaker Grant Whelan **production** 600 **est.** 1991
product range ($12–18 CD) Riesling, Gewurztraminer, Pinot Blanc, Pinot Noir.
summary Ray Watson has established a 2-hectare vineyard on the Banks Peninsula, his interest in wine fired after a 12-month sojourn living on a vineyard in France. The first wines were released from the 1995 vintage; the Pinot Blanc is already a silver medal winner.

black ridge ★★★

Conroys Road, Earnscleugh, Alexandra **region** Otago
phone (03) 449 2059 **fax** (03) 449 2059 **open** 7 days 10–5
winemaker Craig Cooper **production** 3000 **est.** 1981
product range ($12.50–29 R) Riesling, Chardonnay, Gewurztraminer, Pinot Noir.
summary The formidable, rocky vineyard site at Black Ridge is legendary even in New Zealand, where toughness is taken for granted. The 8-hectare vineyard will always be low-producing, but the wines produced to date have all had clear and bracing varietal character. The Pinot Noir is a particularly good example of what the site can produce.

blue rock vineyard ★★☆

Dry River Road, Martinborough **region** Wairarapa
phone (06) 306 9353 **fax** (06) 306 9353 **open** 7 days 11–6
winemaker Jenny Clark **production** 3500 **est.** 1986
product range ($15–30 CD) Chardonnay, Sauvignon Blanc, Riesling Bone Dry, Pinot Noir, Cabernet Sauvignon, Magenta Méthode Traditionelle.
summary Blue Rock is a partnership run by the Clark family in a bid to diversify the activities carried out on its 200-hectare sheep and cattle farm. There are now 16 hectares of windswept vineyards servicing a winery which was built in 1992, and a winery tasting room-cum-café-style restaurant completed in 1994, overlooking a 4-hectare park complete with lake, wildlife habitat and barbecue facilities.

bradshaw estate NR

291 Te Mata Road, Havelock North **region** Hawke's Bay
phone (06) 877 8017 **fax** (06) 876 5494 **open** 6 days Mon–Sat (except during vintage)
winemaker Hans Peet **production** 1700 **est.** 1994
product range Dry White, Medium White, Chardonnay, Cabernet Merlot.
summary Wayne and Judy Bradshaw have established their operation on the historic Vidal's No 1 Vineyard and Homestead, and in 1996 opened a new winery with an attendant restaurant on the vineyard. The winery restaurant is open Friday to Sunday and every day throughout January.

briar vale estate NR

Kelliher Lane, Springvale, Alexandra **region** Otago
phone (03) 448 8221 **open** Weekends and public holidays Nov–Mar 10–5
winemaker Mike Wolter **production** 150 **est.** NA
product range Pinot Gris, Pinot Blanc, Pinot Noir.
summary Alsace was the inspiration for the varieties chosen by John and Judy Currie when they established their 1.75-hectare vineyard on a steep north-facing slope above their cherry orchard. The cool climate carries the threat of spring frosts, however, and until the installation of frost protection (via overhead sprinklers) the crops were significantly reduced; better things are now on the way.

brookfields vineyards ★★★★☆

Brookfields Road, Meeanee, Napier **region** Hawke's Bay
phone (06) 834 4615 **fax** (06) 834 4622 **open** Mon–Sat 9–5, Sun 12–4
winemaker Peter Robertson **production** 8000 **est.** 1937
product range ($16–46 R) Chardonnay, Gewurztraminer, Sauvignon Blanc, Fumé Blanc, Pinot Gris, Cabernet, Reserve Cabernet Sauvignon, Gold Label Cabernet Merlot.
summary Peter Robertson has worked hard since acquiring Brookfields in 1977, producing grassy Sauvignon Blanc, lightly-oaked, understated Chardonnay and – best of all – the powerful, structured Gold Label Cabernet Merlot, now his highly regarded top-of-the-range release. A particular feature of his wines is their ability to age with grace.

Brookfields Gewurztraminer

Like the Pinot Gris, grown on the gravelly soils of Ohiti Estate. An unusual style for New Zealand, made bone-dry and genuinely suited to food.

🍷🍷🍷🍷 **1996** Medium yellow-green; there is a mix of spice, lychee and rose petal aromas leading into a bone-dry, lightly spiced palate which will develop fruit fatness with age. **rating:** 86

⇨ **best drinking** 1998 – 2003 **best vintages** NA **drink with** Asian cuisine • $19

Brookfields Pinot Gris

Produced from vines grown on the stony river flats of Ohiti Estate, and typically harvested mid-April. Stainless steel fermented and early bottled.

🍷🍷🍷🍷 **1996** Light yellow-green; the bouquet is light, crisp and clean with minerally characters; there is much more mouthfeel than the bouquet promises, with light peach/pear flavours together with echoes of fruit spice. **rating:** 85

⇨ **best drinking** 1998 – 1999 **best vintages** NA **drink with** Antipasto • $16.95

Brookfields Chardonnay

Produced from grapes grown on the Potaka Estate, on silty clay loam soil adjacent to the Ngarurora River. The wine is barrel-fermented in a mix of American and French oak, mostly used, but with a few new American barrels. Approximately one-third is taken through malolactic fermentation.

🍷🍷🍷🍷 **1996** Medium yellow-green; a clean and smooth bouquet of light to medium intensity with pleasant peach and melon fruit and minimal oak. The well-balanced and composed palate shows more of that peach and melon fruit with a touch of vanilla and spice from the American oak component. A smooth and pleasant wine. **rating:** 84

⇨ **best drinking** 1998 – 2001 **best vintages** NA **drink with** Grilled chicken • $17

Brookfields Reserve Chardonnay

Draws upon 20-year-old vines at Potaka Estate, and is barrel-fermented in 100% new French oak (Allier from Francois Freres) in which it spends eight months with the usual lees contact and stirring. Two-thirds of the wine is taken through malolactic fermentation.

🍷🍷🍷🍷🍷 **1996** Medium to full yellow-green; notwithstanding all of the oak used, the influence is subtle on soft, peachy buttery fruit on the bouquet. In the mouth the wine is much richer texturally, long, smooth and round, rich yet not cloying. Peach and melon fruit on the excellent mid-palate are followed by a pleasantly drying finish. **rating:** 92

⇨ **best drinking** 1998 – 2003 **best vintages** '89, '91, '95, '96 **drink with** Pan-fried veal • $34

Brookfields Gold Label Cabernet Merlot

Produced from grapes grown on the hillside vineyard of Tukituki, across the road, as it were, from Te Mata. Not produced in lesser years (none made in '92, '93 or '96), with production typically ranging between 300 and 500 cases in the top years. The wine spends 18 months in 95% new Nevers oak. The wine is eggwhite fined but not filtered.

🍷🍷🍷🍷🍷 **1995** Spectacular colour; exceptionally rich, almost voluptuous cassis/berry fruit is the driving force in the bouquet, and has swallowed up the new oak. An excellent palate showing a mix of cassis, spice, a hint of plum and a touch of meatiness. Despite all these flavours, the wine has elegance, finishing with well-balanced tannins. **rating:** 95

⇨ **best drinking** 2000 – 2010 **best vintages** NA **drink with** Fine New Zealand lamb • $46

---

brownlie brothers NR

6 Franklin Road, Bayview **region** Hawke's Bay
phone (06) 836 6250 **open** 7 days 9–6
winemaker Chris Brownlie **production** 180 **est.** 1991
product range Chardonnay, Sauvignon Blanc, Gewurztraminer, Pinot Noir.
summary Chris and Jim Brownlie have progressively established 15 hectares of vineyards, selling most of the grapes to other wineries, but recently taking the plunge and vinifying a small part of the production for mail order and cellar-door sales.

bullrush wines NR

Main Road, Waimauku, Kumeu (PO Box 132) **region** Kumeu and Huapai
phone (09) 358 2952 **fax** (09) 366 7112 **open** Not
winemaker Mark Robertson **production** NA **est.** 1995
product range Sauvignon Blanc, Chardonnay.
summary Bullrush Wines is based on a 16-hectare vineyard owned by Matua Valley winemaker Mark Robertson and wine judge Jane Osborne. So far, the wines have only been marketed through Card Member Wines.

c j pask winery ★★★★☆

1133 Omahu Road, Hastings **region** Hawke's Bay
phone (06) 879 7906 **fax** (06) 879 6428 **open** Mon–Fri 9–5, Sat and public holidays 10–5, Sun 11–4
winemaker Kate Radburnd **production** 24 000 **est.** 1985
product range ($10–25 CD) Sauvignon Blanc, Chardonnay, Reserve Chardonnay, Cabernet Merlot, Cabernet Sauvignon; Roy's Hill White and Red are second label.
summary Ex-cropduster pilot Chris Pask became one of the most highly regarded grape growers in Hawke's Bay; his coup in securing former Vidal winemaker Kate Radburnd (née Marris) has paid the expected dividends. Production has increased rapidly, and the wines have had significant and consistent success in New Zealand and international wine shows thanks to the complexity of the Chardonnays and the supple, sweet fruit of its Cabernet Merlots and Reserve Cabernet Sauvignons.

C J Pask Sauvignon Blanc

Chris Pask was the first vigneron to plant vines in the now famous Gimblett Road region when he moved there in 1982. The deep gravel soils always produce wines with an extra dimension of flavour, even in difficult vintages such as 1995. Gifted winemaker Kate Radburnd uses an interesting approach for the sauvignon blanc, relying on multiple pickings between 18.5 and 21.5° brix to give a range of fruit flavours and a balance of acidity. The wine is cold fermented in stainless steel, and retains around 5.5 grams per litre of residual sugar.

🍷🍷🍷🍷 **1997** Light yellow-green; the bouquet is crisp, and while of light to medium intensity does show a range of passionfruit, citrus and gooseberry aromas. The brisk, tangy and spotlessly clean palate has lemony and gently herbal fruit flavours, the finish giving no hint of the touch of unfermented sugar. **rating:** 85

➾ **best drinking** 1998 – 1999 **best vintages** NA **drink with** Shellfish • $12

C J Pask Chardonnay

The experience of Kate Radburnd shows through in this wine, as does her philosophy that it should be the fruit to shine through, rather than complicated oak handling. Produced from a mix of Mendoza (50%) and clones 6 and 15. The wine is not given any skin contact, but is crushed direct into press and is then tank fermented, employing innerstaves and/or oak chips. No malolactic fermentation, of course.

🍷🍷🍷🍷 **1996** Light to medium yellow-green; light and fresh nectarine fruit of medium intensity together with a touch of spicy oak on the bouquet is followed by a fresh and lively melon and nectarine-flavoured palate; very sensitive use of oak which works well to provide delicate seasoning. **rating:** 84

⇒ **best drinking** 1998 – 2000 **best vintages** '91, '94 **drink with** White-fleshed fish • $17

C J Pask Reserve Chardonnay

As with all the C J Pask wines, estate-grown. The wine was entirely barrel-fermented in Francois Freres French oak, and is given five months lees contact before being racked and cleaned up and returned to barrel for a further five months. Interestingly, and consistently with all of the Pask Chardonnays, does not undergo malolactic fermentation. Runner-up in the Fuller Bodied White Table Wine section at the 1998 Sydney International Wine Competition.

🍷🍷🍷🍷🍷 **1996** Glowing yellow-green; exceptionally sophisticated use of oak is immediately apparent on the complex and powerful bouquet, supported, however, by citrus/melon fruit. That same sophisticated oak use introduces and closes the palate with melon and grapefruit flavours peaking on the mid-palate. Just a fraction more fruit weight and concentration would lift it into the highest category, and if it develops like the '95, may achieve that height anyway. **rating:** 90

⇒ **best drinking** 1998 – 2002 **best vintages** '95, '96 **drink with** Blue-lipped mussels in sauce • $23.50

C J Pask Reserve Cabernet Sauvignon

Typically picked in the last week of April, and after a traditional warm fermentation taken immediately to barrel where it spends 22 months in new American oak. Makes a very powerful case for the use of American oak to provide the element of sweetness and softness absent from many New Zealand Cabernets.

🍷🍷🍷🍷🍷 **1995** Medium red-purple; there is lots of aroma and spice on the sweet plummy berry bouquet which shows some barrel-ferment characters. The palate has the sweetness and suppleness missing from so many New Zealand Cabernets, yet is not egregiously oaky. Good tannins pick up on the finish; the wine should age well. **rating:** 90

⇒ **best drinking** 1999 – 2005 **best vintages** '91, '94, '95 **drink with** Saddle of lamb • $25

cairnbrae wines ★★★★

Jacksons Road, RD3, Blenheim **region** Marlborough
phone (03) 572 8048 **fax** (03) 572 8048 **open** 7 days 9–5
winemaker Kim Crawford (Consultant) **production** 14 000 **est.** 1981
product range ($13–23 R) Riesling, Reserve Riesling, Semillon, Sauvignon Blanc, Reserve Barrel Fermented Sauvignon Blanc, Chardonnay, Reserve Chardonnay.

summary The Brown family (Daphne, Murray and Dion) established 18 hectares of vineyard progressively from 1981, selling the grapes to Corbans until 1992, when part of the production was made for them by Kim Crawford, and the label was launched with immediate success. A fast-growing label to watch, with Pinot Noir and Pinot Gris in the pipeline, likewise exports to Australia.

Cairnbrae Riesling

Estate-grown and showing the technical perfection one would expect given a winemaker with the skills of Kim Crawford; yet another wine to demonstrate just how good Riesling can be when grown in the Marlborough region.

🍷🍷🍷🍷 **1996** Pale green-yellow; an as yet relatively undeveloped bouquet with stony/ minerally/herbal aromas. The palate, too, shows a wine with everything in front of it, crisp, clean and fresh, the citrus, lime and toast flavours of the future waiting to emerge. **rating:** 84

⇨ **best drinking** 2000 – 2005 **best vintages** NA **drink with** Seafood antipasto • $13

Cairnbrae Reserve Riesling

Produced in limited quantities, and not exported to Australia. Was awarded five stars in *Cuisine* magazine, and it is not hard to see why. Very much a manifestation of Kim Crawford's approach to Riesling, with the emphasis on ripe fruit.

🍷🍷🍷🍷🍷 **1997** Light to medium yellow-green; there is wonderful, intense lime juice and passionfruit on the bouquet, the palate intense and full flavoured, with particularly attractive mid-palate richness. In New Zealand terms, dry at 5.5 grams residual sugar per litre. **rating:** 92

⇨ **best drinking** 1999 – 2003 **best vintages** NA **drink with** Sashimi • $18

Cairnbrae Sauvignon Blanc

Attractive, clean and rich wine which has had significant show success.

🍷🍷🍷🍷 **1997** Pale straw-green; the bouquet is full and rich, with abundant ripe gooseberry fruit, the palate living up to the bouquet, with seductive ripe and sweet gooseberry fruit. **rating:** 89

⇨ **best drinking** 1998 – 1999 **best vintages** '93, '94, '97 **drink with** Grilled flounder • $15

Cairnbrae Reserve Chardonnay

As is appropriate, Cairnbrae Reserve Chardonnay is made in diametrically opposed style to the varietal Chardonnay. The Reserve uses the full gamut of barrel fermentation, malolactic fermentation and opulent American oak.

🍷🍷🍷🍷 **1997** Medium yellow-green; both the bouquet and palate are dominated by assertive charry toasty oak which needs to tone down; the wine has fair length, and may conceivably rise above the oak, meriting higher points. **rating:** 84

⇨ **best drinking** 1999 – 2001 **best vintages** NA **drink with** Chinese chicken dishes • $23

canadoro NR

New York Street, Martinborough **region** Wairarapa
phone (04) 387 9761 **fax** (04) 387 9761 **open** Via The Grape Vine
winemaker Chris Lintz, Greg Robins **production** 400 **est.** 1993
product range ($23–28 CD) Chardonnay, Cabernet Sauvignon.
summary Canadoro is a weekend operation for Wellington residents Greg and Lesley Robins. The 1.25-hectare vineyard is planted to cabernet sauvignon and chardonnay, but is due to be expanded over the next few years; Greg Robins makes the wine with assistance from Chris Lintz.

cellier le brun ★★★★

Terrace Road, Renwick **region** Marlborough
phone (03) 572 8859 **fax** (03) 572 8814 **open** 7 days 9–5
winemaker Allan McWilliams **production** 15 000 **est.** 1985
product range ($18–49.95 CD) Méthode Champenoise specialist with a large range of both vintage and non-vintage wines, including NV Brut, NV Rosé, Vintage Brut, Vintage Blanc de Blancs and super Cuvées of Blanc de Noirs and Cuvée Adele. Small quantities of Sauvignon Blanc, Chardonnay and Pinot Noir table wine also made and sold under the Terrace Road label.
summary For almost a decade has produced some of New Zealand's highly rated sparkling wines, initially somewhat erratic, but now much more consistent in style – a style which tends to the baroque, but which seems to be exactly what New Zealanders like and want. The Courtyard Café restaurant is open 7 days from 9 am to 5 pm.

Cellier Le Brun Terrace Road Sauvignon Blanc

Cellier Le Brun branched out into table (i.e. non-sparkling) wines in 1995, and made a fairly inauspicious start. However, the follow-on vintage marked a much surer touch.

🍷🍷🍷🍷 **1996** Light green-yellow; the bouquet is firm with a mix of herbal and more floral blossom notes. The palate is clean, firm and still fresh, with a mix of herbal mineral and some sweeter notes tracking those of the bouquet. Well balanced. **rating:** 87

➾ **best drinking** 1998 – 1999 **best vintages** NA **drink with** Salmon terrine • $16

Cellier Le Brun Methode Traditionnelle

Made from 60% Pinot Noir, 30% Chardonnay and 10% Pinot Meunier, and typically given two years on yeast lees. An extremely bold style.

🍷🍷🍷🍷 **NV** Full straw-yellow; a powerful, but clean, bouquet with toasty butter and butterscotch aromas. The palate has distinctive fruit sweetness and richness with biscuit and butterscotch flavours balanced by strong acidity on the finish. **rating:** 89

➾ **best drinking** 1998 – 1999 **best vintages** NA **drink with** Pan-fried scallops • NA

chancellor wines of waipara ★★★

133 Mt Cass Road, Waipara **region** Canterbury
phone (03) 314 6834 **fax** (03) 314 6894 **open** By appointment
winemaker Paddy Borthwick, Kym Rayner **production** 4300 **est.** 1982
product range ($14.50–25 CD) Waipara Sauvignon, Chardonnay, Cabernet Sauvignon (estate-grown); Riesling and Chardonnay from contract growers in Marlborough.
summary Having been grape growers for 15 years Anthony and Helen Willy took the plunge of establishing the Chancellor Wines brand in 1995, and also almost doubling the estate plantings to 11 hectares, which will see Pinot Noir added to the portfolio in the near future. A winery, cellar door and restaurant are all planned for the future.

Chancellor Waipara Sauvignon

Labelled simply 'Sauvignon' which some argue is the correct nomenclature. Produced from 5 hectares of estate plantings, and made in direct style from vines which are now fully mature.

🍷🍷🍷🍷 **1997** Light to medium yellow-green; the bouquet is crisp, with herbal/asparagus/capsicum aromas; the palate is lively, with minerally rather than fleshy structure and flavour, finishing with fresh acidity. **rating:** 84

➾ **best drinking** 1998 – 1999 **best vintages** NA **drink with** Oysters • $15

Chancellor Waipara Cabernet Sauvignon

Like the Sauvignon, comes from the original plantings established in 1982, and which are now mature. A most interesting wine which demonstrates that with appropriate site selection, the Waipara/Canterbury region can produce ripe cabernet flavours.

🍷🍷🍷🍷 **1996** Medium red-purple; the bouquet has ample fresh red berry/earthy fruit with subtle oak; the palate flavours run through herb, olive and red berry, and while firm, are not green, and the overall structure of the wine is good. **rating:** 86

➾ **best drinking** 2000 – 2004 **best vintages** NA **drink with** Lamb shanks • $25

chard farm ★★★★☆

Chard Road, RD1, Gibbston **region** Otago

phone (03) 442 6110 **fax** (03) 441 8400 **open** 7 days 11–5

winemaker Duncan Forsyth, Rob Hay **production** 8000 **est.** 1987

product range ($12–33 R) Riesling, Gewurztraminer, Sauvignon Blanc, Judge and Jury Chardonnay, Closeburn Chardonnay, Southern Lakes Chardonnay, Pinot Noir, Bragato Reserve Pinot Noir.

summary Perched precariously between sheer cliffs and the fast-flowing waters of the Kawarau River, Chard Farm is a tribute to the vision and courage of Rob and Gregory Hay. At a latitude of 45°S, viticulture will never be easy, but Chard Farm has made every post a winner to date, supplementing production from the 20-hectare vineyard with grapes purchased from Marlborough. The Chardonnay and Pinot Noir are superb, especially the intermittent prestige releases.

Chard Farm Judge And Jury Chardonnay

Strikingly packaged in one of the new generation rocket missile-shaped dark green Italian glass bottles, and taking its name from the prominent outcrops of rock across the Kawarau Gorge; Chard Farm clings precariously on the side of the Gorge. There is a great deal more to the wine than innovative (and no doubt expensive) packaging. Since 1994, has come both from estate-grown and Bannockburn (NZ) vineyard fruit; barrel-fermented in predominantly new French oak.

🍷🍷🍷🍷 **1996** Light to medium yellow-green; a clean and fresh bouquet with tangy citrussy/white peach fruit is followed by a crisp tangy/lemony palate surrounded by ever so slightly fuzzy oak. The acid is quite brisk, and the wine as yet fractionally hard, but should age well. **rating:** 85

➾ **best drinking** 1999 – 2003 **best vintages** NA **drink with** Calamari • $29

Chard Farm Bragato Reserve Pinot Noir

Named in honour of the visionary viticulturist Romeo Bragato who came to New Zealand from Victoria at the end of the nineteenth century, and momentarily took the New Zealand industry by the scruff of the neck, propelling it in the direction in which it has finally headed 90 years later. He departed, and his vision was lost, but not entirely forgotten. This is a fitting tribute to his memory, even more fittingly packaged in an exotic Italian glass bottle.

🍷🍷🍷🍷 **1996** Faint blackish tinges to the purple-red colour raise the ghost of a query. The bouquet is fragrant, with a mix of spicy tobacco leaf and black cherry aromas of light to medium intensity, the palate a curious mix of powerful plum, cherry and spice fruit yet trails away slightly into a fractionally tart, short finish. May fill out and evolve with another year or so in bottle. **rating:** 86

➾ **best drinking** 1998 – 2001 **best vintages** '91, '93 **drink with** Spiced quail • $29

chifney ★★★

Huangarua Road, Martinborough **region** Wairarapa
phone (06) 306 9495 **fax** (06) 306 9495 **open** 7 days 9–5
winemaker Sue Chifney, Michael Mebus **production** 2000 **est.** 1980
product range ($14–25 CD) Gewurztraminer, Chardonnay, Chenin Blanc, Rosé, Cabernet Sauvignon, Tawny Port.
summary After a long reign (he opened Wairarapa's first winery) Stan Chifney died in 1996; the business is being carried on by Rosemary Chifney together with daughter Sue, who has undertaken the winemaking responsibilities. The cabernet-based wines from 1995 and 1996 show pronounced green leaf/green tannin characters.

claddagh vineyards NR

Puruatanga Road, Martinborough **region** Wairarapa
phone (06) 306 9264 **fax** (06) 306 9264 **open** By appointment
winemaker Russell Pearless **production** 300 **est.** 1991
product range Pinot Noir, Cabernet Sauvignon.
summary Presently a weekend and holiday occupation for computer industry executives Russell and Suzanne Pearless, but when the 5-hectare vineyard (also planted to chardonnay and sauvignon blanc) comes into full bearing, the level of involvement will doubtless increase.

clearview estate ★★★★★

Clifton Road, RD2, Te Awanga **region** Hawke's Bay
phone (06) 875 0150 **fax** (06) 875 1258 **open** Thur-Mon 10–6 summer; weekends 10–5 winter
winemaker Tim Turvey **production** 6000 **est.** 1989
product range ($12–65 CD) Beach Head Chardonnay, Reserve Chardonnay, Black Reef Riesling, Te Awanga Sauvignon Blanc, Fumé Blanc, Reserve Fumé Blanc, Reserve Cabernet Franc, Reserve Merlot, Reserve The Old Olive Block (Cabernet blend), Cape Kidnappers Cabernet, Basket Press Cabernet, Blush, Sea Red (dessert red wine), Noble 51 (botrytised Chardonnay).
summary Clearview Estate is situated on a shingly site first planted by Anthony Vidal in 1916 on the coast of Te Awanga; it has been replanted since 1988 with chardonnay, cabernet sauvignon, cabernet franc and merlot, with grapes also coming from a neighbouring vineyard. All of the wines to date have been of exceptional quality, especially the magically concentrated and complex Chardonnay. The icing on the cake is an outstanding restaurant, rated by Bob Campbell as Hawke's Bay's best.

Clearview Estate Beach Head Chardonnay

The second label of Clearview, and the only wine made in any significant volume. In 1996, for example, 4 tonnes of grapes went to make the few hundred cases of Reserve, and 25 tonnes were used in Beach Head. Fifty per cent of the wine is barrel-fermented in American oak, 50% in stainless steel. The second pressing of the Reserve wine and all of the other grapes are used in the wine.

🍷🍷🍷🍷 **1996** Light to medium yellow-green; the bouquet is fresh, with nicely controlled spicy American oak leading on to an elegant and remarkably long-flavoured palate. **rating:** 88

➯ **best drinking** 1998 – 2001 **best vintages** NA **drink with** Clams • $20

Clearview Estate Reserve Chardonnay

Tim Turvey makes the most spectacular Chardonnays in New Zealand. A mini vertical tasting of the '93 to '96 Chardonnays in September 1997 was overwhelmingly impressive. These are monumental wines, whether one looks at the alcohol consistently exceeding 14 degrees, or the sheer volume and complexity of flavour. For the record, 30% to 50% is given between six and eight hours skin contact, and the rest is whole-bunch pressed. The wine is barrel-fermented in a cool room at 11 degrees for up to six weeks, and around 20% is taken through malolactic fermentation. Only a tiny fraction of the total production makes the Reserve label.

🍷🍷🍷🍷🍷 **1996** Light to medium yellow-green; as one would expect, a complex bouquet showing the sophisticated use of spicy oak and excellent melon and citrus fruit. The palate is still relatively tight for a wine of 14.3 degrees alcohol, with a mix of citrus, grapefruit and nectarine flavours running through an extremely long, beautifully balanced finish. **rating:** 97

➾ **best drinking** 1998 – 2003 **best vintages** '94, '95, '96 **drink with** Sweetbreads • $29

Clearview Estate Reserve Merlot

The Clearview vineyards are planted on a free-draining shingle which always limits the yield and protects against dilution through wet weather. The wine was made from low-yielding vines and exhibits tremendous concentration and power. It spends 18 months in predominantly French Nevers oak with a touch of Seguin Moreau American oak. Both the '94 and '95 received gold medals.

🍷🍷🍷🍷🍷 **1995** Very good purple-red; the bouquet is slightly lighter than the '94, but will evolve with more bottle age. The palate is long and intense with lively and fresh mint, leaf and red berry flavours, finishing with fine tannins. **rating:** 92

➾ **best drinking** 1999 – 2004 **best vintages** '94, '95 **drink with** Smoked lamb • $30

Clearview Estate Basket Press Cabernet

The top of the range red from Clearview Estate which throws down the gauntlet to the Reserve Chardonnay in terms of absolute quality, and stands at the very head of the New Zealand quality tree. Token amounts of Merlot (4%) and Cabernet Franc (1%) are incorporated.

🍷🍷🍷🍷🍷 **1994** Strong purple-red; a spotlessly clean and sweet bouquet with fully ripe cabernet fruit is supported by first class oak handling. The palate, similarly, has a mix of luscious cassis/berry fruit together with a touch of mint; supple tannins on the finish. **rating:** 93

➾ **best drinking** 1998 – 2004 **best vintages** NA **drink with** Leg of lamb • $65

clifford bay ★★★★☆

PO Box 1088, Blenheim **region** Marlborough
phone (03) 578 4617 **fax** (03) 578 4619 **open** Not
winemaker Glen Thomas (Vavasour Wines – Contract) **production** 8500 **est.** 1994
product range ($16.95–18.95 R) Sauvignon Blanc.
summary Clifford Bay has made the most spectacular imaginable entry onto the scene, winning 2 gold medals (Air New Zealand Wine Awards and Christchurch Show) with its first wine, a 1997 Sauvignon Blanc. It is the venture of Eric and Beverley Bowers, Graham and Thelma Cains, and Chris Wilson. Viticultural advice has come from Richard Bowling, and the wine is made by the masterful Glen Thomas. Twenty hectares of sauvignon blanc, chardonnay and riesling are under vine.

Clifford Bay Sauvignon Blanc

Grown on river terraces adjoining the Awatere River, and not harvested until 1 May. Fifteen per cent of the wine is barrel-fermented in new French oak barriques, the remainder in stainless steel. A richly deserving winner of gold medals at the 1997 Air New Zealand National Wine Show and at Christchurch.

🍷🍷🍷🍷🍷 **1997** Light to medium yellow-green; delicious, soft gooseberry/passionfruit/tropical aromas are complexed by just a subtle hint of spicy oak on the bouquet. The multiflavoured palate is equally good, with a touch of herb to go along with the tropical fruit, that hint of oak spice, and perfect acidity on the finish. **rating:** 93

⇨ **best drinking** 1998 – 1999 **best vintages** NA **drink with** Sugar-cured tuna • NA

clifton road NR

Clifton Road, Te Awanga **region** Hawke's Bay
phone (06) 875 0748 **fax** (06) 876 6211 **open** Not
winemaker Preston Group (White), Tim Turvey (Red) – both Contract **production** 900 **est.** 1992
product range Sauvignon Blanc, Cabernet Sauvignon.
summary The 2.5-hectare vineyard owned by Wayne Harrison and Terri Coats is established close to the sea on the same shingle soils as Clearview Estate. Not surprisingly, there is a similarity in both the quality and style of the wines. A label to watch, even if production will always be small.

cloudy bay ★★★★★

Jacksons Road, Blenheim **region** Marlborough
phone (03) 572 8914 **fax** (03) 572 8065 **open** 7 days 10–4.30
winemaker Kevin Judd **production** 75 000 **est.** 1985
product range ($23.95–39.50 R) Sauvignon Blanc, Chardonnay, Cabernet Merlot, Pelorus (sparkling).
summary The other arm of Cape Mentelle, masterminded by David Hohnen and realised by Kevin Judd, his trusted lieutenant from day one. A marketing tour de force, it became a world-recognised brand in only a few years, but the wine quality and style should not be underestimated: Hohnen and Judd may share a great sense of humour, but they are perfectionists in every way, the wines consistently great. A warped New World view, perhaps, but I rate the Sauvignon Blanc the best in the world, all vintages taken into account. Kevin Judd, incidentally, could as easily earn a living as a photographer, he has a rare talent.

Cloudy Bay Sauvignon Blanc

The most famous New World Sauvignon Blanc with an international reputation second to none. The creative team of David Hohnen and Kevin Judd are disarmingly modest about the wine, however correctly they may point to the perfect marriage between the variety and the climate and soil of Marlborough. There is also the attention to detail, the discipline and the creative intelligence required to make a wine of such distinction with such consistency.

🍷🍷🍷🍷🍷 **1997** Light to medium yellow-green; the bouquet shows a range of complex gooseberry, passionfruit and more smoky/mineral aromas, the palate lively and fresh with crisp gooseberry, apple and passionfruit. Has the usual impeccable balance and length. Simply outstanding as ever. **rating:** 97

⇨ **best drinking** 1998 – 2003 **best vintages** '92, '94, '96 **drink with** Virtually any seafood dish • $23.95

Cloudy Bay Pelorus

A blend of Pinot Noir and Chardonnay, made with consultancy advice and direction from Californian-born and trained Harold Osborne. The wine is aged for three years on yeast lees, and is given further bottle age prior to release. One of the most positively flavoured and structured sparkling wines from Australasia.

1993 Deep yellow-gold; that utterly idiosyncratic bouquet with its pronounced nutty/bready/yeast autolysis influence leads into an ultra-full-flavoured, rich palate with no primary fruit evident, but lots of nutty bready flavours. Marches to the tune of its own drum. **rating:** 88

best drinking 1998 – 1999 **best vintages** NA **drink with** Medium-weight shellfish or fish dishes • $39.50

collards

303 Lincoln Road, Henderson, Auckland **region** Henderson
phone (09) 838 8341 **fax** (09) 837 5840 **open** Mon-Sat 9–5, Sun 11–5
winemaker Bruce Collard, Geoff Collard **production** 20 000 **est.** 1910
product range ($11.95–28 CD) Riesling, Queen Charlotte Riesling, Chardonnay (Rothesay, Hawke's Bay Reserve, Marlborough, Blakes Mill), Chenin Blanc, Sauvignon Blanc (Rothesay, Marlborough), Private Bin Dry White, Barrel Fermented Semillon, Marlborough Pinot Noir, Rothesay Cabernet Sauvignon, Cabernet Merlot, Tawny Port.
summary At the same time a family-owned and run business which is a bastion of conservatism, adopting a low promotional profile, but which consistently produces fastidiously crafted wines of excellent quality, and which has moved with the times in developing new wines and labels.

Collards Riesling

Typically, Collards Riesling is a blend of Hawke's Bay, Auckland and Marlborough grapes, but in 1996 missing the Marlborough component. Interestingly, there is no price differential between this wine and the Queen Charlotte, and – indeed – looking at the wine in the glass, why should there be?

1996 Light to medium yellow-green; a concentrated bouquet with abundant lime and toast aromas leads on to a smooth but long lime juicy palate, finishing with excellent acidity and perfectly judged residual sugar. **rating:** 90

best drinking 1998 – 2001 **best vintages** '93, '94, '96 **drink with** Seafood salad • $13

Collards Queen Charlotte Riesling

The flag-bearer of the Collards Rieslings, until 1996 known simply as Marlborough Riesling.

1996 Light to medium yellow-green; a potent and concentrated bouquet with what may or may not be some botrytis influence, and a powerful palate with lime, lemon and more herbal flavours running through the mid-palate and into a long, lingering finish. Should develop superbly. **rating:** 90

best drinking 1998 – 2004 **best vintages** '92, '94, '96 **drink with** Sashimi • $13

Collards Marlborough Sauvignon Blanc

Almost diametrically opposed in style to the Collards Rothesay, positively leaping out of the glass and giving the impression that it will, like so many of its counterparts, be quick-developing. That said and done, an utterly delicious wine of the highest quality.

🍷🍷🍷🍷🍷 **1997** Light green-yellow; a fragrant, fresh passionfruit-accented bouquet leads into an utterly seductive palate, with an extra dimension of tropical passionfruit flavours cut and restrained by precisely judged acidity on the finish. **rating:** 93

➡ **best drinking** 1998 – 1999 **best vintages** '92, '94, '97 **drink with** Bluff oysters • $15

Collards Rothesay Sauvignon Blanc

The grapes come from Collards' Rothesay Vineyard in Waimauku in West Auckland, and challenges the notion that Sauvignon Blanc cannot produce the same intense varietal character so far north as it does conspicuously in Marlborough and Wairarapa, and also (in a fuller mode) Hawke's Bay. Made in a typical no-frills Collards fashion, stainless steel fermented and early bottled.

🍷🍷🍷🍷🍷 **1997** Light green-yellow; a spotlessly clean and crisp bouquet of medium intensity with herbal and gooseberry fruit. The tight palate, lively and fresh, with excellent grip and structure, is one of those unusual Sauvignon Blancs which actually give the impression of needing time in bottle. **rating:** 90

➡ **best drinking** 1998 – 2000 **best vintages** '93, '95, '96, '97 **drink with** Crab • $15

Collards Hawke's Bay Chardonnay

An unusual labelling exercise sees the word 'Reserve' included as part of the grand name in better vintages. It is barrel-fermented, but most is removed from oak and held in stainless steel until bottling. All in all, a very elegant, unforced style.

🍷🍷🍷🍷 **1996** Reserve. Medium green-yellow; a complex and intriguing bouquet with echoes of Burgundy. The palate, while elegant and restrained has excellent feel and weight, driven primarily by the citrus/melon fruit, but just a touch of oak there in the background. **rating:** 89

➡ **best drinking** 1998 – 2001 **best vintages** '94, '96, '97 **drink with** Stir-fried prawns • $18

Collards Rothesay Chardonnay

Arguably the most distinguished of the Collards wines, proving that the Auckland region – in this case at Waimauku – can indeed produce high-quality Chardonnay and Sauvignon Blanc. Since it was first made in 1986, the wine has won eight gold medals in New Zealand wine shows, but had its ultimate moment of glory at the 1994 Australian National Wine Show in Canberra, where it topped a field of over 100 medal-winning Chardonnays. One hundred per cent barrel-fermented and lees aged, with varying percentages of malolactic fermentation according to the vintage, but up to 80%.

🍷🍷🍷🍷🍷 **1996** Medium yellow-green; ripe and rich, with obvious barrel-ferment characters over tangy fruit, with more of the same on the stylish palate. Here the fruit veers more to melon and fig, the oak expertly handled and integrated. **rating:** 94

➡ **best drinking** 1998 – 2000 **best vintages** '86, '87, '89, '93, '94, '96 **drink with** Pan-fried breast of chicken • $28

coopers creek NR

State Highway 16, Huapai **region** Kumeu and Huapai
phone (09) 412 8560 **fax** (09) 412 8375 **open** Mon-Fri 9–5.30, weekends 10.30–5.30
winemaker Kim Crawford **production** 40 000 **est.** 1980
product range ($10–27.50 R) Hawke's Bay Riesling, Hawke's Bay Reserve Riesling, Late Harvest Riesling, Hawke's Bay Chardonnay, Swamp Road Reserve Chardonnay, Marlborough Sauvignon Blanc, Marlborough Oak Aged Sauvignon Blanc, Gisborne Fumé Blanc, Gisborne Chardonnay, Hawke's Bay Merlot, Huapai Cabernet Merlot.

summary A long-term producer of stylish white wines sourced from Gisborne, Hawke's Bay and Marlborough, respectively. They are full of character and flavour, but avoid the heavy, coarse phenolics which were once so much part of the white wine scene in New Zealand. Unfortunately, in 1998 became embroiled in accusations of mislabelling varietal wines, with government appointed auditors investigating. A loss of credibility seems inevitable.

Coopers Creek Hawke's Bay Reserve Riesling

A new arrival on the scene, destined to be made only in outstanding vintages. What is more, only 275 cases were made in the initial (1996) vintage, compared to around 2000 for the varietal version. Likewise grown at Jim Scotland's vineyard, the wine has 13.5 degrees alcohol and 13 grams per litre of residual sugar.

🍷🍷🍷🍷🍷 **1996** Light yellow-green; the bouquet is distinctly Alsatian in its complex aroma, and on the palate shares many of the characteristics of Alsatian Vendage Tardive. An extremely rich and striking wine, with some botrytis influence adding to the impact. **rating:** 92

⇨ **best drinking** 1998 – 2003 **best vintages** NA **drink with** Strong Asian food • $20

Coopers Creek Marlborough Sauvignon Blanc

This is the engine-room of the Coopers Creek winery, with 10 000 cases made in a no-frills, unwooded style. However, some complexity comes from the two differently sited vineyards providing the grapes.

🍷🍷🍷🍷 **1997** Light yellow-green; a delicate, crisp and lively bouquet with a mix of passionfruit and herbal aromas, and a similar mix of flavours on the no less crisp, fresh and delicate palate, lengthened by lively acidity. **rating:** 89

⇨ **best drinking** 1998 – 1999 **best vintages** '91, '94, '96, '97 **drink with** Crustacea • $15

Coopers Creek Hawke's Bay Chardonnay

Winemaker Kim Crawford believes in ripe grapes, something fairly readily achieved in the Hawke's Bay climate. Barrel fermentation in American oak, lees contact and 100% malolactic fermentation all add to the impact of a powerful wine style.

🍷🍷🍷🍷🍷 **1997** Medium yellow-green; a tangy bouquet with a mix of mineral and citrus aromas, and a touch of cashew which comes through on the palate. A stylish and restrained wine which will hurry slowly. **rating:** 92

⇨ **best drinking** 1998 – 1999 **best vintages** '86, '89, '91, '92, '95, 96, '97 **drink with** Sweet and sour pork • $19

Coopers Creek Swamp Road Reserve Chardonnay

The somewhat off-putting name should not mislead you; this is the flagship of the excellent Coopers Creek white wine range. One hundred per cent barrel fermentation in all tight-grain, heavy toast French oak (from Francois Freres and Dargaud & Jaegle), 70% of which is new, with malolactic fermentation and ten months in barrel produce a wine which is never to be denied. Not made in poor vintages, incidentally.

🍷🍷🍷🍷🍷 **1996** Medium to full yellow-green; an elegant bouquet, still surprisingly tight, with citrus and melon fruit does not prepare you for the extremely rich, intense Batard Montrachet-like viscosity of the palate. Tangy and lively, with all the weight one could conceivably wish for. **rating:** 95

⇨ **best drinking** 1998 – 2000 **best vintages** '92, '94, '95, '96 **drink with** Creamy pasta • $27.50

corbans (auckland) ★★★★☆

426–448 Great North Road, Auckland **region** Henderson
phone (09) 837 3390 **fax** (09) 836 0005 **open** Mon-Sat 12–5 pm
winemaker Kerry Hitchcock (Chief) **production** In excess of 20 million litres (approx 750 000 plus 3 million casks) **est.** 1902
product range ($11–36 R) Headed by newly introduced flagship range Cottage Block; then the premium varietal ranges of Corbans Private Bin and Cooks Winemaker's Reserve; the negociant-type label Robard & Butler; and the low-priced Corbans White Label Collection. The regional brands are listed under the other Corbans entries.
summary New Zealand's second largest wine group with a turnover exceeding $NZ100 million, 500 hectares of estate vineyards and another 500 hectares of contracted vineyards. Wine quality is exemplary, setting the pace for others to follow.

corbans (gisborne)

Solander Street, Gisborne **region** Gisborne
phone (06) 867 1269 **fax** (06) 867 8467 **open** By appointment
winemaker David Freschi **production** NA **est.** 1970
product range ($8–30 R) The winery supplies Chardonnay, Riesling, Sauvignon Blanc and Müller Thurgau variously used in the Cottage Block, Cooks, Huntaway and Corbans Private Bin ranges.
summary Gisborne unfairly labours under the reputation of simply being a bulk-wine producer, no doubt because the major wine companies have such large holdings there, but do not seek publicity for their wineries, and also no doubt because of the dearth of small, high-profile makers, The Millton Vineyard and Matawhero being the exceptions which prove the rule.

Corbans Cottage Block Gisborne Chardonnay

The grapes for this wine were whole-bunch pressed direct to new and one-year-old French barriques, and the wine was not innoculated, undergoing a natural fermentation. The technique is very evident in the wine, which certainly challenges conventional wisdom and which (in 1995) was a radical departure from the extremely good '94 vintage.

1995 Light to medium yellow-green; a striking, challenging bouquet with very strong French hot solids characters. The palate is less unconventional and challenging, with considerable length and complexity, although there is an echo of the hot solids characters on the finish. Tailor-made for those who love traditional French Burgundies. **rating:** 84

best drinking 1998 – 2002 **best vintages** NA **drink with** Sweetbreads • $29

corbans (hawke's bay) ★★★★☆

Timms Street, Napier **region** Hawke's Bay
phone (06) 835 4333 **fax** (06) 835 9791 **open** By appointment
winemaker Evan Ward **production** NA **est.** 1944
product range ($11–36 R) The principal regionally identified brand is Longridge of Hawke's Bay; Chardonnay, Sauvignon Blanc, Gewurztraminer, Chenin Blanc, Pinot Noir, Cabernet Sauvignon, Cabernet Franc and Merlot are produced for the Longridge, Cooks and Corbans Private Bin ranges. Verde Méthode Traditionelle.
summary Established on what was the original McWilliam's winery, although no longer recognisable as such. Arguably the most important red wine production facility for Corbans.

Corbans Amadeus

Vintaged from Pinot Noir and a little Chardonnay grown not in Marlborough (as I had always supposed) but in Hawke's Bay. The '90, '91 and '93 wines have all been outstanding, and the wine has now escaped from the dreadful packaging which did much to hide its light under a bushel.

🍷🍷🍷🍷🍷 **1993** Medium straw-yellow; there are classic biscuity/toasty/bready Pinot Noir varietal aromas, undercut with some more minerally notes. The palate is very fine, with toasty/biscuity flavours and a long cleansing finish. **rating:** 93

➯ **best drinking** 1998 – 1999 **best vintages** '90, '91, '93 **drink with** Shellfish, oysters • $19

corbans (marlborough) ★★★★☆

Jacksons Road, RD3, Blenheim **region** Marlborough
phone (03) 572 8198 **fax** (03) 572 8199 **open** 7 days 10–4
winemaker David Freschi **production** NA **est.** 1989
product range ($11–36 R) The Marlborough winery flag-bearers are Stoneleigh Vineyard Riesling, Cottage Block Noble Riesling, Cottage Block Marlborough Sauvignon Blanc, Private Bin Marlborough Chardonnay, Cottage Block Pinot Noir, Cottage Block Merlot and Private Bin Amberly Riesling; also the full Stoneleigh range and many others, including the new (1998) varietal Estate range.
summary A much expanded and upgraded winery, some outstanding vineyards, notably the Stoneleigh Vineyard, and some outstanding winemaking skills (notably from former winemaker Alan McCorkindale) have all contributed to the quality of the impressive range of wines coming from Corbans' Marlborough winery.

Corbans Cottage Block Marlborough Sauvignon Blanc

1997 marked the first Cottage Block Marlborough Sauvignon Blanc, making an exceptional auspicious debut. Whole-bunch pressing and partial barrel, partial stainless steel fermentation has produced a brilliant example of oaked Sauvignon Blanc.

🍷🍷🍷🍷🍷 **1997** Light to medium yellow-green; highly fragrant bouquet with spicy nutmeg barrel-ferment aromas evident but not dominant, with strong passionfruit also present. The sophisticated making comes through on the multiflavoured palate with spicy nutmeg oak and lush fruit balanced by acidity. **rating:** 94

➯ **best drinking** 1998 – 1999 **best vintages** '97 **drink with** Chinese prawns • $20

Corbans Estate Marlborough Sauvignon Blanc

The Corbans Estate is a new low-priced range of wines. The '97 made an extraordinarily auspicious debut. For the record it is near dry, with only 5 grams per litre of residual sugar.

🍷🍷🍷🍷 **1997** Light green-yellow; the bouquet is clean, crisp and fresh with direct aromas of light to medium intensity; the usual passionfruit and gooseberry characters are present and correct. The palate has excellent freshness and balance, replicating the characters of the bouquet; good balance. **rating:** 89

➯ **best drinking** 1998 – 1999 **best vintages** '97 **drink with** Mussels • $14

Corbans Private Bin Marlborough Sauvignon Blanc

Straightforward making and early bottling; while the '96 was disappointing, and roundly criticised, the '97 deserves the Private Bin tag, and was the top wine in *Cuisine's* annual review

🍷🍷🍷🍷🍷 **1997** Light to medium yellow-green; the very sophisticated use of a touch of spicy oak works extremely well on both bouquet and palate; the fruit, while not heavy, is perfectly ripened with sweeter passionfruit and gooseberry notes building towards the finish. **rating:** 95

➾ **best drinking** 1998 – 1999 **best vintages** '97 **drink with** Deep-fried calamari • $18

Corbans Cottage Block Pinot Noir

Corbans was the first producer to release a noteworthy Pinot Noir from Marlborough, starring in various Sydney International Wine Competitions. The '94 is a tribute to the skills of its maker, Alan McCorkindale.

🍷🍷🍷🍷🍷 **1994** Medium red; a very fine, elegant and stylish wine on both bouquet and palate, with sappy cherry and plum aromas, and fine spicy plum and cherry flavours on a long, silky palate. Excellent oak balance and integration; they don't come much better in the light to medium weight and style. **rating:** 94

➾ **best drinking** 1998 – 1999 **best vintages** '91, '92, '94 **drink with** Roast pigeon • $33

cottle hill winery NR

Cnr State Highway 10 and Cottle Hill Drive, Kerikeri **region** Northland and Matakana
phone (09) 407 5203 **fax** (09) 407 6808 **open** 7 days 10–5
winemaker Michael Bendit **production** 1000 **est.** 1997
product range ($14–22 CD) Sauvignon Blanc, Chardonnay, Bay Breeze (Sauvignon Blanc Chardonnay), Cabernet Sauvignon, Cabernet Sauvignon Reserve.
summary Michael and Barbara Webb are fugitives from 'the southern California rat-race'. They first arrived in the Bay of Islands on their yacht in 1992, and have now returned to establish Cottle Hill Winery.

covell estate NR

Troutbeck Road, Galatea, RD1, Murupara **region** Waikato and Bay of Plenty
phone (07) 366 4827 **open** 7 days 10–4 by appointment
winemaker Bob Covell **production** 1000 **est.** NA
product range ($12–25 CD) Riesling, Chardonnay, Pinot Noir, Rata Red.
summary Owners Bob and Desarei Covell have established this vineyard using strict biodynamic organic standards, and mature their wines for extended periods in oak, and give them further time in bottle before release. The 1992 Chardonnay and Pinot Noir, tasted in late 1997, can best be described as rich but rustic.

crab farm NR

125 Main Road, Bay View, Hawke's Bay **region** Hawke's Bay
phone (06) 836 6678 **open** 7 days 10–5
winemaker Hamish Jardine **production** 2600 **est.** 1989
product range ($10–17 CD) Gewurztraminer, Sauvignon Blanc, Chardonnay, Pinot Noir, Merlot, Cabernet Sauvignon.
summary Hamish Jardine has worked at both Chateau Reynella and Matawhero; the family vineyards were planted in 1980 and are now mature, so given the equable Hawke's Bay climate there is no reason why the wines should not succeed. A seafood restaurant has recently been added, open from the end of October to Easter.

cross roads winery ★★★★

State Highway 50, Korokipo Road, Fernhill, Napier **region** Hawke's Bay
phone (06) 879 9737 **fax** (06) 879 6068 **open** 7 days 10–5
winemaker Malcolm Reeves, Ken Sanderson **production** 10 000 **est.** 1990
product range ($10–33 CD) Gewurztraminer, Dry Riesling, Late Harvest Riesling, Chardonnay, Reserve Chardonnay, Oak Aged Sauvignon, Sauvignon, Pinot Noir, Cabernet Merlot, Reserve Cabernet Merlot, Talisman, Stormy Ports.
summary A very successful partnership between Malcolm Reeves, wine journalist and Massey University lecturer, and computer entrepreneur Lester O'Brien. Right from vintage, the wines have received widespread critical acclaim, and have enjoyed great success in wine shows. Production has grown as projected, and a new winery facility has been completed. Draws in part on 5 hectares of various of red vinifera varieties which go to produce the super-premium Talisman red. The identity of those varieties (and hence the blend) is deliberately kept confidential.

Cross Roads Reserve Chardonnay

As one would expect, has distinctly more weight and complexity than the varietal release, benefiting from better fruit and obvious winemaker inputs through the full cavalcade of barrel ferment, lees contact and malolactic fermentation.

🍷🍷🍷🍷 **1996** Medium yellow-green; the bouquet is complex, with abundant cashew and melon aromas, the palate likewise complex and structured, with strong cashew/hazelnut barrel-ferment and malolactic-ferment derivatives. **rating:** 86

➾ **best drinking** 1998 – 1999 **best vintages** NA **drink with** Kassler • $20.30

daniel schuster ★★★★

Reeces Road, Omihi, North Canterbury (vineyard only) **region** Canterbury
phone (03) 337 1763 **fax** (03) 337 1762 **open** By appointment
winemaker Danny Schuster **production** 3500 **est.** 1984
product range ($20–30 R) Hawke's Bay Chenin Blanc, Hawke's Bay Pinot Blanc, Marlborough Chardonnay, Canterbury Chardonnay, Petrie Vineyard Selection Chardonnay, Pinot Noir, Canterbury Pinot Noir, Reserve Pinot Noir.
summary Austrian-born, German-trained Danny Schuster must now rank as one of the leading consultant viticulturists in the world, his clients ranging from Stag's Leap, Neibaum Coppola, Moraga and Spotswoode in the Napa Valley to Antinori in Tuscany. The mix is all the more fascinating when one considers that the Napa Valley makers are all producing powerful and dense Cabernet-based red wines; that the climate of Tuscany is as far removed from that of Canterbury as one could imagine; and that at home Danny Schuster is known for his pioneering work in the production of Pinot Noir from the Canterbury/Waipara region. Truly, a man for all seasons, producing wines of equally variable (seasonal) quality, at times exhilarating, at times depressing.

Daniel Schuster Petrie Vineyard Selection Chardonnay

The Petrie Vineyard Selection is drawn from the best blocks on the estate Petrie Vineyard at Rakaia. Hand-harvested grapes are barrel-fermented and lees aged in a mix of new and used Vosges and Troncais barriques for 15 months with a spontaneous malolactic fermentation. Only 250 cases produced.

🍷🍷🍷🍷½ **1996** Medium yellow-green; the gently complex bouquet runs through melon and fig fruit, some subtle cashew barrel-ferment/malolactic-fermentation aromas, with some more buttery/toasty aromas also present. A wine which grows and grows on you as you taste it, with melon, fig and cashew flavours, more of that subtle barrel-ferment oak, and an exceptional mouthfeel to the long finish. **rating:** 92

⇨ **best drinking** 1998 – 2003 **best vintages** NA **drink with** Fresh abalone • $26.95

darjon vineyards NR

North Eyre Road, Swannanoa, North Canterbury **region** Canterbury
phone (03) 312 6054 **fax** (03) 312 6544 **open** Fri–Sun and public holidays 12–5
winemaker John Baker **production** 500 **est.** 1992
product range ($20 CD) The minute estate-produced Swannanoa range of Pinot Noir and Riesling is supplemented by wines from Marlborough, and from other New Zealand and Australian boutique producers.
summary A new arrival on the Christchurch scene, run by former amateur winemaker John Baker and his wife Michelle. The restaurant was opened on-site in 1994, coinciding with the first production from the estate plantings (earlier wines were made from purchased grapes) and all of the Darjon wine will be sold through the restaurant, mail list and cellar-door sales.

de gyffarde NR

Gifford Road, Rapaura, RD3, Blenheim **region** Marlborough
phone (03) 572 8189 **fax** (03) 572 8189 **open** At Marlborough Vintners, Rapaura Road, Blenheim
winemaker Graeme Paul **production** 3500 **est.** 1995
product range ($17 CD) Sauvignon Blanc, Chardonnay under both de Gyffarde and Lofthouse labels.
summary English-born owners Di and Rod Lofthouse were 20-year veterans of the film and television industry before establishing their 6-hectare vineyard in 1989, and moving into winemaking from 1995. They have now taken the process one step further by becoming part-owners of Marlborough Vintners Limited. This operates the new winery, commissioned for the 1998 vintage, which makes the wine for de Gyffarde and three other similar-sized Marlborough wineries. Over 90% of the production is exported to the United Kingdom.

de Gyffarde Sauvignon Blanc

First made in 1995, with the third vintage moving closer to Rod Lofthouse's stated aim of winning a gold medal, the 1997 receiving a silver medal at the 1997 Air New Zealand Wine Awards.

🍷🍷🍷🍷 **1997** Light yellow-green; the bouquet is crisp and clean, on the herbal side, with lemon and capsicum aromas. The palate shows some slightly riper flavours with gooseberry and lemon, and has particularly good mouthfeel and balance, and a long, clean finish. **rating:** 86

⇨ **best drinking** 1998 – 1999 **best vintages** NA **drink with** Thai prawns • $17

delegat's wine estate ★★★★☆

Hepburn Road, Henderson **region** Henderson
phone (09) 836 0129 **fax** (09) 836 3282 **open** Mon–Fri 10–5, weekends 10–6
winemaker Michale Ivicevich **production** NFP **est.** 1947
product range ($16.95–25 R) Estate label of Chardonnay, Sauvignon Blanc and Cabernet Merlot; top-of-the-range Proprietors Reserve label of Chardonnay, Fumé Blanc, Cabernet

Sauvignon and Merlot. Also vineyard-designated Chardonnay from Hawke's Bay, Oyster Bay Chardonnay and Sauvignon Blanc, and Sauvignon Blanc from Marlborough.

summary Delegat's now sources most of its grapes from Hawke's Bay, utilising its own vineyards there and contract growers, but has added the Oyster Bay range from Marlborough to its repertoire. The quality of the wines is seldom less than good, with a number of excellent wines under the Proprietors Reserve label, conspicuously the Chardonnay.

Delegat's Oyster Bay Sauvignon Blanc

The first vintage of Delegat's Oyster Bay Sauvignon Blanc, made from two-year-old vines, had extraordinary success in winning the Marquis de Goulaine Trophy for Best Sauvignon Blanc at the International Wine and Spirit Competition in London in July 1991. Not surprisingly, the Oyster Bay label has spearheaded Delegat's export drive since that time. It is made in a classic, no-frills, bracingly direct Marlborough-style.

🍷🍷🍷🍷 **1997** Light to medium yellow-green; a potent, pungent bouquet with a mix of herbal, minerally/stony and tangy gooseberry fruit aromas is followed by a palate with a similarly powerful and diverse array of flavours. Long, intense, well-balanced finish. **rating:** 89

➾ **best drinking** 1998 – 1999 **best vintages** '90, '91, '92, '94, '97 **drink with** Oysters, mussels • $17

Delegat's Proprietors Reserve Sauvignon Blanc

An outstanding Hawke's Bay Sauvignon Blanc, picked ripe and partially fermented in barrel, part in stainless steel, before being given up to six months barrel maturation. The oak handling is sophisticated and sensitive, and in no way threatens the fruit. One of the relatively rare Sauvignon Blancs which ages well, the '96 winning the only gold medal in the 1996 and Older Sauvignon Blanc Class at the 1997 Liquorland National Wine Show of Australia.

🍷🍷🍷🍷🍷 **1996** Light to medium yellow-green; there is no sign of phenolic break-up, no sign of the weedy vegetable characters which often appear in aged Sauvignon Blanc. Both the bouquet and palate are fresh, with ripe, tropical gooseberry fruit, the oak contributing as much to the structure of the wine as it does to its flavour. **rating:** 92

➾ **best drinking** 1998 – 2000 **best vintages** '92, '94, '96 **drink with** Abalone • $18

Delegat's Oyster Bay Chardonnay

The partner to Oyster Bay Sauvignon Blanc, both so prominently branded and well known that they have a life almost independent of Delegat's. Seventy five per cent of the wine undergoes barrel fermentation in new oak, and spends six months thereafter on yeast lees. Significantly, none of the wine goes through malolactic fermentation, producing a style which (to my palate, at least) works brilliantly well.

🍷🍷🍷🍷🍷 **1996** Medium yellow-green; well-balanced nutty/charry barrel-ferment oak is woven through melon and citrus fruit on the bouquet, a promising start but it is the palate which really takes off. Lively, zesty nectarine, citrus and melon, even a hint of passionfruit, ripple along the palate and into a lingering finish. **rating:** 93

➾ **best drinking** 1998 – 2001 **best vintages** '90, '91, '92, '96 **drink with** Sugar-cured tuna • $20

Delegat's Proprietors Reserve Chardonnay

Made from hand-harvested, estate-grown grapes; 50% is barrel-fermented in a mixture of new and one-year-old French oak barriques, and a sensibly restrained 25% undergoes malolactic fermentation. Consistently one of the highest-rated New Zealand Chardonnays, although I am not sure I do not prefer the more direct appeal of the Oyster Bay-style.

🍷🍷🍷🍷🍷 **1996** Medium to full yellow-green; an extremely rich, full buttery/toasty bouquet leads on to a mouthfilling, solid peachy/buttery palate with an almost unctuously soft finish. **rating:** 90

➪ **best drinking** 1998 – 1999 **best vintages** '86, '89, '91, '92, '94, '96 **drink with** Smoked salmon • $25

Delegat's Proprietors Reserve Merlot

A 100% Merlot, 100% Hawke's Bay wine. Sophisticated winemaking involves warm fermentation (up to 30°C) and 50% of the wine finishing its primary fermentation in barriques. That portion undergoes malolactic fermentation in barrel, the remainder in tank. The components are then blended and spend 12 months in new French oak prior to being eggwhite-fined and bottled. It is an approach which pays considerable dividends.

🍷🍷🍷🍷 **1996** Strong red-purple; a complex bouquet with a mix of ripe plummy fruit and more cedary/dusty/briary/gamey characters is followed by a full-flavoured palate with lush berry fruit, a hint of chocolate, and powerful, ever so slightly green, tannins on the finish. **rating:** 87

➪ **best drinking** 2000 – 2005 **best vintages** '86, '89, '91, '92, '94, '96, '97 **drink with** Seared venison • $25

deredcliffe estates ★★★

Lyons Road, Mangatawhiri Valley, Bombay Hills, near Auckland **region** Waikato and Bay of Plenty

phone (09) 233 6314 **fax** (09) 233 6215 **open** 7 days 9.30–5

winemaker Mark Compton **production** 17 500 **est.** 1976

product range ($12–29 R) Marlborough Riesling, Marlborough Sauvignon Blanc, Mangatawhiri Chardonnay, Hawke's Bay Pinot Noir, Hawke's Bay Cabernet Merlot, Hawke's Bay Cabernet Merlot Franc; 'The Dedication Series' is top-end label, along with Mangatawhiri Chardonnay.

summary The Waikato's answer to the Napa Valley, with the $7 million Hotel du Vin, luxury restaurant, wine tours, lectures, the lot; briefly listed on the Stock Exchange, but now Japanese-owned. Production continues to increase, and deRedcliffe now has vineyards in both Hawke's Bay and Marlborough.

dry river ★★★★★

Puruatanga Road, Martinborough **region** Wairarapa

phone (06) 306 9388 **fax** (06) 306 9275 **open** Not

winemaker Neil McCallum **production** 3500 **est.** 1979

product range ($18–45 CD) Craighall Estate Riesling, Botrytis Selection Riesling, Chardonnay, Gewurztraminer, Sauvignon Blanc, Pinot Gris, Pinot Noir.

summary Winemaker/owner Neil McCallum is a research scientist with a Doctorate from Oxford University, with winemaking very much a part-time occupation. He has justifiably gained an international reputation for the exceptional quality of his wines, which he jealously guards and protects. Each is made in tiny quantities, and sells out immediately on release, but minuscule quantities are now making their way to Australia. Some rate Dry River as New Zealand's best winery, and I'm not sure I would disagree.

Dry River Botrytis Selection Riesling

Acknowledged by all to be a New Zealand classic, produced in tiny quantities from heavily botrytised grapes.

🍷🍷🍷🍷🍷 **1996** Bright, light yellow-green; intense lime/tropical aromas and flavours run through a beautifully made wine, with tremendous length to the palate, and perfect acidity on the finish to balance the luscious botrytised fruit. **rating:** 95

➾ **best drinking** 1998 – 2002 **best vintages** NA **drink with** Fruit tart • $28

Dry River Pinot Noir

For many observers, New Zealand's finest Pinot Noir and certainly its most sought after. Immaculately crafted, as are all of Neil McCallum's wines, but with all of the robust fruit of Martinborough at its best.

🍷🍷🍷🍷🍷 **1996** Strong and dense purple-red; the bouquet is similarly intense, concentrated and complex with abundant ripe plummy fruit. The palate is exceptionally rich and smooth, with masses of dark plum fruit showing absolute ripeness; finishes with fine tannins and subtle oak. Compellingly powerful. **rating:** 96

➾ **best drinking** 1998 – 2000 **best vintages** '89, '90, '91, '93, '94, '96 **drink with** Coq au vin • $36

---

esk valley estate ★★★★☆

745 Main Road, Bay View, Napier **region** Hawke's Bay
phone (06) 836 6411 **fax** (06) 836 6413 **open** 7 days 10–6 summer, 10–5 winter
winemaker Gordon Russell **production** 25 000 **est.** 1933

product range ($13.50–59 CD) Chenin Blanc, Sauvignon Blanc, Riesling, Chardonnay, Reserve Chardonnay, Merlot Rosé, Merlot, Merlot Cabernet Sauvignon, Reserve Merlot Malbec Cabernet Sauvignon; also The Terraces, a super-premium single estate vineyard Bordeaux-blend sold by mail order only, when two years old.

summary The little brother in the Villa Maria-Vidal family, but with the ultra-premium The Terraces standing boldly in the top echelon of New Zealand reds, and making the winery rating difficult. Which is not to say that some of the other wines in the portfolio aren't impressive; they are.

Esk Valley Reserve Chardonnay

Typically sourced from two vineyards, one near the Tutaekurai River, the other from the Gimblett Road area. The wine is barrel-fermented in French oak, taken fully through malolactic fermentation, and aged in barriques for ten months.

🍷🍷🍷🍷 **1996** Medium yellow-green; a powerful and complex bouquet driven by the barrel-ferment and malolactic-ferment inputs is followed by a solidly constructed, well-balanced palate with peach and ripe fig fruit; soft finish. **rating:** 88

➾ **best drinking** 1998 – 1999 **best vintages** '94, '95, '96 **drink with** Chinese pork with cashew nuts • $28

Esk Valley The Terraces

A blend of 40% Merlot, 40% Malbec and 20% Cabernet Franc drawn from a single small terraced vineyard adjacent to the winery. Originally terraced in the 1940s, it was replanted with the Bordeaux varietal mix in 1988. Its spends 21 months in new French barriques. Only 200 cases of this celebrated wine were released, and sold only through cellar door.

🍷🍷🍷🍷🍷 **1995** Almost impenetrable red-purple; an enormously powerful, dense, introverted bouquet fitting the winemaker's description of 'black and tarry'. The palate provides the concentration, structure and ripe tannins so seldom seen in New Zealand, almost to the point of excess. Black fruit, spice and some cedary oak round off a quite extraordinary and unique wine. **rating:** 94

➪ **best drinking** 2000 – 2010 **best vintages** NA **drink with** Char-grilled rump • $59

eskdale winegrowers NR

Main Road, Eskdale **region** Hawke's Bay
phone (06) 836 6302 **open** Mon–Sat 9–5
winemaker Kim Salonius **production** Under 1000 **est.** 1973
product range Gewurztraminer, Chardonnay, Cabernet.
summary Having gained winemaking experience at McWilliam's, Canadian-born Kim Salonius and family have established a small 4-hectare estate operation, making wines in very small quantities sold cellar door which have gained a strong reputation for consistency of style.

fairhall downs estate NR

814 Wrekin Road, RD2, Brancott Valley, Marlborough **region** Marlborough
phone (03) 572 8356 **fax** (03) 572 8357 **open** Not
winemaker John Forrest (Contract) **production** 5500 **est.** 1996
product range ($13.75–16.25 ML) Sauvignon Blanc, Chardonnay.
summary Ken Small and Stuart Smith have been grape growers in Marlborough since 1982, supplying Montana and Villa Maria from their 20-hectare vineyard at the top of the Brancott Valley Road. In 1996 they launched their own label, with John Forrest as contract winemaker, and using the Forrest Estate winery facility. Instant success followed with the 1996 Sauvignon Blanc winning a gold medal and trophy at the Royal Perth Wine Show, and a silver medal in every other competition entered.

Fairhall Downs Estate Sauvignon Blanc

Draws upon 10 hectares of estate sauvignon blanc and 2.25 hectares of estate semillon; it represents only a small part of the vineyard output. Cold fermented in stainless steel, the wine has 4% Semillon included to add structure. A 20-day spread in harvest dates is also used to maximise fruit complexity.

🍷🍷🍷🍷 **1997** Medium yellow-green; a clean bouquet with a most attractive mix of passionfruit, gooseberry and nectarine aromas is followed by a well-balanced, fresh palate with a similar spread of flavours to the bouquet. **rating:** 88

➪ **best drinking** 1998 – 1999 **best vintages** NA **drink with** Tempura • $13.75

fairmont estate NR

Gladstone Road, RD2, Gladstone, Wairarapa **region** Wairarapa
phone (06) 379 8498 **fax** (06) 379 5498 **open** 7 days 9–5
winemaker Jon McNab **production** 700 **est.** 1996
product range Riesling, Sauvignon Blanc, Chardonnay, Pinot Noir.
summary Jon McNab started his wine career at Martinborough Vineyard 'as a general dogsbody', working for Larry McKenna for two years before taking up an assistant winemaker

position in Germany. Thereafter he commuted between Germany and Martinborough Vineyard for several years before coming back to Fairmont Estate and its first on-site vintage in 1997. (The initial vintage was made off-site by Chris Lintz at Lintz Estate.) Fairmont is in the Gladstone subregion of Wairarapa, situated on the free-draining alluvial Ruamahanga River terrace.

felton road wines NR

Bannockburn, RD, Central Otago **region** Otago
phone (03) 445 0885 **fax** (03) 445 0881 **open** 7 days 11–5
winemaker Blair Walter **production** 6500 **est.** 1991
product range ($17–33 CD) Dry Riesling, Riesling, Sauvignon Blanc, Chardonnay, Pinot Noir.
summary Felton Road gives every promise of becoming a major player in the Central Otago wine scene. Twelve hectares of vines were established between 1992 and 1994, with a further 2 hectares to be planted in 1998 or 1999. The grapes from the first two vintages (1995 and 1996) were sold to Gibbston Valley, the first Felton Road wines being produced from the '97 vintage. Winemaker Blair Walter has had an impeccable apprenticeship for making Pinot Noir and Chardonnay, including a lengthy stint at Giesen, followed by Sokol Blosser (Oregon), Tarrawarra (Yarra Valley), Rippon Vineyard (Central Otago) and Domaine de L'Arlot (Nuits St Georges, France). He has designed and built a 200-tonne winery drawing upon this varied yet specialised experience; it will be a major surprise if he doesn't produce excellent wine.

forrest estate

Blicks Road, Renwick, Marlborough **region** Marlborough
phone (03) 572 9084 **fax** (03) 572 9084 **open** Mon-Sun 10–5 Sept-May
winemaker John Forrest **production** 7000 **est.** 1989
product range ($12–28 CD) Chardonnay, Marlborough Chardonnay; Sauvignon Blanc, Semillon, Riesling, Rosé, Gibsons Creek (Cabernet blend), Indian Summer Late Harvest.
summary Former biochemist and genetic engineer John Forrest has had considerable success since his first vintage in 1990, relying initially on purchased grapes but with a 4-hectare vineyard now planted. Wine quality has been remarkably consistent right across the range, perhaps reflecting John Forrest's strong grounding in chemistry.

Forrest Estate Sauvignon Blanc

An interesting wine which is a blend of 96% Sauvignon Blanc and 4% Semillon (1996); a portion of the Semillon is barrel-fermented in French oak barriques and part of the wine is taken through malolactic fermentation. John Forrest is forever looking for ways to add weight and complexity to his Sauvignon Blanc, including multiple pickings over varying degrees of ripeness.

1997 Light green-yellow; the bouquet is clean, firm and rather close, with not a lot of fruit expression, but the wine expands on the palate with excellent, tightly knit structure, and that barrel-fermented semillon component evidencing itself. This is a different style of Sauvignon Blanc from the usual. **rating:** 86

➪ **best drinking** 1998 – 1999 **best vintages** '91, '92, '94, '95, '97 **drink with** Fresh snapper • $15

Forrest Estate Chardonnay

Intensive viticulture (trimming, leaf-plucking and bunch-thinning to limit the yield to 10 tonnes per hectare is followed by 15% barrel fermentation, 30% malolactic fermentation and all of the wine held on yeast lees for six months.

🍷🍷🍷🍷 **1996** Medium yellow-green; there are complex nectarine and spicy fruit characters on the bouquet, moving through nectarine and ripe guava on the powerful palate. An acid bite to the finish provides balance; minimal oak influence throughout. **rating:** 87

🍷🍷🍷🍸 **1996** Marlborough. Light to medium yellow-green, not showing excessive development; the bouquet is clean, of light to medium intensity with light melon fruit and a subtle touch of barrel-ferment oak. The palate is not overly complex, but does have fresh citrus and melon fruit, and a pleasant finish. **rating:** 84

➪ **best drinking** 1998 – 2001 **best vintages** NA **drink with** Pan-fried veal • $17

foxes island wines ★★★★

PO Box 1039, Blenheim **region** Marlborough
phone (03) 572 8299 **fax** (03) 572 8399 **open** 7 days 9–5 at Wairau River Wine Shop
winemaker John Belsham **production** 2500 **est.** 1992
product range ($25–30 R) Chardonnay, Pinot Noir.
summary Former Hunter's winemaker John Belsham runs Rapaura Vintners contract-winemaking business (formerly Vintech), but since 1992 has made small quantities of wine under the Foxes Island label, the name of the pinot noir vineyard he is establishing. The Chardonnay is – and will in the future be – made from purchased grapes.

Foxes Island Chardonnay

John Belsham deliberately adopts a very low profile for Foxes Island, emphasising that his main business is the contract-making of wine for others through Rapaura Vintners (formerly Vintech) and emphatically not Foxes Island. The grapes are purchased from the Rose and Jenkins families. The wine spends 12 months in oak.

🍷🍷🍷🍷🍸 **1996** Glowing yellow-green; a super-smooth, clean bouquet with melon fruit and subtle oak heralds an unusually elegant and harmonious palate, with restrained hazelnut, cashew and melon flavours, which linger long in the mouth. **rating:** 91

➪ **best drinking** 1998 – 2001 **best vintages** '94, '96 **drink with** Blanquette of veal • $30

framingham ★★★★

Conders Bend Road, Marlborough **region** Marlborough
phone (03) 572 8884 **fax** (03) 572 9884 **open** By appointment
winemaker Ant Mackenzie **production** 8000 **est.** 1982
product range ($15.70–18.95 R) Classic Riesling, Dry Riesling, Medium Riesling, Late Harvest Riesling, Sauvignon Blanc, Chardonnay, Reserve Méthode Champenoise.
summary Rex and Paula Brooke-Taylor established their 13-hectare vineyard in 1981, being content to sell the grapes in the intervening years to various makers, most conspicuously Grove Mill and Corbans. In 1994 they had part of their production vinified, immediately striking gold with the Riesling of that year at the 1995 Liquorland Royal Easter Wine Show, following up with a gold medal at the 1995 Air New Zealand Wine Awards for the Classic Dry Riesling.

Framingham Classic Riesling

Classic Riesling is the Jekyll of Jekyll and Hyde, formerly the first part of a single wine called Classic Dry Riesling. As from 1997 the Classic has its own life, produced with 10 grams per litre of residual sugar, just above threshold level.

🍷🍷🍷🍷 **1997** Medium yellow-green; the aromas are quite complex, running through spice, lime and citrus, with similar flavours on the palate. That barely perceptible touch of residual sugar does flesh out the finish. **rating:** 84

➾ **best drinking** 1998 – 2002 **best vintages** NA **drink with** Gravlax • $16.95

Framingham Dry Riesling

The Dr Hyde of the split personality, with 5 grams per litre of residual sugar – a distinction, incidentally, which is nowhere explained on the label (front or back) of the wines, which will no doubt add to the already considerable confusion.

🍷🍷🍷🍷 **1997** Medium yellow-green; the bouquet is clean, with mineral, spice and a hint of lime, of light to medium intensity. The palate is elegant, with light, spicy minerally/toasty flavours, and a particularly long finish. **rating:** 86

➾ **best drinking** 1998 – 2003 **best vintages** NA **drink with** Asparagus • $18.95

Framingham Sauvignon Blanc

Made in a no-frills style, but with some quite excellent fruit.

🍷🍷🍷🍷 **1997** Light to medium yellow-green; a spotlessly clean, crisp bouquet with mineral, herb and lemon aromas is followed by a crisp palate with good length and structure, offering gooseberry and a touch of capsicum on the back palate. **rating:** 88

➾ **best drinking** 1998 – 1999 **best vintages** NA **drink with** Fried oysters • $16.95

fromm winery ★★★★

Godfrey Road, RD2, Blenheim **region** Marlborough

phone (03) 572 9355 **fax** (03) 572 9366 **open** Sat 11–5, summer holidays Tues-Sat 11–5

winemaker Hatsch Kalberer, George Fromm **production** 4000 **est.** 1992

product range ($15–38 R) Released under the La Strada label are Reserve Chardonnay, Pinot Noir, Clayvin Vineyard Pinot Noir, Syrah, Merlot, Merlot Cabernet Syrah, Reserve Malbec, Clayvin Vineyard Cabernet Sauvignon.

summary Swiss-born and resident George Fromm and former Matawhero winemaker Hatsch Kalberer have formed a dynamic team to produce exceptionally full-flavoured wines, with the emphasis on red wines, and in particular Pinot Noir. Fromm has 4 hectares of estate vineyards coming into maturity, and 7 hectares under contract.

fullers NR

86 Candia Road, Swanson, Auckland **region** Henderson

phone (09) 833 7026 **fax** (09) 832 1778 **open** Mon-Sat 9–6, Sun 11–6

winemaker Ray Allen **production** 300 **est.** NA

product range Sauvignon Blanc, Cabernet Merlot and a range of sparkling and fortified wines.

summary A west Auckland landmark specialising in functions for up to 240 people at a time, year round, with all of the estate-produced wine sold through this outlet.

gatehouse wines NR

Jowers Road, RD6, Christchurch **region** Canterbury
phone (03) 342 9682 **open** Mon-Sat 10–5 Nov-Feb, Sat 10–5 Mar-Oct
winemaker Peter Gatehouse **production** 1300 **est.** 1989
product range Chardonnay, Gewurztraminer, Riesling, Pinot Noir, Merlot, Cabernet Sauvignon.
summary The Gatehouse family made its first wines in 1989 from estate plantings commenced in the early 1980s. The initial release was under the Makariri label, but the wines will henceforth be released under the Gatehouse label, and it is planned to increase production through the purchase of additional grapes from contract growers.

gibbston valley ★★★★

State Highway 6, Gibbston, RD1, Queenstown **region** Otago
phone (03) 442 6910 **fax** (03) 442 6909 **open** 7 days 10–5.30
winemaker Grant Taylor **production** 12 000 **est.** 1989
product range ($15–40 R) Five wines from Central Otago: Riesling, Sauvignon Blanc, Chardonnay, Pinot Gris, Pinot Noir, Reserve Pirot Noir; from Marlborough: Chardonnay, Sauvignon Blanc; Wairiti White, Greenstone Chardonnay and Rosé of Pinot are cheaper second labels.
summary A highly professional and attractive winery, restaurant and cellar-door sales facility situated near Queenstown which has been an outstanding success since the day it opened. Viticulture poses special problems, and both varietal selection and determining style will inevitably take time. However, a neat, modern production facility, New Zealand's largest cellar caves (opened December 1995). The arrival of Grant Taylor as winemaker, with significant international experience, has lifted wine quality further, particularly with the elusive Pinot Noir.

Gibbston Valley Marlborough Sauvignon Blanc

Right from the outset, Gibbston Valley has not hesitated to venture outside the confines of Central Otago to supplement its wine intake. In four vintages since 1992 it has made a Sauvignon Blanc from Marlborough grapes, wines which have won four gold, two silver and two bronze medals in New Zealand wine shows, the most recent success going to the '97 which won a gold medal at the 1997 Liquorland Top 100 Wine Competition.

ΥΥΥΥ **1997** Medium yellow-green; the bouquet is intense, with rich, sweet tropical/gooseberry fruit; a rich, mouthfilling and ripe wine on the palate, clean and very well made, and which does not cloy on the finish. **rating:** 88

➩ **best drinking** 1998 – 1999 **best vintages** '92, '94, '96, '97 **drink with** Whitebait • $18.50

Gibbston Valley Central Otago Pinot Gris

Pinot gris was one of the first plantings at Gibbston Valley in 1981, and tiny quantities have been made and released by Gibbston Valley in every vintage other than 1996. Increased plantings will see increased production in the future, as there are now 4 hectares coming into bearing.

ΥΥΥΥ **1997** Light green-yellow; the bouquet is very floral, with spicy pear aromas, and the palate has considerable fruit flavour and intensity, again showing ripe pear flavours. Well balanced. **rating:** 89

➩ **best drinking** 1998 – 2001 **best vintages** NA **drink with** Poached salmon • $20

Gibbston Valley Pinot Noir

Produced in limited quantities from the relatively small estate plantings of the variety. The short growing season carries with it threats at both the start and finish of the season; the yields are low, and the wine is very much subject to vintage conditions.

🍷🍷🍷🍷🍷 **1996** Medium red-purple; solid plummy fruit on the bouquet is cut by a pleasant touch of earth and stem. The palate is of medium to full weight, with relatively tight structure, but ample sweet plummy fruit. Well-made wine. **rating:** 90

➾ **best drinking** 1998 – 2000 **best vintages** '94, '96 **drink with** Spiced quail • $27

Gibbston Valley Reserve Pinot Noir

Californian-trained winemaker Grant Taylor came to Gibbston Valley in 1993, but has since returned to Oregon for the 1995 and 1996 vintages, and to Domaine Dujac in Burgundy for the '97 vintage. Two vintages a year working with Pinot Noir attest to Taylor's passion; the Reserve Pinots from Gibbston Valley attest to his skill. They are outstanding wines.

🍷🍷🍷🍷🍷 **1996** Excellent, strong red-purple; the bouquet is full of ripe, rich and sweet plummy/ cherry fruit, yet avoids Portiness. A powerful wine on the palate, with outstanding structure, length and mouthfeel. Gold medal at the 1997 Air New Zealand Wine Awards. **rating:** 96

➾ **best drinking** 1998 – 2003 **best vintages** NA **drink with** Venison • $40

giesen estate ★★★★☆

Burnham School Road, Burnham **region** Canterbury
phone (03) 347 6729 **fax** (03) 347 6450 **open** Mon–Sat 10–5
winemaker Marcel Giesen, Andrew Blake **production** 35 000 **est.** 1981
product range ($7–30 CD) Müller Thurgau, Riesling, Dry Riesling, Extra Dry Riesling, Late Harvest Riesling, Marlborough Sauvignon Blanc, Canterbury Burnham School Road Chardonnay, Reserve Chardonnay, Pinot Noir and Reserve Pinot Noir (in each case both from Canterbury and Marlborough); Merlot.
summary Determination, skill and marketing flair have seen Giesen grow from obscurity to one of the largest family-owned and run wineries in New Zealand. Given the Giesens' Rhine Valley origins it is not surprising that they have done so well with aromatic, non-wooded white wines, but have also gained acclaim for impressive Chardonnay and Pinot Noir.

Giesen Estate Marlborough Sauvignon Blanc

In recent years Giesen has established its own vineyards in Marlborough, and this wine now comes from its Dillon's Point Vineyard. In typical Giesen fashion, it is also fermented dry, using partial skin contact and extended lees contact to add both complexity and balance.

🍷🍷🍷🍷🍷 **1997** Medium yellow-green; highly aromatic and tangy gooseberry fruit, with faintly minerally undertones, leads into a fresh, well-balanced stylish wine on the palate, with lingering gooseberry and herb flavours. **rating:** 90

➾ **best drinking** 1998 – 1999 **best vintages** NA **drink with** Full-flavoured Asian seafood • $16

Giesen Reserve Canterbury Burnham School Road Chardonnay

Estate-grown, and given the full winemaking treatment before being held back and given an extra year's bottle age to release.

🍷🍷🍷🍷🍷 **1996** Deep yellow; a rich, complex and unexpectedly ripe yellow peach-fruited bouquet is followed by a striking palate, with many flavours and textures. Peach, fig and some more nutty notes, subtle oak and good balancing acid produce a high-flavoured but not overblown wine. **rating:** 90

➾ **best drinking** 1998 – 2000 **best vintages** NA **drink with** Veal parmigiana • $30

Giesen Estate Reserve Canterbury Pinot Noir

Produced from the heart of 4 hectares of estate plantings in the Canterbury region, and the most convincing possible demonstration of the suitability of this region for Pinot Noir. The '94 richly deserved its gold medal at the 1995 Air New Zealand Wine Awards. The '96 was a gold medal winner at the 1997 Liquorland National Wine Show of Australia.

🍷🍷🍷🍷🍷 **1996** Good red-purple; abundant plum and cherry fruit is offset against spicy toasty oak on the bouquet. The palate, like the bouquet, has power and depth, and will evolve yet further with additional time in bottle. **rating:** 90

➾ **best drinking** 1998 – 2002 **best vintages** '94, '96 **drink with** Peking duck • $30

gillan wines ★★★★

Rapaura Road, Blenheim, Marlborough **region** Marlborough

phone (03) 572 9979 **fax** (03) 572 9980 **open** 7 days 10–5 summer or by appointment

winemaker Sam Weaver **production** 7000 **est.** 1992

product range ($16 R) Eastfields Sauvignon Blanc, Chardonnay, Merlot, Brut Reserve.

summary Gillan Wines is a partnership between English-born Toni and Terry Gillan and local vignerons Hamish and Anne Young. A white, Mediterranean-style wine cellar and restaurant (serving tapas-style food) opened in December 1996. While being Mediterranean-style, architect Neil Charles-Jones believes it is also a building 'which belongs in the Marlborough landscape while quietly alluding to the great Champagne cellars of France'. That is quite an achievement.

Gillan Eastfields Sauvignon Blanc

The first release from Gillan, produced from the Eastfields Vineyard of Hamish and Anne Young, had instantaneous success, winning a gold medal at the 1994 Air New Zealand Wine Awards, New Zealand's premier wine show. The 1996 vintage showed well at the 1997 Sydney International Wine Competition.

🍷🍷🍷🍷 **1997** Light to medium yellow-green; the bouquet is clean, crisp, pungently herbal, with hints of gooseberry and redcurrant. The palate is light on entry but builds on the mid to back palate, with riper gooseberry flavours on the finish, attesting to its 13.5 degrees alcohol. Bone-dry. **rating:** 85

➾ **best drinking** 1998 – 1999 **best vintages** '94, '96 **drink with** Shellfish • $15.95

gladstone vineyard ★★★★☆

Gladstone Road, RD2, Carterton, Wairarapa **region** Wairarapa

phone (06) 379 8563 **fax** (06) 379 8563 **open** 7 days 10–12, 2–5 Sept-May; by appointment June-Aug

winemaker Christine Kernahan **production** 2000 **est.** 1987

product range ($13–25 CD) Riesling, Sauvignon Blanc, Fumé Blanc, Chardonnay, Cabernet Sauvignon Merlot, Red Label Cabernet Merlot, Cabernet Sauvignon, Cafe Red.

summary Gladstone Vineyard was acquired from founder Dennis Roberts by Christine and David Kernahan in February 1996, with Christine now in charge of winemaking. That the transition has been without pain is handsomely demonstrated by the quality of the Sauvignon Blanc.

Gladstone Sauvignon Blanc

Made from estate plantings established in 1984 on an ancient riverbed with sandy clay loam over river gravels. Complex winemaking techniques see part of the wine tank-fermented, part barrel-fermented and taken through malolactic fermentation. Superb Sauvignon Blanc has been produced since 1992. The wine always seems to possess an extra degree of richness, without ever being coarse, phenolic or aggressive.

🍷🍷🍷🍷 **1997** Light green-yellow; a clean, crisp and restrained bouquet with lemon/mineral aromas is followed by an equally tight and restrained palate with mineral, herb and lemon flavours; excellent acidity and length. A second-glass style. **rating:** 87

⇨ **best drinking** 1998 – 1999 **best vintages** '92, '94, '97 **drink with** Mussels • $18

glenmark wines ★★★

Mackenzies Road, Waipara **region** Canterbury
phone (03) 314 6828 **fax** (03) 314 6828 **open** 7 days 11–6
winemaker Kym Rayner **production** 2700 **est.** 1981
product range ($11–25 CD) Waipara Riesling, Weka Plains Riesling, Waipara White, Chardonnay, Gewurztraminer, Pinot Noir.
summary Kym Rayner is a very experienced winemaker, and Glenmark is an important part of the Canterbury scene, notwithstanding its relatively small size. Much of the wine is sold cellar door, with the Weka Plains Wine Garden offering a full restaurant service and wine by the glass from October through to April. Bookings are essential.

glover's vineyard ★★☆

Gardner Valley Road, Upper Moutere **region** Nelson
phone (03) 543 2698 **open** 7 days 10–6
winemaker David Glover **production** 1900 **est.** 1984
product range ($11–18 CD) Sauvignon Blanc, Riesling, Late Harvest Riesling, Pinot Noir, Cabernet Sauvignon.
summary David Glover studied winemaking and viticulture at Charles Sturt University in southern New South Wales during a 17-year stay in Australia. He returned with wife Penny to establish their own vineyard in 1984, struggling with birds and other predators before producing their first wines in 1989. The quality of the white wines has been good, although the muscular, brawny Pinot Noir has pleased others more than it has me.

goldwater estate ★★★★★

18 Causeway Road, Putiki Bay, Waiheke Island **region** Waiheke Island
phone (09) 372 7493 **fax** (09) 372 6827 **open** 7 days 11–4 summer
winemaker Kim Goldwater, Martin Pickering **production** 18 000 **est.** 1978
product range ($20–75 CD) Marlborough Roseland Chardonnay, Delamore Chardonnay, Dog Point Marlborough Sauvignon Blanc, Waiheke Island Esslin Merlot, Waiheke Island Cabernet Merlot Franc.
summary Goldwater Estate goes from strength to strength. Having initially forged a reputation for its Waiheke Island Cabernet Merlot Franc, it has built on that with its superb

Waiheke Island Esslin Merlot and a range of beautifully crafted wines made from Marlborough grapes, with the limited volume Waiheke Island-sourced Delamore Chardonnay providing additional support.

Goldwater Estate Marlborough Roseland Chardonnay

An extremely well-made wine in the bold, luscious style which Goldwater Estate seems to have made its own.

🍷🍷🍷🍷🍷 **1996** Medium yellow-green; an extremely stylish bouquet with tangy melon/citrus fruit surrounded by spicy French oak. A potent, powerfully, intensely flavoured wine on the palate, baroque in style but none the worse for that, and with the fruit (rather than oak) leading the charge. **rating:** 92

⇨ **best drinking** 1997 – 1999 **best vintages** '96 **drink with** Poached salmon • $18.30

Goldwater Estate Waiheke Island Esslin Merlot

Waiheke Island continues to unveil extremely impressive red wines, and although it cannot challenge Hawke's Bay in terms of volume, is certainly laying down the gauntlet on quality. The wine may be expensive, but it is of world class.

🍷🍷🍷🍷🍷 **1995** Full purple-red; luscious blackcurrant fruit aromas intermingle with hints of spice, leading into a deliciously sweet and juicy palate. There is abundant red and blackcurrant fruit with perfectly rounded and ripe tannins on a soft finish. **rating:** 95

⇨ **best drinking** 2000 – 2005 **best vintages** '95 **drink with** Venison • $47.50

Goldwater Estate Waiheke Island Cabernet Merlot Franc

Another extremely distinguished red from Goldwater Estate, acknowledged by Bob Campbell as a New Zealand classic, and it is not hard to see why.

🍷🍷🍷🍷🍷 **1995** Full red-purple; the bouquet is of medium to full intensity with a mix of ripe blackberry fruit and more leafy/woody notes. There is a stylish mix of berry, cedar and leaf on the palate, finishing with fine-grained but persistent tannins. **rating:** 91

⇨ **best drinking** 1998 – 2003 **best vintages** '95 **drink with** Lamb fillets • $45

greenhough vineyard ★★★★

Patons Road, RD1, Richmond, Nelson **region** Nelson

phone (03) 542 3868 **fax** (03) 542 3462 **open** Mon-Sat 10–5 Dec-Mar

winemaker Andrew Greenhough **production** 2000 **est.** 1991

product range ($14–20 CD) Riesling, Sauvignon Blanc, Chardonnay, Pinot Noir.

summary Yet another name change for the what was initially Ranzau, then Pelorus and now Greenhough – the last change a sensible one, dictated by the confusion with the Pelorus Méthode Champenoise of Cloudy Bay. Under whatever name, Andrew Greenhough makes appealing wines, notably the Sauvignon Blanc.

Greenhough Vineyard Sauvignon Blanc

Produced from vines grown on the Waimea Plains at Brightwater, with free-draining stony loam soil. Scott Henry trellis and bunch thinning reduce the yield to around 4 tonnes per acre. Cold fermented in stainless steel, with 7 grams per litre of residual sugar and 8.5 grams of acid.

The '97 achieved Top 100 status in the 1998 Sydney International Wine Competition, being very strongly supported by some of the panel.

🍷🍷🍷🍷🍷 **1997** Light yellow-green; the bouquet shows intense varietal character, with excellent ripeness and balance between passionfruit, gooseberry and more herbal characters. The palate is tight, clean, immaculately balanced, particularly good mouthfeel on the finish. **rating:** 91

➾ **best drinking** 1998 – 1999 **best vintages** NA **drink with** Asparagus quiche • $16

grove mill ★★★★★

Waihopai Valley Road, Marlborough **region** Marlborough
phone (03) 572 8200 **fax** (03) 572 8211 **open** 7 days 11–5
winemaker David Pearce, Al Soper **production** 43 000 **est.** 1988
product range ($12.95–30 R) Marlborough Sauvignon Blanc, Chardonnay, Riesling, Dry Riesling, Pinot Gris; Lansdowne Chardonnay and Winemakers Reserve Sauvignon Blanc and Gewurztraminer.
summary Has firmly established itself as a producer of wines of consistently high quality in substantial volumes. Its success in wine shows both in New Zealand and elsewhere (particularly Australia) underlines the continuing achievements of the winemaking team headed by David Pearce.

Grove Mill Marlborough Riesling

Made from grapes grown principally on the Framingham vineyard, and given top ranking by Michael Cooper (five stars), Keith Stewart (*Fine Wines of New Zealand*), and Bob Campbell (*Wine Annual*). The extraordinary feature of the wine is the way it carries its residual sugar, which typically varies between 24 and 30 grams per litre, almost into spätlese levels, yet always seems balanced. It is a further testament to the integrity (as well as the quality of the label) that no Riesling was bottled under the Grove Mill label in 1995.

🍷🍷🍷🍷 **1997** Excellent green-yellow; the bouquet is redolent of lime/tropical fruit, the palate very rich, full and generous, with more of that fleshy/tropical/lime fruit of the bouquet. There may have been a touch of botrytis, but who cares. **rating:** 88

➾ **best drinking** 2000 – 2005 **best vintages** '91, '92, '93, '94 **drink with** Salad of snow peas • $15

Grove Mill Marlborough Sauvignon Blanc

It would seem I rate this wine a little higher than most New Zealand judges and writers, although it certainly receives strong support across the board from the critics. To a lesser degree than the Lansdowne Chardonnay, it is a 'love it or hate it' style, and one certainly needs to know what has gone on in the making of the wine. This is a long way from the straightforward no-frills cutthroat Marlborough Sauvignon Blanc style, utilising partial oak ageing, partial malolactic fermentation, some Semillon if the year is right and, generally speaking, of a lot of thought. If the '96 was outstanding, and it was, the '97 is even more brilliant – a wonderful wine.

🍷🍷🍷🍷🍷 **1997** Light yellow-green; a spotlessly clean, wonderfully fragrant, almost crunchy crisp gooseberry and passionfruit bouquet leads into a wonderfully pure palate, with impeccable balance, outstanding length and glorious varietal definition. **rating:** 96

➾ **best drinking** 1998 – 1999 **best vintages** '92, '94, '96, '97 **drink with** Wairau River trout • $17

Grove Mill Lansdowne Chardonnay

The gold label Lansdowne Chardonnay burst on to the scene with its 1989 vintage which was awarded the trophy as Champion Chardonnay of the Air New Zealand Wine Awards, and hasn't looked back since. The style was opulent to the point of being baroque, although in more recent years it has become (comparatively speaking) more restrained, and offers a more certain cellaring future than the earlier years. One hundred per cent barrel-fermented and matured for 20 months in one-year-old Nevers, Troncais and Bourgogne barriques, with the full gamut of winemaking techniques including prolonged lees ageing without sulphur dioxide and partial malolactic fermentation.

🍷🍷🍷🍷🍷 **1996** Light to medium green-yellow; a clean and fresh bouquet with melon and nectarine fruit surrounded by subtle but nonetheless evident oak. The palate is elegant and delicate, with smooth nectarine and melon flavours and a long, unforced finish. **rating:** 91

➾ **best drinking** 1998 – 2000 **best vintages** '89, '91, '92, '93, '96 **drink with** Smoked pork • $30

Grove Mill Marlborough Chardonnay

A lower-priced version, partially barrel-fermented in French and American oak, and part stainless steel, the wine does not appear to have undergone any malolactic fermentation.

🍷🍷🍷🍷🍷 **1996** Light green-yellow; a light, fresh, clean and crisp bouquet with citrus/grapefruit aromas and the oak almost imperceptible is followed by an intensely flavoured palate with melon and grapefruit running through a long, lingering finish. The oak is no more than a whisper. **rating:** 91

➾ **best drinking** 1998 – 2002 **best vintages** NA **drink with** Slow-cooked salmon • $19

gunn estate NR

85 Ohiti Road, RD9, Hastings **region** Hawke's Bay

phone (06) 874 3250 **fax** (06) 874 3256 **open** Nov-March weekends 10.30–5

winemaker Denis Gunn **production** 2000 **est.** 1994

product range ($16–30 R) Sauvignon Blanc, Chardonnay, Reserve Chardonnay, Merlot Cabernet, Reserve Merlot.

summary Denis and Alan Gunn have been contract grape growers since 1982, with 15 hectares of vines providing grapes for many of the best-known names in the Hawke's Bay region. In the interim, Denis Gunn graduated from Roseworthy College, Australia, and became assistant winemaker at Villa Maria in 1993, moving to Kemblefield in 1995, where the 1995 Gunn Estate wines were made. In 1996 production moved to a newly constructed on-site winery.

harrier rise vineyard ★★★★

748 Waitakere Road, RD1, Kumeu **region** Kumeu and Huapai

phone (09) 412 7256 **fax** (09) 412 7256 **open** Weekends 12–6

winemaker Tim Harris **production** 3600 **est.** 1986

product range ($16–30 CD) Cabernet Sauvignon Cabernet Franc, Merlot Cabernets, Cabernet Franc, Uppercase Merlot.

summary The project of Auckland lawyer and wine-writer Tim Harris and wife Alix. The resolution of some complicated vineyard ownership arrangements in 1996 has led to the change of name from Waitakere Road to Harrier Rise, and to the Harrises acquiring full ownership of the 4-hectare Harrier Rise Vineyard, replete with 15-year-old cabernet sauvignon, merlot and cabernet franc. Wine quality is impressive, with ripe flavours and tannins.

Harrier Rise Cabernet Franc

The 2 hectares of estate Cabernet Franc is used to produce three wines: a 100% varietal, a premium half and half Cabernet Sauvignon Cabernet Franc blend, and as a 30% component in a Merlot (45%) and Cabernet Sauvignon (25%) blend. The varietal Cabernet Franc is now matured in French oak.

🍷🍷🍷🍷 **1996** Medium red-purple; a clean bouquet with a varietally correct mix of cedar, earth, forest and tobacco aromas, leads into an attractive, quite firm palate with red berry notes, tobacco, and soft, ripe tannins – a valuable commodity in New Zealand. **rating:** 84

⇨ **best drinking** 1999 – 2003 **best vintages** NA **drink with** Pastrami • NA

Harrier Rise Uppercase Merlot

As with the Cabernet Franc, the 3 hectares of estate merlot has split usage, partly as a varietal, and partly as the dominant portion of the Merlot Cabernets blend.

🍷🍷🍷🍷 **1996** Medium to full red-purple; the bouquet is deliciously sweet with red berry fruit and perfectly integrated and balanced oak. The palate is similarly soft and sweet, with red berry/raspberry flavours; fully ripe, with no hint of the New Zealand greens. **rating:** 88

⇨ **best drinking** 1999 – 2004 **best vintages** NA **drink with** Baby lamb • NA

hau ariki wines NR

Regent Street, Martinborough **region** Wairarapa
phone (06) 306 9360 **fax** (06) 306 9360 **open** Weekends 9–5
winemaker Chris Lintz (Contract) **production** NA **est.** 1994
product range ($18–28 CD) Sauvignon Blanc, Rosé, Pinot Noir, Cabernet Sauvignon.
summary Hau Ariki is housed in New Zealand's first marae to be making and selling wine on a commercial basis. The 3.5-hectare vineyard was developed by the marae kaumatua (elder) and managing director George Hawkins together with former Mission Vineyard viticulturist Mike Eden who had retired to Martinborough from Hawke's Bay.

Hau Ariki Sauvignon Blanc

Made by Chris Lintz at Lintz Estate for Hau Ariki from estate-grown grapes. The wine is said to have been (partially) barrel-fermented in French oak, but is essentially fruit-driven.

🍷🍷🍷🍷 **1996** Light to medium yellow-green, the wine is of medium intensity, clean, with aromas running through the riper fruit spectrum of characters. The quite tangy and intense palate, with a mix of slightly toasty (possibly oak-derived) and stone fruit characters, has both grip and structure. **rating:** 84

⇨ **best drinking** 1998 – 1999 **best vintages** NA **drink with** Mussels • $18

hawkesbridge wines ★★★★

Hawkesbury Road, Renwick, Marlborough **region** Marlborough
phone (03) 572 8024 **fax** (03) 572 9489 **open** 7 days 10.30–4.30
winemaker Contract **production** 2000 **est.** 1991
product range ($17 R) Willowbank Vineyard Sauvignon Blanc, Sophie's Vineyard Chardonnay.
summary Hawkesbridge Wines and Estates (to give it its full name) is presently chiefly a contract grape grower, but export demand for its wines is likely to see half the production from its 16 hectares of vines vinified under the Hawkesbridge label, with a target 4500 cases or thereabouts.

Hawkesbridge Willowbank Vineyard Sauvignon Blanc

First made in 1994, and very well received. After an indifferent 1995 – not surprising given the vintage – has bounced back with the '96 and '97.

🍷🍷🍷🍷 **1997** Medium yellow-green; a potent bouquet in traditional Marlborough-style, with a mix of ripe gooseberry and more herbaceous fruit is followed by a full, rich flavoursome palate with abundant gooseberry fruit, thickening ever so slightly on the finish. **rating:** 87

⇨ **best drinking** 1998 – 1999 **best vintages** '94, '96, '97 **drink with** Seafood • $17

heron's flight ★★★★☆

Sharp Road, Matakana **region** Northland and Matakana
phone (09) 422 7915 **fax** (09) 422 7915 **open** 7 days 10–6
winemaker David Hoskins **production** 1500 **est.** 1987
product range ($12–27 CD) La Volee (Chardonnay), Barrique Fermented Matakana Chardonnay, La Cerise (Merlot), Matakana Cabernet Sauvignon Merlot, Cabernet Merlot.
summary Having established a small vineyard in 1987, David Hoskins and Mary Evans leased the defunct Antipodean Winery which was the scene of so much marketing hype and excitement in the mid-1980s. (The Antipodean has built a new winery since.) The first Heron's Flight wine (a densely-coloured and flavoured Cabernet Sauvignon) was produced from the 1991 vintage, and was a gold medal winner. The '94 Cabernet Merlot was, if anything, even better, but no wines made in either 1995 or 1996. A small quantity of Sangiovese (New Zealand's first) was made in 1997.

highfield estate ★★★☆

Brookby Road, RD2, Blenheim **region** Marlborough
phone (03) 572 8592 **fax** (03) 572 9257 **open** 7 days 10–5
winemaker Tony Hooper **production** 12 000 **est.** 1990
product range ($13–24.95 CD) Riesling, Late Harvest Riesling, Sauvignon Blanc, Chardonnay, Merlot, Sparkling Merlot; Elstree range of Brut Reserve Riesling (a table wine, not sparkling), Reserve Sauvignon Blanc, Chardonnay, Optima (Chardonnay), Botrytised Semillon Sauvignon Blanc, Czar (dessert Riesling), Cuvée Sparkling.
summary Highfield Estate was purchased by an international partnership in late 1991, the English and Japanese limbs of which are associated with the French Champagne House Drappier. The ornate Tuscan-style winery which has since been built is Marlborough's answer to some of the more bizarre edifices of the Napa Valley. Wine quality has been erratic; the flamboyantly packaged and confusingly labelled Elstree range was introduced onto the market in late 1997 in the super-premium sector, some justifying their price, others not.

Highfield Estate Elstree Reserve Sauvignon Blanc

Part of the newly introduced premium range from Highfield Estate, and a proverbial country mile better than the standard varietal release.

🍷🍷🍷🍷 **1997** Light yellow-green; the bouquet is light, crisp and minerally, not especially fruity, but clean and without volatility. The palate is lively, with an attractive mix of capsicum, gooseberry and some faintly spicy characters. Finishes with bright acidity. **rating:** 87

⇨ **best drinking** 1998 – 1999 **best vintages** NA **drink with** Fresh asparagus with hollandaise sauce • $24

Highfield Estate Elstree Cuvée

A blend of 50% Chardonnay and 50% Pinot Noir which spends three years on yeast lees prior to disgorgement. Another wine in the Elstree range which deserves the premium rating.

1994 Light to medium yellow-green; the bouquet is clean, with gentle autolysis characters and fruit neutral. The wine opens up on the palate, with intense citrus flavours on the back palate, and a classically long, lingering finish. **rating:** 84

⇨ **best drinking** 1998 – 1999 **best vintages** NA **drink with** Fresh shellfish • NA

Highfield Estate Elstree Botrytised Semillon Sauvignon Blanc

The classic blend of Semillon and Sauvignon Blanc (together with a little Muscadelle) of Sauternes is surprisingly rare in Australasia; for some reason, Sauvignon Blanc does not often respond to botrytis. So not only is this an uncommon blend in this part of the world, but is an extremely interesting wine in style terms.

1995 Deep burnished gold; the bouquet ranges through toffee, cumquat and mandarin, a cross between Sauternes and (Hungarian) Tokaji in style. Those cumquat toffee and mandarin flavours also come through on the richly flavoured palate, which is of moderate sweetness and good acidity. **rating:** 85

⇨ **best drinking** 1998 – 2001 **best vintages** NA **drink with** Rich cake • $24.95

---

holmes brothers ★★★

McShane Road, Richmond, Nelson **region** Nelson
phone (03) 544 4230 **fax** (03) 544 4230 **open** 7 days 10–6
winemaker Jane Cooper **production** 1600 **est.** 1991
product range ($14.95–20 CD) Sauvignon Blanc, Chardonnay, Rosé and Pinot Noir; Richmond Plains is second label red wine.
summary The 4-hectare estate vineyard is claimed by David Holmes to be the most southerly in the world to be certified fully organic, having been run on fully organic principles right from the outset. The tasting-room facilities are shared with Te Mania Estate, and are supported by a range of other local handicraft shops.

Holmes Brothers Richmond Plains Sauvignon Blanc

Produced from organically-grown sauvignon blanc planted in 1992 on free-draining stony soils adjacent to the Western Ranges of Nelson Bay. An inoffensive '96 vintage has been followed by an outstanding '97.

1997 Medium yellow-green; the bouquet is redolent of passionfruit and gooseberry, striking even by New Zealand standards. The palate is as high flavoured as the bouquet promises yet avoids heaviness. The flavours ripple through the palate to a long finish. **rating:** 91

⇨ **best drinking** 1998 – 1999 **best vintages** NA **drink with** Seafood • $15.95

---

huia NR

Rapaura Road, RD3, Blenheim **region** Marlborough
phone (03) 572 8326 **fax** (03) 572 8326 **open** 7 days 10–4.30 from December 1998
winemaker Claire Allan, Mike Allan **production** 2600 **est.** 1996
product range ($22.50 CD) Gewurztraminer, Sauvignon Blanc, Chardonnay.

summary Owners Claire and Mike Allan bring a wealth of experience to Huia. Both are winemakers, and both have had outstanding careers in Marlborough, variously working at Cloudy Bay, Corbans Marlborough, Rapaura Vintners, Lawsons Dry Hills and Vavasour Wines – as well as working an 'extended stage' in Champagne, France. They acquired their vineyard in Rapaura Road in late 1990, and have now planted 12 hectares of vines, with new Dijon (Burgundy) clones of pinot noir and chardonnay due to come into full production in 1999.

Huia Sauvignon Blanc

Spotlessly clean, well made but relatively light-bodied.

🍷🍷🍷🍷 **1997** Light green-yellow; the bouquet is light, fresh and spotlessly clean gooseberry and passionfruit aromas in mainstream spectrum. The palate, likewise, is at the dead centre of ripe Marlborough Sauvignon Blanc-style, although not especially concentrated or rich, scoring more for its cleanness and freshness. **rating:** 88

➯ **best drinking** 1998 – 1999 **best vintages** NA **drink with** Shellfish • $22.50

hunter's wines ★★★★★

Rapaura Road, Blenheim **region** Marlborough
phone (03) 572 8489 **fax** (03) 572 8489 **open** 7 days 9.30–4.30
winemaker Gary Duke **production** 40 000 **est.** 1980
product range ($15.95–29.50 R) Chardonnay, Gewurztraminer, Sauvignon Blanc, Oak Aged Sauvignon Blanc, Riesling, Pinot Noir, Cabernet Merlot, Brut; Spring Creek is a newly introduced second label.

summary Hunter's goes from strength to strength, consistently producing flawless wines with tremendous varietal character. Given the quantity and quality of its production, it is a winery of world standing, and certainly among the top dozen in Australasia: it is hard to choose between its long-lived Riesling, Sauvignon Blanc, Oak Aged Sauvignon Blanc (a tour de force) and subtly complex Chardonnay.

Hunter's Riesling

Not a major item in the Hunter's line-up, but an attractive wine, showing typical New Zealand (or, rather, Marlborough) elegance. It ages with grace, showing no tendency to toughen up or coarsen. Part of the grapes, incidentally, are grown by the noted journalist-turned-grape grower Ted Reynolds in the Awatere Valley.

🍷🍷🍷🍸 **1997** Light to medium yellow-green; the bouquet is lifted, with scented tropical lime fruit and hints of spice. The palate is softer than the usual Hunter's Riesling, again with tropical lime fruit flavours. **rating:** 84

➯ **best drinking** 1999 – 2003 **best vintages** '90, '91, '93, '94 **drink with** Asparagus with hollandaise sauce • $15.95

Hunter's Oak Aged Sauvignon Blanc

Having decided to put Sauvignon Blanc in oak, Jane Hunter and her winemaking/consulting team have not done anything by half measures. It is barrel-fermented with a substantial percentage of new wood making a pronounced impact on the wine. Whether it is a better wine than the unoaked version really depends on one's personal view of oak and, for that matter, of Sauvignon Blanc. Universally accepted as a five-star/classic wine.

🍷🍷🍷🍷🍷 **1996** Medium to full yellow-green; the bouquet is driven by the sophisticated use of spicy nutmeg oak, which also is an important part of the palate, although here gooseberry fruit appears early and carries through to the finish. **rating:** 90

⇨ **best drinking** 1998 – 1999 **best vintages** '88, '89, '91, '93, '94, '96 **drink with** Grilled spatchcock • $23.50

Hunter's Chardonnay

Just as the Sauvignon Blanc is so often at the head of the field in New Zealand, so is the Chardonnay. After a slight wobble in '93, bounced back with a vengeance in '94, following up with a marvellous '95 in the face of a challenging vintage. The '96 is in the same class.

🍷🍷🍷🍷🍷 **1996** Medium yellow-green; a complex array of melon, cashew, fig, and even faintly buttery, aromas with just a hint of spicy oak are followed by a smooth, yet textured, palate displaying all the flavours promised by the bouquet. As ever, sensitive use of oak. **rating:** 90

⇨ **best drinking** 1998 – 2002 **best vintages** '90, '91, '92, '94, '95, '96 **drink with** Honey prawns • $25.50

huthlee estate NR

Montana Road, RD5, Hastings, Hawke's Bay **region** Hawke's Bay
phone (06) 879 6234 **fax** (06) 879 6234 **open** Mon-Sat 10–5, Sun 11–4
winemaker Devon Lee **production** 1000 **est.** 1991
product range ($12–25 R) Pinot Gris, Rosé, Kaweka Red, Cabernet Franc, Cabernet Sauvignon Merlot, Merlot, Reserve Merlot, Cabernet Sauvignon.
summary Devon and Estelle Lee commenced planting their 6-hectare vineyard in 1984, and established an on-site cellar door in 1992. The majority of the grapes are sold to other producers; the best is reserved for their own label.

isabel estate vineyard ★★★★☆

Hawkesbury Road, Renwick, Marlborough **region** Marlborough
phone (03) 572 8933 **fax** (03) 572 9797 **open** By appointment
winemaker Jeff Sinnott **production** 5000 **est.** 1982
product range ($18.50–27.50 R) Sauvignon Blanc, Chardonnay, Pinot Noir.
summary The 54-hectare Isabel Estate Vineyard was planted in 1982, and until 1994 was purely and simply a grape growing enterprise (and the largest external supplier to Cloudy Bay). In that time it built up a considerable reputation for the quality of its grapes, and in 1994 introduced the Isabel Estate label. It has now taken a further critical step, constructing a 300-tonne winery which will be in operation for the 1998 vintage, and employing a full-time winemaker, of course. Stage 2 will see the construction of an underground cellar for 500 barrels.

Isabel Estate Marlborough Sauvignon Blanc

Unusually complex winemaking techniques are used to produce this wine, which is made up of a number of different components. The majority is cold fermented with a neutral yeast and aged on lees for three months. Fifteen per cent of the wine is fermented in French oak barriques and underwent a partial malolactic fermentation. A small portion was whole-bunch pressed directly to barrel and fermented warm. The finished wine has over 7 grams of acid and very low (2.3 grams) residual sugar. A classy act.

🍷🍷🍷🍷🍷 **1997** Light yellow-green; the bouquet has amazingly pungent, sweet gooseberry and passionfruit aromas, the palate similarly pungent and penetrating, crammed to the gills with delicious fruit, and finishing bone-dry on the palate. Something special. **rating:** 94

➯ **best drinking** 1998 – 1999 **best vintages** NA **drink with** Sugar-cured tuna • NA

Isabel Estate Marlborough Chardonnay

Thirty per cent of the wine is fermented in new and used French oak barriques, then aged on lees with stirring for 14 months. The balance is cool fermented in tank, aged on lees, and allowed to go through a natural malolactic fermentation.

🍷🍷🍷🍷 **1996** Medium yellow-green; the bouquet shows complex nutty/toasty barrel-ferment and malolactic-ferment influences which come through on the cashew and hazelnut flavoured palate. Concentrated and powerful, with an ever so slight alcohol catch (13.6 degrees) on the finish. **rating:** 89

➯ **best drinking** 1998 – 2000 **best vintages** NA **drink with** Crumbed brains • NA

jackson estate ★★★★☆

Jacksons Road, Blenheim **region** Marlborough

phone (03) 572 8287 **fax** (03) 572 9500 **open** Not

winemaker Martin Shaw (Consultant) **production** 22 000 **est.** 1988

product range ($13.45–30 ML) Riesling, Marlborough Dry Riesling, Sauvignon Blanc, Chardonnay, Botrytis Riesling, Pinot Noir. A top-line maker of Sauvignon Blanc and Chardonnay.

summary Long-term major grape growers John and Warwick Stichbury, with leading viticulturist Richard Bowling in charge, own substantial vineyards in the Marlborough area, and have now established their own winery and brand.

Jackson Estate Sauvignon Blanc

Produced from 15 hectares of estate plantings established in 1988, and producing the first vintage in 1991. The vines are not irrigated, are hand-pruned and utilise the Scott Henry trellis. The quality of the fruit is beyond dispute, and the winemaking skills of international flying winemaker Martin Shaw add the final touch. The most striking feature of this wine is that it is invariably perfectly weighted and proportioned.

🍷🍷🍷🍷🍷 **1997** Light green-yellow; a firm, crisp, fresh and clean bouquet with a mix of herb, mineral and lemon fruit aromas; the palate is distinguished by excellent mouthfeel and length, with perfectly balanced fruit ripeness and flavours. Bang-slap in the best tradition of Jackson Estate. **rating:** 94

➯ **best drinking** 1998 – 1999 **best vintages** '91, '92, '93, '94, '97 **drink with** Calamari • $17

johanneshof cellars NR

State Highway 1, Koromiko, RD3, Blenheim **region** Marlborough

phone (03) 573 7035 **fax** (03) 573 7034 **open** Tues-Sun 10–4

winemaker Edel Everling, Warwick Foley **production** 2500 **est.** 1991

product range ($15–32 R) Riesling, Gewürztraminer, Sauvignon Blanc, Botrytised Sauvignon Blanc Chardonnay, Müller Thurgau, Emmi Méthode Champenoise, Pinot Noir.

summary Marlborough district winemaker Warwick Foley met his wife-to-be Edel Everling in New Zealand and followed her back to Germany (where her family has a winemaking history) to spend five years studying and working, inter alia at Geisenheim. The couple have returned to New Zealand to make European-style wines in an underground cellar blasted into a hillside between Blenheim and Picton.

john mellars of great barrier island NR

Okupu Beach, Great Barrier Island **region** Great Barrier Island
phone (09) 429 0361 **fax** (09) 429 0370 **open** By appointment
winemaker John Mellars **production** 100 **est.** 1990
product range ($35 R) Great Barrier Cabernet.
summary The winery's full name is John Mellars of Great Barrier Island, and indeed the 1 hectare of vines planted on a steep, stony slope facing the nearby sea is the only planting on the island. Output is tiny, and likely to remain so, perhaps fortunate given that access to the cellar door is either a ten-minute beach and track walk or by dinghy from a boat. Judging by the newsletter, those who make the effort will be rewarded by a delightfully eccentric and humorous John Mellars in person.

kaituna valley NR

150 Old Tai Tapu Road, Halswell, Christchurch **region** Canterbury
phone (03) 325 2094 **fax** (03) 322 9272 **open** Not
winemaker Grant Whelan **production** 150 **est.** 1993
product range Pinot Noir.
summary Grant and Helen Whelan bring considerable skills to this tiny venture; Grant Whelan was a tutor in Wine Science and Viticulture at Lincoln University before becoming winemaker for Rossendale Wines in Christchurch, while Helen is a PhD graduate in plant pathology. The vineyard is established on the Banks Peninsula on a north-facing, non-irrigated slope; extensive canopy work paid dramatic dividends with the first vintage (1993) which won the gold medal and trophy for Champion Pinot Noir at the 1995 Liquorland Royal Easter Wine Show.

kanuka forest wines NR

Moore Road, Thornton, RD2, Whakatane **region** Waikato and Bay of Plenty
phone (07) 304 9963 **fax** (07) 304 9963 **open** Weekends 10–6, Tues-Fri 3–6
winemaker Tony Hassall **production** 500 **est.** 1992
product range ($17.95–24.95 CD) Fumé Blanc, Chardonnay, Cabernet Sauvignon Merlot.
summary Tony and Julia Hassall commenced the establishment of their 3-hectare vineyard in 1989, offering their first wine for sale at the end of 1994. The winery and vineyard enjoy spectacular views of the eastern Bay of Plenty. It is the eastern Bay of Plenty's only commercial wine producer; the wines are made exclusively from grapes grown at Thornton.

kawarau estate NR

Cromwell-Wanaka Highway, SH6, Cromwell **region** Otago
phone (03) 215 9311 **fax** (03) 218 7657 **open** By appointment
winemaker Rudi Bauer **production** 1200 **est.** 1992
product range ($15–22 CD) Sauvignon Blanc, Summer Chardonnay, Reserve Chardonnay, Pinot Noir, Reserve Pinot Noir.
summary A venture with two vineyard sites: one at Lake Hayes, the other at Lowburn. The partners claim each enjoys exceptional sunlight interception and warmth, and the entire venture is run on full 'Bio-Gro' organic status, with no herbicides or pesticides being used.

kemblefield estate ★★★☆

Aorangi Road, Hastings **region** Hawke's Bay
phone (06) 874 9649 **fax** (06) 874 9457 **open** Mon–Fri 9–5
winemaker John Kemble **production** 12 000 **est.** 1993
product range ($14.95–19.95 CD) Gewurztraminer, Sauvignon Blanc, Reserve Sauvignon Blanc, Chardonnay, Cabernet Merlot, Merlot; also Terrace View range of Sauvignon Blanc, Chardonnay and Cabernet Merlot.
summary With 8.5 hectares of sauvignon blanc, 7.3 hectares of chardonnay, 4.5 hectares of merlot and 2.9 hectares of cabernet sauvignon, Kemblefield Estate has accelerated out of the blocks since it graduated from grape growing to winemaking in 1994. John Kemble, incidentally, is a graduate of UCLA Davis, and worked in California for 15 years before moving to Hawke's Bay.

Kemblefield Estate Gewurztraminer

Like the Chardonnay, produced from grapes grown near the Tutaekuri River; cold-fermented in stainless steel.

🍷🍷🍷🍷 **1996** Light yellow-green; there is voluminous spice and lychee varietal character on the bouquet, and plenty of weight and flavour on a rich palate; the touch of residual sugar works well in the wine. **rating:** 88

➾ **best drinking** 1998 – 1999 **best vintages** NA **drink with** Chinese prawns • $15

Kemblefield Estate Chardonnay

Produced from the small-berried Mendoza clone of chardonnay grown near the Tutaekuri River. It is 100% barrel-fermented in French oak, 25% new. Seventy-five per cent undergoes malolactic fermentation, and is kept on lees for nine months prior to bottling, with fortnightly lees stirring.

🍷🍷🍷🍷 **1996** Medium yellow-green; the bouquet is clean, smooth, and of medium intensity, with gentle fruit and well-balanced and integrated oak. A quite elegant palate, well weighted and structured, needing just a touch more fruit concentration for higher points. **rating:** 87

➾ **best drinking** 1998 – 2001 **best vintages** NA **drink with** Sautéed veal • $18

kenley vineyard NR

Earnscleugh Road, No 1 RD, Alexandra **region** Otago
phone (03) 449 2674 **fax** (03) 440 2064 **open** Not
winemaker Mike Woltner, Rudi Bauer (Contract) **production** 300 **est.** 1989
product range ($15–17 R) Gewurztraminer, Pinot Noir.
summary Ken and Bev Boddy have taken the slow boat in establishing their 1-hectare Kenley Vineyard. Ken Boddy became interested in the possibility of growing grapes in the Central Otago region in the mid-1960s during his time as a staff bacteriologist at the Oamaru Hospital. He corresponded with institutions around the world as well as New Zealand's Te Kauwhata Research Station, the latter giving him scant encouragement, but eventually supplying him with grape cuttings which formed the nucleus of a back garden nursery vineyard. Another 20 years were to pass before the Boddys acquired their present vineyard site (in 1989), planting half a hectare of pinot noir and half a hectare of gewurztraminer. They have 10 hectares available for planting, and Ken Boddy is currently evaluating the potential for scheurebe and viognier through trial plantings of each. Even after this long time, they appear to be in no great hurry.

kerr farm vineyard NR

48 Dysart Lane, Kumeu, Auckland **region** Kumeu and Huapai
phone (09) 412 7575 **fax** (09) 412 7575 **open** By appointment
winemaker Contract **production** 1000 **est.** 1989
product range ($14.95–18.95 CD) Semillon, Sauvignon Blanc, Chardonnay, Pinotage, Cabernet Sauvignon.
summary Jason and Wendy Kerr have established 5.5 hectares of vines on the site of an old Corbans vineyard, their first wines being made in 1995.

kim crawford wines ★★★★★

Main Road, Kumeu, Auckland **region** Kumeu and Huapai
phone (09) 373 4551 **fax** (09) 379 4541 **open** Not
winemaker Kim Crawford **production** 5000 **est.** 1996
product range ($16–26.95 R) Marlborough Riesling, Marlborough Sauvignon Blanc, Awatere Sauvignon, Marlbourgh Unoaked Chardonnay, Tietjen Gisborne Chardonnay.
summary Kim Crawford first made his reputation as winemaker at Coopers Creek (he continues in that job), then as consultant winemaker for a number of vineyards, and now as the producer of a number of absolutely brilliant wines under his own label, sourced from vineyards in Marlborough, Hawke's Bay and Gisborne. The cascade of trophies and gold medals from wine shows in both New Zealand and Australia seems certain to continue.

Kim Crawford Marlborough Dry Riesling

Winning the top gold medal in Class 1 at the 1997 Liquorland National Wine Show, sweeping aside all of the Australian Rieslings, tells part of the story of a particularly unusual wine. The other part of the story comes from its chemistry: the grapes were left on the vine until 15 May, the Indian summer of 1997 preventing any botrytis infection. Yet the grapes were so ripe the wine has 13 degrees alcohol, very rare for a conventional Riesling, balanced 8 grams per litre of acidity and 7 grams per litre of residual sugar (thus technically dry, even by Australian show standards). The wine was cold-fermented, and fermentation stopped naturally with the subliminal sweetness evident, and coming from that touch of residual sugar.

🍷🍷🍷🍷🍷 **1997** Light green-yellow; a powerful, quite racy bouquet; a similarly intense palate with tastes of citrus, nettle and mineral; considerable structure and depth. A Riesling for Chardonnay drinkers. **rating:** 92

➾ **best drinking** 1998 – 2003 **best vintages** NA **drink with** Calamari • $19.95

Kim Crawford Awatere Sauvignon

An extremely rich and complex oaked style of Sauvignon Blanc. Fifty per cent of the wine is barrel-fermented, lees aged and undergoes malolactic fermentation, with ten months maturation in new American oak. The remaining 50% is tank fermented and held in stainless steel until blending and bottling.

🍷🍷🍷🍷🍷 **1996** Medium yellow-green; ripe gooseberry fruit is interwoven with strong toasty spicy oak on the bouquet; the palate is more fruit than barrel-ferment driven with textural complexity, and the oak spice being most evident on the finish of the wine. Lively and flavoursome. **rating:** 90

➾ **best drinking** 1998 – 1999 **best vintages** '96, '97 **drink with** Seafood chowder • $26.95

Kim Crawford Marlborough Sauvignon Blanc

Produced from grapes grown in Marlborough's Awatere Valley, emanating from low-yielding vines. Straightforward cold fermentation in stainless steel and early-bottling followed, the wine quality coming principally from the vineyard selection, and partly from the choice of yeast strain. Gold medal winner and Top 100 NZ Liquorland International Wine Competition 1997.

🍷🍷🍷🍷🍸 **1997** Light to medium straw-green; the bouquet has both depth and complexity, with ripe gooseberry aromas dominant, but with hints of herb and capsicum. The palate is textured, with an array of flavours, starting with gooseberry, then some hints of lime and passionfruit, finally extending into white peach. A user-friendly wine in every respect. **rating:** 91

⇨ **best drinking** 1998 – 1999 **best vintages** '97 **drink with** Salmon terrine • $16.95

Kim Crawford Marlborough Unoaked Chardonnay

Produced from a single vineyard in Marlborough's cooler Omaka Valley region, and picked with very high levels of natural acidity. Taken through 100% malolactic fermentation in tank before stabilisation and bottling. Has greater structure and texture than most Australian unoaked Chardonnays.

🍷🍷🍷🍷 **1997** Light to medium yellow-green; delicate, fresh nectarine and peach fruit, with just a hint of cashew/hazelnut from the malolactic fermentation on the bouquet. The palate is very fresh and lively, with pure nectarine, peach and citrus fruit, and, once again, a happily subtle touch from the malolactic component. **rating:** 88

⇨ **best drinking** 1998 – 2000 **best vintages** NA **drink with** Chinese prawns • $16.95

Kim Crawford Tietjen Gisborne Chardonnay

Made from grapes grown by Paul Tietjen, one of Gisborne's most respected viticulturists. His vineyard sits below the Ormond Hills, and is one of Gisborne's coolest. Oxidatively handled juice was barrel-fermented in new American oak, and kept in barrel for six months with weekly lees stirring. Malolactic fermentation occurred spontaneously.

🍷🍷🍷🍷🍷 **1997** Medium yellow-green; very well-balanced and integrated fruit, oak and malolactic fermentation components on the bouquet are repeated to perfection on the palate. It has almost buttery viscosity, with subtle oak woven throughout; the malolactic component is judged to perfection, the acid persistent but soft on a long finish. Outstanding winemaking. **rating:** 94

⇨ **best drinking** 1998 – 2000 **best vintages** NA **drink with** New Zealand whitebait • $24.95

kindale wines NR

Falveys Road, Omaka Valley, Blenheim, Marlborough **region** Marlborough
phone (03) 572 8272 **fax** (03) 572 8272 **open** By appointment
winemaker Various **production** 250 **est.** 1993
product range Müller Thurgau, Chardonnay, Pinot Noir.
summary The Hadfield family have been grape growers since 1978, selling their production to Montana Wines. The first wine was made in 1993 for a special occasion; it has now graduated to slightly more commercial levels, with the wine sold through local retail outlets and through the mailing list.

kingsley estate NR

Gimblett Road (PO Box 1110), Hastings **region** Hawke's Bay
phone (025) 454 780 (mobile) **fax** (08) 326 9463 **open** Not
winemaker Kingsley Tobin **production** 300 **est.** 1991
product range ($24–29 ML) Cabernet Merlot, Reserve Cabernet Sauvignon.
summary Kingsley Tobin has established a 6-hectare vineyard at Gimblett Road, with certified Bio-Gro status. Most of the grapes are sold; a small portion is made by C J Pask winemaker Kate Radburnd, but Tobin does have plans to establish his own storage facility at the vineyard and to expand production. The current tiny production is sold by mail order.

kumeu river wines ★★★★★

550 Highway 16, Kumeu **region** Kumeu and Huapai
phone (09) 412 8415 **fax** (09) 412 7627 **open** Mon-Fri 9–5.30, Sat 11–5.30
winemaker Michael Brajkovich **production** 20 000 **est.** 1944
product range ($13–35 CD) At the top end come the limited production Maté Vineyard Chardonnay; then follow the Kumeu River range of Sauvignon Semillon, Chardonnay and Merlot Cabernet; the less expensive wines come under the Brajkovich Signature range, with Chardonnay, Sauvigon Semillon, Cabernet Merlot, Merlot Malbec Cabernet Franc and Cabernet Franc.
summary The wines of Michael Brajkovich defy conventional classification, simply because the highly trained, highly skilled and highly intelligent Brajkovich does not observe convention in crafting them, preferring instead to follow his own French-influenced instincts and preferences. Not surprisingly, the wines have won high praise both in New Zealand and overseas, most notably high in the *Wine Spectator* (US) top 100 annual listing for 1996.

Kumeu River Sauvignon Semillon

A blend of 90% Sauvignon Blanc and 10% Semillon, barrel-fermented, lees-aged and taken through a full malolactic fermentation.

YYYY **1996** Light to medium yellow-green; an intriguing bouquet with ripe stone fruit, ripe pear and apricot aromas, followed by a wine which is round and supple in the mouth, with the flavours even moving into melon. **rating:** 87

⇨ **best drinking** 1998 – 2000 **best vintages** NA **drink with** Braised pork • $21

Kumeu River Chardonnay

Produced from five different vineyard sites around Kumeu. Whole-bunch pressed direct to barrel, and relies upon indigenous yeasts. Twenty to twenty-five per cent new French oak is used, and the wine undergoes malolactic fermentation and lees contact in barrel before being bottled just prior to the following vintage. The Brajkovichs regard the '96 as the best vintage in the past ten years, and it is not hard to see why.

YYYYY **1996** Light green-yellow; a sophisticated bouquet with lively melon and grapefruit surrounded by gently spicy oak. An extremely elegant and intense yet almost delicate palate with exceptional balance and a very long finish; great breeding and class. **rating:** 94

⇨ **best drinking** 1998 – 2003 **best vintages** NA **drink with** Trout • $32

Kumeu River Maté Vineyard Chardonnay

The top-of-the-range Chardonnay from Kumeu River, named by Michael Brajkovich in honour of his late father, Maté Brajkovich – surely one of the all-time great gentlemen of the wine industry anywhere. A single-vineyard wine fermented in French oak, and an outstanding example of the genre. The vineyard, incidentally, was first planted in 1944, but entirely replanted in 1990, with the first wine from the new plantings made in 1993.

🍷🍷🍷🍷🍷 **1996** Light green-yellow; the aromas are extremely complex and concentrated, with impeccable oak balance and integration, and no one aroma dominating. There is an extra dimension of intensity of flavour on the palate, which has the longest finish I have encountered in a Chardonnay for many years. Here, too, it is hard to single out a single taste descriptor, which is no doubt exactly what Michael Brajkovich intended. **rating:** 97

⇨ **best drinking** 1999 – 2004 **best vintages** NA **drink with** Milk-fed veal • $35

Kumeu River Merlot Malbec Cabernet Franc

A blend of 70% Merlot, 15% Malbec and 15% Cabernet Franc, with new clones of merlot providing the major part of the wine.

🍷🍷🍷🍷🍷 **1996** Excellent red-purple colour; the bouquet is fragrant with cedary/spicy notes to the red berry and mint fruit. There is much more fruit weight, extract and tannin on the palate than one would expect from the bouquet, all the components (including the tannins) being ripe. **rating:** 91

⇨ **best drinking** 2000 – 2005 **best vintages** NA **drink with** Osso buco • $32

lake chalice wines

NR

Vintage Lane (Box 66), Renwick **region** Marlborough
phone (03) 572 9327 **fax** (03) 572 9327 **open** Not
winemaker Chris Gambitsis, Matt Thomson **production** 5000 **est.** 1989
product range ($13–26 CD) Riesling, Sauvignon Blanc, Platinum Oak Aged Sauvignon Blanc, Chardonnay, Platinum Chardonnay, Platinum Merlot.
summary Lake Chalice Wines is a partnership of three long-time friends, Chris Gambitsis, Ron Wichman and Phil Binning. In 1989 they purchased the 11.5-hectare Falcon Vineyard; the name of the winery comes from a wilderness lake situated in the Richmond Range which borders the northern side of Marlborough's Wairau Plain. The first wine release was in 1993; the first red wine was released in 1997.

langdale estate

NR

Langdale Road, West Melton, Christchurch **region** Canterbury
phone (03) 342 6266 **fax** (03) 342 6266 **open** Tues-Thur 11–5, Fri-Sat 11–10, Sun 11–5
winemaker Mark Rattray, Dayne Sherwood **production** 3000 **est.** 1989
product range ($14–23 CD) Riesling, Marlborough Sauvignon Blanc, Pinot Gris, Chardonnay, Breidecker, Pinot Noir, Melton Hills Pinot Noir.
summary Based upon 4.5 hectares of estate vineyards planted to pinot noir, riesling, breidecker and pinot gris, with plantings commencing in 1989 and expanded since. Most of the wine is sold through the cellar door and restaurant, and wedding function centre on-site.

larcomb vineyard

★★★☆

Larcombs Road, RD5, Christchurch **region** Canterbury
phone (03) 347 8909 **open** Tues-Sun 11–5 Nov-March, Fri-Sun 11–5 Apr-Oct
winemaker Contract **production** 2000 **est.** 1985
product range ($14–16 CD) Riesling, Breidecker, Gewurztraminer, Pinot Gris, Chardonnay, Pinot Noir.

summary Following its acquisition by Michelle and Warren Barnes in 1995, the winery has apparently obtained a reputation for itself as 'home of Rattle the Rafters Barn Dance', which – if nothing else – is something different.

lawson's dry hills ★★★★

Alabama Road, Blenheim **region** Marlborough
phone (03) 578 7674 **fax** (03) 578 7603 **open** 7 days 10–5
winemaker Mike Just **production** 15 000 **est.** 1992
product range ($16–24.50 R) Gewurztraminer, Sauvignon Blanc, Chardonnay, Riesling, Late Harvest Riesling, Pinot Noir.
summary Lawson's Dry Hills is situated on the Wither Hills, which in turn take their name from their parched mid-summer look. It is part-owned by Barbara and Ross Lawson, recently joined by three shareholders who have contributed vineyards giving a total of 22 hectares. The partners have all graduated from being grape growers to winemakers, with conspicuous success.

leaning rock vineyard NR

Hillview Road, Alexandra **region** Otago
phone (03) 448 9169 **fax** (03) 448 9169 **open** By appointment
winemaker Mark Hesson, Dhana Pillai **production** 450 **est.** 1991
product range ($16–25 CD) Riesling, Chardonnay, Pinot Noir.
summary Notwithstanding bare gravel soils and a northerly slope, spring frosts proved a major problem for geologist owners Mark Hesson and Dhana Pillai, curtailing production until sprinklers were installed prior to the 1996 growing season. Small quantities of strongly flavoured wines were then produced with gradually increasing quantities (particularly Pinot Noir) expected over coming vintages.

limeburners bay NR

112 Hobsonville Road, Hobsonville **region** Kumeu and Huapai
phone (09) 416 8844 **open** Mon–Sat 9–6
winemaker Alan Laurenson **production** 3500 **est.** 1978
product range ($7–19.95 CD) Müller Thurgau, Semillon Chardonnay, Sauvignon Blanc, Chardonnay, Cabernet Merlot, Cabernet Sauvignon.
summary Initially established a reputation for itself in the 1980s with some good Cabernet Sauvignon, but with more variable outcomes in the 1990s. No recent tastings.

lincoln vineyards ★★★

130 Lincoln Road, Henderson **region** Henderson
phone (09) 838 6944 **fax** (09) 838 6984 **open** Mon–Sat 9–6, Sun 11–5
winemaker Ian Trembath **production** 35 000 **est.** 1937
product range ($6.95–21.50 CD) Chardonnay (under a series of labels including Vintage Selection, Gisborne, Show Reserve and Parklands Vineyard), Sauvignon Blanc, Chenin Blanc, Riesling, Müller Thurgau, Cabernet Sauvignon, Merlot. Presidents Selection is newly introduced flagship.
summary A substantial family-owned operation drawing its grapes from Auckland, Gisborne and Hawke's Bay. The labels are avant-garde, but the wines have been variable, good at best but sometimes disappointing, even if the prices are competitive.

Lincoln Marlborough Sauvignon Blanc

First made in the difficult vintage of 1995, with a follow-up from the very nearly as difficult 1996. The '97 must have given Lincoln considerable satisfaction.

🍷🍷🍷🍷🍷 **1997** Light yellow-green; a pungent bouquet with a mix of herbal, sweet capsicum, asparagus and redcurrant aromas leads on to a crisply powerful palate with a long finish and pungent acidity. Excellent fruit intensity. **rating:** 90

⇒ **best drinking** 1998 – 1999 **best vintages** '97 **drink with** Oysters • $14

linden estate NR

Napier-Taupo Road, SH5, Eskdale **region** Hawke's Bay

phone (06) 836 6806 **fax** (06) 836 6806 **open** 7 days 10–6

winemaker Nick Chan **production** 12 000 **est.** 1971

product range ($16–32 CD) Sauvignon Blanc, Oak Aged Sauvignon Blanc, Estate White, Chardonnay, Merlot, Cabernet Sauvignon, Cabernet Franc Merlot.

summary This is the project of retired civil engineer and long-term grape grower Wim van der Linden and family, son John being a tutor in Viticulture at the Polytechnic in Hawke's Bay. The estate vineyard was replanted in 1989 to 30 hectares of premium varieties, including a 2.5-hectare hillside planting producing a Reserve wine first released in 1996. The '97 Sauvignon Blanc is an unusual wine, like a cross between Sauvignon Blanc and Chardonnay, and having a peculiar salty finish.

Linden Estate Esk Valley Chardonnay

Estate-grown, and aged in American oak for eight months; carries the American oak very well.

🍷🍷🍷🍷 **1996** Medium to full yellow-green; the bouquet is complex, with toasty vanilla oak immediately obvious, but with good fruit there to carry that oak. The well-structured palate has melon, fig and cashew flavours, again with some toasty oak. **rating:** 86

⇒ **best drinking** 1998 – 1999 **best vintages** NA **drink with** Chicken cacciatore • $18

lintz estate NR

Kitchener Street, Martinborough **region** Wairarapa

phone (06) 306 9174 **fax** (06) 306 9175 **open** By appointment while stocks last

winemaker Chris Lintz **production** 3000 **est.** 1989

product range ($16–65 CD) Reserve Riesling, Spicy Traminer, Sauvignon Blanc, Optima Noble Selection, Rosé, Pinot Noir, Moy Hall (Pinot), Cabernet Merlot, Vitesse Cabernet Sauvignon, Bottle Fermented Riesling Brut.

summary New Zealand-born Chris Lintz comes from a German winemaking family, and graduated from Geisenheim. The first stage of the Lintz winery, drawing grapes from the 9-hectare vineyard, was completed in 1991, and production is eventually planned to increase to about 13 000 cases. Since 1996 Lintz Estate has enjoyed much show success, winning numerous gold medals across the full range of wines, both white and red.

Lintz Estate Reserve Riesling

Produced from low-yielding estate-grown vines, now approaching ten years of age. The wine is cold fermented, and bottled immediately after fermentation has been stopped (typically with 7.5 grams per litre residual sugar).

🍷🍷🍷🍷🍷 **1997** Bright, light green-yellow; a classically restrained and fine bouquet, crisp and clean, with nuances of lime and passionfruit. The palate delivers all the bouquet promises, with a similar range of flavours, and wonderfully clean, fine fruit; acidity and residual sugar are in perfect balance. **rating:** 95

⇨ **best drinking** 1998 – 2003 **best vintages** NA **drink with** Sashimi • $20

Lintz Estate Chardonnay

Given the full winemaking treatment, with three hours skin contact, overnight cold settling, then simultaneous inoculation for both primary and malolactic fermentation; then transferred to barriques for fermentation and total malolactic fermentation, 80% new barrels are used, 10% American, the remainder from the centre of France. Nine months lees contact with light stirring before bottling. The '96 vintage won a gold medal at its only showing at the 1997 Liquorland Royal Easter Wine Show.

🍷🍷🍷🍷 **1996** Full yellow; an extremely powerful, highly worked and complex bouquet showing the full gamut of barrel-ferment and malolactic-fermentation influences. The palate is rich and big, with creamy/toasty/nutty flavours again tracking and reflecting the winemaking techniques. Less might be better still. **rating:** 89

⇨ **best drinking** 1998 – 1999 **best vintages** NA **drink with** Smoked chicken and avocado salad • $28

Lintz Estate Cabernet Merlot

Made from almost equal quantities of Cabernet Sauvignon and Cabernet Franc, with just a touch of Merlot. Post-fermentation maceration (for seven days) is followed by ten months in oak barriques on fine lees.

🍷🍷🍷🍷 **1994** Medium red-purple; a complex bouquet, showing quite ripe fruit with some gamey/earthy notes. There are very interesting flavours on the palate with red berry fruits softened by distinct gamey barnyard characters which are far from unpleasant. Persistent tannins run through the palate, all in all reflecting an extremely low yield of less than a tonne per acre and unusual levels of ripeness. **rating:** 88

⇨ **best drinking** 1998 – 2003 **best vintages** NA **drink with** Venison in red wine sauce • $28

lombardi wines NR

298 Te Mata Road, Havelock North **region** Hawke's Bay
phone (06) 877 7985 **fax** (06) 877 7816 **open** 7 days 10–5
winemaker Tracy Haslam **production** 1000 **est.** 1948
product range ($9.95–14.95 CD) Riesling Sylvaner, Sauternes, Sherry, Vermouth, Marsala and flavoured fortifieds.
summary The Australian Riverland transported to the unlikely environment of Hawke's Bay, with a half-Italian, half-English family concentrating on a kaleidoscopic array of Vermouths and sweet, flavoured fortified wines. A change of ownership at the end of 1994 has not signalled any fundamental change in direction – except for a desire to have fun while making better wines.

longbush wines NR

State Highway 2, Manutuke, Gisborne **region** Gisborne
phone (06) 862 8577 **fax** (06) 867 8012 **open** Tues-Sun 10–5 Oct-Easter
winemaker John Thorpe **production** 15 000 **est.** 1992

product range ($9–20 CD) Woodlands Chardonnay; the Longbush range of Rhine Riesling, Chardonnay, Sauvignon Blanc, Botrytis Riesling, Pinot Noir, Merlot, Kahurangi; Nicks Head Sauvignon Blanc, Muller Muscat, Sea Breeze Classic Dry, Chardonnay, and Merlot.
summary Part of the ever-changing circus of winemaking and brand ventures of the Thorpe Brothers group. Woodlands is the premium label; Longbush the principal (and mid-range) label; Nicks Head is the third and lowest priced.

longview estate NR

State Highway 1, Whangarei **region** Northland and Matakana
phone (09) 438 7227 **fax** (09) 438 7227 **open** Mon-Sat 8.30–6 summer, winter Sat 8.30–5.30, Sun 9–5
winemaker Mario Vuletich **production** 2500 **est.** 1969
product range ($10–24 R) Chardonnay, Gewurztraminer, White Diamond (sweet), Scarecrow Cabernet Sauvignon, Mario's Merlot, Cabernet Merlot, Gumdigger's Port, Golden Sherry, Dry Sherry.
summary Mario and Barbara Vuletich have been involved in viticulture and winemaking since 1969, but have replanted the 6-hectare vineyard on elevated slopes overlooking Whangarei harbour, with the four principal Bordeaux varieties (and shiraz) with the intention of making full-bodied dry reds. That they have succeeded handsomely in so doing is evident by the fact that both the Cabernet Sauvignon and the Merlot have received four stars in *Cuisine* magazine for the '93, '94 and '96 vintages.

loopline vineyard NR

Loopline Road, RD1, Masterton **region** Wairarapa
phone (06) 377 3353 **fax** (06) 378 8338 **open** 7 days 9–6
winemaker Frank Parker **production** 500 **est.** 1994
product range ($12.50–19.50 CD) Chasselas, Riesling, Chardonnay, Sauvignon Blanc, Chasselas Chenin Blanc, Waipipi Red.
summary Frank and Bernice Parker are pioneer viticulturists on the Opaki Plains, five kilometres north of Masterton. They have established 1 hectare of riesling, and a quarter of a hectare of chasselas, supplementing their intake with limited quantities of grapes grown by other producers in the region.

macmillan wines NR

c/o 19 Gladstone Road, Richmond, Nelson (Contract facilities) **region** Nelson
phone (03) 544 5853 **fax** (03) 544 5853 **open** Summer 7 days 10–5, winter by appointment
winemaker Saralinda MacMillan **production** 400 **est.** 1993
product range ($16–20 CD) Chardonnay.
summary Former Seifried winemaker Saralinda MacMillan left Seifried in 1992 to have her first child. She has since commenced winemaking on her own account in a tiny way using contract facilities, making Chardonnay and Sauvignon Blanc.

margrain vineyard ★★★

Ponatahi Road, (PO Box 97), Martinborough **region** Wairarapa
phone (06) 306 9292 **fax** (04) 569 2698 **open** Weekends and holidays 11–5
winemaker Strat Canning **production** 500 **est.** 1992
product range ($14–26 CD) Riesling, Chardonnay, Pinot Noir, Merlot.

summary Graham and Daryl Margrain planted their first vines in 1992, and produced the first wine (Chardonnay) in 1994. The vineyard is now planted to a total of 24 hectares of chardonnay, pinot noir, merlot and pinot gris; eight luxury accommodation villas have been built on an adjoining ridge; and a woolshed has been converted into a conference facility and tasting room. An underground cellar was constructed in 1994, and a winery (including a restaurant) was commissioned for the 1996 vintage. And what did the Margrains do before they established Margrain Vineyard? They spent 25 years in the building industry, of course.

Margrain Riesling

Winemaker Strat Canning produces wines with abundant character and flavour, at times a little too enthusiastically. There are no problems with this Riesling, however.

🍷🍷🍷🍷 **1997** Light to medium yellow-green; strong lime and toast varietal aromas lead into a wine with good grip and fibre; there are more of those lime and toast flavours, and the sweetness, while evident, provides balance. **rating:** 84

⇒ **best drinking** 1998 – 2003 **best vintages** NA **drink with** Sugar-cured tuna • $16

Margrain Chardonnay

Made in a particularly full-blown, sometimes rustic, style.

🍷🍷🍷🍷 **1996** Medium to full yellow-green; a somewhat inexpressive bouquet, although ripe fruit is evident. There is nothing reticent about the palate, which is full and complex, with abundant ripe, toasty/buttery fruit in a bells-and-whistles style. **rating:** 87

⇒ **best drinking** 1998 – 1999 **best vintages** NA **drink with** Loin of pork • $26

mark rattray vineyards NR

State Highway 1, Waipara **region** Canterbury
phone (03) 314 6710 **fax** (03) 314 6710 **open** 7 days 10–5
winemaker Mark Rattray **production** 3200 **est.** 1992
product range ($22–27 CD) French Farm Chardonnay, Waipara Chardonnay, Marlborough Sauvignon Blanc, Waipara Pinot Noir, Aquilon Pinot.
summary Mark Rattray is a high-profile wine consultant in the Canterbury district, who has enjoyed much success. Initially based at Waipara Springs, with wife Michelle he has now established the Mark Rattray Vineyards label, while continuing to consult to a number of other makers in the region (including Waipara Springs). Has enjoyed particular success in the United Kingdom.

martina vineyard NR

Kopuku Road, Te Kauwhata **region** Waikato and Bay of Plenty
phone (07) 826 7790 **fax** (07) 826 7790 **open** By appointment
winemaker Tony Martin **production** 1000 **est.** 1995
product range ($9–20 ML) Rhine Riesling, Sauvignon Blanc, Chardonnay, Pinot Noir, Syrah, Martined (Light Red), Malbec Cabernet Sauvignon, Dolce Vita (dessert wine).
summary Italian-born and trained Tony Martin was a winemaker at Cooks Te Kauwhata winery for five years before launching his Martina range of wines in 1995, using grapes sourced from both The Waikato and Hawke's Bay, but with changes in the wind.

martinborough vineyard ★★★★★

Princess Street, Martinborough **region** Wairarapa
phone (06) 306 9955 **fax** (06) 306 9217 **open** 7 days 11–5
winemaker Larry McKenna **production** 10 000 **est.** 1980
product range ($16–42.50 CD) Riesling, Riesling Late Harvest, Gewurztraminer, Pinot Gris, Sauvignon Blanc, Chardonnay, Chardonnay Late Harvest, Pinot Noir, Pinot Noir Reserve.
summary Australian-born and trained Larry McKenna has established a firm reputation as New Zealand's most skilled producer of Pinot Noir, and with an ability to produce Chardonnay and Riesling of similarly impressive ilk. It is on these wines that the reputation of Martinborough Vineyard rests, although McKenna also makes classy Sauvignon Blanc. The Pinot Noir Reserve, only made in good vintages, is in a class of its own.

Martinborough Vineyard Chardonnay

Larry McKenna works very hard with all his wines, focusing as much on structure and mouthfeel as on varietal or primary fruit flavours. These are very complex, sophisticated wines, as far removed from the jungle-juice, phenolic, skin-contacted Chardonnays of bygone years or lesser producers as one could imagine. Produced from estate-grown grapes and grapes from the McCreanor Vineyard; barrel-fermented and aged on lees for 12 months, with 50% malolactic fermentation.

1996 Medium yellow-green; the bouquet is clean but tangy with a mix of citrus, lemon and white peach fruit supported by subtle oak. There is layer upon layer of flavour on the palate, with cashew, citrus and melon fruit, and just an echo of gently sweet oak. **rating:** 90

⇨ **best drinking** 1998 – 2003 **best vintages** '88, '89, '91, '94, '96 **drink with** Pan-fried veal • $27.50

Martinborough Vineyard Pinot Noir

For long one of the benchmarks for Pinot Noir in Australasia, although in more recent years (but only in the best vintages) topped by the Reserve Pinot Noir. The Martinborough Vineyard Pinot Noirs are made in much the same style as the Chardonnays, with as much focus on structure and complexity as on fruit. Larry McKenna has never been afraid to experiment, and deliberately walks the razor's edge in the quest for ultimate quality.

1996 Medium red-purple; the bouquet is exemplary, with cherry and plum fruit complexed and cut by some foresty/stemmy characters. The palate, likewise, has a mix of cherry plum fruit and more foresty/stemmy characters giving grip, texture and length. **rating:** 92

⇨ **best drinking** 1998 – 2002 **best vintages** '86, '88, '91, '94, '95 **drink with** Roast quail • $33

---

matariki wines 

Gimblett Road, Havelock North **region** Hawke's Bay
phone (06) 877 8002 **fax** (06) 877 8004 **open** Not
winemaker John O'Connor **production** NA **est.** 1981
product range Sauvignon Blanc, Chardonnay, Anthology (Bordeaux-blend).
summary John and Rosemary O'Connor purchased their Gimblett Road property in 1981, and are now the owners of the largest individual vineyard in that area, with 30 hectares (of a total 60 hectares) under vine, with syrah and sauvignon blanc planted on pure shingle, and cabernet franc, cabernet sauvignon, malbec, merlot, semillon and chardonnay on terraces with a

greater amount of soil. They have also more recently purchased a limestone terrace property below Te Mata Peak, which is cooler and which has been planted to chardonnay. Currently they share the Trinity Hill winery with John Hancock, which houses their own winemaking equipment, but with plans for a large two-storey winery already drawn up. The quality of the first releases (from 1997) is immaculate.

Matariki Sauvignon Blanc

The first release from 1997 of Matariki Sauvignon Blanc holds much promise for the future. Part stainless steel fermentation and a well-judged portion of barrel fermentation produces a genuinely successful food style – a phrase which is often no more than an excuse for lack of flavour, but is certainly not in this instance.

🍷🍷🍷🍷🍸 **1997** Light to medium yellow-green; all of the components are discreet and harmonious, with a mix of smoky barrel-ferment, mineral and herb aromas on the bouquet. The palate has the same harmony and mouthfeel, with the various components working synergistically. **rating:** 90

➾ **best drinking** 1998 – 1999 **best vintages** NA **drink with** Smoked haddock or eel • $19.50

Matariki Chardonnay

Like the Matariki Sauvignon Blanc, first made in 1997. While the full range of winemaking treatments has been used, it is fruit, rather than oak, which drives the wine.

🍷🍷🍷🍷 **1996** Medium yellow-green; melon, peach and fig fruit aromas on the bouquet, move more to melon and cashew on the palate. Light to medium weight; good length and balance. **rating:** 86

➾ **best drinking** 1998 – 2000 **best vintages** NA **drink with** Brains in black butter • $19.50

---

matawhero wines ★★☆

Riverpoint Road, Matawhero **region** Gisborne
phone (06) 868 8366 **fax** (06) 867 9856 **open** Mon–Sat 9–5
winemaker Denis Irwin **production** 6000 **est.** 1975
product range ($16–25 CD) Gewurztraminer, Riesling, Chardonnay, Reserve Chardonnay, Sauvignon Blanc, Chenin Blanc, Pinot Noir, Syrah, Cabernet Merlot.
summary The wines have always been cast in the mould of Matawhero's unpredictable founder and owner Denis Irwin: at their best, in the guise of the Gewurztraminer from a good vintage, they are quite superb, racy and powerful; at their worst, they are poor and exhibit marked fermentation problems.

matua valley ★★★★

Waikoukou Road, Waimauku **region** Kumeu and Huapai
phone (09) 411 8301 **fax** (09) 411 7982 **open** Mon–Sat 8.30–5, Sun 11–4.30
winemaker Ross Spence, Mark Robertson **production** 110 000 **est.** 1974
product range ($10.90–33.00 CD) A very large range running from generic and varietal white and red table wines at the bottom end of the price scale, then to the Shingle Peak Marlborough range of Sauvignon Blanc, Riesling, Pinot Gris, Chardonnay, Cabernet Sauvignon; the Hawke's Bay varietal wines including Gewurztraminer and Sauvignon Blanc;

then to the premium white and red table wines under the Reserve, Ararimu or Judd Estate labels. Waimauku and Smith Cabernet Sauvignons recent illustrious additions.

summary One of the stalwarts of the New Zealand wine industry, producing a wide range of wines of good quality. The Shingle Peak label has been particularly successful, while the presentation of the Ararimu Chardonnay and Cabernet Sauvignon (not to mention the quality of the wines) set new standards of excellence for New Zealand.

Matua Valley Hawke's Bay Gewurztraminer

Gewurztraminer seems to do well wherever it is grown in New Zealand, combining flavour with delicacy when well handled – as this wine is.

🍷🍷🍷🍷 **1997** Light to medium yellow-green; there are strong spicy lychee and peach aromas on the bouquet, and plenty more of that peach and lychee fruit on the palate which avoids the phenolic trap. **rating:** 85

➾ **best drinking** 1998 – 2001 **best vintages** NA **drink with** Ginger prawns • $13

Matua Valley Hawke's Bay Sauvignon Blanc

Sourced from a number of growers in Hawke's Bay, simply cold-fermented in stainless steel and early bottled.

🍷🍷🍷🍷 **1997** Light to medium yellow-green; there is ripe and generous gooseberry fruit on the bouquet which is of medium to full intensity. A nicely weighted and styled wine on the palate, again with predominant gooseberry flavours (and no passionfruit) and a touch of grip to the finish. **rating:** 86

➾ **best drinking** 1998 – 1999 **best vintages** NA **drink with** Vegetable terrine • $16

Matua Valley Shingle Peak Sauvignon Blanc

Shingle Peak is the Marlborough label of Matua Valley, almost a separate brand, so far is it distanced from Matua Valley. Ever reliable, the '97 won a gold medal at the 1997 Liquorland National Wine Show of Australia. Like the Hawke's Bay Sauvignon Blanc, made without artifice or intervention, and, like the Hawke's Bay wine, 100% Sauvignon Blanc. The two wines provide a perfect contrast between the style of Hawke's Bay Sauvignon and that of Marlborough.

🍷🍷🍷🍷🍷 **1997** Light to medium green-yellow; there is a fragrant mix of gooseberry, passionfruit and more herbal notes on the bouquet; the lively, long and well-balanced palate has a nice minerally grip to the finish. Excellent varietal example. **rating:** 92

➾ **best drinking** 1998 – 1999 **best vintages** NA **drink with** New Zealand whitebait • $15

Matua Valley Shingle Peak Pinot Gris

As with all the Shingle Peak wines, produced from nine hectares, and first made in 1995. Partial barrel fermentation and some lees contact, both sensitively used, add texture and interest, without submerging the fairly elusive and hard-to-describe varietal fruit of Pinot Gris.

🍷🍷🍷🍷🍷 **1997** Light yellow-green; the bouquet has good fruit weight and density, with that spicy lemony minerally mix of the grape. There is lots of flavour on the palate, which has weight, richness and real character. **rating:** 90

➾ **best drinking** 1998 – 2000 **best vintages** NA **drink with** Clams or pippies • $15

mazuran's vineyard NR

255 Lincoln Road, Henderson **region** Henderson
phone (09) 838 6945 **open** Mon-Sat 9–6
winemaker Rado Hladilo **production** 1000 **est.** 1938
product range Sherries and Ports.
summary A Sherry and Port specialist, still surviving on the reputation built for its wines by George Mazuran, who died in 1980. The business is continued by his son and son-in-law.

mcdonald winery ★★★★☆

150 Church Road, Taradale **region** Hawke's Bay
phone (06) 844 2053 **fax** (06) 844 3378 **open** 7 days 9–5
winemaker Tony Prichard **production** NFP **est.** 1897
product range ($18.35–35 R) Church Road Sauvignon Blanc, Chardonnay, Noble Semillon, Cabernet Sauvignon Merlot; Church Road Reserve Chardonnay, Merlot, Cabernet Sauvignon Merlot; Twin Rivers Cuvée Brut; super delux Cabernet Cuvée released 1997.
summary Montana's acquisition of the historic McDonald Winery in 1989 and its investment of $2 million on refurbishment followed by the announcement of the Cordier joint venture, together with the acquisition of premium Hawke's Bay vineyards, signalled Montana's determination to enter the top end of the market with high-quality Chardonnay and Cabernet Sauvignon. Legal squabbles have forced the adoption of the Church Road name for the wine label.

McDonald Church Road Chardonnay

Drawn from the full range of Montana's Hawke's Bay vineyards, part hand-harvested and whole-bunch pressed, part machine-harvested, crushed and given short skin contact. Fermented in a mix of new and used French and American oak barrels in the McDonald cool room, with partial malolactic fermentation and prolonged lees contact. Typically given seven months in oak, always producing a rich and complex wine.

🍷🍷🍷🍷🍸 **1996** Medium yellow-green; there is abundant ripe fig and peach fruit with quite obvious barrel-fermentation characters in a solid bouquet. There is a hint of spice, possibly from the American oak, on top of rich, ripe peach and fig fruit on the palate; the malolactic influence is nicely muted. **rating:** 90

➾ **best drinking** 1998 – 1999 **best vintages** '94, '95 **drink with** Creamy fettuccine • $20

McDonald Church Road Reserve Chardonnay

Estate-grown, but selected from various vineyard blocks according to the vintage, the one constant being the Mendoza clone. After brief settling, the wine is taken direct to barrel for fermentation in French oak (two-thirds new) situated in a temperature-controlled cool room. A portion of the wine is taken through malolactic fermentation, and the wine spends seven months on yeast lees before being cleaned up and bottled. Always an outstanding wine at the very top of the New Zealand tree.

🍷🍷🍷🍷🍷 **1996** Medium yellow-green; a wine which continuously evolves and reveals itself as it sits in the glass, tightly constructed but extremely stylish. The palate is beautifully balanced, with gently ripe melon and fig fruit supported by faultless oak handling. It has an exceptionally long carry and finish. **rating:** 97

➾ **best drinking** 1998 – 2003 **best vintages** '94, '95, '96 **drink with** Yellow-fin tuna • $29

McDonald Church Road Reserve Merlot

Sometimes made with a dash of Cabernet Sauvignon (6% in 1995, for example) and sourced from Montana's Fernhill Estate vineyard with a lesser but significant amount coming from the Esk Valley. After 12–14 days post-fermentation maceration the wine is run to new French medium-toast barriques where it spends 14 months, with regular aerobic rackings. It poses the question whether merlot is the grape for Hawke's Bay, but does not answer it.

🍷🍷🍷🍷 **1995** Medium purple-red; the light to medium intensity bouquet shows earthy/berry fruit together with a hint of spicy oak, with rather more sweet berry, plum and cherry fruit coming through on the palate. A good wine, for sure, but not earthshaking. **rating:** 85

➯ **best drinking** 1999 – 2004 **best vintages** '94, '95 **drink with** Braised oxtail • $32

McDonald Church Road Reserve Cabernet Merlot

A blend of Cabernet Sauvignon and Merlot, first made in 1994 with two-thirds Cabernet Sauvignon and one-third Merlot, but with the Cabernet component moving to 83% in 1995. The Esk Valley and Montana's Phoenix Estate are the fruit sources, and the wine spends 14 months in predominantly new French oak barriques.

🍷🍷🍷🍷 **1995** Medium to full red-purple; the bouquet is of medium intensity, with some quite sweet notes, together with hints of chocolate and earth. An elegant wine on the palate, but there is not as much mid-palate fruit as the bouquet promises, and the tannins do threaten the balance. For my palate, the '94 has better balance, with attractive cedary/chocolatey fruit. **rating:** 89

➯ **best drinking** 2000 – 2004 **best vintages** '94, '95 **drink with** Rare beef • $35

---

melness wines NR

1816 Cust Road, Cust, North Canterbury **region** Canterbury

phone (03) 312 5402 **fax** (03) 512 5466 **open** Saturdays and public holidays 10–5

winemaker Mathew Donaldson, Lynette Hudson **production** 1200 **est.** NA

product range ($10–25 CD) Gewurztraminer, Riesling, Chardonnay (spray free), Floral (spray free), Rosé, Pinot Noir.

summary Melness' vineyards are run organically, which makes the utilisation of what is claimed to be the only Lyre Trellis system on the South Island all the more understandable, as it maximises sunlight and wind penetration. Owners Colin and Norma Marshall are establishing the winery and a café in a garden setting due to be opened in April 1998. The 1996 Pinot Noir has won a number of awards.

merlen wines NR

c/o Rapaura Vintners, Cnr Rapaura Road and SH 6, Renwick **region** Marlborough

phone (03) 572 8393 **fax** (03) 572 8472 **open** 7 days 9–5

winemaker Almuth Lorenz **production** 6500 **est.** 1987

product range ($13–22 CD) Riesling, Sauvignon Blanc, Chardonnay, Semillon, Gewurztraminer.

summary In mid-1997 the long-standing winemaking and administration team headed by the colourful and substantial figure of Almuth Lorenz suddenly parted company with the winery which was publicly offered for sale. Almuth Lorenz is the owner of the brand, and has taken it (and herself) to Rapaura Vintners (a major contract crush winery) where she is making the Merlen wines. No information yet on the direction in which the old Merlen winery will head.

Merlen Riesling

Says Almuth Lorenz, 'For me a Riesling should be very delicate, austere, light and very shy, so you will have to look closely to find all the subtleties. Try and age the wine.' In fact the Rieslings are made with between 10 and 12 grams per litre of residual sugar, so they are certainly not dry; on the other hand, the intense fruit and relatively high acid of Marlborough Riesling seems to gobble up the sugar and one cannot accuse these wines of being soft or cloying. Merlen's best wine by some distance, and very age worthy.

🍷🍷🍷🍷🍸 **1997** Light green-yellow; the bouquet is fragrant, with attractive lime and passionfruit aromas. The palate is powerful and concentrated, with more of that lime juice fruit of the bouquet, the impact heightened by the deliberate use of considerable sweetness on the finish. You can go either way with a wine such as this; much will depend on the circumstances of consumption. **rating:** 90

⇨ **best drinking** 1999 – 2003 **best vintages** '89, '91, '94, '96 **drink with** Pork with ginger • $14

mills reef winery ★★★★

143 Moffat Road, Bethlehem, Tauranga **region** Waikato and Bay of Plenty
phone (07) 576 8800 **fax** (07) 576 8824 **open** 7 days 8–5
winemaker Paddy Preston **production** 25 000 **est.** 1989

product range ($11–30 CD) Under the Moffat Road/Mere Road labels Riesling, Sauvignon Blanc, Chardonnay, Pinot Blush and Cabernet Sauvignon; then comes the Reserve range of Riesling, Sauvignon Blanc, Chenin Blanc, Chardonnay, Pinot Noir and Ice Wine Riesling; the top of the range is the Elspeth range of Riesling, Sauvignon Blanc, Chardonnay and Cabernet Merlot; Méthode Champenoise comprises Charisma NV and Vintage.

summary Mills Reef has recently completed a new winery, situated on an 8-hectare chardonnay vineyard within five minutes of Tauranga, incorporating wine tasting and display rooms, a restaurant and a conference/meeting room, together with usual winemaking facilities. The initial releases from Mills Reef were impressive, and after a few intervening disappointments it has returned to top form with its Méthode Champenoise.

Mills Reef Elspeth Chardonnay

The flagship Chardonnay for Mills Reef (ranking above the Reserve), produced from grapes from Mere Road in Hawke's Bay. One hundred per cent barrel-fermented in new French oak, and 100% malolactic fermentation, followed by the usual lees contact and almost a full year in barrel. Despite this no-holds-barred treatment, an elegant style which should age extremely well.

🍷🍷🍷🍷🍸 **1996** Light to medium yellow-green; the bouquet is clean with a nice mix of biscuity/minerally secondary fruit flavours and faintly spicy oak. Tangy melon and citrus fruit comes through on the palate, which has considerable length, and which is neither overblown by the malolactic fermentation nor shrouded with oak. **rating:** 90

⇨ **best drinking** 1999 – 2003 **best vintages** NA **drink with** Turkey • $24

Mills Reef Vintage Traditional Method

Made from 100% Hawke's Bay Chardonnay, fermented and aged in oak for nine months, a very unusual approach, and then tiraged before spending over two years on yeast lees prior to disgorging.

🍷🍷🍷🍷🍷 **1992** Glowing yellow-green; a clean bouquet with strong toasty/bready, yet crisp, fruit. The palate is complex and well balanced with creamy/nutty/toasty flavours, yet not obviously oaky. Good finish and balance. **rating:** 90

➭ **best drinking** 1998 – 1999 **best vintages** '90, '92 **drink with** Most fish or white meat dishes • $27.50

millton vineyard ★★★★☆

Papatu Road, Manutuke, Gisborne **region** Gisborne
phone (06) 862 8680 **fax** (06) 862 8869 **open** By appointment
winemaker James Millton **production** 10 000 **est.** 1984
product range ($15–35 CD) Barrique Fermented Chardonnay, Clos de Ste Anne Chardonnay, Chenin Blanc, Tete du Cuvée (botrytised Chenin Blanc), Te Arai River Sauvignon Blanc, Riesling Opou Vineyard, Clos de Ste Anne Pinot Noir, Te Arai River Cabernet Merlot.
summary The only registered organic vineyards in New Zealand using biodynamic methods and banning insecticides and herbicides; winemaking methods are conventional, but seek to limit the use of chemical additives wherever possible. The white wines, particularly botrytised, can be of the highest quality; the Germanic, lime-flavoured Riesling Opou Vineyard is almost always outstanding, while James Millton is doing some of the most exciting things with Chenin Blanc anywhere in the world outside the Loire Valley.

Millton Riesling Opou Vineyard

As with all of the Millton wines, estate-grown according to strict organic standards. The composition of the finished wine reads like a German Riesling: 10% alcohol, 8.6 grams per litre of acid (natural) and 18.3 grams per litre residual sugar. Just as James Millton endeavours to allow nature to run its course in the vineyard, so he also takes a non-interventionist role in the winery. In fact, the result is a beautifully balanced wine.

🍷🍷🍷🍷🍷 **1996** Medium green-yellow; a quite firm bouquet with lime, passionfruit and some more toasty characters, the palate is smooth, soft, and with the acid and residual sugar in perfect balance. Gently honeyed, lime and peach fruit flavours linger on the finish. **rating:** 90

➭ **best drinking** 1998 – 2005 **best vintages** NA **drink with** Shellfish in creamy sauce • $19

Millton Chenin Blanc

The wine is made from grapes hand-picked over a number of days, barrel-fermented and aged for six months in oak. The '94 was the trophy winner for the Champion Dry White Wine Other Varieties at the 1995 Air New Zealand Wine Awards, and a remarkable wine in all respects. The '96 is a less remarkable vintage, but a good wine.

🍷🍷🍷🍷 **1996** Full yellow, with just a hint of green; the generous bouquet has aromas of soft peach, spice and honey with nicely controlled oak. The palate is soft, fleshy and rounded, though not particularly concentrated; may well build complexity and character with further time in bottle. **rating:** 85

➭ **best drinking** 1999 – 2004 **best vintages** NA **drink with** Seafood bisque • $18.80

Millton Barrique Fermented Chardonnay

A full-blown style which, as the name indicates, is barrel-fermented (in French oak). Estate-grown and hand-picked, it is consistently at the rich end of the spectrum.

🍷🍷🍷🍷 **1996** Full yellow; a solid bouquet with ripe and smooth peachy/buttery fruit dominant; subtle oak. The palate is similarly rich and fat with masses of peachy flavour, and just a hint of botrytis evident. **rating:** 87

⇨ **best drinking** 1998 – 1999 **best vintages** NA **drink with** Pan-fried chicken breast • $27

Millton Tete du Cuvée (375 ml)

Said to be a botrytised berry selection, which may or may not mean the individual picking of berries from the vine or by selection on a sorting table in the winery, but it really doesn't matter very much. The end result is an extraordinarily complex and massively botrytis-influenced wine, 80% of which is barrel-fermented for further complexity.

🍷🍷🍷🍷🍷 **1994** Golden orange; intense mandarin and cumquat aromas, strongly reminiscent of the great sweet wines of the Loire Valley. A powerful, aristocratic and complex palate, with the lusciousness of the fruit balanced by powerful acidity. Marvellous stuff. **rating:** 94

⇨ **best drinking** 1998 – 2003 **best vintages** NA **drink with** Rich desserts • $40

miro NR

Browns Road, Waiheke Island **region** Waiheke Island
phone (09) 372 7854 **fax** (09) 372 7056 **open** By appointment
winemaker Stephen White, Barnett Bond **production** 700 **est.** 1994
product range ($55 R) A single Bordeaux-blend of Cabernet Sauvignon, Merlot, Cabernet Franc and Malbec.
summary Dr Barnett Bond and wife Cate Vosper are the most recent arrivals on the beautiful Waiheke Island scene, planting their first vines in 1994 and extending the vineyard to 3 hectares in 1996. A luxury holiday cottage on-site is available overlooking the steep north-facing slopes of the vines looking out to the Onetangi Bay.

mission estate winery ★★★☆

Church Road, Taradale **region** Hawke's Bay
phone (06) 844 2259 **fax** (06) 844 6023 **open** Mon-Sat 8.30–5.30, Sun 11–4
winemaker Paul Mooney **production** 50 000 **est.** 1851
product range ($7–35 CD) Predominantly varietal designated wines; Sauvignon Blanc, Fumé Blanc, Semillon Sauvignon Blanc, Semillon, Pinot Gris, Chardonnay, Cabernet Merlot, Cabernet Sauvignon. Also proprietary brands including Sugar Loaf Semillon, White Heritage, St Mary's Riesling Sylvaner, St Peter Chanel Chardonnay and Estella Sauternes. Recently introduced premium Jewelstone range.
summary New Zealand's oldest winemaker, owned by the Society of Mary. Once content to make honest, basically unpretentious wines at modest prices, it has developed some top-end wines since 1992, notably the Jewelstone range.

Mission Jewelstone Chardonnay

First made in 1992, and has done much to lift the profile of Mission. Each vintage released (it is not made every year) has justified both price and the premium label.

🍷🍷🍷🍷 **1996** Medium yellow-green; a well-balanced and composed bouquet of considerable complexity with attractive biscuity notes is followed by an elegant palate in which well-judged winemaker inputs into medium weight Chardonnay has produced a stylish drink. **rating:** 86

⇨ **best drinking** 1998 – 1999 **best vintages** '92, '94, '96 **drink with** Veal parmigiana • $26

Mission Jewelstone Franc Cabernet

A most unusual name for a blend of 70% Cabernet Franc and 30% Cabernet Sauvignon, the Cabernet Franc coming from a vineyard in Ohiti Road and the Cabernet Sauvignon from a low-yielding vineyard at Moteo. The wine was fermented in an open fermenter with hand-plunging, and given extended post-fermentation maceration before spending 18 months in French oak barriques.

🍷🍷🍷🍷🍷 **1995** Medium to full red-purple; the bouquet is full and complex, with ripe earthy berry fruit and subtle oak. There is substantial extract evident on the palate, with earthy berry flavours and quite persistent tannins. **rating:** 90

➾ **best drinking** 2000 – 2006 **best vintages** NA **drink with** Rump steak • $30

---

montana wines ★★★★

171 Pilkington Road, Glen Innes, Auckland **region** Auckland and South Auckland
phone (09) 570 5549 **fax** (09) 527 1113 **open** 7 days 9.30–5.30
winemaker Jeff Clarke (Chief) **production** 35 000 tonnes (2.25 million case equivalent)
est. 1977

product range ($10.95–30.00 CD) A vast range headed by Marlborough Sauvignon Blanc, Riesling, Chardonnay and Cabernet Sauvignon; Renwick Estate Chardonnay, Brancott Estate Sauvignon Blanc and Fairhall Estate Cabernet Sauvignon (also all from Marlborough); Saints Marlborough Sauvignon Blanc and Saints Gisborne Chardonnay; Ormond Estate Chardonnay (Gisborne); important sparkling wines headed by Deutz Marlborough Cuvée (Brut and Blanc de Blanc) and Lindauer (Special Reserve Brut de Brut, Brut, Sec and Rosé); large volume Wohnsiedler Müller Thurgau, Blenheimer and Chablisse; Church Road Chardonnay and Cabernet Sauvignon are top-of-the-range. The bright-blue bottle of Azure Bay was a colourful (and commercially significant) addition in 1996.

summary Has a more dominant position than does Southcorp through Seppelts-Penfolds-Lindemans in Australia, as it produces 50% of New Zealand's wine. Having parted company with Seagram many years ago, it formed joint ventures with Deutz for sparkling winemaking and Cordier with its Church Road winery offshoot. As one might expect, the wines are invariably well crafted right across the range, even if most attention falls on its Marlborough Sauvignon Blanc. It has recently decided to tackle the difficult Australian market in earnest, and deserves to succeed.

Montana Sauvignon Blanc

This was the first wine to focus attention on the extraordinarily symbiotic relationship between Marlborough and Sauvignon Blanc. Right from the outset, it has been made in a no-frills fashion, using free-run juice, and simple stainless steel tank fermentation at low temperatures. The price has always been ultra-competitive, and the best vintages have shown a remarkable capacity to age gracefully in bottle, even if the wines do pass through a typically dumb phase after they lose their initial bright fresh fruit, before emerging three or four years later as mature wines.

🍷🍷🍷🍷 **1997** Light green-yellow; crystal clear, razor-sharp varietal fruit on both the bouquet and palate, with a mixture of herb, mineral, capsicum and gooseberry running throughout, and that long, crisp, cleansing finish. Not complex, not concentrated but great value. **rating:** 85

➾ **best drinking** 1998 – 1999 **best vintages** '80, '81, '84, '85, '88, '89, '91, '94, '97 **drink with** Shellfish • $12

Montana Marlborough Reserve Vineyard Selection Sauvignon Blanc

First made in 1996; the name may be more of a mouthful than the wine, but the idea was (and is) to produce a richer, riper style (with higher alcohol) than the cheaper varietal stablemate. As the long name implies, achieved by careful vineyard block selection of the best parcels of fruit. Given the enormous resources available to Montana, and the ever-increasing competition which has long since knocked its varietal wine from the top of the tree, a sensible move. The '97 was the runner up in the Best Lighter Bodied Dry White section of the 1998 Sydney International Wine Competition.

🍷🍷🍷🍷🍷 **1997** Light to medium yellow-green; a clean, crisp and fresh bouquet with classic asparagus, capsicum and gooseberry aromas of medium to full intensity. The palate is spotlessly clean and direct in its impact with a mix of minerally, toasty and riper fruit characters.

rating: 90

⇨ **best drinking** 1998 – 1999 **best vintages** NA **drink with** Asparagus • $17

Montana Saints Marlborough Sauvignon Blanc

The Saints range of wines is a relatively new introduction into the Montana portfolio, pitched towards the upper end of the market. The grapes come from the Brancott Estate in the Wairau Valley and 10% of the wine was fermented in new Demptos American oak barriques, the remainder being cold fermented in stainless steel.

🍷🍷🍷🍷🍷 **1997** Light yellow-green; a wine with an altogether softer profile, rounded and complexed by the touch of barrel fermentation which comes through ever so gently. The palate is equally carefully and cleverly constructed, with a gentle touch of passionfruit, and the oak barely perceptible. Extremely successful winemaking. **rating:** 90

⇨ **best drinking** 1998 – 1999 **best vintages** '96, '97 **drink with** Seafood • $16.95

Montana Saints Gisborne Chardonnay

As will be perfectly evident, I have problems with the oak handling in several of the Montana Chardonnays (including Ormond Estate, for the record) but have no such problem with this wine. A modestly priced wine which showed particularly well in a number of tastings in Australia and New Zealand late in 1997.

🍷🍷🍷🍷🍷 **1996** Medium yellow-green; the bouquet is clean, of medium intensity, smooth and not particularly complex, but with nicely balanced melon and cashew fruit and oak. The palate has good attack and length, with nice citrus melon fruit, and length to the finish. **rating:** 90

⇨ **best drinking** 1998 – 1999 **best vintages** NA **drink with** Herb and fetta cheese in filo pastry • $16.95

morton estate ★★★★

State Highway 2, RD2, Kati Kati **region** Waikato and Bay of Plenty

phone (07) 552 0795 **fax** (07) 552 0651 **open** 7 days 10.30–5

winemaker Steve Bird **production** 90 000 **est.** 1982

product range ($9.50–28.00 CD) At the top end is the Black Label range of Chardonnay, Pinot Noir, Merlot, Late Harvest Chardonnay and Méthode Champenoise; next is the White Label range of Chardonnay, Sauvignon Blanc and Cabernet Merlot (all Hawke's Bay); then follows the Stone Creek range of Riesling, Sauvignon Blanc and Chardonnay; and the budget-priced Mill Road range of Chardonnay, Sauvignon Blanc, Dry White, Müller Thurgau, Dry Red and Cabernet Merlot, with Boars Leap Dry White bringing up the rear.

summary Now owned by John Coney, with Steve Bird in charge of winemaking, long-term winemaker John Hancock having left to head up his new Hawke's Bay winery. It will be interesting to watch the development of wine style; it seems probable that the more restrained approach of recent years will continue.

Morton Estate White Label Hawke's Bay Chardonnay

The style of this wine has oscillated wildly over the years, as has the quality. However, a core of ripe fruit (from Morton's River View Vineyard) and richness is a common thread.

🍷🍷🍷🍷 **1998** Medium yellow-green; a rich and complex bouquet with ripe citrus and melon fruit and sweet oak leads into a richly flavoured palate with abundant white peach fruit, almost to the point of sweet canned fruit, and subtle oak on the close. **rating:** 87

➾ **best drinking** 1998 – 1999 **best vintages** NA **drink with** Braised neck of pork • $17

morworth estate NR

Shands Road, Christchurch **region** Canterbury
phone (03) 349 5014 **fax** (03) 349 4419 **open** By appointment
winemaker Dayne Sherwood **production** 4000 **est.** 1995
product range ($9–17 CD) Riesling, Breidecker, Pinot Noir.
summary Leonie and Chris Morkane have established 9 hectares of vines on the outskirts of Christchurch, with a total of 2 hectares of pinot gris, chardonnay and gewurztraminer to provide their first vintage in 1999, thereby expanding the range of wines on offer.

mount linton wine company NR

Hammerichs Road, Rapaura, Blenheim **region** Marlborough
phone (03) 572 9911 **fax** (03) 572 9486 **open** Not
winemaker Tim Macfarlane **production** 2000 **est.** 1992
product range ($16–19 R) Sauvignon Blanc, Chardonnay.
summary A small and new entrant in Marlborough, employing contract-winemaking of a portion of estate-grown grapes (10 hectares chardonnay and 5 hectares sauvignon blanc) produced on a tiny part of a very large and long-established pastoral business owned by the Macfarlane family.

mount riley NR

Renwick Road, Blenheim **region** Marlborough
phone (09) 486 0286 **fax** (09) 486 0643 **open** By appointment
winemaker Allan Scott (Contract) **production** 10 000 **est.** 1995
product range ($13.00–15.10 R) Sauvignon Blanc, Chardonnay, Cabernet Merlot.
summary Mount Riley is a joint venture between Auckland-based businessmen and wine enthusiasts Steve Hotchin and John Buchanan, and Marlborough vigneron and winemaker Allan Scott. Mount Riley owns three vineyards in the Wairau Valley, and has developed a fourth vineyard in Seventeen Valley, 10 kilometres south of Blenheim planted to clonally selected pinot noir. In all, Mount Riley owns 42 hectares of vineyards, and is in no sense a second label of Allan Scott, even though it shares winemakers and wine facilities with Allan Scott Wines.

Mount Riley Sauvignon Blanc

Made in a classically uncomplicated fashion, night-harvested by machine and cold-fermented in stainless steel at low temperatures for three weeks. Both at juice and wine stage minimal intervention and maximum fruit protection pays handsome dividends.

🍷🍷🍷🍷 **1997** Light to medium yellow-green; an intense, classic Marlborough fruit profile, with a mix of capsicum, redcurrant and gooseberry aromas; the palate is similarly fresh and pure, with all of the flavours promised by the bouquet. A wine which has weight, length and good acidity. **rating:** 89

➾ **best drinking** 1998 – 1999 **best vintages** NA **drink with** Clams • $13

mountford vineyard NR

434 Omihi Road, Waipara, North Canterbury **region** Canterbury
phone (03) 314 6819 **fax** (03) 314 6819 **open** By appointment
winemaker Daniel Schuster (Consultant) **production** 300 **est.** 1990
product range Chardonnay, Pinot Noir.
summary Michael and Buffy Eaton have established 4 hectares of vines on an east-facing slope of the Waipara Valley, producing the first tiny vintage in 1996 and scheduled to come into full production by 1999. They already offer bed and breakfast accommodation and a restaurant, with a winery which was due to be constructed in time for the 1998 vintage. In the meantime, local Pinot Noir doyen Danny Schuster is making the wine for the Eatons.

moutere hills vineyard ★★★☆

Sunrise Valley, RD1, Upper Moutere, Nelson **region** Nelson
phone (03) 543 2288 **fax** (03) 543 2288 **open** October–Easter 11–5
winemaker Simon Thomas **production** 1200 **est.** 1996
product range ($13.50–20 CD) Nelson Riesling, Barrique Fermented Sauvignon Blanc, Chardonnay, Sunrise Valley Red (Rosé), Merlot, Cabernet Merlot.
summary Moutere Hills winery was established in an old shearing shed by owners Simon and Alison Thomas. Overlooking the Moutere Valley, it draws upon 1.5 hectares of estate vineyards supplemented by small quantities of grapes purchased from local growers. Wines are available by the glass matched by light meals.

Moutere Hills Nelson Riesling

Made from contract-grown grapes sourced from the Waimea Plains in the Richmond subdistrict. A silver medal in 1997 at the Christchurch Wine Show.

🍷🍷🍷🍷 **1997** Medium yellow-green; there is a range of aromas running from minerally to spicy, with faintly dusty overtones, but which are clean and show no botrytis influence. The wine has considerable mouthfeel and weight, with the intelligent use of residual sugar to give an almost creamy feel, without compromising the balance. **rating:** 85

➾ **best drinking** 1998 – 2000 **best vintages** NA **drink with** Scallops and ginger • $14.50

mud house

Conders Bend Road, Renwick, Marlborough **region** Marlborough
phone (03) 572 9490 **fax** (03) 572 9491 **open** By appointment
winemaker Simon Waghorn **production** 3900 **est.** 1993
product range ($15.95–31 CD) Sauvignon Blanc, Chardonnay, Pinot Noir offered both under the Le Grys and Mud House labels.

summary Mud House marks the end of an odyssey dating back to 1066; Jennifer Joslin's family name (Le Grys) dates back to that time, and the Marlborough vineyard was purchased by John and Jennifer Joslin at the end of a six-year sailing trip around the world. A mudbrick guesthouse built in 1995 is ultimately to be followed by a mudbrick tasting room and cellar.

mudbrick vineyard NR

Church Bay Road, Oneroa, Waiheke Island **region** Waiheke Island
phone (09) 372 9050 **fax** (09) 372 9052 **open** 7 days 10–6 summer, Fri-Sun 10–6 winter
winemaker Aran Knight **production** 200 **est.** 1996
product range ($25–35 CD) Chardonnay, Cabernet Sauvignon Merlot Malbec Cabernet Franc, Croll Vineyard Cabernet Syrah.
summary The metamorphosis from accountancy to winemaking and restaurateurs/hoteliers is about as radical as they come, but Nick and Robyn Jones have accomplished it. Their 4-hectare vineyard, planted to cabernet sauvignon, merlot, malbec, cabernet franc, shiraz and a little chardonnay, is still coming into production, but the restaurant and accommodation are fully operational.

muirlea rise

50 Princess Street, Martinborough **region** Wairarapa
phone (06) 306 9332 **open** Not
winemaker Willy Brown **production** 700 **est.** 1991
product range Pinot Noir, Justa Red, Apres Wine Liqueur, Sibbald (Rhône-style Cabernet Sauvignon).
summary Former Auckland wine distributor Willy Brown has established a 1.9-hectare vineyard. Since the first wine release of a 1991 Pinot Noir, the accent has remained on that variety, but with an extraordinarily eclectic gaggle of other wines which are decidedly left-of-centre in style, and for that matter, quality.

murdoch james estate ★★★★

c/o Barbara Turner, 15 Cologne Street, Martinborough **region** Wairarapa
phone (06) 306 9193 **fax** (06) 306 9120 **open** Not
winemaker Oliver Masters (Contract) **production** 500 **est.** 1986
product range ($22–33 CD) Pinot Noir, Shiraz.
summary The origin of Murdoch James Estate goes back to 1986 when Roger and Jill Fraser planted 2.5 hectares of shiraz and pinot noir. The Frasers' plans were interrupted in 1989 when Roger was transferred to Melbourne by his employer, and the decision was made to sell the grapes rather than make wine. In 1993 a limited quantity was contract-made at Ata Rangi, and each year since that time around 180 cases of Pinot Noir have been made annually, and will be made until 2003. Tiny quantities of Shiraz are also made each year.

Murdoch James Estate Pinot Noir

The first vintage (of 200 cases) from 1993 won a gold medal at the 1995 Easter Show, and succeeding vintages have done even better. The Wairarapa climate, skilled viticulture and skilled winemaking do the rest.

🍷🍷🍷🍷🍷 **1996** Medium red-purple; generous cherry and plum fruit aromas as complexed by touches of spice and subtle oak on the bouquet. A stylish wine with very good weight and balance, finishing with attractive, soft fruit, and almost milky oak tannins. **rating:** 93

➾ **best drinking** 1998 – 2000 **best vintages** NA **drink with** Venison • $33

nautilus wines ★★★★

Bucks Road, Renwick, Marlborough **region** Marlborough
phone (09) 366 1140 **fax** (09) 366 1141 **open** 7 days 10.30–4.30
winemaker Matt Harrop **production** 50 000 **est.** 1986
product range ($10–30 R) Chardonnay, Sauvignon, Cabernet Sauvignon Merlot, Cuvée Marlborough Brut; Twin Islands is the second label, sold only in New Zealand; also Half Moon Bay Sauvignon Blanc.
summary Nautilus is ultimately owned by Yalumba of Australia. Until 1996 the wines were made by Yalumba winemaker Alan Hoey at Matua Valley, but from that vintage most will be made at Rapaura Vintners (of which Nautilus is now a part-owner) under the direction of former Brokenwood (Australia) winemaker Matt Harrop. Draws both upon estate vineyards (7 hectares at Renwick, 10 hectares at the Awatere River), and contract-grown grapes.

Nautilus Marlborough Sauvignon

Sauvignon Blanc was the first wine to be released under the striking and beautiful Nautilus label, and remains the most important wine in terms of quantity; invariably clearly defined. Principally made from vineyards situated in the Awatere Valley, the remainder from two vineyards in the Wairau Valley.

🍷🍷🍷🍷 **1997** Very light green-yellow; an incredibly voluminous and aromatic bouquet with striking passionfruit aromas is followed by a fresh, clean and almost delicate palate. The flavours do track the bouquet, but (happily) are less intense. Well-balanced acidity; the finish is bone-dry. **rating:** 87

➾ **best drinking** 1998 – 1999 **best vintages** '89, '90, '91, '94 **drink with** Crayfish • $17

Nautilus Reserve Chardonnay

As the name suggests, a vineyard selection of the very best fruit available, and given top-end oak treatment.

🍷🍷🍷🍷 **1996** Medium yellow-green; sophisticated spicy oak is woven through melon and white peach fruit on both bouquet and palate. There is lots of flavour and intensity here, with crisp acidity giving the promise of reasonable longevity. **rating:** 89

➾ **best drinking** 1998 – 2002 **best vintages** NA **drink with** Fresh salmon • $24

neudorf vineyards ★★★★★

Neudorf Road, Upper Moutere, Nelson **region** Nelson
phone (03) 543 2643 **fax** (03) 543 2955 **open** 7 days 10–5 Nov–Easter
winemaker Tim Finn **production** 6000 **est.** 1978
product range ($16–35 CD) The Moutere label is reserved for estate-grown wines, notably Chardonnay and Pinot Noir; Nelson typically indicates a mix of estate-grown and locally purchased grapes from the Nelson region; the second label is Neudorf Village. Wines encompass Chardonnay, Sauvignon Blanc, Semillon, Riesling, Pinot Noir and Cabernet Sauvignon.

summary Tim Finn has produced some of Australasia's most stunningly complex and rich Chardonnays, outstanding in any class. But his skills do not stop there, spanning all varieties, which are consistently of show medal standard.

Neudorf Riesling

Tim Finn creeps up on you with his Riesling, made in tiny quantities from 2 acres of close-planted estate vineyards. Different in style from the Marlborough Rieslings, as one would expect, but out of the same basic family.

🍷🍷🍷🍷🍷 **1997** Light green-yellow; the bouquet is initially quite tight and crisp, but the mineral, herb and lime aromas build in intensity as you go back to the wine. The palate is typically tight, crisp and minerally, with some lime flavours; an absolute certainty for the cellar. **rating:** 90

➭ **best drinking** 2001 – 2005 **best vintages** '91, '93, '94, '97 **drink with** Marinated grilled octopus • $16

Neudorf Sauvignon Blanc

After the odd peregrination, has settled back to Nelson (and a predominantly estate-grown) base. Eighty per cent of the wine is stainless steel fermented; 20% barrel-fermented in old French oak.

🍷🍷🍷🍷🍷 **1997** Medium yellow-green; a richly textured bouquet with a subtle hint of oak and sweet fruit running from conventional aromas into nectarine, but without any flabbiness. The palate, likewise, is rich and fleshy yet not heavy; even the most hardened opponent of Sauvignon Blanc could not fail to enjoy this wine, particularly when you arrive to the richly textured back palate and finish. **rating:** 93

➭ **best drinking** 1998 – 2000 **best vintages** '89, '91, '94, '97 **drink with** Shellfish • $17.30

Neudorf Moutere Chardonnay

Tim Finn has mastered the temperamental Nelson climate, producing consistently rich and opulent Chardonnays of quite exceptional complexity. Part of the answer lies in the non-irrigated vineyard, which is planted on Moutere clays, interspersed with layers of gravel. Part lies in the skilled use of barrel fermentation (50% new oak), malolactic fermentation and extended lees contact.

🍷🍷🍷🍷🍷 **1996** Medium yellow-green; the bouquet is at once more complex yet more reserved and tighter than the Neudorf Nelson Chardonnay of the same vintage; a marvellously elegant wine on the palate, complex yet restrained, with faultless integration of oak and equally faultless fruit and oak balance. Cashew/melon flavours linger on a long finish. **rating:** 94

➭ **best drinking** 1997 – 2001 **best vintages** '87, '89, '91, '92, '93, '94, '96 **drink with** Veal, pasta • $35

Neudorf Moutere Pinot Noir

If Chardonnay presents a challenge in the Nelson climate, Pinot Noir presents an even greater one – the relatively high summer rainfall poses particular difficulties. The contrast between the '91, '92, '93 and '94 vintages shows how big an impact vintage plays, for these are all quite different wines in style, the '91 muscular, the '92 fragrant and cherry-accented, the '93 spicy, the '94 powerful and plummy. The '96 has echoes of the '92.

ŸŸŸŸ **1996** Medium to full red-purple; the bouquet is complex and stylish, with a mix of strawberry and more stemmy fruit backed by subtle oak. A multiflavoured wine on the palate, in an earthy forest-floor style, fractionally hard on the finish. **rating:** 85

➾ **best drinking** 1997 – 1998 **best vintages** '83, '90, '91, '92, '94 **drink with** New Zealand venison • $28

newton forrest estate NR

Cnr State Highway 50 and Gimblett Road, Hawke's Bay **region** Hawke's Bay
phone (06) 879 4416 **fax** (06) 876 6020 **open** Not
winemaker John Forrest (Contract) **production** 1200 **est.** 1988
product range ($28 ML) Cornerstone Vineyard Cabernet Merlot.
summary Newton Forrest is a joint venture between Hawke's Bay grape grower Bob Newton and Marlborough winemaker and vigneron John Forrest of Forrest Estate. It has produced a single Cornerstone Vineyard Cabernet Merlot each year since 1994, the '95 vintage winning a gold medal at the 1997 Auckland Royal Easter Wine Show.

nga waka vineyard ★★★★

Kitchener Street, Martinborough **region** Wairarapa
phone (06) 306 9832 **fax** (06) 306 9832 **open** Weekends 10–5 while stocks last
winemaker Roger Parkinson **production** 3000 **est.** 1988
product range ($18–30 R) Riesling, Sauvignon Blanc, Chardonnay.
summary Roseworthy-trained Roger Parkinson produces the Nga Waka wines from 4 hectares of estate plantings in the heart of the Martinborough Terraces. The early promise of the vineyard came into full flower in the unlikely environment of the 1995 vintage with the performance of the 1995 Sauvignon Blanc at the Air New Zealand Wine Awards of that year. Subsequent vintages have been good, but not quite so exciting as the '95.

Nga Waka Sauvignon Blanc

A most interesting wine with a strong regional identity, recalling the Sauvignon Blancs of Palliser Estate and Martinborough Vineyards. Sensibly, made without the use or intervention of oak. Leapt to national prominence when it was the only '95 vintage white to win a gold medal at the 1995 Air New Zealand Wine Awards, also winning the trophy for Champion Sauvignon Blanc. The '96 was a very full-flavoured wine, rich and tropical, but somewhat controversial, the '97 conventional.

ŸŸŸŸ **1997** Light yellow-green; the bouquet shows nicely ripened and balanced fruit with a mix of gooseberry, passionfruit and herbal aromas. The palate opens with gooseberry fruit, then moves on to a lighter, crisper finish. **rating:** 89

➾ **best drinking** 1998 – 1999 **best vintages** '94, '95 **drink with** Seafood pasta • $22

Nga Waka Chardonnay

Produced from estate-grown grapes, which have been particularly sensitively handled. Barrel-fermented (35% new oak barriques) with 30% taken through malolactic fermentation and given prolonged yeast lees ageing.

ŸŸŸŸY **1996** Medium yellow-green; attractive melon, nectarine and stone fruit aromas are balanced by high-quality but not overly assertive French oak. Altogether an elegant wine on the palate, well balanced and harmonious, with a long finish. **rating:** 90

➾ **best drinking** 1998 – 2000 **best vintages** NA **drink with** Poached salmon • $30

ngatarawa wines ★★★★

Ngatarawa Road, Bridge Pa, RD5, Hastings **region** Hawke's Bay
phone (06) 879 7603 **fax** (06) 879 6675 **open** 7 days 11–5
winemaker Alwyn Corban **production** 30 000 **est.** 1981
product range ($10–60 R) The top wines under the Glazebrook label include Chardonnay and Cabernet Merlot; the lesser-priced Stables range comprises Chardonnay, Sauvignon Blanc, Classic White, and Cabernet Merlot. Also Alwyn Noble Bofrytis.
summary Alwyn Corban is a highly qualified and highly intelligent winemaker from a famous New Zealand wine family, who has elected to grow vines organically and make wines which sometimes (but certainly not always) fall outside the mainstream. Challenging and interesting, and not to be taken lightly.

Ngatarawa Stables Sauvignon Blanc

In 1996 (and again in 1997) Alwyn Corban aged the Stables Sauvignon Blanc in seasoned oak puncheons for two months to add textural and structural complexity to the wine. For the prior decade it had simply been fermented in stainless steel and early bottled. Like all of Corban's wines, restrained, with the accent on secondary characters.

🍷🍷🍷🍷 **1997** Light to medium yellow-green; there is some oak influence evident on the bouquet, but far from dominant, with pleasantly tangy fruit. The palate is complex, with unusual touches of peach and guava together with some nutty characters; well structured, good acidity. **rating:** 85

⇨ **best drinking** 1998 – 2000 **best vintages** NA **drink with** Avocado salad • NA

Ngatarawa Glazebrook Chardonnay

Estate-grown, hand-picked grapes are barrel-fermented in 100% new French oak, with extended time on yeast lees. Eighty per cent of the wine is taken through malolactic fermentation. The aim of Alwyn Corban is to take the wine into secondary flavours and textures, and he succeeds admirably in his aim.

🍷🍷🍷🍷 **1996** Medium yellow-green; a typically complex, rich and toasty bouquet with hazelnut and cashew aromas, the palate likewise predominantly running through the nutty/cashew/creamy/toasty spectrum. Strongly styled and well balanced, though not effusive in terms of varietal fruit. **rating:** 86

⇨ **best drinking** 1998 – 2002 **best vintages** NA **drink with** Smoked salmon • $26

Ngatarawa Alwyn Noble Harvest

Not made every year, but when it is made and when conditions are right, scales the ultimate heights. The grapes are allowed to hang on the vines for long after normal harvest, with a mix of botrytis and raisining lifting the sugar levels over 40 degrees brix. Unusually, the wine is barrel-fermented and held in oak for 18 months, yet shows no sign either of oak or oxidation. Some of the great German botrytis wines are made this way, but relatively few in the New World.

🍷🍷🍷🍷🍷 **1996** Glowing yellow-green; the intensely perfumed bouquet has aromas of cumquat, peach, lime and honey, the palate offering some orange and lime peel flavours as well. Balanced acidity in a classy wine. **rating:** 92

⇨ **best drinking** 2000 – 2004 **best vintages** '92, '94, '96 **drink with** Dappled sunlight • $30

Ngatarawa Glazebrook Cabernet Merlot

A blend of 65% Cabernet Sauvignon and 35% Merlot, which spends 15 months in new oak, 80% new. The fruit power absolutely swallows up that oak, which is not the least intrusive.

🍷🍷🍷🍷 **1996** Bright red-purple; the bouquet is clean, with earthy Cabernet varietal fruit aromas to the fore. The palate is typically restrained, with earthy Cabernet, a touch of briar and forest; the oak is just there, giving some vanilla cedar hints; finishes with balanced tannins. **rating:** 86

➾ **best drinking** 2000 – 2006 **best vintages** '90, '91, '95, '96 **drink with** Rib of veal • $26

nobilo ★★★★

Station Road, Huapai **region** Kumeu and Huapai
phone (09) 412 9148 **fax** (09) 412 7124 **open** Mon-Fri 9–5, Sat 10–5, Sun 11–4
winemaker Greg Foster, Russell Wiggins **production** 300 000 **est.** 1943
product range ($7.95–29.00 R) Marlborough Sauvignon Blanc, Gewurztraminer, Chardonnay and Cabernet Sauvignon; Poverty Bay Chardonnay; Müller Thurgau, White Cloud, Huapai Pinotage and Hawke's Bay Cabernet. More recently (in 1996 and 1997) the Fall Harvest (low price), Icon (mid-price) and Grand Reserve (high price) varietal ranges have been introduced.
summary One of the more energetic and effective wine marketers, with production heavily focused on white wines sourced from Gisborne, Hawke's Bay and Marlborough. A long-time exponent of flamboyant label and packaging redesign, but the quality of the top-of-the-range Grand Reserve wines leaves nothing to be desired.

Nobilo Icon Gewurztraminer

Showed extremely well at the 1997 Sydney International Wine Competition, perfectly made and with all the varietal character one could wish for. Produced from Marlborough grapes, and shows the clearest possible varietal character.

🍷🍷🍷🍷 **1997** Light to medium yellow-green; the bouquet is clean, with generous spice, lychee and apple blossom aromas; the palate crisp and clean, and not quite as intense as the bouquet, but helped by a touch of residual sugar on the finish. **rating:** 85

➾ **best drinking** 1998 – 1999 **best vintages** NA **drink with** Asian food • $18.95

Nobilo Grand Reserve Sauvignon Blanc

The grapes come from a single vineyard in the Awatere Valley in Marlborough. 1996 was not only the first vintage of this flagship wine, but – amazingly – was the first crop from the vineyard. The wine was whole-bunch pressed and then fermented in a mix of French and German oak, thereafter spending nine months on gross lees in barrel. Forty per cent of the wine underwent malolactic fermentation. How such a seemingly heavy-handed approach could produce such a wine as this, particularly from a first crop, is beyond my comprehension, but no one could quibble with the result.

🍷🍷🍷🍷🍷 **1996** Medium yellow-green; the bouquet is complex, with the barrel-ferment and malolactic-ferment components quite evident, yet miraculously restrained and subtle. The palate has marvellous flavour, complexity and structure, with passionfruit and spice running through a long and never heavy finish. Perhaps the relatively high acidity (over 9 grams per litre) is part of the secret. **rating:** 94

➾ **best drinking** 1998 – 1999 **best vintages** '96 **drink with** Japanese seafood • $20

Nobilo Icon Sauvignon Blanc

Marlborough-grown, and the top of the tree of the unoaked style for Nobilo.

🍷🍷🍷🍷🍸 **1997** Light to medium yellow-green; the bouquet is spotlessly clean, and equally precise varietal fruit in a gooseberry and passionfruit mode. The palate has good length, and once again perfect definition of varietal fruit with tangy gooseberry flavours; well-balanced acidity. **rating:** 90

➾ **best drinking** 1998 – 1999 **best vintages** '97 **drink with** Steamed crab with black bean sauce • $15

Nobilo Grand Reserve Chardonnay

Composed of equal portions of Gisborne and Marlborough Chardonnay, all Mendoza clone. Both portions utilised indigenous yeast; the Marlborough Chardonnay was pressed straight into new French oak, while the Gisborne portion was given brief skin contact before being fermented in new American oak. All of the wine went through malolactic fermentation, and was given prolonged lees contact for nine months. As with the Grand Reserve Sauvignon Blanc, what can only be described as a spectacular result.

🍷🍷🍷🍷🍷 **1996** Medium yellow-green; not surprisingly, spicy barrel-ferment oak characters are immediately obvious on the bouquet, but there is excellent melon, grapefruit and fig fruit there too. On the palate, a modern, fresh and lively wine showing the ultra-sophisticated use of oak, with its spicy nutmeg overtones, yet allowing the white peach, melon and cashew-accented fruit to shine through. **rating:** 94

➾ **best drinking** 1998 – 1999 **best vintages** '94 **drink with** Coloubiac of salmon • $29

Nobilo Icon Chardonnay

Not, as one might expect, the ultimate Chardonnay statement from Nobilo, but positioned well under the Grand Reserve. Like the Grand Reserve, a blend of Marlborough and Gisborne fruit; the major part was barrel-fermented, part steel-fermented and 70% underwent malolactic fermentation.

🍷🍷🍷🍷 **1996** Medium yellow-green; the bouquet is complex, with the barrel-fermentation and malolactic-fermentation inputs obvious but not killing the fruit. On the palate, strong winemaker thumbprints appear all over a highly structured wine, which is almost Californian in style. **rating:** 89

➾ **best drinking** 1998 – 1999 **best vintages** NA **drink with** Chicken yakitori • $20

---

obsidian NR

PO Box 345, Waiheke Island **region** Waiheke Island
phone (09) 372 6100 **fax** (09) 372 6100 **open** Not
winemaker Kim Crawford **production** 600 **est.** 1993
product range ($30 R) A single red wine made from 65% Cabernet Sauvignon, 25% Merlot and small quantities of other Bordeaux reds.
summary Although still in its infancy (the first vintage was 1997) destined to be an important part of the Waiheke Island scene. A partnership between Andrew Hendy, owner of Coopers Creek, winemaker Kim Crawford and businessman Lindsay Spilman, it brings together the formidable winemaking skills of Crawford and the largest (10-hectare) vineyard on Waiheke Island, established in a natural amphitheatre.

odyssey wines NR

32 Henderson Valley Road, Henderson **region** Henderson
phone (09) 309 1969 **fax** (09) 309 1969 **open** Not
winemaker Rebecca Salmond **production** 1500 **est.** 1994
product range ($13.95–16.95 R) Hawke's Bay Sauvignon Blanc, Gisborne Chardonnay, Reserve Gisborne Chardonnay, Cabernet Merlot, Reserve Kumeu Cabernet Sauvignon.
summary Rebecca Salmond is winemaker for Pleasant Valley, and makes the wines for her Odyssey brand at that facility. There are no cellar-door sales; the wines are sold via retail and mail order.

ohinemuri estate NR

Moresby Street, Karangahake **region** Waikato and Bay of Plenty
phone (07) 862 8874 **fax** (07) 862 8847 **open** 7 days 10–6
winemaker Horst Hillerich **production** 1000 **est.** 1989
product range ($14.50–19.50 CD) Chardonnay, Classique (Chenin Blanc Chardonnay blend), Gewurztraminer, Riesling, Sauvignon Blanc, Pinotage.
summary German-born, trained and qualified winemaker Horst Hillerich came to New Zealand in 1987, first working at Totara before establishing Ohinemuri Estate. An atmospheric restaurant was duly opened at the newly constructed winery in the Karangahake Gorge in 1993; Hillerich has produced some highly regarded Gewurztraminer and Sauvignon Blanc. All of the grapes, incidentally, are purchased from growers in Hawke's Bay, The Waikato and Gisborne.

okahu estate NR

Okahu Road, Kaitaia **region** Northland and Matakana
phone (09) 408 2066 **fax** (09) 408 2686 **open** 7 days 10–6 summer, weekends 10–6 winter
winemaker Monty Knight **production** 2400 **est.** 1984
product range ($12.95–22.95 CD) 90 Mile White and Red; Clifton Chardonnay, Montgomery Chardonnay, Riesling, Te Hana Pinot Noir, Kaz Shiraz, Old Brother John's Tawny Port.
summary The 90 Mile wines (respectively blends of Chardonnay, Semillon and Arnsburger, and Cabernet Merlot, Pinotage and Pinot Noir) signal the location of Okahu Estate at the bottom end of the 90 Mile Beach. Recently the focus of the estate plantings of 2.5 hectares has switched to semillon and shiraz, which are said to show considerable promise; the other wines are made from grapes purchased from other regions.

olssen's of bannockburn NR

Olsen's Garden Vineyard, 306 Felton Road, Bannockburn, Central Otago **region** Otago
phone (03) 445 1716 **fax** (03) 445 0050 **open** 7 days 10–5
winemaker Duncan Forsythe **production** 5000 **est.** 1989
product range ($17–26.50 CD) Riesling, Gewurztraminer, Sauvignon Blanc, Chardonnay, Pinot Noir.
summary Heather McPherson and John Olssen began the establishment of their 10-hectare vineyard (and now 5 hectares of rural garden and outdoor eating sites) in 1989. For the first three years after the vineyard came into bearing the grapes were sold to Chard Farm, but in 1997 the first wines were made under the Olssens of Bannockburn label. A new but substantial enterprise in the Central Otago scene.

omaka springs estate NR

Kennedys Road, RD2, Blenheim, Marlborough **region** Marlborough
phone (03) 572 9933 **fax** (03) 572 9934 **open** 7 days 12–5
winemaker Ian Marchant **production** 12 500 **est.** 1992
product range ($7.99–15.99 R) Riesling, Semillon, Sauvignon Blanc, Chardonnay, Cabernet Merlot.
summary Omaka Springs is a substantial operation, with a state-of-the-art winery built at the end of 1994 capable of handling up to 20 000 cases of wine, and drawing upon 38 hectares of estate vineyards. The winery also processes the fruit from 10 hectares of olive trees transplanted from Ruby Bay, Nelson, in 1992. While wine quality is not exhilarating, the wines are well priced, and offer excellent value for money.

Omaka Springs Sauvignon Blanc

Made in mainstream Marlborough-style, unoaked but with up to 12% Semillon incorporated to give a little more complexity and depth.

🍷🍷🍷🍷 **1997** Light to medium yellow-green; a fresh and quite aromatic palate with a mix of light gooseberry, passionfruit and peach aromas is followed by a delicate yet flavoursome palate with slightly atypical but enjoyable white peach tastes to go with the more traditional gooseberry and passionfruit. A considerable step up from the pleasant but light '96. **rating:** 88

⇨ **best drinking** 1998 – 1999 **best vintages** '94, '97 **drink with** Sautéed scallops • $11.90

---

omarama vineyard NR

Omarama Avenue, Omarama, North Otago **region** Otago
phone (03) 438 9708 **fax** (03) 438 9708 **open** Summer 11–9, winter 11–6
winemaker Mike Wolter **production** NA **est.** 1991
product range Pinot Gris, Muscat, Müller Thurgau.
summary All of the output of Omarama Vineyard is sold through the cellar door and, more particularly, through the vineyard's wine bar and café.

opihi vineyard NR

Gould's Road, Opihi, Pleasant Point, South Canterbury **region** Canterbury
phone (03) 614 7232 **fax** (03) 614 7234 **open** By appointment
winemaker Tony Coakley (Contract) **production** 180 **est.** 1991
product range ($9.50–12.50 CD) Riesling, Müller Thurgau, Chardonnay, Breidecker, Pinot Noir.
summary Plantings at Opihi Vineyard commenced in 1991 with half a hectare each of müller thurgau, riesling, pinot noir and chardonnay, followed the next year by 2.5 hectares of pinot gris. The vineyard is established on a north-facing slope of Timaru clay loam with superb views across to the snow-clad Two Thumb Range. The tiny production is chiefly sold by mail order, with limited South Canterbury regional distribution.

pacific vineyards ★★★

90 McLeod Road, Henderson **region** Henderson
phone (09) 838 9578 **fax** (09) 838 9578 **open** Mon-Sat 9–6
winemaker Steve Tubic **production** 10 000 **est.** 1936

product range ($13–18 CD) Under the Phoenix label comes Gisborne Gewurztraminer, Marlborough Riesling, Marlborough Sauvignon Blanc, Gisborne Chardonnay, Merlot, Cabernet Sauvignon; also Quail Farm Gisborne Chardonnay and Cabernet Sauvignon.
summary One of the more interesting New Zealand wineries, notwithstanding its low profile, which has at various times produced very large quantities of wine (sold in cask and bulk) but is now refocusing on its bottled wine production (in more limited quantities) utilising grapes from Hawke's Bay and Gisborne, and on the other side of the fence has ventured into beer brewing.

palliser estate ★★★★☆

Kitchener Street, Martinborough **region** Wairarapa
phone (06) 306 9019 **fax** (06) 306 9946 **open** 7 days 10–6
winemaker Allan Johnson **production** 20 000 **est.** 1989
product range ($18–32 CD) Chardonnay, Sauvignon Blanc, Riesling, Late Harvest Riesling, Rosé of Pinot, Pinot Noir; Palliser Bay Admiral's Dry Red is second label.
summary Palliser Estate has produced a series of highly regarded and highly awarded wines from its state-of-the-art winery right from its first vintage in 1989, and which has grown rapidly in recent years. My tasting notes indicate high scores across the full range of the wines produced with the perfumed silky Pinot Noir to the fore.

Palliser Estate Riesling

Produced both as a dry Riesling (as in this case) with occasional delectable late-harvest, botrytised versions. The '93 was the top gold medal winner in its class at the 1994 National Wine Show of Australia in Canberra, outpointing all of the leading Australian Rieslings (as well as numerous New Zealand contenders). The '96 won a gold medal at the Air New Zealand Wine Awards.

🍷🍷🍷🍷🍷 **1996** Bright, intense green-yellow; that intensity is picked up on the bouquet with powerful lime pastille varietal fruit aromas. The palate is more delicate than the bouquet suggests, which is in fact no bad thing; similar flavours are there, but are cut and balanced by slightly minerally characters. **rating:** 93

🍷🍷🍷🍷🍷 **1997** Medium yellow-green; an intensely fragrant bouquet with a mix of passionfruit, lime and peach aromas introduces a long palate, with intense fruit balanced by a slightly minerally grip to the finish. Top-flight wine. **rating:** 90

➡ **best drinking** 2000 – 2005 **best vintages** '93, '96, '97 **drink with** Lightly poached asparagus • $18

Palliser Estate Sauvignon Blanc

The Wellington/Wairarapa region seems to produce excellent Sauvignon Blanc year in, year out, a capacity underlined by the success the region has had in the annual Air New Zealand Wine Awards. Palliser Estate has been one of the most consistent and impressive performers.

🍷🍷🍷🍷🍷 **1997** Light yellow-green; the bouquet is crisp, clean and light, but with a range of fruit characters running from herbal/capsicum through to passionfruit. The palate is clean and lively, again showing a faint grassy cut to the finish, but with some sweet fruit sustaining the middle. **rating:** 90

➡ **best drinking** 1998 – 1999 **best vintages** '91, '92, '94, '95, '96, '97 **drink with** Grilled fish • $18

Palliser Estate Noble Chardonnay (375 ml)

Every now and then New Zealand bobs up with a botrytised Chardonnay; Hunter's have done so with distinction from time to time and now Palliser has done so.

🍷🍷🍷🍷 **1997** Glowing yellow-green; a super-intense bouquet with an exotic array of lime apricot and peach fruit aromas is followed by a palate which is much less powerful and intense than the bouquet. There is plenty of tasty tropical fruit, however, and the acid is relatively soft, which may please some. **rating:** 87

➭ **best drinking** 1998 – 2001 **best vintages** NA **drink with** Fruit tart • NA

Palliser Estate Pinot Noir

Often somewhat lighter than the biggest wines from Wellington/Wairarapa, but always showing bell-clear varietal character. Typically made using extended pre-fermentation cold-soak, a warm primary fermentation and then extended post-fermentation maceration. Matured for 12 months on light lees in a mix of new and older French oak casks. In 1996 the wine achieved 14.5% alcohol, which may or may not be a badge of honour.

🍷🍷🍷🍷 **1996** Medium to full red-purple; the bouquet is full and very ripe, with masses of plum and cherry varietal fruit. The palate is generous and full bodied, with the fruit flavours literally dancing on the tongue and flooding the mouth. There is the faintest echo of that over-ripe fruit character evident on the bouquet, but the wine gets away with it. **rating:** 88

➭ **best drinking** 1998 – 2001 **best vintages** '89, '91, '94, '96 **drink with** Duck risotto • $32

park estate winery NR

2087 Pakowhai Road, RD3, Napier **region** Hawke's Bay
phone (06) 844 8137 **fax** (06) 844 6800 **open** 7 days 10–5.30
winemaker Owen Park **production** 10 000 **est.** 1992
product range ($8–20 CD) Riesling, Gewurztraminer, Sauvignon Blanc, Chardonnay, Merlot, Shiraz, Cabernet Sauvignon, Muscat.
summary Owen and Dianne Park run a thriving and varied enterprise offering both fruit and grape-based wines (and 35 different types of fudge) from a large mission-style winery and restaurant. Wine production (from grapes, that is) constitutes a modest part of the business.

parker méthode champenoise NR

91 Banks Street, Gisborne **region** Gisborne
phone (06) 867 6967 **fax** (06) 867 6967 **open** 7 days 9.30–6
winemaker Phil Parker **production** 1000 **est.** 1987
product range Dry Flint, Classical Brut, Rosé Brut, Light Red.
summary A Méthode Champenoise specialist which has caused much interest and comment. Has not entered the show ring and I have not tasted the wines. The winery also has a restaurant open for lunch and dinner every day of the week.

pegasus bay ★★★★

Stockgrove Road, Waipara **region** Canterbury
phone (03) 314 6869 **fax** (03) 314 6869 **open** 7 days 10–5
winemaker Matthew Donaldson, Lynnette Hudson **production** 15 000 **est.** 1992
product range ($18–31 CD) Chardonnay, Sauvignon Blanc Semillon, Riesling, Aria, Pinot Noir, Maestro (Bordeaux-blend).

summary Leading wine-writer and wine judge Professor Ivan Donaldson (a neurologist) has, together with his wife and family, established the largest winery in Waipara, with 20 hectares of vineyards in bearing and a large and striking cathedral-like winery. Son Matthew is a Roseworthy graduate, and in every respect this is a serious operation. A winery restaurant adds to the attraction for visitors. Wine quality is consistently good, the wines with style and verve.

Pegasus Bay Sauvignon Blanc Semillon

The Sauvignon Blanc component is cold-fermented in stainless steel, the Semillon component barrel-fermented and taken through malolactic fermentation. Both components are aged separately on lees for approximately eight months before blending and bottling.

🍷🍷🍷🍷 **1996** Medium yellow-green; the bouquet is very complex, with ripe, tropical gooseberry fruit and nutty, slightly hessiany, overtones. The palate is similarly complex, with ripe tropical fruit, but treading a little heavily on the finish. **rating:** 84

⇨ **best drinking** 1998 – 2000 **best vintages** NA **drink with** Fettuccini • $22

Pegasus Bay Maestro

Notwithstanding the use of a Scott Henry trellis for this estate-grown wine, and not withstanding its 12.5% alcohol, it makes one question whether the Bordeaux varieties are as well suited to Canterbury as those of Burgundy – this notwithstanding the success of the Sauvignon Blanc Semillon blend. However, it has to be said the end result is an attractive, light-bodied wine. A blend of 60% Cabernet Sauvignon, 30% Merlot and 10% Cabernet Franc, given post-fermentation maceration.

🍷🍷🍷🍷 **1995** Medium to full red-purple; the bouquet is clean, quite intense, with sweet cassis, Ribena fruit. There is similar, attractively sweet fruit on the palate with mulberry and cassis supported by subtle oak. The tannins are soft and ripe; the wine does not taste green. **rating:** 89

⇨ **best drinking** 2000 – 2005 **best vintages** '95 **drink with** Veal • $30

peninsula estate ★★★★

52A Korora Road, Oneroa, Waiheke Island **region** Waiheke Island
phone (09) 372 7866 **fax** (09) 372 7840 **open** Weekends 1–4
winemaker Christopher Lush **production** 1400 **est.** 1986
product range ($23–33 CD) The top-of-the-line release is Peninsula Estate Cabernet Merlot; the intermittent second label is Oneroa Bay Cabernet Merlot. Both in fact include a small percentage of Cabernet Franc and Malbec.
summary The Peninsula Estate Cabernet Merlot comes from a 5.5-hectare estate vineyard situated on a peninsula overlooking Oneroa Bay. The spectacular vineyard has produced some equally spectacular wines.

pierre estate NR

Elizabeth Street, Waikanae **region** Wairarapa
phone (04) 293 4604 **open** Not
winemaker Peter Heginbotham **production** NFP **est.** 1969
product range ($13.95–19 ML) Blanc du Noir (Pinot Noir), Cabernet Sauvignon.
summary Waikanae is situated on the coast north of Wellington; the wines are estate-grown, made and produced in the 'Chateau' and underground cellars completed in 1991 by Wellington optometrist Peter Heginbotham. I have not tasted the wines.

pleasant valley wines ★★★

322 Henderson Valley Road, Waitakere **region** Henderson
phone (09) 838 8857 **fax** (09) 838 8456 **open** Mon-Sat 9–6, Sun 11–6
winemaker Rebecca Salmond **production** 10 000 **est.** 1902
product range ($5.95–19 CD) Gewurztraminer, Sauvignon Blanc, Chenin Chardonnay, Chardonnay, Riesling, Pinotage, together with a range of fortified wines, chiefly Sherries but also Port.
summary A former moribund fortified winemaker, revitalised since 1984 and now complementing its stocks of old fortified wines with well-made table wines sourced from Hawke's Bay, Gisborne and Marlborough, supplementing a 7-hectare estate vineyard at Henderson.

pomona ridge vineyard NR

Pomona Road, Ruby Bay, Nelson **region** Nelson
phone (03) 540 2769 **fax** (03) 540 2769 **open** Weekends and holidays 10–5
winemaker Peter Hancock **production** 330 **est.** 1993
product range ($15–20 CD) Pinot Noir.
summary Pomona Ridge claims to be New Zealand's only Pinot Noir specialist, but I am not sure that is a correct claim. Peter Hancock is a self-taught winemaker; the tiny production is handled in a converted garage with eminently satisfactory results.

ponder estate NR

New Renwick Road, Blenheim **region** Marlborough
phone (03) 572 8642 **fax** (03) 572 9034 **open** 7 days 10.30–4.30
winemaker Graham Paul **production** 5000 **est.** 1987
product range ($15–20 CD) Marlborough Sauvignon Blanc, Chardonnay.
summary With 25 hectares of vineyard, Ponder Estate is primarily a grape grower (supplying chardonnay, sauvignon blanc and riesling to Matua Valley for its Shingle Peak label) but has commenced to vinify part of its output and also to produce olive oil from 3000 olive trees.

Ponder Estate Sauvignon Blanc

Produced from 8.5 hectares of estate planting. Quality has wandered around a bit, but the quality of the '97 is exemplary.

🍷🍷🍷🍷 **1997** Light green-yellow; a lively, light, crisp and fresh bouquet with herbal and mineral aromas is logically followed by an utterly correct, clean and crisp palate with lemon, capsicum and redcurrant nuances, finishing with the expected acidity. **rating:** 87

➯ **best drinking** 1998 – 1999 **best vintages** '94, '97 **drink with** Shellfish • $16

pouparae park NR

Bushmere Road, Gisborne **region** Gisborne
phone (06) 867 7931 **fax** (06) 867 7909 **open** 7 days 10–6
winemaker Alec Cameron **production** 800 **est.** 1994
product range ($7.50–15 R) Riesling, Chardonnay, Solstice Blanc (Müller Thurgau, Dr Hogg Muscat blend), Pinotage, First Light Red (Pinot Noir).
summary Pouparae Park was established on the family's property by Alec and Rachel Cameron in 1994. 'Pouparae' means 'high vantage point', and First Light Red (made from Pinot Noir) is said to be made from vines which are the first to see the light in the world each day.

providence (nz) NR

Cnr Takakatu and Omaha Flats Roads, Matakana **region** Northland and Matakana
phone (09) 422 9300 **open** By appointment
winemaker James Vuletic **production** NA **est.** 1993
product range Merlot Cabernet Franc blend, also Rosé.
summary Former partner in The Antipodean James Vuletic has gone his separate way with the 2-hectare Providence vineyard, but with the same ambition: to produce a high-quality red wine which will command a high price through its scarcity and its quality.

purple heights estate NR

Main West Coast Road, RD6 (PO Box 31110), Christchurch **region** Canterbury
phone (03) 358 2080 **fax** (03) 325 3843 **open** Not
winemaker Dayne Sherwood (Contract) **production** NA **est.** 1996
product range Riesling, Noble Riesling.
summary Partners Delwyn and John Mathieson and David and Diana Jackson named their vineyard after the colour of the nearby foothills, planting 2 hectares to riesling. Having sold the grapes to other makers for many years, the partners ventured into winemaking (via contract at Sherwood Estate) in 1996. There are no sales to the public; all wine is sold wholesale to retailers and restaurants.

quarry road estate NR

Waerenga Road, RD1, Te Kauwhata **region** Waikato and Bay of Plenty
phone (07) 826 3595 **fax** (07) 826 3595 **open** 7 days 8–6
winemaker Toby Cooper, Jenny Gander, Nikki Cooper **production** 4000 **est.** 1996
product range Grape juices, table wines, sparkling wines, fortified wines and liqueurs.
summary 1996 is a nominal year of establishment, for this is the former Aspen Ridge, acquired by the Cooper family in that year. With the aid of consultancy advice, they intend to move more towards the production of premium table wines and to expand the cellar-door facilities.

quartz reef NR

PO Box 63, Cromwell, Central Otago **region** Otago
phone (03) 445 1135 **fax** (03) 445 1180 **open** By appointment
winemaker Rudi Bauer **production** 2000 **est.** 1996
product range ($21–23 R) Pinot Noir, Méthode Champenoise.
summary Quartz Reef is a joint venture between Rudi Bauer and Clotilde Chauvet, both of whom are Rippon winemakers. Three hectares have been planted to pinot noir and chardonnay, with plantings intended to extend to 10 hectares.

redmetal vineyards NR

2006 Maraekakaho Road, RD1, Bridge Pa, Hastings **region** Hawke's Bay
phone (06) 879 8768 **fax** (06) 879 7187 **open** Not
winemaker Grant Edmonds **production** 1000 **est.** 1992
product range ($22–29 R) Rosé, Merlot, Basket Press Merlot Cabernet.

summary A joint venture between the vastly experienced winemaker Grant Edmonds, wife Sue and Diane and Gary Simpson, with an initial planting of 2 hectares (on an 8-hectare block) on an alluvial silt over gravel soil known locally as red metal.

rippon vineyard ★★★★☆

Mount Aspiring Road, Lake Wanaka **region** Otago
phone (03) 443 8084 **fax** (03) 443 8084 **open** 7 days 11.30–5 Aug-May, or by appointment
winemaker Benjamin Kagi **production** 4000 **est.** 1975
product range ($12–45 CD) Gewurztraminer, Riesling, Osteiner, Hotere White, Chardonnay, Gamay Rosé, Pinot Noir, Pinot Noir Selection.
summary Claimed, with some justification, to be the most beautifully sited vineyard in the world, situated on the edge of Lake Wanaka (which is responsible for the remarkable site climate), with the snow-clad New Zealand Alps painting a striking backdrop. Right across the range, Rippon has produced some outstanding wines, none more so than the Pinot Noir. In recent years, Rippon has moved to Bio-Gro™ certified organic status.

Rippon Vineyard Chardonnay

Produced from estate-grown grapes, with Clones 5 and 6. Barrel-fermented in a mix of 80% new and 20% used medium toast French oak barriques; full malolactic fermentation, full lees stirring, maturation in oak for eight months prior to bottling.

🍷🍷🍷🍷🍸 **1996** Medium yellow-green; the bouquet is clean and fresh, with light melon and citrus fruit supported by subtle oak. The palate is fruit-driven, with citrus and melon flavours running through what is a long and intense wine. Excellent mouthfeel, and restrained oak. **rating:** 90

➾ **best drinking** 1998 – 2002 **best vintages** NA **drink with** Smoked trout • $24

Rippon Vineyard Pinot Noir

Eighty per cent of the fruit is destemmed, 20% fermented as whole bunches, with foot stamping (pigeage). The wine spends 11 months in French oak and is racked once, with no filtration prior to bottling.

🍷🍷🍷🍷🍸 **1996** Medium red; the bouquet is distinctive, with predominantly plum and some cherry fruit; no excess carbonic maceration characters. The palate has crystal clean Pinot varietal flavour in a similar plum/cherry spectrum, and is not jammy. Subtle oak; good length. **rating:** 90

➾ **best drinking** 1998 – 2001 **best vintages** '90, '92, '93 **drink with** Coq au vin • $31

riverside wines ★★☆

Dartmoor Road, Puketapu, Napier **region** Hawke's Bay
phone (06) 844 4942 **fax** (06) 844 4671 **open** Summer, Thur-Sun 10.30–5
winemaker Nigel Davies **production** 3500 **est.** 1989
product range ($10–22 CD) Sauvignon Blanc, Barrel Fermented Sauvignon Blanc, Chardonnay, Reserve Chardonnay, Rosé, Merlot, Cabernet Merlot.
summary Ian and Rachel Cadwallader have established 14 hectares of vines on their farm which are coming progressively into production. The wine is made on-site in the small winery above the Dartmoor Valley. It has to be said that overall wine quality is far from exciting.

Riverside Reserve Hawke's Bay Chardonnay

Hand-harvested Hawke's Bay grapes are 100% barrel-fermented in a mix of one and two-year-old French oak barriques, followed by nine months ageing on yeast lees. Part of the wine undergoes malolactic fermentation.

🍷🍷🍷🍷 **1996** Medium yellow-green; the bouquet shows complex barrel-ferment/malolactic-ferment cashew characters, yet is relatively smooth. There are winemaking thumbprints crawling all over the cashew and cream palate, yet they do not subdue some intense fruit which slowly grows on you as you retaste the wine. Good feel and finish. **rating:** 86

⇨ **best drinking** 1998 – 1999 **best vintages** NA **drink with** Salmon terrine • $20

rockwood cellars NR

James Rochford Place, RD5, Hastings **region** Hawke's Bay
phone (06) 879 8760 **fax** (06) 879 4158 **open** By appointment
winemaker Tony Bish **production** 10 000 **est.** 1995
product range (under $15 R) Sauvignon Blanc, Chardonnay, Cabernet Merlot.
summary Rockwood Cellars aims primarily at the export market, with a varied range of modestly priced wines all selling for less than $NZ15 and is in fact part of the Sacred Hill wine group, albeit with its separate brand identity.

rongopai wines ★★★★

Te Kauwhata Road, Te Kauwhata **region** Waikato and Bay of Plenty
phone (07) 826 3981 **fax** (07) 826 3462 **open** Mon–Fri 9–5, Sat 10–5, Sun 11–5
winemaker Tom van Dam **production** 15 000 **est.** 1985
product range ($11–32 CD) Riesling, Sauvignon Blanc, Oak Aged Sauvignon Blanc, Winemakers Selection Sauvignon Blanc, Chenin Blanc, Chardonnay, TK Reserve Chardonnay, Reserve Botrytis Chardonnay, Botrytis Reserve, Pinot Noir, Merlot Malbec, Waerenga (Cabernet blend), TK Reserve Merlot.
summary Now owned solely by Tom van Dam and wife Faith, but going from strength to strength, it would seem. The reputation of Rongopai rests fairly and squarely upon its spectacular botrytised wines which have enjoyed equal quantities of show success and critical acclaim throughout most of the 1990s. Both Chardonnay and the more conventional Riesling are used in these wines; the minimal use of chemicals and herbicides in the vineyards promotes late-season botrytis, countered by vine-trimming, leaf-plucking and bunch-thinning for the conventional table wines. All grapes are hand-picked.

Rongopai Botrytis Reserve

The grapes used to produce this wine are not specified, but we do know it was chiefly grown in Gisborne by D Dodds. Just for the record, it has 125 grams per litre of residual sugar and 10.5 grams per litre of acid.

🍷🍷🍷🍷½ **1996** Golden orange in colour, and pours viscously. A super-rich, intense, raisined cumquat and mandarin bouquet is followed by an equally intense apricot-flavoured bouquet balanced by cleansing acidity. Somewhere along the way, it does lighten off slightly, and I cannot make up my mind whether this is a good thing or not. **rating:** 93

⇨ **best drinking** 1998 – 2001 **best vintages** NA **drink with** Caramelised fruit tart • $31.95

rosebank estate NR

Cnr Johns and Groynes Drive, Belfast, Christchurch **region** Canterbury
phone (03) 323 8539 **fax** (03) 323 8538 **open** 7 days 10–5
winemaker Mark Lennard **production** 3000 **est.** 1993
product range ($8–15 CD) Riesling, Sauvignon Blanc, Chardonnay, Marlborough Chardonnay, Canterbury Chardonnay, Reserve Canterbury Chardonnay, Müller Thurgau, Directors' White, Sparkling Sekt, Pinot Noir, Cabernet Shiraz.
summary Situated only minutes from the city centre and six minutes from Christchurch airport, this is as much an entertainment centre as it is a winery, with a beautiful garden-setting containing hundreds of roses, rhododendrons and camellias and lunch served from the restaurant each day, and à la carte dinner from Wednesday to Sunday from 6 pm. The Waipara vineyard will ultimately provide 50% of the production; in the meantime most of the grapes are being sourced from Marlborough. In 1996 a cricket ground was established at Rosebank in village-green style.

rossendale wines NR

150 Old Tai Tapu Road, Christchurch **region** Canterbury
phone (03) 322 7780 **fax** (03) 332 9272 **open** 7 days 10–5
winemaker Grant Whelan **production** 3250 **est.** 1987
product range Müller Thurgau, Chardonnay.
summary Rossendale is the highly successful venture of beef exporter Brent Rawstron, who ventured into viticulture on his farm in 1987. A 120-year-old gatekeeper's lodge on the farm has been converted into a restaurant and sales area, nestling in a century-old forest. All this, and situated only 15 minutes from the centre of Christchurch, making it the closest winery to that city. The skills of winemaker Grant Whelan brought the initial vintages of 1993 and 1994 gold and silver medals.

ruby bay wines ★★☆

Korepo Road, RD1, Upper Moutere, Nelson **region** Nelson
phone (03) 540 2825 **open** 7 days 10–6
winemaker David Moore **production** 650 **est.** 1976
product range ($10.50–15.80 CD) Chardonnay, Sauvignon Blanc, Riesling, Gewurztraminer, Pinot Noir, Cabernet Sauvignon, Pinot Rosé.
summary The beautifully sited former Korepo winery, purchased by the Moore family in 1989, is well known for its restaurant. Wine quality has been variable, but the 1991 Cabernet Sauvignon won a gold medal and trophy at the Air New Zealand Wine Awards, an outstanding achievement. More recent tastings have not enthralled me.

sacred hill ★★★★

Dartmoor Road, RD6, Napier **region** Hawke's Bay
phone (06) 844 0138 **fax** (06) 844 3271 **open** 7 days Jan, weekends 11–4 Mar-Apr, winter by appointment
winemaker Tony Bish **production** 19 500 **est.** 1986
product range ($12.95–30 CD) There are three ranges of wines; at the very top come intermittent releases of special selection wines, the first to be released being 1995 Rifleman's Chardonnay and 1995 Brokenstone Merlot; then comes the Reserve range, although not necessarily carrying that word in the name (just to confuse the unwary, typically being described as barrel-fermented or basket press); and at the bottom the Whitecliff range.

summary The Mason family are pastoralists-turned-grape growers and thereafter winemakers (Mark Mason is a Roseworthy graduate). Sacred Hill has had its ups and downs since it was founded in 1986, but has steadied significantly since 1995. The top of the range Rifleman's Chardonnay, Brokenstone Merlot, and Basket Press Cabernet Sauvignon are high-quality wines.

Sacred Hill Whitecliff Hawke's Bay Sauvignon Blanc

Produced from the 6-hectare Whitecliff Vineyard, established on a site overlooking white limestone cliffs carved by the Tutaekuri River. Made in a very different style from the Sacred Hill Fumé Blanc, and sometimes there appears to be a faint hint of oak in the background of the wine – although it is said to be straight stainless steel fermented.

🍷🍷🍷🍷 **1997** Light green-yellow; the bouquet is of medium to full intensity with passionfruit and gooseberry aromas; the palate shows excellent richness and fruit weight, with a well-balanced finish. A quantum leap in advance of the '96. **rating:** 88

➾ **best drinking** 1998 – 1999 **best vintages** '97 **drink with** Asian cuisine • $12.95

Sacred Hill Brokenstone Merlot

The inaugural vintage of this wine, which is in fact a blend of 80% Merlot and 20% Malbec. The wine was given post-fermentation maceration for 21 days, and spent 15 months in new French barriques. A very well-made wine.

🍷🍷🍷🍷🍷(half) **1995** Medium purple-red; positive sweet berry and cherry fruit notes and the scent of violets introduce a silky sweet wine on the palate with excellent fruit and structure; the long finish is only gently pushed by French oak. **rating:** 90

➾ **best drinking** 2000 – 2005 **best vintages** '95 **drink with** Venison • $30

saint clair estate ★★★★☆

739 New Renwick Road, RD2, Blenheim **region** Marlborough
phone (03) 578 8695 **fax** (03) 578 8696 **open** Not
winemaker Kim Crawford, Matt Thomson **production** 17 000 **est.** 1978
product range ($14–26 R) Marlborough Riesling, Marlborough Noble Riesling, Marlborough Sauvignon Blanc, Awatere Valley Oak Aged Sauvignon Blanc, Marlborough Chardonnay, Single Vineyard Rapaura Road Chardonnay, Marlborough Merlot, Single Vineyard Rapaura Road Merlot.

summary Neal and Judy Ibbotson have followed the tried-and-true path of growing grapes for 15 or so years before venturing into wine production, which they did with spectacular success in 1994. Since that year, approximately 30% of the output of their 56 hectares of vines (in four different Marlborough locations) have been vinified, with the exceptional skills of Kim Crawford leading to a cascade of show awards.

Saint Clair Estate Marlborough Riesling

Prior to 1997, was made from contract-grown fruit, but in this year the Saint Clair Estate produced its first crop of riesling which will henceforth be the basis of the wine. Thirty per cent of the grapes were botrytis-affected, and (somewhat unusually) the wine was given brief skin contact prior to pressing.

🍷🍷🍷🍷(half) **1997** Light to medium yellow-green; the bouquet is slightly subdued, clean, but not showing a lot of fruit. However, the palate is very different, with powerful tropical/lime flavours, with hints of honey and spice, and the botrytis influence evident but contributing to the complexity of the wine. The residual sugar is well balanced by acidity. **rating:** 84

➪ **best drinking** 1999 – 2004 **best vintages** NA **drink with** Avocado salad • $14

Saint Clair Estate Marlborough Sauvignon Blanc

Produced from the Saint Clair Estate vineyards in the Wairau and Awatere Valleys. The 1994 vintage was a triumphant introduction, and did much to establish the reputation of Saint Clair.

🍷🍷🍷🍷 **1997** Light green-yellow; the bouquet is firm, clean and crisp with tangy capsicum and herbal notes. The palate is very lively, with a tangy lift to the fruit, and braced by some mineral/chalky notes which run through to the finish. **rating:** 88

➪ **best drinking** 1998 – 1999 **best vintages** '94, '96, '97 **drink with** Sashimi • $15

sandihurst wines ★★★☆

Main West Coast Road, West Melton, Canterbury **region** Canterbury
phone (03) 347 8289 **fax** (03) 347 8289 **open** 7 days 11–5 mid-Oct–Apr
winemaker Tony Coakley **production** 7000 **est.** 1992
product range ($11–18 CD) Riesling, Reserve Gewurztraminer, Pinot Gris, Pinot Gris Reserve, Chardonnay, Breidecker, Pinot Noir.
summary Yet another of the ever-expanding number of wineries in the Christchurch region, releasing its first wines in November 1993. It is a substantial operation, with 16 hectares of vineyards in bearing, and production increasing year by year. Its Pinot Gris is one of New Zealand's best.

Sandihurst Pinot Gris Reserve

A special selection of Pinot Gris, which is produced both in a non-Reserve and Reserve form. It is a variety which Sandihurst says is specially suited to the region, and I can but agree.

🍷🍷🍷🍷 **1997** Medium yellow-green; an exotically rich, perfumed bouquet almost into Gewurztraminer aromaticity. The impressively rich and powerful palate is reminiscent of the weight and structure of T'Gallant's Tribute Pinot Gris from the Mornington Peninsula in good vintages; the ripe, exotic fruit fills the back palate. **rating:** 89

➪ **best drinking** 1998 – 1999 **best vintages** '97 **drink with** Delicately spiced seafood • $18

sapich bros NR

152 Forest Hill Road, Henderson, Auckland **region** Henderson
phone (09) 814 9655 **fax** (09) 814 9655 **open** NA
winemaker Ivan Sapich **production** NA **est.** NA
product range Chardonnay, Purple Death (Port-based drink).
summary Until the 1995 Air New Zealand Wine Awards, best known for its 'Purple Death' Port-based drink which the label said was 'rough-as-guts ... but has the distinctive bouquet of horse shit and old tram tickets'. Out of the purple came a 1994 Chardonnay which won a gold medal at the 1995 Air New Zealand Wine Awards, with abundant solid peachy fruit with complex chewy oaky/mealy texture. A full-frontal wine in the older New Zealand style. No recent encounters with death or otherwise.

saxton estate NR

774 Main Road, Stoke, Nelson **region** Nelson
phone (03) 547 7517 **fax** (03) 547 7827 **open** 7 days 10–7
winemaker Wayne Laurie, Graeme Moore **production** 700 **est.** 1968
product range ($12.95–21.95 CD) Richmond Ranges Blend (Breidecker, Reichensteiner, Chasselas blend), Seibel, Pinot Noir, Cabernet Sauvignon.
summary The wines produced from the 2-hectare estate vineyard attest to the fact that this is indeed Nelson's oldest winery, dating back to 1968 when hybrids were an important part of the industry. Saxton Estate, however, remained largely in the shadows until 1995 when it was purchased by Wayne Laurie and Graeme Moore, who have plans to capitalise on its proximity to Nelson by establishing on-site accommodation and a high-quality restaurant.

seibel wines ★★★

113 Sturges Road, Henderson **region** Henderson
phone (09) 836 6113 **fax** (09) 836 6113 **open** Wed-Mon 11–6
winemaker Norbert Seibel **production** 3200 **est.** 1988
product range ($12–20 CD) Limited Edition Hawke's Bay Chardonnay, Hawke's Bay Sauvignon Blanc, Select Noble Late Harvest Chardonnay lead the roster; then come Scheurebe, Barrel Fermented White Riesling, Late Harvest White Riesling, Barrel Fermented Chenin Blanc, Semi-Dry Gewurztraminer, Medium Dry Riesling, Cabernet Franc Merlot Cabernet Sauvignon.
summary Significantly increasing production shows that Norbert Seibel is doing well; the wine styles have been described as innovative, and those I have tasted have been outside the mainstream.

seifried estate ★★★★

Cnr State Highway 60, Redwood Road, Appleby, Nelson **region** Nelson
phone (03) 544 5599 **fax** (03) 544 5522 **open** 7 days 11–5
winemaker Hermann Seifried **production** 40 000 **est.** 1973
product range ($8–22 R) A white specialist with Riesling, Dry Riesling, Oak Aged Riesling, Chardonnay, Sauvignon Blanc, Chablis, Gewurztraminer, Müller Thurgau, Old Coach Road Classic Dry White, Old Coach Road Chardonnay, Late Harvest Riesling, Ice Wine; the two principal red wines are Pinot and Cabernet Sauvignon.
summary With 56 hectares of vineyards established progressively between 1973 and 1988, and a crush in excess of 900 tonnes, Seifried Estate is by far the largest of the Nelson wineries. The production is heavily biased towards white wines, which are of wholly admirable consistency of style and quality. Just prior to vintage in 1996 Seifried moved to its new winery situated in its picturesque Appleby Vineyard, but some of the 1997 wines showed worrying technical problems.

Seifried Estate Sauvignon Blanc

Made without the use of oak from estate-grown grapes. Produced from Seifried's Rabbit Island and Redwood Valley vineyards. Regularly one of New Zealand's better Sauvignon Blancs, and arguably underrated.

🍷🍷🍷🍷🍷 **1997** Light green-yellow; the bouquet is firm and crisp, with attractive herb, capsicum and gooseberry aromas leading on to a very lively and tangy palate with a mix of sweet citrus, gooseberry and passionfruit flavours. Exceptional mouthfeel and balance. **rating:** 92

➾ **best drinking** 1998 – 1999 **best vintages** '91, '92, '93, '94, '96, '97 **drink with** Sugar-cured tuna • $14.50

selaks drylands estate winery ★★★★☆

Hammerichs Road, Rapaura **region** Marlborough
phone (03) 570 5252 **fax** (03) 570 5272 **open** Mon-Fri 9–5, Sat 10–5, Sun 11–4
winemaker Darryl Woolley **production** NFP **est.** 1934
product range ($7.30–32 CD) Sauvignon Blanc, Marlborough Sauvignon Blanc, Matador Estate Oak Aged Sauvignon Blanc, Founders Reserve Matador Estate Sauvignon Blanc, Chardonnay.
summary A state-of-the-art winery drawing upon its own 14 hectares of estate vineyards and a significant part of the adjoining 80-hectare Matador Vineyard owned by John Webber. The Sauvignon Blancs are as good as they come in classic Marlborough-style.

Selaks Drylands Estate Founders Reserve Matador Estate Sauvignon Blanc

A convincing way to celebrate the commissioning of the Marlborough winery, and an equally convincing demonstration that the marriage of Sauvignon Blanc and oak need not end in divorce. Barrel-fermented in new French oak, both the '96 and '97 are outstanding wines of great complexity, the latter topping the Sauvignon Blanc Class at the 1997 Liquorland National Wine Show of Australia.

🍷🍷🍷🍷🍷 **1997** Medium yellow-green; a voluminous, ripe and complex bouquet, with a faultless marriage of fruit and subtle oak. The palate, like the bouquet, is driven by the complex, ripe gooseberry and passionfruit flavours, with just a hint of spicy oak in support. Has all the length one could wish for. **rating:** 94

➾ **best drinking** 1998 – 2000 **best vintages** '96, '97 **drink with** Seafood pasta • $19.95

Selaks Drylands Estate Marlborough Sauvignon Blanc

A new label for Selaks, which made its debut at the 1995 Sydney International Winemakers Competition, being very highly pointed in the Top 100 and duly receiving a gold medal. It utilises grapes grown on Selak's Drylands Vineyard in Marlborough, which adjoins the well-known Matador Vineyard.

🍷🍷🍷🍷 **1997** Light green-yellow; there are pungent lifted passionfruit and tropical fruit aromas with a very slightly sour underlay on the bouquet. There are similar lively punchy passionfruit and peach flavours, yet they sit slightly at odds with the underlying structure of the wine. Tasted twice in different circumstances with similar notes. **rating:** 87

➾ **best drinking** 1998 – 1999 **best vintages** '95, '96 **drink with** Slow-cooked Tasmanian salmon • $12.95

Selaks Marlborough Sauvignon Blanc

Selaks has a multiplicity of Sauvignon Blanc brands and labels these days, but the Marlborough Sauvignon Blanc which started it all continues to be its commercial flagship.

🍷🍷🍷🍷🍸 **1997** Light green-yellow; a clean and fresh bouquet with gentle asparagus, herb and gooseberry aromas is followed by a wine which does not make any dramatic statements, but has perfectly ripened sauvignon blanc in the mid-range of flavours, and excellent length. Rated high simply because it is so classic, and because of its very good finish and length. **rating:** 90

➾ **best drinking** 1998 – 1999 **best vintages** NA **drink with** Stir-fried vegetables • $12.95

Selaks Drylands Estate Chardonnay

Introduced in 1996, and barrel-fermented in a mix of French and American oak, with the usual attendant winemaking inputs, most notably malolactic fermentation and lees contact. A more than useful debut.

1996 Light green-yellow; a classy bouquet with nutty cashew creamy aromas and subtle oak. The palate is long, with nicely controlled malolactic-fermentation inputs on melon, fig and cashew flavours. **rating:** 90

➾ **best drinking** 1998 – 1999 **best vintages** NA **drink with** Chicken pie • $14.95

selaks wines – auckland ★★★★☆

15 Old North Road, Kumeu **region** Kumeu and Huapai
phone (09) 412 8609 **fax** (09) 412 7524 **open** Mon-Fri 9–5, Sat 10–5, Sun 11–4
winemaker Darryl Woolley **production** 100 000 plus **est.** 1934
product range ($7.30–32 CD) Super-premium wines under Founders label including Oak Aged Sauvignon Blanc, Chardonnay, Cabernet Sauvignon and Méthode Traditionelle.
summary With Montana, Selaks first brought Sauvignon Blanc to the attention of overseas markets, especially Australia. Its Sauvignon Blanc and Sauvignon Semillon blends continue to be its forte, always good, frequently outstanding. The opening of its large (2000-tonne) Drylands Estate Winery in Marlborough in March 1996 is compelling evidence of the success of Selaks.

seresin estate 

Bedford Road, Renwick, Marlborough **region** Marlborough
phone (03) 572 9408 **fax** (03) 572 9850 **open** Summer 10–4.30
winemaker Brian Bicknell, Rhyan Wardman **production** 12 000 **est.** 1992
product range ($18.90–29.90 R) Sauvignon Blanc, Pinot Gris, Estate Chardonnay, Reserve Chardonnay, Pinot Noir.
summary Seresin has charged into the Marlborough scene since New Zealand filmmaker Michael Seresin purchased a little over 60 hectares of prime alluvial terrace land adjacent to the Wairau River. Forty hectares of vineyard have been established, and the state-of-the-art winery designed by Ian Athfield (of Te Mata Estate fame) constructed. Brian Bicknell, one of New Zealand's most experienced Flying Winemakers (he has worked in New Zealand, Hungary, France and for three years in Chile) has been installed as chief winemaker. The first vintage in 1996 immediately established Seresin as one of the star performers in the Marlborough scene.

Seresin Estate Sauvignon Blanc

To say sophisticated winemaking techniques have been used with what might seem a straightforward wine style is a masterly understatement. The wine is a blend of Sauvignon Blanc (93%) and Semillon (7%), with the sauvignon blanc picked over an eight-day period. Fourteen per cent of the wine was barrel-fermented and lees aged in a mix of new and one-year-old French oak barriques. Part of the remaining wine was fermented using cultured yeasts, part relying upon indigenous yeast. If this were not enough, a small component of the barrel-fermented portion underwent malolactic fermentation. All this, and yet the end result is a wine in which Marlborough Sauvignon Blanc, rather than winemaker's tricks, does the talking.

🍷🍷🍷🍷🍷 **1997** Medium green-yellow; a crisp and clean bouquet with a mix of asparagus, herb, mineral and a hint of gooseberry all make their mark is followed by a lively, flavoursome palate with textural complexity deriving from the barrel-ferment component, yet with no appreciable oak flavour. Very much a case of less being better. **rating:** 90

➪ **best drinking** 1998 – 1999 **best vintages** NA **drink with** Steamed crab • $18.80

Seresin Estate Chardonnay

As with all the Seresin Estate wines, a complex range of winemaking techniques are used to handle the estate-grown fruit. Forty per cent is barrel-fermented in French oak barriques, the remainder fermented in a large French oak vat. Part is fermented using cultured yeast, part using indigenous yeast; 70% is taken through malolactic fermentation, and all of the wine given extended lees contact.

🍷🍷🍷🍷 **1996** Light to medium yellow-green; a complex bouquet showing the sophisticated use of barrel-ferment and malolactic-ferment influences well integrated with fig, cashew and melon fruit; very stylish. The palate is perhaps just a fraction light on, but is immaculately balanced, reflecting all of the flavours promised by the bouquet. **rating:** 89

➪ **best drinking** 1998 – 2000 **best vintages** NA **drink with** Sweetbreads • $19.80

Seresin Estate Chardonnay Reserve

The best of the estate-grown grapes are selected for the Reserve programme; the wine is barrel-fermented in 100% new French oak barriques, and is all taken through malolactic fermentation, with the usual lees contact and stirring.

🍷🍷🍷🍷🍷 **1996** Medium yellow-green; an extremely complex, full-on bouquet with cashew/hazelnut malolactic and barrel-ferment aromas; there is a cavalcade of nutty, figgy and toasty flavours on the palate which seem to build power and presence on the finish. **rating:** 91

➪ **best drinking** 1998 – 2003 **best vintages** NA **drink with** Corn-fed chicken • $25.80

settler vineyards NR

Crownthorpe Settlement Road, RD9, Hastings **region** Hawke's Bay
phone (06) 874 3244 **fax** (06) 874 3244 **open** Not
winemaker Evert Nijzink **production** 500 **est.** 1993
product range ($14–20 R) Chardonnay, Cabernet Merlot.
summary Evert Nyzink has established a 2.5-hectare biodynamically managed vineyard, and since 1997 has relied entirely upon estate production. A cellar-door and café facility opened in late 1996.

shalimar estate NR

RD2, Ngatapa Road, Gisborne **region** Gisborne
phone (06) 862 7776 **fax** (06) 862 7776 **open** 7 days 10–5
winemaker Alexander Stuart **production** 900 **est.** 1994
product range Sauvignon Blanc, Chardonnay, Pinot Gris, Merlot.
summary Having been grape growers for 25 years, the Stuart family took the plunge into winemaking in 1994, drawing upon a recently established (and in Gisborne, rare) terraced hillside vineyard. Alexander Stuart believes greater flavour and character will follow the lower than normal yields.

sherwood estate NR

Weedons Ross Road, Christchurch **region** Canterbury
phone (03) 347 9060 **fax** (03) 347 8225 **open** 7 days 11–5
winemaker Dayne Sherwood **production** 7800 **est.** 1987
product range ($12.50–26.50 R) Riesling, Müller Thurgau, Sauvignon Blanc, Chardonnay, Unoaked Chardonnay, Reserve Chardonnay, Estate Pinot Noir, Reserve Pinot Noir, Single Vineyard Selection Rivendell Pinot Noir, Cabernet Franc.
summary Sherwood Estate produced its first wines in 1990; situated close to Christchurch (15 minutes drive) it also offers a garden-setting tasting room with snacks and lunches available in the Vineyard Bar throughout summer. Production has risen significantly since the early days, making Sherwood Estate an important part of the Christchurch landscape. After early success, particularly with Pinot Noir, quality seems to have slipped alarmingly in 1996 and 1997.

silverstream vineyard NR

64 Giles Road, Clarkville, Kaiapoi **region** Canterbury
phone (03) 327 5231 **fax** (03) 327 5678 **open** By appointment
winemaker Peter Todd **production** NFP **est.** 1990
product range ($15–20 CD) Chardonnay, Pinot Noir.
summary One of the newest of the Canterbury wineries, situated on the Waimakari Plains north of Christchurch. Owned by Peter and wife Zeke Todd (of Anglo-Italian and Dutch ancestry, respectively), with 4 hectares of estate plantings. No wine was made under the Silverstream label in 1997 or 1998.

smith of martinborough NR

73 Princess Street, Martinborough **region** Wairarapa
phone (06) 306 9280 **fax** (06) 306 9280 **open** Weekends and public holidays
winemaker Roger Smith **production** NA **est.** 1985
product range Riesling, Pinot Noir, Cabernet Sauvignon.
summary The venture of Sam Lamb and Roger Smith, who in the early years were content to sell the production from their 3-hectare vineyard to other makers, but are now in the course of restoring turn-of-the-century buildings on the property into a visitors centre, craft and wine shop.

soljans wines ★★★

263 Lincoln Road, Henderson **region** Henderson
phone (09) 838 8365 **fax** (09) 838 8366 **open** Mon-Sat 9–6, Sun 11–5
winemaker Russell Wiggins **production** 5400 **est.** 1937
product range ($8.85–25 CD) Ivory, Müller Thurgau, Marlborough Riesling, Gisborne Gewurztraminer, Marlborough Sauvignon Blanc, Hawke's Bay Sauvignon Blanc, Hawke's Bay Unoaked Chardonnay, Barrique Reserve Chardonnay, Momento Spumante, Méthode Traditionelle Legacy, Auckland Pinotage, Barrique Reserve Merlot, Barrique Reserve Cabernet Merlot, Ports and Sherries, Dessert Cabernet Sauvignon and Muscat.
summary The traditional but immaculately maintained winery and vineyard constitute a major tourist attraction, and the well-made wines are sold at very modest prices. In 1993 Soljans made a heavy investment importing state-of-the-art sparkling winemaking equipment from France and is now a major contractor for New Zealand Méthode Traditionelle producers.

solstone estate NR

119 Solway Crescent, Masterton **region** Wairarapa
phone (06) 377 7504 **fax** (06) 337 7504 **open** By appointment
winemaker Luc des Bonnets **production** 2500 **est.** 1981
product range ($12–35 CD) Sauvignon Blanc, Pinot Noir, Cabernet Sauvignon Merlot Cabernet Franc under both Solway and Bloomfield labels.
summary Tiny quantities of the wines sold to date have been eagerly snapped up by the local clientele, but wines are now being distributed (sparingly) through Kitchener Wines. The wines draw upon two hectares of estate cabernet sauvignon and a single hectare of pinot noir, sauvignon blanc, merlot and cabernet franc.

spencer hill estate ★★★★

Best Road, Upper Moutere, Nelson **region** Nelson
phone (03) 543 2031 **fax** (03) 543 2031 **open** 7 days 12–4 Dec–Feb
winemaker Philip Jones **production** 10 000 **est.** 1991
product range ($15–30 R) Spencer Hill is the top label from single vineyard sources; Tasman Bay is the second but main label made in larger volume. Chardonnay, Sauvignon Blanc, Pinot Noir, Pinot Gris, Riesling, Gewurztraminer, Merlot.
summary Philip Jones is a graduate in Viticulture from UCLA Davis, California, and also undertook an Oenology degree at Fresno State University. The ornately complex Spencer Hill Chardonnays have won a cascade of trophies and gold medals, joined by the Tasman Bay Chardonnay in 1997, in wine competitions running from New Zealand to London. There can be no doubt that Philip Jones is a highly talented winemaker.

Spencer Hill Tasman Bay Nelson Riesling

Another wine from Philip Jones which strikes off in a very deliberate style of its own. It includes 15% Gewurztraminer, is partially barrel-fermented and is lees aged.

🍷🍷🍷🍷 **1997** Distinct straw tinges; discreet minerally/toasty aromas tinged with citrus merge into a lime blossom palate of light to medium weight with a mix of spice, apple and smoky flavours, with balanced sweetness on the finish. **rating:** 86

➾ **best drinking** 1998 – 1999 **best vintages** NA **drink with** Sugar-cured tuna • $16

Spencer Hill Evan's Vineyard Moutere Chardonnay

Produced in small quantities (375 cases in 1996) and the flagship wine for Spencer Hill. On the evidence of the '96, made with the philosophy that more is best.

🍷🍷🍷🍷 **1996** Full straw-yellow; a very complex, rich and nutty bouquet with strong malolactic-fermentation inputs is followed by a palate in which, once again, malolactic characters seem to drive the wine. There are opulent fruit flavours, with nuances of mandarin, suggesting a touch of botrytis was at work in the vineyard. **rating:** 85

➾ **best drinking** 1998 – 1999 **best vintages** NA **drink with** Chicken fricassee • $31

springvale estates NR

Springvale Road, Alexandra **region** Otago
phone (03) 449 2333 **open** Not
winemaker Mike Wolter (Contract) **production** 90 **est.** 1989
product range Chardonnay, Pinot Noir.

summary Tony and Jo-Anne Brun planted their first hectare of vines in 1989, doubling the area over the 1995 and 1996 seasons. Contract-winemaking by the ubiquitous Mike Wolter does the rest, and a cellar-door sales and tasting facility was opened in December 1997.

st helena estate ★★★☆

Coutts Island Road, Christchurch **region** Canterbury
phone (03) 323 8202 **fax** (03) 323 8252 **open** Mon-Sat 10–4.30, Sun 12–5
winemaker Alan McCorkindale **production** 10 000 **est.** 1978
product range ($7.50–25 CD) Riesling, Canterbury Plains Müller Thurgau, Southern Alps Dry White, Chardonnay, Reserve Chardonnay, Noble Bacchus, Pinot Gris, Pinot Blanc, Pinot Noir, Reserve Pinot Noir, Port Hills Dry Red, Peers Port.
summary Whether in its moments of success or otherwise, controversy has never been far from St Helena's door. After a spectacular debut for its Pinot Noir in 1982, there has been a roller-coaster ride since, but much work in the vineyard (and also winery) is starting to pay dividends. The arrival of the immensely talented Alan McCorkindale as winemaker should see a continuing lift in quality.

st jerome wines NR

219 Metcalfe Road, Henderson **region** Henderson
phone (09) 833 6205 **fax** (09) 833 6205 **open** Mon-Sat 9–6, Sun 12–5
winemaker Davorin Ozich, Miro Ozich **production** 7000 **est.** 1968
product range ($7.50–35 CD) Riesling, Sauvignon Blanc, Chardonnay, Chablis, Gewurztraminer, Cabernet Merlot, Port.
summary The Cabernet Merlots made by Davorin Ozich between 1987 and 1991 reflect his Master of Science degree and practical training at Chateau Margaux and Chateau Cos d'Estournel in Bordeaux. They were hugely powerful wines, the 1991 in particular. It was rated number two in New Zealand's Top Ten Reds of the Year in the September 1994 edition of *Cuisine* magazine, but did not impress the judges at the 1995 Sydney International Wine Competition, being described as 'harsh and over-extractive'. Herein lies the rub: these are wines which demand cellaring and a certain degree of understanding.

st nesbit ★★★★★

Hingaia Road, RD1, Papakura **region** Auckland and South Auckland
phone (09) 379 0808 **fax** (09) 376 6956 **open** Not
winemaker Dr Tony Molloy QC **production** 800 **est.** 1980
product range ($37 CD) A single Cabernet Merlot (Cabernet Sauvignon, Cabernet Franc, Merlot, Malbec, Petit Verdot) Bordeaux-blend has been supplemented more recently by a Rosé, the result of indifferent vintages in 1992 and 1993 and of the effects of leaf roll virus.
summary Tony Molloy is a leading tax lawyer with a weekend passion; his Bordeaux-blend is revered in New Zealand and very well regarded elsewhere. His Cabernet Merlot is produced in minuscule quantities, much of it exported, leaving a mere 250 cases for the New Zealand market. A major replanting programme of the 4-hectare vineyard enforced a hiatus in production between 1994 and 1996.

stonecroft vineyard ★★★★

Mere Road, RD5, Hastings **region** Hawke's Bay
phone (06) 879 9610 **fax** (06) 879 9610 **open** Weekends, public holidays 11–5
winemaker Dr Alan Limmer **production** 2500 **est.** 1987

product range ($16–38 CD) Gewurztraminer, Gewurztraminer Late Harvest, Sauvignon Blanc, Chardonnay, Ruhani, Crofters II, Syrah.

summary Analytical chemist Dr Alan Limmer produces very full-bodied, rich and ripe wines from his 3-hectare vineyard situated on free-draining, gravelly soils which promote early ripening. Most interesting is the almost unprocurable (mailing list only) Syrah, widely regarded as New Zealand's best.

stonyridge vineyard ★★★★★

80 Onetangi Road, Waiheke Island **region** Waiheke Island
phone (09) 372 8822 **fax** (09) 372 8822 **open** Fri-Sun 12–5
winemaker Stephen White **production** 800 **est.** 1982

product range ($30–85 ML) The top label is Larose Cabernets; the second is Airfield Cabernets. Minuscule quantities of Que Sera Syrah are also grown.

summary The winery that justifies the hype about Waiheke Island. Consistently great wines have been produced, albeit in minuscule quantities; small wonder it has established the highest ex-winery price of $50 en primeur, and $85 upon commercial release, with a limit of one bottle per customer! For many, patronising the winery restaurant will be the only means of tasting these exalted wines.

Stonyridge Larose Cabernets

Although Te Mata would vigorously dispute this (and no doubt others, too) I would nominate this wine as New Zealand's best Bordeaux-blend. The blend varies from vintage to vintage in the manner of the great estate wines of Bordeaux, but will typically be not less than 60% Cabernet Sauvignon, with Merlot and Malbec varying between 10% and 18%, and then 5% to 6% of Cabernet Franc and a nominal 1% of Petit Verdot. Prolonged ageing in new French oak allows the wine to be bottled unfiltered.

🍷🍷🍷🍷🍷 **1996** Medium to full red-purple; the bouquet is strikingly different from the '95, fully ripe, with mulberry, prune and plum aromas, and an intriguing edge of lavender. An exceptionally powerful and complex wine on the palate with layer upon layer of flavour and texture; cedar, vanilla, blackcurrant and chocolate announce a wine out of the ordinary. **rating:** 97

➪ **best drinking** 2002 – 2012 **best vintages** '91, '93, '94, '95, '96 **drink with** Fillet of beef • $40

---

tai-ara-rau wines NR

Upper Stout Street, Gisborne **region** Gisborne
phone (06) 867 2010 **fax** (06) 867 2024 **open** 7 days 10–5
winemaker Jeff Sinnott **production** 1000 **est.** 1989

product range Estate Chardonnay and Merlot; Waimata Vineyard Chardonnay, Pinot Noir and Merlot.

summary Tairawhiti Polytechnic has followed in the footsteps of Australia's Charles Sturt University in making commercial quantities of wine as part of the wine industry certificate course which the institute offers. It is the only New Zealand institution to do so, drawing upon 3 hectares of chardonnay and 1.25 hectares each of pinot noir and merlot.

te awa farm winery NR

Roys Hill Road, SH 50 RD5, Hastings **region** Hawke's Bay
phone (06) 879 7602 **fax** (06) 879 77756 **open** Not
winemaker Jenny Dobson **production** 16 000 **est.** 1992

product range ($14–28 R) Longlands Sauvignon Blanc, Chardonnay, Cabernet Merlot; Boundary Chardonnay and Merlot.
summary The Lawson family is yet another to venture into winemaking after being contract grape growers for over 15 years. Unusually, however, when Gus and Ian Lawson decided to venture into winemaking on their own account, they decided to start again, purchasing a 173-hectare sheep property on Roys Hill Road in 1992, establishing 32 hectares of sauvignon blanc, chardonnay, merlot, cabernet franc, cabernet sauvignon and syrah. The first vintage from Te Awa Farm was in 1994 and an on-site production facility (incorporating a cellar-door sales area) was constructed over 1997, with the peripatetic Jenny Dobson now in charge of winemaking.

te awanga estate NR

Parkhill Road, RD2, Te Awanga, Hawke's Bay **region** Hawke's Bay
phone (06) 875 1188 **fax** (06) 875 1188 **open** By appointment
winemaker Kim Crawford (Consultant) **production** 2500 **est.** 1995
product range ($15–23 R) Chardonnay, Sauvignon Blanc, Pinot Noir, Merlot, Cabernet Merlot, Cabernet Sauvignon.
summary Yet another enterprise with spectacular growth planned in the wake of the conversion from contract grape grower for others to self-production and the expansion of the vineyards from 12 to 32 hectares. An on-site winery is planned for the 1998 vintage, and the promising first wines came onto the market in 1997.

te horo estate NR

State Highway 1, Te Horo **region** Wairarapa
phone (06) 364 3392 **fax** (06) 364 3284 **open** 7 days 10–4
winemaker Alastair Pain **production** 6500 **est.** 1985
product range ($12–28 CD) Chardonnay, Sauvignon Blanc, Riesling, Rosé, Gewurztraminer, Merlot, Cabernet Sauvignon; a selection of fruit wines.
summary Formerly called Grape Republic, a marketing and promotion tour-de-force using direct mail and wine club techniques, with a vast array of flavoured wines and smaller quantities of more expensive table wines which are distinctly austere. A winery restaurant opened for business in 1993, and was expanded to seat 200 people in 1994. An underground cellar and sales area was opened in 1995.

te kairanga wines ★★★★

Martins Road, Martinborough **region** Wairarapa
phone (06) 306 9122 **fax** (06) 306 9322 **open** 7 days 10–5
winemaker Chris Buring **production** 13 000 **est.** 1984
product range ($10–30 CD) At the top end is the Reserve range of Chardonnay and Pinot Noir; then the Premium range of Sauvignon Blanc, Chardonnay, Pinot Noir, Cabernet Sauvignon and Cabernet Merlot; at the bottom end Castlepoint range of Müller Thurgau, Dry White, Dry Red and Cabernet Sauvignon.
summary Te Kairanga is an enigma. For a long time its wines were disappointing, but then took a distinct turn for the better, suggesting that all of its problems were behind it. More recent tastings are less conclusive, so close and yet so far from the best of what is undoubtedly a great region.

Te Kairanga Sauvignon Blanc

A blend of Gisborne (90%) and Martinborough (10%) Sauvignon Blanc, steel fermented and which offers excellent value for money.

1997 Light to medium yellow-green; a clean, crisp bouquet of light to medium intensity with a mix of gooseberry, passionfruit and herbal aromas is followed by a palate with more power and attack than the bouquet suggests, with attractive passionfruit flavours and a lingering, lively finish. **rating:** 86

➾ **best drinking** 1998 – 1999 **best vintages** '90, '91, '94, '95, '96 **drink with** Scallops in cream sauce • $18.50

Te Kairanga Chardonnay

Produced entirely from Martinborough grapes; 33% was barrel-fermented in new French oak, and 30% taken through malolactic fermentation. Aged for five months on lees in barrel before bottling.

1996 Light to medium yellow-green; fine and subtle citrus/melon/mineral aromas are followed by a well-structured palate with stone fruit and mineral flavours, supported by just a hint of oak. Unforced and well balanced. **rating:** 84

➾ **best drinking** 1997 – 1999 **best vintages** '90, '91, '94, '95, '96 **drink with** Seared scallops • $21.50

Te Kairanga Reserve Chardonnay

First made in 1994 from the lowest-yielding and best parcels of fruit available to Te Kairanga, and the Reserve range of Chardonnay and Pinot Noir is only produced in better vintages when exceptional levels of fruit ripeness and flavour are achieved in the winery, and which then justify the use of a higher percentage of new oak. The wine spends 11 months in a mix of new and one-year-old French oak barriques and 15% is taken through malolactic fermentation.

1996 Medium yellow-green; a restrained and elegant bouquet with citrus/grapefruit aromas and subtle oak introduces a wine of considerable elegance. The palate has length and persistence, with attractive nectarine/citrus fruit, and nicely restrained oak and malolactic-fermentation inputs. **rating:** 85

➾ **best drinking** 1998 – 2000 **best vintages** '94, '95, '96 **drink with** Sweetbreads • $30

Te Kairanga Reserve Pinot Noir

Produced from a selection of the best estate-grown grapes, the 1995 vintage spent 18 months in a mix of new and second-use French oak.

1995 Medium red, still retaining some traces of purple; the bouquet is of medium intensity, with some secondary, bottle-developed foresty characters starting to appear. The palate has good texture, structure and length, with black cherry and plum fruit of medium weight. Pales slightly against the very opulent '96 vintage wines from other makers which were on the market at the same time. **rating:** 87

➾ **best drinking** 1998 – 2001 **best vintages** NA **drink with** Smoked quail • $30

---

te mania estate

c/o The Grape Escape, McShanes Road, Richmond, Nelson **region** Nelson
phone (03) 544 4541 **fax** (03) 544 4541 **open** Mon–Fri 10–5 in summer
winemaker Jane Cooper **production** 3500 **est.** 1990

product range ($13.95–17.95 R) Riesling, Late Harvest Riesling, Home Block Sauvignon Blanc, Chardonnay, Merlot.

summary Jon and Cheryl Harrey commenced development of their vineyard in 1990, planting 4.5 hectares in that year (which came into production in 1992), and expanded the plantings in 1994 and 1995, with an additional 4 hectares. They previously sold most of their grapes to other Nelson winemakers, but since 1995 have had Jane Cooper as winemaker. Together with another vineyard owner, the Harreys have purchased a property on which they have erected a cellar-door sales facility, café and arts and crafts centre. Has a rapidly growing reputation, particularly for Sauvignon Blanc.

Te Mania Estate Home Block Sauvignon Blanc

Produced from 1.5 hectares of sauvignon blanc estate-grown on the Te Mania home block situated in Pughs Road. The wine is cool fermented for four weeks and bottled in October in the year of vintage.

🍷🍷🍷🍸 **1997** Light green-yellow; a crisp, pungent bouquet with herbal/gooseberry fruit is followed by a powerful, herbal/green capsicum palate, with a quite powerful finish. **rating:** 84

➾ **best drinking** 1998 – 1999 **best vintages** NA **drink with** Marinated scallops • $16

Te Mania Estate Chardonnay

Predominantly from the Pughs Road vineyard, with 1.5 hectares of Mendoza clone chardonnay. The wine spends nine months in predominantly French oak, and 100% is taken through malolactic fermentation.

🍷🍷🍷🍸 **1996** Medium yellow-green; the bouquet is quite complex, with sweet cashew nut and melon aromas; the oak is more evident on the bouquet, with lots of barrel-ferment and malolactic-fermentation characters subduing the primary fruit. Interestingly, the wine has 12 grams of residual sugar but does not taste at all sweet. **rating:** 84

➾ **best drinking** 1998 – 1999 **best vintages** NA **drink with** Yakitori chicken • NA

te mata estate ★★★★★

Te Mata Road, Havelock North **region** Hawke's Bay

phone (06) 877 4399 **fax** (06) 877 4397 **open** Mon-Fri 9–5, Sat 10–5, Sun 11–4

winemaker Peter Cowley **production** 25 000 **est.** 1896

product range ($9.95–39.50 CD) Elston (Chardonnay), Castle Hill Sauvignon Blanc, Cape Crest Sauvignon Blanc, Rosé, Bullnose (Syrah), Coleraine (Cabernet Franc Merlot), Cabernet Merlot, Awatea (Cabernet Merlot – premium).

summary In the eyes of many, New Zealand's foremost producer of Cabernet Merlot, notwithstanding the consistency of the show success of the Vidal/Villa Maria group. The wines of Te Mata are made in a different style, restrained and elegant but always packed with fine fruit. Nor should the consistently stylish and varietally correct white wines be ignored; these too are of the highest quality.

Te Mata Estate Cape Crest Sauvignon Blanc

A single vineyard Sauvignon Blanc which is entirely barrel-fermented (20% new oak) and given lees contact but no malolactic fermentation. It is the richer and fuller of the two Te Mata Sauvignon Blancs.

🍷🍷🍷🍷🍸 **1996** Bright, light green-yellow; a quite complex bouquet with obvious barrel-ferment inputs into ripe fruit which could almost be mistaken for a cool-climate Chardonnay, with hints of melon and fig. The oak is less assertive on the relatively delicate palate which is crisp and clean, with a tight, faintly smoky/spicy finish. **rating:** 93

⇨ **best drinking** 1998 – 1999 **best vintages** '91, '94, '95, '96 **drink with** Pan-fried whitebait • $18.85

Te Mata Estate Castle Hill Sauvignon Blanc

Another single vineyard Sauvignon Blanc, usually fermented in stainless steel, although in 1997 a percentage was barrel-fermented in old oak. Quite deliberately, a lighter, fresher style.

🍷🍷🍷🍷 **1996** Light green-yellow; a crisp, clean and tangy bouquet of medium intensity with herbaceous overtones to the fruit. The wine has good mouthfeel, with some citrus, a touch of passionfruit and just an echo of sweetness on the finish. **rating:** 89

⇨ **best drinking** 1998 – 1999 **best vintages** NA **drink with** Mussels • $14.95

Te Mata Estate Elston Chardonnay

One of New Zealand's most highly rated Chardonnays, drawn primarily from the Elston Vineyard, but also in part from a vineyard at Havelock North. It is given the full treatment in the winery, with 100% barrel fermentation in French oak, and 100% malolactic fermentation.

🍷🍷🍷🍷🍷 **1996** Medium yellow-green; fine, elegant and classic were the first three words on my tasting sheet; then melon fruit with a background touch of oak spice. The palate has grip and focus, with a very complex array of cashew, mineral, melon and citrus flavours, with an almost piercing finish. **rating:** 94

⇨ **best drinking** 1998 – 2003 **best vintages** '93, '94, '95, '96 **drink with** High-quality fish • $29.50

Te Mata Estate Bullnose Syrah

Introduced in 1995, and both in that year and in 1996 added a dimension to the understanding of Syrah in New Zealand, in much the same way as the first Coleraine did back in 1982.

🍷🍷🍷🍷🍷 **1996** Medium red-purple; a fine and elegant bouquet with a dash of spice and pepper on top of classic black cherry varietal fruit on the bouquet. That same varietal character comes lancing through the palate, with liquorice, spice and pepper flavours, and an elegance which is missing from all of the other Hawke's Bay Syrahs I have tasted. **rating:** 92

⇨ **best drinking** 1999 – 2005 **best vintages** NA **drink with** Spiced lamb • $30

Te Mata Estate Coleraine Cabernet Franc Merlot

A blend of Merlot, Cabernet Sauvignon and Cabernet Franc, clearly the flagship of Te Mata and, in the view of many, of New Zealand's red wines. No longer a single-vineyard wine (which it was between 1982 and 1988) but drawn from the best grapes grown predominantly on the north-facing slopes of Te Mata Peak. Given more new oak than its sister wine, Awatea, and not made every year. (None was made in either 1992 or 1993.)

🍷🍷🍷🍷🍷 **1995** Deep red-purple; a complex and concentrated mix of cassis, mint and green olive is supported by strong, sweetly charry oak on the bouquet. The palate delivers all the flavour the bouquet promises, with both oak and fruit tannins adding power and length to the finish. Retasted end 1997, and evolving slowly but surely, with virtually no change in the notes. **rating:** 95

⇨ **best drinking** 2000 – 2010 **best vintages** '89, '91, '94, '95 **drink with** New Zealand lamb • $39.50

Te Mata Estate Awatea Cabernet Merlot

Like the Coleraine, no longer a single vineyard-based wine. It is made in a slightly lighter, more accessible style, although one would never guess that from the varietal mix, which is more strongly based on Cabernet Sauvignon, typically with only around 10% Merlot and a little Cabernet Franc from time to time. The oak input is, relatively speaking, less, but the wine has the same breed and finesse of the Te Mata Coleraine.

1995 Strong purple-red; abundant, sweet blackcurrant and blackberry fruit aromas with hints of mint and cherry on the bouquet leads on to a round and supple palate, with more of the sweet, fleshy fruit of the bouquet; spicy, toasty oak adds interest and structure throughout. Retasted end 1997, and evolving slowly but surely, with vitrually no change in the notes. **rating:** 93

best drinking 1999 – 2007 **best vintages** '89, '91, '94, '95 **drink with** New Zealand lamb • $36

te motu waiheke vineyards ★★★★

76 Onetangi Road, Onetangi, Waiheke Island **region** Waiheke Island
phone (09) 486 3859 **fax** (09) 486 2341 **open** Not
winemaker Paul Dunleavy, John Dunleavy, Mark Roberton **production** 1300 **est.** 1990
product range ($35 R) Te Motu (Cabernet Merlot), Dunleavy Merlot Franc and a proposed third label for a Cabernet Sauvignon Merlot Franc blend.
summary The venture of the Dunleavy family headed by long-term, but now-retired, Wine Institute of New Zealand chief executive Terry Dunleavy. Produced outstanding wines in 1993 and 1994, providing yet further evidence (if any was needed) of the suitability of Waiheke Island for the production of ripe, full-bodied, Cabernets.

te papa wines NR

Martinborough-Pirinoa Road, Martinborough **region** Wairarapa
phone (06) 306 9899 **open** Not
winemaker John Trethewey **production** 500 **est.** NA
product range ($17–28 ML) Riesling, Sauvignon Blanc, Pinot Gris, Chardonnay, Pinot Noir.
summary With 7 hectares of sauvignon blanc, chardonnay, pinot noir, pinot gris and riesling under vine, the production of Te Papa Wines will increase significantly in the years ahead. The professed aim of John Trethewey is for minimal intervention in vineyard and winery alike.

te whare ra 

Anglesea Street, Renwick, Marlborough **region** Marlborough
phone (03) 572 8581 **fax** (03) 572 8581 **open** 6 days 9–4
winemaker Roger Smith **production** 2500 **est.** 1979
product range ($16–25 CD) Duke of Marlborough Semillon, Gewürztraminer and Chardonnay; Riesling, Berry Selection Gewürztraminer Riesling.
summary Te Whare Ra was purchased from the founding Hogan family by Roger and Christine Smith in October 1997. Christine has taken charge of the vineyard, and Roger the winery; they intend to continue to maintain the winemaking style of the past.

thainstone wines NR

Giffords Road, RD3, Blenheim **region** Marlborough
phone (03) 572 8823 **fax** (03) 572 8823 **open** Not
winemaker Contract **production** 1200 **est.** 1990
product range Sauvignon Blanc, Chardonnay.
summary Jim and Viv Murray acquired their 7-hectare vineyard in 1990; already planted to sauvignon blanc, the decision was later taken to graft part over to chardonnay, which came into production in 1997. Until 1995 all the grapes were sold, but with gradually increasing amounts of wine made under contract since that time.

the antipodean NR

PO Box 5, Matakana **region** Northland and Matakana
phone (09) 422 7957 **fax** (09) 422 7656 **open** Not
winemaker Michelle Chignell-Vuletic **production** 300 **est.** 1977
product range ($90 CD) The Antipodean (a blend of Cabernet Sauvignon, Merlot and Malbec), Pot a Pat (non-vintage blended red), 'A' (Sauvignon Blanc, Semillon-blend), The Iconoclast (Shiraz), Obiter (Cabernet Sauvignon), Matakana Day (a non-vintage blend).
summary More words have been written about this tiny winery than almost any other in New Zealand, and almost certainly more words than bottles produced. After a hugely publicised burst of production from 1985 to 1987, production ceased until 1990 with fierce family disputes, and sales recommenced in 1994 with the 1991 vintage of The Antipodean. As the product range testifies, not your run-of-the-mill winery.

the brothers vineyards NR

Brancott Road, RD2, Blenheim **region** Marlborough
phone (04) 386 3873 **fax** (04) 386 3853 **open** By appointment
winemaker Allen Hogan (and Consultants) **production** 3000 **est.** 1991
product range ($14.50–20 R) Chardonnay, Sauvignon Blanc Semillon, Semillon, Merlot.
summary A new arrival drawing upon 25 hectares of vineyards, with much of the grape production sold to other makers. It has wasted no time in establishing export markets in the United Kingdom, Canada and Australia.

the denton winery NR

Awa Awa Road, Ruby Bay **region** Nelson
phone (03) 540 3555 **open** 7 days 11–6 October to April
winemaker Richard Denton **production** 500 **est.** 1997
product range ($15–25 CD) Riesling, Sauvignon Blanc, Chardonnay, Pinot Noir.
summary Richard, and wife Alexandra, Denton discovered Nelson while on a world tour and some years later moved from their native England to Nelson to purchase the property in 1995. The first 2 hectares of vines were planted, and a winery – and the seemingly obligatory café and art gallery – appeared in time for the 1997 vintage. Richard Denton was an amateur brewer for many years, and graduated to amateur winemaking before taking the final plunge into commercial winemaking. A further 3 hectares of vineyard are to be planted, and increased production will follow.

the village winery NR

417 Mount Eden Road, Mount Eden, Auckland **region** Auckland and South Auckland
phone (09) 638 8780 **fax** (09) 638 9782 **open** Mon–Sat 10–9
winemaker Ken Sanderson **production** 1100 **est.** 1994
product range ($10.95–32.95 R) Windmill Road range, notably Syrah.
summary Enterprises such as this are not uncommon in California, but it is the only one I know of in either Australia or New Zealand, with the winery established in the main street of suburban Mount Eden, for good measure, until owner Peter Schinckel found a loophole in the law – a 'dry' area. (New Zealand, like Australia, still has areas in which alcohol may not be sold.) The wines are made under the Windmill Road label, the winery-cum-shop stocking a broad range of wines from other producers as well as Windmill Road.

torlesse 

Waipara Village, Waipara, Canterbury **region** Canterbury
phone (03) 377 1595 **fax** (03) 377 1595 **open** By appointment
winemaker Kym Rayner **production** 3900 **est.** 1990
product range ($8.45–19.90 R) Müller Thurgau, Riesling (Dry and Medium), Southern Blush, Breidecker Dry, Gewurztraminer, Marlborough Sauvignon Blanc, Marlborough Chardonnay, South Island Chardonnay, Waipara Reserve Chardonnay, Marlborough Cabernet Franc.
summary Torlesse was effectively reborn in 1990 when its existing shareholders purchased the business from a receiver. They include Dr David Jackson, author of several books on viticulture, and winemaker Kym Rayner; all have vineyards in the Canterbury region which supply Torlesse with grapes, supplemented by grapes purchased from the Stonier Vineyard in Marlborough. The plans are for production to increase to about 13 000 cases.

totara vineyards 

Main Road, Thames **region** Waikato and Bay of Plenty
phone (07) 868 6798 **fax** (07) 868 8729 **open** Mon–Sat 9–5.30
winemaker Gilbert Chan **production** 10 000 **est.** 1950
product range ($10–16 R) Müller Thurgau, Chardonnay, Reserve Chardonnay, Sauvignon Blanc, Chenin Blanc, Cabernet Sauvignon.
summary A substantial operation which, however, has had its share of problems, leading to a decision to remove all its vineyards in 1986 under the Vine Pull scheme; it now relies on local growers to provide the grapes for its wines. Had its moment of glory in the 1992 Air New Zealand Wine Awards when the '90 Reserve Chardonnay won the Chardonnay Trophy.

trinity hill 

2396 State Highway 50, RD5, Hastings **region** Hawke's Bay
phone (06) 879 7778 **fax** (06) 879 7770 **open** 7 days 10–5
winemaker John Hancock, Warren Gibson **production** 20 000 **est.** 1996
product range ($13.95–22.95 R) Wairarapa Riesling, Wairarapa Chardonnay (unoaked), Shepherds Croft Chardonnay, Shepherds Croft Sauvignon Blanc, Shepherds Croft Syrah Merlot Cabernet Franc.
summary A fast-rising star in the New Zealand firmament. A joint venture between former Morton Estate winemaker John Hancock, an Auckland businessman and a pair (a couple actually) of London restaurateurs. The venture began with the establishment of a 20-hectare

vineyard on a prime Gimblett Road site, followed by the erection of a state-of-the-art winery in 1996, completed just prior to the first vintage. All of the wines so far released have achieved great critical acclaim.

Trinity Hill Wairarapa Riesling

A one-off release from 1997. The grapes were hand-picked, trucked to Hawke's Bay from the Wairarapa region and whole-bunch pressed. It is ironic that it should be one of the best, if not the best, of the '96 and '97 vintage wines from Trinity Hill.

1997 Light to medium yellow-green; an extremely fragrant bouquet with rich lime blossom and passionfruit aromas. The long palate replicates those flavours finishing with acidity (rather than the flick of residual sugar) uppermost. **rating:** 90

➭ **best drinking** 1998 – 2002 **best vintages** NA **drink with** Japanese Nori rolls • $13.95

Trinity Hill Shepherds Croft Sauvignon Blanc

The Shepherds Croft Vineyard, belonging to Jeff and Judy Whittaker, is situated in the cool Ngatarawa area, with light alluvial soils over deep river shingle. It produces one of the lighter styles of Sauvignon Blanc from Hawke's Bay, tending more to that of Marlborough in all except the warmest vintages.

1997 Bright, light green-yellow; a light, spotlessly clean and crisp bouquet is followed on a crisp, clean palate with a mix of tangy citrus and gooseberry flavours which build on the back palate. Overall, in restrained style. **rating:** 86

➭ **best drinking** 1998 – 1999 **best vintages** NA **drink with** Crab • $15.95

Trinity Hill Shepherds Croft Chardonnay

While Trinity Hill has three distinct areas within Hawke's Bay – Gimblett Road, Ngatarawa and Te Awanga – the majority of the initial releases came from the Shepherds Croft Vineyard at Ngatarawa. Seventy-five per cent of the wine is barrel-fermented, and given the usual lees contact, although it is not easy to tell how much was taken through malolactic fermentation.

1996 Glowing yellow-green; a stylish bouquet with spicy nutmeg oak leads into a lively wine with citrus, herb and melon flavours, finishing with bright acidity. Restrained malolactic influence throughout. **rating:** 86

➭ **best drinking** 1998 – 1999 **best vintages** NA **drink with** Tuna • $22.95

Trinity Hill Wairarapa Chardonnay

Like the Riesling, a one-off wine from the 1997 vintage, made simply because some high-quality fruit from a vineyard near Masterton became available. John Hancock says that Trinity Hill is a Hawke's Bay operation and that's where all of its wines will come from in the future.

1997 Medium yellow-green; citrussy, slightly herbaceous, fruit aromas are supported by subtle oak and a hint of nutty malolactic-fermentation character on the clean bouquet. The lively, tangy citrus and melon fruit of the palate are similarly supported by a hint of cashew and subtle oak. **rating:** 85

➭ **best drinking** 1998 – 2001 **best vintages** NA **drink with** Smoked eel • $17.95

twin bays vineyard NR

56 Koroa Road, Oneroa, Waiheke Island **region** Waiheke Island
phone (09) 372 6450 **open** By appointment
winemaker Contract **production** 200 **est.** 1989
product range Premium label is Fenton Cabernet Merlot; second label is The Red.
summary Despite its tiny size (2 hectares) Twin Bays has already made its contribution to the international reputation enjoyed by Waiheke Island, for the 1994 Stonyridge Airfield Cabernet Merlot which won the trophy for Best New Zealand Cabernet Merlot Blend at the Air New Zealand Wine Awards was made from Twin Bays' grapes. Since 1995 the wine has been made and released by Twin Bays' owners Barry and Meg Fenton, who have plans to double the vineyards to 4 hectares.

unison vineyard NR

2163 Highway 50, RD5, Hastings **region** Hawke's Bay
phone (06) 879 7913 **fax** (06) 879 7915 **open** By appointment
winemaker Anna-Barbara and Bruce Helliwell **production** 1800 **est.** 1993
product range ($25–35 R) Two wines only are produced: Unison and Unison Reserve, both being blends of Merlot, Cabernet Sauvignon and Syrah.
summary Bruce Helliwell a New Zealand winemaker with MSc Honours degree met his German-born and trained viticulturist and winemaker wife Anna-Barbara while she was managing a small estate in Chianti Classico hill country. Between them, they have winemaking and viticultural experience in New Zealand, Germany, California, Italy, Switzerland and France. The vines on the 6-hectare estate are close-planted at a density of 5000 vines per hectare, with the yield reduced to only 1 kilo per vine. Small wonder their first vintage (1996) sold out in two months.

vavasour wines ★★★★★

Redwood Pass Road, Awatere Valley, Marlborough **region** Marlborough
phone (03) 575 7481 **fax** (03) 575 7240 **open** Mon-Fri 9–5, weekends 10–5
winemaker Glenn Thomas **production** 25 000 **est.** 1986
product range ($16–28.75 CD) At the top end come Vavasour Single Vineyard Sauvignon Blanc, Chardonnay; then Awatere Valley Sauvignon Blanc, Chardonnay, Pinot Noir and Cabernet Sauvignon; then Dashwood Chardonnay, Sauvignon Blanc and Pinot Noir; and Stafford Brook Chardonnay and Cabernet.
summary A high-profile newcomer which has quickly fulfilled the expectations held for it. The drier, slightly warmer climate of the Awatere Valley and the unique river-terrace stony soils on which the 12.5-hectare vineyard is established are producing grapes of great intensity of flavour, which are in turn being skilfully handled in the winery by Glenn Thomas.

Vavasour Awatere Valley Sauvignon Blanc

Selected from the three finest estate blocks, some being hand-harvested and whole-bunch pressed, others crushed in the conventional manner. Eight per cent is fermented in older French oak and kept on lees until blending and bottling.

🍷🍷🍷🍷🍷 **1997** Light green-yellow; the bouquet is quite tight and powerful, with secondary mineral aromas, and just a touch of passionfruit. The palate is much more tightly constructed and longer than the Dashwood, with layered flavours. Classy and sophisticated. **rating:** 94

⇨ **best drinking** 1998 – 1999 **best vintages** '97 **drink with** Shellfish • NA

Vavasour Dashwood Sauvignon Blanc

In contrast to the Vavasour Reserve, 40% of which is barrel-fermented and which is drawn solely from the Awatere Valley vineyard, the Dashwood Sauvignon Blanc is fermented in steel and usually comes from a mix of Awatere and Wairau Valley grapes. In some vintages a small percentage of Semillon is added.

🍷🍷🍷🍷 **1997** Light green-yellow; a fragrant bouquet with passionfruit, mineral, herb and gooseberry aromas is followed by a crisp, passionfruit and gooseberry-flavoured palate, finishing with tingling acidity. **rating:** 87

➾ **best drinking** 1998 – 2000 **best vintages** '89, '90, '91, '94, '96, '97 **drink with** Pickled octopus • $17

Vavasour Single Vineyard Sauvignon Blanc

When first released in 1989, this wine was simply called 'Vavasour Reserve'. In the years it has been made since 1994 (there was no 1995) it has been called 'Single Vineyard', but no name ascribed, simply because Glenn Thomas wishes to have freedom to select what he considers to be the very best block or blocks of grapes in any given vintage. Fifty per cent of the wine was barrel-fermented and taken through malolactic fermentation, the remainder steel-fermented. An exceptional wine, driven by the intense, ripe, low-yield fruit.

🍷🍷🍷🍷🍷 **1996** Light to medium yellow-green; intense lime, nettle, herb and gooseberry fruit on the bouquet is supported by almost subliminal oak. An intensely rich yet not blowsy wine in the mouth, with more of those lime, herb and gooseberry flavours on a long, lingering, faintly spicy finish. **rating:** 95

➾ **best drinking** 1998 – 2000 **best vintages** '89, '91, '94, '96 **drink with** Mussel soup • $27

Vavasour Awatere Valley Chardonnay

Produced from Mendoza clone chardonnay grown in the Awatere Valley, hand-picked and part whole-bunch pressed. Fermentation is completed in French oak barriques, 15% new; 100% malolactic fermentation. The wine spends nine months in oak before being bottled.

🍷🍷🍷🍷 **1997** Medium to full yellow-green; the bouquet is complex with citrus, nectarine and apple fruit aromas. The palate is of medium weight, with some spicy oak evident, and fractionally less luscious than the bouquet promises, tending more to citrus and mineral. **rating:** 85

➾ **best drinking** 1998 – 2000 **best vintages** NA **drink with** Milk-fed veal • NA

Vavasour Awatere Valley Cabernet Sauvignon

Normally a blend of Cabernet Sauvignon and Cabernet Franc which is matured for 18 months in French oak barriques, and drawn entirely from the Awatere Valley. It has been Vavasour's contention since the outset that the Awatere Valley – and, in particular, the rocky alluvial vineyard site – is capable of producing red wines every bit as good as the whites. So far that remains to be proven, although not so much through the fault of the reds as for the sheer quality of the top-end whites.

🍷🍷🍷🍷 **1996** The colour is exceptionally deep for Marlborough Cabernet Sauvignon; the bouquet is powerful, with strident leafy cabernet varietal fruit, the palate likewise powerful and concentrated, all in the green-forest spectrum, but does have structure. Plum and cassis are to be found on the back label. **rating:** 84

➾ **best drinking** 2000 – 2005 **best vintages** '89, '90, '91, '94 **drink with** Moroccan lamb • $28.75

---

vidal estate ★★★★☆

913 St Aubyns Street East, Hastings **region** Hawke's Bay
phone (06) 876 8105 **fax** (06) 876 5312 **open** Mon-Sat 11–6, Sun 10.30–5
winemaker Elise Montgomery **production** 46 000 **est.** 1905
product range ($15–40 CD) Constant revamping of the product range (new brand managers?) keeps everyone on their toes. The Private Bin range has been replaced by the Estate Range; the Bays range introduced for restaurants; only the East Coast (at the bottom) and the Reserve range (at the top) continue (for the time being). The usual spread of varietals are covered by each range.
summary Together with Te Mata, Villa Maria and Esk Valley, consistently produces New Zealand's finest red wines; they have ripeness, richness and balance, a far cry from the reds of bygone years. Elise Montgomery seems to have put the white wines on a similar path, much improved from earlier years.

Vidal Hawke's Bay Sauvignon Blanc

The 'Estate Range' replaces the old 'Private Bin' range. From the 1997 vintage the words 'lightly oaked' were added to the label. The '96 was a wine which did extremely well at the 1997 Sydney International Wine Competition, showing Hawke's Bay Sauvignon Blanc to maximum advantage. Perhaps also a tribute to one of the few viticulturists in the world to have a Master of Wine degree – Steve Smith.

🍷🍷🍷🍷 **1997** Light to medium yellow-green; quite intense passionfruit and gooseberry aromas in soft Hawke's Bay style supported by light spicy oak. The palate shows more of those passionfruit and gooseberry flavours in a soft cushion; all in all, a flavoursome Hawke's Bay version of Sauvignon Blanc. **rating:** 86

➾ **best drinking** 1998 – 1999 **best vintages** '94, '96 **drink with** Poached scallops • NA

Vidal Estate Hawke's Bay Chardonnay

An extraordinarily impressive wine given its price, but perhaps benefiting from a less-tricky approach to the winemaking. Oak-aged for only three months, with the fruit allowed to do the work.

🍷🍷🍷🍷½ **1996** Light to medium green-yellow; the bouquet is of medium intensity with melon and fig fruit supported by just a hint of oak. A stylish, elegant and understated wine on the palate, but excellent fruit and varietal character build on a long carry and finish. **rating:** 90

➾ **best drinking** 1998 – 1999 **best vintages** NA **drink with** Creamy pasta • $13

Vidal Estate Reserve Chardonnay

One of the most highly regarded of the Hawke's Bay Chardonnays, even if overshadowed in the eyes of some by its sister wine from Villa Maria. The style is moving along with the mainstream of New Zealand Chardonnay, away from overblown, over-extractive making to a more restrained mode, but without sacrificing drinkability and accessibility. Barrel-fermented in French oak (two-thirds new), part of the ferment in a cool room, and part ambient. Fifty per cent of the wine was taken through malolactic fermentation, and it was given the usual lees contact.

🍷🍷🍷🍷 **1996** Medium yellow-green; a complex bouquet, which is quite intense, with good fruit and oak balance and integration. A multilayered, multiflavoured wine on the palate with cashew, butter and cream flavours running through the mid to back palate, finishing with well-balanced acidity. **rating:** 89

➾ **best drinking** 1998 – 1999 **best vintages** '90, '91, '94 **drink with** Veal fricassee • $27

Vidal Estate Pinot Noir

I remain to be convinced that anyone should be planting pinot noir in Hawke's Bay, particularly if they have the option of anywhere from Martinborough through to Central Otago. However, I have to admit to a sneaking regard for this wine.

🍷🍷🍷🍷 **1996** Medium red-purple; the bouquet is fresh and bright, with fairly straightforward cherry and plum fruit, but the wine grabs attention on the well-structured palate, with ripe plum and cherry fruit, and a nice stemmy cut to the firm finish. **rating:** 87

➯ **best drinking** 1998 – 2000 **best vintages** NA **drink with** Quail • $19

Vidal Estate Reserve Cabernet Sauvignon

Now produced from Vidal's own vineyard at Ngakirkiri, planted between 1992 and 1995 on gravelly soil. Universally regarded as one of New Zealand's greatest Cabernets, and I am not about to challenge that rating. It spends 20 months in oak, 90% French and 70% new, and incorporates just a touch of Malbec.

🍷🍷🍷🍷🍷 **1995** Medium to full red-purple; the bouquet is extremely classy, with rippling aromas running through earth to cassis, but predominantly sweet, and with a subtle touch of lifted oak. A powerful wine in the mouth with classic Cabernet varietal flavours of cassis, chocolate and earth skilfully supported by sweet vanillin oak. **rating:** 94

➯ **best drinking** 1999 – 2006 **best vintages** '87, '89, '90, '91, '94, '95 **drink with** Rack of New Zealand lamb • $28

vilagrad wines NR

Rukuhia Road, RD2, Ohaupo **region** Waikato and Bay of Plenty
phone (07) 825 2893 **open** Tues-Sat 10–6
winemaker Peter Nooyen **production** 2000 **est.** 1922
product range Recently introduced Nooyen Reserve range of Riesling, Gewurztraminer, Chardonnay, Pinot Noir and Cabernet Merlot Malbec head the range.
summary A low-profile operation making wines of modest but consistently acceptable quality that age surprisingly well, but aspiring to greater things with the Nooyen Reserve wines. A winery restaurant is open on Sundays (and for functions at other times by arrangement).

villa maria ★★★★★

5 Kirkbridge Road, Mangere, Auckland **region** Auckland and South Auckland
phone (09) 275 6119 **fax** (09) 275 6618 **open** 7 days 10.15–6
winemaker Michelle Richardson **production** 120 000 **est.** 1961
product range ($7.50–40 CD) A large range of wines under the Private Bin label, basically varietally identified, stands at the bottom end of the portfolio; next comes the Cellar Selection range of Chardonnay, Sauvignon Blanc, Cabernet Merlot; then Wairau Valley Reserve Sauvignon Blanc; at the top end the Reserve Bin range of Barrique Fermented Chardonnay, Marlborough Chardonnay, Sauvignon Blanc, Gewurztraminer, Noble Riesling, Cabernet Merlot and Cabernet Sauvignon.
summary Whether viewed on the basis of its performance at the 1997 and 1998 Sydney International Winemakers Competition, or on any other show result over the last few years, Villa Maria has to be rated one of New Zealand's best large wineries. The quality of the wines, both white and red, is exemplary, the flavours magically full without going over the top.

Villa Maria Cellar Selection Sauvignon Blanc

Yet another good Villa Maria Sauvignon Blanc, drawn from the Rapaura and Awatere Valley regions, and with just a small percentage given a touch of oak.

🍷🍷🍷🍷🍷 **1997** Light green-yellow; a fresh and crisp bouquet with a mix of lemon, citrus and mineral aromas leads into a well-balanced moderately ripe citrus and gooseberry-flavoured palate. **rating:** 90

➪ **best drinking** 1998 – 1999 **best vintages** NA **drink with** Fish soup • $17

Villa Maria Private Bin Sauvignon Blanc

A blend of Marlborough, Te Kauwhata and Hawke's Bay grapes simply cold fermented in stainless steel, and with no tricks of any kind.

🍷🍷🍷🍷🍷 **1997** Light to medium yellow-green; stylish and fragrant with overtones of passionfruit on both bouquet and palate, complementing the more citrussy elements. Lively, fresh and well balanced. **rating:** 94

➪ **best drinking** 1998 – 1999 **best vintages** NA **drink with** Gazpacho • $14.95

Villa Maria Reserve Clifford Bay Sauvignon Blanc

A wine which made its first appearance in 1996 from grapes grown in the Awatere Valley. Both the '96 and '97 are notable for their depth and intensity of flavour, but do give all the signs of being fast-developing styles. The '97 was runner-up to its sister wine Reserve Wairau Valley Sauvignon Blanc in the Medium Bodied Dry White Table section of the 1998 Sydney International Wine Competition.

🍷🍷🍷🍷🍷 **1997** Medium yellow-green; powerful, ripe gooseberry, passionfruit, banana and melon fruit aromas on the bouquet lead into an extremely rich, full-flavoured succulent wine on the palate. Strikingly different from many Marlborough Sauvignon Blancs. **rating:** 94

➪ **best drinking** 1998 – 1999 **best vintages** NA **drink with** Prawn and avocado salad • $19

Villa Maria Wairau Valley Reserve Sauvignon Blanc

Keeping up with the veritable cascade of Sauvignon Blanc labels from Villa Maria is no easy task. This wine sits alongside the Clifford Bay, and is essentially a regional selection, coming as it does from three Marlborough vineyards. This wine, incidentally, used to be labelled 'Reserve Sauvignon Blanc' and, for the record, part is barrel-fermented, although the oak makes relatively little impact. The '97 was a winner of three trophies at the 1998 Sydney International Wine Competition including Best White Table Wine of Show.

🍷🍷🍷🍷🍷 **1997** Light green-yellow; a voluminous, perfumed bouquet is driven by passionfruit and gooseberry fruit aromas, with a mix of passionfruit, gooseberry and more grassy characters on the long palate. **rating:** 94

➪ **best drinking** 1998 – 1999 **best vintages** '92, '94, '96, '97 **drink with** Smoked haddock • $19

Villa Maria Cellar Selection Chardonnay

A neat blend of Gisborne and Marlborough grapes, 30% barrel-fermented and matured in oak for six months. The oak input has the typical Villa Maria stamp on it, and, for my palate at least, teeters on the edge of being overdone.

🍷🍷🍷🍷 **1996** Medium yellow-green; the bouquet is quite complex with strong toasty barrel-ferment oak quite evident, but the palate is generously flavoured with ripe melon fruit and, inevitably, dollops of oak. **rating:** 86

➾ **best drinking** 1998 – 1999 **best vintages** NA **drink with** Ginger pork • $18

Villa Maria Reserve Barrique Fermented Chardonnay

One can legitimately argue about the level of oak in this wine; whether one really likes it or not is a question of personal style preference, but there is no doubting the complexity and power of the wine. A gold medallist and Top 100 finalist in both the 1994 and 1995 Sydney International Wine Competition, and a medal winner at the 1994 Australian National Wine Show in Canberra. A Bob Campbell Classic and five stars from Michael Cooper.

🍷🍷🍷🍷🍷 **1996** Medium to full yellow-green; a rich, ripe voluptuous bouquet with fruit almost veering into the tropical spectrum, and oak evident but under much better control than in prior years. The palate is tremendously rich, sweet and concentrated, with more of those tropical fruit flavours, supported by well-handled oak. Rapid-developing style, however. **rating:** 90

➾ **best drinking** 1998 – 1999 **best vintages** '90, '91, '94, '96 **drink with** Moroccan chicken stuffed with raisins and pine nuts • $29

Villa Maria Reserve Marlborough Chardonnay

As the label suggests, made entirely from Marlborough region grapes drawn from Villa Maria's two best vineyards in the region, predominantly hand-picked. The wine is 100% barrel-fermented in a mix of new (60%) and one-year-old (40%) oak. Given eight months lees contact, with partial barrel stirring, and 25% malolactic fermentation. Sophisticated winemaking, to say the least.

🍷🍷🍷🍷 **1996** Medium yellow-green; a complex and stylish wine with attractive melon and nectarine fruit woven through spicy nutmeg oak. A similarly stylish and well-balanced palate of medium weight, with the oak obvious, and perhaps just a fraction too much so on the mid to back palate where the fruit lightens off fractionally. **rating:** 89

➾ **best drinking** 1998 – 1999 **best vintages** '94, '96, '97 **drink with** Coquilles St Jacques • $23

Villa Maria Reserve Merlot Cabernet

A blend of Cabernet Sauvignon and Merlot grown on the Villa Maria Ngakirikiri vineyard blended with Merlot from Bridge Pa. The percentage of Merlot and Cabernet respectively is not stated, but is necessarily Merlot-dominant. The wine spends 18 months in a mix of predominantly French, and a little American, oak, part new, part used. The '95 won a gold medal at the 1997 Liquorland Royal Easter Wine Show and the gold medal and trophy at the 1997 Air New Zealand Wine Awards.

🍷🍷🍷🍷 **1995** Medium red-purple; sweet berry fruit aromas are supported by pronounced oak on the bouquet; the palate, too, shows a lot of oak influence which is not yet fully integrated, and which tends to overshadow the unquestionably sweet plum and cassis fruit. A splashy show style which could well mature into something quite special. **rating:** 87

➾ **best drinking** 2000 – 2004 **best vintages** '85, '87, '90, '91, '92, '94, '95 **drink with** Rich, soft ripened cheese • $32

voss estate ★★★★

Puruatanga Road, Martinborough **region** Wairarapa
phone (06) 306 9668 **fax** (06) 306 9668 **open** 7 days 10–6 summer
winemaker Gary Voss **production** 1900 **est.** 1988
product range ($16–25 CD) Reserve Chardonnay, Sauvignon Blanc, Pinot Noir, Waihenga Cabernet Merlot Franc.
summary Voss Estate has been established by Annette Atkins, Gary Voss and Murray Voss, with 3 hectares of vineyards (1 hectare each of chardonnay, pinot noir and cabernet sauvignon/merlot) still coming into bearing after a disastrous frost in 1992. In the meantime, grapes are purchased from other regions.

Voss Estate Reserve Chardonnay

One hundred per cent barrel-fermented in a blend of new and three-year-old French oak barriques, with 20% taken through malolactic fermentation. Rigorous fruit selection and skilled winemaking have done the rest.

🍷🍷🍷🍷🍷 **1996** Medium yellow-green; a stylish and complex bouquet with a compelling mix of toasty/creamy/cashew aromas leads into a perfectly balanced and structured wine on the palate, with fine melon varietal fruit woven through cashew notes and subtle, toasty oak. A lot of winemaker's thumbprints, but cleverly placed. **rating:** 92

⇒ **best drinking** 1998 – 2000 **best vintages** NA **drink with** Corn-fed chicken • $24

Voss Estate Pinot Noir

1996 was an outstanding vintage in Wellington/Wairarapa, particularly Pinot Noir. The wines are extraordinarily generous, and are continuing to develop very well in bottle. The subtle use of French oak helps a wine which is admittedly at the baroque end of the spectrum, but which cannot be denied.

🍷🍷🍷🍷🍷 **1996** Very deep red-purple; the bouquet is full, rich and ripe, with opulent dark plum fruit and just a hint of spicy oak. In the mouth, very rich, concentrated and voluptuous; at the far end of the scale but will mature well in bottle, for it has the requisite balance, with foresty characters certain to come through with age. **rating:** 91

⇒ **best drinking** 1998 – 2003 **best vintages** NA **drink with** Venison • $25

wai-iti river vineyard NR

PO Box 86, Brightwater, Nelson **region** Nelson
phone (03) 542 3205 **fax** (03) 542 3205 **open** By appointment
winemaker Dave Glover (Contract) **production** 500 **est.** 1993
product range ($16–24 R) Chardonnay, Pinot Noir, Cabernet Sauvignon.
summary Chan and Philip Woollaston planted their small (6-hectare) vineyard on the Waimea Plains near Nelson in the winter of 1993 on old riverbed gravels. Cellar-door sales and tastings, together with a picnic area, will be open by the end of 1998.

waimarama estate NR

31 Waimarama Road, Havelock North **region** Hawke's Bay
phone (06) 877 6794 **fax** (06) 877 6789 **open** At 264 Te Mata-Mangateretere Road, Hastings
winemaker Dr John Loughlin, Jenny Dobson **production** 2400 **est.** 1988

product range ($19–26.50 ML) Cabernet Sauvignon, Cabernet Merlot, Dessert Cabernet; Undercliffe is the second label.
summary An exciting newcomer which has had consistent show success since day one. Owner (and eye surgeon) Dr John Loughlin has had a lifetime interest in wine, and the origins of Waimarama Estate go back to 1972, when the property was purchased, although it was not until 1988 that vineyard development began. Son John Loughlin also has a part-time interest in the venture.

waipara downs NR

Bains Road, RD3, Amberley **region** Canterbury
phone (03) 314 6873 **fax** (03) 314 6873 **open** By appointment
winemaker Mark Rattray (Contract) **production** 500 **est.** 1989
product range Chardonnay, Pinot Noir, Cabernet Sauvignon, Port.
summary Four hectares of vines on a 320-hectare farm puts Waipara Downs into perspective, but does not diminish the enjoyment Ruth and Keith Berry derive from producing their wines from the limestone soils of the Waipara Valley. The wines have been consistent bronze and silver medal winners in New Zealand wine shows.

waipara springs wines ★★★★

State Highway 1 North, Waipara, North Canterbury **region** Canterbury
phone (03) 314 6777 **fax** (03) 314 6777 **open** 7 days 11–5
winemaker Kym Rayner **production** 6000 **est.** 1990
product range ($13–25 CD) Sauvignon Blanc, Chardonnay, Riesling (Dry and Medium), Pinot Noir, Cabernet Sauvignon.
summary Owned by Bruce and Jill Moore, who commenced planting the vineyard way back in 1982, establishing 4 hectares of chardonnay, the grapes of which were initially sold to Corbans. Plantings now extend to 23 hectares, providing all of the grapes for the rapidly expanding production. The wines enjoy an excellent reputation.

Waipara Springs Riesling

Estate-grown; conventionally cool fermented at the on-site winery. Fermentation stopped with barely perceptible residual sugar (6.5 grams per litre).

🍷🍷🍷🍷 **1996** Light green-yellow; the clean bouquet shows clear varietal character with tight mineral lime fruit, the palate precisely tracking the bouquet. Plenty of depth and length; well balanced. **rating:** 85

➪ **best drinking** 1998 – 2003 **best vintages** NA **drink with** Globe artichokes and hollandaise sauce • $14

Waipara Springs Sauvignon Blanc

Direct, no-frills winemaking places the primary emphasis on the very good fruit base. A silver medal winner at the 1997 Air New Zealand Wine Awards.

🍷🍷🍷🍷🍷 **1997** Light to medium yellow-green; the clean, fruit-driven bouquet ranges through citrus, gooseberry and passionfruit aromas; the palate is lively, crisp and fresh with a mix of citrus and nectarine flavours running through to a most attractive finish. **rating:** 90

➪ **best drinking** 1998 – 1999 **best vintages** NA **drink with** Deep-fried calamari • $15

Waipara Springs Chardonnay

One hundred per cent barrel-fermented in French oak, followed by eight months on lees, with partial malolactic fermentation. Reflects the cool climate and the strong winemaker inputs; wines such as this from New Zealand share many characteristics in common with those of the Mornington Peninsula of Australia.

🍷🍷🍷🍷 **1996** Medium yellow-green; the bouquet shows strong nutty barrel-ferment/cashew aromas which are, however, quite stylish. An elegant wine in the mouth, albeit with the flavours all secondary, and with relatively little primary fruit still evident. **rating:** 85

➾ **best drinking** 1998 – 1999 **best vintages** NA **drink with** Blanquette of veal • $21

waipara west NR

376 Ram Paddock Road, Amberley, RD2, North Canterbury **region** Canterbury
phone (03) 314 8699 **fax** (03) 314 8692 **open** By appointment
winemaker Petter Evans **production** 6000 **est.** 1989
product range ($14.80–20.50 CD) Riesling, Sauvignon Blanc, Chardonnay, Pinot Noir, Ram Paddock Red (Cabernet-blend).
summary Waipara West is situated at the gorge of the Waipara River. The vineyard is surrounded by steep banks and planted on naturally sloping terraces which vary in height and aspect. Seventeen hectares of chardonnay, sauvignon blanc, riesling, merlot, cabernet sauvignon, cabernet franc and pinot noir have been planted, with the very experienced Petter Evans (ex-St Helena) in charge of winemaking. Almost all of the wine is exported, chiefly to the United Kingdom.

wairau river wines ★★★★

Cnr Rapaura Road and SH 6, Blenheim **region** Marlborough
phone (03) 572 9800 **fax** (03) 572 9885 **open** 7 days 9–5
winemaker John Belsham (Contract) **production** 20 000 **est.** 1978
product range ($16–30 CD) Riesling, Botrytised Riesling Reserve, Sauvignon Blanc, Sauvignon Blanc Reserve, Chardonnay, Chardonnay Reserve; Philip Rose Estate is the second label introduced in 1995.
summary Phil and Chris Rose have been long-term grape growers in the Marlborough region, having established a 60-hectare vineyard progressively since 1978. The first wines were made under the Wairau River label in 1991 by contract-winemaker John Belsham, and all of the vintages to date have been of exemplary quality, particularly the tropical-accented Sauvignon Blanc.

Wairau River Sauvignon Blanc

The Sauvignon Blanc accounts for 8000 cases of the total Wairau River production, and is exported to both the United Kingdom and Australia with great success. The consistency of the wine over the '91 to '97 vintages shows why, if you except the very difficult '95 vintage.

🍷🍷🍷🍷½ **1997** Medium yellow-green; a clean almost gentle bouquet with an appealing range of flowery, tropical and citrus notes leads into a palate again showing some slightly unusual but enormously appealing floral frangipani, lime, lime blossom flavours. A clean, long-lingering finish adds to the appeal. **rating:** 91

➾ **best drinking** 1998 – 1999 **best vintages** '91, '92, '93, '94, '96, '97 **drink with** Deep-fried calamari • $18

Wairau River Chardonnay

First made in 1992, and has evolved and improved over the ensuing vintages, particularly with the introduction in 1994 of 40% of clone 6 to ameliorate the excessive power (and acid) of the Mendoza clone. Scott Henry trellising also helps; barrel-fermented and 30% taken through malolactic fermentation.

🍷🍷🍷🍷 **1996** Medium to full yellow, very advanced for age. The bouquet is quite complex and rich, with buttery/toasty/nutty aromas deriving in part from malolactic fermentation and in part from oak. The palate is soft and fleshy, with buttery flavours in emphatic drink-now style. Retasted September 1997 and showing good character. **rating:** 87

⇨ **best drinking** 1997 – 1998 **best vintages** '93, '94, '96 **drink with** Smoked trout • $22

walker estate NR

Puruatanga Road, PO Box 124, Martinborough, Wairarapa **region** Wairarapa
phone (06) 306 9615 **fax** (06) 306 9615 **open** Not
winemaker James Walker, Chris Lintz (Contract) **production** NA **est.** 1988
product range ($14.50–22 CD) Riesling, Rosé, Notre Vigne.
summary The Walker family (Liz, Brendan and son James) established what they believe to be a two-variety vineyard, riesling and shiraz, in 1988. Until 1993 the grapes were sold to other Martinborough winemakers, but since that time have been vinified under the Walker Estate label. The intriguingly named Notre Vigne (our vine) stems from the fact that the vines thought to be shiraz are in fact of an as-yet unidentified variety, with DNA testing failing to reveal the answer. The wines made from the mystery grape are extremely powerful, densely coloured and most unusual.

walnut ridge ★★★★

159 Regent Street, Martinborough **region** Wairarapa
phone (06) 306 9323 **fax** (06) 306 9323 **open** 7 days 11–5
winemaker Bill Brink **production** 1500 **est.** 1986
product range ($16–24 CD) Sauvignon Blanc, Botrytised Sauvignon Blanc, Pinot Noir, Cabernet Sauvignon.
summary While Bill Brink produces both Pinot Noir and Cabernet Sauvignon, he falls on the Pinot Noir side of the argument so far as Martinborough is concerned. That view, mind you, is not so surprising when you find that the first release from Walnut Ridge was the 1994 Pinot Noir which was awarded a silver medal at the 1995 Air New Zealand Wine Awards. As to the rest, I should quote Bill Brink, who says that he 'came to New Zealand via the somewhat circuitous route of Samoa and the Peace Corps in 1973. After a number of years in public service and doing the Dominion crossword, and a change-of-pace year at Victoria University deliberating the obfuscatory logic of "existential deterrence", I came to Martinborough and began the development of what has become Walnut Ridge'.

Walnut Ridge Botrytised Sauvignon Blanc

I suspect that necessity was the mother of invention, and that nature decreed that part of the 1996 Sauvignon Blanc vintage should be made as a botrytised version. It is in fact of only intermediate sweetness, but has been very well handled.

🍷🍷🍷🍷🍷 **1996** Glowing yellow-green, an intensely fragrant bouquet with rich tropical fruit aromas; the palate has excellent flavour though one would be hard-pressed to guess the grape variety. The sweetness is balanced by acidity, and the wine works very well. Retasted

September 1997. Ageing well with attractive apricot peach flavours dominant, and still no sign of the Sauvignon Blanc base. **rating:** 90

➾ **best drinking** 1997 – 2000 **best vintages** NA **drink with** Fresh fruit • $20

Walnut Ridge Pinot Noir

Significantly the best of the Pinot Noirs made between 1994 and 1996, and a very attractive wine.

🍷🍷🍷🍷🍷 **1996** Light to medium red-purple; lively, clearly accented cherry and plum varietal fruit aromas lead into a well-made, nicely balanced palate with more of that cherry and plum fruit; soft tannins and subtle oak in support. **rating:** 90

➾ **best drinking** 1998 – 2000 **best vintages** NA **drink with** Fresh salmon • $22

west brook winery ★★★☆

34 Awaroa Road, Henderson **region** Henderson
phone (09) 838 8746 **fax** (09) 838 5021 **open** Mon-Sat 9–6, Sun 12–5
winemaker Anthony Ivicevich **production** 10 000 **est.** 1937
product range ($8–17 CD) Blue Ridge Sauvignon Blanc, Sauvignon Blanc Semillon, Semillon, Barrique Fermented Chardonnay, Chenin Blanc, Traminer Riesling, Cabernet Sauvignon, Cabernet Merlot, Henderson Merlot (with increasing quantities sourced from Hawke's Bay and Marlborough).
summary Unpretentious producer of wines of reliable quality, seldom aspiring to greatness but – with the white wines in particular – capable of a very pleasant surprise from time to time.

West Brook Blue Ridge Sauvignon Blanc

The top-of-the-line Sauvignon Blanc from West Brook, particularly good in 1996 (a gold medal at the 1997 Auckland Easter Show), but also good in 1997.

🍷🍷🍷🍷 **1997** Light to medium yellow-green; clean, tropical gooseberry fruit of medium intensity with a hint of spice, possibly from a touch of oak. The palate has the tropical gooseberry and passionfruit flavours of the '96, but is not by any means as intense. **rating:** 84

➾ **best drinking** 1998 – 1999 **best vintages** '96 **drink with** Prosciutto and melon • $16

West Brook Barrique Fermented Chardonnay

The '95 vintage of this wine was made from Gisborne fruit, but the '96 comes from Henderson. Barrel-fermented in a mix of French and American oak, it shows highly skilled winemaking, although there is an echo of something in the wine which just holds it back a touch.

🍷🍷🍷🍷 **1996** Light to medium yellow-green; the bouquet is of medium intensity, with cashew, melon and fig fruit supported by subtle oak. The palate has fresh nectarine fruit, some cashew characters and good balance; there is just an errant touch of burnt-matchstick character which haunts the end of the bouquet and the very finish of the palate. **rating:** 84

➾ **best drinking** 1998 – 1999 **best vintages** NA **drink with** Sweetbreads • $19

whitehaven wine company NR

1 Dodson Street, Blenheim, Marlborough **region** Marlborough
phone (03) 577 8861 **fax** (03) 577 8868 **open** 7 days 9–5
winemaker Simon Waghorn **production** 14 000 **est.** 1993
product range ($13–24 R) Riesling, Sauvignon Blanc, Chardonnay, Pinot Noir.

summary Whitehaven is a joint venture between Greg and Sue White, and winemaker Simon Waghorn. Waghorn qualified as a winemaker at Roseworthy in Australia, first becoming assistant winemaker at Cooks Wines and thereafter spending five years as senior winemaker at Corbans Gisborne winery, where he is responsible for production of a string of gold medal winning wines. A 200-tonne state-of-the-art winery has been built, which includes a restaurant and wine shop as part of the complex. As one would expect, the initial releases under the Whitehaven label have had great show success.

Whitehaven Sauvignon Blanc

Multiple vineyard sites and multiple pickings are used by Simon Waghorn to add complexity to a wine which is then simply fermented in stainless steel and early bottled.

1997 Light green-yellow; a clean, crisp, lemon-scented bouquet with some herbal notes also evident leads into a capsicum, lemon and lime-flavoured palate with a crisp, dry finish. No frills, but it doesn't need any. **rating:** 85

best drinking 1998 – 1999 **best vintages** NA **drink with** Crustacea • $16

william hill winery

NR

Dunstan Road, RD1, Alexandra **region** Otago
phone (03) 448 8436 **fax** (03) 448 8434 **open** Mon-Sat 9–4
winemaker Jerry Rowland **production** 1330 **est.** 1982
product range ($16–20 CD) Riesling, Gewurztraminer, Chardonnay, Pinot Noir.
summary Notwithstanding that the William Hill vineyards extend to 7 hectares, production grew painfully slowly in the early years. A new winery was commissioned for 1995 (happily an exceptional vintage for Central Otago) which offers contract-winemaking services for other wineries in the region.

winslow wines

NR

Princess Street, Martinborough **region** Wairarapa
phone (06) 306 9648 **fax** (06) 306 9271 **open** 7 days 10–6
winemaker Ross Turner **production** 650 **est.** 1987
product range ($15–32 CD) Riesling, Sauvignon Blanc, Chardonnay, Cabernet Sauvignon Franc, Reserve Cabernet Sauvignon Franc, Petra Cabernet Sauvignon.
summary The Bio-Gro™ managed estate plantings of 2.2 hectares are devoted to cabernet sauvignon (75%), cabernet franc (15%) and merlot (10%); the riesling and chardonnay are contract-grown. It is with the Cabernet Franc Merlot that Winslow's aspirations rest.

wither hills vineyards

c/o 172 Hepburn Road, Henderson, Auckland **region** Marlborough
phone (09) 836 0129 **fax** (09) 836 3282 **open** Not
winemaker Brent Marris **production** 600 **est.** 1992
product range ($18–25 ML) Chardonnay, Sauvignon Blanc.
summary The family venture for Delegat's winemaker Brent Marris, who has established a 16-hectare vineyard in Marlborough, selling most of the fruit to Delegat's, and making a small portion under the evocative Wither Hills brand, which takes its name from the range of hills to the south of Marlborough's Wairau Valley. Sumptuous gooseberry Sauvignon Blanc and delicately textured Chardonnay are the outcome.

Wither Hills Sauvignon Blanc

First made in 1994; I may have been a bit hard in my judgment of the '96, but the '97 is a marvellous wine.

🍷🍷🍷🍷🍷 **1997** Light green-yellow; the bouquet is fragrant with gooseberry, redcurrant and tropical fruits which come again on the lush gooseberry/passionfruit-flavoured palate. **rating:** 94

⇨ **best drinking** 1998 – 1999 **best vintages** '94, '97 **drink with** Sashimi • $18

Wither Hills Chardonnay

First made in 1992, with the follow-on vintage from '94. An extremely distinguished wine; the latter was a gold medal winner at the 1995 Air New Zealand Wine Awards.

🍷🍷🍷🍷🍷 **1996** Medium to full yellow-green; the stylish and tangy bouquet shows obvious barrel-ferment characters; the palate, however, is marvellously soft yet not flabby, with a textured silky delicacy surrounded by nectarine fruit and some cashew characters. **rating:** 90

⇨ **best drinking** 1998 – 1999 **best vintages** '92, '94, '96 **drink with** Prawns with walnuts • $25

woodfield estate NR

57 Duncan Road, Hamilton **region** Waikato and Bay of Plenty
phone (07) 827 7170 **fax** (07) 827 7140 **open** Tues-Sun 10–5
winemaker Brian Mahoney **production** 750 **est.** 1994
product range Chardonnay, Cabernet Merlot.
summary June and Brian Mahoney have established a small winery and cellar-door facility in an architect-designed farmhouse style, and use natural winemaking methods (minimal additives, minimal filtration, no stabilisation) in handling the Waikato-grown grapes they use to make their wines.

more titles by james halliday from harpercollins*publishers*

James Halliday's Australian and New Zealand Interactive Wine Companion

The new interactive CD-ROM for PC and Mac features James Halliday's detailed assessments of more than 2200 wines and 1000 wineries; vertical tasting notes of over 90 classic wines, many going back 40 or 50 years; a revamped cellar holdings and tasting notes program (compatible with previous versions); interactive wine regions maps; and 'Ask James' – a video interview with the author. With search and print facilities throughout, the *Interactive Wine Companion* is the perfect addition to every wine lover's collection.

Wine Atlas of Australia and New Zealand

New revised edition

Due out late 1998, this new edition offers all the detail and research of the previous edition and more. Including maps of Australia's new wine regions, profiles on Australia and New Zealand's top winemakers and wineries and stunning photographs, the *Wine Atlas of Australia and New Zealand* is an indispensable reference tool.

Classic Wines of Australia

This unique book provides a comprehensive insight into the greatest wines made in Australia over the past 50 or more years. James Halliday's notes on vertical tastings of these wines cover all the most famous names; equally absorbing are the notes for the classics of tomorrow, wines known only to a chosen few. A brief introductory background is given to each of the 82 wines chosen, and tastings range far and wide across sparkling wines, white table wines – both dry and sweet – dry reds and fortified wines.

Some readers will already have cellars that include a number of these wines. Hopefully others will be inspired to start collecting wines and experiencing first hand the magical transformation of a vibrant young wine into a seriously graceful old wine.

Collecting Wine: You and Your Cellar

A necessity for every wine enthusiast, this book contains valuable information on how to start and maintain a cellar, how to choose white and red wines for cellaring, the most efficient cellar racking systems and the problems a bottle may encounter during its life. It also provides Australian and imported wine vintage charts and recommends wine merchants, auction houses, societies and literature.